Rick

LONDON

Rick Steves & Gene Openshaw

2016

CONTENTS

Introduction 1
  Planning 4
  Traveling as a
    Temporary Local 10

**Orientation
  to London** 12

Sights in London 43

**Self-Guided Walks
  and Tours**
▶ **Central London**
  Westminster Walk 114
  Westminster Abbey Tour 131
  Houses of Parliament Tour . . . 142
  National Gallery Tour 149
  National Portrait
    Gallery Tour 168
  West End Walk 184
  Courtauld Gallery Tour 194
▶ **North London**
  British Museum Tour 201
  British Library Tour 227
▶ **The City**
  The City Walk 239

St. Paul's Cathedral Tour . . . 263
Tower of London Tour 276
▶ **The South Bank**
  Bankside Walk 290
  Tate Modern Tour 306
▶ **West London**
  Victoria and Albert
    Museum Tour 319
  Tate Britain Tour 334
▶ **East London**
  Greenwich Tour 349
  The Docklands Walk 364

**Sleeping in
  London** 374
  Victoria Station
    Neighborhood 375
  South Kensington 380
  North of Kensington
    Gardens 382
  Elsewhere in Central
    London 388
  Other Sleeping Options 390

Eating in London 394
  Eating Tips 394

CITY OF LONDON

D0027237

Central London.............. 395
West London............... 408
Elsewhere in London 413
Taking Tea in London 414

**London with
   Children**................. **417**

**Shopping in
   London**................. **426**

**Entertainment
   in London** **441**

**London
   Connections** **457**

**Day Trips from
   London**.................. **471**
▶ Windsor 472
▶ Cambridge 488
▶ Stonehenge 506

**Britain: Past
   and Present**.......... **513**

Practicalities............ **534**
Tourist Information 534
Travel Tips 535
Money 536
Sightseeing 542
Sleeping 544
Eating 552
Staying Connected 560
Transportation............. 567
Resources................. 571

Appendix **575**
Useful Contacts 575
Holidays and Festivals 576
Recommended
   Books and Films 577
Conversions and Climate 581
Packing Checklist.......... 584
British-Yankee
   Vocabulary 585

Index..................... **590**
Map Index **607**

LEGEND

- - - - - Rail Line
Pedestrian-Friendly Area
Popular Shopping Area
- - - - Pedestrian Path
⊖ Underground/Tube Station
≠ Train Station
■ Point of Interest
ℹ Tourist Information

SIGHTS

1 10 Downing Street
2 Apsley House (Wellington Museum)
3 Banqueting House
4 British Museum
5 Buckingham Palace & Queen's Gallery
6 Changing of the Guard
7 Churchill War Rooms
8 Covent Garden
9 Horse Guards
10 Houses of Parliament & Big Ben
11 Leicester Square
12 National Gallery

To Marylebone Station

HARROW RD.

N. WHARF RD.

PADDINGTON STATION (TRAINS TO HEATHROW)

Paddington

BAYSWATER

CRAVEN RD.
PRAED ST.
SPRING ST.
SUSSEX PL.
SUSSEX GDNS.
LANCASTER TERR.
Lancaster Gate

CONNAUGHT ST.

EDGWARE RD.

HYDE PARK ST.

CUMBERLAND GATE

BAYSWATER RD.

N. CARRIAGE DR.

WIGMORE ST.

Marble Arch

MARBLE ARCH ⊖ OXFORD ST.

SPEAKERS' CORNER ■ 18

To Wallace Collection & Madame Tussauds

SELFRIDGES

N. AUDLEY ST.
DUKE ST.
PARK ST.
UPPER BROOK ST.
Grosvenor Square
UPPER GROSVENOR ST.
US EMBASSY
MOUNT ST.
S. AUDLEY ST.

500 Meters
500 Yards

N

Hyde Park

To Kensington Palace

Kensington Gardens

The Serpentine

SERPENTINE GALLERY

DIANA FOUNTAIN

W. CARRIAGE DR.

ROTTEN ROW

BANDSTAND ■

ROSE GARDEN

PARK LN.

APSLEY HOUSE 2

ALBERT MEMORIAL

S. CARRIAGE DR.

KENSINGTON RD.

KNIGHTSBRIDGE

WELLINGTON ARCH

Hyde Park Corner ⊖

GROSVENOR CRESCENT

16 ROYAL ALBERT HALL

PRINCE CONSORT RD.

PRINCE'S GDNS.

ENNISMORE GDNS.

RUTLAND GATE

Knightsbridge ⊖

HARVEY NICHOLS

THE CAPITAL HOTEL ■

LOWNDES SQ.

CRESCENT
WILTON

Belgrave Square

CHAPEL ST.

IMPERIAL COLLEGE RD.
EXHIBITION RD.

SCIENCE MUSEUM

NATURAL HISTORY MUSEUM 14

VICTORIA & ALBERT MUSEUM 22

BROMPTON RD.

BEAUCHAMP PL.

HARRODS

BASIL ST.

PONT ST.

SLOANE ST.

PAVILION RD.

CADOGAN LN.

BELGRAVIA

EATON PL.

BELGRAVE PL.

CROMWELL ROAD

THURLOE PL.

Thurloe Square

THURLOE ST.

WALTON ST.

HASKER ST.

MOORE ST.

CADOGAN ST.

DRAYCOTT PL.

KING'S RD.

CHESTER ROW
LYALL ROW

S. EATON PL.

South Kensington ⊖

PELHAM ST.

DRAYCOTT AVE.

SLOANE AVE.

ELYSTAN ST.

Sloane Square ⊖

LOWER SLOANE ST.

BOURNE ST.

EBURY ST.

OLD BROMPTON RD.

SUMNER PL.

Onslow Square

ONSLOW GDNS.

FULHAM RD.

IXWORTH PL.

CALE ST.

SOUTH KENSINGTON

CHELSEA

To National Army Museum ↓

KING'S RD.

HOLBEIN PL.

PIMLICO RD.

West London

13 National Portrait Gallery
14 Natural History & Science Museums
15 Piccadilly Circus
16 Royal Albert Hall
17 Royal Mews
18 Speakers' Corner
19 St. Martin-in-the-Fields
20 Tate Britain
21 Trafalgar Square
22 Victoria & Albert Museum
23 Westminster Abbey

To British Library & St. Pancras, Euston & King's Cross Staions

BLOOMSBURY

BRITISH MUSEUM

Bedford Square

CARTOON MUSEUM

Tottenham Court Road

NEW OXFORD ST.

HIGH HOLBORN

ST. GILES

Bond Street

OXFORD ST.

Oxford Circus

Hanover Square

Soho Square

SOHO

DENMARK ST.

Covent Garden

COVENT GARDEN

SOTHEBY'S AUCTION HOUSE

CHINATOWN

Leicester Square

Berkeley Square

PICCADILLY CIRCUS

ROYAL ACADEMY OF ARTS

Leicester Square

NATIONAL GALLERY

STRAND

Charing Cross Station

MAYFAIR

Green Park

FORTNUM & MASON

ST. JAMES

Trafalgar Square

RITZ HOTEL

CHRISTIE'S

St. James's Square

ADMIRALTY ARCH

ST. JAMES'S PALACE

MARLBOROUGH ST.

THE MALL

HORSE GUARDS PARADE

WHITEHALL PLACE

Green Park

QUEEN VICTORIA MEMORIAL

St. James's Park

DOWNING ST.

CENOTAPH

CONSTITUTION HILL

BUCKINGHAM PALACE

STATE APARTMENTS ENTRANCE

BIRDCAGE WALK

WELLINGTON BARRACKS

KING CHARLES ST.

Westminster

Buckingham Palace Gardens (private)

ROYAL MEWS

PALACE ST.

BUCKINGHAM GATE

St. James's Park

GREAT GEORGE ST.

ST. MARGARET'S

Parliament Square

BIG BEN

HOUSES OF PARLIAMENT

PETTY FRANCE

WESTMINSTER ABBEY

WESTMINSTER

LITTLE BEN

VICTORIA STREET

Dean's Yard

JEWEL TOWER

GREAT PETER ST.

WESTMINSTER CATHEDRAL

Smith Square

ST. JOHN'S

VICTORIA STATION (TRAINS TO GATWICK)

VICTORIA COACH STATION

Eccleston Square

Warwick Square

BELGRAVE RD.

Westminster School Playing Fields

HORSEFERRY RD.

PAGE ST.

LAMBETH BRIDGE

River

Thames

PIMLICO

TATE BRITAIN

MILLBANK PIER

East London

Barbican
BEECH ST.
CHISWELL ST.
SUN ST.
LONG LN.
ALDERSGATE
SILK ST.
MOORE LN.
MOORGATE
ELDON ST.
LIVERPOOL STREET STATION
SPITALFIELDS MARKET
COMMERCIAL ST.
BRICK LN.
BARBICAN CENTRE
BRUSHFIELD
EAST END
BARBICAN
MOORFIELDS
FINSBURY CIRCUS
Moorgate
LIVERPOOL ST.
Liverpool Street
MIDDLESEX ST.
WENTWORTH ST.
Aldgate East
MUSEUM OF LONDON
20
LONDON WALL
LONDON WALL
PETTICOAT LANE MARKET
GOULSTONE ST.
ANGEL ST.
WOOD ST.
OLD BROAD ST.
HOUNDSDITCH
CUTLER ST.
WHITECHAPEL HIGH ST.
GRESHAM ST.
ALIE ST.
LEADENHALL MARKET
St. Paul's
THE CITY
BANK OF ENGLAND
TOWER 42
30 ST. MARY AXE ("THE GHERKIN")
DUKES PL.
ST. MARY AXE
Aldgate
BRAHAM ST.
ST. PAUL'S
28
CHEAPSIDE
ONE NEW CHANGE
THREADNEEDLE ST.
KING WILLIAM ST.
LOMBARD ST.
CORNHILL
LEADENHALL ST.
LLOYD'S OF LONDON
WHITE-CHAPEL
MINORIES
MANSELL ST.
ST. MARY-LE-BOW
Bank
GRACECHURCH ST.
14
LEADENHALL MARKET
COOPERS ROW
VICTORIA ST.
Mansion House
MANSION HOUSE
CANNON ST.
FENCHURCH ST.
20 FENCHURCH ("WALKIE-TALKIE")
Tower Hill
18
MILLENNIUM BRIDGE
UPPER THAMES ST.
CANNON STREET STATION
Cannon Street
Monument
THE MONUMENT
19
LOWER THAMES ST.
BYWARD ST.
TOWER HILL
BANKSIDE PIER
30
TATE MODERN
SOUTHWARK BRIDGE
LOWER THAMES
ALL HALLOWS
33
TOWER OF LONDON
ST. KATHARINE DOCK
SIDE
24
SHAKESPEARE'S GLOBE
PARK ST.
8
4
LONDON BRIDGE
LONDON BRIDGE PIER
TOWER PIER
HMS BELFAST
9
ST. KATHARINE'S PIER
SUMNER ST.
London Bridge
Tooley St.
TOWER BRIDGE
32
SOUTHWARK ST.
SOUTH-WARK
26
BATTLE BRIDGE LN.
THE SCOOP
CITY HALL
3
BOROUGH MARKET
1
22
29
LONDON BRIDGE STATION
UNION ST.
THE SHARD
ST. THOMAS ST.
UNICORN THEATRE
TOOLEY ST.
NEWCOMEN ST.
SNOWSFIELDS
BERMONDSEY
SOUTHWARK BRIDGE RD.
MARSHALSEA
REDCROSS WY.
BOROUGH HIGH ST.
TABARD ST.
GREAT DOVER ST.
Borough
TRINITY ST.
N
RD.
HARPER RD.
500 Meters
500 Yards
NEW KENT RD.
HEYGATE ST.
RODNEY RD.
WALWORTH RD.
BROWNING ST.

SIGHTS

1. Borough Market
2. BFI Southbank (Cinema)
3. City Hall
4. The Clink Prison Museum
5. Courtauld Gallery
6. Covent Garden
7. To Geffrye Museum
8. Golden Hinde Replica
9. HMS Belfast
10. Houses of Parliament & Big Ben
11. Imperial War Museum
12. The Inns of Court
13. Jubilee Walkway
14. Leadenhall Market
15. London Duck (Land & Sea) Tours
16. London Eye
17. London Transport Museum
18. Millennium Bridge
19. The Monument
20. Museum of London
21. Old Bailey
22. Old Operating Theatre Museum & Herb Garret
23. Royal Courts of Justice
24. Shakespeare's Globe
25. Sir John Soane's Museum
26. Southwark Cathedral
27. St. Bride's Church
28. St. Paul's Cathedral
29. The Shard (Observation Decks)
30. Tate Modern
31. Temple Church
32. Tower Bridge
33. Tower of London

MAYOR OF LONDON

Turnpike Lane
Crouch Hill
Manor House
Upper Holloway
Arsenal
Holloway Road
Caledonian Road
Highbury & Islington ≷
Caledonian Road & Barnsbury
Canonbury
Angel
Farringdon
Old Street ≷
Barbican
≷ Liverpool Street
≷ Moorgate
St. Paul's
Bank
Cannon Street ≷
Monument
Tower Hill
≷ Fenchurch Street
Tower Gateway
≷ London Bridge
Bermondsey
Borough

Harringay Green Lanes
South Tottenham
Seven Sisters ≷
Finsbury Park ≷
Tottenham Hale ≷
Walthamstow Queen's Road
Dalston Kingsland
Hackney Central
Dalston Junction
Homerton
Hackney Wick
Haggerston
Hoxton
Bethnal Green
Mile End
Shoreditch High Street
Aldgate East
Aldgate
Stepney Green
Whitechapel
Shadwell
Limehouse ≷
Wapping
Rotherhithe
Canada Water
Surrey Quays

Woodford
South Woodford
Snaresbrook
Blackhorse Road
Walthamstow Central ≷
Redbridge
Wanstead
Gants Hill
Leytonstone
Leytonstone High Road
Leyton Midland Road
Leyton
Wanstead Park
≷ Stratford International
Stratford
Woodgrange Park
Stratford High Street
Barking
Pudding Mill Lane
Abbey Road
East Ham
Upton Park
Bow Road
Plaistow
Bromley-by-Bow
West Ham ≷
Bow Church
Devons Road
Star Lane
Langdon Park
All Saints
East India
Canning Town
Royal Victoria
Westferry
Poplar
Blackwall
Emirates Royal Docks
West India Quay
Canary Wharf
North Greenwich
Emirates Greenwich Peninsula
West Silvertown
Heron Quays
South Quay
Crossharbour
Mudchute
Island Gardens
Cutty Sark for Maritime Greenwich
≷ Queens Road Peckham
New Cross Gate ≷
New Cross ≷
Greenwich ≷
Deptford Bridge
Eleverson Road
Lewisham ≷
≷ Peckham Rye
Honor Oak Park

River Thames

Bakerloo
Central
Circle
District
District open weekends, public holidays and some Olympia events
Northern
Hammersmith & City
Jubilee
Metropolitan
Piccadilly
Victoria
Waterloo & City
DLR
London Overground
Emirates Air Line

Correct at time of going to print

Reg. user No. 15/2836/P

Version B 12.2014

© Transport for London

UNDERGROUND

TRANSPORT FOR LONDON

EVERY JOURNEY MATTERS

England

LEGEND

═══**A-24**═══	Freeway/Motorway
─────	Major Rail Line
✈	Airport
▲	National Park/Natural Wonder
■	Ruin, Museum, Other Point of Interest
⌂	Castle/Monument/Palace

50 Kilometers
50 Miles

North Sea

• Berwick-upon-Tweed
Holy Island
Beal
■ BAMBURGH CASTLE
• Alnwick
R'S
WALL
Newcastle-upon-Tyne
BEAMISH MUSEUM ■ • Durham
A-1 • Middlesbrough
YORKSHIRE DALES ▲ • Staithes
NORTH YORK MOORS ▲ • Grosmont
RIEVAULX ABBEY ■ • Whitby
• Thirsk • Goathland • Robin Hood's Bay
• Hutton-le-Hole • Pick. • Scarborough
CASTLE HOWARD ■ EDEN CAMP ■
Leeds • • York • Bridlington
M-62 • Doncaster
• Sheffield • Kingston-upon-Hull
M-1 • Grimsby
GLAND MIDLANDS
• Lincoln
• Derby • Newark • Skegness
• Nottingham • Boston
M-1 The Wash
Leicester • • Stamford • King's Lynn • Cromer
• Coventry • Peterborough • Norwich
• Warwick • Northampton • Ely EAST • Great Yarmouth
Stratford • ANGLIA
WOLDS • Cambridge
• Moreton
BLENHEIM PALACE ⌂ Luton ✈ • Ipswich To Amsterdam, Netherlands
• Oxford • Hertford Stansted ✈ • Harwich
M-40 • Leavesden **M-11** • Colchester To Hoek van Holland, Netherlands
• Didcot Thames
• Reading London ✈ ✈ Southend Zeebrugge
HIGHCLERE ■ • Windsor City ✈ • Southend-on-Sea
M-3 Heathrow Greenwich Ostende • Bruges
• Winchester Gatwick ✈ Whitstable
SISSINGHURST GARDENS ■ • Ramsgate
Southampton • ARUNDEL ⌂ KENT Canterbury ⌂ Dunkerque E-40
Portsmouth • • Battle • Ashford WHITE CLIFFS OF DOVER
FISHBOURNE ROMAN PALACE ■ PEVENSEY ■ Folkestone • Dover BELGIUM
Newport • • Brighton • Hastings Channel Tunnel Calais E-17
Isle of Wight Newhaven • Alfriston Rye
• Eastbourne Lille
Channel BEACHY HEAD FRANCE E-42
To St-Malo, France To Ouistreham, France To Dieppe, France A-16 A-26
To Paris To Paris To Brussels

Rick Steves

LONDON

2016

INTRODUCTION

Blow through the city on a double-decker bus, and take a pinch-me-I'm-in-London walk through the West End. Ogle the crown jewels at the Tower of London, hear the chimes of Big Ben, and see the Houses of Parliament in action. Cruise the Thames River, and take a spin on the London Eye. Hobnob with the tombstones in Westminster Abbey, visit with Leonardo, Botticelli, and Rembrandt in the National Gallery, and explore Harry Potter's magical realm at the film studio in Leavesden. Enjoy Shakespeare in a replica of the Globe Theatre and marvel at a glitzy, fun musical at a modern-day theater. Whisper across the dome of St. Paul's Cathedral, then rummage through our civilization's attic at the British Museum. And sip your tea with pinky raised and clotted cream dribbling down your scone.

You can enjoy some of Europe's best people-watching at Covent Garden, and snap to at Buckingham Palace's Changing of the Guard. Just sit in Victoria Station, Piccadilly Circus, or a major Tube station and observe. Tip a pint in a pub with a chatty local, and beach-comb the Thames. Spend one evening at a theater and the other nights catching your breath.

London is more than its museums and landmarks. It's the L.A., D.C., and N.Y.C. of Britain—a living, breathing, thriving organism...a coral reef of humanity. The city has changed dramatically in recent years, and many visitors are surprised to find how "un-English" it is. ESL (English as a second language) seems like the city's first language, as white people are now a minority in major parts of the city that once symbolized white imperialism. Arabs have nearly bought out the area north of Hyde Park. Chinese takeouts outnumber fish-and-chips shops. Eastern Europeans pull pints in British pubs, and Italians express your espresso. Many hotels are run by people with foreign accents (who hire English

Map Legend

Viewpoint	Prehistoric Sight		Tunnel
Entrance	Taxi Stand		Railway
Tourist Info	Tram		Mtn. Rail
Restroom	Bus Stop		Ferry/Boat Route
Castle, Manor House	Parking		Airport
Church	Tube		Stairs
Statue/Point of Interest	Pedestrian Zone		Walk/Tour Route
Pub	Park		Trail

Use this legend to help you navigate the maps in this book.

chambermaids), while outlying suburbs are home to huge communities of Indians and Pakistanis. London is a city of eight million separate dreams, inhabiting a place that tolerates and encourages them. With the English Channel Tunnel and discount airlines making travel between Britain and the Continent easier than ever, London is learning—sometimes fitfully—to live as a microcosm of its formerly vast empire.

The city, which has long attracted tourists, seems perpetually at your service, with an impressive slate of sights, entertainment, and eateries, all linked by a great transit system. Come prepared to celebrate all the tradition and fanfare of yesterday while catching the buzz of a city that's trumpeting its future.

ABOUT THIS BOOK

Rick Steves London 2016 is a personal tour guide in your pocket. Better yet, it's actually two tour guides in your pocket: The co-author of this book is Gene Openshaw. Since our first "Europe through the gutter" trip together as high school buddies in the 1970s, Gene and I have been exploring the wonders of the Old World. An inquisitive historian and lover of European culture, Gene wrote most of this book's self-guided museum tours and neighborhood walks. Together, Gene and I keep this book current and accurate (though, for simplicity, from this point "we" will shed our respective egos and become "I").

In this book, you'll find the following chapters:

Orientation to London has specifics on public transportation, helpful hints, local tour options, easy-to-read maps, and tourist information. The "Planning Your Time" section suggests a schedule for how to best use your limited time.

Sights in London describes the top attractions and includes their cost and hours.

The **Self-Guided Walks** cover Westminster (from Big Ben

Key to This Book

Updates

This book is updated every year—but things change. For the latest, visit www.ricksteves.com/update.

Abbreviations and Times

I use the following symbols and abbreviations in this book: Sights are rated:

▲▲▲	Don't miss
▲▲	Try hard to see
▲	Worthwhile if you can make it
No rating	Worth knowing about

Tourist information offices are abbreviated as **TI,** and bathrooms are **WC**s. To categorize accommodations, I use a **Sleep Code** (described on page 375).

Like Europe, this book uses the **24-hour clock.** It's the same through 12:00 noon, then keeps going: 13:00, 14:00, and so on. For anything over 12, subtract 12 and add p.m. (14:00 is 2:00 p.m.).

When giving **opening times,** I include both peak season and off-season hours if they differ. So, if a museum is listed as "May-Oct daily 9:00-16:00," it should be open from 9:00 a.m. until 4:00 p.m. from the first day of May until the last day of October (but expect exceptions).

A 📖 symbol in a sight listing means that the sight is described in greater detail elsewhere—either with its own self-guided tour, or as part of a self-guided walk. A 𝛀 symbol indicates that a free, downloadable self-guided audio tour is available.

For **transit** or **tour departures,** I first list the frequency, then the duration. So, a train connection listed as "2/hour, 1.5 hours" departs twice each hour, and the journey lasts an hour and a half.

to Trafalgar Square); the West End (it's the thee-ah-ter district, dahling, with restaurants and shops galore, from Leicester Square and Covent Garden to Soho and Piccadilly Circus); The City (the financial district—banks, churches, and courts busy with barristers and baristas); Bankside (on the South Bank, through Shakespeare's world to the Tate Modern); and the Docklands (London's new and creatively planned urban district).

The **Self-Guided Tours** lead you through London's most fascinating museums and sights: Westminster Abbey, the Houses of Parliament, the National Gallery, the National Portrait Gallery, the Courtauld Gallery, the British Museum, the British Library, St. Paul's Cathedral, the Tower of London, the Tate Modern, the Victoria and Albert Museum, and the Tate Britain. The Greenwich Tour ties together the major sights of that London borough.

Sleeping in London describes my favorite hotels, from good-value deals to cushy splurges.

Eating in London serves up a buffet of options, from inexpensive pubs to fancy restaurants.

London with Children includes my top recommendations for keeping your kids (and you) happy in London.

Shopping in London gives you tips on how to enjoy London's celebrated shops, bustling markets, and symbolic souvenirs, without letting it overwhelm your vacation or ruin your budget.

Entertainment in London is your guide to fun, including theater, music, walks, and wintertime activities.

London Connections lays the groundwork for your smooth arrival and departure, covering transportation by train (including the Eurostar to Paris and Brussels) and by plane (with detailed information on London's major airports), plus connections to the cruise-ship ports of Southampton and Dover.

Day Trips from London include Windsor, Cambridge, and Stonehenge.

Great Britain: Past and Present gives the background of this country, including a timeline of London history, information about British architecture, and a rundown of contemporary events and current challenges.

Practicalities is a traveler's tool kit, with my best tips about money, sightseeing, sleeping, eating, staying connected, and transportation (trains, buses, car rentals, driving, and flights).

The **appendix** has the nuts-and-bolts: useful phone numbers and websites, a holiday and festival list, recommended books and films, a climate chart, a handy packing checklist, and a fun British-Yankee dictionary.

Browse through this book and select your favorite sights. Then have a brilliant trip! Traveling like a temporary local, you'll get the absolute most out of every mile, minute, and dollar. As you visit places I know and love, I'm happy you'll be meeting my favorite Londoners.

Planning

This section will help you get started planning your trip—with advice on trip costs, when to go, and things to know before you take off.

TRAVEL SMART

Your trip to London is like a complex play—it's easier to follow and really appreciate on a second viewing. While no one does the same trip twice to gain that advantage, reading this book in its entirety before your trip accomplishes much the same thing.

Design an itinerary that enables you to visit sights at the best possible times. For example, don't do The City Walk on a weekend when the neighborhood's completely dead if you can visit on a lively weekday. Note festivals, holidays, specifics on sights, and days when sights are closed or most crowded (all covered in this book). Treat Saturday as a weekday, except for transportation connections outside of London (which can be less frequent than on Mon-Fri, and downright meager on Sun). To connect the dots smoothly, read the tips in Practicalities on taking trains and buses, or renting a car and driving. A smart trip is a puzzle—a fun, doable, and worthwhile challenge.

Make your itinerary a mix of intense and relaxed stretches. Every trip—and every traveler—needs slack time (laundry, picnics, people-watching, and so on). Pace yourself. Assume you will return.

Even with the best-planned itinerary, you'll need to be flexible. Update your plans as you travel. Get online or call ahead to double-check tourist information, learn the latest on sights (special events, tour schedules, and so on), book tickets and tours, make reservations, reconfirm hotels, and research transportation connections.

London Almanac

Population: Approximately 8.3 million people

Currency: British pound (GBP)

City Layout: London is divided into the City of London (the main financial district) and 32 administrative boroughs—12 in inner London.

Tallest Building: The Shard stands at 1,020 feet, making it the tallest building in Western Europe—for now.

Tourist Tracks: Each year London hosts 16 million tourists, most of whom stop to take a photo at Trafalgar Square. London's most popular attraction, the British Museum, sees 6 million visitors annually.

Popular Misconception: "Big Ben" refers not to the clock, but instead to its 13-ton bell.

Culture Count: While the Queen's English is still the language of the land, fewer than half the residents of inner London speak English as their first language. Nearly 300 different languages are spoken in London's schools. About 60 percent of Londoners are white (many of them Continental Europeans rather than Brits), but the incredible diversity of the rest of the population make this city a global melting pot. Some 17 percent of Londoners are Asian (including 7 percent who are Indian and Bangladeshi), and 13 percent are black, including many from African countries (7 percent of Londoners) and the Caribbean (4 percent). Six in 10 Brits call themselves Christian (half of those are Anglican), but in any given week, more Londoners visit a mosque than an Anglican church.

Fun Food Facts: Traditionally, London's most popular takeaway foods have been fish-and-chips and minced-meat pie (the pies were originally filled with eels...so minced-meat is an improvement). But it's not all about meat; PETA recently named London the world's most vegan-friendly city. These days you'll find more gourmet sandwich and prepackaged-meals shops than "chippies."

Need a Restroom? Ask for the toilet, loo, lavatory, or bog.

Oldest Pub: The Lamb and Flag in Covent Garden. First licensed in 1623, it was once known as the Bucket of Blood, thanks to rowdy, bare-knuckle fights held there.

Average Londoner: The average Londoner is about 34 years old, has 1.7 children, and will live until the age of 80. He/she earns 20 percent more than those in other parts of Great Britain, but pays almost twice as much for housing. He/she will drink 75,000 cups of tea in a lifetime and consumes less alcohol per week than the average Brit.

Enjoy the friendliness of the British people. Connect with the culture. Set up your own quest for the best pub, silly sign, or chocolate bar. Slow down and be open to unexpected experiences. You speak the language—use it! Ask questions—most locals are eager to point you in their idea of the right direction. Keep a notepad in your pocket for noting directions, organizing your thoughts, and confirming prices. Wear your money belt, learn the currency, and figure out how to estimate prices in dollars. Those who expect to travel smart, do.

TRIP COSTS

Five components make up your trip costs: airfare, surface transportation, room and board, sightseeing and entertainment, and shopping and miscellany.

Airfare: A basic round-trip flight from the US to London can cost on average, about $1,000-2,000 total, depending on where you fly from and when (cheaper in winter). If London is part of a longer trip, consider saving time and money in Europe by flying into one city and out of another; for instance, into London and out of Paris. Overall, Kayak.com is the best place to start searching for flights on a combination of mainstream and budget carriers.

Surface Transportation: For a typical one-week visit, allow about $55 for the Tube and buses (for a Seven-Day Travelcard transportation pass). Round-trip train rides to day-trip destinations cost about $30 for Windsor, $40 for Cambridge, and $60 for Salisbury, where you can catch a $22 bus to Stonehenge. You can save money by taking buses instead of trains. Add $95 if you plan to take a taxi between London's Heathrow Airport and your hotel (or save money by taking the Tube, train, bus, or airport shuttle).

Room and Board: London is one of Europe's most expensive major capitals. But if you're careful, you can manage comfortably in London in 2016 on $135 a day per person for room and board. A $135-a-day budget allows $15 for lunch, $30 for dinner, and $90 for lodging (based on two people splitting the cost of a basic $180 double room that includes breakfast). Students and tightwads can do it for as little as $70 a day ($45 for hostel bed, $25 for groceries).

Sightseeing and Entertainment: You'll pay more in London for sights that charge admission than you will anywhere else in Europe. Fortunately, most of London's best sights are free (although many request a donation), including the British Museum, National Gallery, National Portrait Gallery, Tate Britain, Tate Modern, British Library, and the Victoria and Albert Museum. (For a list of free museums—and advice on saving money on sightseeing—see "Affording London's Sights" on page 70.)

Figure on paying roughly $25-35 each for the major sights that charge admission (e.g., Westminster Abbey-$31, Tower of

London-$38), $12-20 for guided walks, and $50 for bus tours and splurge experiences (plays range $25-100). An overall average of $50-60 a day works for most people. Don't skimp here. After all, this category is the driving force behind your trip—you came to sightsee, enjoy, and experience London.

Shopping and Miscellany: Figure roughly $2 per postcard, $3 for tea or an ice cream cone, and $6 per pint of beer. Shopping can vary in cost from nearly nothing to a small fortune. Good budget travelers find that this category has little to do with assembling a trip full of lifelong memories.

WHEN TO GO

July and August are peak season—my favorite time—with long days, the best weather, and the busiest schedule of tourist fun. Prices and crowds don't go up in summer as dramatically in Britain as they do in much of Europe, except for holidays and festivals (see page 576). Still, travelers during "shoulder season" (May, early June, Sept, and early Oct) enjoy lower prices, smaller crowds, decent weather, and the full range of sights and tourist fun spots.

Winter travelers find fewer crowds and soft room prices, but shorter sightseeing hours. The weather can be cold and dreary, and nightfall draws the shades on sightseeing well before dinnertime. While England's rural charm falls with the leaves, London sightseeing is fine in the winter, and is especially popular during the Christmas season. For more on planning a winter holiday visit, read "Winter Diversions" (in the Entertainment in London chapter).

Plan for rain no matter when you go. Just keep traveling and take full advantage of "bright spells." The weather can change several times a day, but rarely is it extreme. As the locals say, "There's no bad weather, only inappropriate clothing." Bring a jacket, and dress in layers. Temperatures below 32°F cause headlines, and days that break 80°F—while more common in recent years—are still infrequent in London. (For more information, see the climate chart in the appendix.) Weather-wise, July and August are not much better than shoulder months. May and June can be lovely. While sunshine may be rare, summer days are very long. The midsummer sun is up from 6:30 to 22:30. It's not uncommon to have a gray day, eat dinner, and enjoy hours of sunshine afterward.

KNOW BEFORE YOU GO

Check this list of things to arrange while you're still at home.

You need a **passport**—but no visa or shots—to travel in Great Britain. You may be denied entry into certain European countries if your passport is due to expire within three months of your ticketed date of return. Get it renewed if you'll be cutting it close. It can take up to six weeks to get or renew a passport. (For more on pass-

How Was Your Trip?

Were your travels fun, smooth, and meaningful? If you'd like to share your tips, concerns, and discoveries, please fill out the survey at www.ricksteves.com/feedback. I value your feedback. Thanks in advance.

ports, see www.travel.state.gov.) Pack a photocopy of your passport in your luggage in case the original is lost or stolen.

Book rooms well in advance if you'll be traveling during peak season or any major holidays or festivals (see page 576).

For simplicity, I **book plays** while in London (but if you have your heart set on a hot show, buying tickets in advance online or by phone is safer). For the current schedule, visit www.officiallondontheatre.co.uk. For more information, see the Entertainment in London chapter.

Advance reservations are required or advantageous for a few of London's major attractions. Booking ahead is not compulsory for the **Churchill War Rooms** or **St. Paul's Cathedral,** but it will let you skip the wait of up to 30 minutes at each sight. The only way to guarantee entrance to **Stonehenge** is by reserving in advance (see page 507); and if you want to go inside the stone circle, book your visit as soon as you know the date you'll be there.

Call your **debit- and credit-card companies** to let them know the countries you'll be visiting, to ask about fees, request your PIN code (it will be mailed to you), and more. See page 538 for details.

Do your homework if you want to buy **travel insurance.** Compare the cost of the insurance to the cost of your potential loss. Also, check whether your existing insurance (health, homeowners, or renters) covers you and your possessions overseas. For more information, see www.ricksteves.com/insurance.

If you plan to hire a **local guide,** reserve ahead by email. Popular guides can get booked up.

If you're bringing a **mobile device,** consider signing up for an international plan for cheaper calls, texts, and data (see page 561). Download any apps you might want to use on the road, such as maps, transit schedules, and **Rick Steves Audio Europe** (see page 5).

You won't want to drive in London because of the traffic and congestion charge (covered on page 32), but if you'll be **renting a car** for touring Britain, you'll need your driver's license.

If you'll be taking the **Eurostar train,** consider buying your ticket in advance; for details, see page 467.

Traveling as a Temporary Local

We travel all the way to Europe to enjoy differences—to become temporary locals. You'll experience frustrations. Certain truths that we find "God-given" or "self-evident," such as cold beer, ice in drinks, bottomless cups of coffee, "the customer is king," and bigger being better, are suddenly not so true. One of the benefits of travel is the eye-opening realization that there are logical, civil, and even better alternatives. A willingness to go local ensures that you'll enjoy a full dose of British hospitality.

Europeans generally like Americans. But if there is a negative aspect to the image the British have of Americans, it's that we are loud, wasteful, ethnocentric, too informal (which can seem disrespectful), and a bit naive.

The British (and Europeans in general) place a high value on speaking quietly in restaurants and on trains. Listen while on the bus or in a restaurant—the place can be packed, but the decibel level is low. Try to adjust your volume accordingly to show respect for the culture.

Although the British look bemusedly at some of our Yankee excesses—and worriedly at others—they nearly always afford us individual travelers all the warmth we deserve.

Judging from all the happy feedback I receive from travelers who have used this book, it's safe to assume you'll enjoy a great, affordable vacation—with the finesse of an independent, experienced traveler.

Thanks, and have a brilliant holiday!

Rick Steves

Back Door Travel Philosophy

From *Rick Steves Europe Through the Back Door*

Travel is intensified living—maximum thrills per minute and one of the last great sources of legal adventure. Travel is freedom. It's recess, and we need it.

Experiencing the real Europe requires catching it by surprise, going casual..."through the Back Door."

Affording travel is a matter of priorities. (Make do with the old car.) You can eat and sleep—simply, safely, and enjoyably—anywhere in Europe for $100 a day plus transportation costs. In many ways, spending more money only builds a thicker wall between you and what you traveled so far to see. Europe is a cultural carnival, and time after time, you'll find that its best acts are free and the best seats are the cheap ones.

A tight budget forces you to travel close to the ground, meeting and communicating with the people. Never sacrifice sleep, nutrition, safety, or cleanliness to save money. Simply enjoy the local-style alternatives to expensive hotels and restaurants.

Connecting with people carbonates your experience. Extroverts have more fun. If your trip is low on magic moments, kick yourself and make things happen. If you don't enjoy a place, maybe you don't know enough about it. Seek the truth. Recognize tourist traps. Give a culture the benefit of your open mind. See things as different, but not better or worse. Any culture has plenty to share. When an opportunity presents itself, make it a habit to say "yes."

Of course, travel, like the world, is a series of hills and valleys. Be fanatically positive and militantly optimistic. If something's not to your liking, change your liking.

Travel can make you a happier American, as well as a citizen of the world. Our Earth is home to seven billion equally precious people. It's humbling to travel and find that other people don't have the "American Dream"—they have their own dreams. Europeans like us, but with all due respect, they wouldn't trade passports.

Thoughtful travel engages us with the world. It reminds us what is truly important. By broadening perspectives, travel teaches new ways to measure quality of life.

Globetrotting destroys ethnocentricity, helping us understand and appreciate other cultures. Rather than fear the diversity on this planet, celebrate it. Among your most prized souvenirs will be the strands of different cultures you choose to knit into your own character. The world is a cultural yarn shop, and Back Door travelers are weaving the ultimate tapestry. Join in!

ORIENTATION TO LONDON

London is more than 600 square miles of urban jungle—a world in itself and a barrage on all the senses. On my first visit, I felt extremely small. To grasp London more comfortably, see it as the old town in the city center without the modern, congested sprawl. (Even from that perspective, it's still huge.)

The Thames River (pronounced "tems") runs roughly west to east through the city, with most of the visitor's sights on the North Bank. Mentally, maybe even physically, trim down your map to include only the area between the Tower of London (to the east), Hyde Park (west), Regent's Park (north), and the South Bank (south). This is roughly the area bordered by the Tube's Circle Line. This four-mile stretch between the Tower and Hyde Park (about a 1.5-hour walk) looks like a milk bottle on its side (see map on next page), and holds 80 percent of the sights mentioned in this book.

With a core focus and a good orientation, you'll get a sampling of London's top sights, history, and cultural entertainment, and a good look at its ever-changing human face.

The sprawling city becomes much more manageable if you think of it as a collection of neighborhoods.

Central London: This area contains Westminster and what Londoners call the West End. The Westminster district includes Big Ben, Parliament, Westminster Abbey, and Buckingham Palace—the grand government buildings from which Britain is ruled. Trafalgar Square, London's gathering place, has many major museums. The West End is the center of London's cultural life, with bustling squares: Piccadilly Circus and Leicester Square host cinemas, tourist traps, and nighttime glitz. Soho and Covent Garden are thriving people zones with theaters, restaurants, pubs, and boutiques. And Regent and Oxford streets are the city's main shopping zones.

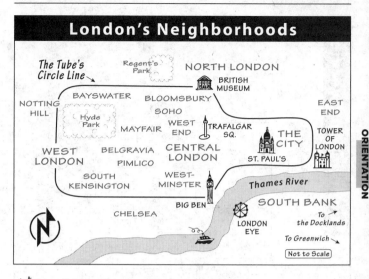

London's Neighborhoods

The Tube's Circle Line

Regent's Park

NORTH LONDON

BRITISH MUSEUM

BAYSWATER · BLOOMSBURY

NOTTING HILL

Hyde Park

SOHO

MAYFAIR · WEST END

EAST END

TRAFALGAR SQ.

WEST LONDON

BELGRAVIA

PIMLICO

CENTRAL LONDON

THE CITY

TOWER OF LONDON

ST. PAUL'S

SOUTH KENSINGTON

WEST-MINSTER

BIG BEN

Thames River

CHELSEA

LONDON EYE

SOUTH BANK

To the Docklands

To Greenwich

Not to Scale

ORIENTATION

North London: Neighborhoods in this part of town—including Bloomsbury, Fitzrovia, and Marylebone—contain such major sights as the British Museum and the overhyped Madame Tussauds Waxworks. Nearby, along busy Euston Road, is the British Library, plus a trio of train stations (one of them, St. Pancras International, is linked to Paris by the Eurostar "Chunnel" train).

The City: Today's modern financial district, called simply "The City," was a walled town in Roman times. Gleaming skyscrapers are interspersed with historical landmarks such as St. Paul's Cathedral, legal sights (Old Bailey), and the Museum of London. The Tower of London and Tower Bridge lie at The City's eastern border.

East London: Just east of The City is the East End—the increasingly gentrified former stomping ground of Cockney ragamuffins and Jack the Ripper.

The South Bank: The South Bank of the Thames River offers major sights (Tate Modern, Shakespeare's Globe, London Eye) linked by a riverside walkway. Within this area, Southwark (SUTH-uck) stretches from the Tate Modern to London Bridge. Pedestrian bridges connect the South Bank with The City and Trafalgar Square.

West London: This huge area contains neighborhoods such as Mayfair, Belgravia, Pimlico, Chelsea, South Kensington, and Notting Hill. It's home to London's wealthy and has many trendy shops and enticing restaurants. Here you'll find a range of museums (Victoria and Albert Museum, Tate Britain, and more), my top hotel recommendations, lively Victoria Station, and the vast green expanses of Hyde Park and Kensington Gardens.

Outside the Center: The Docklands, London's version of

London Map Overview

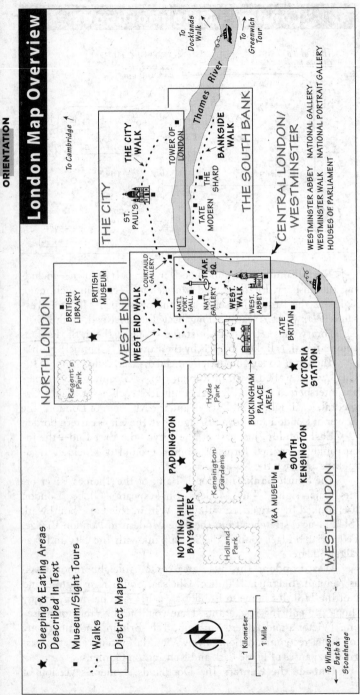

- ★ Sleeping & Eating Areas Described In Text
- ■ Museum/Sight Tours
- ⋯ Walks
- ☐ District Maps

1 Kilometer
1 Mile

NORTH LONDON

WEST END

THE CITY

THE SOUTH BANK

CENTRAL LONDON/ WESTMINSTER

WEST LONDON

Thames River

To Cambridge

To Docklands Walk
To Greenwich Tour

BRITISH LIBRARY
BRITISH MUSEUM

Regent's Park

WEST END WALK

COURTAULD GALLERY

NATL. PORT. GALL.
NATL GALLERY
TRAF. SQ.

ST. PAUL'S

THE CITY WALK

TOWER OF LONDON

THE SHARD

TATE MODERN

BANKSIDE WALK

WEST. WALK
WEST. ABBEY

PADDINGTON

NOTTING HILL/ BAYSWATER

Kensington Gardens

Hyde Park

BUCKINGHAM PALACE AREA

Holland Park

V&A MUSEUM

SOUTH KENSINGTON

VICTORIA STATION

TATE BRITAIN

WESTMINSTER ABBEY   NATIONAL GALLERY
WESTMINSTER WALK   NATIONAL PORTRAIT GALLERY
HOUSES OF PARLIAMENT

To Windsor, Bath & Stonehenge

Manhattan, is farther east than the East End; Olympic Park is just north of the Docklands. Historic Greenwich is southeast of London and across the Thames. Kew Gardens and Hampton Court Palace are southwest of London. North of London is Hampstead Heath and the Warner Bros. Studio Tour for Harry Potter fans.

PLANNING YOUR TIME

London is a super one-week getaway. Its sights can keep even the most fidgety traveler well entertained for seven days. After con-

sidering London's major tourist destinations, I've covered just my favorites in this book. You won't be able to see all of these, so don't try. You'll keep coming back to London. After dozens of visits myself, I still enjoy a healthy list of excuses to return.

For a one-week visit, buy a 7-Day Travelcard (see page 24) and study up on "Affording London's Sights" (see page 70). Armed with this information and your Travelcard, you'll feel more like a Londoner, forget the high cost of sightseeing, and experience the city with a better attitude.

Here's a suggested schedule for London's best seven days:

Day 1

9:00	Tower of London (crown jewels first, then Beefeater tour and White Tower; note that on Sun-Mon, the Tower opens at 10:00).
13:00	Grab a picnic, catch a boat at Tower Pier, and relax with lunch on the Thames while cruising to Westminster Pier.
14:30	Tour Westminster Abbey, and consider their evensong service (usually at 17:00, at 15:00 on Sun and off-season Sat, never on Wed).
17:00 (or after evensong)	Follow my self-guided Westminster Walk. When you're finished, you could return to the Houses of Parliament and possibly pop into see the House of Commons in action (but check their schedule first—see page 44).

Day 2

8:30	Take a double-decker hop-on, hop-off London sightseeing bus tour (from Victoria Station or Green Park), and hop off for the Changing of the Guard.
11:00	Buckingham Palace (guards change most days May-

July at 11:30, alternate days Aug-April—confirm online).

12:00 Walk through St. James's Park to enjoy London's delightful park scene.

13:00 After lunch, tour the Churchill War Rooms.

16:00 Tour the National Gallery.

Evening Have dinner—maybe at a pub?—before a play, concert, or evening walking tour. For ideas, see the Entertainment in London chapter; consider these activities for any evening over the following days.

Day 3

9:00 Follow the first two-thirds of my self-guided walk through The City (as far as St. Paul's), then follow my St. Paul's Cathedral Tour.

15:00 Cross London Bridge and follow my self-guided Bankside Walk along the South Bank of the Thames. Tour Shakespeare's Globe or the Tate Modern if you're interested (or, if it's a day that the Tate Modern is open late, circle back here later). Then walk the Jubilee Walkway from the Millennium Bridge to the London Eye.

Evening Cap your day with South Bank sights and experiences that are open late (a ride on the London Eye—last ascent 20:30-21:30 depending on season; a

Shakespeare play at the Globe—usually at 19:30 in summer; or Tate Modern—open Fri-Sat until 22:00).

Day 4

10:00   Tour the British Museum, then have lunch.

14:00   Tube to Leicester Square to take my self-guided West End Walk to see Covent Garden and Soho, then browse through Regent Street with my Regent Street Shopping Walk.

17:00   Enjoy afternoon tea (at Fortnum & Mason, The Wolseley, or the Orangery at Kensington Palace).

Day 5

Spend the morning exploring a street market (try to make today coincide with the day that your market of choice is busiest—see the Shopping in London chapter for details).

Spend the rest of your day at your choice of major sights. Depending on your interests, choose from the British Library, Tate Britain, Museum of London, Imperial War Museum, or Kew Gardens (consider a cruise to Kew, return to London by Tube).

Day 6

10:00   Cruise from Westminster Pier to Greenwich.

11:15   Tour the salty sights of Greenwich.

16:00   Ride the Docklands Light Railroad (DLR) to the Docklands for my self-guided Docklands Walk and a look at London's emerging "Manhattan."

18:30   Take the DLR or Tube back to London.

Day 7

10:00   Tour the Victoria and Albert Museum.

After lunch (or a picnic in the park), stroll through Hyde Park and visit Kensington Palace. Spend the afternoon at Harrods or other shopping venues.

With More Time

To get a break from big-city London, you can easily spend a day or two side-tripping. Windsor, Cambridge, and Stonehenge each make a satisfying one-day visit.

ORIENTATION

ORIENTATION

Overview

TOURIST INFORMATION

It's amazing how hard it can be to find unbiased sightseeing information and advice in London. You'll see "Tourist Information" offices advertised everywhere, but most of them are private agencies that make a big profit selling tours and advance sightseeing and/or theater tickets; others are run by Transport for London (TFL) and are primarily focused on providing public-transit advice.

The City of London Information Centre next to St. Paul's Cathedral (to the right of the church) is the only publicly funded—and therefore impartial—"real" TI (Mon-Sat 9:30-17:30, Sun 10:00-16:00; Tube: St. Paul's, tel. 020/7332-1456, www.visitthecity.co.uk).

While officially a service of The City (London's financial district), this office also provides information about the rest of London. It sells Oyster cards, London Passes (see page 543), advance "Fast Track" sightseeing tickets (described next), and some National Express bus tickets. It also stocks various free publications: *London Planner* (a free monthly that lists all the sights, events, and hours), some walking-tour brochures, the *Official London Theatre Guide,* a free Tube and bus map, the *Guide to River Thames Boat Services,* and brochures describing self-guided walks in The City (various themes, including Dickens, modern architecture, and film locations).

The TI gives out a free map of The City and sells several citywide maps; ask if they have yet another, free map with a coupon good for 20 percent off admission to St. Paul's. I'd skip their room-booking service (charges a commission) and theater box office (may charge a commission).

Visit London, which serves the greater London area, doesn't have an office you can visit in person—but does have an information-packed website (www.visitlondon.com).

Fast Track Tickets: To skip the ticket-buying queues at certain London sights, you can buy Fast Track tickets in advance—and they can be cheaper than tickets sold right at the sight. They're particularly smart for the Tower of London, the London Eye, and Madame Tussauds Waxworks, all of which get very busy in high season. They're available through various sales outlets around London (including the City of London TI, souvenir stands, and faux-TIs scattered throughout touristy areas).

ARRIVAL IN LONDON

For more information on getting to or from London by train, bus, and plane, see the London Connections chapter.

By Train: London has nine major train stations, all connected by the Tube (subway). All have ATMs, and many of the larger stations also have shops, fast food, exchange offices, and luggage storage. From any station, you can ride the Tube or taxi to your hotel. For more info on train travel, see www.nationalrail.co.uk.

By Bus: The main intercity bus station is Victoria Coach Station, one block southwest of Victoria train/Tube station. For more on bus travel, see www.nationalexpress.com.

By Plane: London has six airports. Most tourists arrive at Heathrow or Gatwick airport, although flights from elsewhere in Europe may land at Stansted, Luton, Southend, or London City airport. For specifics on getting from London's airports to downtown, see the London Connections chapter; for hotels near Heathrow and Gatwick, see the Sleeping in London chapter.

ORIENTATION

HELPFUL HINTS

Theft Alert: Wear your money belt. The Artful Dodger is alive and well in London. Be on guard, particularly on public transportation and in places crowded with tourists, who, considered naive and rich, are targeted. The Changing of the Guard scene is a favorite for thieves. And more than 7,500 purses are stolen annually at Covent Garden alone.

Pedestrian Safety: Cars drive on the left side of the road—which can be as confusing for foreign pedestrians as for foreign drivers. Before crossing a street, I always look right, look left, then look right again just to be sure. Most crosswalks are even painted with instructions, reminding foreign guests to "Look right" or "Look left." While locals are champion jaywalkers, you shouldn't try it; jaywalking is treacherous when you're disoriented about which direction traffic is coming from.

Medical Problems: Local hospitals have good-quality 24-hour-a-day emergency care centers, where any tourist who needs help can drop in and, after a wait, be seen by a doctor. Your hotel has details. St. Thomas' Hospital, immediately across the river from Big Ben, has a fine reputation.

Getting Your Bearings: London is well-signed for visitors. Through an initiative called Legible London, the city has erected thoughtfully designed, pedestrian-focused maps around town—especially handy when exiting Tube stations. In this sprawling city—where predictable grid-planned streets are relatively rare—it's also smart to buy and use a good map.

Maps: Bensons MapGuides' *London Street Map,* sold at many newsstands and bookstores, is my favorite for efficient sightseeing and might be the best £3 you'll spend. I also like *The Handy London Map & Guide* version, which shows every little lane and all the sights, and comes with a transit map.

Getting Online with a Mobile Device: In addition to the Wi-Fi

Daily Reminder

Sunday: The Tower of London and British Museum are both especially crowded today. Speakers' Corner in Hyde Park rants from early afternoon until early evening. These places are closed: Sir John Soane's Museum, and legal sights (Houses of Parliament, City Hall, and Old Bailey; the neighborhood called The City is dead). Westminster Abbey and St. Paul's are open during the day for worship but closed to sightseers. With all these closures, this morning is a good time to take a bus tour. Most big stores open late (around 11:30) and close early (18:00).

Street markets are flourishing at Camden Lock, Spitalfields (at its best today), Petticoat Lane, Brick Lane, and Greenwich, but Portobello Road and Brixton markets are closed (though the Brixton farmers market is open 10:00-14:00). Because of all the market action, it's a good day to take the East End Walk (see page 79). Theaters are quiet, as most actors take today off. (There are a few exceptions, such as Shakespeare's Globe, which offers Sunday performances in summer, and theaters with family-oriented fare, including *The Lion King*, offered year-round.)

Monday: Virtually all sights are open, except Apsley House, Sir John Soane's Museum, and a few others. The Houses of Parliament may be open as late as 22:30.

Tuesday: Virtually all sights are open, except Apsley House. The British Library is open until 20:00, and the Houses of Parliament may be open as late as 22:00. On the first Tuesday of the month, Sir John Soane's Museum is open until 21:00.

Wednesday: Virtually all sights are open. Houses of Parliament

that's likely available at your hotel, many major museums, sights, and even entire boroughs also offer free access. If that's still not enough, consider signing up for a free account with **The Cloud,** a Wi-Fi service found in many convenient spots around London, including most train stations and many museums, coffee shops, cafés, and shopping centers (though the connection can be slow). When you sign up at www.thecloud.net/free-wifi, you'll have to enter a street address and postal code; it doesn't matter which one (use your hotel's, or the Queen's: Buckingham Palace, SW1A 1AA).

Most **Tube stations** and trains have Wi-Fi, but it's free only to those with a British Virgin Media account. However, the Tube's Wi-Fi always lets you access Transport for London's "Journey Planner" (www.tfl.gov.uk), making it easy to look up your city transit options—and get real-time updates on delays—once you're in a station. To use the Tube's pay Wimay be open as late as 22:00.

Thursday: All sights are open, plus evening hours at the National Portrait Gallery (until 21:00).

Friday: All sights are open, except the Houses of Parliament. Sights open late include the British Museum (selected galleries until 20:30), National Gallery (until 21:00), National Portrait Gallery (until 21:00), Victoria and Albert Museum (selected galleries until 22:00), and Tate Modern (until 22:00).

Saturday: Most sights are open, except legal ones (Old Bailey, City Hall; skip The City). The Houses of Parliament are open only with a tour. Tate Modern is open until 22:00. The Tower of London is especially crowded today. Today's the day to hit the Portobello Road street market; the Camden Lock and Greenwich markets are also good.

Notes: St. Martin-in-the-Fields church offers concerts at lunchtime (Mon, Tue, and Fri at 13:00) and in the evening (several nights a week at 19:30, jazz Wed at 20:00).

Evensong occurs nearly daily at St. Paul's (Sun at 15:15 and Tue-Sat at 17:00), Westminster Abbey (Sun at 15:00, Mon-Tue and Thu-Sat at 17:00 except Sat at 15:00 Sept-April), and Southwark Cathedral (Sun at 15:00, Tue-Fri 17:30, Sat at 16:00).

London by Night Sightseeing Tour buses leave from Victoria Station each evening (two departures nightly 20:00 and 21:30 in summer, 19:00 and 21:00 in autumn and winter).

The London Eye spins nightly (last departure 20:30 or 21:30, or even later, depending on the season).

Fi, you can spend £2 for a one-day pass, or £5 for a one-week pass (http://my.virginmedia.com/wifi).

Useful Apps: Tube travelers might want to download MX Apps' free **Tube Map London Underground** (www.mxapps.co.uk), which shows the easiest way to connect station A to station B. While you can always get Tube info on the Web (with Transport for London's "Journey Planner," www.tfl.gov.uk), the app works even when you're not online. When you are online, the app provides live updates about Tube delays and closures. (It doesn't, however, look up bus connections, and sometimes there are fake navigation buttons at the bottom of the screen which are actually ads. Unfortunately, MX Apps' "Bus London" map isn't very useful offline.) The handy **Citymapper** app for London covers every mode of public transit in the city. **City Maps 2Go** lets you download searchable offline maps; their London version is quite good. **Time Out London**'s free app has reviews and listings for theater, museums, movies, and more (download the "Make Your City Amazing" version, which is updated weekly, rather than the boilerplate "Travel Guide" version).

🎧 For free audio versions of some of the self-guided tours in this book (the Westminster Walk, the City Walk, and tours of the British Museum, British Library, and St. Paul's Cathedral), get the Rick Steves Audio Europe app (for details, see page 5).

Travel Bookstores: Located between Covent Garden and Leicester Square, the very good **Stanfords Travel Bookstore** stocks a huge selection of guidebooks (including current editions of nearly all of mine), travel-related novels, maps, and gear (Mon-Sat 9:00-20:00, Sun 11:30-18:00, 12-14 Long Acre, second entrance on Floral Street, Tube: Leicester Square, tel. 020/7836-1321, www.stanfords.co.uk).

Two impressive **Waterstones** bookstores have the biggest collection of travel guides in town: on Piccadilly (Mon-Sat 9:00-22:00, Sun 12:00-18:30, café, great views from top-floor bar—see sidebar on page 88, 203 Piccadilly, tel. 0843-290-8549) and on Trafalgar Square (Mon-Fri 9:00-21:00, Sat 9:30-21:00, Sun 12:00-18:00, Costa Café on second floor, tel. 020/7839-4411).

Baggage Storage: Train stations have replaced lockers with more secure left-luggage counters. Each bag must go through a scanner (just like at the airport). Expect long waits in the morning to check in (up to 45 minutes) and in the afternoon to pick up (each item-£10/24 hours, most stations daily 7:00-23:00). You can also store bags at the airports (similar rates and hours, www.left-baggage.co.uk).

Updates to This Book: For the latest, see www.ricksteves.com/update.

GETTING AROUND LONDON

To travel smart in a city this size, you must get comfortable with public transportation. London's excellent taxis, buses, and subway (Tube) system can take you anywhere you need to go—a blessing for travelers' precious vacation time, not to mention their feet. It's also the most expensive public transit in the world.

While single-ride and paper tickets still exist, for most visitors the Oyster card is simply the only way to go—saving precious time and money.

Public Transit Tickets and Passes

While the transit system has six zones, almost all tourist sights are within Zones 1 and 2, so those are the prices I've listed.

Individual tickets: Individual paper tickets for the Tube are ridiculously expensive (£4.80 per Tube ride). You can buy them at any Tube station, either at (often-crowded) ticket windows or at easy-to-use self-service machines (hit "Adult Single" and enter your destination). Tickets are valid only on the day of purchase. Unless you're literally taking only one Tube ride your entire visit, you'll save money (and time) by buying one of the following multiple-ride passes.

Oyster Card: A pay-as-you-go Oyster card (a plastic card embedded with a computer chip) allows you to ride the Tube, buses, Docklands Light Railway (DLR), and Overground (mostly suburban trains), for about half the rate of individual tickets. To use the card, you simply touch the card against the yellow card reader at the turnstile or entrance, it flashes green, and the fare is automatically deducted. (You must also tap your card again to "touch out" as you exit.)

Buy the card at any Tube station ticket window, or look for nearby shops displaying the Oyster logo, where you can purchase a card or add credit without the wait. You'll pay a £5 deposit up front, then load it with as much credit as you'll need. One ride in Zones 1 and 2 during peak time costs £2.90; off peak is a little cheaper (£2.30 per ride). The system comes with an automatic price cap that guarantees you'll never pay more than £6.40 in one day for riding

within Zones 1 and 2. If you think you'll take more than two rides in a day, £6.40 of credit will cover you, but it's smart to add a little more if you expect to travel outside the city center. If you're staying five or more days, it may be smart to add a 7-Day Travelcard to your Oyster card (see below for details).

Note that Oyster cards are not shareable among companions taking the same ride; each traveler will need his or her own. If your balance gets low, simply add credit—or "top up"—at a ticket window, machine, or shop. You can always see how much credit remains on your card (along with a list of where you've traveled) by touching it to the pad at any ticket machine.

At the end of your trip, you can reclaim your deposit and unused balance (up to £5) by selecting "Pay as you go refund" on any ticket machine that gives change. This will deactivate your card. For balances of more than £5, you'll have to wait in line at a ticket window for your refund. If you do not deactivate your card, the credit never expires—you can use it again on your next trip.

Visitor Oyster Travel Cards, aimed specifically at tourists, have some advantages. But you must purchase them online in advance and have them delivered by mail before your trip, making them more expensive than a regular Oyster card. For more information, visit www.tfl.gov.uk/tickets.

Travelcards: Paper Travelcards let you ride as many times as you want within a one- or a seven-day period for one fixed price, but are only a good deal in limited instances. The card works like a traditional paper ticket: Buy it at any Tube station ticket window or machine, then feed it into a turnstile (and retrieve it) to enter and exit the Tube. On a bus, just show it to the driver when you get on.

Your options are the **Anytime Day Travelcard** (covers Zones 1-4, valid for one day of travel anytime, £12), **Off-Peak Day Travelcard** (covers Zones 1-6, valid for one day of travel after 9:30 on weekdays, anytime on weekends, £12), and **7-Day Travelcard** (£32.10 for Zones 1-2; £58.60 for Zones 1-6). Skip the Anytime or Off-Peak Travelcards unless you're taking full advantage of the discounts that come with them (see below); an Oyster card with its daily cap is almost always a better deal.

The 7-Day Travelcard, which can be added to an Oyster card, is the best option if you're staying five or more days and plan to use public transit a lot. For most travelers, the Zone 1-2 pass works best. Heathrow Airport is in Zone 6, but there's no need to buy the Zones 1-6 version if that's the only ride outside the city center you plan to take—instead you can pay a small supplement to cover the difference.

The Bottom Line

Wondering which pass works best for your trip? On a short visit (three days or fewer), consider purchasing an Oyster card and adding £20-25 of credit (£6.40 daily cap times three days, plus a little extra for any rides outside Zones 1-2). If you'll be taking fewer rides, £15 will be enough, and if not you can always top up. If you're in London for five days or longer, the 7-Day Travelcard—either the paper version or on an Oyster card—will likely pay for itself. Note that certain Travelcards come with sightseeing discounts (see below) that might make them a worthwhile option.

Discounts

Families: A paying adult can take up to four kids (ages 10 and under) for free on the Tube, Docklands Light Railway (DLR), Overground, and buses. Explore other child and student discounts at www.tfl.gov.uk/tickets or ask a clerk at a Tube ticket window which deal is best.

River Cruises: A Travelcard gives you a 33 percent discount on most Thames cruises (see page 39). The Oyster card gives you a 10 percent discount on Thames Clippers (including the Tate Boat museum ferry).

Sightseeing Deal: If you buy a paper Anytime Day or Off-

Peak Day Travelcard at a National Rail train station (not a Tube station), you get same-day, two-for-one discounts at some sights, including the pricey Tower of London (not valid July-Aug), Churchill War Rooms, and Madame Tussauds. For more information, visit www.daysoutguide.co.uk.

By Tube

London's subway system is called the Tube or Underground (but never "subway," which, in Britain, refers to a pedestrian underpass).

The Tube is one of this planet's great people-movers and usually the fastest long-distance transport in town (runs Mon-Sat about 5:00-24:00, Sun about 7:00-23:00; Central, Jubilee, Northern, Piccadilly, and Victoria lines also run Fri-Sat 24 hours). Two other commuter rail lines are tied into the network and use the same tickets: the Docklands Light Railway (called DLR) and the Overground.

Get your bearings by studying a map of the system. At the front of this book, you'll find a Tube map of the city center, with color-coded lines and names. You can also pick up a free, more extensive Tube map at any station, or download a transit app (described earlier).

Each line has a name (such as Circle, Northern, or Bakerloo) and two directions (indicated by the end-of-the-line stops). Find the line that will take you to your destination, and figure out roughly which direction (north, south, east, or west) you'll need to go to get there.

At the Tube station, there are two ways to pass through the turnstile. With a paper ticket or Travelcard, you'll feed it into the turnstile, reclaim it, and hang on to it—you'll need it later. With an Oyster card, touch it flat against the turnstile's yellow card reader,

both when you enter and exit the station.

Find your train by following signs to your line and the (general) direction it's headed (such as Central Line: east). Since some tracks are shared by several lines, double-check before boarding a train—make sure your destination is one of the stops listed on the sign at the platform. Also, check the electronic signboards that announce which train is next, and make sure the destination (the end-of-the-line stop) is the direction you want. Some trains, particularly on the Circle and District lines, split off for other directions, but each train has its final destination marked above its windshield.

Trains run about every 3-10 minutes. For a rough idea of how long it takes to get from point A to point B by Tube, estimate five minutes per stop (which includes time to walk into and out of stations, and to change trains). So a destination six stops away will take you about 30 minutes.

When you leave the system, "touch out" with your Oyster card at the electronic reader on the turnstile, or feed your paper ticket into the turnstile (it will eat your now-expired ticket). With a Travelcard, it will spit out your still-valid card. When leaving a station, save walking time by choosing the best street exit—check the maps on the walls or ask any station personnel.

The system can be fraught with construction delays and breakdowns. Pay attention to signs and announcements explaining necessary detours. Rush hours (8:00-10:00 and 16:00-19:00) can be packed and sweaty. If one train is stuffed—and another is coming in three minutes—wait to avoid the sardine routine. If you get confused, ask for advice from a local, a blue-vested staff person, or at the information window located before the turnstile entry. Online, get help from the "Journey Planner" at www.tfl.gov.uk, which is accessible (via free Wi-Fi) on any mobile device within most Tube stations before you go underground.

Tube Etiquette

- When your train arrives, stand off to the side and let riders exit before you try to board.
- Avoid using the hinged seats near the doors of some trains when the car is jammed; they take up valuable standing space.
- If you're blocking the door when the train stops, step out of the car and off to the side, let others off, then get back on.
- Talk softly in the cars. Listen to how quietly Londoners communicate and follow their lead.
- On escalators, stand on the right and pass on the left. But note that in some passageways or stairways, you might be directed to walk on the left (the direction Brits go when behind the wheel).
- Discreet eating and drinking are fine (nothing smelly); drinking alcohol and smoking are not.

By Bus

If you figure out the bus system, you'll swing like Tarzan through the urban jungle of London (see sidebar for a list of handy routes).

Get in the habit of hopping buses for quick little straight shots, even just to get to a Tube stop. However, during bump-and-grind rush hours (8:00-10:00 and 16:00-19:00), you'll usually go faster by Tube.

You can't buy single-trip tickets for buses, and you can't use cash to pay for your fare when boarding. Instead, you must have an Oyster card, a Travelcard, or a one-day Bus and Tram Pass (£5, buy paper pass from the ticket machine or window in any Tube station). If you're using your Oyster card, any bus ride in downtown London costs £1.50 (with a cap of £4.40 per day).

The first step in mastering London's bus system is learning how to decipher the bus-stop signs. The accompanying photo shows a typical sign listing the various buses (the N91, N68, etc.) that come by here and the destinations they go to (Oakwood, Old Coulsdon, etc). In the first column, find your destination on the list—e.g., to Paddington (Tube and rail station). In the next column, find a bus that goes there—the #23 (routes marked "N" are night-only). In the final column, a letter within a circle (e.g., "H") tells you exactly which nearby bus stop is yours. Find where that stop is on the accompanying bus-stop map, then make your way to that stop—you'll know it's yours

O			
Oakwood ⊖	N91	● ⊗	
Old Coulsdon	N68	Aldwych	
Old Ford	N8	Oxford Circus	
Old Kent Road Canal Bridge	53, N381	●	
	453	● ●	
	N21	●	
Old Street ⊖ ≉	243	Aldwych	
Orpington ≉	N47	●	
Oxford Circus ⊖	Any bus	●	
	N18	●	
P			
Paddington ⊖ ≉	23, N15	● ● ●	
Palmers Green ≉	N29	●	
Park Langley	N3	● ●	
Peckham	12	● ●	
	N89, N343	●	
	N136	● ●	
	N381	●	
Penge Pawleyne Arms	176	●	
	N3	● ●	
Petts Wood ≉	N47	●	
Pimlico Grosvenor Road	24	● ●	
Plaistow Greengate	N15	● ●	
Plumstead ≉	53	●	
Plumstead Common	53	●	

because it will have the same letter on its pole.

When your bus approaches, it's wise to hold your arm out to let the driver know you want on. Hop on and confirm your destination with the driver (often friendly and helpful).

As you board, touch your Oyster card to the card reader, or show your paper Travelcard or Bus and Tram Pass to the driver. Unlike on the Tube, there's no need to show or tap your card when

Handy Bus Routes

Ever since London instituted a congestion charge for cars, the bus system has gotten faster, easier, and cheaper. Tube-oriented travelers need to get over their tunnel vision, learn the bus system, and get around fast and easy. The best views are upstairs on a double-decker.

Here are some of the most useful routes:

Route #9: High Street Kensington to Knightsbridge (Harrods) to Hyde Park Corner to Trafalgar Square to Aldwych (Somerset House).

Route #11: Victoria Station to Westminster Abbey to Trafalgar Square to St. Paul's and Liverpool Street Station and the East End.

Route #15: Trafalgar Square to St. Paul's to Tower of London (sometimes with heritage "Routemaster" old-style double-decker buses).

Routes #23 and #159: Paddington Station (#159 begins at Marble Arch) to Oxford Circus to Piccadilly Circus to Trafalgar Square; from there, #23 heads east to St. Paul's and Liverpool

Street Station, while #159 heads to Westminster and the Imperial War Museum. In addition, several buses (including #6, #13, and #139) also make the corridor run between Marble Arch, Oxford Circus, Piccadilly Circus, and Trafalgar Square.

Route #24: Pimlico to Victoria Station to Westminster Abbey to Trafalgar Square to Euston Square, then all the way north to Camden Town (Camden Lock Market) and Hampstead Heath.

Route #38: Victoria Station to Hyde Park Corner to Piccadilly Circus to British Museum.

Route #RV1 (a scenic South Bank joyride): Tower of London to Tower Bridge to Southwark Street (five-minute walk behind Tate Modern/Shakespeare's Globe) to London Eye/Waterloo Station, then over Waterloo Bridge to Aldwych and Covent Garden.

Route #148: Westminster Abbey to Victoria Station to Notting Hill and Bayswater (by way of the east end of Hyde Park and Marble Arch).

Check the bus stop closest to your hotel—it might be convenient to your sightseeing plans.

LEGEND

———	#9
▬▬▬	#11
··········	#15
▬▬▬	#23
– – –	#24
▬ ▬ ▬	#38
▥▥▥▥	#RV1
● ● ●	#148
• • •	#159
#15	Terminus Points

Not to Scale

you hop off. On the older heritage "Routemaster" buses without card-readers (used on the #15 route), you simply take a seat, and the conductor comes around to check cards and passes.

To alert the driver you want to get off, press one of the red buttons (on the poles between the seats) before your stop.

With a mobile phone, you can find out the arrival time of the next bus by texting your bus stop's five-digit code (posted at the stop, above the timetable) to 87287 (if you're using your US phone, text the code to 011-44-7797-800-287). Or try the helpful London Bus Checker app, with route maps and real-time bus info.

For more information about public transit (bus and Tube), the best single source is the helpful *Hello London* brochure, which includes both a Tube map and a handy schematic map of the best bus routes (available free at TIs, museums, hotels, and at www.tfl.gov. uk). For specific directions on how to get from point A to point B on London's transit, detailed bus maps, updated prices, and general information, check www.tfl.gov.uk or call the automated info line at 0843-222-1234.

By Taxi

London is the best taxi town in Europe. Big, black, carefully regulated cabs are everywhere—there are about 25,000 of them. (While

historically known as "black cabs," London's official taxis are sometimes covered with wildly colored ads.)

I've never met a crabby cabbie in London. They love to talk, and they know every nook and cranny in town. I ride in a taxi each day just to get my London questions answered. Drivers must pass a rigorous test on "The Knowledge" of London geography to earn their license.

If a cab's top light is on, just wave it down. Drivers flash lights when they see you wave. They have a tight turning radius, so you can hail cabs going in either direction. If waving doesn't work, ask someone where you can find a taxi stand. Telephoning a cab will get you one in a few minutes, but costs a little more.

Rides start at £2.40. The regular tariff #1 covers most of the day (Mon-Fri 6:00-20:00), tariff #2 is during "unsociable hours" (Mon-Fri 20:00-22:00 and Sat-Sun 6:00-22:00), and tariff #3 is for nighttime (22:00-6:00) and holidays. Rates go up about 20 percent with each higher tariff. All extra charges are explained in writing on the cab wall. Tip a cabbie by rounding up (maximum 10 percent).

Connecting downtown sights is quick and easy, and will cost

you about £8-10 (for example, St. Paul's to the Tower of London, or between the two Tate museums). For a short ride, three adults in a cab generally travel at close to Tube prices—and groups of four or five adults should taxi everywhere. All cabs can carry five passengers, and some take six, for the same cost as a single traveler.

Don't worry about meter cheating. Licensed British cab meters come with a sealed computer chip and clock that ensures you'll get the correct tariff. The only way a cabbie can cheat you is by taking a needlessly long route. One serious pitfall, however, is taking a cab when traffic is bad to a destination efficiently served by the Tube. On one trip to London, I hopped in a taxi at South Kensington for Waterloo Station and hit bad traffic. Rather than spending 20 minutes and £2 on the Tube, I spent 40 minutes and £16 in a taxi.

If you overdrink and ride in a taxi, be warned: Taxis charge £40 for "soiling" (a.k.a., pub puke). If you forget this book in a taxi, call the Lost Property office and hope for the best (tel. 0845-330-9882).

By Bike

London is keeping up its push to become more bike-friendly. It operates a citywide bike-rental program similar to ones in other major European cities, and new bike lanes are still cropping up around town.

Still, London isn't (yet) ideal for biking. Although the streets are relatively uncongested, the network of designated bike lanes is far from complete, and the city's many one-way streets (not to mention the need to bike on the "wrong" side) can make biking here a bit more challenging than it sounds. If you're accustomed to urban biking, it can be a good option for connecting your sightseeing stops, but if you're just up for a joyride, stick to London's large parks.

Santander Cycles, intended for quick point-to-point trips, are fairly easy to rent and a giddy joy to use, even for the most jaded London tourist. These "Boris Bikes" (as they are affectionately called by locals, after cycle enthusiast and mayor Boris Johnson) are cruisers with big, cushy seats, a bag rack with elastic straps, and three gears.

Approximately 700 bike-rental stations are scattered throughout the city, each equipped with a computer kiosk. To rent a bike, you need to pay an access fee (£2/day). The first 30 minutes are free; if you hang on to the bike for longer, you'll be charged £2 for every additional 30-minute period.

When you're ready to ride, press "Hire a Cycle" and insert your credit card when prompted. You'll then get a ticket with a five-digit code. Take the ticket to any bike that doesn't have a red light (those are "taken") and punch in the number. After the yellow light blinks, a green light will appear: Now you can (firmly) pull the bike out of the slot.

When your ride is over, find a station with an empty slot, then push your bike in until it locks and the green light flashes.

You can hire bikes as often as you like (which will start your free 30-minute period over again), as long as you wait five minutes between each use. There can be problems, of course—stations at popular locations (such as entrances to parks) can temporarily run out of bikes, and you may have trouble finding a place to return a bike—but for the most part, this system works great. To make things easier, get a map of the docking stations—pick one up at any major Underground station. It's also available online at www.tfl.gov.uk (click on "Santander Cycles") and as a free app (http://cyclehireapp.com).

Helmets are not provided, so ride carefully. Stay to the far-left side of the road and watch closely at intersections for *left*-turning cars. Be aware that in most parks (including Hyde Park/Kensington Gardens) only certain paths are designated for bike use—you can't ride just anywhere. Maps posted at park entrances identify bike paths, and non-bike paths are generally clearly marked.

Some bike tour companies also rent bikes—for details, see page 38.

By Car

If you have a car, stow it—you don't want to drive in London. If you need convincing, here's one more reason: A £10 **congestion charge** is levied on any private car entering the city center during peak hours (Mon-Fri 7:00-18:00, no charge Sat-Sun and holidays, fee payable at gas stations, convenience stores, and self-service machines at public parking lots, or online at www.cclondon.com). There are painfully stiff penalties for late payments. The system has cut down traffic jams, bolstered London's public transit, and made buses cheaper and more user-friendly. Today, the vast majority of vehicles in the city center are buses, taxis, and service trucks.

Tours in London

☊ To sightsee on your own, download my **free audio tours** that illuminate some of London's top sights and neighborhoods, including my Westminster Walk, Historic London: "The City," and tours of the British Museum, British Library, and St. Paul's Cathedral (see sidebar on page 5 for details).

▲▲▲BY HOP-ON, HOP-OFF DOUBLE-DECKER BUS

Two competitive companies (**Original** and **Big Bus**) offer essentially the same two tours of the city's sightseeing highlights, with nearly 30 stops on each route. Big Bus tours are a little more expensive (£32, cheaper if you book in advance online), while Original tours are cheaper (£26 with this book).

These two-to-three hour, once-over-lightly bus tours drive by all the famous sights, providing a stress-free way to get your bearings and see the biggies. They stop at the same core group of sights regardless of which overview tour you're on: Piccadilly Circus, Trafalgar Square, Big Ben, St. Paul's, the Tower of London, Marble Arch, Victoria Station, and elsewhere. With a good guide and nice weather, I'd sit back and enjoy the entire tour. (If you don't like your guide, you can hop off and try your luck with the next departure.) On a recent trip, I had a livelier, more informative guide on the Original tour than the Big Bus tour, though guides can vary even within the same company.

Each company offers at least one route with live (English-only) guides, and a second (sometimes slightly different route) comes with recorded, dial-a-language narration. In addition to the overview tours, both Original and Big Bus include the Thames River boat trip by City Cruises (between Westminster and the Tower of London) and three 1.5-hour walking tours.

Pick up a map from any flier rack or from one of the countless salespeople, and study the color-coded system. Sunday morning—when the traffic is light and many museums are closed—is a fine time for a tour. Traffic is at its peak around lunch and during the evening rush hour (around 17:00). Unless you're using the bus tour mainly for hop-on, hop-off transportation, consider saving time and money by taking a night tour (described later).

Buses run daily about every 10-15 minutes in summer, every 10-20 minutes in winter. They start at about 8:00 or 8:30 and run until early evening in summer or late afternoon in winter. The last full loop usually leaves Victoria Station at about 19:00 in summer, and at about 17:00 in winter (confirm by checking the schedule or asking the driver).

You can buy tickets online in advance, or on the day of your trip from drivers or from staff at street kiosks (credit cards accepted at kiosks at major stops such as Victoria Station, ticket good for 24 hours, or 48 hours in winter).

Combining a London Bus Tour and the Changing of the Guard

For a grand and efficient intro to London, consider catching an 8:30 departure of a hop-on, hop-off overview bus tour, riding 90 percent of the loop (which takes just over two hours, depending on traffic), and hopping off at Buckingham Palace in time to find a good spot to watch the Changing of the Guard ceremony at 11:30. If you miss the first bus, you could take the next one (generally about 20 minutes later), though it may get you to the ceremony late (check with the driver).

Original London Sightseeing Bus Tour

They offer two versions of their basic highlights loop: **The Original Tour** (live guide, marked with a yellow triangle on the front of the bus) and the **City Sightseeing Tour** (essentially the same route but with recorded narration, a kids' soundtrack option, and a stop at Madame Tussauds; bus marked with a red triangle). Other routes include the blue-triangle **Museum Tour** (connecting far-flung museums and major shopping stops), and green, black, and purple triangle routes (linking major train stations to the central route). All routes are covered by the same ticket. Keep it simple and just take one of the city highlights tours (£30, £4 less with this book, limit four discounts per book, they'll rip off the corner of this page—raise bloody hell if the staff or driver won't honor this discount; also online deals, info center at 17 Cockspur Street, tel. 020/8877-1722, www.theoriginaltour.com).

Big Bus London Tours

For £32 (up to 30 percent discount online—print tickets or have them delivered to your phone), you get the same basic overview tours: Red buses come with a live guide, while the blue route has a recorded narration and a one-hour longer path that goes around Hyde Park. These pricier Big Bus tours tend to have more departures—meaning shorter waits for those hopping on and off (tel. 020/7808-6753, www.bigbustours.com).

BY BUS OR CAR
London by Night Sightseeing Tour

This tour offers a 1.5-hour circuit, but after hours, with no extras (e.g., walks, river cruises), and at a lower price. While the narration can be pretty lame, the views at twilight are grand—though note that it stays light until late on summer nights, and London just doesn't do floodlighting as well as, say, Paris (£20, £15 online). June through September, open-top buses depart at 20:00 and 21:30 from Victoria Station (Jan-May and late Sept-late Dec departs at 19:00

and 21:00, only with closed-top bus, no tours between Christmas and New Year). Buses leave from near Victoria Station, in front of Grosvenor Hotel on Buckingham Palace Road (or you can board at any stop, such as Marble Arch, Trafalgar Square, London Eye, or Tower of London; tel. 020/8545-6110, www.london-by-night. net). For a memorable and economical evening, munch a scenic picnic dinner on the top deck. (There are plenty of take-away options within the train stations and near the various stops.)

Land and Sea Tours

A bright-yellow amphibious WWII-vintage vehicle (the model that ferried supplies and wounded soldiers on Normandy's beaches on D-Day) takes a gang of 30 tourists past some famous sights on land—Big Ben, Trafalgar Square, Piccadilly Circus—then splashes into the Thames for a cruise. All in all, it's good fun at a rather steep price. The live guide works hard, and it's kid-friendly to the point of goofiness. Beware: These book up in advance (£24, April-Sept daily, first tour 9:30 or 10:00, last tour usually 18:00, shorter hours Oct-March, 2-6/hour, 1.25 hours—45 minutes on land and 30 minutes in the river, £3 booking fee by phone or online, departs from Chicheley Street—you'll see the big, ugly vehicle parked 100 yards behind the London Eye, Tube: Waterloo or Westminster, tel. 020/7928-3132, www.londonducktours.co.uk).

Driver-Guides

These three guides have cars or a minibus (particularly helpful for travelers with limited mobility), and they also do walking-only tours: **Robina Brown** (£345/half-day, £515/day, £600 outside London, £40 more for groups of 4-6 people, also does overnight tours farther afield, tel. 020/8675-2810, www.driverguidetours.com, robina@driverguidetours.com), **Janine Barton** (£370/half-day, £490/day within London, £550 outside London, tel. 020/7402-4600, http://seeitinstyle.synthasite.com, jbsiis@aol.com), and **David Stubbs** (£195/half-day, £295/day, about £50 more for groups of 4-6 people, also does tours to the Cotswolds, Stonehenge, and Stratford, mobile 07775-888-534, www.londoncountrytours. co.uk, info@londoncountrytours.co.uk).

▲▲ON FOOT

Several times a day, top-notch local guides lead (sometimes big) groups on walking tours through specific slices of London's past. Look for brochures at TIs or ask at hotels, although the latter usually push higher-priced bus tours. *Time Out,* the weekly entertainment guide, lists some, but not all, scheduled walks. Check with the various tour companies by phone or online to get their full picture.

To take a walking tour, simply show up at the announced location and pay the guide. Then enjoy two chatty hours of Dickens, Harry Potter, the Plague, Shakespeare, street art, the Beatles, Jack the Ripper, or whatever is on the agenda.

London Walks

This leading company lists its extensive and creative daily schedule on their amusing website, as well as in a beefy, plain *London Walks* brochure (available at hotels and in racks all over town, including one at St. Martin-in-the-Fields' Café in the Crypt on Trafalgar Square). Just perusing their fascinating lineup of tours opens me up to dimensions of the city I never considered and inspires me to stay longer in London. Their two-hour walks, led by top-quality professional guides (ranging from archaeologists to actors), cost £10 (cash only, walks offered year-round, private tours for groups-£140, tel. 020/7624-3978 for a live person, tel. 020/7624-9255 for a recording of today's or tomorrow's walks and the Tube station they depart from, www.walks.com).

London Walks also offers day trips into the countryside, a good option for those with limited time and transportation (£18 plus £36-59 for transportation and admission costs, cash only: Stonehenge/Salisbury, Oxford/Cotswolds, Cambridge, Bath, and so on). These are economical in part because everyone gets group discounts for transportation and admissions.

Sandemans New London "Free Royal London Tour"

This company employs students (rather than licensed guides) who recite three-hour spiels covering the basic London sights. While the youthful tours are light and irreverent, and can be both entertaining and fun, it's misleading to call the tours "free," as tips are expected (the guides actually pay the company for the privilege of asking for tips). You'll spend a lot of time at the start as they collect emails and take a group photo (not doing you a favor but establishing the size of the group so the guide can be charged accordingly). Given that London Walks offers daily tours at a reasonable price, taking this "free" tour makes no sense to me (daily at 10:00, 11:00, and 14:00; meet at Covent Garden Piazza by the Apple Store, Tube: Covent Garden). Sandemans also has other guided tours for a charge, including a Pub Crawl (£20, nightly at 19:30, meet at Slug and Lettuce Bar in Leicester Square, Tube: Leicester Square, www.newlondon-tours.com).

Beatles Walks

Fans of the still-Fab Four can take one of three Beatles walks (London Walks has two that run 5 days/week; for more on Beatles sights, see page 69).

Jack the Ripper Walks

Each walking tour company seems to make most of its money with "haunted" and Jack the Ripper tours. Many guides are historians and would rather not lead these lightweight tours—but, in tourism as in journalism, "if it bleeds, it leads" (which is why the juvenile London Dungeon is one of the city's busiest sights).

Back in 1888—in the decade of Sherlock Holmes and Dr. Jekyll and Mr. Hyde, when London was still a Dickensian Tale of Two Cities—locals were terrorized by the murder of five prostitutes within a few weeks. In the wee hours, the murderer (who was given his name by local newspapers, which made a fortune on this sensational series of events) slit the throats and cut out the guts of his victims in the poor and wretched side of town. These were desperate women—so desperate they took their customers not to a bed, but up against a wall for a "four-penny knee trembler." While almost no hint of the dark and scary London of that period survives, guides do a good job of spinning the story. Think of this mile-long walk, starting at the Tower of London, as a cheap night out with a few laughs. It's still light out in summer, so the scary factor is limited to the tales of the victims' miserable lot in life and the gory way in which they were killed.

Two reliably good two-hour tours start every night at the Tower Hill Tube station exit. **London Walks** leaves nightly at 19:30 (£10, pay at the start, tel. 020/7624-3978, recorded info tel. 020/7624-9255, www.jacktheripperwalk.com). **Ripping Yarns,** which leaves earlier, is guided by off-duty Yeoman Warders—the Tower of London "Beefeaters" (£8, pay at end, nightly at 18:30, no tours between Christmas and New Year, mobile 07813-559-301, www.jack-the-ripper-tours.com). After taking both, I found the London Walks tour more entertaining, informative, and with a better route (along quieter, once hooker-friendly lanes, with less traffic), starting at Tower Hill and ending at Liverpool Street Station. Groups can be huge for both, and one group can be nearly on top of another, but there's always room—just show up.

Private Walks with Local Guides

Standard rates for London's registered Blue Badge guides are about £150-165 for four hours and £250 or more for nine hours (tel. 020/7611-2545, www.guidelondon.org.uk or www.britainsbestguides.org). I know and like five fine local guides: **Sean Kelleher** (tel. 020/8673-1624, mobile 07764-612-770, sean@seanlondonguide.com); **Britt Lonsdale** (£230/half-day, £330/day, great with families, tel. 020/7386-9907, mobile 07813-278-077, brittl@btinternet.com); **Joel Reid**, an imaginative guide who specializes in off-the-beaten-track London (mobile 07887-955-720, joelyreid@gmail.com); and two others who work in London when they're not on the road leading my Britain tours: **Tom Hooper** (mobile 07986-048-047, tomh@ricksteves.net), and **Gillian Chadwick** (mobile 07889-976-598, gillychad@hotmail.co.uk). If you have a particular interest, London Walks (see earlier) has a huge selection of guides and can book you one for your exact focus (£180/half-day).

BY BIKE

London is committed to creating more bike paths, and many of its best sights can be laced together with a pleasant pedal through its parks. A bike tour is a fun way to see the sights and enjoy the city on two wheels.

London Bicycle Tour Company

Three tours covering London are offered daily from their base at Gabriel's Wharf on the South Bank of the Thames. Sunday is the best, as there is less car traffic (**Central Tour**—£24, daily at 10:30, 6 miles, 3 hours, includes Westminster, Buckingham Palace, Covent Garden, and St. Paul's; **West End Tour**—£24, April-Oct daily at 14:30, Nov-March daily at 12:00 as long as at least 4 people show up, 7 miles, 3 hours, includes Westminster, Buckingham Palace, Hyde Park, Soho, and Covent Garden; **East Tour**—£27.50, April-Oct Sat-Sun at 14:00, Nov-March Sat-Sun at 12:00, 9 miles, 3.5 hours, includes south side of the river to Tower Bridge, then The City to the East End; book ahead for off-season tours). They also rent bikes (£3.50/hour, £20/day; office open daily April-Oct 9:30-18:00, Nov-March 10:00-16:00, west of Blackfriars Bridge on the South Bank, 1 Gabriel's Wharf, tel. 020/7928-6838, www. londonbicycle.com).

Fat Tire Bike Tours

Nearly daily bike tours cover the highlights of downtown London, on two different itineraries (£2 discount with this book): **Royal London** (£22, April-Oct daily at 11:00, mid-May-mid-Sept also at 15:30, Nov-March Thu-Mon at 11:00, 7 miles, 4 hours, meet at Queensway Tube station; includes Parliament, Buckingham Palace, Hyde Park, and Trafalgar Square) and **River Thames** (£28, nearly daily in summer at 10:30, March-Nov Thu-Sat at 10:30, 4.5 hours, meet just outside Southwark Tube Station; includes London Eye, St. Paul's, Tower of London, and London Bridge). Their guiding style wears its learning lightly, mixing history with humor. Reservations are easy online, and required for River Thames tours and kids' bikes (off-season tours can be arranged, mobile 078-8233-8779, www.fattirebiketourslondon.com). Confirm the schedule online or by phone. They also offer a range of walking tours that include a fish-and-chips dinner, a beer-tasting pub tour, and theater packages (details online or by phone).

▲▲BY CRUISE BOAT

London offers many made-for-tourist cruises, most on slow-moving, open-top boats accompanied by entertaining commentary

about passing sights. Several companies offer essentially the same trip. Generally speaking, you can either do a **short city-center cruise** by riding a boat 30 minutes from Westminster Pier to Tower Pier (particularly handy if you're interested in visiting the Tower of London anyway), or take a **longer cruise** that includes a peek at the East End, riding from Westminster all the way to Greenwich (save time by taking the Tube back).

Each company runs cruises daily, about twice hourly, from morning until dark; many reduce frequency off-season. Boats come and go from various docks in the city center (see sidebar). The most popular places to embark are Westminster Pier (at the base of Westminster Bridge across the street from Big Ben) and Waterloo Pier (at the London Eye, across the river).

A one-way trip within the city center costs about £10; going all the way to Greenwich costs about £2 more. Most companies charge around £3 more for a round-trip ticket, and others sell hop-on, hop-off day tickets (around £19). But I'd rather just savor one cruise, then zip home by Tube—making these return tickets not usually worthwhile.

You can buy tickets at kiosks on the docks. A Travelcard can snare you a 33 percent discount on most cruises (just show the card when you pay for the cruise); the pay-as-you-go Oyster card nets you a discount only on Thames Clippers. Because companies vary in the discounts they offer, always ask. Children and seniors generally get discounts. You can purchase drinks and scant, overpriced snacks on board. Clever budget travelers pack a picnic and munch while they cruise.

The three dominant companies are **City Cruises** (handy 30-minute cruise from Westminster Pier to Tower Pier; www.citycruises.com), **Thames River Services** (fewer stops, classic boats, friendlier and more old-fashioned feel; www.thamesriverservices.co.uk), and **Circular Cruise** (full cruise takes about an hour, operated by Crown River Services, www.crownriver.com). I'd skip the **London Eye**'s River Cruise from Waterloo Pier—it's about the same price as Circular Cruise, but 20 minutes shorter. The speedy **Thames Clippers** (described later) are designed more for no-nonsense transport than lazy sightseeing.

Thames Boat Piers

While Westminster Pier is the most popular, it's not the only dock in town. Consider all the options (listed from west to east, as the Thames flows—see the color maps in the front of this book):

Millbank Pier (North Bank), at the Tate Britain Museum, is used primarily by the Tate Boat service (express connection to Tate Modern at Bankside Pier).

Westminster Pier (North Bank), near the base of Big Ben, offers round-trip sightseeing cruises and lots of departures in both directions (though the Thames Clippers boats don't stop here). Nearby sights include Parliament and Westminster Abbey.

Waterloo Pier (a.k.a. **London Eye Pier,** South Bank), right at the base of the London Eye, is a good, less-crowded alternative to Westminster, with many of the same cruise options (Waterloo Station is nearby).

Embankment Pier (North Bank) is near Covent Garden, Trafalgar Square, and Cleopatra's Needle (the obelisk on the Thames). This pier is used mostly for special boat trips (such as some RIB—rigid inflatable boat—trips, and lunch and dinner cruises).

Festival Pier (South Bank) is next to the Royal Festival Hall, just downstream from the London Eye.

Blackfriars Pier (North Bank) is in The City, not far from St. Paul's.

Bankside Pier (South Bank) is directly in front of the Tate Modern and Shakespeare's Globe.

London Bridge Pier (a.k.a. **London Bridge City Pier,** South Bank) is near the HMS *Belfast* and the start of my Bankside Walk.

Tower Pier (North Bank) is at the Tower of London, at the east edge of The City and near the East End.

St. Katharine's Pier (North Bank) is just downstream from the Tower of London.

Canary Wharf Pier (North Bank) is at the Docklands, London's new "downtown."

In outer London, you might also use the piers at **Greenwich, Kew Gardens,** and **Hampton Court.**

For details—including prices, schedules, and exactly which piers each company uses—check their websites or look for ticket kiosks at the docks. If you'd like to compare all of your options in one spot, head to Westminster Pier, which has a row of kiosks for all of the big outfits.

Cruising Downstream, to Greenwich: Both **City Cruises** and **Thames River Services** head from Westminster Pier to Greenwich. The cruises are usually narrated by the captain, with most commentary given on the way to Greenwich. The companies' prices are the same, though their itineraries are slightly different (Thames River Services makes only one stop en route and takes just an hour, while City Cruises makes two stops and adds about 15 minutes). The **Thames Clippers** boats, described later, are cheaper and faster (about 20-45 minutes to Greenwich), but have no commentary and no seating up top. To maximize both efficiency and sightseeing, I'd take a narrated cruise to Greenwich one way, and go the other way on the DLR (Docklands Light Railway), with a stop in the Docklands (Canary Wharf station; ⏍ see The Docklands Walk chapter).

Cruising Upstream, to Kew Gardens and Hampton Court Palace: Boats operated by the Westminster Passenger Service Association leave for Kew Gardens from Westminster Pier (£12 one-way, £18 round-trip, cash only, discounts with Travelcard, 2-4/day depending on season, 1.5 hours, boats sail April-Oct, about half the trip is narrated, www.wpsa.co.uk). Most boats continue on to Hampton Court Palace for an additional £3 (and another 1.5 hours). Because of the river current, you can save 30 minutes cruising from Hampton Court back into town (depends on the tide—ask before you commit to the boat). Romantic as these rides sound, it can be a long trip...especially upstream.

Commuting by Clipper

The sleek, 220-seat catamarans used by **Thames Clippers** are designed for commuters rather than sightseers. Think of the boats as express buses on the river—they zip through London every 20-30 minutes, stopping at most of the major docks en route (including Canary Wharf/Docklands and Greenwich). They're fast: roughly 20 minutes from Embankment to Tower, 10 more minutes to Docklands, and 10 more minutes to Greenwich. However, the boats are less pleasant for joyriding than the cruises described earlier, with no commentary and no open deck up top (the only outside access is on a crowded deck at the exhaust-choked back of the boat, where you're jostling for space to take photos). Any one-way ride costs £7.15, and a River Roamer all-day ticket costs £17.35 (discounts with Travelcard and Oyster card, www.thamesclippers.com).

Thames Clippers also offers two express trips. The **Tate Boat** ferry service, which directly connects the Tate Britain (Millbank Pier) and the Tate Modern (Bankside Pier), is made for art lovers (£7.15 one-way, covered by River Roamer day ticket; buy ticket at self-service machines before boarding or use Oyster Card; for frequency and times, see the Tate Britain and Tate Modern tour chapters or www.tate.org.uk/visit/tate-boat). The **O2 Express** runs only on nights when there are events at the O2 arena (departs from Waterloo Pier).

Other Cruise Options

Careening at Top Speed Along the Thames: Two competing companies invite you aboard a small, 12-person, high-speed rigid inflatable boat (RIB—similar to a Zodiac) for a pricey, adrenaline-fueled tour of the city (**London RIB Voyages** departs Waterloo Pier, www.londonribvoyages.com; **Thames RIB Experience** boats depart Embankment Pier, www.thamesribexperience.com).

Away from the Thames, on Regent's Canal: Consider exploring London's canals by taking a cruise on historic Regent's Canal in north London. Several companies offer trips through Regent's Park, Little Venice, and Camden Lock Market. Check out **London Waterbus Company** (www.londonwaterbus.com), **Jason's Trip** (www.jasons.co.uk), or the good ship *Jenny Wren,* which offers 1.5-hour guided canal boat cruises from Walker's Quay in Camden Town through scenic Regent's Park to Little Venice (£12.50; 2-3/day April-Oct, weekends only in March, Walker's Quay, 250 Camden High Street, 3-minute walk from Tube: Camden Town; tel. 020/7485-4433, www.walkersquay.com). While in Camden Town, stop by the popular, punky Camden Lock Market to browse through trendy arts and crafts (open daily, busiest on weekends, a block from Walker's Quay, www.camdenlockmarket.com; for more on the market, see page 431).

TOUR PACKAGES FOR STUDENTS

Andy Steves (my son) runs **Weekend Student Adventures (WSA Europe),** offering three-day and longer guided and unguided packages—including accommodations, sightseeing, and unique local experiences—for student travelers in 12 top European cities, including London (guided trips from €199, see www.wsaeurope. com).

SIGHTS IN LONDON

These sights are arranged by neighborhood for handy sightseeing. When you see a 📖 in a listing, it means the sight is covered in much more depth in a self-guided walk or self-guided tour. A 🎧 means the walk or tour is available as a free audio tour (via my Rick Steves Audio Europe app—see page 5). Some walks and tours are available in both formats—take your pick.

Check www.ricksteves.com/update for any significant changes that have occurred since this book was published. For money-saving tips, see "Affording London's Sights" on page 70.

"Voluntary Donations": Some London sights automatically add a "voluntary donation" of about 10 percent to their admission fees. The prices posted and quoted in this book include the donation, though it's perfectly fine to pay the base price without the donation. Some of London's free museums also ask for donations as you enter, but again, it's completely optional.

Central London

WESTMINSTER

These sights are listed in roughly geographical order from Westminster Abbey to Trafalgar Square, and are linked in the 📖 Westminster Walk chapter and the 🎧 free Westminster Walk audio tour.

▲▲▲Westminster Abbey

The greatest church in the English-speaking world, Westminster Abbey is the place where England's kings and queens have been crowned and buried since 1066. Like a stony refugee camp huddled outside St. Peter's Pearly Gates, Westminster Abbey has many stories to tell. The steep admission includes a fine audioguide, worthwhile if you have the time and interest. To experience the church more vividly, take a live tour, or attend evensong or an organ concert.

Cost and Hours: £20, £40 family ticket (covers 2 adults and 1 child), includes cloisters, audioguide, and Abbey Museum; abbey—Mon-Fri 9:30-16:30, Wed until 19:00 (main church only), Sat 9:30-14:30, last entry one hour before closing, closed Sun to sightseers but open for services, guided tours available; museum—daily 10:30-16:00; cloisters—daily 8:00-18:00; Tube: Westminster or St. James's Park, tel. 020/7222-5152, www. westminster-abbey.org.

Music: The church hosts evensong performances daily except Wednesday, when it's spoken instead of sung (Mon-Sat at 17:00 except Sept-April Sat at 15:00, Sun year-round at 15:00). A free 30-minute organ recital is usually held on Sunday at 17:45.

📖 See the Westminster Abbey Tour chapter.

▲▲Houses of Parliament (Palace of Westminster)

This Neo-Gothic icon of London, the site of the royal residence from 1042 to 1547, is now the meeting place of the legislative branch of government. Like the US Capitol in Washington, DC, the complex is open to visitors. You can gain access one of two ways. While Parliament is in session, wait in line to enter for free and watch debates in one or both of the public galleries (either the bickering House of Commons or the sleepy House of Lords). Or reserve a tour of

the historic building held on Saturdays year-round, and also on weekdays from August to September (during Parliamentary recess, tour via audioguide or organized group—it's your choice).

Whichever you choose, your visit will include the cavernous and historic Westminster Hall, St. Stephen's Hall, and the Central Lobby—each impressive in its own right.

Cost and Hours (Public Galleries): Free, open only when parliament is in session; House of Commons—Oct-July Mon 14:30-22:30, Tue-Wed 11:30-19:30, Thu 9:30-17:30; House of Lords—Oct-July Mon-Tue 14:30-22:00, Wed 15:00-22:00, Thu 11:00-19:30; last entry depends on the debates; get the exact schedule at www.parliament.uk.

Tours: Audioguide-£18, guided tour-£25, Saturdays year-round 9:00-16:30 and most weekdays during recess (Aug-Sept), 1.5 hours. Confirm the tour schedule and book ahead online at www.parliament.uk or by calling 020/7219-4114. The ticket office sells tour tickets, but there's no guarantee there will be same-day spaces available (open weekdays 10:00-16:00, Sat 9:00-17:00, closed Sun, located in Portcullis House, entrance on Victoria Embankment).

Crowd-Beating Tips: For the public galleries, lines tend to be longest at the start of each session, particularly on Wednesdays; for the shortest wait, try to show up later in the afternoon (but don't push it, as things sometimes close down early).

☐ See the Houses of Parliament Tour chapter.

Nearby: Across the street from the Parliament building's St. Stephen's Gate, the **Jewel Tower** is a rare remnant of the old Palace of Westminster, used by kings until Henry VIII. The crude stone tower (1365-1366) was a guard tower in the palace wall, overlooking a moat. It contains a fine exhibit on the medieval Westminster Palace and the tower (£4.70, April-Sept daily 10:00-18:00; Oct daily 10:00-17:00; Nov-March Sat-Sun 10:00-16:00, closed Mon-Fri; tel. 020/7222-2219). Next to the tower (and free) is a quiet courtyard with picnic-friendly benches.

Big Ben, the 315-foot-high clock tower at the north end of the Palace of Westminster is named for its 13-ton bell, Ben. The light above the clock is lit when Parliament is in session. The face of the clock is huge—you can actually see the minute hand moving. For a good view of it, walk halfway over Westminster Bridge.

▲▲▲Churchill War Rooms

This excellent sight offers a fascinating walk through the underground headquarters of the British government's fight against the

Nazis in the darkest days of the Battle for Britain. It has two parts: the war rooms themselves, and a top-notch museum dedicated to the man who steered the war from here, Winston Churchill. For details on all the blood, sweat, toil, and tears, pick up the excellent, essential, and included audioguide at the entry, and dive in. Advance reservations are not compulsory, but if you book ahead you can skip the line; otherwise on busy days you may find yourself waiting up to 30 minutes. Allow yourself 1-2 hours for this sight.

Cost and Hours: £18 includes audioguide, daily 9:30-18:00, last entry one hour before closing, guidebook-£5; on King Charles Street, 200 yards off Whitehall, follow the signs, Tube: Westmin-

SIGHTS

To Stratford-upon-Avon

To North Wales & Glasgow

To Camden Lock Market & Hampstead Heath

London

ST. JOHN'S WOOD

ABBEY ROAD

LORD'S CRICKET GROUND

ZOO

Regent's Park

To Wembley

MAIDAVALE

HARROW RD.

EDGWARE ROAD

PARK RD.

MADAME TUSSAUDS

MARYLEBONE STATION

MARYLEBONE RD.

FITZROVIA

(M-40) WESTWAY

To Heathrow Airport & Bath

LITTLE VENICE

FLYOVER

BAKER ST.

WALLACE COLLECTION

OXFORD ST.

NEW BOND

REGENT ST.

PORTOBELLO ROAD MARKET

PADDINGTON STATION

Norfolk Square

BAYSWATER

MARBLE ARCH

NOTTING HILL

BAYSWATER

SPEAKERS' CORNER

MAYFAIR

OLD BOND

To Heathrow Airport & Windsor

NOTTING HILL GATE

Kensington Gardens

Hyde Park

PICCADILLY

KENSINGTON PALACE

ALBERT MEMORIAL

KNIGHTS-BRIDGE

Green Park

THE

Holland Park

ROYAL ALBERT HALL

VICTORIA & ALBERT MUSEUM

HARRODS

BUCKINGHAM PALACE

KENSINGTON HIGH ST.

KENSINGTON

CROMWELL RD.

BROMPTON RD.

SLOANE

VICTORIA

VICTORIA STATION

WARWICK RD.

EARL'S COURT RD.

FULHAM RD.

SOUTH KENSINGTON

BELGRAVIA

COACH STATION

A-4

OLD BROMPTON

KING'S RD.

Sloane Square

EARL'S COURT

CHELSEA

To London Bridge (Arizona)

CHELSEA EMBANKMENT

To Wimbledon

To Kew Gardens & Hampton Court Palace

To Gatwick Airport, Canterbury, Dover & Brighton

ster, tel. 020/7930-6961, www.iwm.org.uk/churchill. The museum's gift shop is great for anyone nostalgic for the 1940s.

Cabinet War Rooms: The 27-room, heavily fortified nerve center of the British war effort was used from 1939 to 1945. Churchill's room, the map room, and other rooms are just as they were in 1945. As you follow the one-way route, be sure to take advantage of the audioguide, which explains each room and offers first-person accounts of wartime happenings here. Be patient—it's

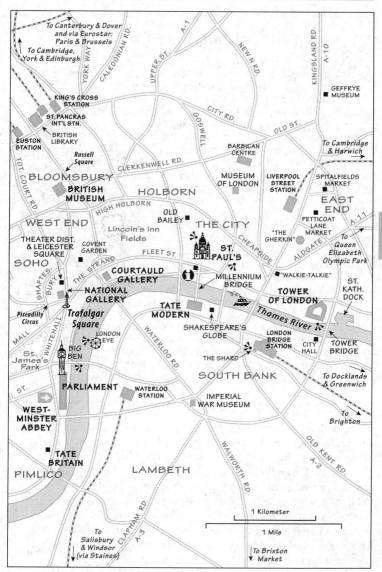

SIGHTS

well worth it. While the rooms are spartan, you'll see how British gentility survived even as the city was bombarded—posted signs informed those working underground what the weather was like outside, and a cheery notice reminded them to turn off the light switch to conserve electricity.

Churchill Museum: Don't bypass this museum, which occupies a large hall amid the war rooms. It dissects every aspect of the man behind the famous cigar, bowler hat, and V-for-victory sign.

Winston Churchill (1874-1965)

As the 20th century dawned, 25-year-old Winston Churchill was making a name for himself in Britain. Working as a newspaper reporter embedded with British troops in South Africa, he was on a train attacked by Boers. Churchill was captured and held as a POW. Meanwhile, back home, the London papers were praising

the young man's heroism for saving fellow train passengers. After two weeks, Churchill escaped from the Boer camp—he slipped through a bathroom window, scaled a wall, walked nonchalantly through an enemy town, hopped a freight train, and was smuggled out of the country. He emerged to find himself famous.

Churchill later entered politics. He first followed in his father's (Lord Randolph Churchill) Conservative Party footsteps, but his desire for social reform drove him to switch to the Liberal Party. (He would later flip back to Conservative.) For three decades, Churchill held numerous government posts,

serving as Chancellor of This, Undersecretary of That, and Minister of The Other. He earned praise for prison reform and for developing newfangled airplanes for warfare; he was criticized for the heavy-handed way he broke labor strikes and for bungling the pacification of Iraq. During World War I, he took a break from politics to personally command British troops on the Western Front.

It's extremely well-presented and engaging, using artifacts, quotes, political cartoons, clear explanations, and high-tech interactive exhibits to bring the colorful statesman to life. You'll get a taste of Winston's wit, irascibility, work ethic, passion for painting, American ties, writing talents, and drinking habits. The exhibit shows Winston's warts as well: It questions whether his party-switching was just political opportunism, examines the basis for his opposition to Indian self-rule, and reveals him to be an intense taskmaster who worked 18-hour days and was brutal to his staffers (who deeply respected him nevertheless).

A long touch-the-screen timeline lets you zero in on events in his life from birth (November 30, 1874) to his first appointment as prime minister in 1940. Many of the items on display—such as a European map divvied up in permanent marker, which Churchill brought to England from the postwar Potsdam Conference—drive home the remarkable span of history this man lived through. Imagine: Churchill began his military career riding horses in the cavalry and ended it speaking out against the proliferation of nuclear ar-

In 1929, Churchill-the-career-bureaucrat retired from politics. He wrote books *(History of the English-Speaking Peoples)* and spoke out about the growing threat of fascist Germany. When World War II broke out, Prime Minister Chamberlain's appeasement policies were discredited, and—on the day that Germany invaded the Netherlands—the king appointed Churchill as prime minister. Churchill guided the nation through its darkest hour (see sidebar on page 272). His greatest contribution may have been his stirring radio speeches that galvanized the will of the British people.

Despite the Allies' victory over the Nazis, Churchill lost the 1945 election. Though considered the ideal man to lead Britain during war, many believed that he and his Conservative Party colleagues were not the best choice to lead the country in peace and during rebuilding. Never one to be idle, he remained active in politics (especially in world affairs) as Leader of the Opposition. In 1946, he gave a speech at a Missouri college, which included the famous Cold War line, "From Stettin in the Baltic to Trieste in the Adriatic, an Iron Curtain has descended across the Continent." In 1951, Churchill was again elected prime minister and served for four years before he retired in 1955. When he died at the age of 90 in 1965, his state funeral in St. Paul's attracted leaders from around the world. Churchill, a legend in his own time, was buried in the family plot at Bladon, a mile from Blenheim Palace, the place of his birth.

maments. It's all the more amazing considering that, in the 1930s, the man who would become my vote for greatest statesman of the 20th century was considered a washed-up loony ranting about the growing threat of fascism.

Eating: Get your rations at the Switch Room café (until 17:00, in the museum), or for a nearby pub lunch, try Westminster Arms

(food served downstairs, on Storey's Gate, a couple of blocks south of the museum).

Horse Guards
The Horse Guards change daily at 11:00 (10:00 on Sun), and a colorful dismounting ceremony takes place daily at 16:00. The rest of the day, they just stand there—terrible for video cameras (at Horse Guards Parade on Whitehall, directly across from the Banqueting House, between Trafalgar Square and 10 Downing Street, Tube: Westminster, www.royal.gov.uk—search "Changing the Guard").

London at a Glance

▲▲▲**Westminster Abbey** Britain's finest church and the site of royal coronations and burials since 1066. **Hours:** Mon-Fri 9:30-16:30, Wed until 19:00, Sat 9:30-14:30, closed Sun to sightseers except for worship. See page 43.

▲▲▲**Churchill War Rooms** Underground WWII headquarters of Churchill's war effort. **Hours:** Daily 9:30-18:00. See page 45.

▲▲▲**National Gallery** Remarkable collection of European paintings (1250-1900), including Leonardo, Botticelli, Velázquez, Rembrandt, Turner, Van Gogh, and the Impressionists. **Hours:** Daily 10:00-18:00, Fri until 21:00. See page 53.

▲▲▲**British Museum** The world's greatest collection of artifacts of Western civilization, including the Rosetta Stone and the Parthenon's Elgin Marbles. **Hours:** Daily 10:00-17:30, Fri until 20:30 (selected galleries only). See page 63.

▲▲▲**British Library** Fascinating collection of important literary treasures of the Western world. **Hours:** Mon-Fri 9:30-18:00, Tue until 20:00, Sat 9:30-17:00, Sun 11:00-17:00. See page 64.

▲▲▲**St. Paul's Cathedral** The main cathedral of the Anglican Church, designed by Christopher Wren, with a climbable dome and daily evensong services. **Hours:** Mon-Sat 8:30-16:30, closed Sun except for worship. See page 72.

▲▲▲**Tower of London** Historic castle, palace, and prison housing the crown jewels and a witty band of Beefeaters. **Hours:** Tue-Sat 9:00-17:30, Sun-Mon 10:00-17:30; Nov-Feb closes one hour earlier. See page 77.

▲▲▲**Victoria and Albert Museum** The best collection of decorative arts anywhere. **Hours:** Daily 10:00-17:45, Fri until 22:00 (selected galleries only). See page 101.

▲▲**Houses of Parliament** London landmark famous for Big Ben and occupied by the Houses of Lords and Commons. **Hours:** When Parliament is in session, generally open Mon-Thu, closed Fri-Sun and most of Aug-Sept. Guided tours offered year-round on Sat and most weekdays during Aug-Sept. See page 44.

▲▲**Trafalgar Square** The heart of London, where Westminster, The City, and the West End meet. **Hours:** Always open. See page 52.

▲▲**National Portrait Gallery** A *Who's Who* of British history, featuring portraits of this nation's most important historical figures. **Hours:** Daily 10:00-18:00, Thu-Fri until 21:00, first and second floors open Mon at 11:00. See page 53.

▲▲Covent Garden Vibrant people-watching zone with shops, cafés, street musicians, and an iron-and-glass arcade that once hosted a produce market. **Hours:** Always open. See page 55.

▲▲Changing of the Guard at Buckingham Palace Hour-long spectacle at Britain's royal residence. **Hours:** Generally May-July daily at 11:30, Aug-April every other day. See page 60.

▲▲London Eye Enormous observation wheel, dominating—and offering commanding views over—London's skyline. **Hours:** Daily 10:00-20:30, later in July and Aug. See page 84.

▲▲Imperial War Museum Exhibits examining the military history of the bloody 20th century. **Hours:** Daily 10:00-18:00. See page 86.

▲▲Tate Modern Works by Monet, Matisse, Dalí, Picasso, and Warhol displayed in a converted powerhouse. **Hours:** Daily 10:00-18:00, Fri-Sat until 22:00. See page 89.

▲▲Shakespeare's Globe Timbered, thatched-roofed reconstruction of the Bard's original "wooden O." **Hours:** Theater complex, museum, and actor-led tours generally daily 9:00-17:30; in summer, morning theater tours only. Plays are also staged here. See page 90.

▲▲Tate Britain Collection of British painting from the 16th century through modern times, including works by William Blake, the Pre-Raphaelites, and J. M. W. Turner. **Hours:** Daily 10:00-18:00. See page 95.

▲▲Natural History Museum A Darwinian delight, packed with stuffed creatures, engaging exhibits, and enthralled kids. **Hours:** Daily 10:00-18:00. See page 104.

▲▲Greenwich Seafaring borough just east of the city center, with *Cutty Sark* tea clipper, Royal Observatory, other maritime sights, and a pleasant market. **Hours:** Most sights open daily, typically 10:00-17:00; market closed Mon. See page 105.

▲Wallace Collection One of the finest private family art collections anywhere—free and open to the public—with paintings by such masters as Rembrandt, Rubens, and Velázquez. **Hours:** Daily 10:00-17:00. See page 64.

▲Courtauld Gallery Fine collection of paintings filling one wing of the Somerset House, a grand 18th-century palace. **Hours:** Daily 10:00-18:00. See page 58.

SIGHTS

Buckingham Palace pageantry is canceled when it rains, but the Horse Guards change regardless of the weather.

▲Banqueting House
England's first Renaissance building (1619-1622) is still standing. Designed by Inigo Jones, built by King James I, and decorated by his son Charles I, the Banqueting House came to symbolize the Stuart kings' "divine right" management style—the belief that God himself had anointed them to rule. The house is one of the few London landmarks spared by the 1698 fire and the only surviving part of the original Palace of Whitehall. Today it opens its doors to visitors, who enjoy a restful 10-minute audiovisual history, a 45-minute audioguide, and a look at the exquisite banqueting hall itself. As a tourist attraction, it's basically one big room, with sumptuous ceiling paintings by Peter Paul Rubens. At Charles I's request, these paintings drove home the doctrine of the legitimacy of the divine right of kings. Ironically, in 1649—divine right ignored—King Charles I was famously executed right here.

Cost and Hours: £6 includes audioguide, daily 10:00-17:00, may close for government functions—though it promises to stay open at least until 13:00 (call ahead for recorded information about closures), WC, immediately across Whitehall from the Horse Guards, Tube: Westminster, tel. 020/3166-6155, www.hrp.org.uk.

For a brief self-guided tour of the Banqueting House—and more details about the history of the place—see page 124 in the Westminster Walk. The Banqueting House is also covered on my free Westminster Walk audio tour.

ON TRAFALGAR SQUARE
▲▲Trafalgar Square
London's renovated central square, the climax of most marches and demonstrations, is a thrilling place to simply hang out. Lord

Nelson stands atop his 185-foot-tall fluted granite column, gazing out toward Trafalgar, where he lost his life but defeated the French fleet. Part of this 1842 memorial is made from his victims' melted-down cannons. He's surrounded by spraying fountains, giant lions, hordes of people, and—until recently—even more pigeons. A former London mayor decided that London's "flying rats" were a public nuisance and evicted Trafalgar Square's venerable seed salesmen (Tube: Charing Cross).

📖 For more on Trafalgar Square, see page 128 in the Westminster Walk. It's also covered on my 🎧 free Westminster Walk audio tour.

▲▲▲National Gallery

Displaying an unsurpassed collection of European paintings from 1250 to 1900—including works by Leonardo, Botticelli, Ve-

lázquez, Rembrandt, Turner, Van Gogh, and the Impressionists—this is one of Europe's great galleries. The collection is huge; following the route suggested in my self-guided tour will give you the best quick visit. For a more thorough tour, use the gallery's excellent audioguide. Or pick out just one masterpiece or a handful of great artists using the gallery's online "Short of Time" suggestions. Whatever time you spend here is worth it.

Cost and Hours: Free, but suggested donation of £5, special exhibits extra, daily 10:00-18:00, Fri until 21:00, last entry to special exhibits 45 minutes before closing; daily free guided tours available, worthwhile audioguide-£4, floor plan-£1; on Trafalgar Square, Tube: Charing Cross or Leicester Square, recorded info tel. 020/7747-2885, switchboard tel. 020/7839-3321, www.nationalgallery.org.uk. The excellent-but-pricey museum restaurant called the National Dining Rooms is a good spot for afternoon tea (see page 415); the museum has cheaper eateries as well.

📖 See the National Gallery Tour chapter.

▲▲National Portrait Gallery

Put off by halls of 19th-century characters who meant nothing to me, I used to call this "as interesting as someone else's yearbook." But a selective walk through this 500-year-long *Who's Who* of British history is quick and free, and puts faces on the story of England.

Some highlights: Henry VIII and wives; portraits of the "Virgin Queen" Elizabeth I, Sir Francis Drake, and Sir Walter Raleigh; the only real-life portrait of William Shakespeare; Oliver Cromwell and Charles I with his head on; portraits by Gainsborough and Reynolds; the Romantics (William Blake, Lord Byron, William Wordsworth, and company); Queen Victoria and her era; and the present royal family, including the late Princess Diana and the current Duchess of Cambridge—Kate.

The collection is well-described, not huge, and in historical sequence, from the 16th century on the second floor to today's royal family on the ground floor.

Cost and Hours: Free, but suggested donation of £5, special exhibits extra; daily 10:00-18:00, Thu-Fri until 21:00, first and second floors open Mon at 11:00, last entry to special exhibits one hour before closing; audioguide-£3, floor plan-£1; entry 100 yards off Trafalgar Square (around the corner from National Gallery, opposite Church of St. Martin-in-the-Fields), Tube: Charing Cross or Leicester Square, tel. 020/7306-0055, recorded info tel. 020/7312-2463, www.npg.org.uk.

☐ See the National Portrait Gallery Tour chapter.

▲St. Martin-in-the-Fields

The church, built in the 1720s with a Gothic spire atop a Greek-type temple, is an oasis of peace on wild and noisy Trafalgar Square. St. Martin cared for the poor. "In the fields" was where the first church stood on this spot (in the 13th century), between Westminster and The City. Stepping inside, you still feel a compassion for the needs of the people in this neighborhood—the church serves the homeless and houses a Chinese community center. The modern east window—with grillwork bent into the shape of a warped cross—was installed in 2008 to replace one damaged in World War II.

A freestanding glass pavilion to the left of the church serves as the entrance to the church's underground areas. There you'll find the concert ticket office, a gift shop, brass-rubbing center, and the recommended support-the-church Café in the Crypt.

Cost and Hours: Free, but donations welcome; hours vary but generally Mon-Fri 8:30-13:00 & 14:00-18:00, Sat 9:30-18:00, Sun 15:30-17:00; services listed at entrance; Tube: Charing Cross, tel. 020/7766-1100, www.smitf.org.

Music: The church is famous for its concerts. Consider a free lunchtime concert (suggested £3.50 donation; Mon, Tue, and Fri at 13:00), an evening concert (£8-28, several nights a week at 19:30), or Wednesday night jazz at the Café in the Crypt (£5.50-12 at 20:00). See the church's website for the concert schedule.

THE WEST END AND NEARBY

☐ The following areas are linked (and further described) in the West End Walk chapter.

▲Piccadilly Circus

Although this square is slathered with neon billboards and tacky attractions (think of it as the Times Square of London), the surrounding streets are packed with great shopping opportunities and swimming with youth on the rampage.

Nearby Shaftesbury Avenue and Leicester Square teem with fun-seekers, theaters, Chinese restaurants, and street singers. To the northeast is London's Chinatown and, beyond that, the funky Soho neighborhood (described next). And curling to the northwest from Piccadilly Circus is genteel Regent Street, lined with exclusive shops.

▲Soho

North of Piccadilly, seedy Soho has become trendy—with many recommended restaurants—and is well worth a gawk (📖 see the West End Walk chapter). It's the epicenter of London's thriving, colorful youth scene, a fun and funky *Sesame Street* of urban diversity.

Soho is also London's red light district (especially near Brewer and Berwick Streets), where "friendly models" wait in tiny rooms up dreary stairways, voluptuous con artists sell strip shows, and eager male tourists are frequently ripped off. But it's easy to avoid trouble if you're not looking for it. In fact, the sleazy joints share the block with respectable pubs and restaurants, and elderly couples stroll past neon signs that flash *Licensed Sex Shop in Basement.*

▲▲Covent Garden

The centerpiece of this boutique-ish shopping district is an iron-and-glass arcade. The "Actors' Church" of St. Paul, the Royal Opera

House, and the London Transport Museum (described next) all border the square, and theaters are nearby. The area is a people-watcher's delight, with cigarette eaters, Punch-and-Judy acts, food that's not good for you (or your wallet), trendy crafts, and row after row of boutique shops and market stalls. For more on this square, see page 187. Better Covent Garden lunch deals can be found by walking a block or two away from the eye of this touristic hurricane (check out the places north of the Tube station, along Endell and Neal Streets, and see my suggestions on page 405).

West End & Nearby

FITZROVIA

Cavendish Square

GREAT PORTLAND ST.

REGENT ST.

MARGARET ST.

BERNERS ST.

NEWMAN ST.

OXFORD

Oxford Circus

STREET

PRINCES ST.

POLAND ST.

BERWICK ST.

WARDOUR ST.

DEAN ST.

SOHO

NEW BOND ST.

Hanover Square

HANOVER ST.

GREAT MARLBOROUGH ST.

LIBERTY DEP'T STORE

BROADWICK ST.

HOPKINS ST.

BOURCH.

BROOK ST.

MADDOX ST.

GEORGE ST.

HAMLEYS

CARNABY ST.

REGENT STREET

KINGLY ST.

MARSHALL ST.

BEAK ST.

LEXINGTON ST.

G. PULTENEY ST.

BREWER ST.

TISBURY CT.

SOTHEBY'S AUCTION HOUSE

CONDUIT ST.

WARWICK ST.

BRIDLE LN.

JAMES ST.

SHERWOOD ST.

GROSVENOR ST.

SAVILE ROW

OLD BURLINGTON ST.

Golden Square

DEN-MAN

RUPERT

SHAFTESBURY AVE.

BRUTON ST.

CLIFFORD ST.

GLASSHOUSE ST.

COVENTRY

MAYFAIR

OLD BOND ST.

BURLINGTON GARDENS

VIGO ST.

REGENT ST.

Piccadilly Circus

Piccadilly Circus

Berkeley Square

ABEMARLE ST.

BURLINGTON ARCADE

SACKVILLE ST.

EROS STATUE

ROYAL ACADEMY OF ARTS

ST. JAMES

DOVER ST.

BERKELEY ST.

PICCADILLY

JERMYN ST.

LOWER REGENT ST.

DUKE OF YORK ST.

FORTNUM & MASON

CURZON ST.

Green Park

ST. JAMES'S

St. James's Square

RITZ HOTEL

CHRISTIE'S AUCTION HOUSE

ST. JAMES ST.

KING ST.

PALL MALL

Green Park

PICCADILLY

200 Meters

200 Yards

MARLBOROUGH RD.

THE MALL

ST. JAMES'S PALACE

▲London Transport Museum

This modern, well-presented museum, located right at Covent Garden, is fun for kids and thought-provoking for adults (if a bit overpriced). Whether you're cursing or marveling at the buses and Tube, the growth of Europe's third-biggest city (after Moscow and Istanbul) has been made possible by its public transit system. Kids enjoy picking up the "stamp card," then punching it with old-fashioned ticket punchers at the different exhibits.

Cost and Hours: £16, ticket good for one year, kids under 18 free, Sat-Thu 10:00-18:00, Fri 11:00-18:00, last entry 45 minutes

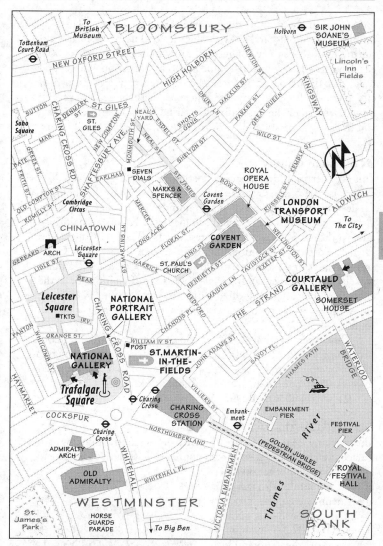

before closing; pleasant upstairs café with Covent Garden view; in southeast corner of Covent Garden courtyard, Tube: Covent Garden, switchboard tel. 020/7379-6344, recorded info tel. 020/7565-7299, www.ltmuseum.co.uk.

Visiting the Museum: After you enter, take the elevator up to the top floor...and the year 1800, when horse-drawn vehicles ruled the road. London invented the notion of a public bus traveling a set route that anyone could board without a reservation. Next, you descend to the first floor and the world's first underground Metro system, which used steam-powered locomotives (the Circle Line,

c. 1865). On the ground floor, horses and trains are replaced by motorized vehicles (cars, taxis, double-decker buses, streetcars), resulting in 20th-century congestion. How to deal with it? In 2003, car drivers in London were slapped with a congestion charge, and today, a half-billion people ride the Tube every year. Learn how city planners hope to improve efficiency with better tracks and more coverage of the expanding East End. Finally, an exhibit lets you imagine futuristic modes of transportation waiting to become real.

▲Courtauld Gallery

This wonderful and compact collection of paintings is a joy. The gallery is part of the Courtauld Institute of Art, and the thoughtful description of each piece of art reminds visitors that the gallery is still used for teaching. You'll see medieval European paintings and works by Rubens, the Impressionists (Manet, Monet, and Degas), Post-Impressionists (Cézanne and an intense Van Gogh self-portrait), and more. Besides the permanent collection, a quality selection of loaners and special exhibits are often included in the entry fee. The gallery is located within the grand Somerset House; enjoy the riverside eateries and the courtyard featuring a playful fountain.

Cost and Hours: £7 (£3 on Mon); open daily 10:00-18:00, occasionally open Thu until 21:00—check website; in Somerset House on the Strand, Tube: Temple or Covent Garden, recorded info tel. 020/7848-2526, www.courtauld.ac.uk.

📖 See the Courtauld Gallery Tour chapter.

BUCKINGHAM PALACE AREA

The working headquarters of the British monarchy, Buckingham Palace is where the Queen carries out her official duties as the head of state. She and other members of the royal family also maintain apartments here. The property hasn't always been this grand—James I (1603-1625) first brought the site under royal protection as a place for his mulberry plantation, for rearing silkworms.

Ticketing Options: Three palace sights require admission—the State Rooms (Aug-Sept only), Queen's Gallery, and Royal Mews. You can pay for each separately (prices below), or buy a combo-ticket: A £35.60 "Royal Day Out" combo-ticket admits you to all three sights; a £17.10 version covers the Queen's Gallery and Royal Mews. For more information or to book tickets online, see www.royalcollection.org.uk. Many tourists are more interested in the Changing of the Guard, which costs nothing at all to view. For locations, see map on page 60.

▲State Rooms at Buckingham Palace

This lavish home has been Britain's royal residence since 1837, when the newly ascended Queen Victoria moved in. When to-day's Queen is at home, the royal standard flies (a red, yellow, and blue flag); otherwise, the Union Jack flaps in the wind. The Queen opens her palace to the public—but only in August and September, when she's out of town.

Cost and Hours: £21 for lavish State Rooms and throne room, includes audioguide; Aug-Sept only, daily 9:30-18:30, until 19:00 in Aug, last admission 17:15 in Aug, 16:15 in Sept; limited to 8,000 visitors a day by timed entry; come early to the palace's Visitor Entrance (opens 9:00), or book ahead in person, by phone, or online; Tube: Victoria, tel. 020/7766-7300.

Queen's Gallery at Buckingham Palace

A small sampling of Queen Elizabeth's personal collection of art is on display in five rooms in a wing adjoining the palace. Her 7,000 paintings, one of the largest private art collections in the world, are actually a series of collections built upon by each successive monarch since the 16th century. The Queen rotates the paintings, enjoying some privately in her many palatial residences while sharing others with her subjects in public galleries in Edinburgh and London. The exhibits change two or three times a year and are lovingly described by the included audioguide.

Because the gallery is small and security is tight (involving lines), I'd suggest visiting this gallery only if you're a patient art lover interested in the current exhibit.

Cost and Hours: £10 but can change depending on exhibit, daily 10:00-17:30, opens at 9:30 Aug-Sept, last entry one hour before closing, Tube: Victoria, tel. 020/7766-7301—but Her Majesty rarely answers. Men shouldn't miss the mahogany-trimmed urinals.

Royal Mews

A visit to the Queen's working stables is likely to be disappointing unless you follow the included audioguide or the hourly guided tour (April-Oct only, 45 minutes), in which case it's fairly entertaining—especially if you're interested in horses and/or royalty. You'll see only a few of the Queen's 30 horses (most active between 10:00 and 12:00), a fancy car, and a bunch of old carriages, finishing with the Gold State Coach (c. 1760, 4 tons, 4 mph). Queen Victoria said absolutely no cars. When she died, in 1901, the mews got its first Daimler. Today, along with the hay-eating transport,

SIGHTS

Buckingham Palace Area

Green Park

To Hyde Park Corner →

CONSTITUTION HILL

FENCE

Buckingham Palace Gardens (Private)

BUCKINGHAM PALACE

QUEEN'S GALLERY

STATE ROOMS ENTRANCE

ROYAL MEWS

GROSVENOR PL.

PALACE ROAD

PALACE ST.

BUCKINGHAM GATE

WILFRED ST.

CASTLE LN.

BRESSENDEN

ALLINGTON

VICTORIA STATION

Victoria

LITTLE BEN

VICTORIA STREET

ST. JAMES'S PALACE

MARLBOROUGH ROAD

To 5 & Trafalgar Square →

THE MALL

CLARENCE HOUSE

LANCASTER HOUSE

THE MALL

QUEEN VICTORIA MEMORIAL

Courtyard

SPUR RD.

Park Lake

BIRDCAGE WALK

Parade Ground

WELLINGTON BARRACKS

GUARDS' CHAPEL

GUARDS' MUSEUM

PETTY FRANCE

PALMER ST.

CAXTON ST.

BROADWAY

St. James's Park

St. James's Park

To 5 & Big Ben →

200 Meters

200 Yards

Note: Numbers correspond to chart on opposite page

----- Guards' Route

the stable is home to five Bentleys and Rolls-Royce Phantoms, with at least one on display.

Cost and Hours: £9, April-Oct daily 10:00-17:00, Nov-March Mon-Sat 10:00-16:00, closed Sun; last entry 45 minutes before closing, generally busiest immediately after changing of the guard, guided tours on the hour in summer; Buckingham Palace Road, Tube: Victoria, tel. 020/7766-7302.

▲▲Changing of the Guard at Buckingham Palace

This is the spectacle every visitor to London has to see at least once: stone-faced, red-coated (or in winter, gray-coated), bearskin-hatted guards changing posts with much fanfare, in an hour-long ceremony accompanied by a brass band.

It's 11:00 at Buckingham Palace, and the on-duty guards (the "Queen's Guard") are ready to finish their shift. Nearby at St. James's Palace (a half-mile

Changing of the Guard Timeline

When	What
10:30	Tourists begin to gather; arrive now for a spot front and center by the ❶ fence outside Buckingham Palace.
11:00	❷ Victoria Memorial gets crowded.
11:00-11:15	"New Guard" gathers for inspection at ❸ Wellington Barracks. "Old Guard" gathers for inspection at ❹ St. James's Palace.
11:00 (10:00 Sun)	Changing of the Horse Guard at ❺ Horse Guards Parade, opposite end of St. James's Park.
11:13	Tired St. James's Palace guards march down ❻ the Mall, heading for Buckingham Palace.
11:27	Fresh replacement troops head from Wellington Barracks down ❼ Spur Road to Buckingham Palace.
11:30	All guards gradually converge around the Victoria Memorial in front of the palace.
11:30-12:00	Changing of the Guard ceremony takes place ❽ inside the fenced courtyard of Buckingham Palace.
12:10	Tired "Old Guard" heads up Spur Road for Wellington Barracks. Fresh "New Guard" heads up the Mall for St. James's Palace.
12:15	Smaller changing of the guard ceremony takes place in front of St. James's Palace.

SIGHTS

northeast), a second set of guards is also ready for a break. Meanwhile, fresh replacement guards (the "New Guard") gather for a review and inspection at Wellington Barracks, 500 yards east of the palace (on Birdcage Walk).

At 11:13, the tired St. James's "Old Guard" heads out to the Mall, and then takes a right turn for Buckingham Palace. At 11:27, the "New Guard" replacement troops, led by the band, also head for Buckingham Palace from the Wellington Barracks. Meanwhile, a fourth group—the Horse Guard—passes by along the Mall on its way back to Hyde Park Corner from its own changing-of-the-guard ceremony on Whitehall (which just took place at Horse Guards Parade at 11:00, or 10:00 on Sun).

At 11:30, the tired and fresh guards converge on Buckingham Palace in a perfect storm of red-coat pageantry. Everyone parades around, the guard changes (passing the regimental flag, or "colour") with much shouting, the band plays a happy little concert, and then they march out. Just after noon, two bands escort two detachments of guards away: the tired "Old Guard" to Wellington Barracks and the fresh "New Guard" to St. James's Palace. As the fresh guards set up at St. James's Palace and the tired ones dress down at the barracks, the tourists disperse.

Cost and Hours: Free, daily May-July at 11:30, every other day Aug-April, no ceremony in very wet weather; exact schedule subject to change—call 020/7766-7300 for the day's plan, or check www.royal.gov.uk (search "Changing the Guard"); Buckingham Palace, Tube: Victoria, St. James's Park, or Green Park. Or hop into a big black taxi and say, "Buck House, please."

Sightseeing Strategies: Most tourists just show up and get lost in the crowds, but those who anticipate the action and know where to perch will enjoy the event more. The action takes place in stages over the course of an hour, at several different locations, see map on page 60. There's several ways to experience the pageantry. Get out your map (or download the official app at www.royalcollection.org.uk) and strategize. Here are a few options to consider:

Watch from One Location: Pick one event and find a good, unobstructed place from which to view it. The key is to get either right up front along the road or fence, or find some raised elevation to stand or sit on—a balustrade or a curb—so you can see over people's heads. The main event is in the forecourt right in front of Buckingham Palace (between Buckingham Palace and the fence) from 11:30 to 12:00. To see it close up, you'll need to get here no later than 10:30 to get a place front and center, next to the fence.

If you get there too late to score a premium spot right along the fence, head for the high ground on the circular Victoria Memorial, which provides the best overall view (come before 11:00 to get a place). From a high spot on the memorial, you have good (if more distant) views of the palace as well as the arriving and departing parades along The Mall and Spur Road. The actual Changing of the Guard in front of the palace is a nonevent. It is interesting, however, to see nearly every tourist in London gathered in one place at the same time.

If you arrive too late to get any good spot at all, or you just don't feel like jostling for a view, stroll down to St. James's Palace and wait near the corner for a great photo-op. At about 12:15, the parade marches up The Mall to the palace and performs a smaller changing ceremony—with almost no crowds. Afterward, stroll through nearby St. James's Park.

Follow the Procession: You won't get the closest views, but you'll get something even better—the thrill of participating in the action. Start with the "Old Guard" mobilizing in the courtyard of St. James's Palace (11:00). Arrive early, and grab a spot just across the road (otherwise you'll be asked to move when the inspection begins). Just before they prepare to leave (at 11:13), march ahead of them down Marlborough Street to The Mall. Pause here to watch them parade past, band and all, on their way to the Palace, then cut through the park and head to the Wellington Barracks—where the "New Guard" is getting ready to leave for Buckingham (11:27). March along with full military band and fresh guards from the barracks to the Palace. At 11:30 the two guard groups meet in the courtyard, the band plays a few songs, and soldiers parade and finally exchange compliments before returning to Wellington Barracks and St. James Palace (12:10). Use this time to snap a few photos of the guards—and the crowds—before making your way across the Mall to Clarence House (on Stable Yard Road), where you'll see the "New Guard" pass one last time on their way to St. James' Palace. On their way, the final piece of ceremony takes place—one member of the "Old Guard" and one member of the first-relief "New Guard" change places here.

SIGHTS

Join a Tour: Local tour companies such as **Fun London Tours** more or less follow the self-guided route above but add in history and facts about the guards, bands, and royal family to their already entertaining march. These walks add color and good value to what can otherwise seem like a stressful mess of tourists (£15, Changing of the Guard tour starts at Piccadilly Circus at 10:00, must book online in advance, www.funlondontours.com).

North London

▲▲▲British Museum

Simply put, this is the greatest chronicle of civilization...anywhere. A visit here is like taking a long hike through *Encyclopedia Britannica* National Park. The vast British Museum wraps around its Great Court (the huge entrance hall), with the most popular sections filling the ground floor: Egyptian, Assyrian, and ancient Greek, with the famous frieze sculptures from the Parthenon in Athens. The museum's stately Reading Room—famous as the place where Karl Marx hung out while formulating his ideas on communism and writing *Das Kapital*—sometimes hosts special exhibits.

Cost and Hours: Free but a £5 donation requested, special exhibits usually extra (and with timed ticket); daily 10:00-17:30, Fri until 20:30 (selected galleries only), least crowded weekday late afternoons; free guided tours offered, multimedia guide-£5; Great Russell Street, Tube: Tottenham Court Road, general info tel. 020/7323-8299, ticket desk tel. 020/7323-8181, www.britishmuseum.org.

📖 See the British Museum Tour chapter or 🎧 download my free audio tour.

▲▲▲British Library

Here, in just two rooms, are the literary treasures of Western civilization, from early Bibles, to Shakespeare's *Hamlet,* to Lewis Carroll's *Alice's Adventures in Wonderland.* You'll see the Lindis-farne Gospels transcribed on an illuminated manuscript, as well as Beatles lyrics scrawled on the back of a greeting card. You might even glimpse the *Magna Carta*—though after celebrating its 800th birthday it may be taking part of 2016 off from public view. The British Empire built its greatest monuments out of paper; it's through literature that England made her most lasting and signifi-cant contribution to civilization and the arts.

Cost and Hours: Free, but £5 suggested donation, admis-sion charged for some special exhibits; Mon-Fri 9:30-18:00, Tue until 20:00, Sat 9:30-17:00, Sun 11:00-17:00; 96 Euston Road, Tube: King's Cross St. Pancras or Euston, tel. 019/3754-6060 or 020/7412-7676, www.bl.uk.

📖 See the British Library Tour chapter or 🎧 download my free audio tour.

▲Wallace Collection

Sir Richard Wallace's fine collection of 17th-century Dutch Mas-ters, 18th-century French Rococo, medieval armor, and assorted

aristocratic fancies fills the sumptuously furnished Hertford House on Man-chester Square. From the rough and intimate Dutch lifescapes of Jan Steen to the pink-cheeked Ro-coco fantasies of François Boucher, a wander through this little-visited mansion makes you nostalgic for the days of the empire. This collection would be a big deal in a mid-sized city, but here in London it gets lost. It's thoroughly enjoyable and affords a classic old-time museum-going experience.

Cost and Hours: Free, daily 10:00-17:00, audioguide-£4 (consider the cost a donation to a great cause), free guided tours or lectures almost daily at 11:30, 13:00, and 14:30—call to confirm times, just north of Oxford Street on Manchester Square, Tube: Bond Street. Tel. 020/7563-9500, www.wallacecollection.org.

Visiting the Museum: The manageable collection is displayed on three floors—not much in the basement; fine arts, medieval

North London

treasures, and armor on the ground floor; and the fine painting collection on the top floor.

As you enter the ground floor, on the right you'll find drawing rooms filled with medieval relics, and to the left (through the gift shop) are the collections of Oriental and European armor—one of the finest such collections in Britain. Then head up the red-carpeted grand staircase to the upper floor, packed with paintings.

The Oval Drawing Room is busy with Boucher and Fragonard—pink, giddy, and Rococo. A highlight is the small but symbolism-packed Rococo masterpiece *The Swing* (1767), by Jean-Honoré Fragonard. The woman is being pulled on the swing by her husband. He's on the right, hidden in shadows, literally "in the dark"—unaware that his wife is having an affair with the man hiding in the bushes on the left. The rascal holds his arm erect as he peeps up this swinging lady's skirt and watches her shoe fly off, symbolizing sexual abandon.

The Great Gallery contains paintings by the big names of the 17th century: Rembrandt, Rubens, Velázquez, Titian, Van Dyck, Murillo, and Hals. One of the museum's best-known paintings is *The Laughing Cavalier* (1624) by Frans Hals (see photo at left). With his hat perched at a jaunty angle, the man smirks enigmatically with unhappy eyes...more of a polite chuckle or a bemused snort.

The Boudoir Cabinet is a tiny room that glitters with exquisite bits of 18th-century French luxury: jeweled snuff boxes, miniatures (a sign of friendship or political allegiance), and spanky pornography for the upper class.

The West Gallery takes you on a trip to 18th-century Venice. It's filled with romantically staged scenes painted by Canaletto and Guardi—purchased as souvenirs by aristocrats on the Grand Tour before the age of postcards.

The East Gallery is interesting for its small-scale 17th-century Dutch paintings by Jan Steen and others who could paint quiet, intimate, and rowdy slices of life—usually conveying a folk moral rather than a religious lesson.

Then head back down to the main floor and go out the door behind the staircase, into the building's gorgeous, glassed-in atrium, filled with light and a restaurant (with slow service and overpriced food).

▲Madame Tussauds Waxworks

This waxtravaganza is gimmicky, crass, and crazily expensive, but dang fun...a hit with the kind of tourists who skip the British Museum. The original Madame Tussaud did wax casts of heads lopped off during the French Revolution (such as Marie-Antoinette's). She took her show on the road and ended up in London in 1835. These days, they've dumped anything really historical (except for what they claim is the blade that beheaded Marie-Antoinette) because "there's no money in it and we're a business." Now it's all about squeezing Leonardo DiCaprio's bum, singing with Lady Gaga, and partying with Brangelina, Benedict Cumberbatch, and the Beatles. The gallery, which sprawls through several rooms of a huge building, is one giant photo-op—the whole point is jockeying for position to snap the best picture of your travel buddy with a famous "person." It's extremely crowded and chaotic, as everyone clamors to press the wax with their heroes, while dodging tourist-trinket kiosks and photographers standing by to overcharge you for a print. These wax sculptures are eerily realistic—count how many times you say "excuse me" after bumping into a dummy.

Cost: £33, kids-£28.80 (kids under 5-free), family passes available; up to 25 percent discount and shorter lines if you buy tickets on their website (also consider a combo-deal with the London Eye), often even bigger discount—up to 50 percent—if you get

"Late Saver" tickets at the door after 17:30, but be aware that some experiences close at 18:00; two-for-one rail vouchers accepted (see page 24).

Hours: July-Aug and school holidays daily 8:30-19:00, Sept-mid-July Mon-Fri 9:30-17:30, Sat-Sun 9:00-18:00, these are last entry times—place stays open roughly two hours later; Marylebone Road, Tube: Baker Street, tel. 0871-894-3000, www. madametussauds.com.

Crowd-Beating Tips: This popular attraction can be swamped. The ticket-buying line can be an hour or more (believe the posted signs about the wait). Once inside, there can be more waits for some popular exhibits. To avoid the ticket line, buy an Online Saver and reserve a time slot at least a day in advance. The place is less crowded (for both buying tickets at the door and for simply enjoying the place) if you arrive after 15:00.

Visiting the Waxworks: First you'll join the paparazzi on the red carpet with A-list stars, then you'll head through several themed sections, featuring Hollywood stars new and old, sports heroes (including some unfamiliar-to-Americans cricket players and footballers), the royal family (pose with the Queen, Will, and Kate...or settle for Charles and Camilla), scientists, artists, writers, musicians, and world leaders. (Even Hitler has a wax figure. Ouch.)

Downstairs are exhibits that sometimes have lines—pick and choose if it's worth the wait. "Scream!" is a hokey but gory haunted-house exhibit where you walk through a dark hallway while actors jump out and grab at you. A small exhibit explains the casting process and the history of Madame Tussaud and her waxy army. Then you'll board a Disney-type people-mover and cruise through a kid-pleasing "Spirit of London" once-over-very-light history of this city. Finally, you reach a nine-minute-long Marvel Super Heroes "4-D" show—a 3-D movie heightened by wind, "back ticklers," and other special effects. It's totally silly, requires a wait in line, and leaves the crowd buzzing with sensory overload—a fitting finale to the entire Waxworks experience.

▲Sir John Soane's Museum

Architects love this quirky place, as do fans of interior decor, eclectic knickknacks, and Back Door sights. Tour this furnished home on a bird-chirping square and see 19th-century chairs, lamps, wood-paneled nooks and crannies, sculptures, and stained-glass skylights. As professor of architecture at the Royal Academy, Soane created his home to be a place of learning, cramming it floor to ceiling with ancient relics, curios, and famous paintings, including several excellent Canalettos and Hogarth's series on *The Rake's Progress* (which is hidden behind a panel in the Picture Room and opened randomly at the museum's discretion, usually twice an hour). In 1833, just before his death, Soane established his house as a museum, stipulating that it be kept as nearly as possible in the state he left it. If he visited today, he'd be entirely satisfied by the diligence with which the staff safeguards his treasures. You'll leave wishing you'd known the man.

Cost and Hours: Free, but donations much appreciated; Tue-Sat 10:00-17:00, open and candlelit the first Tue of the month 18:00-21:00, closed Sun-Mon, long entry lines on Sat; guidebook-£5, guided tour-£10 Tue, Thu, Fri, and Sat 12:00; 13 Lincoln's Inn Fields, quarter-mile southeast of British Museum, Tube: Holborn, tel. 020/7405-2107, www.soane.org.

Cartoon Museum

This humble but interesting museum is located in the shadow of the British Museum. While its three rooms are filled with British cartoons unknown to most Americans, the satirical takeoffs on famous bigwigs and politicians—including Napoleon, Margaret Thatcher, the Queen, and Tony Blair—show the power of parody to deliver social commentary. Upstairs are panels of well-known comics that will interest only diehard fans.

Cost and Hours: £7, Mon-Sat 10:30-17:30, Sun 12:00-17:30, 35 Little Russell Street—go one block south of the British Museum on Museum Street and turn right, Tube: Tottenham Court Road, tel. 020/7580-8155, www.cartoonmuseum.org.

Pollock's Toy Museum

This rickety old house, with glass cases filled with toys and games lining its walls and halls, is a time-warp experience that brings back childhood memories to people who grew up without batteries or computer chips. It also gives a sense of the history of childhood itself, starting from when "childhood" as we know it now first came to be. Though the museum is small, you could spend a lot of time here, squinting at the fascinating toys and well-loved dolls that entertained the children of 19th- and early 20th-century England.

The included information is great. The story of Theodore Roosevelt refusing to shoot a bear cub while on a hunting trip was celebrated in 1902 cartoons, resulting in a new, huggable toy: the Teddy Bear. It was popular for good reason: It could be manufactured during World War I without rationed products; it coincided with the new belief that soft toys were good for a child's development; it was an acceptable "doll for boys"; and it was *the* toy children kept long after they'd grown up.

Cost and Hours: £6, kids-£3, Mon-Sat 10:00-17:00, closed Sun, 1 Scala Street, Tube: Goodge Street, tel. 020/7636-3452, www.pollockstoys.com. A fun retro toy shop is attached.

Beatles Sights

London's city center is surprisingly devoid of sights associated with the famous '60s rock band. To see much of anything, consider taking a guided walk (see page 36).

For a photo op, go to **Abbey Road** and walk the famous crosswalk pictured on the *Abbey Road* album cover (Tube: St. John's

Wood, get information and buy Beatles memorabilia at the small kiosk in the station). From the Tube station, it's a five-minute walk west down Grove End Road to the intersection with Abbey Road. The Abbey Road recording studio is the low-key, white building to the right of Abbey House (it's still a working studio, so you can't go inside). Ponder the graffiti on the low wall outside, and... imagine. To re-create the famous cover photo, shoot the crosswalk from the roundabout as you face north up Abbey Road. Shoes are optional.

Nearby is **Paul McCartney's current home** (7 Cavendish Avenue): Continue down Grove End Road, turn left on Circus Road, and then right on Cavendish. Please be discreet.

The **Beatles Store** is at 231 Baker Street (Tube: Baker Street). It's small—some Beatles-logo T-shirts, mugs, pins, and old vinyl like you might have in your closet—and has nothing of historic value (open eight days a week, 10:00-18:30, tel. 020/7935-4464, www.beatlesstorelondon.co.uk; another rock memorabilia store is across the street).

Sherlock Holmes Museum

A few doors down from the Beatles Store, this meticulous re-creation of the (fictional) apartment of the (fictional) detective sits at the (real) address of 221b Baker Street. The first-floor replica (so to speak) of Sherlock's study delights fans with the opportunity to play Holmes and Watson while sitting in authentic 18th-century chairs. The second and third floors offer fine exhibits on daily Victorian life, showing off furniture, clothes, pipes, paintings, and chamber pots; in other rooms,

Affording London's Sights

London is one of Europe's most expensive cities, with the dubious distinction of having some of the world's steepest admission prices. Fortunately, many sights are free.

Free Museums: Free sights include the British Museum, British Library, National Gallery, National Portrait Gallery, Tate Britain, Tate Modern, Wallace Collection, Imperial War Museum, Victoria and Albert Museum, Natural History Museum, Science Museum, National Army Museum, Sir John Soane's Museum, the Museum of London, the Geffrye Museum, the Guildhall, and on the outskirts of town, the Royal Air Force Museum London.

About half of these museums request a donation of a few pounds, but whether you contribute or not is up to you. If you feel like supporting these museums, renting audioguides, using their café, and buying a few souvenirs all help.

Free Churches: Smaller churches let worshippers (and tourists) in free, although they may ask for a donation. The big sightseeing churches—Westminster Abbey and St. Paul's—charge higher admission fees, but offer free evensong services nearly daily (though you can't stick around afterward to sightsee). Westminster Abbey also offers free organ recitals most Sundays.

Other Freebies: London has plenty of free performances, such as lunch concerts at St. Martin-in-the-Fields (see page 449) and summertime movies at The Scoop amphitheater near City Hall (see page 452). For other freebies, check out www.whatsfree-inlondon.co.uk. There's no charge to enjoy the pageantry of the Changing of the Guard, rants at Speakers' Corner in Hyde Park (on Sun afternoon), displays at Harrods, the people-watching scene at Covent Garden, and the colorful streets of the East End. It's free to view the legal action at the Old Bailey and the legislature at work in the Houses of Parliament. And you can get into a bit of the Tower of London and Windsor Castle by attending Sunday services in each place's chapel (chapel access only).

Greenwich makes for an inexpensive outing. Many of its sights are free, and the journey there is covered by a cheap Zones 1-2 Tube pass.

Sightseeing Deals: Certain One-Day Travelcards (for the Tube) come with discounts at some popular and pricey sights, such as the Churchill War Rooms, Tower of London, and Madame Tussauds. (There are many restrictions—must be purchased at a train station, see page 24 for details.)

Good-Value Tours: The London Walks tours with professional guides (£10) are one of the best deals going. (Note that the guides for the "free" walking tours are unpaid by their companies, and they expect tips—I'd pay up front for an expertly guided tour instead.) Hop-on, hop-off big-bus tours, while expensive (£26-32), provide a great overview and include free boat tours as well as city walks. (Or, for the price of a transit ticket, you could get similar views from the top of a double-decker public bus.) A one-hour Thames ride to Greenwich costs about £12 one-way, but most boats come with entertaining commentary. A three-hour bicycle tour is about £20.

Pricey...but Worth It? Big-ticket sights worth their hefty admission fees (£14-18) are Kew Gardens, Shakespeare's Globe, and the Churchill War Rooms.

The London Eye has become a London must-see—but you may feel differently when you see the prices (£21.50). St. Paul's Cathedral (£18) becomes more worthwhile if you climb the dome for the stunning view. While Hampton Court Palace is expensive (£19.30), it is well-presented and a reasonable value if you have an interest in royal history. The Queen charges royally for a peek inside Buckingham Palace (£21, open Aug-Sept only) and her fine art gallery and carriage museum (adjacent to the palace, £9-10 each). Madame Tussauds Waxworks is pricey but still hard for many to resist (£33, see page 66 for info on discounts). Harry Potter fans gladly pay the Hagrid-sized £33 fee to see the sets and props at the Warner Bros. Studio Tour (but those who wouldn't know a wizard from a Muggle needn't bother).

The Courtauld Gallery and the Wellington Museum at Apsley House are small but affordable (under £10).

Totally Pants (Brit-speak for Not Worth It): The London Dungeon, at £26, is gimmicky, overpriced, and a terrible value... despite the long line at the door.

Theater: Compared with Broadway's prices, London's theater is a bargain. Seek out the freestanding TKTS booth at Leicester Square to get discounts from 25 to 50 percent on good seats (and full-price tickets to the hottest shows with no service charges; see page 444). Buying direct at the theater box office can score you a great deal on same-day tickets, and even the most popular shows generally have some seats under £20 (possibly with obstructed views)—ask. A £5 "groundling" ticket for a play at Shakespeare's Globe is the best theater deal in town (see page 448). Tickets to the Open Air Theatre at north London's Regent's Park start at £25 (see page 449).

London doesn't come cheap. But with its many free museums and affordable plays, this cosmopolitan, cultured city offers days of sightseeing thrills without requiring you to pinch your pennies (or your pounds).

models are posed to enact key scenes from Sir Arthur Conan Doyle's famous books (but not the recently popular BBC series).

Cost and Hours: £15, daily 9:30-18:00, expect to wait 15 minutes or more—up to 2 hours in peak season; large gift shop for Holmes connoisseurs, including souvenirs from the BBC TV series; Tube: Baker Street, tel. 020/7935-8866, www.sherlock-holmes.co.uk.

The City

When Londoners say "The City," they mean the one-square-mile business center in East London that 2,000 years ago was Roman Londinium. The outline of the Roman city walls can still be seen in the arc of roads from Blackfriars Bridge to Tower Bridge. Within The City are 23 churches designed by Sir Christopher Wren, mostly just ornamentation around St. Paul's Cathedral. Today, while home to only 10,000 residents, The City thrives with around 400,000 office workers coming and going daily. It's a fascinating district to wander on weekdays, but since almost nobody actually lives there, it's dull in the evenings and on Saturday and Sunday.

□ See The City Walk chapter or ∩ download my free audio tour.

ST. PAUL'S CATHEDRAL AND NEARBY
▲▲▲St. Paul's Cathedral
Wren's most famous church is the great St. Paul's, its elaborate interior capped by a 365-foot dome. Since World War II, St. Paul's has been Britain's symbol of resilience. Despite 57 nights of bombing, the Nazis failed to destroy the cathedral, thanks to St. Paul's volunteer fire watchmen, who stayed on the dome. Today you can climb the dome for a great city view. The crypt (included with admission) is a world of historic bones and memorials, including Admiral Nelson's tomb and interesting cathedral models.

Cost and Hours: £18, £15.50 if purchased in advance on the website, includes church entry, dome climb, crypt, tour, and au-

dioguide; Mon-Sat 8:30-16:30 (dome opens at 9:30), closed Sun except for worship; book ahead online to skip the line or you might be waiting 15-30 minutes at busy times, guided tours offered; Tube: St. Paul's, recorded info tel. 020/7246-8348, reception tel. 020/7246-8350, www.stpauls.co.uk.

Music: The evensong services are free (Sun 15:15, Tue-Sat

17:00, not on Mon), but nonpaying visitors are not allowed to linger afterward (see page 263 for details).

Cheap Trick: To get a free cityscape view nearly as good as the expensive view from St. Paul's dome, head for the rooftop terrace at One New Change, just behind the church. To reach it, walk through the churchyard (to the left of the church as you face it), cross the busy street, turn right and head toward the modern shopping mall at One New Change. Behind the escalators, you'll find glass elevators where you can ride to the top floor for an amazing view of St Paul's and the rest of the city.

📖 See the St. Paul's Cathedral Tour chapter or 🎧 download my free audio tour.

▲Old Bailey

To view the British legal system in action—lawyers in little blond wigs speaking legalese with an upper-crust accent—spend a few minutes in the visitors' gallery at the Old Bailey courthouse, called the "Central Criminal Court." Don't enter under the dome; continue up the block about halfway to the modern part of the building—the entry is at Warwick Passage.

Cost and Hours: Free, generally Mon-Fri 10:00-13:00 & 14:00-17:00 depending on caseload, last entry at 12:40 and 15:40 but often closes an hour or so earlier, closed Sat-Sun, fewer cases in Aug; no kids under 14; 2 blocks northwest of St. Paul's on Old Bailey Street (down a tunnel called Warwick Passage, follow signs to public entrance), Tube: St. Paul's, tel. 020/7248-3277 www.cityoflondon.gov.uk.

Bag Check: Old Bailey has a strictly enforced policy of no bags, mobile phones, cameras, iPods, or food. Small purses are OK (but no phones or cameras inside). You can check bags at the Capable Travel agency just down the street at 4 Old Bailey for £5/bag and £1/phone or camera; or at the nearby Museum of London for £1.

The Guildhall

Hiding out in The City, the Guildhall offers visitors a grand medieval hall and a delightful painting gallery for free. This area has been a gathering place since ancient Roman times (on the square, note the circular outline of the Roman amphitheater that once stood here). The meeting spot for guilds in medieval times, it still hosts about 100 professional associations today. The venerable hall, which survived both the Great Fire of 1666 and bombing in World War II, dates from the 15th century and is a rare bit of civil architecture surviving from the Middle Ages.

Adjoining the old hall is the Guildhall Art Gallery, giving insight into old London society with mostly Victorian paintings of numerous London scenes. One of best Victorian collections in

The City, The Tower & East London

London, it's well-described and organized into themes (home, beauty, faith, leisure, work, love, and imagination), and includes dreamy Pre-Raphaelite works. In the basement is a well-presented exhibit on a Roman amphitheater discovered during a building project in 1988.

Cost and Hours: Free, Mon-Sat 10:00-17:00, Sun 12:00-16:00, 6 blocks northeast of St. Paul's on Gresham Street, Tube: St. Paul's or Bank, www.guildhall.cityoflondon.gov.uk.

▲Museum of London

This museum tells the fascinating story of London, taking you on a walk from its pre-Roman beginnings to the present. It features London's distinguished citizens through history—from Neanderthals, to Romans, to Elizabethans, to Victorians, to Mods, to today. The displays are chronological, spacious, and informative without being overwhelming. Scale models and costumes help you visualize everyday life in the city at different periods. There are enough whiz-bang multimedia displays (including the Plague and the Great Fire) to spice up otherwise humdrum artifacts. This

regular stop for the local school kids gives the best overview of London history in town.

Cost and Hours: Free, daily 10:00-18:00, last admission an hour before closing, see the day's events board for special talks and tours, café, luggage lockers, 150 London Wall at Aldersgate Street, Tube:

London for Early Birds and Night Owls

Most sightseeing in London is restricted to the hours between 10:00 and 18:00. Here are a few exceptions:

Sights Open Early

Westminster Cathedral: Daily at 7:00

St. Paul's Cathedral: Mon-Sat at 8:30

Shakespeare's Globe: Daily at 9:00

Madame Tussauds Waxworks: Daily at 8:30 or 9:30

Tower of London: Tue-Sat at 9:00

Churchill War Rooms: Daily at 9:30

Westminster Abbey: Mon-Sat at 9:30

British Library: Mon-Sat at 9:30

Buckingham Palace: Aug-Sept daily at 9:30

Sights Open Late

Keep in mind that many of these sights stop admitting visitors well before their posted closing times.

London Eye: Last ascent daily at 20:30, later in July and Aug

Madame Tussauds: Daily until 20:30, and until 21:30 or later in July and August

Clink Prison Museum: July-Sept daily until 21:00, Oct-June Sat-Sun until 19:30

British Library: Tue until 20:00

British Museum (some galleries): Fri until 20:30

National Portrait Gallery: Thu-Fri until 21:00

National Gallery: Fri until 21:00

Victoria and Albert Museum (some galleries): Fri until 22:00

Tate Modern: Fri-Sat until 22:00

Barbican or St. Paul's plus a five-minute walk, tel. 020/7001-9844, www.museumoflondon.org.uk.

Visiting the Museum: The first part of the tour zips quickly through a half-million years, when Britain morphed from peninsula to island, Neanderthals speared mammoths, and Stone Age humans huddled in crude huts on the South Bank of the Thames.

In 54 b.c., Julius Caesar invaded, and the Romans built "Londinium" on the north bank. The settlement quickly became the hub of Britain and a river-trade town, complete with arenas, forums, baths, a bridge across the Thames, and a **city wall.** That wall—arcing from the present Tower of London to St. Paul's—defined the city's boundaries for the next 1,500 years. The Museum of London sits on the northwest perimeter of the city wall—look out the windows to see a crumbling remnant along the street, now called "London Wall."

When Rome could no longer defend the city (A.D. 410), it fell to the Saxons (becoming "Lundenburg") and, later, the Normans (in 1066), who built the Tower of London. Medieval London was devastated by the Black Death plague of 1348. As the city recovered and grew even bigger, it became clear to wannabe kings that whoever controlled London controlled Britain.

When Queen Elizabeth I brought peace to the land, London thrived as a capital of theaters (the Globe and Rose), arts, and ideas. Then, just when things were going so well, the Great Fire of 1666 destroyed the city, leaving London a blank slate.

Next, take a stroll through a recreated Georgian **"pleasure garden"** to experience a day in the life of 18th-century high society, and take a **"Victorian walk"** through a re-creation of a London street to see what it was like to live in the world's greatest city. The interesting costume section helps humanize all the history.

Two world wars and the car changed 20th-century London into a concrete jungle. But it remained a cultural capital of elegance (see an Art Deco elevator from Selfridge's) and a global trendsetter (Beatles-era memorabilia).

In the last room, you'll see the museum's prized possession—an example of the opulence of rebuilt Georgian London. The **Lord Mayor's Coach,** a golden carriage pulled by six white horses, looks as if it pranced right out of the pages of *Cinderella.* At the back of this room, a touching memorial to the victims of the terrorist bombings of July 7, 2005, weaves contemporary London into the tapestry of history.

The Monument

Wren's 202-foot-tall tribute to London's 1666 Great Fire was recently restored. Climb the 311 steps inside the column for a monumental view of The City.

Cost and Hours: £4, £10.50 combo-ticket with Tower Bridge, daily 9:30-18:00, until 17:30 Oct-March, junction of Monument Street and Fish Street Hill, Tube: Monument, tel. 020/7626-2717, www.themonument.info.

TOWER OF LONDON AND NEARBY

▲▲▲Tower of London

The Tower has served as a castle in wartime, a king's residence in peacetime, and, most notoriously, as the prison and execution site of rebels. You can see the crown jewels, take a witty Beefeater tour, and ponder the executioner's block that dispensed with troublesome heirs to the throne and a couple of Henry VIII's wives.

Note that lines can be long for this sight; see page 276 for tips on getting in quickly. After your visit, consider taking the boat to Greenwich from here (see cruise info on page 39).

Cost and Hours: £24.50, family-£61; Tue-Sat 9:00-17:30, Sun-Mon 10:00-17:30; Nov-Feb closes one hour earlier; free Beefeater tours available, skippable audioguide-£4, Tube: Tower Hill, tel. 0844-482-7788, www.hrp.org.uk.

📖 See the Tower of London Tour chapter.

Tower Bridge

The iconic Tower Bridge (often mistakenly called London Bridge) has been recently painted and restored. The hydraulically powered drawbridge was built in 1894 to accommodate the growing East End. While fully modern, its design was a retro Neo-Gothic look.

The bridge is most interesting when the drawbridge lifts to let ships pass, as it does a thousand times a year (best viewed from the Tower side of the Thames). For the bridge-lifting schedule, check the website or call.

You can tour the bridge at the **Tower Bridge Exhibition,** with a history display and a peek at the Victorian engine room that lifts the span. Included in your entrance is the chance to cross the bridge—138 feet above the road along a see-through glass walkway. As an exhibit, it's overpriced, though the adrenaline rush and spectacular city views from the walkways may help justify the cost.

Cost and Hours: £9, £10.50 combo-ticket with Monument, daily 10:00-18:00 in summer, 9:30-17:30 in winter, enter at northwest tower, Tube: Tower Hill, tel. 020/7403-3761, www.towerbridge.org.uk.

Nearby: The best remaining bit of London's **Roman Wall** is just north of the Tower (at the Tower Hill Tube station). The chic **St. Katharine Dock,** just east of Tower Bridge, has private yachts and mod shops. Across the bridge, on the South Bank, is the upscale Butlers Wharf area, as well as City Hall, museums, the Jubilee Walkway, and, towering overhead, the Shard. Or you can head north to Liverpool Street Station and follow my **East End Walk** (see next page).

East London

Every great city needs an "East End"—the downwind-from-industry, poor workers' quarter where rents are cheap, immigrants with different religions and customs can find comfort in numbers, and

SIGHTS

the everyday people who power the economic engine of that city find a humble home.

London's East End has a long history as London's poorer side of town—even in medieval times, this was the less desirable end, in part because it was downwind from the noxious hide-tanning district. London's east/west disparity was exacerbated in Victorian times, when the wind carried the pollution of a newly industrialized London. These days, there's a new energy here, and it's well-worth exploring.

▲East End Walk: Markets, Banglatown, and Jack the Ripper

This walk—which takes about an hour without stopping to slurp a curry or shop the markets—is basically a big rectangle. Liverpool Street Station marks the end of The City—everything beyond is "East End." From Bishopsgate we'll walk down Brushfield Street (dip into Spitalfields Market and visit Christ Church along the way) to Brick Lane (the "Banglatown" Bangladeshi neighborhood), then return to Liverpool Street Station through some characteristic Jack-the-Ripper-type lanes and the Petticoat Lane Market. The walk works best on Sunday afternoons, when the Spitalfields, Petticoat Lane, and Truman markets thrive (for more on these markets, see page 432).

Getting There: Ride the Tube to Liverpool Street, and head into the train station. Exit the busy station through the Bishopsgate exit (facing the train tracks, it's on the far end to your right, up the stairs/escalators).

◑ Self-Guided Walk: Outside the train station, cross Bishopsgate Street and turn left. Continue two blocks ahead to the glassy, modern RBS building, then turn right on Brushfield Street; from here you can see the steeple of Christ Church. The first third of this walk is basically a straight line from here to Brick Lane (with stops at Spitalfields Market and Christ Church). Head for the church, but half a block or so before you get there, detour left into the market.

Spitalfields Market: This lively, inviting, modern-feeling market hall boasts a combination of colorful restaurants, shops, and—on many days—market stalls selling upscale crafts, designer clothes, collectables, and vintage curiosities. Like so many markets, it's liveliest on Sunday (dating back to when it was a Jewish market closed Saturday for the Sabbath). While the eateries here are tempting, consider waiting for the Bangladeshi curry joints coming up soon on this walk. Exit the market through the "Spitfire" gate at the east end and head for the big church on the right.

Christ Church and Fournier Street: This stony church, with its towering 225-foot steeple, has a mysterious heritage. Many find occult symbolism in its curious design (without a cross on top). It also evokes London's most famous serial killer, as many Jack the Ripper witnesses could help pinpoint the time of the crimes by remembering the church bells' chimes.

The interior of the church dates to 1711. That's when Queen Anne decided to build a place for the "God-less thousands who had no place to worship"—meaning to give immigrants a proper Protestant place to worship. It's stripped down to suit Protestant tastes (but the fine 19th-century windows were added during the "Romantic Age").

The Ten Bells is just across Fournier Street from the church (on the corner of busy Commercial Street and Fournier Street). This classic working-class pub, established in 1753, was the hangout of one of Jack the Ripper's victims.

It makes sense that there were lots of watering holes in this neighborhood because pubs have always filled a need for the working class. A beer on the corner was the closest humble workers could get to a comfortable living room, a place to entertain, and a vacation.

This neighborhood is in transition—a battle zone between the 19th century and the 21st century. One way to confront economic hard times is to build. London is building itself out of the Great Recession with a frenzy, and all the construction is threatening characteristic old neighborhoods like this one. The East End Preservation Society is working overtime to protect and preserve the Spitalfields area.

Continue walking east (between the pub and the church) down Fournier Street, which is lined with classic brick tenement houses (though "tenement" now carries a negative connotation, it originally just described any urban apartment building). In the 1700s, Fournier Street was home to lots of Huguenots—French-Protestant religious refugees—who settled here as weavers. With the old lampposts and few signs of modern life, it's not hard to imagine how this gaslit street would have looked on a foggy night in Jack the Ripper's time. This long line of former weaving houses leads to Brick Lane and London's Bangladeshi neighborhood. Walk to the end of the street, marked by the modern metal minaret of a mosque.

Bangladeshi Town and Brick Lane: When you reach Brick Lane, you're suddenly immersed in **"Banglatown,"** London's highest concentration of Bangladeshi residents. Immediately on your left is the neighborhood mosque, **Jamme Masjid.** This building has a history as dynamic as London itself: It was built as a Huguenot chapel and then used as a Methodist chapel and a Jewish synagogue before being converted into a mosque in 1976.

Brick Lane stretches right and left. We'll venture left a block or so, and then head right a couple blocks before turning right again and returning to Liverpool Street Station.

Even back in ancient Roman times, London's bricks were made here, on Brick Lane. As mentioned, this gritty workers' quarter is the engine of a great city (every city needs one). It was once Jewish, then French, now Bangladeshi. That pattern is now in jeopardy: Listen to the sound of construction over the cacophony of languages.

Wander left up **Brick Lane,** window-shopping for lunch or dinner. Here in "the curry capital of Europe," neon signs advertise cheap meals, and out front, pitchmen jockey for your business. The slightest hesitation on your part will result in an offer of a 20 percent discount. This is a great place to sample "Ruby Murray" (Cockney rhyming slang for "curry"—see page 258). Just like the US has "Tex-Mex," England has "Balti," a British-invented "Indian food" that suits English tastes. After all, chicken tikka masala has replaced fish-and-chips as the national dish.

After two blocks is the former Truman Brewery. The brewery, established in 1666, now houses the **Truman Markets**—a collection of eclectic markets and funky shops, a creative and colorful food hall, and Café 1001 (good coffee). A half-block farther north, you'll find the old brewery smokestack. This is the epicenter of a youthful, trendy scene with several lively pub/café/nightclubs.

Now turn around and backtrack south on Brick Lane, passing the mosque at Fournier Street (where you entered this street). The alleyway 30 yards past the minaret (opposite Monsoon at #80) leads to a graffiti-filled courtyard. Check out this new street-based art form.

Jack the Ripper Streets: Continue down Brick Lane another block and turn right (west) on **Fashion Street.** When you hit busy Commercial Street, cross it, go a few steps, and then veer left on Toynbee Street—past a hair salon called "Jack the Clipper." Then head right on **Brune Street,** where you'll see more Industrial Age tenements and the "Soup Kitchen for the Jewish Poor" (sign above the doorways on right, at #9). At the end of the block, turn right onto Tenter Ground, the street where weavers once dried cloth "on tenterhooks," giving us the phrase that means "uneasy." Look up to see the iron racks still rigged to the building.

At the end of Tenter Ground, look across Crispin Street for a big building with a "Women" sign. This is the women's entrance to a Victorian workhouse. Cross Crispin/Bell Lane and walk down narrow **Artillery Lane.** Notice the men's entrance to the same workhouse above you on the right. The name of this street dates to around 1500, when Henry VIII used this as a practice zone for his artillery.

Artillery Lane soon shrinks to become atmospheric **Artillery Passage,** lined with tiny eateries—giving you an idea of how densely packed this neighborhood was when it was filled with grimy-faced 19th-century factory workers. Jack the Ripper films always use this characteristic street.

At the intersection with Sandy's Row are the **bollards** (black-white-red stakes in the pavement), alerting you that you're officially leaving the East End and entering the City of London. (You could end the walk here by continuing straight ahead to Liverpool Street Station.)

Petticoat Lane Market: For a side-trip to Petticoat Lane Market, turn left. Go three blocks (down Sandy's Row and then Middlesex Street) to Wentworth Street, which leads left into the market. One of the oldest markets in Britain, this one has existed here for 400 years selling cheap stuff for poor working people. It's fun daily and packed on Sunday; enticing food stalls line Goulston Street.

Return to Liverpool Street Station by following Middlesex

Street back to your starting point. Middlesex is the border between The City (on your left) and the East End (on your right). Consider again the juxtaposition of these two equally characteristic parts of London: The City, also called "One Square Mile," is the richest square mile on earth. This banking district towers like a rich monster while far below, in the East End, people scrummage for "pants, 3 for a tenner."

Back at the **Liverpool Street** train and Tube stations, take a moment to recall the reason you don't see many garbage cans—and you can't check a bag at the station. At 8:45 on July 7, 2005, a Tube train had just pulled out of Liverpool Street Station when it was rocked by a terrorist bomb—the first of four to hit London that day. But the next day, Londoners were back on the Tube.

▲Geffrye Museum

This low-key but well-organized museum—housed in an 18th-century almshouse—is located north of Liverpool Street Station. It's a strip of 11 rooms, each furnished as a living room from a different age and each very well-described. It's an intimate peek at the middle class as its comforts evolved from 1600 to 2000. In summer, explore the fragrant herb garden.

Cost and Hours: Free, Tue-Sun 10:00-17:00, closed Mon, garden open April-Oct, 136 Kingsland Road, tel. 020/7739-9893, www.geffrye-museum.org.uk.

Getting There: Take the Tube to Liverpool Street, then ride the bus 10 minutes north (bus #149 or #242—leave station through Bishopsgate exit and head left a few steps to find stop; hop off at the Pearson Street stop, just after passing the brick museum on the right). Or take the East London line on the Overground to the Hoxton stop, which is right next to the museum (Tube tickets and Oyster cards also valid on Overground).

The South Bank

The South Bank of the Thames is a thriving arts and cultural center, tied together by the riverfront Jubilee Walkway.

▲Jubilee Walkway

This riverside path is a popular, pub-crawling pedestrian promenade that stretches all along the South Bank, offering grand views of the Houses of

SIGHTS

Parliament and St. Paul's. On a sunny day, this is the place to see Londoners out strolling. The Walkway hugs the river except just east of London Bridge, where it cuts inland for a couple of blocks. It has been expanded into a 60-mile "Greenway" circling the city, including the 2012 Olympics site.

▲▲London Eye

This giant Ferris wheel, towering above London opposite Big Ben, is one of the world's highest observational wheels and London's

answer to the Eiffel Tower. Riding it is a memorable experience, even though London doesn't have much of a skyline, and the price is borderline outrageous. Whether you ride or not, the wheel is a sight to behold.

Designed like a giant bicycle wheel, it's a pan-European undertaking: British steel and Dutch engineering, with Czech, German, French, and Italian mechanical parts. It's also very "green," running extremely efficiently and virtually silently. Twenty-five people ride in each of its 32 air-conditioned capsules (representing the boroughs of London) for the 30-minute rotation (you go around only once). From the top of this 443-foot-high wheel—the second-highest public viewpoint in the city—even Big Ben looks small. Built to celebrate the new millennium, the Eye has become a permanent fixture on the London skyline.

After buying your ticket inside, you'll be aggressively ushered into the *London Eye 4-D Experience*, a brief (four-minute) and

engaging show combining a 3-D movie with wind and water effects. This bombastic ad for the attraction you already bought a ticket for, in some ways, is more exciting than riding the Eye itself. You can politely skip the show if you just want to get on the wheel, and you have the option of coming back

later to see the movie (which is free to enter, even if you don't buy a ticket for the Eye).

Cost: £21.50, family ticket available, about 10 percent cheaper if bought online. Combo-tickets save money if you plan on visiting Madame Tussauds. Buy tickets in advance at www.londoneye.com, by calling 0870-500-0600, or in person at the box office (in the corner of the County Hall building nearest the Eye).

Hours: Daily 10:00-20:30, until 21:30 or later in July and August, check the website for latest schedule, these are last-ascent times, closed Dec 25 and a few days in Jan for annual maintenance, Tube: Waterloo or Westminster. Thames boats come and go from Waterloo Pier at the foot of the wheel.

Crowd-Beating Tips: The London Eye is busiest between 11:00 and 17:00, especially on weekends year-round and every day in July and August. You might have to wait up to 30 minutes to buy your ticket, then another 30-45 minutes to board your capsule—it's best to call ahead or go online to prebook your ticket during these times. To retrieve your ticket at the sight, punch your confirmation code into the machine in the ticket office (or pick it up in the short "Groups and Ticket Collection" line at desks #15-16). Even if you pre-reserve, you still have to wait a bit to board the wheel. You can pay an extra £10 for a Fast Track ticket that lets you jump the queue, but it's probably not worth the expense.

By the Eye: The area next to the London Eye has developed a cotton-candy ambience of kitschy, kid-friendly attractions. There's a game arcade, an aquarium, and the Shrek's Adventure amusement ride.

▲▲Imperial War Museum

This impressive museum covers the wars of the last century—from World War I biplanes, to the rise of fascism, the Cold War, the

 Cuban Missile Crisis, the Troubles in Northern Ireland, the wars in Iraq and Afghanistan, and terrorism. Rather than glorify war, the museum encourages an understanding of the history of modern warfare and the wartime experience, including the effect it has on the everyday lives of people back home. The museum's coverage never neglects the human side of one of civilization's more uncivilized, persistent traits.

Allow plenty of time, as this powerful museum—with lots of artifacts and video clips—can be engrossing. The highlights are the new WWI galleries (renovated to commemorate the 100-year anniversary of that conflict) and the WWII area, the "Secret War" section, and the Holocaust exhibit. War wonks love the place, as do general history buffs who enjoy patiently reading displays. For the rest, there are enough interactive experiences and multimedia exhibits and submarines for the kids to climb in to keep it interesting.

The museum (which sits in an inviting park equipped with

an equally inviting café) is housed in what had been the Royal Bethlam Hospital. Also known as "the Bedlam asylum," the place was so wild that it gave the world a new word for chaos. Back in Victorian times, locals—without reality shows and YouTube—paid admission to visit the asylum on weekends for entertainment.

Cost and Hours: Free, £5 suggested donation, daily 10:00-18:00, special exhibits extra, various free audioguides may be available—ask at the info desk, Tube: Lambeth North or Elephant and Castle; buses #3, #12, and #159 come here from Westminster area; tel. 020/7416-5000, www.iwm.org.uk.

Visiting the Museum: Start with the atrium to grasp the massive scale of warfare as you wander among and under notable battle machines, then head directly for the museum's latest pride and joy: the recently renovated WWI galleries. Here firsthand accounts connect the blunt reality of a brutal war with the contributions, heartache, and efforts of a nation. Exhibits cover the various theaters and war at sea, as well as life on the home front.

As you escape unscathed, pause to ponder the irony of how different this museum would be if the war to end all wars had lived up to its name. Instead, the museum, much like history, builds on itself. Ascending to the first floor, you'll find the permanent **Turning Points** galleries progressing up to and through World War II and including sections explaining the Blitzkrieg and its effects (see an actual Nazi parachute bomb like the ones that devastated London). For a deeper understanding of life during these decades, visit the **Family in Wartime** exhibit to see London through the eyes of an ordinary family.

The second floor houses the **Secret War** exhibit, which peeks into the intrigues of espionage in World Wars I and II through present-day security. You'll learn about MI5 (Britain's domestic spy corps), MI6 (their international spies—like the CIA), and the Special Operations Executive (SOE), who led espionage efforts during World War II. The exhibit features actual surveillance equipment and poses challenging questions about the role of secrecy in government.

The third floor houses various (and often rotating) temporary art and film exhibits speckled with military-themed works including **John Singer Sargent's** *Gassed* (1919), showing besieged troops in World War I, and other giant canvases.

The fourth-floor section on the **Holocaust**, one of the best on the subject anywhere, tells the story with powerful videos, ar-

London's Best Views

Though London is a height-challenged city, you can get lofty perspectives on it from several high-flying places. For some viewpoints, you need to pay admission, and at the bars or restaurants, you'll need to buy a drink; the only truly free spots are Primrose Hill, the rooftop terrace of One New Change shopping mall (behind St. Paul's Cathedral), the Sky Garden at 20 Fenchurch, and the viewpoint in front of Greenwich's Royal Observatory.

London Eye: Ride the giant Ferris wheel for stunning London views. See page 84.

St. Paul's Dome: You'll earn a striking, unobstructed view by climbing hundreds of steps to the cramped balcony of the church's cupola. See the St. Paul's Cathedral Tour chapter.

One New Change Rooftop Terrace: Get fine, free views of St. Paul's Cathedral and surroundings—nearly as good as those from St. Paul's Dome—from the rooftop terrace of the shopping mall just behind and east of the church. See page 72.

Tate Modern: Take in a classic vista across the Thames from the restaurant/bar on the museum's sixth level. See page 307.

20 Fenchurch (a.k.a. "The Walkie-Talkie"): Get 360-degree views of London from the mostly enclosed Sky Garden, complete with a thoughtfully planned urban garden, bar, restaurants, and lots of locals. It's free to access but you'll need to make reservations in advance and bring photo ID (Mon-Fri 10:00-18:00, Sat-Sun 11:00-21:00, 20 Fenchurch Street, Tube: Monument, www.skygarden.london). If you can't get a reservation, try arriving before 10:00 (or 11:00 on weekends) and ask to go up. Once in, you can stay as long as you like.

National Portrait Gallery: A mod top-floor restaurant peers over Trafalgar Square and the Westminster neighborhood. See the

tifacts, and fine explanations. While it's not the same as actually being at one of Europe's many powerful Holocaust sites, the exhibits are compelling enough to evoke the same emotions.

Crowning the museum on the fifth floor is the Lord Ashcroft Gallery and the **Extraordinary Heroes** display. Here, more than 250 stories celebrate Britain's highest military award for bravery with the world's largest collection of Victoria Cross medals. Civilians who earned the George Cross medal for bravery are also honored.

FROM TATE MODERN TO CITY HALL

These sights are in Southwark (SUTH-uck), the core of the tourist's South Bank. Southwark was for centuries the place Londoners would go to escape the rules and decency of the city and let their hair down. Bearbaiting, brothels, rollicking pubs, and

National Portrait Gallery Tour chapter.

Waterstones Bookstore: Its hip, low-key, top-floor café/bar has reasonable prices and sweeping views of the London Eye, Big Ben, and the Houses of Parliament (see page 22, on Sun bar closes one hour before bookstore, www.5thview.co.uk).

OXO Tower: Perched high over the Thames River, the building's upscale restaurant/bar boasts views over London and St. Paul's, with al fresco dining in good weather (Barge House Street, Tube: Blackfriars, tel. 020/7803-3888, www.harveynichols.com/restaurants/oxo-tower-london).

London Hilton, Park Lane: You'll spot Buckingham Palace, Hyde Park, and the London Eye from Galvin at Windows, a 28th-floor restaurant/bar in an otherwise nondescript hotel (22 Park Lane, Tube: Hyde Park Corner, tel. 020/7208-4021, www.galvinatwindows.com).

The Shard: The observation decks that cap this 1,020-foot-tall skyscraper offer London's most commanding views, but at an outrageously high price. See page 93.

Primrose Hill: For dramatic 360-degree city views, head to the huge grassy expanse at the summit of Primrose Hill, just north of Regent's Park (off Prince Albert Road, Tube: Chalk Farm or Camden Town, www.royalparks.org.uk/parks/the-regents-park).

The Thames River: Various companies run boat trips on the Thames, offering a unique vantage point and unobstructed, ever-changing views of great landmarks (see page 39).

Royal Observatory Greenwich: Enjoy sweeping views of Greenwich's grand buildings in the foreground, the Docklands' skyscrapers in the middle ground, and The City and central London in the distance.

SIGHTS

theater—you name the dream, and it could be fulfilled just across the Thames. A run-down warehouse district through the 20th century, it's been gentrified with classy restaurants, office parks, pedestrian promenades, major sights (such as the Tate Modern and Shakespeare's Globe), and a colorful collection of lesser sights. The area is easy on foot and a scenic—though circuitous—way to connect the Tower of London with St. Paul's.

📖 You'll find more information on these sights in the Bankside Walk chapter.

▲▲Tate Modern

Dedicated in the spring of 2000, the striking museum fills a derelict old power station across the river from St. Paul's—it opened the new century with art from the previous one. Its powerhouse collection includes Dalí, Picasso, Warhol, and much more. Of

equal interest are the many temporary exhibits featuring more current,
cutting-edge art. Each year, the main
hall features a different monumental
installation by a prominent artist.

Cost and Hours: Free, but £4
donation appreciated, fee for special exhibitions; open daily 10:00-
18:00, Fri-Sat until 22:00, last entry
to special exhibits 45 minutes before closing, especially crowded
on weekend days (crowds thin out on Fri and Sat evenings); free
guided tours available, videoguide-£4.50, view restaurant on top
floor, across the Millennium Bridge from St. Paul's; Tube: Southwark, London Bridge, St. Paul's, Mansion House, or Blackfriars
plus a 10-15-minute walk; or connect by Tate Boat museum ferry
from Tate Britain—see page 41; tel. 020/7887-8888, www.tate.
org.uk.

 See the Tate Modern Tour chapter.

▲Millennium Bridge

The pedestrian bridge links St. Paul's Cathedral and the Tate
Modern across the Thames. This is London's first new bridge in
a century. When it opened, the $25 million bridge wiggled when
people walked on it, so it promptly closed for repairs; 20 months
and $8 million later, it reopened. Nicknamed the "blade of light"
for its sleek minimalist design (370 yards long, four yards wide,
stainless steel with teak planks), its clever aerodynamic handrails
deflect wind over the heads of pedestrians.

▲▲Shakespeare's Globe

This replica of the original Globe Theatre was built, half-timbered
and thatched, as it was in Shakespeare's time. (This is the first
thatched roof constructed in London since they were outlawed
after the Great Fire of 1666.) The Globe originally accommodated
2,200 seated and another 1,000 standing. Today, slightly smaller
and leaving space for reasonable aisles, the theater holds 800 seated
and 600 groundlings.

Its promoters brag that the theater melds "the three A's"—actors, audience, and architecture—with each contributing to the
play. The working theater hosts authentic performances of Shakespeare's plays with actors in period costumes, modern interpreta-
tions of his works, and some works by other playwrights.

The Globe complex has four parts: the Globe theater itself,
the box office, a museum (called the Exhibition), and the Sam
Wanamaker Playhouse (an indoor Jacobean theater around back).
The Playhouse, which hosts performances through the winter, is
horseshoe-shaped, intimate (seating fewer than 350), and some-

times uses authentic candle-lighting for period performances. The repertoire focuses less on Shakespeare and more on the work of his contemporaries (Jonson, Marlow, Fletcher), as well as concerts. (For details on getting tickets, see page 448.)

Cost: £13.50 ticket (good all day) includes Exhibition, audioguide, and 40-minute tour of the Globe; when theater is in use, you can tour the Exhibition only for £6.

Hours: The complex is open daily 9:00-17:30. Tours start every 30 minutes; during Globe theater season (late April-mid-Oct), last tour Mon at 17:00, Tue-Sat at 12:30, Sun at 11:30—it's safest to arrive for a tour before noon; located on the South Bank over the Millennium Bridge from St. Paul's, Tube: Mansion House or London Bridge plus a 10-minute walk; tel. 020/7902-1400, box office tel. 020/7401-9919, www.shakespearesglobe.com.

Visiting the Globe: You browse on your own in the **Exhibition** (with the included audioguide) through displays of Eliza-

bethan-era costumes and makeup, music, script-printing, and special effects (the displays change). There are early folios and objects that were dug up on site. Videos and scale models help put Shakespearean theater within the context of the times. (The Globe opened one year after England mastered the seas by defeating the Spanish Armada. The debut play was Shakespeare's *Julius Caesar*.) You'll also learn how they built the replica in modern times, using Elizabethan materials and techniques. Take advantage of the touch screens to delve into specific topics.

You must **tour the theater** at the time stamped on your ticket, but you can come back to the Exhibition museum afterward. A

guide (usually an actor) leads you into the theater to see the stage and the various seating areas for the different classes of people. You take a seat and learn how the new Globe is similar to the old Globe (open-air performances, standing-room by the stage, no curtain) and how it's different (female actors today, lights for night performances, concrete floor). It's not a backstage tour—you don't see dressing rooms or costume shops or sit in on rehearsals—but the guides are energetic, theatrical, and knowledgeable, bringing the Elizabethan period to life.

Eating: The Swan at the Globe café offers a sit-down res-

Crossing the Thames on Foot

You can cross the Thames on any of the bridges that carry car traffic over the river, but London's two pedestrian bridges are more fun. The Millennium Bridge (see photo) connects the sedate St. Paul's Cathedral with the great Tate Modern. The Golden Jubilee Bridge, well-lit and with a sleek, futuristic look, links bustling Trafalgar Square on the North Bank with the London Eye and Waterloo Station on the South Bank.

SIGHTS

taurant (for lunch and dinner, reservations recommended, tel. 020/7928-9444), a drinks-and-plates bar, and a sandwich-and-coffee cart (daily 9:00-closing, depending on performance times).

The Clink Prison Museum

Proudly the "original clink," this was, until 1780, where law-abiding citizens threw Southwark troublemakers. Today, it's a low-tech torture museum filling grotty old rooms with papier-mâché gore. There are storyboards about those unfortunate enough to be thrown in the Clink, but little that seriously deals with the fascinating problem of law and order in Southwark, where 18th-century Londoners went for a good time.

Cost and Hours: Overpriced at £7.50; July-Sept daily 10:00-21:00; Oct-June Mon-Fri 10:00-18:00, Sat-Sun until 19:30; 1 Clink Street, Tube: London Bridge, tel. 020/7403-0900, www.clink.co.uk.

Golden Hinde Replica

This is a full-size replica of the 16th-century warship in which Sir Francis Drake circumnavigated the globe from 1577 to 1580. Commanding the original ship (now long gone), Drake earned his reputation as history's most successful pirate. This replica, however, has logged more than 100,000 miles, including a voyage around the world. While the ship is fun to see, its interior is not worth touring.

Cost and Hours: £6, daily 10:00-17:00, Tube: London Bridge, ticket office just up Pickfords Wharf from the ship, tel. 020/7403-0123, www.goldenhinde.com.

▲Southwark Cathedral

While made a cathedral only in 1905, it's been the neighborhood church since the 13th century, and comes with some interesting history. The enthusiastic docents give impromptu tours if you ask.

Cost and Hours: Free, but £4 donation requested, Mon-Fri

8:00-18:00, Sat-Sun 8:30-18:00, guidebook-£4.50, Tube: London Bridge. Tel. 020/7367-6700, http://cathedral.southwark.anglican. org.

Music: The cathedral hosts evensong Sun at 15:00, Tue-Fri 17:30, Sat at 16:00; they also host organ recitals Mon at 13:00 and music recitals Tue at 15:15 (call or check website to confirm times of evensong and recitals).

▲Old Operating Theatre Museum and Herb Garret

Climb a tight and creaky wooden spiral staircase to a church attic where you'll find a garret used to dry medicinal herbs, a fascinating exhibit on Victorian surgery, cases of well-described 19th-century medical paraphernalia, and a special look at "anesthesia, the defeat of pain." Then you stumble upon Britain's oldest operating theater, where limbs were sawed off way back in 1821. (See page 296 for a full description.)

Cost and Hours: £6.50, borrowable laminated descriptions, daily 10:30-17:00, closed Dec 15-Jan 5, 9a St. Thomas Street, Tube: London Bridge, tel. 020/7188-2679, www.thegarret.org.uk.

The Shard

Rocketing dramatically 1,020 feet above the south end of the London Bridge, this addition to London's skyline is by far the tallest building in Western Europe. Designed by Renzo Piano (best known as the co-architect of Paris' Pompidou Center), the glassclad pyramid shimmers in the sun and its prickly top glows like the city's nightlight after dark. Its uppermost floors are set aside as public viewing galleries, but the ticket price is as outrageously high as the building itself, especially given that it's a bit far from London's most exciting landmarks. The Aqua Shard bar on the 31st floor offers views from half the height for the price of a fancy drink (free to ride up, but if they're at capacity they can turn you away, bar open 12:00-24:00; no sportswear, shorts, or flip-flops; access the bar from separate entrance on St. Thomas Street, www.aquashard. co.uk). For a list of cheaper view opportunities in London, see the sidebar on page 88.

Cost and Hours: £25 if booked at least a day in advance, £30 for same-day reservations; book as soon as you have reasonable chance of assuring decent weather, least crowded on weekday mornings, but perhaps better photo opportunities in the early evening (less haze); daily 10:00-22:00, last entry slot at 21:00; Tube: London Bridge—use London Bridge exit and follow signs, tel. 0844-499-7111, www.theviewfromtheshard.com.

Visiting the Shard: From the entrance on Joiner Street (just off St. Thomas Street) you'll take a two-part elevator ride up to the 68th floor, then climb up one story to the main observation platform. It's equipped with cool telescopes that label major landmarks,

SIGHTS

and even let you see how the view from here would appear at other times of the day. From here you've got great views of St. Paul's, the Tower of London, Southwark Cathedral (straight down), and, in the distance, the 2012 Olympic stadium in one direction, and the Houses of Parliament in the other (find Buckingham Palace, just left of the Eye). On the clearest days, you can see 40 miles out, and a few people say they've been able to make out ships on the North Sea. Even in bad weather it's mesmerizing to watch the constant movement of the city's transit system, which looks like a model-train set from this height. Ascending to the 72nd floor gets you to the open-air deck, where the wind roars over the glass enclosure. As you look up, try to picture Prince Andrew rappelling off the very top, which he and 40 others did in 2012 as a charity fundraising stunt.

SIGHTS

HMS *Belfast*

The last big-gun armored warship of World War II clogs the Thames just upstream from the Tower Bridge. This huge vessel—now manned with wax sailors—thrills kids who always dreamed of sitting in a turret shooting off their imaginary guns. If you're into WWII warships, this is the ultimate. Otherwise, it's just lots of exercise with a nice view of the Tower Bridge.

Cost and Hours: Adult-£16, kids 5-15-£8, kids under 5-free, includes audioguide, daily March-Oct 10:00-18:00, Nov-Feb 10:00-17:00, last entry one hour before closing, Tube: London Bridge, tel. 020/7940-6300, www.iwm.org.uk/visits/hms-belfast.

City Hall

The glassy, egg-shaped building near the south end of Tower Bridge is London's City Hall, designed by Sir Norman Foster, the

architect who worked on London's Millennium Bridge and Berlin's Reichstag. Nicknamed "the Armadillo," City Hall houses the office of London's mayor—it's here that the mayor consults with the Assembly representatives of the city's 25 districts. An interior spiral ramp allows visitors to watch and hear the action below in the Assembly Chamber—ride the lift to floor 2 (the highest visitors can go) and spiral down. On the lower ground floor is a large aerial photograph of London and a handy cafeteria. Next to City Hall is the outdoor amphitheater called The Scoop (see page 452 for info on performances).

Cost and Hours: Free, open to visitors Mon-Thu 8:30-18:00,

Fri 8:30-17:30, closed Sat-Sun; Tube: London Bridge station plus 10-minute walk, or Tower Hill station plus 15-minute walk; tel. 020/7983-4000, www.london.gov.uk.

West London

▲▲Tate Britain

One of Europe's great art houses, Tate Britain specializes in British painting from the 16th century through modern times. The recently renovated museum has a good representation of William Blake's religious sketches, the Pre-Raphaelites' naturalistic and detailed art, Gainsborough's aristocratic ladies, and the best collection anywhere of J. M. W. Turner's swirling works.

Cost and Hours: Free but £4 donation requested, admission fee for special exhibits; daily 10:00-18:00, last entry 45 minutes before closing; free tours generally daily; on the Thames River, south of Big Ben and north of Vauxhall Bridge, Tube: Pimlico, Tate Boat museum ferry goes directly to the museum from Tate Modern—see page 41; switchboard tel. 020/7887-8888, www.tate.org.uk.

📖 See the Tate Britain Tour chapter.

Victoria Station

From underneath this station's iron-and-glass canopy, trains depart for the south of England and Gatwick Airport. While Victoria Station is famous and a major Tube stop, few tourists actually take trains from here—most just come to take in the exciting bustle. It's a fun place to just be a "rock in a river" teeming with commuters and services. The station is surrounded by big red buses and taxis, travel agencies, and lousy eateries. It's next to the main intercity bus station (Victoria Coach Station) and the best inexpensive lodgings in town.

Westminster Cathedral

This cathedral, the largest Catholic church in England and just a block from Victoria Station, is strikingly Neo-Byzantine, but not very historic or important to visit. Opened in 1903, the church has an unfinished interior, with a spooky, blackened ceiling waiting for the mosaics that are supposed to be placed there.

SIGHTS

While it's definitely not Westminster Abbey, half the tourists wandering around inside seem to think it is. Take the lift to the top of the 273-foot bell tower for a view of the glassy office blocks of Victoria Station.

Cost and Hours: Free entry, £6 for the lift; church—daily 7:00-19:00; tower—daily 9:30-17:00, Sat-Sun until 18:00; 5-minute walk from bus terminus in front of Victoria Station, just off Victoria Street at 42 Francis Street, Tube: Victoria, www.westminstercathedral.org.uk.

National Army Museum

This museum—undergoing renovation and expected to reopen sometime in late 2016—tells the story of the British army from 1415 through the Bosnian conflict and Iraq, with lots of Redcoat lore and a good look at Waterloo. Kids enjoy trying on a Cromwellian helmet, seeing the skeleton of Napoleon's horse, and peering out from a WWI trench through a working periscope.

Cost and Hours: When it reopens, it will likely be free, daily 10:00-17:30, Royal Hospital Road, Chelsea, Tube: Sloane Square, tel. 020/7730-0717, www.national-army-museum.ac.uk.

HYDE PARK AND NEARBY

A number of worthwhile sights border this grand park, from Apsley House on the east to Kensington Palace on the west.

▲Apsley House (Wellington Museum)

Having beaten Napoleon at Waterloo, Arthur Wellesley, the First Duke of Wellington, was once the most famous man in Europe.

He was given a huge fortune, with which he purchased London's ultimate address, Number One London. His refurbished mansion offers a nice interior, a handful of world-class paintings, and a glimpse at the life of the great soldier and two-time prime minister. Those who know something about Wellington ahead of time will appreciate the place much more than those who don't, as there's scarce biographical background. The place is well-described by the included audioguide, which has sound bites from the current Duke of Wellington (who still lives at Apsley).

Cost and Hours: £9.20, Wed-Sun 11:00-17:00, closed Mon-Tue year-round, no photos, 20 yards from Hyde Park Corner Tube station, tel. 020/7499-5676, www.english-heritage.org.uk.

Visiting the House: An 11-foot-tall marble statue of Napoleon, clad only in a fig leaf, greets you. Napoleon commissioned the sculptor Canova to make it for him but didn't like it, and after Napoleon's defeat, Wellington acquired it as a war trophy. It's one of several images Wellington acquired of his former foe to have in his home. The two great men were polar opposites—Napoleon the daring general and champion of revolution, Wellington the play-it-safe strategist and conservative politician—but they're forever linked in history.

The core of the collection is a dozen first-floor rooms decorated with fancy wallpaper, chandeliers, a few pieces of furniture, and wall-to-wall paintings from Wellington's collection. You'll see fancy dinnerware and precious objects given to the Irish-born general by the crowned heads of Europe, who were eternally grateful to him for saving their necks from the guillotine. The highlight is the large ballroom, the Waterloo Gallery, decorated with Anthony van Dyck's *Charles I on Horseback* (over the main fireplace), Diego Velázquez's earthy *Water-Seller of Seville* (to the left of Van Dyck), Jan

Steen's playful *Dissolute Household* (to the right). Just outside the door, in the Portico Room, is a large portrait of Wellington by Francisco Goya.

Downstairs is a small gallery of Wellington memorabilia, including a pair of Wellington boots, which the duke popularized—

Brits today still call rubber boots "wellies" (sometimes on loan to the Wellington Arch, see below).

Nearby: **Hyde Park**'s pleasant rose garden is picnic-friendly. **Wellington Arch,** which stands just across the street, is open to the public but not worth the £5.20 charge (or £10 combo-ticket with Apsley House; elevator up, lousy views and boring exhibits).

▲Hyde Park and Speakers' Corner

London's "Central Park," originally Henry VIII's hunting grounds, has more than 600 acres of lush greenery, Santander Cycles rental stations, the huge man-made Serpentine Lake (with rental boats and a lakeside swimming pool), the royal Kensington Palace (described next), and the ornate Neo-Gothic Albert Memorial across from the Royal Albert Hall (for more about the park, see www. royalparks.org.uk/parks/hyde-park). The western half of the park is known as Kensington Gardens. The park is huge—study a Tube map to choose the stop nearest to your destination.

On Sundays, from just after noon until early evening, **Speakers' Corner** offers soapbox oratory at its best (northeast corner of the park, Tube: Marble Arch). Characters climb their stepladders, wave their flags, pound emphatically on their sandwich boards, and share what they are convinced is their wisdom. Regulars have resident hecklers who know their lines and are always ready with a verbal jab or barb. "The grass roots of democracy" is actually a holdover from when the gallows stood here and the criminal was allowed to say just about anything he wanted to before he swung. I dare you to raise your voice and gather a crowd—it's easy to do.

The **Princess Diana Memorial Fountain** honors the "People's Princess," who once lived in nearby Kensington Palace. The low-key circular stream, great for cooling off your feet on a hot day, is in the south-central part of the park, near the Albert Memorial and Serpentine Gallery (Tube: Knightsbridge). A similarly named but different sight, the **Diana, Princess of Wales Memorial Playground,** in the park's northwest corner, is loads of fun for kids (Tube: Queensway).

Kensington Palace

For nearly 150 years (1689-1837), Kensington was the royal residence, before Buckingham Palace became the official home of the monarch. Sitting primly on its pleasant parkside grounds, the palace gives a glimpse into royal life, especially Queen Victoria, who was born and raised here. It's strange to think that, in this city that was so shaped by Victoria, this relatively paltry exhibit is London's first and only museum that's truly *about* Victoria. (For more on Victoria's life and times, see the sidebar on page 102.)

After Queen Victoria moved the monarchy to Buckingham Palace, lesser royals bedded down at Kensington. Princess Diana lived here both during and after her marriage to Prince Charles (1981-1997). More recently, Will and Kate moved into a thoroughly renovated Apartment 1A (the southern flank of the palace complex, with four stories and 20 rooms). And Prince Harry lives in their old digs, a "cottage" on the other side of the main building. However— as many disappointed visitors discover—none of these more recent apartments are open to the public.

Cost and Hours: £17.50, daily 10:00-18:00, Nov-Feb until 17:00, last entry one hour before closing, least crowded in mornings; £5 guidebook but friendly and knowledgeable "explainers" will answer questions for free, cloakroom available for bags and luggage; a long 10-minute stroll through Kensington Gardens from either High Street Kensington or Queensway Tube stations, tel. 0844-482-7788, www.hrp.org.uk.

◑ Self-Guided Tour: Before entering the building, notice the statue of Queen Victoria facing Hyde Park and welcoming you to her birth palace. After buying your ticket, head through the foyer into the vestibule with the circular couch. This humble spot is the hub for visitors: From here, you can reach any of the three main exhibits. To see them chronologically, head to the right, pass through a long hallway, and go up the stairs to start with the...

Queen's State Apartments: In 1689 an optimistic England welcomed King William, a Protestant from the Netherlands, to take the throne with his English-born wife, Queen Mary. Almost immediately, William hired Sir Christopher Wren to build this new palace in what was then the peaceful village of Kensington as an escape from grimy central London. William moved the royal residence from Whitehall to what became Kensington Palace. These next few rooms focus on the palace's first royal resident: Queen Mary. Entering the **queen's gallery,** you get a sense of the

SIGHTS

grandeur of the palace—the dances and banquets held here, with expansive views over landscaped gardens. When it wasn't used for entertaining, this was simply the queen's living room, used for everyday activities. Find portraits of William and Mary. Parliament had recently overthrown the Catholic King James II in the "Glorious Revolution," and William and Mary represented a new, more democratic start.

But things would not end well. As you head into the **queen's closet,** you'll read about Mary's impending death from smallpox. When Mary died—childless—she was eventually succeeded by her sister, Anne. After many failed pregnancies, Queen Anne finally had one child who survived. But on his 11th birthday, he danced so heartily that he came down with a fever and dropped dead. Who would rule after Anne?

Pass through the **dining room,** where William and Mary enjoyed meals in private, and the **drawing room,** where Mary kept her collection of porcelain, into the last room, the **queen's bedroom,** where the plan of succession of would-be kings and queens is explained. Parliament solved the dilemma by inviting the German-born Hanover dynasty (the "King Georges")—whose apartments we see next.

• *Retrace your steps back down to the vestibule hall, then up the grand King's Staircase to the...*

King's State Apartment: After climbing the staircase (with its colorful murals of courtiers gazing down at you), you enter

the **presence chamber,** where the king would receive visitors on a raised throne. Even when the throne was empty, visitors had to bow—and exit the room backward. The **privy chamber, cupola room,** and **king's drawing room** showcase court life during the palace's heyday in the 1700s—the salons attended by wits and intellectuals; the parties, music, card games, and dancing; the clothes of the day—serious men in ruffled sleeves, courtly ladies in wide skirts, and the elaborate costume of the prestigious Order of the Garter. The large **king's gallery** ends the visit with paintings by Tintoretto *(Esther Before Ahaserus)* and Veronese *(Adoration of the Kings).*

• *Now head back downstairs to the vestibule, and up the stone stairs to the third main exhibit...*

Victoria Revealed: The artifacts here tell the story of Queen Victoria's life, displayed in the rooms where she grew up. As Victoria was an avid journal-keeper, you'll see many excerpts from her own accounts.

The Red Saloon recreates the day in 1837 when she ascended the throne and the first meeting with her Privy Council. You see the dress the 4'11", 18-year-old monarch wore. A painting on the wall shows the young queen facing down a room full of nobility assigned to advise her. Standing at the far right end of the table, find Robert "Bobbie" Peel, who's credited with starting the first professional police force—the "bobbies." As you can see from the painting, the meeting took place in this very room.

The next room commemorates Victoria's marriage to her beloved Prince Albert (see their portraits). The carpets, mirrors, and screen are decorated with passages from their love letters, and Victoria's wedding gown is on display (she began the fashion of brides wearing white). The room to the left is where, most likely, Victoria was born. It has objects from her own childhood (such as her original doll collection) and portraits of her nine children. Continue on through two rooms to a room that celebrates Prince Albert's Great Exhibition of 1851. Its centerpiece was the Crystal Palace—the wonder of its age—that once stood in the park just in front of you.

The next rooms, shrouded in dark, recall Albert's sudden and tragic death from typhoid fever: You see the heart-shaped locket that holds a lock of Albert's hair. Victoria would dress in black for the rest of her life. She lived to be 82, and you can watch footage of her Diamond Jubilee celebration (marking 60 years as reigning monarch from 1837 to 1897). Finally, the exhibit ends with an eclectic collection of items belonging to the royal couple, including Albert's dressing case (with his tongue scraper), and Victoria's watercolor box and Transylvanian jewelry.

Outside: Garden enthusiasts enjoy popping into the secluded Sunken Garden, 50 yards from the exit. Consider afternoon tea at the nearby Orangery (see page 414), built as a greenhouse for Queen Anne in 1704. On the south side of the palace are the golden gates that became famous in 1997 as the backdrop to the sea of flowers left here by Princess Diana's mourners.

▲▲▲Victoria and Albert Museum

The world's top collection of decorative arts encompasses 2,000 years of art and design (ceramics, stained glass, fine furniture, clothing, jewelry, carpets, and more), displaying a surprisingly interesting and diverse assortment of crafts from the West, as well as Asian and Islamic cultures. There's much to see, including

Queen Victoria (1819-1901)

Plump, pleasant, and barely five feet tall, Queen Victoria, with her regal demeanor and 64-year reign, came to symbolize the global dominance of the British Empire during its greatest era.

Born in Kensington Palace, Victoria was the granddaughter of "Mad" King George III, the tyrant who sparked the American Revolution. Her domineering mother raised her in sheltered seclusion, drilling into her the strict morality that would come to be known as "Victorian." At 18, she was crowned queen. Victoria soon fell madly, deeply in love with Prince Albert, a handsome German nobleman with mutton-chop sideburns. They married and set up house in Buckingham Palace (the first monarchs to do so) and at Windsor Castle. Over the next 17 years, she and Albert had nine children, whom they eventually married off to Europe's crowned heads. Victoria's royal descendants include Kaiser Wilhelm II of Germany (who started World War I); the current monarchs of Spain, Norway, Sweden, and Denmark; and England's Queen Elizabeth II, who is Victoria's great-great-granddaughter.

Victoria and Albert promoted the arts and sciences, organizing a world's fair in Hyde Park (1851) that showed off London as *the* global capital. Just as important, they were role models for an entire nation; this loving couple influenced several generations with their wholesome middle-class values and devoted parenting. Though Victoria is often depicted as dour and stuffy—she supposedly coined the phrase "We are not amused"—in private she was warm, easy to laugh, plainspoken, thrifty, and modest, with a talent for sketching and journal writing.

In 1861, Victoria's happy domestic life ended. Her mother's death was soon followed by the sudden loss of her beloved Albert to typhoid fever. A devastated Victoria dressed in black for the funeral—and for her remaining 40 years never again wore any other color. She hunkered down at Windsor with her family. Critics complained she was an absentee monarch. Rumors swirled that her kilt-wearing servant, John Brown, was not only her close friend but also her lover. For two decades, she rarely appeared in public.

Over time, Victoria emerged from mourning to assume her role as one of history's first constitutional monarchs. She had inherited a crown with little real power. But beyond her ribbon-cutting ceremonial duties, Victoria influenced events behind the scenes. She studiously learned politics from powerful mentors (especially Prince Albert and two influential prime ministers) and kept well-informed on what Parliament was doing. Thanks to Victoria's personal modesty and honesty, the British public never came to disdain the monarchy, as happened in other countries.

Victoria gracefully oversaw the peaceful transfer of power from the nobles to the people. The secret ballot was introduced during her reign, and ordinary workers acquired voting rights (though this applied only to men—Victoria opposed women's suffrage). The traditional Whigs and Tories morphed into today's Liberal and Conservative parties. Victoria personally promoted progressive charities, and even paid for her own crown.

Most of all, Victoria became the symbol of the British Empire, which she saw as a way to protect and civilize poorer peoples. Britain enjoyed peace at home, while its colonial possessions included India, Australia, Canada, and much of Africa. Because it was always daytime someplace under Victoria's rule, it was often said that "the sun never sets on the British Empire."

The Victorian era saw great changes. The Industrial Revolution was in full swing. When Victoria was born, there were no trains. By 1842, when she took her first train trip (with much fanfare), railroads crisscrossed Europe. The telegraph, telephone, and newspapers further laced the world together. The popular arts flourished—it was the era of Dickens novels, Tennyson poems, Sherlock Holmes stories, Gilbert and Sullivan operettas, and Pre-Raphaelite paintings. Economically, Britain saw the rise of the middle class. Middle-class morality dominated—family, hard work, honor, duty, and sexual modesty.

By the end of her reign, Victoria was wildly popular, both for her personality and as a focus for British patriotism. At her Golden Jubilee (1887), she paraded past adoring throngs to Westminster Abbey. For her Diamond Jubilee (1897), she did the same at St. Paul's Cathedral. Cities, lakes, and military medals were named for her. When she passed away in 1901, it was literally the end of an era.

Raphael's tapestry cartoons, five of Leonardo da Vinci's notebooks, the huge Islamic Ardabil Carpet (4,914 knots in every 10 square centimeters), and a cast of Trajan's Column that depicts the emperor's conquests—not to mention the catsuit Mick Jagger wore for the Rolling Stones' 1972 world tour.

Cost and Hours: Free, but £4 donation requested, extra for some special exhibits, daily 10:00-17:45, some galleries open Fri until 22:00, free tours daily, on Cromwell Road in South Kensington, Tube: South Kensington, from the Tube station a long tunnel leads directly to museum, tel. 020/7942-2000, www.vam.ac.uk.

📖 See the Victoria and Albert Museum Tour chapter.

▲▲Natural History Museum

Across the street from the Victoria and Albert, this mammoth museum is housed in a giant and wonderful Victorian, Neo-Romanesque building. It was built in the 1870s specifically for the huge collection (50 million specimens). Exhibits are wonderfully explained, with lots of creative, interactive displays. It covers everything from life ("creepy crawlies," human biology, our place in evolution, and awe-inspiring dinosaurs) to earth science (meteors, volcanoes, and earthquakes).

Cost and Hours: Free, but £5 donation requested, fees for (optional) special exhibits, daily 10:00-18:00, helpful £1 map, open later last Fri of the month, long tunnel leads directly from South Kensington Tube station to museum (follow signs), tel. 020/7942-5000, exhibit info and reservations tel. 020/7942-5011, www.nhm.ac.uk. Free visitor app available via the "Visit" section of the website.

Visiting the Museum: Enter by the main Cromwell Road entrance (in the middle of the long building), which is easiest for getting oriented. You step into Hintze Hall, with a big *Diplodocus* skeleton, bookended by a massive slice of sequoia tree and Charles Darwin sitting as if upon a throne overseeing it all. Review the "What's on Today" board for special events and tours, and note which sections are closed. For more information, ask one of the many helpful guards scattered throughout the museum.

The building is organized into several color-coded "zones." The Blue Zone (to the left) has the biggest animals and biggest crowds: dinosaurs (may have a line), a life-size blue whale model, and other stuffed-and-mounted mammals.

Straight ahead, up the stairs behind Darwin, is the Treasures

Gallery, housing a rotating display of the museum's greatest hits, including a dodo skeleton, moon rock, stuffed specimen of the extinct great auk, and the *Iguanodon* tooth that kicked off human awareness of dinosaurs.

To the right is the Green Zone, tracing the evolution of the earth and its creatures. Don't miss its minerals section, with rare and precious stones, including a meteorite from Mars, the Aurora Pyramid of Hope—displaying 296 diamonds showing their full range of natural colors—and this description of some microscopic cosmic diamonds: "These are the oldest things you will ever see."

Keep exploring. The Orange Zone (far left) lets you see today's scientists at work in their labs. In the Red Zone (far right), you can ride a dramatic escalator up one floor to experience an earthquake.

Even with limited time to spend here, pop in, if only for the dinosaur collection—including a realistic animatronic *T. rex*—and to hear English children exclaim, "Oh, my goodness!"

▲Science Museum

Next door to the Natural History Museum, this sprawling wonderland for curious minds is kid-perfect, with themes such as measuring time, exploring space, climate change, and the evolution of modern medicine. It offers hands-on fun, from moonwalks to deep-sea exploration, with trendy technology exhibits, a state-of-the-art IMAX theater (shows-£11, £9 for kids, £27/£30 for families of 3 or 4), and the Garden, a cool play area for children up to age seven.

Cost and Hours: Free, daily 10:00-18:00, until 19:00 during school holidays, last entry 45 minutes before closing, Exhibition Road, Tube: South Kensington, tel. 0870-870-4868, www.sciencemuseum.org.uk.

Greater London

EAST OF LONDON
▲▲Greenwich

This borough of London—an easy boat trip or DLR (light rail) journey from downtown—combines majestic, picnic-perfect parks; the stately trappings of Britain's proud nautical heritage (the restored *Cutty Sark* clipper, the over-the-top-ornate retirement home for sailors at the **Old Royal Naval College,** and the comprehensive **National Maritime Museum**); and the **Royal Observatory Greenwich,** with a fine museum on the evolution of seafaring and a chance to straddle the eastern and western hemispheres at the Prime Meridian. An affordable jaunt from central London, and boasting several top-notch museums (including some free ones),

Greenwich is worth considering and easy to combine with a look at the Docklands (described next).

□ See the Greenwich Tour chapter.

▲▲The Docklands

Once the primary harbor for the Port of London, the Docklands has been transformed into a vibrant business center, with ultra-tall skyscrapers, subterranean supermalls, trendy pubs, and peaceful parks with pedestrian bridges looping over canals. It also boasts the very good **Museum of London Docklands,** which illuminates the gritty and fascinating history of the port. While not full of the touristy sights that many are seeking in London, the Docklands offers a refreshing look at the British version of a 21st-century city. It's best at the end of the workday, when it's lively with office workers. It's ideal to see on your way back from Greenwich, since both line up on the same train tracks.

□ See The Docklands Walk chapter.

Queen Elizabeth Olympic Park

London refashioned this park—the biggest new park to open in the city in a century—from the site of the 2012 Olympic Games. You'll find miles of parkland trails and waterways, kids' play areas, an array of sporting venues (London Aquatics Centre, Lee Valley VeloPark, Copper Box Arena), quirky sculpture, and places to eat. The park is huge—bigger than Hyde Park/Kensington Gardens. It's also quite beautiful, laced with canals and tributaries of the Lea River. The best overview of the park is along a 500-yard-long berm called the **Greenway,** which sits at the park's southern perimeter. The easiest landmark to head for is the **View Tube,** a covered shelter with a free lookout tower, café, WC, and maps. There's also the hard-to-miss red, 350-foot viewing tower called the **Orbit,** which was designed as an Eiffel-Tower-like landmark for London and has been compared to a giant hookah and a vertical roller coaster. (Plans to add the world's longest, tallest tunnel slide in 2016 promise to make good on its amusement-park vibe.) For help in planning your visit, drop by the "Information Point" near the Aquatics Centre, where you can also ask about a tour with a Blue Badge guide (£10, Wed, Sat, and Sun at 11:00).

Cost and Hours: Free and always open, toll-free tel. 0800-0722-110, www.queenelizabetholympicpark.co.uk.

Getting There: From central London by Tube, it's a 30-minute ride to the Stratford station. Take the escalator up to "The Street" (which is actually the outdoor part of the Westfield shopping center), bear left past The Cow pub, and the park is directly ahead of you, across the road.

WEST OF LONDON
▲▲Kew Gardens

For a fine riverside park and a palatial green-house jungle to swing through, take the Tube or the boat to every botanist's favorite escape, Kew Gardens. While to most visitors the Royal Botanic Gardens of Kew are simply a delightful opportunity to wander among 33,000 different types of plants, to the hard-working organization that runs them, the gardens are a way to promote the understanding and preservation of the botanical diversity of our planet.

Cost and Hours: £16.50, June-Aug £11 after 16:00, kids 4-16-£3.50, kids under 4-free; April-Aug Mon-Fri 10:00-18:30, Sat-Sun 10:00-19:30, closes earlier Sept-March—check schedule online, glasshouses close at 17:30 in high season—earlier off-season, free one-hour walking tours daily at 11:00 and 13:30, Tube: Kew Gardens, boats run April-Oct between Kew Gardens and Westminster Pier—see page 41, tel. 020/8332-5000, for recorded messages call 020/8332-5655, www.kew.org.

Getting There: From the Kew Tube station, cross the foot-bridge over the tracks, which drops you in a little community of plant-and-herb shops, a two-block walk from Victoria Gate (the main garden entrance).

Visiting the Gardens: Pick up a map brochure and check at the gate for a monthly listing of the best blooms. Garden lov-ers could spend days explor-ing Kew's 300 acres. For a quick visit, spend a fragrant hour wandering through three buildings: the Palm House, a humid Victorian world of iron, glass, and tropical plants that was built in 1844; a Waterlily

House that Monet would swim for; and the Princess of Wales Conservatory, a meandering modern greenhouse with many dif-ferent climate zones growing countless cacti, bug-munching car-nivorous plants, and more. With extra time, check out the Xstrata Treetop Walkway, a 200-yard-long scenic steel walkway that puts you high in the canopy 60 feet above the ground. Young kids will love the Climbers and Creepers indoor/outdoor playground and little zip line, as well as a slow and easy ride on the hop-on, hop-off Kew Explorer tram (adults-£4.50, kids-£1.50 for narrated 40-min-ute ride, departs Victoria Gate, ask for schedule when you enter).

Eating: For a sun-dappled lunch or snack, walk 10 minutes from the Palm House to the Orangery Cafeteria (£4 sandwiches, £8-12 lunches, Mon-Fri 10:00-18:30, Sat-Sun 10:00-19:30, until 16:15 in winter, closes early for events).

▲Hampton Court Palace

Fifteen miles up the Thames from downtown, the 500-year-old palace of Henry VIII is worth ▲▲ for palace aficionados. Actually, it was originally the palace of his minister, Cardinal Wolsey. When Wolsey, a clever man, realized Henry VIII was experiencing a little palace envy, he gave the mansion to his king. The Tudor palace was also home to Elizabeth I and Charles I. Sections were updated by Christopher Wren for William and Mary. The stately palace stands overlooking the Thames and includes some fine Tudor rooms, including a Great Hall with a magnificent hammer-beam ceiling. The industrial-strength Tudor kitchen was capable of keeping 600 schmoozing courtiers thoroughly—if not well—fed. The sculpted garden features a rare Tudor tennis court and a popular maze.

The palace tries hard to please, but it doesn't quite sparkle. From the information center in the main courtyard, you can pick up audioguides for self-guided tours of various wings of the palace (free but slow, aimed mostly at school-age children). For more in-depth information, strike up a conversation with the costumed characters or docents posted in each room. The Tudor portions of the castle, including the rooms dedicated to the young Henry, are most interesting; the Georgian rooms are pretty dull. The maze in the nearby garden is a curiosity some find fun (maze free with palace ticket, otherwise £4.40).

Cost and Hours: £19.30, family-£48.20; online discounts, daily April-Oct 10:00-18:00, Nov-March 10:00-16:30, last entry one hour before closing, café, tel. 0844-482-7777 or 020/3166-6000, www.hrp.org.uk.

Getting There: The train (2/hour, 35 minutes, Oyster cards OK) from London's Waterloo Station drops you across the river from the palace (just walk across the bridge). Consider arriving at or departing from the palace by boat (connections with London's Westminster Pier, see page 41); it's a relaxing and scenic three- to four-hour cruise past two locks and a fun new/old riverside mix.

Kew Gardens/Hampton Court Blitz: Because these two sights are in the same general direction (about £20 for a taxi between the two), you can visit both in one day. Here's a game plan: Start your morning at Hampton Court, tour the palace and garden, and have a Tudor-style lunch in the atmospheric dining hall. After lunch, take bus #R68 from Hampton Court Station to Richmond (40 minutes), then transfer to bus #65, which will drop you off at the Kew Gardens gate (5 minutes). After touring the gardens, have tea in the Orangery, then Tube or boat back to London.

NORTH OF LONDON

Royal Air Force Museum London

A hit with aviation enthusiasts, this huge aerodrome and airfield contain planes from World War II's Battle of Britain up through the Gulf War. You can climb inside some of the planes, try your luck in a cockpit, and fly with the Red Arrows in a flight simulator.

Cost and Hours: Free, but £3 suggested donation, flight simulator-£3, daily 10:00-18:00, café, shop, parking-£3 for up to 3 hours, Grahame Park Way, 30-minute ride from downtown London plus another 15 minutes by foot, Tube: Colindale—top of Northern Line Edgware branch, tel. 020/8205-2266, www.rafmuseum.org.uk.

Hampstead Heath

This surprisingly vast expanse of greenery sprawls over a square mile and a quarter at the northern edge of downtown London.

It features rolling, scrubby pastures ("heath") as well as tranquil wooded areas. Its most popular viewpoint, Parliament Hill, offers distant views of London's fast-growing skyline. At the northeast corner of the park is a chunk of land owned by English Heritage, where a stately palace called Kenwood House overlooks a pasture, pond, and gentle wood; inside is a fine art collection, plus an inviting café (and WCs). Maps posted at each entrance to the park help get you oriented. On a sunny day, the park is crammed with Londoners communing with nature—relieved to escape from their bustling burg. The adjoining village of Hampstead is quaint and cute; a stroll through here is almost as pleasant as the park itself.

Getting There: Hampstead Heath is just a 20-minute Tube ride from downtown London. The handiest Tube stop is the one called Hampstead (on the convenient Northern line/Edgware branch, which runs north to south through London's city center). This stop is in the middle of the charming village of Hampstead, from which it's about a 10-minute walk to the park (turn left out of the station to head one block down Hampstead High Street, then turn left on Flask Walk—across from Starbucks—and follow

SIGHTS

Harry Potter's London

Harry Potter's story is set in a magical Britain, and all of the places mentioned in the books, except London, are fictional, but you can visit many real film locations. Many of the locations are closed to visitors, though, or are an unmagical disappointment in person, unless you're a huge fan. For those diehards, here's a sampling.

Spoiler Warning: The information below will ruin surprises for the three of you who haven't yet read or seen the Harry Potter series.

Harry's story begins in suburban London, in the fictional town of Little Whinging. In the first film, *The Sorcerer's Stone* (2001), the gentle giant Hagrid touches down on his flying motorcycle at #4 Privet Drive. There, baby Harry—who was orphaned by the murder of his wizard parents—is left on the doorstep to be raised by an antimagic aunt and uncle. The scene was shot in the town of **Bracknell** (pop. 50,000, 10 miles west of Heathrow) on a street of generic brick rowhouses called Picket Close. Later, 10-year-old Harry first realizes his wizard powers when talking with a boa constrictor, filmed at the **London Zoo's Reptile House** in Regent's Park (Tube: Great Portland Street). Harry soon gets invited to Hogwarts School of Witchcraft and Wizardry, where he'll learn the magical skills he'll need to eventually confront his parents' murderer, Lord Voldemort.

Big Ben and **Parliament,** along the Thames, welcome Harry to the modern city inhabited by Muggles (nonmagic folk). London bustles along oblivious to the parallel universe of wizards. Hagrid takes Harry shopping for school supplies. They enter the glass-roofed **Leadenhall Market** (Tube: Bank) and approach the **storefront** at 42 Bull's Head Passage—the entrance to The Leaky Cauldron pub (which, in the books, is placed among the bookshops of Charing Cross Road). The pub's back wall parts, opening onto the magical Diagon Alley, where Harry shops for wands, cauldrons, and wizard textbooks. He pays for them with gold Galleons from goblin-run Gringotts Wizarding Bank, filmed in the marble-floored and chandeliered Exhibition Hall of **Australia House** (Tube: Temple), home of the Australian Embassy.

Harry catches the train to Hogwarts at **King's Cross Station.** (The fanciful exterior shown in the 2002 *Chamber of Secrets* was actually shot in nearby **St. Pancras International Station.**)

Inside the glass-roofed train station, on a **pedestrian sky bridge** over the tracks, Hagrid gives Harry a train ticket. Harry heads to platform 9¾, where he and his new buddy Ron magically push their luggage carts through a brick pillar between the platforms, emerging onto a hidden platform. (For a fun photo-op, head to King's Cross Station's track 9 to find the *Platform 9¾* sign, the luggage cart that looks like it's disappearing into the wall, a Harry Potter gift shop, and a 30-minute wait in line to snap a photo.)

A red steam train—the Hogwarts Express—speeds the boys through the (Scottish) countryside to Hogwarts, where Harry will spend the next seven years. The steam engine used in filming is on display at a Platform 9¾ exhibit at Harry Potter Warner Bros. Studio Tour.

In *The Prisoner of Azkaban* (2004), Harry careens through London's lamp-lit streets on a purple three-decker bus (also on display at the Harry Potter Warner Bros. Studio Tour) that dumps him at The Leaky Cauldron pub. In this film, the pub's exterior was shot on rough-looking Stoney Street at the southeast edge of **Borough Street Market,** by The Market Porter pub, with trains rumbling overhead (Tube: London Bridge).

In *The Order of the Phoenix* (2007), the Order takes to the night sky on broomsticks, zooming down the Thames and over London, passing over plenty of identifiable landmarks, including the **Tower Bridge, London Eye, Big Ben,** and **Buckingham Palace.** They arrive at Sirius Black's home at "Twelve Grimmauld Place," filmed at a park-like square called Lincoln's Inn Fields, near Sir John Soane's Museum (Tube: Holborn).

The **Millennium Bridge** is attacked by Death Eaters and collapses into the Thames in the dramatic finale to *The Half-Blood Prince* (2009).

For *Order of the Phoenix* and the first *Deathly Hallows* (2010), the real government offices of Whitehall serve as exteriors for the Ministry of Magic. Also for the first *Deathly Hallows*, Harry, Ron, and Hermione fight off disguised Death Eaters in a Muggle café, filmed in the West End's bustling **Piccadilly Circus.** Other London settings, like Diagon Alley, only exist at Warner Bros. Studio in Leavesden (20 miles north of London), where most of the films' interiors were shot. Leavesden welcomes Harry Potter pilgrims, who come to see many of the original sets and props.

Finally, cinema buffs can visit **Leicester Square** (Tube: Leicester Square), where Daniel Radcliffe and other stars have strolled past paparazzi and down red carpets to the Odeon Theater to attend the movies' premieres.

it until it becomes Well Walk and eventually runs into East Heath Road; the park is in front of you, with Parliament Hill still a ways in and to the right). The station called Hampstead Heath, directly at the southern tip of the park and closer to Parliament Hill, is on the less convenient Overground line; however, bus #24 easily (though slowly) connects Victoria Station and downtown London (including Trafalgar Square) with the Hampstead Heath stop.

Hampstead Heath combines well with a visit to the fun and funky Camden Lock Market (see page 431), which is on both the Northern Tube line and the bus #24 route.

Highgate Cemetery

Located in the tea-cozy-cute village of Highgate, north of the city, this Victorian cemetery represents a fascinating, offbeat piece of London history. Built as a private cemetery, this was the fashionable place to bury the wealthy dead in the late 1800s. It has themed mausoleums, professional mourners, and several high-profile residents in its East Cemetery, including Karl Marx, George Eliot, and Douglas Adams. The tomb of "Godfather of Punk" Malcolm McLaren (former manager of the Sex Pistols) is often covered with rotten veggies.

Cost and Hours: East Cemetery—£4, Mon-Fri 10:00-17:00, Sat-Sun 11:00-17:00; older, creepier West Cemetery—viewable by £12 guided tour only, price includes entrance to East Cemetery, Mon-Fri at 13:45—must book in advance; Sat-Sun 2/hour, 11:00-15:00, no reservations taken but space is limited; Tube: Archway on the Northern Line/High Barnet branch or—slower—bus #C2 from Victoria Station or Oxford Circus, tel. 020/8340-1834, www.highgatecemetery.org.

The Making of Harry Potter:
Warner Bros. Studio Tour London

While you can visit several real-life locations in Britain where the Harry Potter movies were filmed (see sidebar on page 110), there's only one way to see imaginary places like Hogwarts' Great Hall, Diagon Alley, Dumbledore's office, and the interior of #4 Privet Drive: by visiting the Warner Bros. Studio in Leavesden, where Daniel Radcliffe and company brought the tale of the boy wizard to life. You'll begin with a brief guided tour, then be set free to explore on your own.

Attractions include the actual sets used for the films (Hogwarts bridge, Hagrid's hut), several familiar costumes and props (such as the Nimbus 2000, the Sorting Hat, the Sword of Gryffindor, Hagrid's motorcycle, and a Hogwarts Express attraction), video interviews with the actors and filmmakers, and exhibits about how the films' special effects were created.

Your visit starts with an intro film and brief overview by a live guide. Then you're free to wander through large halls with the sets, props, and costumes. You may be impressed by the level of detail the super-enthusiastic designers put into even the simplest of props. The visit culminates with a stroll down Diagon Alley and a room-sized 1:24-scale model of Hogwarts that will bring young Potter fans to tears.

As this attraction is understandably popular, it's essential to reserve your visit online as far ahead as you can (entrance possible only with reserved time slot). Allowing about three hours for your time at the studio, plus nearly three hours to get there and back, this experience will eat up the better part of a day.

Cost and Hours: £33, kids ages 5 to 15-£25.50, family ticket for 2 adults and 2 kids-£101; opening hours flex with season—first tour at 9:00 or 10:00, last tour as early as 16:30 or as late as 18:30, if you miss your appointment time you can still get in with the next batch admitted; audio/videoguide-£5, café, still photography allowed, tel. 0845-084-0900, www.wbstudiotour.co.uk.

Getting There: Leavesden is about 20 miles northwest of London. Reaching the studio is easy, requiring a **train and shuttle bus** connection. Give yourself at least 90 minutes to get from your central London hotel to the studio for your appointed time. First, take the frequent train from London Euston (platforms 8-11) to Watford Junction (about 5/hour, 15-20 minutes). At Watford Junction, exit the station and look left to find the bus stop. Catch the Mullany's Coaches shuttle bus (instantly recognizable by its bright paint job) to the studio tour (2-4/hour, 15 minutes, £1.50 one-way, £2 round-trip, buy ticket from driver).

More direct (and more expensive), Golden Tours runs 3-4 **buses** per day between their office near Victoria Station in central London and the studio (price includes round-trip bus and studio entrance: adults-£57, kids-£52; generally leaves London at 8:00, 10:00, 11:00, and 14:00, tour begins 2 hours after bus departs, reserve ahead at www.goldentours.com).

WESTMINSTER WALK

From Big Ben to Trafalgar Square

Just about every visitor to London strolls along historic Whitehall from Big Ben to Trafalgar Square. This quick nine-stop walk gives meaning to that touristy ramble. Under London's modern traffic and big-city bustle lie 2,000 fascinating years of history. You'll get a whirlwind tour as well as a practical orientation to London.

Orientation

Length of This Walk: Allow one hour for a leisurely walk, and add more time if you tour the Churchill War Rooms (1-2 hours) and the Banqueting House (30-60 minutes). Other nearby sights include the Houses of Parliament, Westminster Abbey, National Gallery, National Portrait Gallery, and St. Martin-in-the-Fields.

Getting There: Take the Tube to Westminster, then take the Westminster Pier exit. The walk ends at Trafalgar Square (nearest Tube stop: Charing Cross).

Churchill War Rooms: £18, daily 9:30-18:00, last entry one hour before closing.

Supreme Court: Free, Mon-Fri 9:30-16:30, closed Sat-Sun, £1 guidebooklet, requires security check, tel. 020/7960-1900, www.supremecourt.uk.

Banqueting House: £6, includes audioguide, daily 10:00-17:00; may close for government functions—though it always stays open at least until 13:00.

Horse Guards: Free to see Changing of the Guard Mon-Sat at 11:00, Sun at 10:00, dismounting ceremony daily at 16:00.

Tours: ⌂ Download my free Westminster Walk **audio tour.**

Services: WCs along this walk are at Westminster Pier (pay), in Supreme Court (free), at the intersection of Bridge Street and

Whitehall (underground, pay), and at Trafalgar Square (free, in square, at National Gallery, and downstairs at St. Martin-in-the-Fields).

Eateries: See page 403 for recommended eateries near Trafalgar Square, and page 131 for recommendations near Westminster Abbey.

The Walk Begins

• *Start halfway across Westminster Bridge.*

❶ Westminster Bridge
Views of Big Ben and Parliament
• *First look upstream, toward the Parliament.*

Ding dong ding dong. Dong ding ding dong. Yes, indeed, you are in London. **Big Ben** is actually "not the clock, not the tower, but the bell that tolls the hour." How-ever, since the 13-ton bell is not visible, everyone just calls the whole works Big Ben. Named for a fat bureaucrat, Ben is scarce-ly older than my great-

grandmother, but it has quickly become the city's symbol. The tower—officially named the "Elizabeth Tower" in honor of Queen Elizabeth II's Diamond Jubilee—is 315 feet high. The clock faces are 23 feet across, and the 13-foot-long minute hand sweeps the length of your body every five minutes. For fun, call home from near Big Ben at about three minutes before the hour to let your loved one hear the bell ring.

Big Ben hangs out in the north tower of a long building (the Houses of Parliament) that stretches along the Thames. Britain is ruled from this building, which for five centuries was the home of kings and queens. Then, as democracy was foisted on tyrants, a par-liament of nobles was allowed to meet in some of the rooms. Soon, commoners were elected to office, the neighborhood was shot, and the royalty moved to Buckingham Palace. While most of the cur-rent building looks medieval with its prickly flamboyant spires, it was actually built after a fire gutted the old Westminster Palace in 1834.

Today, the House of Commons meets in one end of the build-ing. The rubber-stamp House of Lords grumbles and snoozes in the other end of this 1,000-room complex, and provides a tem-pering effect on extreme governmental changes. The two houses

Westminster Walk

1 Westminster Bridge
2 Statue of Boadicea
3 Parliament Square
4 Start of Whitehall
5 Cenotaph

6 10 Downing Street & Ministry of Defence
7 Banqueting House
8 Horse Guards
9 Trafalgar Square

are very much separate: Notice the riverside tea terraces with the color-coded awnings—royal red for lords, common green for commoners. Alluding to the traditional leanings of the two chambers, locals say, "Green for go...red for stop" (for tips on visiting the Houses of Parliament, see page 142). The modern Portcullis Building (with the tube-like chimneys), across Bridge Street from Big Ben, holds offices for the 650 members of the House of Commons. They commute to the Houses of Parliament by way of an underground passage.

• *Now look north (downstream).*

Views of the London Eye, The City, and the Thames

Built in 2000 to celebrate the millennium, the London Eye—originally nicknamed "the London Eyesore," but now generally appreci-

ated by locals—is a giant Ferris wheel standing 443 feet tall. It slowly spins 32 capsules (also the number of boroughs in London), each filled with a maximum of 25 visitors, up to London's best viewpoint (with up to 25 miles' visibility on a rare clear day). Aside from Big Ben, Parliament, St. Paul's Cathedral (not visible from here), and the wheel itself, central London's skyline is not overwhelming; it's a city that wows from within.

Next to the wheel sprawls the huge former County Hall building, now a hotel and tourist complex. The London Eye marks the start of the Jubilee Walkway, a pleasant one-hour riverside promenade along the South Bank of the Thames, through London's vibrant, gentrified arts-and-cultural zone. Along the way, you have views across the river of St. Paul's stately dome and the financial district, called The City.

London's history is tied to the **Thames,** the 210-mile river linking the interior of England with the North Sea. The city got its start in Roman times as a trade center along this watery highway. As recently as a century ago, large ships made their way upstream

to the city center to unload. Today, the major port is 25 miles downstream, and tourist cruise boats ply the waters.

Look for the **boat piers** on either bank of the Thames. Several tour-boat companies offer regular departures from Westminster Pier (on the left) or Waterloo Pier (on

WESTMINSTER

the right, near the London Eye). This is an efficient, scenic way to get from here to the Tower of London or Greenwich (downstream) or Kew Gardens (upstream). For details, see page 39.

Lining the river, beneath the lampposts, are little green copper **lions' heads** with rings for tying up boats. Before the construction of the Thames Barrier in 1982 (the world's second-largest movable flood barrier, downstream near Greenwich), high tides from the nearby North Sea made floods a recurring London problem. The police kept an eye on these lions: "When the lions drink, the city's at risk."

Until 1750, only London Bridge crossed the Thames. Then a bridge was built here. Early in the morning of September 3, 1802, William Wordsworth stood where you're standing and described what he saw:

> *This City now doth, like a garment, wear*
> *The beauty of the morning; silent, bare,*
> *Ships, towers, domes, theatres, and temples lie*
> *Open unto the fields, and to the sky;*
> *All bright and glittering in the smokeless air.*

• *Near Westminster Pier is a big statue of a lady on a chariot (nicknamed "the first woman driver"...no reins).*

❷ Statue of Boadicea, Queen of the Iceni

Riding in her two-horse chariot, daughters by her side, this Celtic Xena leads her people against Roman invaders. Julius Caesar was

the first Roman general to cross the Channel, but even he was weirded out by the island's strange inhabitants, who worshipped trees, sacrificed virgins, and went to war painted blue. Later, Romans subdued and civilized them, building roads and making this spot on the Thames—"Londinium"—into a major urban center.

But Boadicea refused to be Romanized. In A.D. 60, after Roman soldiers raped her daughters, she rallied her people and "liberated" London, massacring its 60,000 Romanized citizens. However, the brief revolt was snuffed out, and she and her family took poison to avoid surrender.

• *There's a civilized public toilet down the stairs behind Boadicea. Cross the street to just under Big Ben and continue one block inland to the busy intersection of Parliament Square. Pause here for the view.*

WESTMINSTER

❸ Parliament Square

To your left are the sandstone-hued **Houses of Parliament.** If Parliament is in session, the entrance (midway down the building) is lined with tourists, enlivened by political demonstrations, and staked out by camera crews interviewing Members of Parliament (MPs) for the evening news. Only the core part, Westminster Hall, survives from the circa-1090s original. While the Houses of Parliament are commonly described as "Neo-Gothic" (even in this book), this uniquely English style is more specifically called Neo-Perpendicular Gothic. For a peek at genuine Perpendicular Gothic (the fanciest and final stage of that style), simply look across the street at the section of Westminster Abbey closest to the Houses of Parliament—it dates from 1484.

Kitty-corner across the square, the two white towers of **Westminster Abbey** rise above the trees. The broad boulevard of Whitehall (here called Parliament Street) stretches to your right up to Trafalgar Square.

This square is the heart of what was once a suburb of London—the medieval City of Westminster. Like Buda and Pest (later Budapest), London is two cities that grew into one. In Roman and medieval times, the city was centered farther east, near St. Paul's Cathedral. But in the 11th century, King Edward the Confessor moved his court here, and the center of political power shifted to this area. Edward built a palace and a church (minster) here in the west, creating the city of "West Minster." Over time, the palace evolved into a meeting place for debating public policy—a parliament. Today's Houses of Parliament sit atop the remains of Edward's original palace. To this day, the Houses of Parliament are known to Brits as the "Palace of Westminster."

Across from Parliament, the cute little church with the blue sundials, snuggling under the Abbey "like a baby lamb under a ewe," is **St. Margaret's Church.** Since 1480, this has been *the* place for politicians' weddings, including Winston and Clementine Churchill's.

Parliament Square, the expanse of green between Westminster Abbey and Big Ben, is filled with statues of famous statesmen (and sometimes with protesters). The statue of **Winston Churchill,** the man who saved Britain from Hitler, shows him in the military overcoat he was fond of wearing. According to tour guides, the statue has a current of electricity running through it to honor Churchill's wish that if a statue were made of him, his head wouldn't be soiled

WESTMINSTER

by pigeons. Other statues honor politicians (including a few non-Brits) for their contributions, not to Britain, but to mankind. At the

opposite corner of the square from Churchill stands **Nelson Mandela** (erected in 2007), who battled South African apartheid. Nearby is the robed statue of **Mahatma Gandhi** (erected in 2015), who helped liberate India from the British. And behind them (across the street) stands the man who liberated America's slaves, **Abraham Lincoln** (erected in 1920, patterned after a similar statue in Chicago's Lincoln Park).

The white building (flying the Union Jack) at the far end of the square houses Britain's **Supreme Court.** You can wander the building after going through security, see a small exhibit on this recently sanctioned legal body, and observe any courts currently in session (it also has a café and WCs).

In 1868, the world's first traffic light was installed on the corner where Whitehall now spills double-decker buses into the square. Another reminder of a bygone era is the little yellow "Taxi" lantern atop the fence on the street corner closest to Parliament. In pre-mobile phone days, when an MP needed a taxi, this lit up to hail one. And here's one more ancient artifact: Along the north side of Parliament Square are some nearly obsolete remnants of 20th-century technology—red phone booths, mainly used today by tourists wanting a photo-op with Big Ben.

• *Consider touring Westminster Abbey (📖 see the Westminster Abbey Tour chapter). Otherwise, turn right (north), walk away from the Houses of Parliament and the Abbey, and continue up Parliament Street, which becomes Whitehall.*

❹ Walking Along Whitehall

Today, Whitehall is choked with traffic, but imagine the effect this broad street must have had on out-of-towners a little more than

a century ago. In your horse-drawn carriage, you'd clop along a tree-lined boulevard past well-dressed lords and ladies, dodging street urchins. Gazing left, then right, you'd try to take it all in, your eyes dazzled by the bone-white walls of this man-made marble canyon.

Whitehall is now the most important street in Britain, lined with the ministries of finance, treasury, and so on. You may see limos and camera crews as important dignitaries enter or exit. Political demonstrators wave signs and chant slogans—sometimes about issues foreign to most Americans (Britain's former colonies still resent the empire's continuing influence), and sometimes about issues very familiar to us (the wars in the Middle East and the economy). Notice the security measures. Iron grates seal off the concrete ditches between the buildings and sidewalks for protection against explosives.

The black, ornamental arrowheads topping the iron fences were once colorfully painted. In 1861, Queen Victoria ordered them all painted black when her beloved Prince Albert ("the only one who called her Vickie") died. Possibly the world's most determined mourner, Victoria wore black for the standard two years of mourning—and then tacked on 38 more. (For more on Victoria, see the sidebar on page 102.)

• *Continue down Whitehall. On your right is a colorful pub, the Red Lion. Across the street, a 700-foot detour down King Charles Street leads to the Churchill War Rooms, the underground bunker of 27 rooms that was the nerve center of Britain's campaign against Hitler (see page 45 for details). Farther along, you reach a tall, square, stone monument in the middle of the boulevard.*

❺ Cenotaph

This monument honors those who died in the two events that most shaped modern Britain—World Wars I and II. The monumental

devastation of these wars helped turn a colonial superpower into a cultural colony of an American superpower.

The actual cenotaph is the slab that sits atop the pillar—a tomb. You'll notice no religious symbols on this memorial. The dead honored here came from many creeds and all corners of Britain's empire. It looks lost in a sea of noisy cars, but on each Remembrance Sunday (closest to November 11), Whitehall is closed to traffic, the royal family fills the balcony overhead in the foreign ministry, and a memorial service is held around the cenotaph.

The year 2014 marked the centennial of the start of what Brits call "the Great War"—World War I. It's hard for an American to understand the war's long-term impact on Europe. On a single day (at the Battle of the Somme, 1916), the British suffered nearly 60,000 casualties. It's said that if the roughly one million WWI dead from the British Empire were to march four abreast past the cenotaph, the sad parade would last for seven days.

WESTMINSTER

Eternally pondering the cenotaph (from *way* up the street—barely visible from here) is an equestrian statue. **Field Marshal Douglas Haig** (marked with his honorary title, *Earl Haig*) was commander-in-chief of the British army from 1916 to 1918. He was responsible for ordering so many brave and not-so-brave British boys out of the trenches and onto the killing fields of World War I.

• *Just past the cenotaph is a crosswalk. On the other (west) side of Whitehall is a black iron security gate guarding the entrance to Downing Street.*

❻ 10 Downing Street and the Ministry of Defence

Britain's version of the White House is where the prime minister and his family live, at #10. It's the black-brick building 100 yards down the blocked-off street, on the right; there's a lantern and usually a security guard.

Like the White House's Rose Garden, the black door marked #10 is a highly symbolic point of power, popular for photo ops to mark big occasions. This is where suffragettes protested in the early 20th century, where Neville Chamberlain showed off his regrettable peace treaty with Hitler, and where Winston Churchill made famous the V-for-Victory sign. It's where President Barack Obama came to discuss global economic issues with the previous prime minister, and where Prime Minister David Cameron and his wife Samantha try to raise their young family like normal people.

It looks modest, but #10's entryway does open up into fairly impressive digs—the prime minister's offices (downstairs), his residence (upstairs), and two large formal dining rooms. The PM's staff has offices here. Many on the staff are permanent bureaucrats, staying on to serve as prime ministers come and go. The cabinet meets at #10 on Tuesday mornings. This is where foreign dignitaries come for official government dinners, where the prime minister receives honored schoolkids and victorious soccer teams, and where he gives monthly addresses to the nation. Next door, at #11, the chancellor of the exchequer (finance minister) lives with his family, and #12 houses the PM's press office.

This has been the traditional home of the prime minister since the position was created in the early 18th century. But even before that, the neighborhood (if not the building itself) was a center of power, where Edward the Confessor and Henry VIII had palaces. The facade is, frankly, quite cheap, having been built as part of a middle-class cul-de-sac of homes by American-born George

Prime Minister David Cameron

David Cameron succeeded Gordon Brown as prime minister in May 2010, and lives at 10 Downing Street with his wife, Samantha, and their young children. Elected at age 43, Cameron was the youngest PM in two centuries. He heads the Conservative Party (the "Tories"), but has never quite fit the stodgy Conservative image. Rumors still swirl of wild parties and illicit drugs in his student days at Oxford. He's known as "Dave" to his friends, and he developed a habit of riding his bike to work. Cameron rose quickly through the political ranks: He worked to re-elect Conservative PM John Major (1992), assisted the finance minister at 11 Downing Street (1992-1994), and was himself elected to Parliament in 2001, becoming head of the Conservative Party in 2005. By 2008, he was on the cover of *Time* magazine, which hailed him as the future of conservatism.

In 2010, Cameron's Conservative Party came to power, but it was hardly a sweeping Conservative mandate: Three parties split the vote, forcing Cameron's Conservatives to form a coalition with the (more left-leaning) Liberal Democrat Party. The Labour Party, which had held power in Britain for 13 years under Gordon Brown and Tony Blair, is the coalition's chief opposition.

Politically, Cameron is a moderate Conservative who is more pragmatic than ideological. Socially, he's "liberal" in the classical sense, advocating for personal freedoms—gay rights, decriminalization of drugs, allowing hunting and smoking, and ensuring citizens' privacy against government intrusion. Fiscally, he rails against big-government waste. His fiscal policies have emphasized austerity and belt-tightening in order to get the budget under control. The immediate result was a double-dip recession, but now Britain's economy is on the upswing. His most right-of-center stance is his support for distancing Britain from the euro and the European Union; he's pledged to negotiate new terms with the EU and then hold a vote on Britain's EU membership before the end of 2017.

Despite his personal appeal, Cameron can't quite shake the Conservatives' image as the party of the upper class. Cameron was born rich, married rich, and has worked within the corporate culture. His colleagues form an old boys' network from his days at Eton, England's most exclusive prep school. Fellow politician (and mayor of London until mid-2016) Boris Johnson is not only an old Oxford frat buddy but also a distant cousin. Cameron's reputation has been tarnished by his links to discredited media mogul Rupert Murdoch, and some have questioned his handling of riots in London and other urban centers in the summer of 2011.

As the Conservatives try to unite the country to solve Britain's severe economic and cultural problems, it remains to be seen whether David Cameron has brought a fresh enough approach to #10. Thanks to a successful re-election campaign in 2015, Cameron's party has one more chance to deliver.

WESTMINSTER

Downing in the 1680s. When the first PM moved in, the humble interior was combined with a mansion in back. During a major upgrade in the 1950s, they discovered that the facade's black bricks were actually yellow—but had been stained by centuries of Industrial Age soot. To keep with tradition, they now paint the bricks black.

The guarded metal gates were installed in 1989 to protect against Irish terrorists. Even so, #10 was hit and partly damaged in 1991 by an Irish Republican Army mortar launched from a van. These days, there's typically not much to see unless a VIP happens to drive up. Then the bobbies snap to and check credentials, the gates open, the car is inspected for bombs, the traffic barrier midway down the street drops into its bat cave, the car drives in, and... the bobbies go back to mugging for the tourists.

The huge building across Whitehall from Downing Street is the **Ministry of Defence** (MOD), the "British Pentagon." This bleak place looks like a Ministry of Defence should. In front are statues of illustrious defenders of Britain. "Monty" is **Field Marshal Bernard Law Montgomery** of World War II, who beat the Nazis in North Africa (defeating Erwin "The Desert Fox" Rommel at El Alamein), which gave the Allies a jumping-off point to retake Europe. Along with Churchill, Monty breathed confidence back into a demoralized British army, persuading them they

THE WOMEN OF WORLD WAR II

could ultimately beat Hitler. A **memorial** honoring the women who fought and died in World War II stands in the middle of the street. Its empty uniforms evoke the often-overlooked sacrifices of Britain's female war heroes.

You may be enjoying the shade of London's **plane trees.** They do well in polluted London: roots that work well in clay, waxy leaves that self-clean in the rain, and bark that sheds and regenerates so the pollution doesn't get into the trees' vascular systems.

• *At the equestrian statue of Haig (described earlier), you'll be flanked by the Welsh and Scottish government offices. At the corner (same side as the Ministry of Defence), you'll find the...*

❼ Banqueting House

This two-story building is just about all that remains of what was once the biggest palace in Europe—Whitehall Palace, which once stretched from Trafalgar Square to Big Ben. Henry VIII started building it when he moved out of the Palace of Westminster (now the Parliament) and into the residence of the archbishop of York. Queen Elizabeth I and other monarchs added on as England's worldwide prestige grew.

Today, the exterior of Greek-style columns and pediments looks rather ho-hum, much like every other white, marble building in London. But in 1620, it was a one-of-a-kind wonder—a big, white temple rising above small, half-timbered huts. Built by architect Inigo Jones, it sparked London's interest in the classical style. Within a century, London was awash in Georgian-style architecture, the English version of Neoclassical.

Facing the Banqueting House, look at the first-floor windows (with the balustrade)—the site of one of the pivotal events of English history. On January 30, 1649, a man dressed in black appeared at one of the windows and looked out at a huge crowd that surrounded the building. He stepped out the window and onto a wooden platform. It was King Charles I. He gave a short speech to the crowd, framed by the magnificent backdrop of the Banqueting House. His final word was "Remember." Then he knelt and laid his neck on a block as another man in black approached. It was the executioner—who cut off the king's head.

Plop—the concept of divine monarchy in Britain was decapitated. But there would still be kings after Oliver Cromwell, the Protestant antimonarchist who brought about Charles I's death and then became England's leader. Soon after Cromwell's death, royalty was restored, and Charles' son, Charles II, got his revenge here in the Banqueting Hall...by living well. But, from then on, every king knew that he ruled by the grace of Parliament.

Charles I is remembered today with a statue at one end of Whitehall (in Trafalgar Square at the base of the tall column), while his enemy, Oliver Cromwell, is given equal time with a statue at the other end (at the Houses of Parliament).

• *You can pop into the Banqueting House, following the self-guided tour below. Otherwise, skip to "Horse Guards."*

Banqueting House Interior

Start with the 10-minute video on the history of the House, which shows the place in banqueting action. History buffs might consider the included, 45-minute audioguide. The low-ceilinged ground floor, a.k.a. the Undercroft, was King James I's personal wine cellar and tasting room. Climb to the first floor to find a portrait of the doomed king.

The main hall is impressive—two stories high, white with gold trim, full of light, and topped with colorful paintings in a gold-coffered ceiling. At 55 feet wide, 55 feet high, and 110 feet long, it's a perfect double cube. The chandeliers can be raised and lowered to accommodate any event. The throne is a modern reconstruction, but it gives an idea of the king's canopied throne that once stood here.

Ceiling Paintings: Charles I, who inherited the Banqueting House from his father, commissioned the famed Peter Paul Rubens to complete the decor. The paintings glorify Charles' dad, James I, the man who built the Banqueting House and who once told Parliament: "Kings are called gods...even by God himself."

To view the large oval painting in the center, *The Apotheosis of James I*, approach from the entrance, like a visiting ambassador, and watch the scene unfold. King James I (in red robe, with gray beard) rests his foot on a globe, as king of the whole world. Lady Faith (with a torch) and Miss Justice (with scales) lead him up into heaven, where baby angels blow trumpets and the goddess Minerva crowns him with the laurel wreath of wisdom. Minerva sticks her foot in our face, a triumph of illusion three centuries before 3-D glasses.

The painting above the throne, *The Peaceful Reign of King James*, shows wise King James seated on his throne, flanked by corkscrew columns from the temple of wise King Solomon. To the left, Peace embraces Plenty. Two angels swoop down at dramatic angles to adorn James with laurels, while a cherub holds his royal crown. Below, the Roman gods—Mercury, Mars, Minerva—arrive to help James subdue the serpents of rebellion.

In the painting above the entrance, *The Union of the Crowns,* James points his scepter at two ladies—England and Scotland—warning them to get along. James united the two bickering countries, having been crowned both King of Scots (in 1567) and King of England (1603). Smoke clouds of peace rise in the background as Cupid (bottom left corner) torches the weapons of war. The ladies place a crown on a baby's head and lead him to the throne. It's James' son, the future Charles I. When Charles grew up, he had this painting hung so that he could see it (right-side up) while seated on the Banqueting House throne.

The Banqueting House Through History

Imagine the many events this place has hosted over the centuries. Originally built as the royal dining hall for the sprawling

Whitehall Palace, the Banqueting House also served as its de facto throne room. Picture ambassadors arriving here and walking the length of this hall lined with courtiers to pay homage to the king on his canopied throne. Loyal subjects knelt here to be made knights and nobles.

In the 1600s, the hall was famous throughout Europe as an occasional theater. Plays called "masques" were performed by torchlight and featured mask-wearing actors, singers and dancers, and elaborate costumes, sets, and special effects.

Picture the scene in 1622, when the brand-new Banqueting House was inaugurated with a performance of *The Masque of Augurs,* by Shakespeare protégé Ben Jonson (with set design by the hall's architect, Inigo Jones). King James and his courtiers crowded the balcony and tiered seats, and watched in awe as a parade of goofy commoners in masks entered the hall, singing and reveling, accompanied by two dancing bears. The comic chaos was suddenly interrupted by Greek gods who descended magically from the ceiling, eventually bringing harmony to the realm—just as a wise king does. And behind one of the masks, one of the actors was none other than 21-year-old Prince "I just can't wait to be king" Charles.

In 1649, the Banqueting House served a much more serious purpose—as an execution site for the public beheading of Charles I. Oliver Cromwell subsequently used this symbolic spot to legitimize his own leadership as Lord Protector. When Charles' son, Charles II, restored the monarchy in 1660, it was here that they celebrated.

In 1698, a massive fire destroyed Whitehall Palace, leaving only the name and the Banqueting House. The monarchs moved their residence elsewhere, eventually to Buckingham Palace. The Banqueting House became the Royal Chapel, complete with organ and pews.

Today, besides being a museum, the Banqueting House still functions much as it did in its heyday—hosting government receptions for foreign dignitaries or for parliament. World-renowned classical musicians perform for the paying public. And it's a rent-a-hall for parties and dinners. You could hold your daughter's wedding reception here, with 400 guests and full catering, for as little as $100,000.

WESTMINSTER

• *When you're finished ogling the paintings, head back outside. Continue up Whitehall on the left (west) side, where you'll see (and smell) the building known as Horse Guards, guarded by traditionally dressed soldiers—who are also called Horse Guards.*

❽ Horse Guards

For 200 years, soldiers in cavalry uniforms have guarded this arched entrance along Whitehall that leads to Buckingham Palace

and one of its predecessors as royal residence, St. James's Palace.

Two different squads alternate, so depending on the day you visit, you'll see soldiers in either red coats with white plumes in their helmets (the Life Guards), or blue coats with red plumes (the Blues and Royals). Together, they constitute the Queen's personal bodyguard. Besides their ceremonial duties here in old-time uniforms, these elite troops have fought in Iraq and Afghanistan. Both Prince William and Prince Harry have served in the Blues and Royals.

Stroll between the two guards, into the courtyard. The Horse Guards building was the headquarters of the British army from the time of the American Revolution until the Ministry of Defence was created in World War II. Back when this archway was the only access point to The Mall (the street leading to Buckingham Palace), it was a security checkpoint. Anyone on horseback had to dismount before passing through. Today, by tradition, you must dismount your bicycle, Vespa, or Segway and walk it through. During the 2012 Olympics, the broad expanse of Horse Guards Parade was covered in sand to host the beach volleyball matches.

The Horse Guards Museum offers a glimpse at the stables and a collection of uniforms and weapons.

• *Continue up Whitehall, passing the Old Admiralty (#26, on left), headquarters of the British navy that once ruled the waves. Across the street, behind the old Clarence Pub, stood the original Scotland Yard, headquarters of London's crack police force in the days of Sherlock Holmes. Finally, Whitehall opens up into the grand, noisy, traffic-filled Trafalgar Square.*

To reach the center of the square, cross a few streets at the crosswalks.

❾ Trafalgar Square

London's central meeting point bustles around the world's biggest Corinthian column, where **Admiral Horatio Nelson** stands 170 feet off the ground, looking over London in the direction of one of the greatest naval battles in history. Nelson saved England at

Trafalgar Square Area

COVENT GARDEN

LISLE ST.

CRANBOURN

Leicester Square

GARRICK

KING ST.

NEW ROW

ST. MARTINS LANE

CHARING CROSS ROAD

BEDFORD

WHITCOMB STREET

PANTON

TKTS

IRVING

ORANGE ST.

CHANDOS PL.

To Courtauld Gallery & The City

THE CHANDOS PUB

THE HARP PUB

WILLIAM IV ST.

NATIONAL PORTRAIT GALLERY

ST. MARTIN'S PL.

CRYPT, CAFÉ & SHOP ENTRANCE

ST. MARTIN-IN-THE-FIELDS

THE STRAND

To Piccadilly

NATIONAL GALLERY

SAINSBURY WING

GEORGE WASH.

DUNCANNON

To Embankment

HAYMARKET

FOURTH PLINTH

SOUTH AFRICA HOUSE

Charing Cross

VILLIERS

Trafalgar Square

NELSON'S COLUMN

Charing Cross

CHARING CROSS STATION

PALL MALL

COCKSPUR ST.

CANADA HOUSE

CHARLES I

Charing Cross

SHERLOCK HOLMES PUB

To St. James's Palace

ADMIRALTY ARCH

NORTHUMBERLAND

SITE OF OLD SCOTLAND YARD

GREAT SCOTLAND YARD

To Buckingham Palace

THE MALL

OLD ADMIRALTY

WHITEHALL

WHITEHALL PL.

Green Park

To Big Ben & Westminster

200 Meters

200 Yards

WESTMINSTER

a time as dark as World War II. In 1805, Napoleon was poised on the other side of the Channel, threatening to invade England. Meanwhile, more than 900 miles away, the one-armed, one-eyed, and one-minded Lord Nelson attacked the French fleet off the coast of Spain at Trafalgar. The French were routed, Britannia ruled the waves, and the once-invincible French army was slowly

worn down, then defeated at Waterloo. Nelson, while victorious, was shot by a sniper in the battle. He died, gasping, "Thank God, I have done my duty."

At the top of Trafalgar Square (north) sits the domed **National Gallery** with its grand staircase, and, to the right, the steeple of **St. Martin-in-the-Fields,** built in 1722, inspiring the steeple-over-the-entrance style of many town churches in New England (free lunch concerts—see page 449).

At the base of Nelson's column are bronze reliefs cast from melted-down enemy cannons, and four huggable lions dying to have their photo taken with you. In front of the column, Charles I sits on horseback, with his head still on his shoulders. In the pavement just behind the statue is a plaque marking the center of London, from which all distances are measured. Of the many statues that dot the square, the pedestal on the northwest corner

(the "fourth plinth") is periodically topped with contemporary art. The fountains, lit by colored lights, can shoot water 80 feet in the air.

Trafalgar Square is the center of modern London, connecting Westminster, The City, and the West End. A 2003 remodeling of the square rerouted car traffic, helping reclaim the area for London's citizens. Spin clockwise 360 degrees and survey the city:

To the south (down Whitehall) is the center of government, Westminster. Looking southwest, down the broad boulevard called The Mall, you see Buckingham Palace in the distance. (Down Pall Mall is St. James's Palace and Clarence House, where Prince Charles lives when in London.) A few blocks northwest of Trafalgar Square is Piccadilly Circus. Directly north (a block behind the National Gallery) sits Leicester Square, the jumping-off point for Soho, Covent Garden, and the West End theater district (see the West End Walk chapter).

The boulevard called the Strand takes you past Charing Cross Station, then eastward to The City, the original walled town of London and today's financial center. In medieval times, when people from The City met with the Westminster government, it was here. And finally, Northumberland Street leads southeast to the Golden Jubilee pedestrian bridge over the Thames. Along the way, you'll pass the Sherlock Holmes Pub (just off Northumberland Street, on Craven Passage), housed in Sir Arthur Conan Doyle's favorite watering hole, with an upstairs replica of 221b Baker Street.

Soak it in. You're smack-dab in the center of London, a thriving city atop two millennia of history.

WESTMINSTER ABBEY TOUR

Westminster Abbey is more than just an "abbey"—it's the most famous English church in Christendom, where royalty has been wedded, crowned, and buried since the 11th century. Indeed, the histories of Westminster Abbey and England are almost the same. A thousand years of English history—3,000 tombs, the remains of 29 kings and queens, and hundreds of memorials to poets, politicians, scientists, and warriors—lie within its stained-glass splendor and under its stone slabs.

Orientation

Cost: £20, £40 family ticket (covers 2 adults and 1 child), includes fine audioguide and entry to the cloisters and Abbey Museum. Praying is free, thank God. It's also free to enter just the cloisters and Abbey Museum (through Dean's Yard, around the right side as you face the main entrance), but if it's too crowded inside, the marshal at the cloister entrance may not let you in.

Hours: Abbey—Mon-Fri 9:30-16:30, Wed until 19:00 (main church only), Sat 9:30-14:30, last entry one hour before closing, closed Sun to sightseers but open for services; Abbey Museum—daily 10:30-16:00; cloisters—daily 8:00-18:00. Special events can shut down all or part of the Abbey.

When to Go: The place is most crowded every day at midmorning and all day Saturdays and Mondays. Visit early, during lunch, or late to avoid tourist hordes. Weekdays after 14:30—especially Wed—are less congested; come after that time and stay for the 17:00 evensong (but keep in mind the Wed 17:00 evensong is generally spoken, not sung). The main entrance, on the Parliament Square side, often has a sizable line—skip it by booking tickets in advance via the Abbey's website.

Dress Code: There is none, even for services.

Getting There: Near Big Ben and the Houses of Parliament (Tube: Westminster or St. James's Park).

Information: Because special events and services can shut out sightseers, check the website or call ahead to confirm that the Abbey is open, and get the latest schedule for guided tours, concerts, or services (tel. 020/7222-5152, www.westminster-abbey.org). If you have questions about the cathedral, ask any marshal in red or volunteer verger in green. There's surprisingly little posted information on the Abbey's sights, so you must rely on the audioguide, the vergers, or this book.

Music and Church Services: Mon-Fri at 7:30 (prayer), 8:00 (communion), 12:30 (communion), 17:00 evensong (except on Wed, when the evening service is generally spoken—not sung); **Sat** at 8:00 (communion), 9:00 (prayer), 15:00 (evensong; May-Aug it's at 17:00); **Sun** services generally come with more music: at 8:00 (communion), 10:00 (sung Matins), 11:15 (sung Eucharist), 15:00 (evensong), 18:30 (evening service). Services are free to anyone, though visitors who haven't paid church admission aren't allowed to linger afterward. Free **organ recitals** are usually held Sun at 17:45 (30 minutes). For a schedule of services or recitals on a particular day, look for posted signs with schedules or check the Abbey's website.

Tours: The included **audioguide** is excellent, taking some of the sting out of the steep admission fee. To add to the experience, you can take an entertaining **guided tour** from a verger—the church equivalent of a museum docent (£5, schedule posted both outside and inside entry, up to 5/day in summer, 4/day in winter, 1.5 hours).

Length of This Tour: Allow 1.5 hours. If you have less time, focus on the main part of the church, skipping the cloisters and Abbey Museum.

Services: WCs are inside near Poets' Corner and next to the café. Outside the Abbey, the nearest public pay WCs are in front of Methodist Central Hall, the grand domed building across the street from the Abbey's west entrance.

Photography: Photos are prohibited, except in the Little Cloister and College Garden.

Eating: A **café** with table service and simple fare (£7-10 salads and sandwiches, £16 afternoon tea) is in the abbey's cellar; enter through the cloisters. Other options are nearby: **Wesley's Café,** the cafeteria in the basement of Methodist Central Hall across the street, serves £7-9 lunches (Mon-Sun 9:00-16:00, good free WC). The **Supreme Court** building on Parliament Square has a basic basement café and free WCs (but you have to go through a security checkpoint to get there; Mon-Fri

9:30-16:30, closed Sat-Sun). **The Westminster Arms** pub is just past the Methodist Central Hall on Storey's Gate (£9-11 pub grub including fish-and-chips, food served daily 12:00-20:00, eat downstairs). Picnickers can find benches at the nearby Jewel Tower, a half-block south of the Abbey.

Starring: Edwards, Elizabeths, Henrys, Annes, Marys, and poets.

The Tour Begins

You'll have no choice but to follow the steady flow of tourists through the church, along the route laid out for the audioguide. It's all one-way, and most days the crowds are a real crush. Here are the Abbey's top 10 (plus one) stops.

• *Walk straight in, entering the north transept. Pick up the map flier that locates the most illustrious tombs and borrow the included audioguide. Follow the crowd flow to the right, passing through* **"Scientists' Corner,"** *with memorials to Isaac Newton (left side of the choir screen), Michael Faraday, Charles Darwin (on the floor), and others. Enter the spacious...*

❶ Nave

Look down the long and narrow center aisle of the church. Lined with the praying hands of the Gothic arches, glowing with light from the stained glass, it's clear that this is more than a museum. With saints in stained glass, heroes in carved stone, and the bodies of England's greatest citizens under the floor stones, Westminster Abbey is the religious heart of England.

The Abbey was built in 1065. Its name, Westminster, means Church in the West (west of St. Paul's Cathedral). The king who built the Abbey was Edward the Confessor. Find him in the stained glass windows on the left side of the nave ("left" as you face the altar). He's in the third bay from the end (marked *S: Edwardus rex...*), with his crown, scepter, and ring. Take some time to thank him for this Abbey.

For the next 250 years, the Abbey was redone and remodeled to become essentially the church you see today, notwithstanding an extensive resurfacing in the 19th century. Thankfully, later architects—ignoring building trends of their generation—honored the vision of the original planner, and the building was completed in one relatively harmonious style.

The Abbey's 10-story nave is the tallest in England. The chan-

Westminster Abbey Tour

1 Nave
2 Choir
3 Coronation Spot
4 Shrine of Edward the Confessor
5 Tomb of Elizabeth I & Mary I
6 Chapel of King Henry VII
7 Royal Air Force Chapel
8 Tomb of Mary, Queen of Scots
9 Poets' Corner
10 Cloisters & Abbey Museum
11 Coronation Chair

deliers, 10 feet tall, look small in comparison (16 were given to the Abbey by the Guinness family).

On the floor near the west entrance of the Abbey is the flower-lined **Grave of the Unknown Warrior,** one ordinary WWI soldier buried in soil from France with lettering made from melted-down weapons from that war. Take time to contemplate the million-man army from the British Empire, and all those who gave their lives. Their memory is so revered that, when Kate Middleton walked up the aisle on her wedding day, by tradition she had to step around the tomb (and her wedding bouquet was later placed atop this tomb, also in accordance with tradition). Hanging on a column next to the tomb is the US Medal of Honor, presented by General John J. Pershing in 1921 to honor England's WWI dead. Closer to the door, also on the floor, is a memorial to a hero of World War II, Winston Churchill.

• *Now walk straight up the nave toward the altar. This is the same route every future monarch walks on the way to being crowned. Midway up the nave, you pass through the colorful screen of an enclosure known as the...*

2 Choir

These elaborately carved wood and gilded seats are where monks

once chanted their services in
the "quire"—as it's known in
British churchspeak. Today, it's
where the Abbey boys' choir
sings the evensong. You're approaching the center of a cross-
shaped church. The **"high"
(main) altar**—which usually
has a cross and candlesticks

atop it—sits on the platform up the five stairs in front of you.
• *It's on this platform—up the five steps—that the monarch is crowned.*

❸ Coronation Spot

The area immediately before the high altar is where every English coronation since 1066 has taken place. Imagine the day when
Prince William becomes king. (Or you can picture Prince Charles,
who'll come first if his mother doesn't manage to outlive him.)

The nobles in robes and powdered wigs look on from the carved
wooden stalls of the choir. The Archbishop of Canterbury stands at
the high altar. The coronation chair (which we'll see later) is placed
before the altar on the round, brown pavement stone representing
the earth. Surrounding the whole area are temporary bleachers for
8,000 VIPs, going halfway up the rose windows of each transept,
creating a "theater."

Long silver trumpets hung with banners sound a fanfare as the
monarch-to-be enters the church. The congregation sings, "I will
go into the house of the Lord," as William parades slowly down the
nave and up the steps to the altar. After a church service, he sits in
the chair, facing the altar, where the crown jewels are placed. William is anointed with holy oil, then receives a ceremonial sword,
ring, and cup. The royal scepter is placed in his hands, and—dut,
dutta dah—the archbishop lowers the Crown of St. Edward the
Confessor onto his royal head. Finally, King William V stands up,
descends the steps, and is presented to the people. As cannons roar
throughout the city, the people cry, "God save the king!"

Royalty are also given funerals here. Princess Diana's coffin was carried to this spot for her funeral service in 1997. The
"Queen Mum" (mother of Elizabeth II) had her funeral here in
2002. This is also where most of the last century's royal weddings
have taken place, including the unions of Queen Elizabeth II and
Prince Philip (1947), her parents (1923), her sister Princess Margaret (1973), and her son Prince Andrew (to Sarah Ferguson, 1986).
Most recently, of course, in April 2011, Prince William and Kate
Middleton strolled up the nave, passed through the choir, climbed
the five steps to the high altar, and became husband and wife—and
the future King and Queen of the United Kingdom and its Com-

monwealth. Though royal marriages and funerals can happen any-where, only one church can hold a coronation—the Abbey.

• *Now veer left and follow the crowd. You'll walk past the statue of Rob-ert ("Bob") Peel, the prime minister whose policemen were nicknamed "bobbies." Stroll a few yards into the land of dead kings and queens. Use the audioguide to explore the* **side chapels**—*the Chapel of St. John the Baptist and Chapel of St. Michael. There you'll see effigies of the dead lying atop their tombs of polished stone. They lie on their backs or recline on their sides. Dressed in ruffed collars, they relax on pillows, clasping their hands in prayer, many buried side by side with their spouses.*

After exploring the chapels, pause at the wooden staircase on your right.

❹ Shrine of Edward the Confessor

The holiest part of the church is the raised area behind the altar (where the wooden staircase leads—sorry, no tourist access except with verger tour). Step back and peek over the dark coffin of Ed-ward I to see the tippy-top of the green-and-gold wedding-cake tomb of King Edward the Confessor—the man who built West-minster Abbey.

God had told pious Edward to visit St. Peter's Basilica in Rome. But with the Normans thinking conquest, it was too dangerous for him to leave England. Instead, he built this grand church and dedicated it to St. Peter. It was finished just in time to bury Edward and to crown his foreign successor, William the Con-queror, in 1066. After Edward's death, people prayed at his tomb, and, after getting good results, Pope Alexander III canonized him. This elevated, central tomb—which lost some of its luster when Henry VIII melted down the gold coffin-case—is surrounded by the tombs of eight kings and queens.

• *Continue on. At the top of the stone staircase, veer left into the private burial chapel of Queen Elizabeth I.*

❺ Tomb of Queens Elizabeth I and Mary I

Although only one effigy is on the tomb (Elizabeth's), there are actually two queens buried beneath it, both daughters of Henry VIII (by different mothers). Bloody Mary—meek, pious, sickly, and Catholic—enforced Catholicism during her short reign (1553-1558) by burning "heretics" at the stake.

Elizabeth—strong, clever, and Protestant—steered England on an Anglican course. She holds a royal orb symbolizing that she's queen of the whole globe. When 26-year-old Elizabeth was crowned in the Abbey, her right to rule was questioned (especially by her Catholic subjects) because she was considered the bastard seed of Henry VIII's unsanctioned marriage to Anne Boleyn. But Elizabeth's long reign (1559-1603) was one of the greatest in English history, a time when England ruled the seas and Shakespeare explored human emotions. When she died, thousands turned out for her funeral in the Abbey. Elizabeth's face on the tomb, modeled after her death mask, is considered a very accurate take on this hook-nosed, imperious "Virgin Queen."

The two half-sisters disliked each other in life—Mary even had Elizabeth locked up in the Tower of London for a short time. Now they lie side by side for eternity. The Latin inscription ends, "Here we lie, two sisters in hope of one resurrection."

• *Continue into the ornate, flag-draped room up a few more stairs, directly behind the main altar.*

❻ Chapel of King Henry VII (The Lady Chapel)

The light from the stained-glass windows; the colorful banners overhead; and the elaborate tracery in stone, wood, and glass give this room the festive air of a medieval tournament. The prestigious Knights of the Bath meet here, under the magnificent ceiling studded with gold pendants. The ceiling—of carved stone, not plaster (1519)—is the finest English Perpendicular Gothic and fan vaulting you'll see (unless you're going to King's College Chapel in Cambridge). The ceiling was sculpted on the floor in pieces, then jigsaw-puzzled into place. It capped the Gothic period and signaled the vitality of the coming Renaissance.

The knights sit in the wooden stalls with their coats of arms on the back, churches on their heads, their banner flying above, and the graves of dozens of kings beneath their feet. When the Queen worships here, she sits in the southwest corner chair under the carved wooden throne with the lion crown (immediately to the left as you enter).

Behind the small altar is an iron cage housing tombs of the old warrior Henry VII of Lancaster and his wife, Elizabeth of York. Their love and marriage finally settled the Wars of the Roses between the two clans. The combined red-and-white rose symbol decorates the top band of the ironwork. Henry VII, the first Tudor king, was the father of Henry VIII and the grandfather of Elizabeth I. This exuberant chapel heralds a new optimistic postwar era as England prepares to step onto the world stage.

• *Go to the far end of the chapel and stand at the banister in front of the modern set of stained-glass windows.*

❼ Royal Air Force Chapel

Saints in robes and halos mingle with pilots in parachutes and bomber jackets. This tribute to WWII flyers is for those who earned their angel wings in the Battle of Britain (July-Oct 1940). Hitler's air force ruled the skies in the early days of the war, bombing at will, and threatening to snuff Britain out without a fight. But while determined Londoners hunkered down underground, British pilots in their Spitfires and Hurricanes took advantage of newly invented radar to get the jump on the more powerful Luftwaffe. These were the fighters about whom Churchill said, "Never...was so much owed by so many to so few."

The Abbey survived the Battle and the Blitz, but this window did not. As a memorial, a bit of bomb damage has been preserved—the little glassed-over hole in the wall below the windows in the lower left-hand corner. The book of remembrances lists each of the 1,497 airmen (including one American) who died in the Battle of Britain.

You're standing on the grave of Oliver Cromwell, leader of the rebel forces in England's Civil War. Or, rather, what had been his grave, when Cromwell was buried here from 1658 to 1661. Then his corpse was exhumed, hanged, drawn, quartered, and decapitated, and the head displayed on a stake as a warning to anarchists.

• *Exit the Chapel of Henry VII. Turn left into a side chapel with the tomb (the central one of three in the chapel).*

❽ Tomb of Mary, Queen of Scots

Historians get dewy-eyed over the fate of Mary, Queen of Scots (1542-1587). The beautiful, French-educated queen was held under

house arrest for 19 years by Queen Elizabeth I, who considered her a threat to her sovereignty. Elizabeth got wind of an assassination plot, suspected Mary was behind it, and had her first cousin (once removed) beheaded. When Elizabeth—who was called the "Virgin Queen"—died heirless, Mary's son, James VI, King of Scots, also became King James I of England and Ireland. James buried his mum here (with her head sewn back on) in the Abbey's most sumptuous tomb.

• *Exit Mary's chapel. Ahead of you, again, is the tomb of the church's founder, Edward the Confessor. Continue on, until you emerge in the south transept. You're in...*

❾ Poets' Corner

England's greatest artistic contributions are in the written word.

Here the masters of arguably the world's most complex and expressive language are remembered. (Many writers are honored with plaques and monuments; relatively few are actually buried here.)

• *Start with Chaucer, buried in the wall under the blue windows, marked with a white plaque reading* Qui Fuit Anglorum...

Geoffrey Chaucer (c. 1343-1400) is often considered the father of English literature. Chaucer's *Canterbury Tales* told of earthy people speaking everyday English, not French or Latin. He was the first great writer buried in the Abbey (thanks to his job as a Westminster clerk). Later, it became a tradition to bury other writers here, and Poets' Corner was built around his tomb. The blue windows have blank panels awaiting the names of future poets.

• *The plaques on the floor before Chaucer are gravestones and memorials to other literary greats.*

Lord Byron, the great lover of women and adventure: "Though the night was made for loving, / And the day returns too soon, / Yet we'll go no more a-roving / By the light of the moon."

Dylan Thomas, alcoholic master of modernism, with a Romantic's heart: "Oh as I was young and easy in the mercy of his means, / Time held me green and dying / Though I sang in my chains like the sea."

W. H. Auden, Brit-turned-American modernist on love, politics, and religion: "He was my North, my South, my East and West / My working week and Sunday rest / My noon, my midnight, my talk, my song / I thought that love would last forever: I was wrong."

Lewis Carroll, creator of *Alice's Adventures in Wonderland* and *Through the Looking-Glass:* "'Twas brillig, and the slithy toves / Did gyre and gimble in the wabe..."

T. S. Eliot, American-turned-British author of the influential *Waste Land:* "April is the cruellest month, breeding / Lilacs out of the dead land, mixing / Memory and desire, stirring / Dull roots with spring rain."

Alfred, Lord Tennyson, conscience of the Victorian era: "'Tis better to have loved and lost / Than never to have loved at all."

Robert Browning: "Oh, to be in England / Now that April's there."

• *Farther out in the south transept, you'll find a statue of...*

William Shakespeare: Although he's not buried here, this greatest of English writers is honored by a fine statue that stands near the end of the transept, overlooking the others: "Life's but a walking shadow, a poor player that struts and frets his hour upon the stage and then is heard no more."

George Frideric Handel: High on the wall opposite Shakespeare is the German immigrant famous for composing the *Messiah* oratorio: "Hallelujah, hallelujah, hallelujah." The statue's features are modeled on Handel's death mask. Musicians can read the vocal score in his hands for "I Know That My Redeemer Liveth." His actual tomb is on the floor, next to...

Charles Dickens, whose serialized novels brought literature to the masses: "It was the best of times, it was the worst of times."

On the floor near Shakespeare, you'll also find the tombs of **Samuel Johnson** (who wrote the first English dictionary) and the great English actor **Laurence Olivier.** (Olivier disdained the "Method" style of experiencing intense emotions in order to portray them. When co-star Dustin Hoffman stayed up all night in order to appear haggard for a scene, Olivier said, "My dear boy, why don't you simply try acting?")

And finally, near the center of the transept, find the small, white floor plaque of **Thomas Parr** (marked *THO: PARR*). Check the dates of his life (1483-1635) and do the math. In his (reputed) 152 years, he served 10 sovereigns and was a contemporary of Columbus, Henry VIII, Elizabeth I, Shakespeare, and Galileo.

• *Exit the church (temporarily) at the south door, which leads to the...*

⓾ Cloisters and Abbey Museum

The buildings that adjoin the church housed the monks. (The church is known as the "abbey" because it was the headquarters of the Benedictine Order until Henry VIII kicked them out in 1540.) Cloistered courtyards gave them a place to meditate on God's creations.

The **Chapter House** is where the monks had daily meetings. It features fine architecture and stained glass, some faded but well-described medieval paintings and floor tiles, and—in the corridor—Britain's oldest door. A few steps farther down the hall is the **Pyx Chamber.** This old, thick-walled room once safeguarded the coins used to set the silver standard of the realm (a pyx is a small box that held gold and silver coins).

The small **Abbey Museum,** formerly the monks' lounge, is worth a peek for its fascinating and well-described exhibits. Look into the impressively realistic eyes of Elizabeth I, Charles II, Admiral Nelson, and a dozen others, part of a compelling series of wax-and-wood statues that, for three centuries, graced coffins during funeral processions. Also see exhibits on royal coronations, funerals, Abbey history, a close-up look at medieval stained glass, and replicas of the crown jewels used for coronation practice. The once-exquisite, now-fragmented Westminster Retable, which decorated the high altar in 1270, is the oldest surviving altarpiece in England. The image of Christ in the central panel is time-worn, but it retains the essentials: his face, the orb of power, and his blessing hand. Beyond the Abbey Museum, passageways lead to the

Little Cloister and picturesque College Garden (open Tue-Thu).

As you return to the church, look back through the cloister courtyard to the church exterior, and meditate on the **flying buttresses.** These stone bridges that push in on the church walls allowed Gothic architects to build so high.

If you need a bite or drink, or the WC, head for the abbey café.

• *Go back into the church for the last stop.*

⓫ Coronation Chair

A gold-painted oak chair waits here under a regal canopy for the next coronation. For every English coronation since 1308 (except two), it's been moved to its spot before the high altar to receive the royal buttocks. The chair's legs rest on lions, England's symbol. The space below the chair originally held a big sandstone rock from Scotland called the Stone of Scone (pronounced "skoon"), symbolizing Scotland's unity with England's monarch. But in the 1990s, Britain gave Scotland more sovereignty, its own Parliament, and the Stone, which Scotland has agreed to loan to Britain for future coronations (the rest of the time, it's on display in Edinburgh Castle).

Next to the chapel with the chair hangs a 600-year-old portrait of King Richard II. The boy king is holding the royal orb and scepter, wearing the crown, and seated upon this very chair.

Finally, take one last look down the nave. Listen to and ponder this place, filled with the remains of the people who made Britain a world power—saints, royalty, poets, musicians, scientists, soldiers, politicians. Now step back outside into a city filled with the modern-day poets, saints, and heroes who continue to make Britain great.

HOUSES OF PARLIAMENT TOUR

With an epic history, the Houses of Parliament (home to the House of Commons and the House of Lords) remains the site of fierce verbal tussles among members of the UK's Conservative, Labour, and smaller parties. "Westminster" (as Brits call the place) appears almost nightly on TV, as the impressive backdrop to the latest political news. A visit here gives both UK residents and foreign tourists alike a chance to tour a piece of living history and see the British government in action.

There are two ways to enter the Houses of Parliament: Attend a debate, or join a tour—either way, once you're through security you'll have time to explore its grand halls. The public galleries of both the House of Commons and the House of Lords are open—and free—to visitors whenever Parliament is in session (if you see a light above Big Ben's clock, it's in session). When Parliament is recessed, the only way to visit is with a reserved tour (see "Tours," next page). This self-guided tour assumes you'll watch live debates while Parliament is in session.

Orientation

Cost: Free.

Hours: Parliament is in session generally from October to July, Monday through Thursday (House of Commons—Mon 14:30-22:30, Tue-Wed 11:30-19:30, Thu 9:30-17:30; House of Lords—Mon-Tue 14:30-22:00, Wed 15:00-22:00, Thu 11:00-19:30; last entry depends on debates; exact schedule at www.parliament.uk).

When to Go: No matter when you go, expect lines—it may take a while to get through security, then another 20-60 minutes to be admitted to the House chambers. You'll have the best chance of viewing both chambers if you arrive at around 14:00. Lines are longest at the start of each day's session, but that's when the most fiery debates often occur (and it's almost impossible to enter on Wed, when the prime minister normally attends). The later in the day you enter, the less crowded (and less exciting) it is. Avoid going at 16:00, when parliamentary functions make things extra busy. Visiting after 18:00 is risky, as sessions tend to end well before their official closing time, and visitors aren't allowed in after the politicians call it a day.

Getting There: You can't miss this gigantic, riverside, Neo-Gothic temple of government—it's London's most recognized symbol. The visitors entrance is around the back side (away from the river) on Cromwell Green, facing the buttresses of Westminster Abbey. Tube: Westminster.

Information: Tel. 020/7219-4272 or 020/7219-3107. See www.parliament.uk for schedule, or visit www.parliamentlive.tv for a preview. To preview a debate from home, tune into "Prime Minister's Questions"; in the US, the 30-minute broadcast airs live Wed mornings at 7:00 (ET) on C-SPAN2, re-airing Sun at 21:00 (ET) on regular C-SPAN (www.c-span.org).

Choosing a House: If you only visit one of the bicameral legislative bodies, I'd choose the House of Lords. Though less important politically, the Lords meet in a more ornate room, and the wait time is shorter (likely less than 30 minutes). The House of Commons is where major policy is made, but the room is sparse, and wait times are longer (30-60 minutes or more).

Tours: On Saturdays and whenever Parliament is in recess (including much of Aug and Sept), the only way to enter is by taking a behind-the-scenes tour—either with an audioguide or a live guide. The advantage is that you can linger and see a few more rooms while learning about the history of Britain's political system (audioguide-£18, guided tour-£25, 1.5 hours, Sat 9:00-16:30 and most weekdays during recess—days and times vary, so confirm schedule at www.parliament.uk). Book ahead online or by calling 020/7219-4114 to guarantee a tour (ticket office open Mon-Fri 10:00-16:00, Sat 9:00-17:00, closed Sun, Portcullis House, entrance on Victoria Embankment).

Length of This Tour: Aside from the sometimes lengthy lines and security rigmarole (which can eat up an hour or more), it takes less than an hour to tour the interior and drop in—briefly—on a parliamentary session.

Photography: Allowed only in Westminster Hall and St. Stephen's Hall.

Starring: A grand building and a gaggle of chattering parliamentarians.

HOUSES OF PARLIAMENT

BACKGROUND

The Palace of Westminster has been the center of political power in England for nearly a thousand years. Around 1050, King Edward the Confessor moved here to be next to his newly constructed "minster" (church) in the "west"—Westminster Abbey. The Palace became the monarch's official residence, the meeting place of his noble advisors (or parliament), and the supreme court of the land. In the 1500s, Henry VIII moved down the block to Whitehall Palace (now destroyed, see page 127), and later monarchs chose to live at Kensington and Buckingham Palaces. But Westminster Palace remained home to the increasingly powerful Parliament.

In 1834, a horrendous fire gutted the Palace. It was rebuilt in a retro, Neo-Gothic style that recalled England's medieval Christian roots—pointed arches, stained-glass windows, spires, and saint-like statues. At the same time, Britain was also retooling its government. Democracy was on the rise, the queen became a constitutional monarch, and Parliament emerged as the nation's ruling body. The Palace of Westminster became a symbol—a kind of cathedral—of democracy.

The Tour Begins

• *Enter midway along the west side of the building (across the street from Westminster Abbey), where a tourist ramp leads to the...*

❶ Visitors Entrance

As you enter, you'll be asked if you want to visit the House of Commons or the House of Lords. I choose "Lords" (because the line is shorter), but it really doesn't matter. Once inside the building, you'll be able to see all the public spaces described in this tour as you transit to the chamber you intend to visit. If you have questions, the attendants are extremely helpful.

• *At the airport-style security, collect your visitor badge. Continue past the Jubilee Café (which has live video feeds of Parliament in session), pick up helpful brochures at the information desk, and take in the cavernous...*

❷ Westminster Hall

This vast hall—covering 16,000 square feet—survived the 1834 fire, and is one of the oldest and most important buildings in England. Begun in 1097, the hall was extensively remodeled around 1390 by Richard II, who made it the grand-

Houses of Parliament

To Whitehall &
Trafalgar Square

PARLIAMENT
SHOP

PORTCULLIS HOUSE

Westminster

BRIDGE ST.

PARL. ST.

FENCE

CHURCHILL
STATUE

*Parliament
Square*

CARRIAGE
GATES

BIG
BEN

VICTORIA EMBANKMENT

WESTMINSTER
PIER

STATUE OF
BOADICEA

STAIRS DOWN
TO RIVERSIDE

WESTMINSTER
BRIDGE

Speaker's
Green

New
Palace
Yard

BROAD SANCTUARY

FENCE

ST.
MARGARET'S

Cromwell
Green

CROMWELL
STATUE

**WESTMINSTER
ABBEY**

CHAPTER
HOUSE

BARRIER

Old
Palace
Yard

SPEAKER'S
HOUSE

THE TERRACE

*Thames
River*

**HOUSES OF
PARLIAMENT**

ABINGDON STREET

JEWEL
TOWER

VICTORIA
TOWER

❶ Visitors Entrance
❷ Westminster Hall
❸ St. Stephen's Hall
❹ Central Lobby
❺ House of Lords
❻ House of Commons
❼ Portcullis House
   Ticket Office

Victoria
Tower
Gardens

BURGHERS
OF CALAIS
STATUE

N

50 Meters

50 Yards

HOUSES OF PARLIAMENT

est space in Europe. His self-supporting oak-timber roof (1397) wowed everyone. Unlike earlier roofs that spanned the hall with long beams, this "hammer-beam" roof uses short beams that jut horizontally out from the walls. They're part of a complex system of curved braces and arches that distribute the weight of the roof outward to the walls, not downward to the floor, so there's no need for supporting pillars. The 26 carved angels also do their part to hold up the 650-ton roof.

Stroll the room to read various plaques about the hall's history. The King's Table (c. 1250) originally sat on a raised platform at the south end of the hall. Here the king presided—dispensing justice, welcoming ambassadors, hosting his coronation banquet, toasting revelers.

England's vaunted legal system was invented in this hall, as this was the major court of the land for 700 years. King Charles I was tried and sentenced to death here. Guy Fawkes was condemned for plotting to blow up the Halls of Parliament in 1605. (He's best remembered today for the sly-smiling "Guy Fawkes mask" that has become the symbol of 21st-century anarchists.)

In more recent times, the hall has hosted the lying-in-state of Winston Churchill, G-G-G-George VI, and the Queen Mother. And in 2011, Britain's bigwigs gathered here for a speech by Barack Obama.

• *Walking through the hall and up the stairs, you'll enter the busy world of today's government. You soon reach St. Stephen's Hall, where visitors wait to enter the House of Commons Chamber.*

❸ St. Stephen's Hall

This long, beautifully lit room was the original House of Commons for three centuries (from 1550 until the fire of 1834). MPs sat in church pews on either side of the hall—the ruling party on one side, the opposition on the other—a format they'd keep when they moved into the new chambers.

It was here that British history turned forever. On January 4, 1642, King Charles I marched into this room with 400 soldiers and demanded that Parliament turn over five rebels. The Speaker bluntly refused. The standoff between King and Parliament eventually snowballed into the English Civil War, the king was decapitated, and Parliament emerged triumphant.

After the fire of 1834, the hall was rebuilt. The stained glass windows—forming a tall, rectangular grid—are a textbook example of the "Perpendicular" Gothic style used by architect Charles Barry.

• *Next, you reach the...*

❹ Central Lobby

This ornate, octagonal, high-vaulted room is often called the "heart of British government," because it sits in the geographical center of the Palace, midway between the House of Commons (to the left) and the House of Lords (right). Clerks bustle about. Constituents come to this lobby to petition, or "lobby," their MPs (from which the term may derive). Video monitors list the schedule of meetings and events going on in this 1,100-room governmental hive.

This is the best place to admire the Palace's interior decoration—carved wood, chandeliers, statues, and floor tiles—designed by Barry's partner, Augustus Pugin.

• *This lobby marks the end of the public space where you can wander freely. To see the House of Lords or House of Commons you must wait in line. You must also check your belongings—bag, camera, phone, even this guidebook—so read the following section before entering. While you wait, ask the attendant for any brochures.*

❺ House of Lords

When you're called, you'll walk to the Lords Chamber by way of the long Peers' Corridor. Paintings on the corridor walls depict the antiauthoritarian spirit brewing under the reign of Charles I: You'll see Parliament rebuffing Charles' demands for the five MPs, and the freedom-seeking Pilgrims leaving England for America on the Mayflower. When you reach the House of Lords Chamber, you'll watch the proceedings from the upper-level visitors gallery. Each day opens with a 30-minute session where four questions are posed to the government, usually followed by legislation and then debate.

The House of Lords consists of around 800 members, called "Peers." They are not elected by popular vote. Some are nobles who've inherited the position; others are appointed by the Queen. These days, their role is largely advisory. They can propose, revise, and filibuster laws, but they have no real power to pass laws on their own. On any typical day, only a handful of the lords actually shows up to debate.

The Lords Chamber is church-like and impressive, with stained glass and intricately carved walls. The benches where the Lords sit are always upholstered red (the ones in the House of Commons are green). At the far end is the Queen's gilded throne. She's the only one who may sit there, and only once a year, when she gives a speech to open Parliament.

In front of the throne sits the woolsack—a cushion stuffed with wool. Here the Lord Speaker presides, with a ceremonial mace behind the backrest. To the Lord Speaker's right (our left) are the members of the ruling party (a.k.a. "government"). The first two rows in the seats closest to the woolsack are filled with bishops. To the Lord Speaker's left (our right) are the members of the opposition (the Labour Party). Unaffiliated Crossbenchers sit in between.

❻ House of Commons

The Commons Chamber may be much less grandiose than the Lords', but this is where the sausage gets made. The House of Commons is as powerful as the Lords, prime minister, and Queen combined.

This seat of power is surprisingly small—barely 3,000 square feet. The chamber was destroyed in the Blitz, and Churchill rebuilt it with the same cube-shaped floor plan. Of today's 650-plus MPs, only 450 can sit—the rest have to stand at the ends. On any given day, most MPs are in their offices, located elsewhere in the complex or in nearby, modern buildings.

As in the House of Lords, the ruling party sits on the right of the Speaker (our left), opposition on the left (our right). Television screens on the wall show the topic and who is speaking; the press box is to the left, above the government MPs. Members stand when they want to speak, waiting patiently to be called on by the Speaker.

Keep an eye out for two red lines on the floor, which cannot be crossed when debating the other side. (They're supposedly two sword-lengths apart, to prevent a literal clashing of swords.) Between the benches is the canopied Speaker's Chair, for the chairman who keeps order and chooses who can speak next. The clerks sit at a central table that holds the ceremonial mace, a symbol of the power given Parliament by the monarch. Also on the table are the two "dispatch boxes"—old wooden chests that serve as lecterns, one for each side.

The Queen is not allowed in the Commons Chamber. The last monarch to enter a Commons Chamber was Charles I, and you know what happened to him. When the prime minister visits, he speaks from one of the boxes. His ministers (or cabinet) join him on the front bench, while lesser MPs (the "backbenchers") sit behind. It's often a fiery spectacle, as the prime minister defends his policies, while the opposition grumbles and harrumphs in displeasure. It's not unheard-of for MPs to get out of line and be escorted out by the Serjeant at Arms (who calls in to his doorkeepers—think of them as Parliamentary bouncers—for the heavy lifting). One furious MP even grabbed the Serjeant's hallowed mace and threw it to the ground. His career was over.

• *And so is our tour. Heading back out of the sprawling complex, be sure to get a good look at—if you haven't already—the Houses of Parliament's best-known symbol, its giant clock tower. For a full description of what tourists call "Big Ben," see the start of the* 📖 *Westminster Walk. Big Ben is also covered on my* 🎧 *free Westminster Walk audio tour.*

NATIONAL GALLERY TOUR

The National Gallery lets you tour Europe's art without ever crossing the Channel. With so many exciting artists and styles, it's a fine overture to art if you're just starting a European trip, and a pleasant reprise if you're just finishing. The "National Gal"—with Britain's greatest collection of paintings—is always a welcome interlude from the bustle of London sightseeing.

This tour gives you a quick chronological sweep through art history: medieval holiness, Renaissance realism, Dutch detail, Baroque excess, British restraint, and the colorful French Impressionism that leads to the modern world. Cruise like an eagle with wide eyes for the big picture, seeing how each style progresses into the next. Enjoy the biggies quickly, leaving yourself with enough time to circle back and browse.

Orientation

Cost: Free, but suggested donation of £5 (consider depositing your loose change here); fee for optional special exhibits.

Hours: Daily 10:00-18:00, Fri until 21:00, last entry to special exhibits 45 minutes before closing.

Getting There: It's as central as can be, overlooking Trafalgar Square, a 15-minute walk from Big Ben and 10 minutes from Piccadilly. The closest Tube stop is Charing Cross or Leicester Square. Handy buses #9, #11, #15, and #24 (among others) pass by (see page 28).

Information: The information desk in the lobby has a £1 floor plan (similar to this book's map, but with a few masterpieces highlighted) and a schedule of upcoming events and lunchtime lectures. The National Gallery loans out many paintings, so some of the canvases mentioned in this tour may not be on display.

Special exhibitions sometimes force paintings in the permanent collection to be moved, usually temporarily. If you can't find a particular piece, ask the attendants stationed in each room. Info tel. 020/7747-2885, switchboard tel. 020/7839-3321, www.nationalgallery.org.uk.

Tours: Free one-hour **overview tours** leave from the Sainsbury Wing info desk daily at 11:30 and 14:30, plus Fri at 19:00 and Sat-Sun at 16:00. Ask the info desk about 10-minute talks on individual paintings, Mon-Fri at 16:00.

The **audioguides** are excellent. Choose from the one-hour highlights tour, several theme tours, or a tour option that lets you dial up info on any painting in the museum (£4).

The museum is surprisingly family-friendly (especially on Sunday mornings). Check their website for a variety of **kids' activities** or look for the "Family Fun" brochure at the information desk.

Length of This Tour: Allow 1.5 hours. If you have less time, the can't-miss pieces are Van Eyck's *Arnolfini Portrait*, Leonardo's *Virgin and Child with St. Anne and St. John the Baptist*, Rembrandt's *Belshazzar's Feast* and self-portraits, Velázquez's *Rokeby Venus*, Turner's *Fighting Téméraire*, the Impressionists, and Van Gogh's *Sunflowers*.

Cloakroom: Cloakrooms are at each entrance (£1 for bags). You can take a small bag into the museum.

Photography: Photos are allowed without flash.

Cuisine Art: There are three eateries in the Gallery. The National Dining Rooms, located on the first floor of the Sainsbury Wing, has a classy, table-service restaurant menu (£15-18 main dishes), cheaper bakery section (£8-9 meals), and offers afternoon tea (see page 414). The National Café, located near the Getty Entrance, has a table-service restaurant (£14-18 entrées) and an adjoining sandwich/soup/salad/pastry café (£5-7). Seek out the Espresso Bar, near the Portico and Getty entrances, for sandwiches, pastries, and soft couches. Outside the Gallery, several options are on or near Trafalgar Square (see page 403).

Starring: You name it—Leonardo, Raphael, Titian, Rembrandt, Monet, and Van Gogh.

The Tour Begins

The National Gallery has three entrances facing Trafalgar Square:

The main Portico Entrance (under the dome, in the center), the low-key Getty Entrance (to the right as you face the building), and the Sainsbury Entrance (in the smaller building to the left of the main entrance).

• *Enter through the Sainsbury Entrance. Pick up the handy map (£1) and climb the stairs. At the top, turn left, then left again through* Room 51, *and enter Room 52.*

MEDIEVAL AND EARLY RENAISSANCE (1260-1440)

In Rooms 52 and 53, shiny gold paintings of saints, angels, Madonnas, and crucifixions float in an ethereal gold never-never land. One thing is very clear: Medieval heaven was different from medieval earth. The holy wore gold plates on their heads. Faces were serene and generic. People posed stiffly, facing either directly out or to the side, never in between. Saints are recognized by the symbols they carry (a key, a sword, a book), rather than by their human features.

Art in the Middle Ages was religious, dominated by the Church. The illiterate faithful could meditate on an altarpiece and visualize heaven. It's as though they couldn't imagine saints and angels inhabiting the dreary world of rocks, trees, and sky they lived in.

• *One of the finest medieval altarpieces is in a glass case in Room 53.*

❶ Anonymous—*The Wilton Diptych* (c. 1395-1399)

Two saint/kings and St. John the Baptist present King Richard II (left panel) to the Virgin Mary and her rosy-cheeked baby (right

panel), who are surrounded by angels with flame-like wings. Despite the gold-leaf background, a glimmer of human realism peeks through. The kings have distinct, down-to-earth faces. And the outside shows not a saint, not a god, but a real-life deer lying down in the grass of this earth.

But the anonymous artist is

MEDIEVAL & EARLY RENAISSANCE
- ❶ ANONYMOUS – The Wilton Diptych
- ❷ UCCELLO – Battle of San Romano
- ❸ VAN EYCK – The Arnolfini Portrait

EARLY ITALIAN RENAISSANCE
- ❹ LEONARDO – The Virgin of the Rocks
- ❺ BOTTICELLI – Venus and Mars
- ❻ CRIVELLI – The Annunciation, with Saint Emidius
- ❼ LEONARDO – Virgin and Child with St. Anne and St. John the Baptist

HIGH RENAISSANCE
- ❽ MICHELANGELO – The Entombment
- ❾ RAPHAEL – Pope Julius II
- ❿ BRONZINO – An Allegory with Venus and Cupid
- ⓫ TINTORETTO – The Origin of the Milky Way

NORTHERN PROTESTANT ART
- ⓬ VERMEER – A Young Woman Standing at a Virginal
- ⓭ VAN HOOGSTRATEN – A Peepshow with Views of the Interior of a Dutch House
- ⓮ REMBRANDT – Belshazzar's Feast
- ⓯ REMBRANDT – Self-Portrait at the Age of 63

BAROQUE & FRENCH ROCOCO
- ⓰ RUBENS – The Judgment of Paris
- ⓱ VELÁZQUEZ – The Rokeby Venus
- ⓲ VAN DYCK – Equestrian Portrait of Charles I
- ⓳ CARAVAGGIO –The Supper at Emmaus
- ⓴ BOUCHER – Pan and Syrinx

BRITISH ROMANTIC ART
- ㉑ CONSTABLE – The Hay Wain
- ㉒ TURNER – The Fighting Téméraire
- ㉓ DELAROCHE – The Execution of Lady Jane Grey

To Leicester Square (5 min. walk)

SAINSBURY WING

ENTRANCE ON LEVEL 0

SELF-GUIDED TOUR STARTS ON LEVEL 2

TOUR BEGINS

SAINSBURY ENTRANCE

NATIONAL GALLERY

struggling with reality. John the Baptist is holding a "lamb of God" that looks more like a Chihuahua. Nice try. Mary's exquisite fingers hold an anatomically impossible little foot. The figures are flat, scrawny, and sinless, with cartoon features—far from flesh-and-blood human beings. Still, Richard II himself (king of England from 1377 to 1399) knelt before this portable altarpiece to inspire his personal devotions to the Virgin.

• *Continuing into Room 54, you'll leave this gold-leaf peace and find...*

National Gallery

ORANGE ST.
ENTRANCE

Not to Scale

⊠ Elevator/Lift

30 Meters
30 Yards

21   22
20   18   23 **15**
19   **14** 24   25   **12**
26   27   28   **13**
17   15   **16**   31 **18**
16   29   **17**   30   32   33 **20**
WOHL
ROOM   14   SUNLEY   37   **19**
9   ROOM
LINK   13   CENTRAL 39   38   36   35   **22**
10   11   12   HALL   34   **21**
5   SHOP   40
10   6   4   2   **30**   44   43 **25**   41
9
8   8   45   **29**   **28**   **26 27**   42   **23**
7 **11**   46   **24**

PORTICO
ENTRANCE

GETTY
ENTRANCE
(LEVEL 0)

STAIRS DOWN
TO NAT'L
CAFÉ & WC

Trafalgar Square   NELSON'S
COLUMN

To Charing Cross ⊖
(2 min. walk) →

IMPRESSIONISM & BEYOND

24 MONET – Gare St. Lazare
25 MONET – The Water-Lily Pond
26 MANET – Corner of a
     Café-Concert
27 RENOIR – The Skiff

28 SEURAT – Bathers at
     Asnières
29 VAN GOGH – Sunflowers
30 CÉZANNE – Bathers

NATIONAL GALLERY

❷ Uccello—*Battle of San Romano* (c. 1438-1440)

This colorful battle scene shows the victory of Florence over Siena in 1432—and the battle for literal realism on the canvas. It's an early Renaissance attempt at a realistic, nonreligious, three-dimensional scene.

Uccello challenges his ability by posing the horses and soldiers at every conceivable angle. The background of farmyards, receding hedges, and tiny soldiers creates an illusion of distance. The artist actually constructs a grid of fallen lances in the foreground, then places the horses and warriors within it. Still, Uccello hasn't quite worked out the bugs—the figures in the distance are far too big, and the fallen soldier on the left isn't much larger than the fallen shield on the right.

• *In Room 56, you'll find...*

❸ Van Eyck—*The Arnolfini Portrait* (1434)

Called by some "The Shotgun Wedding," this painting was once thought to depict a wedding ceremony forced by the lady's swelling belly. Today it's understood as a portrait of a solemn, well-dressed, well-heeled couple, the Arnolfinis of Bruges, Belgium. It is a masterpiece of down-to-earth details.

Van Eyck has built a medieval dollhouse, inviting us to linger over the furnishings. Feel the texture of the fabrics, count the ter-

rier's hairs, trace the shadows generated by the window. Each object is painted at an ideal angle, with the details you'd see if you were standing directly in front of it. So the strings of beads hanging on the back wall are as crystal clear as the bracelets on the woman.

To top it off, look into the round mirror on the far wall—the whole scene is reflected backward in miniature, showing the loving couple and a pair of mysterious visitors. Is one of them Van Eyck himself at his easel? Or has the art-

ist painted you, the home viewer, into the scene?

The surface detail is extraordinary, but the painting lacks true Renaissance depth. The tiny room looks unnaturally narrow, cramped, and claustrophobic.

In medieval times (this was painted only a generation after *The Wilton Diptych*), everyone could read the hidden meaning of certain symbols—the chandelier with its one lit candle (love), the fruit on the windowsill (fertility), the dangling whisk broom (the woman's domestic responsibilities), and the terrier (Fido—fidelity).

By the way, the woman likely is not pregnant. The fashion of the day was to gather up the folds of one's extremely full-skirted dress. At least, that's what they told her parents.

• *Return to Room 55, turn left into Room 57, and enter the...*

EARLY ITALIAN RENAISSANCE (1400-1500)

The Renaissance—or "rebirth" of the culture of ancient Greece and Rome—was a cultural boom that changed people's thinking about every aspect of life. In politics, it meant democracy. In religion, it meant a move away from Church dominance and toward the assertion of man (humanism) and a more personal faith. Science and secular learning were revived after centuries of superstition and ignorance. In architecture, it was a return to the balanced columns and domes of Greece and Rome.

In painting, the Renaissance meant realism. Artists rediscovered the beauty of nature and the human body. With pictures of beautiful people in harmonious, 3-D surroundings, they expressed the optimism and confidence of this new age.

❹ Leonardo—*The Virgin of the Rocks* (c. 1491-1508)

In this painting, Mary, the mother of Jesus, plays with her son and little Johnny the Baptist (with cross, at left) while an androgynous angel looks on. Leonardo brings this holy scene right down to earth by setting it among rocks, stalactites, water, and flowering plants. But looking closer, we see that Leonardo has deliberately posed his people into a pyramid shape, with Mary's head at the peak, creating an oasis of maternal stability and serenity amid the hard rock of the earth. Leonardo, who was born illegitimate, may have sought in his art the young mother he never knew. Freud thought so.

• *In Room 58 is...*

❺ Botticelli—*Venus and Mars* (c. 1485)

Mars takes a break from war, succumbing to the delights of love (Venus), while impish satyrs play innocently with the discarded tools of death. In the early spring of the Renaissance, there was an optimistic mood in the air—the feeling that enlightened Man could solve all problems, narrowing the gap between mortals and the Greek gods. Artists felt free to use the pagan Greek gods as symbols of human traits, virtues, and vices. Venus has sapped man's medieval stiffness; the Renaissance has arrived.

• *Continue to Room 59.*

❻ Crivelli—*The Annunciation, with Saint Emidius* (1486)

Mary, in green, is visited by the dove of the Holy Spirit, who beams down from the distant heavens in a shaft of light.

Like Van Eyck's wedding, this is a brilliant collection of realistic details. Notice the hanging rug, the peacock, the architectural minutiae that lead you way, way back, then bam!—you have a giant pickle in your face.

It combines meticulous detail with Italian spaciousness. The floor tiles and building bricks recede into the distance. We're sucked right in, accelerating through the alleyway, under the arch, and off into space. The Holy Spirit spans the entire distance, connecting heavenly background with earthly foreground. Crivelli creates an Escheresque labyrinth of rooms and walkways that we want to walk through, around, and into—or is that just a male thing?

Renaissance Italians were interested in—even obsessed with—portraying 3-D space. Perhaps they focused their spiritual passion away from heaven and toward the physical world. With such restless energy, they needed lots of elbow room. Space, the final frontier.

• *Continue into Room 60, then turn right into Room 51, where we first entered. Tucked in an adjoining room labeled* The Leonardo Cartoon *is...*

❼ Leonardo—*Virgin and Child with St. Anne and St. John the Baptist* (c. 1499-1500)

At first glance, this chalk cartoon (a full-size preparatory drawing

for a painting) looks like a simple snapshot of two loving moms and two playful kids. The two children play—oblivious to the violent deaths they'll both suffer—beneath their mothers' Mona Lisa smiles.

But follow the eyes: Shadowy-eyed Anne turns toward Mary, who looks tenderly down to Jesus, who blesses John, who gazes back dreamily. As your eyes follow theirs, you're led back to the literal and psychological center of the composition—Jesus—the Alpha and Omega. Without resorting to heavy-handed medieval symbolism, Leonardo drives home a theological concept in a natural, human way. Leonardo the perfectionist rarely finished paintings. This sketch—pieced together from two separate papers (see the line down the middle)—gives us an inside peek at his genius.

• *From Room 51, cross to the main building (the West Wing) and enter the large Room 9, filled with big, colorful canvases. Turn right and exit at the far end into Room 8.*

HIGH RENAISSANCE (1500-1600)

The Renaissance was born in Florence, but it flowered in Venice and Rome, before spreading north to the rest of Europe. The "Big Three" of the High Renaissance—Leonardo (whom we saw earlier), Michelangelo, and Raphael—were all Florence-trained. Like Renaissance architects (which they also were), they carefully composed their figures on canvas, "building" them into geometrical patterns that reflected the balance and order they saw in nature.

In Venice—a city grown wealthy by trading with the luxurious and exotic East—artists forged a happy-go-lucky art style that shows a taste for the finer things in life. Madonnas and saints were replaced by smooth-skinned, sexy, golden centerfolds. Venetian artists revived the classical world in all its pagan glory, creating beautiful scenes of sensuous Nature.

❽ Michelangelo—*The Entombment* (c. 1500-1501)

Michelangelo, the greatest sculptor ever, proves it here in this "painted sculpture" of the crucified Jesus being carried to the tomb.

Florentine artists like Michelangelo were inspired by ancient statues of balanced, anatomically perfect, nude Greek gods. Like a chiseled Greek god, this musclehead in red ripples beneath his clothes. Christ's naked body, shocking to the medieval Church, was completely acceptable in the Renaissance world, where classical nudes were admired as an expression of the divine.

Renaissance balance and symmetry reign. Christ is the center of the composition, flanked by two people leaning equally, who support his body with strips of cloth. They, in turn, are flanked by two others.

The painting is not damaged, but it is unfinished. Michelangelo, 25 years old at the time, moved on to other projects before he got around to adding crucial details, even leaving a blank space in the lower right where Mary would have been.

Regardless of the lack of detail, Michelangelo lets the bodies do the talking. The two supporters strain to hold up Christ's body, and in their tension we, too, feel the great weight and tragedy of their dead god. Michelangelo expresses the divine through the human form.

❾ Raphael—*Pope Julius II* (1511)

The new worldliness of the Renaissance even reached the Church. Pope Julius II, who was more a swaggering conquistador than a

pious pope, set out to rebuild Rome in Renaissance style, hiring Michelangelo to paint the ceiling of the Vatican's Sistine Chapel.

Raphael gives a behind-the-scenes look at this complex leader. On the one hand, the pope is an imposing pyramid of power, with a velvet shawl, silk shirt, and fancy rings boasting of wealth and success. But at the same time, he's a bent and broken man, his throne backed into a corner, with an expression that seems to say, "Is this all there is?"

• *And now for something completely different. In Room 8, find...*

❿ Bronzino—*An Allegory with Venus and Cupid* (c.1545)

You may not recognize this painting, but you might recognize a foot. Look closely at the figure of boy Cupid, on the left. His right foot became famous on TV in the 1970s and 1980s in the comedy show *Monty Python's Flying Circus*. As the show opened and circus music played, the credits would come to an end on the last note, with Cupid's giant foot coming down from above to squash the scene with a flatulent *ffft!* The Pythons used collage-style graphics to end sketches abruptly (rather than fumble for a punch line), thus making a seamless (if surreal) transition to the next bit.

• *From Room 8, pass through Room 7 and enter Room 6 for...*

⓫ Tintoretto—*The Origin of the Milky Way* (c. 1575)

In this scene from a classical myth, the god Jupiter places his illegitimate son, baby Hercules, at his wife's breast. Juno says, "Wait a

Painting: From Tempera to Tubes

The technology of painting has evolved over the centuries.

1400s Artists used tempera (pigments dissolved in egg yolk) on wood.

1500s Still painting on wood, artists mainly used oil (pigments dissolved in vegetable oil, such as linseed, walnut, or poppy).

1600s Artists applied oil paints to canvases stretched across wooden frames.

1850 Paints in convenient, collapsible tubes are invented, making open-air painting feasible.

The Frames: Although some frames are original, having been chosen by the artist, most are selected by museum curators. Some are old frames from other paintings, others are Victorian-era reproductions in wood, and still others are recent reproductions made of a composite substance to look like gilded wood.

minute. That's not my baby!" Her milk spurts upward, becoming the Milky Way.

Tintoretto places us right up in the clouds, among the gods, who swirl around at every angle. Jupiter appears to be flying almost right at us. An X composition unites it all—Juno slants one way while Jupiter tilts the other.

• *Backtrack into the big Room 9. Exit this room at the far end and turn right, entering the long Room 29 (with forest-green wallpaper). Midway through Room 29, turn left and find Room 25.*

NORTHERN PROTESTANT ART (1600-1700)

We switch from CinemaScope to a tiny TV—smaller canvases, subdued colors, everyday scenes, and not even a bare shoulder.

Money shapes art. While Italy had wealthy aristocrats and the powerful Catholic Church to purchase art, the North's patrons were middle-class, hardworking, Protestant merchants. They wanted simple, cheap, no-nonsense pictures to decorate their homes and offices. Greek gods and Virgin Marys were out, hometown folks and hometown places were in—portraits, landscapes, still lifes, and slice-of-life scenes. Painted with great attention to detail, this is art meant not to wow or preach at you, but to be enjoyed and lingered over. Sightsee.

⑫ Vermeer—*A Young Woman Standing at a Virginal* (c. 1670)

Inside a simple but wealthy Dutch home, a prim virgin plays an early piano called a "virginal." We've surprised her, and she pauses to look up at us.

By framing off such a small world to look at—from the blue chair in the foreground to the wall in back—Vermeer forces us to appreciate the tiniest details, the beauty of everyday things. We can meditate on the tiles lining the floor, the subtle shades of the white wall, and the pale, diffused light that seeps in from the window. Amid straight lines and rectangles, the woman's billowing dress adds a soft touch. The painting of a nude cupid on the back wall only strengthens this virgin's purity.

• *Also in Room 25, you'll find...*

⑬ Van Hoogstraten—*A Peepshow with Views of the Interior of a Dutch House* (c. 1655-1660)

Look through the open end of this ingenious device to make the painting of a house interior come to three-dimensional life. Compare the twisted curves of the painting with the illusion it creates and appreciate the painstaking work of the dedicated artist. Painted on the top of the box is another anamorphic projection.

• *Enter the adjoining Room 24.*

⑭ Rembrandt—*Belshazzar's Feast* (c. 1635)

Belshazzar, the wicked king of Babylon, has been feasting with God's sacred dinnerware when the meal is interrupted. The king turns to see the hand of God, burning an ominous message into the wall that Belshazzar's number is up. As he turns, he knocks over a goblet of wine. We see the jewels and riches of his decadent life.

Rembrandt captures the scene at the most ironic moment. Belshazzar is about to be ruined. We know it, his guests know it, and, judging by the look on his face, he's coming to the same conclusion.

Rembrandt's flair for the dramatic is accentuated by the strong contrast between light and dark. Most of his canvases are a rich, dark brown, with a few crucial details highlighted by a bright light.

Before leaving this room, notice the self-portrait of Rembrandt at age 34, just to the left. Remember this face.

• *Nearby (either in Room 24 or in the adjoining Room 23), you'll find...*

⓯ Rembrandt—*Self-Portrait at the Age of 63* (1669)

Rembrandt throws the light of truth on...himself. He made this craggy self-portrait in the year he would die, at age 63. Contrast it with one done three decades earlier (which we just saw in the previous room). Rembrandt, the greatest Dutch painter, started out as the successful, wealthy young genius of the art world. But he refused to crank out commercial works. Rembrandt painted things that he believed in but no one would invest in—family members, down-to-earth Bible scenes, and self-portraits like these.

Here, Rembrandt surveys the wreckage of his independent life. He was bankrupt, his mistress had just died, and he had also buried several of his children. We see a disillusioned, well-worn, but proud old genius.

• *Backtrack to the long, forest-green Room 29.*

BAROQUE (1600-1700)

This room holds big, colorful, emotional works by Peter Paul Rubens and others from Catholic Flanders (Belgium). While artists in Protestant and democratic Europe painted simple scenes, those in Catholic and aristocratic countries turned to the style called Baroque. Baroque art took what was flashy in Venetian art and made it flashier, what was gaudy and made it gaudier, what was dramatic and made it shocking.

⓰ Rubens—*The Judgment of Paris* (c. 1636-1639)

Rubens painted anything that would raise your pulse—battles, miracles, hunts, and, especially, fleshy women with dimples on all four cheeks. For instance, *The Judgment of Paris* (one of two versions by Rubens in this museum) is little more than an excuse for a study of the female nude, showing front, back, and profile all on one canvas.

• *Exit Room 29 at the far end. In Room 30 (with red wallpaper), on the left-hand wall, you'll find...*

⓱ Velázquez—*The Rokeby Venus* (c. 1647-1651)

Like a Venetian centerfold, Venus lounges diagonally across the canvas, admiring herself, with flaring red, white, and gray fabrics to highlight her rosy white skin and inflame our passion. Horny

NATIONAL GALLERY

Spanish kings loved Titianesque nudes despite Spain's strict Inquisition, the Church tribunal that rooted out bad behavior. This work by the king's personal court painter is a rare Spanish nude from that ultra-Catholic country. About the sole concession to Spanish modesty is the false reflection in the mirror—if it really showed what the angle should show, Velázquez would have needed two mirrors...and a new job.

In 1914, the painting was slashed seven times by a knife-wielding vandal. She claimed she'd attacked "the most beautiful woman in mythological history" to protest the arrest of "the most beautiful character in modern history"—a fellow suffragette.

• *From Room 30, turn left into the big, red Room 31, where you'll see a large canvas.*

⓲ Van Dyck—*Equestrian Portrait of Charles I* (c. 1637-1638)

King Charles sits on a huge horse, accentuating his power. The horse's small head makes sure that little Charles isn't dwarfed.

Charles was a soft-on-Catholics king in a hard-core Protestant country until England's Civil War (1648), when his genteel head was separated from his refined body by Cromwell and company.

Kings and bishops used the grandiose Baroque style to impress the masses with their power. Van Dyck's portrait style set the tone for all the stuffy, boring portraits of British aristocrats who wished to be portrayed as sophisticated gentlemen—whether they were or not.

• *Return to Room 30 and turn left, exiting at the far end, and entering Room 32. On the right wall, find...*

⓳ Caravaggio—*The Supper at Emmaus* (1601)

After Jesus was crucified, he rose from the dead and appeared without warning to some of his followers. Jesus just wants a quiet meal, but the man in green, suddenly realizing who he's eating with, is about to jump out of his chair in shock. To the right, a man spreads his hands in amazement, bridging the distance between Christ and us by sticking his hand in our faces.

The Baroque took reality and exaggerated it. Most artists amplified prettiness, but Caravaggio exaggerated grittiness, using real, ugly, unhaloed people in Bible scenes. Caravaggio's paintings look like how a wet dog smells. Reality.

We've come a long way since the first medieval altarpieces that wrapped holy people in gold foil. From the torn shirts to the five o'clock shadows, from the blemished apples to the uneven part in Jesus' hair, we are witnessing a very human miracle.

• *Leave Room 32 at the far end, and enter Room 33.*

FRENCH ROCOCO (1700-1800)

As Europe's political and economic center shifted from Italy to France, Louis XIV's court at Versailles became its cultural hub. Every aristocrat spoke French, dressed French, and bought French paintings. The Rococo art of Louis' successors was as frilly, sensual, and suggestive as the decadent French court. We see their rosy-cheeked portraits and their fantasies: lords and ladies at play in classical gardens, where mortals and gods cavort together.

• *One of the finest examples is the tiny...*

⑳ Boucher—*Pan and Syrinx* (1759)

Curious Pan seeks a threesome, but to elude him, Syrinx eventually changes into reeds, leaving him all wet.

Rococo art is like a Rubens that got shrunk in the wash—smaller, lighter pastel colors, frillier, and more delicate than the Baroque style. Same dimples, though.

• *Enter Room 34. The most eye-catching painting is of **Whistlejacket**, a late 18th-century prime minister's famous racehorse, captured on a blank background by George Stubbs. Mentally hop on and prance around Room 34, taking in the English country-garden ambience.*

BRITISH ROMANTIC ART (1800-1850)
㉑ Constable—*The Hay Wain* (1821)

The reserved British were more comfortable cavorting with nature than with the lofty gods. Come-as-you-are poets like Wordsworth found the same ecstasy just in being outside.

John Constable set up his easel out-of-doors, making quick sketches to capture the simple majesty of billowing clouds, spreading trees, and everyday rural life. Even British portraits (by Thomas Gainsborough and others) placed refined lords and ladies amid idealized greenery.

This simple style—believe it or not—was considered shocking in its day. The rough, thick, earth-toned paint and crude country settings scandalized art lovers used to the highfalutin, prettified sheen of Baroque and Rococo.

㉒ Turner—*The Fighting Téméraire* (1839)

Constable's landscape was about to be paved over by the Industrial Revolution. Soon, machines began to replace humans, factories belched smoke over Constable's hay cart, and cloud-gazers had to punch the clock. Romantics tried to resist it, lauding the forces of nature and natural human emotions in the face of technological "progress." But alas, here a modern steamboat symbolically drags a famous but obsolete sailing battleship off into the sunset to be destroyed.

Turner's messy, colorful style gives us our first glimpse into the modern art world—he influenced the Impressionists. Turner takes an ordinary scene (like Constable), captures the play of light with messy paints (like Impressionists), and charges it with mystery (like, wow).

• *To view more Constables, Stubbs horses, an enormous collection of Turners, and other British art, visit London's Tate Britain (*📖 *see the Tate Britain Tour). For now, continue ahead to Room 41.*

㉓ Delaroche—*The Execution of Lady Jane Grey* (1833)

It's 1554. The teenage queen's nine-day reign has reached its curfew. This innocent girl, manipulated into power politics by cunning advisors, is now sent to the execution site in the Tower of London. As her friends swoon with grief, she's blindfolded and forced to kneel at the block. Legend has it that the confused, humiliated girl was left kneeling on the scaffold. She crawled around, groping for the chopping block, crying out, "Where is it? What am I supposed to do?" The executioner in scarlet looks on with as much compassion as he can muster.

Britain's distinct contribution to art history is this Pre-Raphaelite style, showing medieval scenes in luminous realism with a mood of understated tragedy.

• *Exit Room 41 and enter Room 43. The Impressionist paintings are scattered throughout Rooms 43-46.*

NATIONAL GALLERY

IMPRESSIONISM AND BEYOND (1850-1910)

For 500 years, a great artist was someone who could paint the real world with perfect accuracy. Then along came the camera, and, click, the artist was replaced by a machine. But unemployed artists refused to go the way of *The Fighting Téméraire*.

They couldn't match the camera for painstaking detail, but they could match it—even beat it—in capturing color, the fleeting moment, the candid pose, the play of light and shadow, the quick impression. A new breed of artists burst out of the stuffy confines of the studio. They donned scarves and berets and set up their canvases in farmers' fields or carried their notebooks into crowded cafés, dashing off quick sketches in order to catch a momentary... impression.

• *Start with the misty Monet train station.*

㉔ Monet—*Gare St. Lazare* (1877)
Claude Monet, the father of Impressionism, was more interested in the play of light off his subject than the subject itself. He uses smudges of white and gray paint to capture how sun filters through the glass roof of the train station and is refiltered through the clouds of steam.

㉕ Monet—*The Water-Lily Pond* (1899)

In his Giverny home, near Paris, Monet planned an artificial garden, rechanneled a stream, built a bridge, and planted water lilies. Various paintings in the Gallery collection show scenes from Monet's garden— a living work of art, an oasis of order and calm in a hectic world.

㉖ Manet—*Corner of a Café-Concert* (1878-1880)
Imagine just how mundane (and therefore shocking) Manet's quick

"impression" of this café must have been to a public that was raised on Greek gods, luscious nudes, and glowing Madonnas.

㉗ Renoir—*The Skiff* (1875)
It's a nice scene of boats on sun-dappled water. Now move in close. The "scene" breaks up into almost random patches of bright colors. The "blue" water is actually separate brushstrokes of blue, green, pink, purple, gray, and white. The rower's hat is a blob of green, white, and

blue. Up close, it looks like a mess, but when you back up to a proper distance, *voilà!* It shimmers. This kind of rough, coarse brushwork (where you can actually see the brushstrokes) is one of the telltale signs of Impressionism. Renoir was not trying to paint the water itself, but the reflection of sky, shore, and boats off its surface.

• *In Room 44, you'll find...*

㉘ Seurat—*Bathers at Asnières* (1884)

Viewed from about 15 feet away, this is a bright, sunny scene of people lounging on a riverbank. Up close it's a mess of dots, show-

ing the Impressionist color technique taken to its logical extreme. The "green" grass is a shag rug of green, yellow, red, brown, purple, and white brushstrokes. The boy's "red" cap is a collage of red, yellow, and blue.

Seurat has "built" the scene dot by dot, like a newspaper photo, using small points of different, bright colors. Only at a distance do the individual brushstrokes blend. Impressionism is all about color. Even people's shadows are not dingy black, but warm blues, greens, and purples.

• *In Room 45, you'll see...*

㉙ Van Gogh—*Sunflowers* (1888)

In military terms, Van Gogh was the point man of his culture. He went ahead of his cohorts, explored the unknown, and caught

a bullet young. He added emotion to Impressionism, infusing his love of life even into inanimate objects. These sunflowers, painted with characteristic swirling brushstrokes, shimmer and writhe in either agony or ecstasy —depending on your own mood.

Van Gogh painted these during his stay in southern France, a time of frenzied creativity, when he hovered between despair and delight, bliss and madness. A year later, he shot himself.

In his day, Van Gogh was a penniless nobody, selling only one painting in his whole career. In 1987, a different *Sunflowers* painting (he did a half-dozen versions) sold for $40 million (a salary of about $2,500 a day for 45 years), and could probably fetch five times that today.

NATIONAL GALLERY

③⓪ Cézanne—*Bathers* (c. 1894-1905)

We've traveled from medieval spirituality to Renaissance realism to Baroque elegance and Impressionist colors. Before you spill out into the 21st-century hubbub of London, relax for a second with this gaggle of bathing nudes. These bathers are arranged in strict triangles à la Leonardo—the five nudes on the left form one triangle, the seated nude on the right forms another, and even the background trees and clouds are triangular patterns of paint.

Cézanne uses the Impressionist technique of building a figure with dabs of paint (though his "dabs" are often larger-sized "cube"

shapes) to make solid, 3-D geometrical figures in the style of the Renaissance. In the process, his cube shapes helped inspire a radical new style—Cubism—bringing art into the 20th century.

• *Exiting Room 45, you find yourself in the stairwell of the Gallery's main entrance (under the dome) on Trafalgar Square. If you want to return to the Sainsbury Entrance, cross the stairwell and pass through several rooms (eventually you'll see Michelangelo, Raphael, etc.). When you reach Room 9, turn left to reach the Sainsbury Wing.*

After perusing 700 years of art—from gold-backed Madonnas to Cubistic bathers—you've earned a well-deserved break.

NATIONAL PORTRAIT GALLERY TOUR

Rock groupies, book lovers, movie fans, gossipmongers, and even historians all can find at least one favorite celebrity here. From Elizabeth I to Elizabeth II, Byron to Bowie, Keats to Kate, the National Portrait Gallery puts a face on 500 years, making "history" the simple story of flesh-and-blood people. Consider that, for the most part, these portraits were painted in the presence of their subjects—providing us with a tangible link to the real person in the painting. The Gallery is a great rainy-day museum for serious students, or a quick (and free) peek at the eccentric inhabitants of the British Isles.

Orientation

Cost: Free, but suggested donation of £5; fee for optional special exhibits.

Hours: Daily 10:00-18:00, Thu-Fri until 21:00—often with music and drinks offered in the evening, first and second floors open Mon at 11:00, last entry to special exhibits one hour before closing.

Getting There: It's at St. Martin's Place, 100 yards off Trafalgar Square (around the corner from the National Gallery and opposite the Church of St. Martin-in-the-Fields). The closest Tube stops are Charing Cross and Leicester Square.

Information: A floor plan costs £1. The first-floor mezzanine level (just up the stairs from the main lobby) houses a new bookshop and computer kiosks; construction may still be underway during your visit. Tel. 020/7306-0055, recorded info tel. 020/7312-2463, www.npg.org.uk.

Tours: The well-done £3 audioguide lets you choose from several theme tours, or you can dial up any of 300 individual works.

Look for "Portrait Explorer" computers that give info on virtually any portrait or artist in the extensive collection.

Length of This Tour: Allow 1.5 hours. If you're in a rush, focus on your favorite Brits through history.

Services: WCs are in the basement and on the third floor. Lockers (£1) and coatcheck (£2 donation) are both in the basement.

Photography: Photos are allowed without flash.

Cuisine Art: The elegant Portrait Restaurant on the top floor is pricey but offers afternoon tea, and has a fine view over the rooftops of Westminster (£12-15 lunches, £15-20 dinner entrées, reservations wise, tel. 020/7312-2490); you can also just enjoy a drink at the bar with the same view. The Portrait Café in the basement is cheaper and offers sandwiches, salads, and pastries. For more eateries near Trafalgar Square, see page 403.

Starring: Royalty (Henry VIII, Elizabeth I, Victoria), writers (Shakespeare, the Brontës), scientists (Newton, Darwin), politicians (Churchill), and musicians (Handel, McCartney).

OVERVIEW

The Gallery covers 500 years of history from top to bottom—literally. Start on the second floor and work chronologically down to modern times on the ground floor. Historians should linger at the upper floor; celebrity hunters will lose elevation quickly and head to the contemporary section. There are many, many famous people from all walks of life, so use this chapter as an overview, then follow your interests, either with an audioguide or by reading the museum's informative labels.

The Tour Begins

• *From the lobby (which is up on the first floor), ride the long escalator up to the second floor and start in Room 1, marked* The Tudors.

Second Floor

1500s—DEBUT

The small, isolated island of Britain (pop. four million) enters the world stage. The Tudor kings—having already settled family feuds (the Wars of the Roses), balanced religious factions, and built England's navy—bring wealth from abroad.

• *Find the large black-and-white sketch (cartoon) of Henry VIII with his hands on his hips.*

National Portrait Gallery—
Second Floor

To Room 20

ORANGE STREET ENTRANCE (BELOW)

19 18 16 14 ⑬ ⑫ 13 ⑪ 12 11
⑮ ⑭ 15 8 ⑧ 9 ⑨ 10 ⑩
17 7 6 ⑤ 5 ⑤ ④ ③ 4
⑦ ⑥
REST.
STAIRS TO FIRST FLOOR
TOUR BEGINS
① 1 2 ② 3 **ELEV.**

Not to Scale

ST. MARTIN'S PLACE ENTRANCE (BELOW)

- ① Henry VIII & Wives
- ② Elizabeth I (3 Versions)
- ③ William Shakespeare
- ④ James I (England) & VI (Scotland)
- ⑤ Charles I
- ⑥ Oliver Cromwell
- ⑦ Charles II
- ⑧ Isaac Newton & John Locke
- ⑨ Christopher Wren
- ⑩ George Frideric Handel
- ⑪ James Watt
- ⑫ George III
- ⑬ George Washington
- ⑭ Admiral Horatio Nelson & Emma, Lady Hamilton
- ⑮ The Romantics

① Henry VIII (1491-1547), The Whitehall Mural Cartoon

Young, athletic, intense, and charismatic, with jeweled hands, gold dagger, and bulging codpiece (the very image of kingly power),

Henry VIII carried England on his broad shoulders from political isolation to international power.

In middle age, he divorced his older, dull-eyed, post-childbearing queen, Catherine of Aragon (see her portrait on the nearby wall), for the younger, shrewd, sparkling-eyed Anne Boleyn (near Catherine; see photo, next page), in search of love, sex, and a male heir. Nine months later, the future Elizabeth I was born, and the pope excommunicated adulterous Henry. Defiant, Henry started the (Protestant) Church of England, sparking a century-plus of religious strife between the country's Protestants and Catholics.

By the time Henry died—400

NATIONAL PORTRAIT GALLERY

National Portrait Gallery Tour 171

pounds of stinking, pus-ridden paranoia—he had wed six wives (see the
sixth, sweet young **Catherine Parr,** opposite her predecessors), executed several
of them (including Anne Boleyn), killed
trusted advisors, and pursued costly wars
(for more on Henry, see the sidebar,
later).

After all that, he'd produced only
one male heir—**Edward VI** (see an
image of him nearby). Nine-year-old
Edward (son of Henry's third wife, Jane Seymour) ruled for only
six years (1547-1553) before dying young, leaving England in religious and economic turmoil. (One of the Edward VI portraits
often on display is an optical illusion. View it through the hole at
the right end to put the enigmatic boy king into perspective.)
• *Go to Room 2, with portraits of the next generation of Tudors. Among
them, you'll always find at least one image of...*

❷ Elizabeth I (1533-1603)

Elizabeth I was pale, stern-looking, red-haired (like her father,
Henry VIII), and wore big-shouldered power dresses. During her
reign, she kept Protestant/Catholic
animosity under control and made
England a naval power and cultural
capital.

Three different portraits (the
displays change) depict the span of
her life. The one with the most elaborate frame (with a crown on the
top) shows her coronation at age 26,
with the crown, scepter, and orb.
At age 42 (see photo), she exudes a
regal bearing. The largest painting
(The Ditchley Portrait) captures her
standing on a map of England, age
60. She looks ageless, always aware
of her public image, resorting to
makeup, dye, wigs, showy dresses, and pearls to dazzle courtiers.

The "Virgin Queen" was married only to her country, but she
flirtatiously wooed opponents to her side. ("I know I have the body
of a weak and feeble woman," she'd coo, "but I have the heart and
stomach of a king.") When England's navy sank 72 ships of the
Spanish Armada in a single, power-shifting battle (1588), Britannia ruled the waves, feasting on New World spoils. Elizabeth surrounded herself with intellectuals, explorers, and poets.

Henry VIII (1491-1547)

The notorious king who single-handedly transformed England was a true Renaissance Man—six feet tall, handsome, charismatic, well-educated, and brilliant. He spoke English, Latin, French, and Spanish. A legendary athlete, he hunted, played tennis, and jousted with knights and kings. He played the lute and wrote folk songs; his "Pastime with Good Company" is still being performed. When 17-year-old Henry, the second monarch of the House of Tudor, was crowned king in Westminster Abbey, all of England rejoiced.

Henry left affairs of state in the hands of others, and filled his days with sports, war, dice, women, and the arts. But in 1529, Henry's personal life became a political atom bomb, and it changed the course of history. Henry wanted a divorce, partly because his wife had become too old to bear him a son, and partly because he'd fallen in love with Anne Boleyn, a younger woman who stubbornly refused to be just the king's mistress. Henry begged the pope for an annulment, but—for political reasons, not moral ones—the pope refused. Henry went ahead and divorced his wife anyway, and he was excommunicated.

The event sparked the English Reformation. With his defiance, Henry rejected papal authority in England. He forced monasteries to close, sold off some church land, and confiscated everything else for himself and the Crown. Within a decade, monastic institutions that had operated for centuries were left empty and gutted (many ruined sites can be visited today, including the abbeys of Glastonbury, St. Mary's at York, Rievaulx, and Lindisfarne). Meanwhile, the Catholic Church was reorganized into the (Anglican) Church of England, with Henry as its head. Though Henry himself basically adhered to Catholic doctrine, he discouraged the veneration of saints and relics, and commissioned an English translation of the Bible. Hard-core Catholics had to assume a low profile. Many English welcomed this break from Italian religious influence, but others rebelled. For the next few generations, England would suffer through bitter Catholic-Protestant differences.

Henry famously had six wives. The issue was not his love life (which could have been satisfied by his numerous mistresses), but the politics of royal succession. To guarantee the Tudor family's dominance, he needed a male heir born by a recognized queen.

Henry's first marriage, to Catherine of Aragon, had been arranged to cement an alliance with her parents, Ferdinand and Isabel of Spain. Catherine bore Henry a daughter, but no sons. Next came Anne Boleyn, who also gave birth to a daughter. After a turbulent few years with Anne and several miscarriages, a frustrated Henry had her beheaded at the Tower of London. His next wife, Jane Seymour, finally had a son (but Jane died soon after giving birth). A blind-marriage with Anne of Cleves ended quickly when she proved to be both politically useless and ugly—the "Flanders Mare." Next, teen bride Catherine Howard ended up cheating on Henry, so she was executed. Henry finally found comfort—but no children—in his later years with his final wife, Catherine Parr.

In 1536 Henry suffered a serious accident while jousting. His health would never be the same. Increasingly, he suffered from festering boils and violent mood swings, and he became morbidly obese, tipping the scales at 400 pounds with a 54-inch waist.

Henry's last years were marked by paranoia, sudden rages, and despotism. He gave his perceived enemies the pink slip in his signature way—charged with treason and beheaded. (Ironically, Henry's own heraldic motto was "Coeur Loyal"—true heart.) Once-wealthy England was becoming depleted, thanks to Henry's expensive habits, which included making war on France, building and acquiring palaces (he had 50), and collecting fine tapestries and archery bows.

Henry forged a large legacy. He expanded the power of the monarchy, making himself the focus of a rising, modern nation-state. Simultaneously, he strengthened Parliament—largely because it agreed with his policies. He annexed Wales, and imposed English rule on Ireland (provoking centuries of resentment). He expanded the navy, paving the way for Britannia to soon rule the waves. And—thanks to Henry's marital woes—England would forever be a Protestant nation.

When Henry died at age 55, he was succeeded by his nine-year-old son by Jane Seymour, Edward VI. Weak and sickly, Edward died six years later. Next to rule was Mary, Henry's daughter from his first marriage. A staunch Catholic, she tried to brutally reverse England's Protestant Reformation, earning the nickname "Bloody Mary." Finally came Henry's daughter with Anne Boleyn— Queen Elizabeth I, who ruled a prosperous, expanding England, seeing her father's seeds blossom into the English Renaissance.

London abounds with "Henry" sights. He was born in Greenwich (at today's Old Royal Naval College) and was crowned in Westminster Abbey. He built a palace along Whitehall and enjoyed another at Hampton Court. At the National Portrait Gallery, you can see portraits of some of Henry's wives, and at the Tower you can see where he executed them. Henry is buried alongside his final wife at Windsor Castle.

• *Pass through Room 3, through the stairwell, and into Room 4.*

❸ William Shakespeare (1564-1616)

Though famous in his day, Shakespeare's long hair, beard, earring, untied collar, and red-rimmed eyes make him look less the celebrity and more the bohemian barfly he likely was (for more on Shakespeare's life and influence, see the sidebar on page 236). This unassuming portrait captures 45-year-old Shakespeare just before he retired from his career as actor, poet, and world's greatest playwright. The shiny, domed forehead is a beacon of intelligence. (I suspect Shakespeare liked this plain-spoken portrait.)

The museum attributes this portrait to a Shakespeare contemporary, John Taylor, and claims it's the only one that could have been painted during the Bard's lifetime. But other scholars insist it was done long after the writer's death. Compare this version with the one you can see in the British Library (see page 235.) One recently discovered portrait (not in the museum) depicts a 46-year-old Shakespeare looking like a matinee idol, with a full head of hair. The search goes on for the "real" Will.

• *Also in Room 4, find the portrait of James I that marks the end of the Elizabethan Age and the beginning of the...*

1600s—RELIGIOUS AND CIVIL WARS

Catholic kings bickered with an increasingly vocal Protestant Parliament until Civil War erupted (1642-1651), killing thousands, decapitating the king, and eventually establishing Parliament as the main power.

❹ James I of England and VI of Scotland (1566-1625)

When the "Virgin Queen" died childless, her cousin—an arrogant Scotsman—moved to genteel London and donned the royal robes. Deeply religious, he launched the "King James" translation of the Bible, but he alienated Anglicans (Church of England), harder-line Protestants (Puritans), and democrats everywhere by insisting that he ruled by divine right, directly from God. He passed on this attitude to his son, Charles.

• *Enter Room 5, with portraits of Civil War veterans.*

❺ Charles I (1600-1649)

Picture Charles' sensitive face (with scholar's eyes and artist's long hair and beard) severed from his elegant body (in horse-riding finery), and you've arrived quickly at the heart of the Civil War.

The short, shy, stuttering Charles angered Protestants and democrats by dissolving Parliament, raising taxes, and marrying a Catholic. Parliament formed an army, fought the king's supporters, arrested and tried Charles, and—outside the Banqueting House on Whitehall—beheaded him.

• *The man responsible was...*

❻ Oliver Cromwell (1599-1658)

Cromwell, with armor, sword, command baton, and a determined look, was the Protestant champion and military leader. The Civil

War pitted Parliamentarians (Parliament, Protestant Puritans, industry, and urban areas) against Royalists (King, Catholics, nobles, traditionalists, and rural areas). After Charles' execution, Cromwell led kingless England as "Lord Protector."

Stern Cromwell hated luxury and ordered a warts-and-all portrait (see wart on his left temple and scar between his eyebrows). He has a simple, bowl-cut hairstyle adorning his 82-ounce brain (49 is average). Speaking of heads, three years after Cromwell's death, vengeful Royalists exhumed his body, cut off the head, stuck it on a stick, and placed it outside Westminster Abbey, where it rotted publicly for 24 years.

• *Pass through Room 6 and into Room 7. Facing you is...*

❼ Charles II (1630-1685)

After two decades of wars, Cromwell's harsh rule, and Puritanical excesses (no dancing, theater, or political incorrectness), Parliament welcomed the monarchy back (with tight restrictions) under Charles II. England was ready to party.

Looking completely ridiculous, with splayed legs, puffy face, big-hair wig, garters, and ribbons on his shoes, Charles II became a king with nothing to do, and he did it with grace and a sense of humor. Charles' picture is sandwiched between portraits of his devoted wife,

Catherine of Braganza, and one of his well-known mistresses, the actress Nell Gwyn.

• *Make a U-turn right, entering Room 8. In the right corner are the bewigged and unamused...*

❽ Isaac Newton (1642-1727) and John Locke (1632-1704)

The 1600s, the Age of Enlightenment, saw scientific discoveries suggesting that the world operates in an orderly, rational way. Isaac Newton explained the universe's motion with the simplest of formulas (f = ma, etc.), and John Locke used human reason to plan a democratic utopia, coining phrases like "life, liberty..." that would inspire America's revolutionaries.

• *Walk straight ahead (through Room 9) to Room 10. Along the right wall, find...*

❾ Christopher Wren (1632-1723)

Christopher Wren—leaning on blueprints with a compass in hand—designed St. Paul's Cathedral, a glorious demonstration of mathematics in stone.

• *In Room 11, make a U-turn left, entering Room 12, with painters, writers, actors, and musicians of the 1700s.*

1700s—DOMESTIC STABILITY, WARS WITH FRANCE

Blossoming agriculture, the first factories, overseas colonization, and political stability from German-born kings (George I, II, III) allowed the arts to flourish. Overseas, England financed wars against Europe's No. 1 power, France.

❿ George Frideric Handel (1685-1759)

In London, an old form of art became something new—modern theater. Handel, a German who wrote Italian operas in England, had several smash hits in London (especially with the oratorio *Messiah,* on his desk), making musical theater popular with ordinary folk. Hallelujah.

• *Walk on, to Room 13, for the portrait of...*

⓫ James Watt (1736-1819)

Deep-thinking Watt pores over plans to turn brainpower into work power. His steam engines (with a separate condenser to capture formerly wasted heat energy) soon powered gleaming machines, changing the focus of England's economy from grain and ships to iron and coal.

• *Head to Room 14, where you'll find George III over your left shoulder and George Washington along the right wall.*

⓬ George III (1738-1820) and
⓭ George Washington (1732-1799)

Just crowned at 23, King George III gives little hint in this portrait that he will lead England into the drawn-out, humiliating "Ameri-

can War" (Revolutionary War) against a colony demanding independence. George III, perhaps a victim of an undiagnosed disease, closed out the stuffy "Georgian" era (in Percy Shelley's words) "an old, mad, blind, despised, dying king."

Perhaps it was the war that drove him mad, or perhaps it was that his enemy, George Washington (portrait nearby), had the same hairdo. Washington was born in British-ruled Virginia and fought for Britain in the French and Indian War, but sided with the colonies in what the British called the "American War." This famous portrait of Washington is one of several versions of a 1796 portrait by Gilbert Stuart.

1800s—COLONIAL AND INDUSTRIAL GIANT

Britain defeated France (Napoleon) and emerged as the world's top power. With natural resources from overseas colonies (Australia, Canada, India, West Indies, China), good communications, and a growing population of seven million, Britain became the first industrial powerhouse, dotted with smoke-belching factories and laced with railroads.

• *Exit Room 14 into Room 8 and turn right, ending up in the bright aqua Room 17, featuring a red-jacketed man flanked by portraits of brave Brits who battled Napoleon.*

⓮ Admiral Horatio Nelson (1758-1805) and
Emma, Lady Hamilton (1761-1815)

While the Duke of Wellington fought Napoleon on land (the final victory at Waterloo, near Brussels, 1815), Admiral Nelson battled France at sea (Battle of Trafalgar, off Spain, 1805).

At Nelson's side is Emma, Lady Hamilton, dressed in white, with her famously beautiful face turned coyly. She first met dashing Nelson on his way to fight the French in Egypt. She used the influence of her husband, Lord Hamilton, to restock Nelson's ships. Nelson's daring victory at the Battle of the Nile made him an instant celebrity, though the battle cost him an arm and an eye. The hero— a married man—returned home to woo, bed, and impregnate Lady H., with sophisticated Lord Hamilton's patriotic tolerance.

• *Step into Room 18.*

ⓕ The Romantics

Not everyone worshipped industrial progress. Romantics questioned the clinical detachment of science, industrial pollution, and the personal restrictions of modern life. They reveled in strong emotions, non-Western cultures, personal freedom, opium, and the beauties of nature.

• *Scattered around the room, you may see...*

John Keats (1795-1821) broods over his just-written "Ode to a Nightingale." ("My heart aches, and a drowsy numbness pains/My sense, as though of hemlock I had drunk.")

Samuel Taylor Coleridge (1772-1834), at 23, is open-eyed, open-mouthed, and eager. ("And all should cry, Beware! Beware!/His flashing eyes, his floating hair!/...For he on honey-dew hath fed,/And drunk the milk of Paradise."—"Kubla Khan")

Mary Wollstonecraft Shelley (1797-1851), in telling ghost stories with husband Percy Shelley and friend Lord Byron, conceived a tale of science run amok—*Frankenstein*—imitated by many. ("Ahhhhhhh, sweet mystery of life, at last I've found you!")

William Wordsworth (1770-1850): "The world is too much with us.../Little we see in Nature that is ours;/We have given our hearts away, a sordid boon!"

Percy Bysshe Shelley (1792-1822), political radical, sexual explorer (involving Mary and Claire Clairmont), traveler, and poet. ("O wild West Wind, thou breath of Autumn's being,.../If Winter comes, can Spring be far behind?")

George Gordon, **Lord Byron** (1788-1824), was athletic, exotic, and passionate about women and freedom. Famous and scandalous in his day, he became a Kerouacian symbol of the Romantic movement. ("She walks in beauty, like the night/Of cloudless climes and starry skies...")

Jane Austen (1775-1817) wrote of the landed-gentry class that surrounded her—its manners, love lives, and lifestyle. ("The person, be it gentleman or lady, who has not pleasure in a good novel, must be intolerably stupid.")

• *After browsing Rooms 19 and 20, backtrack to Room 15 and head downstairs one flight to the* **first floor.** *Turn right at the bottom of the stairs, pass through the long hall lined with busts (Room 22), and enter Room 21.*

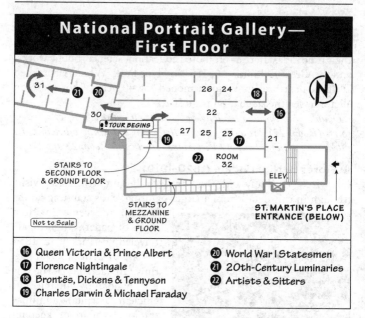

**National Portrait Gallery—
First Floor**

TOUR BEGINS

STAIRS TO
SECOND FLOOR
& GROUND FLOOR

STAIRS TO
MEZZANINE
& GROUND
FLOOR

Not to Scale

ROOM
32

ELEV.

ST. MARTIN'S PLACE
ENTRANCE (BELOW)

16 Queen Victoria & Prince Albert
17 Florence Nightingale
18 Brontës, Dickens & Tennyson
19 Charles Darwin & Michael Faraday

20 World War I Statesmen
21 20th-Century Luminaries
22 Artists & Sitters

First Floor

1837-1901—THE VICTORIANS

As the wealthiest nation on earth with a global colonial empire, Britain during Queen Victoria's long reign embraced modern technology, contributing to the development of power looms, railroads, telephones, motorcars, and electric lights. It was a golden age of science, literature, and middle-class morality, though pockets of extreme poverty and vice lurked in the heart of London itself.

• Find a statue of a happy couple, titled Queen Victoria and Prince Albert in Anglo-Saxon Dress. *Flanking the statue are paintings of...*

16 Queen Victoria (1819-1901) and Prince Albert (1819-1861)

Crowned at 18, the short (4'11"), plump, bug-eyed, quiet girl in-

herited a world empire. The next year, she proposed marriage (the custom) to the German Prince Albert. They were a perfect match—lovers, friends, and partners—a model for middle-class couples.

(See the white statue of the pair as genteel knight and adoring lady.) Albert co-ruled, especially when "Vickie" was pregnant with their nine kids. "Bertie" promoted education, science, public works, and the Great Exhibition of 1851 in Hyde Park. When Albert died at 42, a heartbroken Victoria moped for 40 years. (For more on Victoria, see the sidebar on page 102.)

• *Double back through the long hall lined with stuffy busts of starched shirts (Room 22), browsing around the rooms branching off, which are filled with many prominent Victorians. Start with Room 23 and...*

⑰ Florence Nightingale (1820-1910)

Known as "the Lady with the Lamp" for her nightly nursing visits (though in this detail from a larger painting, she's standing lamp-

less, in the center, with a piece of paper), Nightingale traveled to Turkey in 1854 to tend to Crimean War victims. In fact, her forte was not hands-on nursing but efficient hospital administration (sanitation, keeping supplies stocked, transporting wounded), which ended up saving lives and raising public awareness about health issues. To learn more about her, you can visit the Florence Nightingale Museum, just across the Thames from Big Ben (in Gassiot House at 2 Lambeth Palace Road, Tube: Westminster, Waterloo, or Lambeth North).

• *Across the hall, in Room 24, you'll find several...*

⑱ Writers

Anne, Emily, and Charlotte Brontë (left to right, youngest to oldest, painted by brother Branwell), three teenage country girls, grew up to write novels such as *Wuthering Heights* (Emily, 1818-1848) and *Jane Eyre* (Charlotte, 1816-1855), about the complex family and love lives of England's rural gentry.

To the left of the Brontës is a youthful **Charles Dickens** (1812-1870). He was only 12 years old when his dad was sent to a debtor's prison, forcing young Charles to work in a factory. The experience gave him a working-class perspective on British society. He became phenomenally successful writing popular novels *(Oliver*

Twist, A Tale of Two Cities, A Christmas Carol) for Britain's educated middle-class.

To the right of the Brontës is **Alfred, Lord Tennyson** (1809-1892), the poet laureate of Victorian earnestness. ("Theirs not to reason why,/Theirs but to do and die;/Into the Valley of Death/Rode the six hundred.")

• *Head to Room 27.*

⓳ Science and Technology
Charles Darwin (1809-1882), with basset-hound eyes and long white beard, looks tired after a lifetime of reluctantly defending his controversial theory of evolution, which shocked an entire generation.

Michael Faraday (1791-1867), across from Darwin, shocked himself from time to time, harnessing electricity as the work force of the next century.

• *The long hall (Room 22) leads into Room 30, dedicated to World War I.*

1900s—WORLD WARS
Two devastating world wars and an emerging US superpower shrank Britain from global empire to island nation. But the country remained a cultural giant, producing writers, actors, composers, painters, and Beatles.

⓴ World War I Statesmen
Fighting Germans from trenches in France and Belgium, the British Army lost nearly a million men. In the big group portrait titled *Some Statesmen of the Great War,* find a bored-looking Winston Churchill.

• *The large Room 31 contains 20th-century portraits. These exhibits change frequently, and some of the portraits mentioned here may not be on display during your visit. Be prepared to put the book aside and browse.*

㉑ 20th-Century Luminaries

The **Duchess of Windsor** (see photo) caught the eye of **Edward, Duke of Windsor.** The Duchess' smug smile tells us she got her man.

Edward VIII (1894-1972), great-grandson of Queen Victoria, became king in 1936 as a bachelor dating a common-born (gasp),

twice-divorced (double gasp) American (oh no!) named Wallis Simpson (1896-1986). Rather than create a constitutional stink, Edward quietly abdicated, married Wallis, and the two moved to the Continent, living happily ever after. They hosted cocktail parties, played golf, and listened to servants call them "Your Majesty"—though they were now just plain Duke and Duchess of Windsor. (His brother "Bertie" took over as King George VI, and George VI's daughter became Queen Elizabeth II. Elizabeth—and all the other royals—essentially snubbed their disgraced aunt and uncle for the rest of their lives.)

George Bernard Shaw (1856-1950)—playwright, critic, and political thinker—brought socialist ideas into popular discussion with plays such as *Man and Superman* and *Major Barbara*. **Virginia Woolf** (1882-1941) wrote feminist essays ("A woman must have money and a room of her own if she is to write fiction.") and experimental novels (*Mrs. Dalloway* jumps back and forth in time) before filling her pockets with stones and drowning herself in a river to silence the voices in her head.

In the darkest days at the beginning of World War II, with Nazi bombs raining on a wounded London, Sir **Winston Churchill** (1874-1965) rallied his people with stirring speeches from the Houses of Parliament. ("We shall fight on the beaches...We shall never surrender!") Britain's military chief, Field Marshall **Bernard Montgomery, 1st Viscount** (1887-1976, known as "Monty") points out the D-Day beaches of the decisive Allied assault.

Sir **Laurence Olivier** (1907-1989), movie and stage actor, played everything from romantic leads and Shakespeare heavies to character parts with funny accents. Sir **Noel Coward** (1899-1973) continued the British tradition of writing witty, sophisticated comedies about the idle rich. **Henry Moore** (1898-1986), the most famous 20th-century sculptor, combined the grandeur of Michelangelo, the raw stone of primitive carvings, and the simplified style of abstract art. **Dylan Thomas** (1914-1953) wrote abstract imagery with a Romantic's heart ("Do not go gentle into that good

night..."). American-born poet **T. S. Eliot** (1888-1965; see photo) captured the quiet banality of modern life: "This is the way the world ends/Not with a bang but a whimper."
• *Backtrack to the staircase. Before going downstairs, continue past the stairwell into the long Room 32, filled with an exhibit called...*

㉒ Artists and Sitters: Britain 1960-1990

This ever-changing collection high-

lights the relationship between portraitist and subject. Often included in this section are contemporary royals (including Queen Elizabeth II, Prince Charles, and the late Princess Di), politicians (Margaret Thatcher), and fixtures of British popular culture (Sir Paul McCartney and Mick Jagger, among others).
• *Now head down to the **ground floor**.*

1990 TO THE PRESENT

London since the Swinging '60s has been a major exporter of pop culture. The contemporary collection, located in Rooms 32-42, changes often depending on who's hot, but you may find royal youngsters (William and Harry, plus a famously creepy-looking Kate), politicians (Tony Blair), entrepreneurs (Sir Richard Branson), classic-rock geezers (Sir Elton John, David Bowie), and actors (Sir Michael Caine, Dame Judi Dench), as well as those in lower-profile professions—writers (Sir Salman Rushdie, Doris Lessing, Germaine Greer), scientists (Stephen Hawking), composers, painters, and intellectuals.

We've gone from battles to Beatles, seeing Britain's history in the faces of its major players.

WEST END WALK

From Leicester Square to Piccadilly Circus

The West End, the area just west of the original walled City of London, is London's liveliest neighborhood. It's easy to get caught up in fantasies of jolly olde England, but the West End is where you'll feel the pulse of the living, breathing London of today, from genteel shopping to raunchy red light districts, and everything in between. Theaters, pubs, restaurants, bookstores, ethnic food, markets, and boutiques attract rock stars, punks, tourists, and ladies and gentlemen stepping from black cabs for a night on the town.

Most of this book's walks and tours focus on history, art, and museums. But this walk is about appreciating the London lifestyle: the entertainment energy at Leicester Square; the thriving popular hum of Covent Garden; the rock-and-roll history of Denmark Street; the bohemian, creative, hedonistic groove of Soho; and the bustling neon hub of Piccadilly Circus. Use the walk to get the lay of the land, then go explore—especially in the evening, when the neon glitters and London sparkles.

Orientation

Length of This Walk: Allow two hours to lace together these highlights.

When to Go: Take your pick—sightseeing by day, or nightlife after dark. Early evenings are ideal, since most pubs and squares are carbonated with locals enjoying a post-work pint. After that, join the bustle of people who should probably be grabbing a cab home.

Getting There: Take the Tube to the Leicester Square stop, which is a block from the square itself.

Finding Your Way: If you have a more detailed map than the one provided here, it may help you find your way more quickly through the maze of irregular streets.

The Walk Begins

• *Start at Leicester Square. Stand at the top of the square and take in the scene.*

❶ Leicester Square

Leicester (LESS-ter) Square is a small park surrounded by glitzy cinema houses. This space was modernized and spiffed up in anticipation of the 2012 Olympics crowds. It sits smack in the middle of the theater district—ground zero for London's enticing offerings of flashy musicals, intimate plays starring big-name actors, and much more (for details, see the Entertainment in London chapter). Here, at the entertainment center of London, a statue of Shakespeare looks out, as if pondering the quote chiseled into his pedestal: "There is no darkness but ignorance."

The square's **movie theaters**—the Odeon (Britain's largest cinema), Empire, and Vue—are famous for hosting red-carpet

movie premieres. When Bradley Cooper, Benedict Cumberbatch, Keira Knightley, or Jennifer Lawrence need a publicity splash, it'll likely be here. (Search online for "London film premieres" to find upcoming events.) On any given night, this entire area is a mosh-pit of clubs and partying teens in town from the suburbs.

Leicester Square is the central clearinghouse for daytime theater ticket sales. Check out the **TKTS booth** (see page 444) and ignore all the other establishments that bill themselves as "half-price" (they're just normal booking agencies). It's often cheaper still to buy tickets directly from one of the theaters we'll pass on this walk.

Capital Radio London (next to the Odeon) plays a role in British rock-and-roll history. Back in the 1960s, the BBC was the only radio station in town, and it was mostly talk and Bach, with a smattering of pop. The British Invasion was in full swing—Beatles, Rolling Stones, The Who—but Brits couldn't hear much of it on the BBC. They had to resort to "pirate" radio stations, beamed from

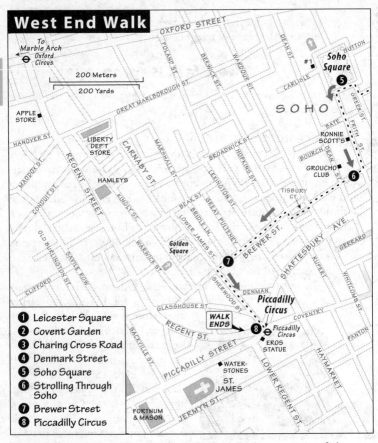

West End Walk

To Marble Arch / Oxford Circus

200 Meters
200 Yards

OXFORD STREET

SOHO

Soho Square

1 Leicester Square
2 Covent Garden
3 Charing Cross Road
4 Denmark Street
5 Soho Square
6 Strolling Through Soho
7 Brewer Street
8 Piccadilly Circus

APPLE STORE
LIBERTY DEP'T STORE
HAMLEYS
RONNIE SCOTT'S
GROUCHO CLUB
Golden Square
Piccadilly Circus
WALK ENDS
EROS STATUE
WATER-STONES
ST. JAMES
FORTNUM & MASON

Luxembourg or from ships at sea. Capital Radio was one of the first commercial stations allowed to play rock and roll—and that was in 1973! Ironically, within a few years, Capital had itself become mainstream. (The Clash struck back with their song "Capital Radio," which starts, "Yes, it's time for the Dr. Goebbels Show...") Today, FM 95.8 carries on as a major top-40 broadcasting power.

• Exit Leicester Square from its top corner, heading east (past the Vue cinema) on Cranbourn Street. Cross Charing Cross Road and continue along Cranbourn to the six-way intersection.

Pause here to notice two things: traffic and chain outlets. London has a "Congestion Zone" plan that fights downtown traffic by charging regular vehicles £11.50 to enter the center. Sure there's still lots of traffic, but it could be far worse. The traffic you do see is limited to residents, taxis, service vehicles, city buses...and those willing to pay that fee to drive here. Also, take a moment to survey the various eateries. London keeps countless restaurants busy, and the vast majority are chains. Most places that look like one-offs

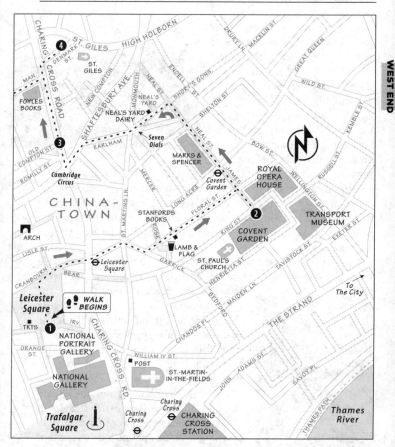

are just chain outlets dressed up to look like one-offs. In our globalized, corporate world, the economy of scale is hard to compete with, and London's food scene (like its hotel scene) is brutal on the mom-and-pop shop. If you don't factor in the intangible social issues, they have simply a better economic value.

• *Now, angle right onto Garrick Street. Shortly afterward, turn left onto calm, brick-lined Floral Street. Soon you'll see (on the left) the back door of Stanfords, an excellent travel book and map shop—pop in (see page 19). A few steps further, across the street and down the tiny lane called Lazenby Court, is the Lamb & Flag pub, with good atmosphere and grub (kitchen open 12:00-20:00). Farther along Floral Street, you'll be immersed in a scintillating array of fashion boutiques. When Floral Street opens onto traffic-free James Street, turn right and head for...*

❷ Covent Garden

Covent Garden (only tourists pluralize the name) is a large square teeming with people and street performers—jugglers, sword swallowers, and guitar players. London's buskers (including those in the Tube) are auditioned, licensed, and assigned times and places where they are allowed to perform.

The square's centerpiece is a covered marketplace. A market has been here since medieval times, when it was the "convent" garden owned by Westminster Abbey. In the 1600s, it became a housing development with this courtyard as its center, done in the Palladian style by Inigo Jones. Today's fine iron-and-glass structure was built in 1830 (when such buildings were all the Industrial Age rage) to house the stalls of what became London's chief produce market.

A tourist market thrives here today (for details, see page 434). Go inside the market hall and poke around. As you enter

through the brick passage, notice the posted diagram on the right identifying shops. Inside the market, you'll hit the so-called Apple Market zone. Picture it in full Dickensian color, lined with fruit and vegetable stalls. Covent Garden remained a produce market until 1973 (look for photos from these days in the middle side aisles). After 1973, its venerable arcades were converted to boutiques, cafés, and antique shops. For a drink overlooking all the action on the square below, The Punch & Judy pub has a view terrace on the rooftop.

Back outside, across from the west end of the market hall, stands **St. Paul's Church** (not the famous cathedral), with its Greek temple-like facade and blue clock face (and pay WCs just to the left). Known as the Actors' Church, it's long been a favorite of nervous performers praying for success. To go inside, pass through one of the gates on either side of the facade, and find the entrance around back. If the gates are closed, you can duck down the streets on either side of the church and look for the passage leading to the tranquil churchyard—a nice escape from the busker bustle on Covent Garden. Inside, the walls are lined with memorials to theater folk, some of whom (Chaplin, Karloff) you might recognize (irregular hours, generally daily 8:30-17:30).

At the bottom (southeast) corner of the square is the **London Transport Museum,** which gives a well-presented look at the evolution of this city's famously well-planned mass transit system (see page 56).

Tucked into the top (northeast) corner of the square is the **Royal Opera House,** which showcases top-notch opera and ballet.

• *Now browse your way northwest, along some lively and colorful streets.*

❸ From Covent Garden to Charing Cross Road

First backtrack two blocks up St. James Street, then continue straight (along the side of the Marks & Spencer department store) up narrow Neal Street. Head two blocks up Neal Street, passing through an up-and-coming shopping zone.

Turn left on Short's Gardens, where Neal's Yard Dairy (at #17) sells a wide variety of cheeses from the British Isles. This is the original shop of what is now a thriving chain. Everything is well-described, and they'll slice off a sample if you ask nicely.

Continue along Short's Gardens to the next intersection—called **Seven Dials**—where seven sundials atop a pole mark the meeting of seven small streets. Built in 1694, this once served the timekeeping needs of this busy merchants' quarter. Continue straight ahead onto Earlham Street.

Then, bearing left, you'll spill out into **Cambridge Circus**—the busy intersection of Shaftesbury Avenue and Charing Cross Road—with its fine red-brick Victorian architecture and classic theaters. **Charing Cross Road** is the traditional home of London's bookstores. Turn right up Charing Cross and walk two blocks to reach one of the biggest, **Foyles Books,** which puts on free events several nights a week—from book signings to jazz in their gallery (usually around 18:00, bookstore is on left at 107 Charing Cross Road, www.foyles.co.uk).

• *A few steps up from Foyles, turn right onto...*

❹ Denmark Street

This seemingly nondescript little street is a musician's mecca. In the

1920s, it was known as "Britain's Tin Pan Alley"—the center of the UK's music-publishing industry, when songwriters here cranked out popular tunes printed as sheet music.

Later, in the 1960s, Denmark Street was ground zero for rock and roll's British Invasion, which brought so much great pop music to the US. Regent Sound Studio (at #4, on the right, now a guitar store with a similar name) was a low-budget recording studio. It was here in 1964 that the Rolling Stones recorded the song that raised them from obscurity, "Not Fade Away". Other acts that recorded on Denmark Street

include The Who ("Happy Jack"), The Kinks (who wrote a song called "Denmark Street"), the Beatles ("Fixing a Hole"), David Bowie, and Black Sabbath (who made their first two records here—including the track "Iron Man"). Today, Regent is a music store, and the former studio's walls are lined with a wonderland of guitars.

The storefront at #20 (on the left, now Wunjo Guitars) was formerly a music publishing house that employed a lowly office boy named Reginald Dwight. In 1969, on the building's rooftop, he wrote "Your Song" and went on to become famous as Sir Elton John. In the 1970s, the Sex Pistols lived in apartments above #6. The 12 Bar Café at #25, on the left (now closed) helped launch the careers of more recent acts: Damien Rice, KT Tunstall, Jeff Buckley, and Keane.

Today, Denmark Street offers one-stop shopping for the modern musician. Without leaving this short street, you could buy a vintage Rickenbacker guitar, get your sax repaired, take piano lessons, lay down a bass track, have a few beers, or tattoo your name across your fist like Ozzy Osbourne. Notice the bulletin board in the alley alongside the 12 Bar Café (through doorway #27). If you're a musician looking for a band to play in, this could be your connection.

• *From Denmark Street, go back across Charing Cross Road and head down Manette Street. After a short block, on the right (down the lane called Orange Yard) you'll see The Borderline, where R.E.M. and Oasis have played. Continue down Manette Street and under the "Pillars of Hercules" passage, then turn right up Greek Street to...*

❺ Soho Square

The Soho neighborhood is London's version of New York City's Greenwich Village. It's a ritzy, raffish, edgy, and colorful area. Because of its eccentric 1970s landlord, porn publisher Paul Raymond, the Soho district escaped late 20th-century development. So, rather than soulless office towers, it retains its characteristic charm. And because the square has no real through-roads, it's almost traffic-free—strangely quiet and residential-feeling for being in the center of such a huge city.

Soho Square Gardens is a favorite place for a nap or picnic on a sunny afternoon (pick up picnic goodies from nearby shops). The little house in the middle of the square is the gardener's hut. History plaques at each entrance tell the area's story, which dates back to 1731. Originally a "key garden," this was once a yard shared by the wealthy people who lived on this square. And speaking of wealthy people, at #1, on the west (left) side of

the square, the MPL building (McCartney Publishing Limited) houses offices of Britain's richest musician, Sir Paul McCartney.

• *At the bottom of the square, wander down Frith Street (which runs parallel to Greek Street).*

❻ Strolling Through Soho

The restaurants and boutiques here and on adjoining streets (such as Greek, Dean, and Wardour streets) are trendy and creative, the kind that attract high society when they feel like slumming it. Bars with burly, well-dressed bouncers abound. Private clubs, like the low-profile **Groucho Club** (a block over, at #45 Dean Street), cater to the late-night rock crowd.

Ronnie Scott's Jazz Club (#47 Frith Street) has featured big-name acts for more than 50 years. In 1970, Jimi Hendrix jammed here with Eric Burdon and War; it was the last performance before his death in a London apartment a few days later.

Frith Street hits **Old Compton Street** at the center of the neighborhood. This street is the center of London's gay scene. Stroll a block to the right on Old Compton Street to take in the eclectic variety of people going by. You're surrounded by the buzz of Soho.

At the corner of Dean Street, look left for the pagoda-style arch down the street. South of here, on the other side of Shaft-

esbury Avenue, is London's underwhelming **Chinatown.** With Gerrard Street as its spine, it occupies what was once just more of Soho, with the same Soho artsy vibe. In the 1960s, the Chinese community gathered here, eventually dominated this zone, and non-Asian businesses moved out. The Chinese population swelled when the former British colony of Hong Kong was returned to China in 1997, but the neighborhood's identity is now threatened by developers eyeing this high-rent real estate.

• *Continue along Old Compton Street to where it hits Wardour Street (with a string of enticing restaurants just to the right). Crossing Wardour, Old Compton squeezes down into a narrow alley (Tisbury Court). Penetrate this sleazy passage of sex shows and blue-video shops, tolerate the barkers' raunchy come-ons, then jog a half-block right and turn on Brewer Street.*

❼ Brewer Street: Sleaze, Porn Shops, and Prostitutes

Soho was a bordello zone in the 19th century. A bit of that survives today in this area. Sex shops, video arcades, and prostitution

mingle with upscale restaurants here in west Soho. While it's illegal in Britain to sell sex on the street, well-advertised "models" entertain (profitably) in their tiny apartments. And these days massage parlors that promise memorable endings are harder for the police to bust.

Crossing Brewer Street, Berwick Street hosts a daily produce market.

• *Our walk is nearly finished. Continue a few short blocks along Brewer Street, observing the fascinating metamorphosis of a neighborhood from sleaze to gentrification. When you reach The Crown tavern, at the intersection of Brewer Street and Sherwood Street (also called Lower James Street), it's time to plan your next move. Dedicated rock fans could turn right here and detour a couple of blocks to Carnaby Street (see page 435).*

Otherwise, turn left onto Sherwood Street and walk one block down, emerging into the bustling intersection known as...

❽ Piccadilly Circus

London's most touristy square got its name from the fancy ruffled shirts—*picadils*—made in the neighborhood long ago. In the late 20th century, the square veered to-ward the gimmicky and tacky—look no further than the gargantuan Rip-ley's Believe-It-or-Not Museum.

The square's center features a statue-on-a-pillar of a tipsy-but-perfectly balanced Eros. (Actually, scholars say it's Anteros, the love god's brother, but Londoners call it Eros.) Until just a couple of years ago, Piccadilly was a famously busy traffic circle, with cars and big red buses spinning around the statue. Now—though still busy with cars—it's also a packed people zone. At night it's as bright as day—with neon pulsing and the 20-foot-high video ads painting the classic Georgian facades in a rainbow of colors. Black cabs honk, tourists crowd the attractions, and Piccadilly shows off big-city London at its glitziest.

• *Our walk is done. If you're up for more sightseeing, it's easy to connect from here to my Regent Street Shopping Walk (page 435). Several of my recommended restaurants are nearby (see page 396). If you're ready to move on, the Piccadilly Tube stop is here, and handy buses #15, 23, 38, and 148 stop near here (see page 28). It's all ready for you—you're at the center of London.*

COURTAULD GALLERY TOUR

The Courtauld Gallery (part of the Courtauld Institute of Art) is just small enough that you can see it all in a single visit, which makes for a pleasant experience. The collection spans the history of Western painting, from medieval altarpieces through the Italian Renaissance to the 20th century. But its highlight is Impressionist and Post-Impressionist works, some of which you'll recognize. Besides the pieces I've featured, you'll likely see many other well-known Post-Impressionist, Fauvist, and early modern paintings, part of the museum's rotating collection of loaners. For some, the Van Gogh self-portrait alone is worth the price of admission.

The gallery is located at Somerset House, a grand 18th-century civic palace that offers a marvelous public space (housing temporary exhibits) and a riverside terrace with several eateries (between the Strand and the Thames). The palace once held the national registry that recorded Britain's births, marriages, and deaths: "...where they hatch 'em, match 'em, and dispatch 'em." Step into the courtyard to enjoy the fountain. Go ahead...walk through it. The 55 jets get playful twice an hour. In the winter, this becomes a popular ice-skating rink with a toasty café for viewing.

Orientation

Cost: £7 (£3 on Mon); extra fee for special exhibits.

Hours: Daily 10:00-18:00, occasionally open late on Thu (until 21:00, usually the first and second Thu of the month—check their website) when there may be concerts or other events.

Getting There: The Courtauld is located in Somerset House, a major arts and cultural center on the Strand. It's a 10-minute walk from Trafalgar Square. Tube: Temple or Covent Garden, or catch bus #6, #9, #11, #13, #15, or #23 from Trafalgar

Square. The gallery is right at the Strand entrance to the huge Somerset House.

Information: Lunchtime art talks are generally offered Mon and Fri at 13:15 (15 minutes, included in ticket). Recorded info tel. 020/7848-2526, gallery shop tel. 020/7848-2579, www. courtauld.ac.uk.

Length of This Tour: Allow one hour. With limited time, don't miss Manet's *A Bar at the Folies-Bergère* and Van Gogh's *Self-Portrait with Bandaged Ear*.

Services: Free lockers and WCs are in the basement.

Photography: Permitted without flash in the permanent exhibit.

Cuisine Art: The café (serving soups, salads, sandwiches, pastries, and drinks), with the same hours as the gallery, is in the basement. The recommended Sitar Indian Restaurant is next door (see page 406).

Starring: Van Gogh, Manet, Cézanne, Degas, and many other artists spanning the centuries.

OVERVIEW

The museum is arranged more or less chronologically, from the bottom up. Wealthy collectors created this museum by donating

their personal collections. Samuel Courtauld (1876-1947)—a philanthropist, industrialist, and wealthy great-nephew of a textile magnate—gave his paintings (Van Gogh, Manet, Cézanne, and others on the first floor) and his name to the budding museum.

If you don't see a particular painting where this chapter says it should be, don't fret—it may be a few rooms farther along. Occasionally, the paintings described in this tour are loaned to other museums. If there's a piece you really want to see, check with a guard or at the front desk (the ticket seller has a notebook that lists pieces currently on loan).

This tour covers just enough to introduce you to the wide range of art in the collection. Take time to explore the gallery's many other masterpieces.

The Tour Begins

COURTAULD GALLERY

• *Start on the ground floor, in Room 1 (a.k.a. Gallery I, directly across from the ticket counter), filled with religious paintings.*

Robert Campin—*The Seilern Triptych: The Entombment* (c. 1425)

As the earliest known work of this pioneering artist, the altarpiece is a mix of medieval piety and proto-Renaissance techniques.

Christ's followers prepare to lower him into the tomb. In medieval fashion, it's set on a gold-leaf background with intricate vines and flowers hammered in. Christ's body is spindly, weightless, and presented at an unnatural angle. But the faces! With knit brows, they bear their sorrow solemnly. Even the angels are choked up. The man kneeling at left (who donated the money for the altarpiece) has a day's growth of beard—that's spot-on realism.

• *Climb the stairs two flights up to the "first" floor. Here you'll survey the rooms clockwise, in chronological order. Begin by turning left from the top of the stairs into Room 2 (with large painted chests). Rooms 2-4 generally showcase the Courtauld's old masters.*

Lucas Cranach the Elder—*Adam and Eve* (1526)

Eve—having taken a bite of Knowledge—gazes into the distance, and passes the forbidden fruit to a puzzled Adam, standing in a lush garden amid peaceful animals. Strategically-placed branches fuzz out their genitals, but otherwise they're nude, with the pale, thin bodies of the aristocrats for whom Cranach painted. (Adam, beware of antlers.) Though the subject is biblical, it captures the worldly spirit of Germany's Renaissance. The northern version of humanism saw humans not as noble Greek gods (as the Italian Renaissance did), but as fallible, lusty, and even a bit cynical.

Peter Paul Rubens—*The Family of Jan Brueghel the Elder* (1613-1615)

Rubens paints his close friend and occasional collaborator, along with his wife and two kids. Rubens and Brueghel, Antwerp's two best painters, tag-teamed a couple of dozen works. Brueghel focused on his specialty—background, flowers, animals, and garlands—and Rubens did the people. Also in this room is Rubens' dreamy *Landscape by Moonlight* (1635-1640).

• *Proceed into Rooms 5-7, which feature Impressionism and Post-Impressionism.*

Edgar Degas—*Two Dancers on the Stage* (1874)

Degas differs from his Impressionist peers in that he often painted interiors with people, especially dancers, rather than landscapes. These two ballerinas look at each other while we observe them from above, perhaps from balcony seating. The dancers are most likely performing the *Ballet des Roses* at the Paris Opera company's rendition of Mozart's *Don Giovanni*.

Edouard Manet—*A Bar at the Folies-Bergère* (1882)

While we look at the barmaid and her wares, Manet also shows us the barmaid's-eye view of the crowded nightclub, reflected in the

(slightly tilted) mirror behind her. We see the glittering chandeliers rendered in Impressionist smudges, the bottles of wine, the swirl of activity, and even a trapeze artist (upper left). From the barmaid's own reflection, we see that she's facing a mustachioed man in a top hat. This may be a self-portrait, but whoever he is, he's standing right where we are.

Manet, in his last major painting, places us in the center of the scene, surrounded with glitter. Reflected in the mirror, the gaiety all looks a bit fake, and, judging from her blank expression, that's the way the barmaid sees it.

Edouard Manet—*Le Dejeuner sur l'Herbe* (c. 1863-1868)

This is a smaller, cruder version Manet did of his famous painting (now in Paris' Orsay Museum, pictured here) that launched

the Impressionist revolution. The nude woman in a classical pose wasn't shocking. It was the presence of the fully clothed men in everyday dress that suddenly made the nude naked. Manet and the Impressionists rejected goddesses and romance for the landscapes, café scenes, and still lifes of the real world.

Edgar Degas—*Study in the Nude for Dressed Ballet Dancer* (1879-1917)

This famous sculpture is sometimes on display. The naked 14-year-old girl splays her feet out (fourth position), bends her arms back, and turns her face up, exuding the sheer joy of dancing. Like a stripped Barbie doll, this is a smaller-scale, nude version of the famous statue Edgar Degas exhibited in Paris in 1881. The original was made of wax and plaster over a wire frame. (The Courtauld's version is a bronze cast of a wax statue, done after Degas' death.) Degas dressed his original wax statue in a cloth tutu and ballet slippers and attached real human hair to the wax head, creating a modern collage of materials that shocked and intrigued the Parisians. Critics of the day both praised its modernism and lambasted the angular, adolescent body and "ugly" face.

The model for the statue was an aspiring dancer who, like so many adolescent girls then and now, dreamed of finding a career on stage. Degas sketched and painted her many times. But this well-known painter was also a closet sculptor, fashioning dozens of small-scale statues in the privacy of his studio, especially in his later years as his eyesight failed and painting became more difficult. Only *The Little Fourteen-Year-Old Dancer* was exhibited.

Paul Gauguin—*Nevermore* (1897)

A nude Tahitian woman lies daydreaming. The curves of her body and of the headboard soften the horizontal lines of the bed and the verticals of the wall.

Gauguin—who quit his stockbroker job, abandoned his wife and family, and moved to Tahiti—paints in the "primitive" style he found there. With complete simplicity, he draws the girl with a thick outline (so different from Impressionists who "built" a figure with a mosaic of brushstrokes) and then fills it in with solid Crayola colors. Gauguin emphasizes only the two dimensions of height and width, so that the women and clouds in the "background" blend into the flowery wallpaper in the "foreground." Gauguin rejected the camera-eye literalness of Western art. His simple style requires the viewer's imagination to fill in the blanks, perhaps evoking the romance of a bygone world that is...nevermore.

By the way, Gauguin insisted that the title and the raven were not from Poe's poem, but "a bird of the devil who watches." Hmm.

Vincent van Gogh—*Self-Portrait with Bandaged Ear* (1889)

On the night of December 23, 1888, Vincent van Gogh went ballistic. Drunk, self-doubting, clinically insane, and enraged at his friend Gauguin's smug superiority, he waved a knife in Gauguin's face, and later that night cut off a piece of his own ear and gave it to a prostitute. Gauguin hightailed it back to Paris, and the locals in Arles persuaded the mad Dutchman to get help. A week later, just released from the hospital, Vincent stood in front of a blank canvas and looked at himself in the mirror.

What he saw looking back was a calm man with an unflinching gaze, dressed in a heavy coat (painted with thick, vertical strokes of blue and green) and fur-lined hat. The slightly stained bandage over his ear is neither hidden in shame nor worn as a badge of honor—it's just another accessory. The scene is evenly lit, with no melodramatic shadows.

Vincent must have been puzzled and unnerved by his "artist's fit," as he called it. Does this man suspect it would be only the first of many he'd suffer over the next year and a half before finally taking his own life?

• *Linger awhile in Rooms 5-7, with their ever-changing array of works by well-known Impressionists and Post-Impressionists (Toulouse-Lautrec, Seurat, and so on). When you're ready for an encore, head upstairs to the top floor and Room 8, where you'll find several Cézanne paintings, including...*

Paul Cézanne—*La Montagne Sainte-Victoire* (1882)

Cézanne could look out his studio window at this 3,300-foot-high mountain in Provence. Over a 20-year span, he painted the same mountain 60 different ways, each with its own color scheme and mood. This one—with a windblown branch framing the mountain from above—may reflect the turmoil of the fortysomething's life (father's death, stalled Impressionist career, shuttling between Paris and hometown Aix-en-Provence, the recent humiliation of having his childhood friend Emile Zola parody him in a novel).

The mountain is realistic, but the scene is carefully composed. The tree branch echoes the curving ridgeline, uniting foreground and background. A patch of paint forming a house (in the foreground) is the same size as a patch depicting a rock formation (in the background), further flattening this "distant" scene into a wall of brushstrokes. (Cézanne's "cube"-shaped brushstrokes inspired the Cubists, a decade later, to build figures using geometric shapes, to mix foreground and background, and to emphasize style over realism.) Cézanne juggles many technical balls of modern painting—a roughed-up surface texture done with thick brushwork, a self-imposed color scheme, abstract composition—and still manages to stay true to his Impressionist roots, painting the mountain he sees.

• *Move onward to see...*

The Rest of the Courtauld

Rooms 9-13 contain paintings by the pioneers of Modernism—20th-century artists Derain, Dufy, Kandinsky, Jawlensky, Modigliani, Vlaminck, and more. Many have the bright, bold colors and thick brushstrokes of the Fauvist style, from the time when Impressionism was merging into abstract. The museum rotates its large collection, so you may see a different mix.

You may also see works by members of Britain's own Bloomsbury Group—Roger Fry, Vanessa Bell, and Duncan Grant. This group of intellectual friends also included Virginia Woolf (Bell's sister), E. M. Forster, and the economist John Maynard Keynes. During the 1910s and 1920s, they met for cocktails, flirting, and high-minded discussions in their Bloomsbury neighborhood (east of the British Museum), and went on to fame in their respective fields.

BRITISH MUSEUM TOUR

In the 19th century, the British flag flew over one-fourth of the world. London was the empire's capital, where women in saris walked the streets with men in top hats. And England collected art as fast as it collected colonies.

The British Museum is *the* chronicle of Western civilization. History is a modern invention. Three hundred years ago, people didn't care about crumbling statues and dusty columns. Nowadays, we value a look at past civilizations, knowing that "those who don't learn from history are condemned to repeat it."

The British Museum is the only place I can think of where you can follow the rise and fall of three great civilizations—Egypt, Assyria (ancient Iraq), and Greece—in a few hours, with a coffee break in the middle. And, while the sun never set on the British Empire, it will on you, so on this tour we'll see just the most exciting two hours.

Orientation

Cost: Free, but a £5 donation is requested. (Take this opportunity to unload your spare change.) Interesting temporary exhibits usually require a separate admission (and a timed ticket).

Hours: The museum is open daily 10:00-17:30, Fri until 20:30 (not all galleries are open Fri night, but most of our tour is). The **Great Court**—the grand entrance with eateries, gift shops, and an exhibit gallery—is open daily 9:00-18:00, Fri until 20:30.

When to Go: Rainy days and Sundays are the most crowded times; the same goes for school holidays. The museum is least crowded late on weekday afternoons.

Getting There: The main entrance is on Great Russell Street. From

British Museum Overview

MONTAGUE PLACE

MONTAGUE PLACE
ENTRANCE

Russell
Square

← To Fitzrovia &
Charlotte Place
Eateries

UP TO
MUMMIES

CAFÉ

CAFÉ

E G Y P T

PARTHENON GALLERIES

G R E E C E

A S S Y R I A

ROSETTA
STONE

READING
ROOM
& SHOP

THE KING'S
GALLERY

MONTAGUE ST.

WC

WC

THE
GREAT
COURT

WINGED
LIONS

INFO

INFO

BOUTIQUE

BLOOMSBURY ST.

CLOAK-
ROOM

BOOK-
SHOP

CAFÉ

COLUMNS

Not to Scale

MAIN
ENTRANCE

GREAT RUSSELL STREET

To Tottenham
Court Road ⊖ (10 min. walk)

To Holborn ⊖
(10 min. walk)

BRITISH MUSEUM

the Tottenham Court Road Tube stop, take exit #3, then with the tall Centrepoint building on your right, walk to Museum Street and hang a left. If exit #3 is closed, take exit #1, cross the street and head up Tottenham Road (with the Dominion Theater on your right). Turn right on Greet Russell Street and follow all the way to the main entrance. The Holborn and Russell Square Tube stops are also nearby. Buses #38 and #24 are among the many that stop here (see page 28).

Information: Information desks are just inside the Great Court. You can pick up the basic map (£2 donation), but it's not essential for this tour. The *Visitor's Guide* (£3.50) offers 15 different tours and skimpy text. The main bookstore is inside the entrance on the left. General info tel. 020/7323-8299, ticket desk tel. 020/7323-8181, www. britishmuseum.org.

Tours: Free 30-minute **eyeOpener tours** are led by volunteers, who focus on select rooms (daily 11:00-15:45, generally every 15 minutes). Free 45-minute **gallery talks** on specific subjects are offered Tue-Sat at 13:15; a free 20-minute highlights tour is available on Friday evening.

The £5 **multimedia guide** offers dial-up audio commentary and video on 200 objects, as well as several theme tours (for example, 1.5-hour highlights tour or Parthenon sculptures tour). They're substantial and cerebral (must leave photo ID). There's also a fun children's multimedia guide (£3.50).

🎧 Download my free British Museum **audio tour.**

Length of This Tour: Allow at least two hours. If you have less time, be sure to see the Parthenon Galleries (㉖); you can skip the long upstairs detour to the mummies (❻) and go quickly through the Assyrian collection (⓬-⓳).

Cloakroom: £1.50 per item. You can carry a daypack in the galleries, but big backpacks must be checked.

Photography: Photos allowed without flash or tripod (but photos prohibited in the temporary exhibits).

Eateries: You have three choices inside the complex. The self-service Court Café (£4-5 sandwiches and salads) is in the Great Court ground floor. The pricier Court Restaurant (£15-18 entrées) is on the upper level atop the Reading Room. The cafeteria-style Gallery Café (£9-11 hot dishes; kids under 12 eat free with each paying adult) is deeper into the museum, near the Greek art in Room 12.

Near the museum, there are lots of fast, cheap, and colorful cafés, pubs, and markets along Great Russell Street and Museum Street. For other recommendations and some handy sit-down chains, see page 407. The sumptuous Princess Louise Pub is nearby (see page 400). No picnicking is allowed indoors, except on weekends and holidays, when the museum opens a family area in the basement under the Great Court. Karl Marx picnicked on the benches near the museum entrance and in nearby Russell Square.

Starring: Rosetta Stone, Egyptian mummies, Assyrian lions, and the Parthenon sculptures.

The Tour Begins

The main entrance on Great Russell Street spills you into the Great Court, a glass-domed space with the round Reading Room in the center. From the Great Court, doorways lead to all wings. To the left are the exhibits on Egypt, Assyria, and Greece—our tour. You'll notice that this tour does not follow the museum's numbered sequence of rooms. Instead, we'll try to hit the highlights as we work chronologically.

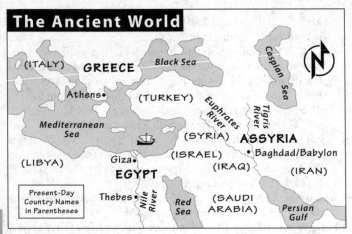

The Ancient World

(ITALY) GREECE Black Sea Caspian Sea
Athens• (TURKEY) Euphrates River Tigris River
Mediterranean Sea (SYRIA) ASSYRIA
(LIBYA) Giza• (ISRAEL) •Baghdad/Babylon
EGYPT (IRAQ) (IRAN)
Present-Day Country Names in Parentheses Thebes• Nile River Red Sea (SAUDI ARABIA) Persian Gulf

Enjoy the Great Court, Europe's largest covered square, which is bigger than a football field. This people-friendly court—delightfully spared from the London rain—was for 150 years one of London's great lost spaces...closed off and gathering dust. Since the year 2000, it's been the 140-foot-wide hub of a two-acre cultural complex.

The stately Reading Room now hosts special exhibitions, but in years past, it was a study hall for Oscar Wilde, Arthur Conan Doyle, Rudyard Kipling, T. S. Eliot, Virginia Woolf, W. B. Yeats, Mark Twain, and V. I. Lenin. Karl Marx formulated his ideas on communism and wrote *Das Kapital* here.

• *The Egyptian Gallery is in the West Wing, to the left of the round Reading Room. Enter the Egyptian Gallery. The Rosetta Stone is directly in front of you.*

ANCIENT EGYPT

Egypt was one of the world's first "civilizations"—a group of people with a government, religion, art, free time, and a written language. The Egypt we think of—pyramids, mummies, pharaohs, and guys who walk funny—lasted from 3000 to 1000 B.C. with hardly any change in the government, religion, or arts. Imagine two millennia of Nixon.

❶ The Rosetta Stone

When this rock was unearthed in the Egyptian desert in 1799, it was a sensation in Europe. This black slab, dating from 196 B.C., caused a quantum leap in the study of ancient history. Finally, Egyptian writing could be decoded.

The hieroglyphic writing in the upper part of the stone was indecipherable for a thousand years. Did a picture of a bird mean "bird"? Or was it a sound, forming part of a larger word, like "bur-

British Museum—Egypt

Not to Scale

To **5** & **6**

GREAT COURT & READING ROOM

1 Rosetta Stone
2 King Ramesses II
3 Egyptian Gods as Animals
4 Colossal Scarab
5 Up to Nebamun Hunting in the Marshes
6 Up to Mummies & Coffins
7 Head & Arm of Amenhotep III
8 Four Figures of Sekhmet
9 Beard Piece of Great Sphinx
10 False Door & Architrave of Ptahshepses
11 Statue of Nenkheftka

ASSYRIA

WINGED LIONS

CLOAKROOM

BRITISH MUSEUM

den"? As it turned out, hieroglyphics are a complex combination of the two, surprisingly more phonetic than symbolic. (For example,

ple, the hieroglyph that looks like a mouth or eye is the letter "R.")

The Rosetta Stone allowed linguists to break the code. It contains a single inscription repeated in three languages. The bottom third is plain old Greek (find your favorite frat or sorority), while the middle is medieval Egyptian. By comparing the two known languages with the one they didn't know, translators figured out the hieroglyphics.

The breakthrough came when they discovered that the large ovals (such as in the sixth line from the top) represented the name of the ruler, Ptolemy. Simple.

• *In the gallery to the right of the Stone, find the huge head of Ramesses.*

❷ King Ramesses II

When Moses told the king of Egypt, "Let my people go!" this was the stony-faced look he got. Ramesses II ruled for 66 years (c. 1290-1223 B.C.) and may have been in power when Moses cursed Egypt with plagues, freed the Israeli slaves, and led them out of Egypt to their homeland in Israel (according to the Bible, but not exactly corroborated by Egyptian chronicles).

This seven-ton statue (c. 1250 B.C.), made from two different colors of granite, is a fragment from a temple in Thebes. It shows Ramesses with the traditional features of a pharaoh—goatee, cloth headdress, and cobra diadem on his forehead. Ramesses was a great builder of temples, palaces, tombs, and statues of himself. There are probably more statues of him in the world than there are cheesy fake *David*s. He was so concerned about achieving immortality that he even chiseled his own name on other people's statues. Very cheeky.

Picture what the archaeologists saw when they came upon this: a colossal head and torso separated from the enormous legs and toppled into the sand—all that remained of the works of a once-great pharaoh. Kings, megalomaniacs, and workaholics, take note.

• Say, *"Ooh, heavy,"* and climb the ramp behind Ramesses, looking for animals.

❸ Egyptian Gods as Animals

Before technology made humans the alpha animal on earth, it was easier to appreciate our fellow creatures. Animals were stronger, swifter, and fiercer than feeble *Homo sapiens*. The Egyptians worshipped animals as incarnations of the gods.

Though the displays here change, you may see the powerful ram—the god Amun (king of the gods)—protecting a puny pharaoh under his powerful chin. The falcon is Horus, the god of the living. The speckled, standing hippo (with lion head) is Tawaret, protectress of childbirth. Her stylized breasts and pregnant belly are supported by ankhs, symbols of life. (Is Tawaret grinning or grimacing in labor?) Finally, the cat (with ear- and nose-rings) served Bastet, the popular goddess of stress relief.

Scattered around the floor are huge stone boxes. The famous mummies of ancient Egypt were wrapped in linen and then encased in finely decorated wooden coffins, which were then placed in these massive stone outer coffins.

• *At the end of the Egyptian Gallery is a big stone beetle.*

❹ Colossal Scarab

This species of beetle would burrow into the ground, then reappear—it's a symbol of resurrection, like the sun rising and setting,

or death and rebirth. Scarab amulets were placed on mummies' chests to protect the spirit's heart from acting impulsively. Pharaohs wore the symbol of the beetle, and tombs and temples were decorated with them (this one, from c. 332 B.C., probably once sat in a temple). The hieroglyph for scarab meant "to come into being."

Like the scarab, Egyptian culture was buried—first by Greece, then by Rome. Knowledge of the ancient writing died, condemning the culture to obscurity. But since the discovery of the Rosetta Stone, Egyptology has boomed, and Egypt has come back to life.

• *You can't call Egypt a wrap until you visit the mummies upstairs. Continue to the end of the gallery and up the West Stairs (four flights or elevator) to Floor 3. At the top, turn left into Room 61, with objects and wall paintings from the tomb of Nebamun.*

❺ Painting of Nebamun Hunting in the Marshes

Nebamun stands in a reed boat, gliding through the marshes. He raises his arm, ready to bean a bird with a snakelike hunting stick. On the right, his wife looks on, while his daughter crouches between his legs, a symbol of fatherly protection.

This nobleman walks like Egyptian statues look— stiff and flat, like he was just run over by a pyramid. We see the torso from the front and everything else—arms, legs, face—in profile, creating the funny walk that has become an Egyptian cliché. (Like an early version of Cubism, we see various perspectives at once.)

But the stiffness is softened by a human touch. It's a family snapshot of loved ones from a happy time. The birds, fish, and plants are painted realistically, like encyclopedia entries. (The first "paper" came from papyrus plants like the bush on the left.) The only unrealistic element is the house cat (thigh-high, in front of the man) acting as a retriever—possibly the only cat in history that ever did anything useful.

When Nebamun passed into the afterlife, his awakening soul could look at this painting (c. 1350 B.C.) on the tomb wall and think of his wife and daughter—doing what they loved for all eternity.

• *Browse through Rooms 62-63, filled with displays in glass cases.*

❻ The Egyptian Funeral

To mummify a body, you first disembowel it (but leave the heart inside), then pack the cavities with pitch, and dry it with natron, a natural form of sodium carbonate (and, I be-

lieve, the active ingredient in Twinkies). Then carefully bandage it head to toe with hundreds of yards of linen strips. Let it sit 2,000 years, and...*voilà!* Or just dump the corpse in the desert and let the hot, dry, bacteria-killing Egyptian sand do the work—you'll get the same results.

The mummy was placed in a wooden coffin, which was put in a stone coffin, which was placed in a tomb. (The pyramids were super-sized tombs for the rich and famous.) The re-

sult is that we now have Egyptian bodies that are as well preserved as Larry King.

The internal organs were preserved alongside the mummy in canopic jars, and small-scale statuettes of the deceased *(shabtis)* were scattered around. Written in hieroglyphs on the coffins and the tomb walls were burial rites from the Book of the Dead. These were magical spells to protect the body and crib notes for the waking soul, who needed to know these passwords to get past the guardians of eternity.

Many of the mummies here are from the time of the Roman occupation, when fine memorial portraits painted in wax became popular. X-ray photos in the display cases tell us more about these people.

Don't miss the animal mummies. Cats (Room 62) were popular pets. They were also considered incarnations of the cat-headed goddess Bastet. Worshipped in life as the sun god's allies, preserved in death, and memorialized with statues, cats were given the adulation they've come to expect ever since.

• *Linger in Rooms 62 and 63, but remember that eternity is about the amount of time it takes to see this entire museum. In Room 64, in a glass case, you'll find what's left of a visitor who tried to see it all...*

Gebelein Man, Known as "Ginger"

This man died 5,400 years ago, a thousand years before the pyramids. His people buried him in the fetal position, where he could

"sleep" for eternity. The hot sand naturally dehydrated and protected the body. With him are a few of his possessions: bowls, beads, and the flint blade next to his arm. His grave was covered with stones. Named "Ginger" by scientists for his wisps of red hair, this man from a distant time seems very human.

• *Backtrack to Room 61 and head back down the stairs to the Egyptian Gallery and the Rosetta Stone. Just past the Rosetta Stone, find a huge head (facing away from you) with a hat like a bowling pin.*

❼ Head and Arm of a Statue of Amenhotep III

Art served as propaganda for the pharaohs, kings who called themselves gods on earth. Put this red granite head (c. 1370 B.C.) on

top of an enormous body (which still stands in Egypt), and you have the intimidating image of an omnipotent ruler who demands servile obedience. Next to the head is, appropriately, the pharaoh's powerful fist—the long arm of the law.

Amenhotep's crown is actually two crowns in one. The pointed upper half is the royal cap of Upper Egypt. This rests on the flat, fez-like crown symbolizing Lower Egypt. A pharaoh wearing both crowns together is bragging that he rules a combined Egypt. As both "Lord of the Two Lands" and "High Priest of Every Temple," the pharaoh united church and state.

• *Along the wall to the left of the red granite head (as you're facing it) are four black lion-headed statues.*

❽ Four Figures of the Goddess Sekhmet

The lion-headed goddess Sekhmet looks pretty sedate here (in these sculptures dating c. 1360 B.C.), but she could spring into a fierce crouch when crossed. She was the pharaoh's personal bodyguard, who could burn his enemies to a crisp with flaming arrows.

The gods ruled the Egyptian cosmos like dictators in a big banana republic (or the US Congress). Egyptians bribed their gods for favors, offering food, animals, or money, or erecting statues like these.

Sekhmet holds an ankh. This key-shaped cross was the hieroglyph meaning "life" and was a symbol of eternal life. Later, it was adopted as a Christian symbol because of its cross shape and religious overtones.

• *Continuing down the Egyptian Gallery, a few paces directly in front of you and to the left, find a glass case containing a...*

❾ Beard Piece of the Great Sphinx

The Great Sphinx—a statue of a pharaoh-headed lion—crouches in the shadow of the Great Pyramids in Cairo. Time shaved off

the sphinx's soft, goatee-like limestone beard, and a piece is now preserved here in a glass case. This hunk of stone is only a whisker—about three percent of the massive beard—giving an idea of the scale of the six-story-tall, 250-foot-long statue.

The Sphinx is as old as the pyramids (c. 2500 B.C.), built during the time known to historians as the Old Kingdom (2686-2181 B.C.), but this beard may have been added later, during a restoration (c. 1420 B.C., or perhaps even later under Ramesses II).

• *Ten steps past the Sphinx's soul patch is a 10-foot-tall, red-tinted "building" covered in hieroglyphics.*

❿ False Door and Architrave of Ptahshepses

This limestone "false door" (c. 2400 B.C.) was a ceremonial entrance (never meant to open) for a sealed building, called a *mastaba*, that marked the grave of a man named Ptahshepses. The hieroglyphs of eyes, birds, and rabbits serve as his epitaph, telling his life story, how he went to school with the pharaoh's kids, became an honored vizier, and married the pharaoh's daughter.

The deceased was mummified, placed in a wooden coffin that was encased in a stone coffin, then in a stone sarcophagus (like the **red-granite sarcophagus** in front of Ptahshepses' door), and buried 50 feet beneath the *mastaba* in an underground chamber.

Mastabas like Ptahshepses' were decorated inside and out with statues, steles, and frescoes like those displayed nearby. These pictured things that the soul would find useful in the next life—magical spells, lists of the deceased's accomplishments, snapshots of the deceased and his family while alive, and secret passwords from the Egyptian Book of the Dead. False doors like this allowed the soul (but not grave robbers) to come and go.

• *Just past Ptahshepses' false door is a glass case with a red-tinted statue.*

⑪ Statue of Nenkheftka

Painted statues such as this one (c. 2400 B.C.) represented the soul of the deceased. Meant to keep alive the memory and personality of the departed, this image would have greeted Nenkheftka's loved ones when they brought food offerings to place at his feet to nourish his soul. (In the mummification rites, the mouth was ritually opened, to prepare it to eat soul food.)

In ancient Egypt, you *could* take it with you. The Egyptians believed that after death, your soul lived on, enjoying its earthly possessions—sometimes including servants, who might be walled up alive with their dead master. (Remember that even the great pyramids were just big tombs for Egypt's most powerful.)

Statues functioned as a refuge for the soul on its journey after death. The rich scattered statues of themselves everywhere, just in case. Statues needed to be simple and easy to recognize, mug shots for eternity: stiff, arms down, chin up, nothing fancy. This one has all the essential features, like the simplified human figures on international traffic signs. To a soul caught in the fast lane of astral travel, this symbolic statue would be easier to spot than a more detailed one.

With their fervent hope for life after death, Egyptians created calm, dignified art that seems built for eternity.

• *Relax. One civilization down, two to go. Near the end of the gallery, on the right, are two huge, winged Assyrian lions (with bearded human heads) standing guard over the Assyrian exhibit halls.*

ANCIENT ASSYRIA

Long before Saddam Hussein, Iraq was home to other palace-building, iron-fisted rulers—the Assyrians.

Assyria was the lion, the king of beasts of early Middle Eastern civilizations. These Semitic people from the agriculturally challenged hills of northern Iraq became traders and conquerors, not farmers. They conquered their southern neighbors and dominated the Middle East for 300 years (c. 900-600 B.C.).

Their strength came from a superb army (chariots, mounted cavalry, and siege engines), a policy of terrorism against enemies ("I tied their heads to tree trunks all around the city," reads a royal inscription), ethnic cleansing and mass deportations of the vanquished, and efficient administration (roads and express postal service). They have been called the "Romans of the East."

The British Museum's valuable collection of Assyrian artifacts has become even more priceless since the recent destruction of ancient sites in Iraq by ISIS terrorists.

⑰ Two Human-Headed Winged Lions

These stone lions guarded an Assyrian palace (11th-8th century B.C.). With the strength of a lion, the wings of an eagle, the brain of a man, and the beard of ZZ Top, they protected the king from evil spirits and scared the heck out of foreign ambassadors and left-wing newspaper reporters. (What has five legs and flies? Take a close look. These winged quintupeds, which appear complete from both the front and the side, could guard both directions at once.)

Carved into the stone between the bearded lions' loins, you can see one of civilization's most impressive achievements—writing. This wedge-shaped **(cuneiform)** script is the world's first written language, invented 5,000 years ago by the Sumerians (of southern Iraq) and passed down to their less-civilized descendants, the Assyrians.

• *Walk between the lions, glance at the large reconstructed wooden gates from*

British Museum—Assyria

ROOM 8

ROOM 23

⑯

N I M R U D

G R E E C E

⑰

⑱

⑲

ROOM 10

E G Y P T

⑮

⑭

ROOM 7

G A L L E R Y

⑬

WINGED LIONS

⑫

Not to Scale

⑫ Winged Lions
⑬ Ashurnasirpal II's Palace at Nimrud
⑭ Battle Scene Panels
⑮ Plaque of the Northwest Palace & Symbolic Scene Panel
⑯ Two Winged Bulls
⑰ Royal Lion Hunts
⑱ The Lion-Hunt Room
⑲ Dying Lioness

BRITISH MUSEUM

an Assyrian palace, and turn right into the long, narrow red gallery (Room 7) lined with stone relief panels.

⑬ Ashurnasirpal II's Palace at Nimrud

This gallery is a mini version of the throne room and royal apartments of King Ashurnasirpal II's Northwest Palace at Nimrud (9th century B.C.). Entering, you would have seen the king on his throne at the far end, surrounded by these pleasant, sand-colored, gypsum relief panels (which were, however, originally painted and varnished).

That's Ashurnasirpal himself in the **first panel on your right,** with braided beard, earring, and fez-like crown, flanked by his

supernatural hawk-headed henchmen, who sprinkle incense on him with pinecones. The bulging forearms tell us that Ashurnasirpal II (r. 883-859 B.C.) was a conqueror's conqueror who enjoyed his reputation as a merciless warrior, using torture and humiliation as part of his distinctive management style. The room's panels chronicle his bloody career.

Under Ashurnasirpal's reign, the Assyrians dominated the Mideast from their capital at Nineveh (near modern Mosul). Ashurnasirpal II proved his power by building a brand-new palace in nearby Nimrud (called "Calah" in the Bible).

The cuneiform inscription running through the center of the panel is Ashurnasirpal's résumé: "The king who has enslaved all mankind, the mighty warrior who steps on the necks of his enemies, tramples all foes and shatters the enemy; the weapon of the gods, the mighty king, the King of Assyria, the king of the world, B.A., M.B.A., Ph.D., etc...."

• *A dozen paces farther down, on the left wall, are several relief panels (among many in this room) that are worth focusing on.*

⓮ Panels with Battle Scenes

Many "nations" conquered by the Assyrians consisted of little more than a single walled city. Find the panel in which the Assyrians lay siege with a crude "tank" that shields them as they advance to the city walls to smash down the gate with a battering ram. The king stands a safe distance away behind the juggernaut and bravely shoots arrows.

Nearby, another panel shows enemy soldiers fleeing the slings and arrows of outrageous Assyrians by swimming across the Euphrates, using inflated animal bladders as life preservers. Their friends in the castle downstream applaud their ingenuity.

After that, prisoners are paraded before the Assyrian king, who is shaded by a parasol. Ashurnasirpal II sneers and tells the captured chief, "Drop and give me 50." Above the prisoners' heads, we see the rich spoils of war—elephant tusks, metal pots, and so on. The Assyrians, whose economy depended on booty, depopulated conquered lands by slavery and ethnic cleansing, then moved in Assyrian settlers.

• *On the opposite wall is an artist's rendering of what the palace would have looked like.*

⓯ Plaque of the Northwest Palace and Symbolic Scene Panel

The plaque shows the king at the far end of the throne room, shaded by a parasol and flanked by winged lions. (In the diagram of the palace's floor plan, the throne room is Room B.) The 30,000-square-foot palace was built atop a 50-acre artificial mound. The new palace was inaugurated with a 10-day banquet (according to an inscription), where the king picked up the tab for 69,574 of his closest friends.

The relief panel (immediately to the right) labeled **Symbolic**

Scene stood behind the throne. It shows the king (and his double) tending the tree of life while reaching up to receive the ring of kingship from the winged sun god.
• *Exit the gallery at the far end, then hang a U-turn left. Pause at the entrance of Room 10c to see the impressive...*

⓰ Two Winged Bulls from the Palace of Sargon

These marble bulls (c. 710-705 B.C.) guarded the entrance to the city of Dur-Sharrukin ("Sargonsburg"), a new capital (near Nineveh/Mosul) with vast palaces built by Sargon II (r. 721-705 B.C.). The 30-ton bulls were cut from a single block, tipped on their sides, then dragged to their place by POWs. (In modern times, when the British transported them here, they had to cut them in half; you can see the horizontal cracks through the bulls' chests.)

Sargon II gained his reputation as a general by subduing the Israelites after a three-year siege of Jerusalem (2 Kings 17:1-6). He solidified his conquest by ethnically cleansing the area and deporting many Israelites (inspiring legends of the "Lost" Ten Tribes).

In 710 B.C., while these bulls were being carved for his palace, Sargon II marched victoriously through the streets of Babylon (near present-day Baghdad), having put down a revolt there against him. His descendants would also have to deal with the troublesome Babylonians.
• *Sneak between these bulls and veer right (into Room 10), where horses are being readied for the big hunt.*

⓱ Royal Lion Hunts from the North Palace of Ashurbanipal

Lion hunting was Assyria's sport of kings. On the right wall are horses; on the left are the hunting dogs. And next to them, lions, resting peacefully in a garden, unaware that they will shortly be rousted, stampeded, and slaughtered.

Lions lived in Mesopotamia up until modern times, and it was the king's duty to keep the lion population down to protect farmers and herdsmen. This duty soon became sport, with staged hunts and zoo-bred lions, as the kings of men proved their power by taking on the king of beasts.

• *Continue ahead into the larger lion-hunt room. Reading the panels like a comic strip, start on the right and gallop counterclockwise.*

⑱ The Lion-Hunt Room

In these panels (c. 650 B.C.), the king's men release lions from their cages, then riders on horseback herd them into an enclosed arena.

The king has them cornered. Let the slaughter begin. The chariot carries King Ashurbanipal, the great-grandson of Sargon II (not to be confused with Ashurnasirpal II, who ruled 200 years earlier, mentioned previously).

The last of Assyria's great kings, Ashurbanipal has reigned now for 50 years. Having left a half-dozen corpses in his wake, he moves on, while spearmen hold off lions attacking from the rear.

• *At about the middle of the long wall...*

The fleeing lions, cornered by hounds, shot through with arrows, and weighed down by fatigue, begin to fall. The lead lion carries on even while vomiting blood.

This low point of Assyrian cruelty is, perhaps, the high point of their artistic achievement. It's a curious coincidence that civilizations often produce their greatest art in their declining years. Hmm.

• *On the wall opposite the vomiting lion is the...*

⑲ Dying Lioness

A lion roars in pain and frustration. She tries to run, but her body is too heavy. Her muscular hind legs, once a source of power, are now paralyzed.

Like these brave, fierce lions, Assyria's once-great warrior nation was slain. Shortly after Ashurbanipal's death, Assyria was conquered, and its capital at Nineveh was sacked and looted by an ascendant Babylon (612 B.C.). The mood of tragedy, dignity, and proud struggle in a hopeless cause makes this dying lioness one of the most beautiful of human creations.

• *Exit the lion-hunt room at the far end and make your way back to the huge, winged lions at the start of the Assyrian exhibit. To reach the Greek section, exit Assyria between the winged lions and make a U-turn to the right, into Room 11.*

*You'll walk past (**20**) early Greek Barbie and Ken dolls from the Cycladic period (2500 B.C.). Continue into Room 12 (the hungry can go straight to the Gallery Café), and turn right, into Room 13, filled with Greek vases in glass cases.*

ANCIENT GREECE

The history of ancient Greece (600 B.C.–A.D. 1) could be subtitled "making order out of chaos." While Assyria was dominating the Middle East, "Greece"—a gaggle of warring tribes roaming the Greek peninsula—was floundering in darkness. But by about 700 B.C., these tribes began settling down, experimenting with democracy, forming self-governing city-states, and making ties with other city-states. Scarcely two centuries later, they would be a relatively united community and the center of the civilized world.

During its Golden Age (500-430 B.C.), Greece set the tone for all of Western civilization to follow. Democracy, theater, literature, mathematics, philosophy, science, gyros, art, and architecture, as we know them, were virtually all invented by a single generation of Greeks in a small town of maybe 80,000 citizens.

• *Roughly in the middle of Room 13 is a Z-shaped glass case marked #8. On the lower shelf, the item marked #137 is a...*

21 Black-Figured Amphora with Achilles Killing Penthesilea

Greeks poured wine from jars like this one, which is painted with a legend from the Trojan War. The Trojan War (c. 1200 B.C.)—part fact but mostly legend—symbolized Greece's long struggle to rise above war and chaos.

On the vessel (540-530 B.C.), Achilles of Greece faces off against the Queen of the Amazons, Penthesilea, who was fighting for Troy. (The Amazons were a legendary race of warrior women who cut off one breast to facilitate their archery skills.) Achilles bears down, plunging a spear through her neck, as blood spurts. In her dying moment, Penthesilea looks

British Museum—Greece

PARTHENON GALLERIES

Not to Scale

ROOM 17
ROOM 18
ROOM 15
ROOM 14
ROOM 13
ROOM 12

ASSYRIA
EGYPT

WINGED LIONS
CLOAKROOM

WC
GALLERY CAFE
RM 11

20 Cycladic Figures
21 Black-Figured Amphora
22 Map of the Greek World
23 Idealized Youth
24 Wine Cooler
25 Nereid Monument
26 Parthenon Galleries

up, her gaze locking on Achilles. His eyes bulge wide, and he falls instantly in love with her. She dies, and Achilles is smitten.

Greek pottery was a popular export product for the sea-trading Greeks. Their earliest pots featured geometric patterns (8th century B.C.), then evolved into painted black silhouettes on the natural orange clay, before switching to red figures on black backgrounds. On this jar, see the names of the two enemies/lovers ("AXILEV" and "PENOESIIEA") as well as the signature of the craftsman, Exekias.

• Continue to Room 15, then relax on a bench and read, surrounded by statues and vases in glass cases. On the entrance wall, find a...

22 Map of the Greek World, 520-430 B.C.

After Greece drove out Persian invaders in 480 B.C., the city of Athens became the most powerful of the city-states and the center of the Greek world. Golden Age Greece was never really a full-fledged empire, but more a common feeling of unity among Greek-speaking people.

A century after the Golden Age, Greek culture was spread still farther by Alexander the Great, who conquered the Mediterranean world and beyond (including Persia). By 300 B.C., the "Greek" world stretched from Italy and Egypt to India (including most of what used to be the Assyrian Empire). Two hundred years later, this Greek-speaking Hellenistic Empire was conquered by the Romans.

• There's a nude male statue (missing his arms and legs) on the left side of the room.

㉓ Torso of an Idealized Youth (Kouros)

The Greeks saw their gods in human form...and human beings were godlike. They invented a statue type—the kouros (literally, "youth")—to showcase idealized bod-
ies. In this example (c. 520-510 B.C.), the youth would have exemplified the divine orderliness of the universe with his once perfectly round head (it's now missing), symmetrical pecs, and navel in the center. The ideal man was geometri-cally perfect, a balance of opposites, the Golden Mean. In a statue, that meant finding the right balance between move-ment and stillness, between realistic human anatomy (with human flaws) and the perfection of a Greek god. Our youth is still a bit uptight, stiff as the rock from which he's carved. But—as we'll see—in
just a few short decades, the Greeks would cut loose and create realistic statues that seemed to move like real humans.

• *Two-thirds of the way down Room 15 (on the left) is a glass case containing a vase.*

㉔ Red-Figured Wine Cooler Signed by Douris as Painter

This clay vessel (490 B.C.), called a *psykter,* would have been topped off with wine and floated in a bowl of cooling water. Its red-

figure drawings show satyrs at a *symposium,* or drinking party. These half-man/half-animal creatures (notice their tails) had a reputation for lewd behavior, reminding the balanced and moderate Greeks of their rude roots.

The reveling figures painted on this jar are realistic and three-dimensional; their move-ments are more naturalistic than the literally three-dimensional but quite stiff kouros. The Greeks are beginning to conquer the natural world in art. The art, like life, is more in balance. And speaking of "balance," if that's a Greek sobriety test, revel on.

• *Carry on into Room 17 and sit facing the Greek temple at the far end.*

㉕ Nereid Monument

Greek temples (like this reconstruction of a temple-shaped tomb from Xanthos, c. 390-380 B.C.) housed a statue of a god or goddess. Unlike Christian churches, which serve as meeting places, Greek temples were the gods' homes. Worshippers gathered outside, so the most impressive part of the temple was its exterior. Temples were rectangular buildings surrounded by rows of columns and topped by slanted roofs.

The triangle-shaped space above the columns—the pediment—is filled with sculpture. Supporting the pediment are decorative relief panels, called metopes. Now look through the columns to the building itself. Above the doorway, another set of relief panels—the frieze—runs around the building (under the eaves).

The statues between the columns are Nereids—friendly sea nymphs with dramatic wave-like poses and wind-blown clothes; some appear to be borne aloft by sea animals. Notice the sculptor's delight in capturing the body in motion, and the way the wet clothes cling to the figures' anatomy.

Next, we'll see pediment, frieze, and metope decorations from Greece's greatest temple.

• *Enter through the glass doors labeled* Parthenon Galleries. *(The rooms branching off the entryway usually have helpful exhibits that reconstruct the Parthenon and its once-colorful sculptures.)*

㉖ Parthenon Galleries

If you were to leave the British Museum, take the Tube to Heathrow, and fly to Athens, there, in the center of the old city, on top of

the high, flat hill known as the Acropolis, you'd find the Parthenon—the temple dedicated to Athena, goddess of wisdom and the patroness of Athens. It was the crowning glory of an enormous urban-renewal plan during Greece's Golden Age. After Athens was ruined in a war with Persia, the city—under the bold leadership of Pericles—constructed the greatest building of its day (447-432 B.C.). The Parthenon was a model of balance, simplicity, and harmonious elegance, the symbol of the Golden Age. Phidias, the greatest Greek sculptor, decorated the exterior with statues and relief panels.

While the building itself remains in Athens, many of the Parthenon's best sculptures are right here in the British Museum—the so-called Elgin Marbles, named for the shrewd British ambassador

British Museum—Parthenon Galleries

Not to Scale

PEDIMENT

6

7

8 METOPES

FRIEZE

2
3

FRIEZE

1

4
5

NEREID MONUMENT

To Egypt →

ROOM 17

ROOM 18

1 Panel #136
2 Panel #67
3 Panel #61
4 Panel #35
5 Panel #29
6 Pediment Sculptures
7 Metope Panels #XXXI & #XXX
8 Metope Panels #XXVIII & #XXVII

BRITISH MUSEUM

who had his men hammer, chisel, and saw them off the Parthenon in the early 1800s. Though the Greek government complains about losing its marbles, the Brits feel they rescued and preserved the sculptures. The often-bitter controversy continues.

The marble panels you see lining the walls of this large hall are part of the frieze that originally ran around the exterior of the Parthenon, under the eaves. The statues at either end of the hall once filled the Parthenon's triangular-shaped pediments. Near the pediment sculptures, we'll also find the relief panels known as metopes.

The Frieze: These 56 relief panels show Athens' "Fourth of July" parade, celebrating the birth of the city. On this day, citizens marched up the Acropolis to symbolically present a new robe to the 40-foot-tall gold-and-ivory statue of Athena housed in the Parthenon. The

grand parade featured chariots, musicians, children, animals for sacrifice, and young maidens with offerings.

• *Start at the panels by the entrance (#136), and work counterclockwise.*

Men on horseback lead the parade, all heading in the same direction—uphill. Prance on.

Notice the muscles and veins in the horses' legs and the intricate folds in the cloaks and dresses. Some panels have holes drilled in

them, where gleaming bronze reins were fitted to heighten the festive look. All of these panels were originally painted in realistic colors. As you move along, notice that, despite the bustle of figures posed every which way, the frieze has one unifying element—all the people's heads are at the same level, creating a single ribbon around the Parthenon.

• *Cross to the opposite wall.*

A three-horse chariot **(#67)**, cut from only a few inches of marble, is more lifelike and three-dimensional than anything the Egyptians achieved in a freestanding statue.

Enter the girls (five yards to the left, **#61**), the heart of the procession. Dressed in pleated robes, they shuffle past the parade marshals, carrying incense burners and jugs of wine and bowls to pour out an offering to the thirsty gods.

The procession culminates **(#35)** in the presentation of the robe to Athena. A man and a child fold the robe for the goddess while the rest of the gods look on. There are Zeus and Hera **(#29)**, the king and queen of the gods, seated, enjoying the fashion show and wondering what length hemlines will be this year.

• *Head for the set of pediment sculptures at the far right end of the hall.*

The Pediment Sculptures: These statues were originally nes-

Centaurs Slain Around the World

Dateline 500 B.C.—Greece, China, India: Man no longer considers himself an animal. Bold new ideas are exploding simultaneously around the world. Socrates, Confucius, Buddha, and others are independently discovering a nonmaterial, unseen order in nature and in man. They say man has a rational mind or soul. He's separate from nature and different from the other animals.

tled nicely in the triangular pediment above the columns at the Parthenon's main (east) entrance. The missing statues at the peak of the triangle once showed the birth of Athena. Zeus had his head split open, allowing Athena, the goddess of wisdom, to rise from his brain fully grown and fully armed, inaugurating the Golden Age of Athens.

The other gods at this Olympian banquet slowly become aware of the amazing event. The first to notice is the one closest to them, Hebe, the cupbearer of the gods (tallest surviving fragment). Frightened, she runs to tell the others, her dress whipping behind her. A startled Demeter (just left of Hebe) turns toward Hebe.

The only one who hasn't lost his head is laid-back Dionysus (the cool guy farther left). He just raises another glass of wine to his lips. Over on the right, Aphrodite, goddess of love, leans back into her mother's lap, too busy admiring her own bare shoulder to even notice the hubbub. A chess-set

horse's head screams, "These people are nuts—let me out of here!"

The scene had a message. Just as wise Athena rose above the

lesser gods, who were scared, drunk, or vain, so would her city, Athens, rise above her lesser rivals.

This is amazing workmanship. Compare Dionysus, with his natural, relaxed, reclining pose, to all those stiff Egyptian statues standing eternally at attention.

Appreciate the folds of the clothes on the female figures (on the right half), especially Aphrodite's clinging, rumpled robe.

Some sculptors would first build a nude model of their figure, put real clothes on it, and study how the cloth hung down before actually sculpting in marble. Others found inspiration at the *taverna* on wet T-shirt night.

Even without their heads, these statues, with their detailed anatomy and expressive poses, speak volumes.

Wander behind. The statues originally sat 40 feet above the ground. The backs of the statues, which were never intended to be seen, are almost as detailed as the fronts.

• *The metopes are the panels on the walls to either side. Start with the three South Metope panels on the right wall.*

The Metopes: In the central panel of the three **(#XXXI),** a centaur grabs a man by the throat while the man pulls his hair. The humans have invited some centaurs—wild half-man/half-horse creatures—to a wedding feast. All goes well until the brutish centaurs, the original party animals, get too drunk and try to carry off the women. A battle ensues.

The centaur does the hair-pulling, and begins to drive the man to his knees **(#XXX).**

The Greeks prided themselves on creating order out of chaos. Within just a few generations, they went from nomadic barbarism to the pinnacle of early Western civilization. These metopes tell the story of this struggle between the forces of human civilization and animal-like barbarism.

On the opposite wall (center, **#XXVIII**), the centaurs take control of the party, as one rears back and prepares to trample the helpless man. The leopard skin draped over the centaur's arm roars a taunt. The humans lose face.

To the left (**#XXVII**), the humans finally rally and drive off the brutish centaurs. A centaur tries to run, but the man grabs him by the neck and raises his (missing) right hand to run him through. The man's folded cloak sets off his smooth skin and graceful figure.

The centaurs have been defeated. Civilization has triumphed over barbarism, order over chaos, and rational man over his half-animal alter ego.

Why are the Parthenon sculptures so treasured? The British of the 19th century saw themselves as the new "civilized" race, subduing "barbarians" in their far-flung empire. Maybe these carved stones made them stop and wonder—will our great civilization also turn to rubble?

THE REST OF THE MUSEUM

You've toured only the foundations of Western civilization on the ground floor of the West Wing. Upstairs you'll find still more artifacts from these ancient lands, plus Rome and the medieval civilization that sprang from it. Locate the rooms with themes you find interesting (Etruscan, Persian, Roman Britain, Dark Age Europe, and so on) and explore. Some highlights:

Lindow Man (a.k.a. the Bog Man): This victim of a Druid human-sacrifice ritual, with wounds still visible, was preserved for 2,000 years in a peat bog (Room 50, upper floor, via East Stairs).

Sutton Hoo Ship-Burial: Finds from a seventh-century Anglo-Saxon burial site (Room 41, upper floor, via East Stairs).

Treasures of the Persian Civilization: The collection here is far better than what remains to be seen in Iran (Room 52, upper floor).

Michelangelo's Drawings: The museum owns a complete cartoon (a full-scale preliminary drawing for another work of art) by Michelangelo—it's one of only two that survive (Room 90, level

4, accessed via the North Stairs or from the top of the Reading Room).

Enlightenment Gallery: Formerly known as the King's Library, this room held the British Library's treasures when it was founded in 1753. Today it displays objects that reveal the learning and wonder of the Age of Discovery (Room 1; the long hall to the right of the main entry).

And, of course, history doesn't begin and end in Europe. Look for remnants of the sophisticated, exotic cultures of Asia and the Americas (in North Wing, ground floor) and Africa (lower floor)—all part of the totem pole of the human family.

BRITISH LIBRARY TOUR

The British Empire built its greatest monuments out of paper. It's through literature that England has made her lasting contribution to history and the arts. These national archives of Britain include more than 150 million items. A copy of every publication in the UK and Ireland is sent here. It's all housed on 380 miles of shelving in the deepest basement in London.

But everything that matters for your visit is in the delightful Sir John Ritblat Gallery and an adjacent room containing the Magna Carta. We'll concentrate on a handful of documents—literary and historical—that changed the course of history. Start with these top stops, then stray according to your interests.

Orientation

Cost: Free (£5 suggested donation); admission charged for some special exhibits.

Hours: Mon-Fri 9:30-18:00, Tue until 20:00, Sat 9:30-17:00, Sun 11:00-17:00.

Getting There: From the King's Cross St. Pancras Tube station, exit to Euston Road, turn right, and walk a block west to 96 Euston Road, where you'll see a humble brick building dating from 1998. Euston Tube station is also nearby. Buses #10, #30, #59, #63, #73, and #91 (among others) also stop nearby.

Rotating Exhibits: Exhibits change often, and many of the museum's old, fragile manuscripts need to "rest" periodically in order to stay well-preserved. Even some of the major items I describe here could be napping out of view (likely candidates are *The Canterbury Tales* and *Alice's Adventures in Wonderland*). Items usually on view include the Magna Carta (which may take a short snooze after celebrating its 800th anniversary in

2015), Shakespeare's First Folio, Leonardo da Vinci's note-books, and at least one book by Jane Austen. If your heart's set on seeing that one particular rare Dickens book or letter penned by Gandhi, call ahead to make sure it's on display.

Information: Tel. 019/3754-6060; general info tel. 020/7412-7676, www.bl.uk.

Tours: There are no guided tours or audioguides for the permanent collection. There are, however, guided tours of the building itself—the archives and reading rooms (for details, call 020/7412-7639 or see the website). Touch-screen computers in the permanent collection let you page virtually through some of the rare books.

🎧 Download my free British Library **audio tour.**

Length of This Tour: Allow one hour.

Cloakroom: Free. Pay lockers (no large bags). For security, bags may be searched at the library entrance.

Services: There's free Wi-Fi throughout the library.

Photography: No photos allowed.

Eating: The upper-level restaurant has good hot meals. The ground-floor café (sandwiches and drinks) is next to the vast and fun pull-out stamp collection.

Starring: Bibles, Shakespeare, English Lit 101, Magna Carta, and—ladies and gentlemen—the Beatles.

The Tour Begins

Entering the library courtyard, you'll see a big statue of a naked Isaac Newton bending forward with a compass to measure the universe. The statue symbolizes the library's purpose: to gather all knowledge and promote humanity's endless search for truth.

Stepping inside, you'll find the information desk and shop (the cloakroom and WC are down a short staircase to the right). A 50-foot-tall wall of 65,000 books teasingly exposes its shelves in the middle of the building. In 1823 King George IV gifted the collection to the people under the condition the books remain on display for all to see. The high-tech bookshelf—with moveable lifts to reach the highest titles—sits behind glass, inaccessible to commoners but ever-visible. Likewise, the reading rooms upstairs are not open to the public. The PACCAR Gallery, down a few steps to the left, houses temporary exhibits (sometimes requiring an admission charge).

Our tour is of the tiny but exciting area variously called "The Sir John Ritblat Gallery," "Treasures of the British Library," or just "The Treasures." This priceless literary and historical collection is held in one large, carefully designed, dimly lit room.

• *The entrance to the Treasures room is directly ahead, up the stairs to the*

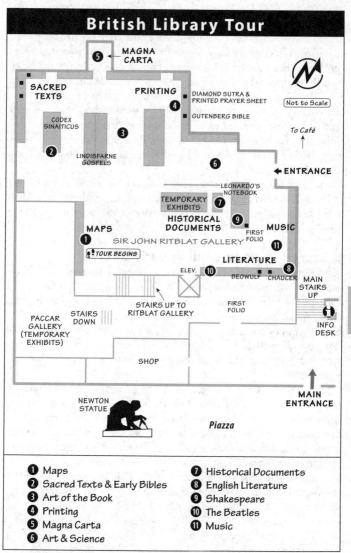

British Library Tour

- **1** Maps
- **2** Sacred Texts & Early Bibles
- **3** Art of the Book
- **4** Printing
- **5** Magna Carta
- **6** Art & Science
- **7** Historical Documents
- **8** English Literature
- **9** Shakespeare
- **10** The Beatles
- **11** Music

left. Enter and let your eyes adjust. The room has display cases grouped according to themes: maps, sacred texts, music, and so on. Focus on the big picture, and don't be too worried about locating every specific exhibit in this tour. Start at the far side of the room with the display case of...

❶ Maps

The historic maps show how humans' perspective of the world expanded over the centuries. These pieces of paper, encoded with information gleaned from travelers, could be passed along to future generations—each building upon the knowledge of the last.

The collection changes year to year, but you may see maps similar to these: A crude 13th-century map of Britain put medieval man in an unusual position—looking down on his homeland from 50 miles in the air. A few centuries later, maps of Britain were of such high quality they could still be used today to plan a trip. And only a few generations after Columbus' first journey, the entire globe was fairly well mapped, except for the mysterious expanse of unknown land that lay beyond America's east coast—"Terra Incognita."

• *Move into the area dedicated to sacred texts from several cultures—the Hebrew Torah, Muslim Quran, Buddhist sutras, and Hindu Upanishads. Start by browsing the different versions of the sacred text of Christians, the Bible.*

❷ Sacred Texts (Including Early Bibles)

My favorite excuse for not learning a foreign language is "If English was good enough for Jesus Christ, it's good enough for me!" I don't know what that has to do with anything, but obviously Jesus didn't speak English—nor did Moses or Isaiah or Paul or any other Bible author or character. As a result, our present-day English Bible came not directly from the mouths and pens of these religious figures, but is instead the fitful product of centuries of evolution and translation.

The Bible is not a single book; it's an anthology of books by many authors from different historical periods writing in various languages (usually Hebrew or Greek). So there are three things that editors must do in compiling the most accurate Bible: 1) decide which books actually belong, 2) find the oldest and most accurate version of each book, and 3) translate it accurately.

The **Codex Sinaiticus,** from A.D. 350, is one of the oldest complete Bibles in existence ("codex" means it's an ancient, bound manuscript). It's one of the first attempts to collect various books by different authors into one authoritative anthology. The parchment is made from animal skin. It's in Greek, the language in which most of the New Testament was written. The Old Testament portions are Greek translations from the original Hebrew. This particular Bible, and the nearby **Codex Alexandrinus** (A.D. 425), both contain some books not included in most modern English Bibles. (Even today, Catholic Bibles contain books not found in Protestant Bibles.)

These accounts of Jesus of Nazareth are about as old as any in existence, but even so, they weren't written down until several generations after Jesus' death. Today, Bible scholars pore diligently over every word in the New Testament, trying to separate Jesus' authentic words from those that seem to have been added later.

• *Nearby, you'll find more early Bibles (along with other texts) in the display cases called...*

❸ Art of the Book

After the fall of Rome, the Christian message was preserved by monks, who reproduced ancient Bibles by hand. This was a painstaking process, usually done for a rich patron. You'll see various "Bibles" (collections of sacred writings), "Gospels" (histories of Jesus), "Psalters" (songs from the Bible), and "Books of Hours" (prayers and inspiring Bible quotes). Many of these are beautifully illustrated, or "illuminated," and are some of the finest works of art from what we call the Dark Ages. The little intimate details offer a rare and fascinating peek into medieval life.

The **Lindisfarne Gospels** (A.D. 698) are the most magnificent of medieval British monk-uscripts. The text is in Latin, the language of scholars ever since the Roman Empire, but the illustrations—with elaborate tracery and interwoven decoration—mix Irish, classical, and even Byzantine forms. (Read an electronic copy using the touch-screen computers.)

These Gospels are a reminder that Christianity almost didn't make it in Europe. After the fall of Rome (which had established Christianity as the empire's official religion), much of Europe reverted to its pagan ways. People worshipped woodland spirits and terrible Teutonic gods.

Lindisfarne was an obscure monastery of Irish monks on an island off the east coast of England. In that chaotic era, it was one of the few beacons of light, tending the embers of civilization through the long night of the Dark Ages. It took 500 years before Christianity was fully re-established in Europe.

While browsing the displays in Art of the Book (and in Sacred Texts), you'll likely see some **Early English Bibles.**

By the year 1400, England was mostly Christian. But the Bible was still written in Latin, even though only a small percentage of the population understood that language. A few brave reformers risked death to translate the sacred books into English and print them using Gutenberg's new invention, the printing press. Within two centuries, English translations were both legal and popular.

These Bibles are written in the same language you speak, but try reading them. The strange letters and archaic words clearly show how quickly languages evolve. Jesus spoke Aramaic, a form of Hebrew. His words were written down in Greek. Greek manuscripts were translated into Latin, the language of medieval monks and scholars. In the 1400s, English scholars began translating the Greek and Latin into the King's English.

The **King James version** (made during his reign) has been the most widely used English translation. Fifty scholars worked for four years, borrowing heavily from previous translations, to produce the work. Its impact on the English language was enormous. It made Elizabethan English something of the standard, even after ordinary people had long since stopped saying "thee," "thou," and "verily, verily."

Recent translations are not only more readable but also more accurate, based on better scholarship and original manuscripts. But scholars still encounter problems when trying to translate old phrases to fit contemporary viewpoints (case in point: our generation's debate over whether the God of the Bible should be a he or a she).

• *Move on to the wall of glass cases featuring early...*

❹ Printing

Printing was invented by the Chinese (what wasn't?). The **Diamond Sutra** (c. 868) is the world's earliest, complete printed book bearing a date. It's written in Chinese even though the Buddhist faith originated in India. Considered one of Buddhism's most important sacred works, it addresses the nature of perception, reality, enlightenment, and impermanence. The **Printed Prayer Sheet** (c. 618-907) was made seven centuries before the printing press

was "invented" in Europe. A bodhisattva (an incarnation of Buddha) rides a lion, surrounded by a prayer in Chinese characters. The faithful gained a blessing by saying the prayer, and so did the printer by reproducing it. Texts such as this were printed using wooden blocks carved with Chinese characters, then dipped into paint or ink.

The **Gutenberg Bible** looks like just another monk-made Latin manuscript, but it was the first book printed in Europe using movable type (c. 1455). Printing is one of the most revolutionary inventions in history.

Johann Gutenberg (c. 1397-1468), a German silversmith, devised a convenient way to reproduce written materials quickly, neatly, and cheaply—by printing with movable type. You scratch each letter onto a separate metal block, then arrange them into words, ink them up, and press them onto paper. When one job was done you could reuse the same letters for a new one.

This simple idea had immediate and revolutionary consequences. Suddenly, the Bible was available for anyone to read, fueling the Protestant Reformation. Knowledge became cheap and accessible to a wide audience, not just the rich. Books became the mass medium of Europe, linking people by a common set of ideas.

• *Through a doorway near the Printing and Art of the Book displays is a small room with, if it's not "resting" in 2016, the...*

❺ Magna Carta

How did Britain, a tiny island with a few million people, come to rule a quarter of the world? Not by force, but by law. The 1215 Magna Carta was the basis for England's constitutional system of government. Though historians talk about *the* Magna Carta, several different versions of the document exist, some of which are kept in this room.

The Articles of the Barons (labeled *King John*): In 1215, England's barons rose in revolt against the slimy King John. (The same King John appears as a villain in the legends of Robin Hood.) After losing London, John was forced to negotiate. The barons presented him with this list of demands. John, whose rule was worthless without the barons' support, had no choice but to affix his seal to it.

Magna Carta: A few days after John agreed to this original document, it was rewritten in legal form, and some 35 copies of the final version of the "Great Charter" were distributed around the kingdom.

This was a turning point in the history of government. Before, kings had ruled by God-given authority, above the laws of men. Now, for the first time, there were limits—in writing—on how a king could treat his subjects. More generally, it established the idea of "due process"—the notion that a government can't infringe on citizens' freedom without a legitimate legal reason. This small step became the basis for all constitutional governments, including yours.

So what did this radical piece of paper actually say? Not much, by today's standards. The specific demands had to do with things such as inheritance taxes, the king's duties to widows and orphans, and so on. It wasn't the specific articles that were important, but the simple fact that the king had to abide by them as law.

• *Now return to the main room to find display cases featuring…*

❻ Art and Science

Books also spread secular knowledge. During the Renaissance, men turned their attention away from heaven and toward the nuts and bolts of the material world around them.

Pages from **Leonardo da Vinci's note-book** show his powerful curiosity, his genius for invention, and his famous backward and inside-out handwriting, which makes sense only if you know Italian and have a mirror. Leonardo's restless mind pondered diverse subjects (the displays change), from how birds fly, to the flow of the Arno River, to military fortifications, to an early helicopter, to the "earthshine" reflecting onto the moon.

One person's research inspired another's, and books allowed knowledge to accumulate. Galileo championed the counter-commonsense notion that the Earth spun around the sun, and Isaac Newton later explained the mathematics of those moving celestial bodies.

❼ Historical Documents

Nearby are many more historical documents. The displays change frequently, but you may see letters by Henry VIII, Queen Elizabeth I, Darwin, Freud, Gandhi, and others. But for now, let's trace the evolution of…

❽ English Literature

Four out of every five English words have been borrowed from other languages. The English language, like English culture (and London today), is a mix derived from foreign invaders. Some of the historic ingredients that make this cultural stew:

• The original Celtic tribesmen
• Latin-speaking Romans (A.D. 1-500)
• Germanic tribes called Angles and Saxons (English is a Germanic language, and the name England comes from "Angle-land"—island of the Angles)
• Vikings from Denmark (A.D. 800)
• French-speaking Normans under William the Conqueror (1066-1250)

Beowulf is the first English literary masterpiece. The Anglo-Saxon epic poem, written in Old English (the earliest version of our language), almost makes the hieroglyphics on the Rosetta Stone look easy. The manuscript is from A.D. 1000, although the story itself dates to about 750. In this epic story, the young hero Beowulf defeats two half-human monsters threatening the kingdom. Beowulf symbolizes England's emergence from the chaos and barbarism of the Dark Ages.

Now find **The Canterbury Tales.** Six hundred years later, England was Christian, but it was hardly the pious, predictable, Sunday-school world we might imagine. Geoffrey Chaucer's bawdy collection of stories (c. 1410), told by pilgrims on their way to Canterbury, gives us the full range of life's experiences—happy, sad, silly, sexy, and devout. (Late in life, Chaucer wrote an apology for those works of his "that tend toward sin.")

While most serious literature of the time was written in scholarly Latin, the stories in *The Canterbury Tales* were written in Middle English, the language that developed after the French invasion of 1066 added a Norman twist to Old English.

The Literature wall is often a greatest-hits sampling of literature in English, from Brontë to Kipling to Woolf to Joyce to Dickens, whose novels were as popular in his time as blockbuster movies are today. Jane Austen's novels of upper-class young women seeking suitable husbands, though set in the 19th century, have become enormously popular in the 21st. The original *Alice's Adventures in Wonderland* by Lewis Carroll created a fantasy world, where grown-up rules and logic were turned upside down. Also on display are superb works by contemporary writers, making it clear that Britain continues to be a powerful force in the world of ideas and imagination.

• *The most famous of England's writers generally gets his own display case.*

❾ Shakespeare

Shakespeare wrote his plays to be performed, not read. He published a few, but as his reputation grew, unauthorized "bootleg" versions began to circulate. Some of these were written by actors who were trying (with faulty memories) to re-create plays they had

William Shakespeare (1564-1616)

William Shakespeare is the greatest author in any language, period. He expanded and helped define modern English. In one fell swoop, he made the language of everyday people as important as Latin. In the process, he gave us phrases like "one fell swoop," which we quote without knowing they're Shakespeare. (Without him, no one would ever "vanish into thin air," "play fast and loose," "have seen better days," do anything "without rhyme or reason," become a "laughingstock," or wish anything "good riddance.")

Shakespeare was born in Stratford-up-on-Avon in 1564 to John Shakespeare and Mary Arden. Though his parents were probably illiterate, Shakespeare is thought to have attended Stratford's grammar school, finishing his education at age 14. When he was 18, he married a 26-year-old local girl, Anne Hathaway, who was three months pregnant at the time with their daughter Susanna.

The next few years are a blank—following his marriage, Shakespeare disappeared from any historical record, not turning up again until seven years later. By this point, he was a budding poet and playwright in London. He soon hit the big time, writing and performing for royalty, founding (along with his troupe) the Globe Theatre (a replica of which now sits along the Thames' South Bank—see page 90), and raking in enough dough to buy New Place, a swanky mansion back in his hometown. Around 1611, the rich-and-famous playwright retired from the theater, moving back to Stratford, where he died at the age of 52.

With plots that entertained both the highest and the lowest minds, Shakespeare taught the theater-going public about human nature. His tool was an unrivaled mastery of the English language. Using borrowed plots, outrageous puns, and poetic language,

appeared in years before. Publishers also put out different versions of his plays.

It wasn't until seven years after his death, in 1623, that a complete collection of Shakespeare's plays was published, commonly known as the First Folio. Of the 700 printed, about 150 survive (most are in the US). Western literature owes much to this folio, which collects 36 of the 37 known Shakespeare plays (*Pericles* missed out). If the First Folio is not out for viewing, the library should have other Shakespeare items on display.

The engraving of Shakespeare on the title page

Shakespeare wrote comedies (c. 1590—*Taming of the Shrew, As You Like It*), tragedies (c. 1600—*Hamlet, Othello, Macbeth, King Lear*), and fanciful combinations (c. 1610—*The Tempest*), exploring the full range of human emotions and reinventing the English language.

Perhaps as important was his insight into humanity. His father was a glove maker and wool merchant, and his mother was the daughter of a landowner from a Catholic family. Some scholars speculate that Shakespeare's parents were closet Catholics, practicing their faith during the rise of Protestantism. It is this tug-of-war between two worlds, some think, that helped enlighten Shakespeare's humanism. Think of his stock of great characters and great lines: Hamlet ("To be or not to be, that is the question"), Othello and his jealousy ("It is the green-eyed monster"), ambitious Mark Antony ("Friends, Romans, countrymen, lend me your ears"), rowdy Falstaff ("The better part of valor is discretion"), and the star-crossed lovers Romeo and Juliet ("But soft, what light through yonder window breaks"). Shakespeare probed the psychology of human beings 300 years before Freud. Even today, his characters strike a familiar chord.

The scope of his brilliant work, his humble beginnings, and the fact that no original Shakespeare manuscripts survive raise a few scholarly eyebrows. Some have wondered if maybe Shakespeare had help on several of his plays. After all, they reasoned, how could a journeyman actor with little education have written so many masterpieces? And he was surrounded by other great writers, such as his friend and fellow poet, Ben Jonson. Most modern scholars, though, agree that Shakespeare did indeed write the plays and sonnets attributed to him.

His contemporaries had no doubts about Shakespeare—or his legacy. As Jonson wrote in the preface to the First Folio, "He was not of an age, but for all time!"

is reportedly one of only two portraits done during his lifetime. Is this what he really looked like? No one knows. The best answer probably comes from Ben Jonson, in the introduction on the facing page. Jonson concludes, "Reader, look not on his picture, but his book."

⑩ The Beatles

Bach, Beethoven, Brahms, Bizet...Beatles. Future generations will have to judge whether this musical quartet ranks with such artists, but no one can deny their historical significance. The Beatles burst onto the scene in the early 1960s to unheard-of popularity. With their long hair and loud music, they brought counterculture and revolutionary ideas to the middle class, affecting the values of a whole generation. Touring the globe, they served as a link between young people everywhere. Look for photos of John Lennon, Paul McCartney, George Harrison, and Ringo Starr before and after their fame.

Most interesting are the manuscripts of song lyrics written by Lennon and McCartney, the two guiding lights of the group. "I Want to Hold Your Hand" was the song that launched them to superstardom in America. "A Hard Day's Night" and "Help" were title songs of two films capturing the excitement and chaos of their hectic touring schedule. Some call "Ticket to Ride" the first heavy-metal song. "Michelle," with a line in French, seemed oh-so-sophisticated. "Yesterday," by Paul, was recorded with guitar and voice backed by a string quartet—a touch of class from producer George Martin. Also, glance at the rambling, depressed, and cynical but humorous "untitled verse" by a young John Lennon. Is that a self-portrait at the bottom?

⓫ Music

Kind of an anticlimax after the Fab Four, I know, but there are manuscripts by Mozart, Beethoven, Schubert, and others. George Frideric Handel's famous oratorio, **the** *Messiah* (1741), is often on display. Handel, a German, became the toast of London in the early 1700s, where musical theater was all the rage. Increasingly, he left Italian-language operas behind in favor of productions in English. The *Messiah* was written in a flash of inspiration—three hours of music in 24 days. When it got its London premiere in Covent Garden, King George II reportedly stood in respect during its most famous tune, the "Hallelujah" chorus. Here are the final bars. Hallelujah.

THE CITY WALK

From Trafalgar Square to London Bridge

In Shakespeare's day, London consisted of a one-square-mile area surrounding St. Paul's. Today, that square mile, the neighborhood known as "The City," is still the financial heart of London, densely packed with history and bustling with business.

This two-mile walk from Trafalgar Square to London Bridge parallels the Thames, on the same main road that's been used for centuries. Along the way, you'll see sights from The City's storied past, such as St. Paul's Cathedral, the steeples of other Wren churches, historic taverns, a Crusader church, and narrow alleyways with faint remnants of the London of Shakespeare and Dickens.

But you'll also catch The City in action today, especially if you visit on a weekday at lunchtime, when workers spill out onto the streets and The City is at its liveliest. See lawyers and judges in robes and wigs taking cigarette breaks, brokers in pin-striped power suits buying newspapers from Cockneys, and the last of a dying breed—elderly gentlemen with bowler hats and brollies (umbrellas) browsing for tailored shirts and Cuban cigars. Sip a pint in the same pub where Dickens did, and eavesdrop on a power lunch. Use this walk to help resurrect the London that was, then let The City of today surprise you with what is.

Orientation

Length of This Walk: Allow three or more hours, depending on what you visit. If you have less time, you could skip a mile's worth of the Strand by taking the Tube directly to Temple, picking up the walk at St. Clement Danes, then ending at St. Paul's. Less-important stops along the way include the Temple Church, Inns of Court, and Dr. Johnson's House.

Getting There: Start at Trafalgar Square (Tube: Charing Cross or Embankment). You'll head east on the Strand and end at London Bridge (where the Bankside Walk begins). Handy buses #15 and #11 (see page 28) travel along the Strand and Fleet Street from Trafalgar Square.

Tourist Information: The City of London TI is located next to St. Paul's; open Mon-Sat 9:30-17:30, Sun 10:00-16:00.

Courtauld Gallery: £7 (£3 on Mon), daily 10:00-18:00.

St. Clement Danes: Free, daily 9:00-16:00, closed to sightseers during worship (generally Sun at 11:00, Wed and Fri at 12:30); tel. 020/7242-2380, www.raf.mod.uk/stclementdanes.

Royal Courts of Justice: Free, Mon-Fri 10:00-16:30, closed Sat-Sun, no photos, on the Strand; tel. 020/7947-6000, www.justice.gov.uk/courts/rcj.

Twinings Tea Shop: Mon-Fri 9:30-17:00, Sat 10:00-17:00, Sun 10:30-16:30.

Temple Church: £5, irregular visiting hours, often 10:00-16:00, not open every day, confirm schedule at www.templechurch.com.

St. Dunstan-in-the-West: Mon-Fri 9:30-17:00, free 45-minute recital on Wed at 13:15; you're welcome to bring a bag lunch; confirm schedule at www.stdunstaninthewest.org.

Dr. Johnson's House: £4.50, Mon-Sat 11:00-17:30, closed Sun, closes at 17:00 Oct-April, audioguide-£2, tel. 020/7353-3745, www.drjohnsonshouse.org.

St. Bride's Church: Free, Mon-Fri 8:00-17:00, Sat hours generally 11:00-15:00, Sun 10:00-18:30; free lunch concerts usually Tue and Fri at 13:15; Sun choral Eucharist at 11:00 and evensong at 17:30; tel. 020/7427-0133, www.stbrides.com.

Old Bailey: Free, public galleries only; opening hours depend on court schedule, but generally Mon-Fri 10:00-13:00 & 14:00-17:00, last entry at 12:40 and 15:40 but often closes an hour or so earlier, closed Sat-Sun, reduced hours in Aug, no kids under 14, on Old Bailey Street. No bags, mobile phones, cameras, iPods, or food, but small purses OK; you can check bags at the Capable Travel agency just down the street at 4 Old Bailey for £5/bag and £1 per phone or camera, or at nearby Museum of London for £1.

St. Paul's Cathedral: £18, includes church entry, dome climb, crypt, tour, and audioguide; Mon-Sat 8:30-16:30, dome opens at 9:30, closed Sun except for worship.

St. Mary-le-Bow: Free, Mon-Wed 7:30-18:00, Thu 7:30-18:30, Fri 7:30-16:00, closed Sat-Sun.

The Guildhall: Free, Mon-Sat 10:00-17:00, Sun 12:00-16:00.

Bank Museum: Free, Mon-Fri 10:00-17:00, closed Sat-Sun; tel. 020/7601-5545, www.bankofengland.co.uk/museum.

The Monument: £4 to climb the steps for the view, daily 9:30-18:00, Oct-March until 17:30.

Tours: 🎧 Download my free Historic London: "The City" **audio tour.**

Services: You'll find pay WCs toward the back of the terrace café at Somerset House, in front of the Royal Courts of Justice (in a traffic island), and free ones in the basement of St. Paul's (around the left side).

OVERVIEW

The City stretches from Temple Church (near Blackfriars Bridge) to the Tower of London. This was the London of the ancient Ro-

WELCOME TO THE CITY OF LONDON

mans, William the Conqueror, Henry VIII, Shakespeare, and Elizabeth I.

But The City has been stripped of its history by the Great Fire (1666), the WWII Blitz (1940-1941), and modern economic realities. Today, it's a neighborhood of modern bank buildings and retail stores. Only about 10,000 people actually live here, but The City is a hive of business activity on workdays—packed with almost half a million commuting bankers, legal assistants, and coffee-shop baristas.

The route is simple—a two-mile walk east along a single street that changes names as you go. The Strand becomes Fleet Street, which becomes Cannon Street.

The Walk Begins

• *From Trafalgar Square (Tube: Charing Cross or Embankment), head east on the Strand. (Or you can skip a mile's worth of the Strand by taking the Tube directly to Temple and starting the walk at St. Clement Danes.)*

The Strand

This busy boulevard, home to theaters and retail stores, was formerly a high-class riverside promenade, back before the Thames was tamed with retaining walls in the 19th century.

The venerable **Charing Cross Sta-**

THE CITY

The City Walk

To British Museum ←

SIR JOHN SOANE'S MUSEUM

Lincoln's Inn Fields

THE OLD BANK OF ENGLAND PUB

ROYAL COURTS OF JUSTICE

AUSTRALIA HOUSE

BUSH HOUSE

COVENT GARDEN

GIBRALTAR HOUSE

KING'S COLLEGE

SOMERSET HOUSE

THE TEMPLE

FLEET ST.

TUDOR ST.

VICTORIA EMBANKMENT

BLACKFRIARS PIER

Thames

To Trafalgar Square &

WALK BEGINS

CHARING CROSS STATION

Charing Cross

Embankment

EMBANKMENT PIER

WATERLOO BRIDGE

ROYAL NATIONAL THEATRE

Jubilee Walkway

OXO TOWER

SOUTH BANK

❶ Savoy Hotel & Theatre
❷ Courtauld Gallery
❸ St. Mary-le-Strand
❹ St. Clement Danes
❺ Royal Courts of Justice
❻ Twinings Tea Shop
❼ Temple Bar Monument
❽ 17 Fleet Street
❾ Temple Church
❿ The Inns of Court
⓫ St. Dunstan-in-the-West
⓬ Dr. Johnson's House
⓭ Ye Olde Cheshire Cheese Tavern
⓮ View of St. Paul's
⓯ St. Bride's Church

THE CITY

tion still has a terminus hotel (a standard part of station design in the early days of rail travel) and remains a busy transportation hub.

The station is named for the **Charing Cross monument,** which stands quietly out of place amid all the commotion in front of the station. This monument is a Victorian Age replacement of the original, medieval "Eleanor Cross." When Queen Eleanor died in 1290, her body was carried from Nottingham to Westminster Abbey. King Edward I had a memorial "Eleanor Cross" built at each of the 12 places his wife's funeral procession spent the night during that long, sad trek. Charing Cross marks the final overnight stop.

A few blocks up the Strand on the left is Southampton Street, which leads to **Covent Garden** (described on page 55).

Ahead on the right is the drive-up entrance to the ❶ **Savoy Hotel** and **Savoy Theatre.** The hotel sparkles after a recent £100 million renovation. Its shiny gold knight represents the Earl of Savoy, who built the original riverside palace here in 1245. This is one of London's ritziest locales, with Rolls-Royces, fancy shops,

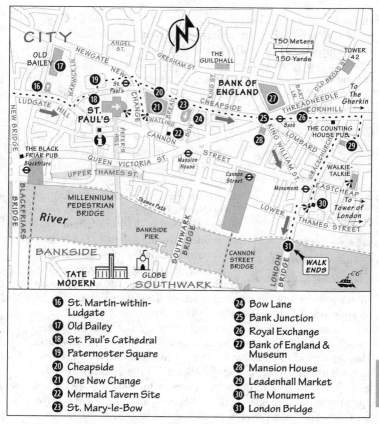

16 St. Martin-within-Ludgate
17 Old Bailey
18 St. Paul's Cathedral
19 Paternoster Square
20 Cheapside
21 One New Change
22 Mermaid Tavern Site
23 St. Mary-le-Bow
24 Bow Lane
25 Bank Junction
26 Royal Exchange
27 Bank of England & Museum
28 Mansion House
29 Leadenhall Market
30 The Monument
31 London Bridge

Simpson's Restaurant, Donald Trump-style luxury, and the doorman in top hat and tails. Everyone has stayed here. Monet painted the Thames at the Savoy; Oscar Wilde romanced Lord Douglas; Chaplin, Sinatra, and Burton-and-Taylor made the scene; as did the Beatles, The Who, and Bob Dylan, who filmed his cue-card-flipping film for *Subterranean Homesick Blues* in an alley around back—one of the earliest examples of a music video. Step inside to see the spiffy foyer under the pretext of asking about their (overpriced) afternoon tea under the glass cupola or visiting the tea shop.

At the next major intersection, a side-trip out onto **Waterloo Bridge** affords one of the best London views, overlooking the city in both directions.

A half-block farther down the Strand is **Gibraltar House** (at 150 Strand), a quasi-embassy and visitors center for one of Britain's last little "colonies," located on the southern tip of Spain.

Next up is **Somerset House,** the last of the many great riverside mansions that once lined the Strand. Today, it has a people-friendly courtyard with playful fountains, a riverside terrace, a choice of cafés (with WCs), an exhibition hall, and the ❷ **Cour-tauld Gallery**—a fine art collection including Impressionist and Post-Impressionist gems (📖 see the Courtauld Gallery Tour chapter). The courtyard is a busy public space all year long, with ice skating in the winter and concerts in the summer.

You'll encounter two different churches left Strand-ed in the middle of traffic when the road was widened around them. The

first, ❸ **St. Mary-le-Strand,** with its clean, white interior lit by blue-and-green stained glass, is an oasis of quiet (see photo). Charles Dickens' parents were married here. To the right of the church (in the ugly concrete building) is **King's College,** one of the world's top universities, with 20,000 current students and a distinguished list of former students that includes John Keats, Florence Nightingale, and Desmond Tutu. During school term, the college welcomes visitors and even provides self-guided campus tours at the reception desk (Mon-Fri 9:00-17:00).

Straight ahead and across the street is **Bush House,** former home of the BBC's World Service. And just beyond is **Australia House,** a kind of embassy for that member of the British Commonwealth. It's most famous for its role as the goblin-run Gringotts Wizarding Bank in the *Harry Potter* movies. Though it's not open to visiting Muggles, you can step into the lobby—enter at the far side—and gaze through glass doors at the chandeliered room they filmed in (no photos allowed). The building sits on a multibranched intersection where the flow of traffic is a marvel to watch.
• *Also in the intersection, behind the statue of William Gladstone—Queen Victoria's longest-serving prime minister—is the second traffic-island church of...*

❹ St. Clement Danes

Built by Christopher Wren (1682), the church was blitzed heavily in World War II. Today, it's a busy Royal Air Force chapel and a memorial to the 125,000 RAF servicemen who gave their lives in both world wars. Outside stand statues of brave airmen. Inside, hundreds of gray medallions in the stone floor are dedicated to various squadrons. Lining the walls are Books of Remembrance—10 thick volumes (with a page respectfully turned each day). This is the first of several Wren-built churches (steeple added later) we'll see on the walk. Of the 50-some he originally built, 23 Wren churches still dot London. Pick up the tourist guide at the entry for more information on the church.

THE CITY

• *Past St. Clement Danes, on the left side of street are the...*

❺ Royal Courts of Justice

When former Spice Girls sue tabloids for libel, when media mogul Rupert Murdoch is called to testify in a corruption inquiry, or when ex-Beatles pay $50 million divorce settlements to gold diggers, the trial is likely to be held here, at Britain's highest civil court. (Criminal cases are heard down the street at the Old Bailey.) Paparazzi often litter the entrance, awaiting a celeb or a lawyer (many of whom are celebrities themselves). The 76 courtrooms in this Neo-Gothic complex are open to the public. At least step into the lobby to see the vast Gothic entry hall (submit to a security check to go farther in). This is just one of several legal buildings in the neighborhood.

• *Across the street is...*

❻ Twinings Tea Shop (216 Strand)

When this slender store first opened its doors ("established 1706"), tea was an exotic concoction from newly explored lands. (The Chi-

nese statues at the entrance remind us that tea came first from China, then India.) This store has been in the Twining family for nearly 300 years. The Twinings shop is narrow, but explore its depths—there's a small museum exhibit and tea-tasting room in the back (help yourself to a sample of whichever tea you like, whether bagged or loose, and enjoy the tea tips of the chatty hostess).

In the 1700s, London was in the grip of a coffee craze, and "coffee houses" were everywhere. These were rather seedy places, where "gentlemen" went for coffee, tobacco, and female companionship. Tea offered a refreshing change of pace, and the late-in-the-day "cuppa" (as well as "afternoon tea") soon became a national institution. These days—as you'll see on this walk—coffee has made a comeback in London in the form of modern Starbucks-style coffee shops.

• *Pass a Thai restaurant at #229, which used to be a pub called The Wig and Pen. There's a small plaque on the front of the wood-and-stained-glass facade that commemorates the old pub—the only building on the*

Strand to survive the Great Fire of 1666. Up ahead, in the middle of the street, is a small statue of a winged creature.

❼ Temple Bar Monument

A statue of a griffin, a mythological beast with an eagle's wings and a lion's body, marks the official border between the City of West-

minster and The City of London. The Queen, who presides over Westminster, does not pass this point without ceremonial permission of The City's Lord Mayor. The relief at its base shows Queen Victoria submitting to this ritual in 1837.

• Cross the border, leaving Westminster and entering The City. Ahead on the left (194 Fleet Street) is The Old Bank of England pub—a former bank with a lavish late-Victorian interior that serves lunches to the 9-to-5 crowd. (To imagine a fancy 19th-century bank, pop inside.) Up a few storefronts, on the right side of the street, look above the street-level shops to find an old building with black-framed, stained-glass bay windows.

❽ 17 Fleet Street

This half-timbered, three-story, Tudor-style building (1610) is one of the few to survive the Great Fire. In Shakespeare's day, the en-

tire City was packed, rooftop to rooftop, with wood and plaster buildings like this. Many were five and six stories high, with narrow frontage. Little wonder that a small fire could spread so quickly and become the Great Fire of 1666.

The building flies the red-and-yellow flag of Spain's Catalan region, as it now houses the Catalan tourist board.

• Pass underneath the house, through the passageway called Inner Temple Lane that leads a half-block to the exotic...

❾ Temple Church

Exterior: The round, crenellated, castle-turret roof and tiny statue of a knight on horseback (on a pillar in the courtyard) mark this as a Crusader church (1185) from the days of King Richard the Lionheart. The church was the headquarters of the Knights Templar, a band of heavily armed, highly trained monks who dressed in long white robes (decorated with red crosses) beneath heavy armor. In their secret rituals, the knights were sworn to chastity and to the protection of pilgrims on their way to the Muslim-held Holy Land.

Interior: Inside, some honored knights lie face-up on the floor under the rotunda of the circular "nave," patterned after the Church of the Holy Sepulchre in Jerusalem. A knight's crossed legs indicate that he probably died peacefully at home. Surrounding the serene knights are grotesque faces, perhaps the twisted expressions seen in distant wars. Fans of *The Da Vinci Code* (book and movie) will recognize the Temple Church as a place the protagonist comes to find clues leading to a special tomb.

By 1300, the Knights Templars' mission of protecting pilgrims had become a corrupt "protection" racket, and they'd grown rich loaning money to kings and popes. Those same kings and popes condemned the monks as heretics and sodomites, and confiscated their lands (1312). The Temple Church was rented to lawyers, who built the Inns of Court around it.

• *Abutting, surrounding, and extending from the Temple Church is a vast complex of buildings covering a full city block between the Strand/Fleet Street and the Thames, known collectively as...*

❿ The Inns of Court

Wander through the peaceful maze of buildings, courtyards, narrow lanes, nooks, gardens, fountains, and century-old gas lamps, where lawyers take a break from the Royal Courts. The complex is a self-contained city of lawyers, with offices, lodgings, courtrooms, chapels, and dining halls. Law students must live here (and are even required to eat a number of meals on the premises) to complete their legal internship.

You'll see barristers in modern business suits and ties, plus a few in traditional wigs and robes, as they prepare to do legal battle. The wigs are a remnant of French manners of the 1700s, when every self-respecting European gentleman wore one.

• *Get lost. Don't worry—when you go uphill, you'll eventually spill back out onto the busy street. Return to 17 Fleet Street, which marks the spot where the Strand becomes...*

Fleet Street

"The Street" was the notorious haunt of a powerful combination—lawyers and the media. In 1500, Wynkyn de Worde moved here with a newfangled invention, a printing press, making this area

the center of an early Information Age. In
1702, the first daily newspaper appeared. Soon
you had the *Tatler,* the *Spectator,* and many
others pumping out both hard news and paparazzi gossip for the hungry masses. Just past
St. Dunstan church (described next), you'll
see a building decorated with mosaic signs
with the names of some bygone newspapers:
the *Dundee Evening Telegraph,* the *People's
Journal,* and so on.

London became the nerve center of a
global, colonial empire, and Fleet Street was where every twitch
found expression. Hard-drinking, ink-stained reporters gathered
in taverns and coffeehouses, pumping lawyers for juicy pretrial information, scrambling for that choice bit of must-read gossip that
would make their paper number one. They built an industry that
still endures. Even in this digital age, Britain supports about a
dozen national newspapers, selling more than 9 million papers a
day.

Today, busy Fleet Street bustles with almost every business
except newspapers. The industry made a mass exodus in the 1980s
for offices elsewhere, replaced by financial institutions. As you walk
along, you'll see the former offices of the *Daily Telegraph* (135 Fleet
Street) and the *Daily Express* (#121-128—peek into the lobby to
see its classic 1930s Art Deco interior). The last major institution to
leave (in the summer of 2005) was the Reuters news agency (#85,
opposite the *Daily Express*).

• *Heading 50 yards east past 17 Fleet Street, you'll find...*

⓫ St. Dunstan-in-the-West

This church stands where the Great Fire of September 1666 finally
ended. The fire started near London Bridge. For three days it swept

westward, fanned by hot and blustery
weather, leveling everything in its path.
As it approached St. Dunstan, 40 theol-
ogy students battled the blaze, holding
it off until the wind shifted, and the fire
slowly burned itself out.

From here to the end of our walk
(1.5 miles), we'll be passing through the
fire's path of destruction. It left London
a Sodom-and-Gomorrah wasteland so
hot it couldn't be walked on for weeks.
(For more on the fire, 📖 see the end of
the Bankside Walk chapter.)

Today, St. Dunstan is one of the few churches with a thriving congregation (of Orthodox Romanians) in this now depopulated and secularized district. An unbroken line of vicars dating back to 1237 is listed in the vestibule. The clock on the bell tower outside (1670) features London's first minute hand and has two slaves gonging two bells four times an hour.

The church usually hosts Wednesday lunch-time concerts from 13:15-14:00; you can bring a bag lunch.

Alongside the church is a rare contemporary statue of Queen Elizabeth I. Surviving from her reign, this 1586 depiction of Elizabeth is as accurate as anything we have. The scepter and orb symbolize her religious and secular authority.

• *Continue east on Fleet Street. A half-block past Fetter Lane, turn left through a covered alleyway at #167. (Don't take the alleyway called Red Lion Court; you want the alleyway 20 paces farther, immediately across from #54.) Follow signs through the narrow lanes directing you to* Dr. Johnson's House.

Narrow Lanes—1700s London

"Sir, if you wish to have a just notion of the magnitude of this city, you must...survey the innumerable little lanes and courts," said the

writer Samuel Johnson in 1763 to his young friend and biographer, James Boswell. These twisting alleyways and cramped buildings that house urban hobbits give a faint glimpse of rebuilt 1700s London, a crowded city of half a million people. After the Great Fire, London was resurrected in brick and stone instead of wood, but they stuck to the same medieval street plan, resulting in narrow lanes of brick buildings like these.

• *The narrow lanes eventually spill out onto Gough Square, about a block north of Fleet Street, where* you'll find...

⓬ Dr. Johnson's House (17 Gough Square)

"When a man is tired of London, he is tired of life," wrote Samuel Johnson, "for there is in London all that life can afford." Johnson (1709-1784) loved to wander these twisting lanes, looking for pungent slices of London street life that he could pass along in his weekly columns called "The Rambler" and "The Idler."

At age 28, Johnson arrived in London with one of his former students, David Garrick, who went on to revolutionize London

THE CITY

The Great Fire

The stones of St. Paul's flew from the building, the lead melting down the streets in a stream... God grant mine eyes may never behold the like... Above 10,000 homes all in one flame, the noise and crackling and thunder of the impetuous flames, the shrieking of women and children, the hurry of the people, the fall of the towers, houses, and churches was like a hideous storm.
—John Evelyn, eyewitness

theater. Dr. Johnson prowled the pubs, brothels, coffeehouses, and illicit gaming pits where terriers battled cornered rats while men bet

on the outcome. Johnson—described as "tall, stout," and "slovenly in his dress"—became a well-known eccentric and man-about-town, though he always seemed to live on the fringes of poverty. At the far end of Gough Square is a statue of Johnson's beloved cat Hodge, who dined on oysters.

Johnson inhabited this house from 1748 to 1759. He prayed at St. Clement Danes, drank in Fleet Street pubs, and, in the attic of the house, produced his most famous work, *A Dictionary of the English Language*. Published in 1755, it was the first great English-language dictionary, starring Johnson's 42,773 favorite words culled from all the books he'd read. It took Johnson and six assistants more than six years to sift through all the alternate spellings and Cockney dialects of the world's most complex language. He standardized spelling and pronunciation, explained each word's etymology, and occasionally put his own droll spin on words. ("Oats: a grain, which is generally given to horses, but in Scotland supports the people.")

Today, the house is a museum. While the exhibits are fascinating for hard-core Johnson fans (I met one once), the old house is interesting in itself, even for the casual visitor. See a video and climb four stories through period furniture, passing a first edition of Johnson's dictionary and pictures of Johnson, Garrick, and Boswell. Nothing is roped off or behind glass, and you can browse at will. See objects Johnson once owned: his walking stick, a chair,

London's Great Plague of 1665

The Grim Reaper—in the form of the bacteria *Yersinia pestis* (bubonic plague)—rode through London on fleas atop a black rat. It killed one in six people, while leaving the buildings standing. (The next year, the Great Fire consumed the buildings.) It started in the spring as "the Poore's Plague," neglected until it spread to richer neighborhoods. During the especially hot summer, 5,000 died each week. By December, the congregation at St. Bride's (you'll see the church later) was 2,111 souls fewer.

Victims passed through several days of agony: headaches, vomiting, fever, shivering, swollen tongue, and swollen buboes (lumps) on the groin glands. After their skin turned blotchy black (the "Black Death"), they died. "Searchers of the Dead" carted bodies off to mass graves, including one near St. Bride's. Both the victims and their families were quarantined under house arrest, with a red cross painted on the door and a guard posted nearby, and denied access to food, water, or medical attention for 40 days—a virtual death sentence even for the uninfected.

The disease was blamed on dogs and cats, and paid dog-killers destroyed tens of thousands of pets—which brought even more rats. People who didn't die tried to leave. The Lord Mayor quarantined the whole city within the walls, so the only way out was to produce (or purchase) a "certificate of health."

By fall, London was a ghost town, and throughout England, people avoided Londoners like the Plague. It took the Great Fire of 1666 to fully cleanse the city of the disease. Some scholars have suggested that a popular nursery rhyme refers to the dreaded disease (while others brush this off as bunk):

Ring around the rosie (flower garlands
    to keep the Plague away)
A pocket full of posies (buboes on the groin)
Ashes, ashes (your skin turns black)
We all fall down (dead).

a letter carrier, and a brick from something that fascinated him—the Great Wall of China. Portraits bring to life his urbane circle of friends, which, in addition to Boswell and Garrick (pictured in the role of Richard III), included actress Sarah Siddons, painter Sir Joshua Reynolds, and writer Oliver Goldsmith, many of whom socialized at the home of the sophisticated Elizabeth Montagu. Finally you arrive in the top-floor garret where literary history was made—the birthplace of the dictionary that standardized our English language.

• *At the other end of Gough Square, turn right at the statue of Hodge and head back toward Fleet Street, noticing the lists of barristers (trial lawyers) on the doorways (e.g., next to the door at 9 Gough Square). They work not as part of a firm, but as freelancers sharing offices and clerks. Stay to the left as you wind downhill through the alleys, and look near Fleet Street for the entrance of...*

⓭ Ye Olde Cheshire Cheese Tavern

Johnson often—and I do mean often—popped 'round here for a quick one, sometimes with David Garrick and his sleazy actor friends.

"The Cheese" dates from 1667, when it was rebuilt after the Great Fire, but it's been a tavern since 1538. It's a four-story warren of small, smoky, wood-lined rooms, each offering different menus, from pub grub to white-tablecloth meals. A traditional "chop house," it serves hearty portions of meats to power-lunching businessmen.

Sit in Charles Dickens' favorite seat, next to a coal fireplace (in the "Chop Room," main floor) and order a steak-and-kidney pie and some spotted dick (sponge pudding with currants, served in winter). Sip a pint of Samuel Smith (the house beer of the current owners) and think of Samuel Johnson, who drank here pondering various spellings: "pint" or "pynte," "color" or "colour," "theater" or "theatre." Immerse yourself in a world largely unchanged for centuries, a world of reporters scribbling the news over lunch, of Alfred Lord Tennyson inventing rhymes and Arthur Conan Doyle solving crimes, of W. B. Yeats, Teddy Roosevelt, and Mark Twain.

• *Back out on Fleet Street, you're met with a cracking...*

⓮ View of St. Paul's

If you were standing here on December 30, 1940, the morning after a German Luftwaffe firebomb raid, you'd see nothing but a flat, smoldering landscape of rubble, with St. Paul's rising above it almost miraculously intact. (For more on the Blitz, see the sidebar on page 272.)

Christopher Wren (1632-1723)

After London burned, King Charles II turned to his childhood friend Christopher Wren to rebuild it. The 33-year-old Wren was not an architect, but he'd proven his ability in every field he'd touched: astronomy (mapping the moon and building a model of Saturn), medicine (using opium as a general anesthetic, making successful blood transfusions between animals), mathematics (a treatise on spherical trigonometry), and physics (his study of the laws of motion influenced Newton's "discovery" of gravity). Wren also invented a language for the deaf, studied refraction and optics, and built weather-watching instruments.

Though domed St. Paul's is Wren's most famous church, the smaller churches around it better illustrate his distinctive style: a steeple over the west entrance; an uncluttered, well-lit interior; Neoclassical (Greek-style) columns; a curved or domed plaster ceiling; geometrical shapes (e.g., round rosettes inside square frames); and fine carved woodwork, often by his favorite whittler, Grinling Gibbons.

Standing here in September of 1666, you'd see nothing but smoke and ruins. The Great Fire razed everything, including the original St. Paul's Cathedral. And standing here a year earlier, in September of 1665, you'd hear "Bring out yer dead!" as they carted away 70,000 victims of the bubonic plague. After the double-whammy of plague and fire, the architect Christopher Wren was hired to rebuild St. Paul's and The City.

Even today, we see the view that Wren intended—a majestic dome hovering above the hazy rooftops, surrounded by the thin spires of his lesser churches. In the foreground below St. Paul's (between you and the dome) is the slender, lead-covered steeple of St. Martin-within-Ludgate, perfectly offsetting the more massive dome. Wren's 23 surviving churches are more than plenty for today's secular ghost town of a city.

• *Go a block downhill from Ye Olde Cheshire Cheese, cross the street, and walk a half-block down St. Bride's Avenue to see the stacked-tier steeple of...*

⓯ St. Bride's Church

The 226-foot steeple, Wren's tallest, is stacked in layers as it tapers to a point.

THE CITY

It's said to have inspired the wedding cake. Supposedly, a Fleet Street baker named Mr. Rich gazed out his shop window at St. Bride's as he made the first multitiered cake. (By the way, the word "Bride" in St. Bride's is only coincidental. The church was dedicated to St. Bridgit—or Bride—of Kildare long before the steeple or any wedding cakes.)

St. Bride's, built between 1671 and 1675, was one of the first of Wren's churches to open its doors after the Fire. St. Bride's is nicknamed both "The Cathedral of Fleet Street" and "The Printer's Church." Notice that the pews bear the names of departed journalists. It has been home to newspaper reporters, scholars, and literati ever since 1500, when Wynkyn de Worde set up his printing press here on church property. De Worde's press first served the literate clergy of St. Bride's, but was soon adopted by secular scholars, bookmakers, and newspapers, as Fleet Street became a global center for printed information.

During World War II, St. Bride's suffered terribly in the Blitz. (Today's structure was largely rebuilt after the war.) But thanks to Hitler's bombs, St. Bride's was instantly excavated down to its sixth-century Saxon foundations. Layers of previously unknown history were revealed from six previous churches that stood on this spot, including items such as Roman coins, medieval stained glass, and 17th-century tobacco pipes.

Also in the crypt is a wedding dress—worn by the wife of the Fleet Street baker whose wedding cake was inspired by St. Bride's steeple.

• *A block past St. Bride's Church on Fleet Street is **The Punch Tavern**, draped with memories of the venerable London political magazine famous for its satirical cartoons. Peek in to see Punch and his twin wife Judy looking down on a perfectly Victorian scene. These characters from a popular puppet show came onto the London scene 350 years ago. The characters gave the magazine its name, and the pub became the magazine staff's hangout. In the back room hang huge, colorful Victorian-era pastels of Punch and Judy. Don't be shy—the tavern is proud of their history and welcomes curious visitors popping in for a quick look. It's also a friendly place to order a drink or a meal (respected for their gins and pies, good £6-15 lunches, 99 Fleet Street). The valley between St. Bride's and St. Paul's is the...*

Fleet River and Ludgate

The Fleet River—now covered over by Farringdon Road—still flows southward, crossing underneath Fleet Street on its way to the Thames at Blackfriars Bridge. In medieval times, the river formed the western boundary of the walled city. Between you and the towering dome of St. Paul's stands Wren's steeple-topped church of ⑯ **St. Martin-within-Ludgate.** It incorporates the old city wall into its west wall, at the old city entrance known as Ludgate.

• *A block after crossing Farringdon Road, look left down Old Bailey Street to see a dome crowned by a golden statue of justice, which marks the...*

⑰ Old Bailey—Central Criminal Court

England's most infamous criminals—from the king-killers of the Civil War to the radically religious William Penn, from the "criminally homosexual" Oscar Wilde to the Yorkshire Ripper—were tried here, in Britain's highest criminal court. On top of the copper dome stands the famous golden Lady who weighs and executes Justice with scale and sword. The Old Bailey is built on the former site of Newgate Prison, with its notorious execution-by-hanging site. Inside, you can visit courtrooms and watch justice doled out the old-fashioned way to modern-day offenders (see page 73). Bewigged barristers argue before stern judges while the accused sit in the dock.

• *Continue up Ludgate Hill to...*

⑱ St. Paul's Cathedral

The greatest of Wren's creations is the rebuilt St. Paul's, England's national church and the heart of The City. Wren labored for more than 40 years on the church, both designing and overseeing construction of what was then the second-largest dome in the world. Unlike many church architects, Wren lived long enough to see his masterpiece completed.

📖 See the St. Paul's Cathedral Tour chapter or 🎧 download my free audio tour.

If you're not paying to enter the great church, you can pop into the basement (entry to left of front) for a café, fine WCs, a shop, and a peek at the memorials in the crypt. Belly up to the iron Churchill Gates. Standing on a plaque honoring Churchill, you can see the tomb of Admiral Lord Nelson directly below the dome.

• *A right turn at St. Paul's would take you to the Millennium Bridge, leading across the Thames to the Tate Modern and Bankside area. Instead, look for the Temple Bar gate—a white stone archway—directly to the left of the church. The gate was once the west entrance to the City of London. Relocated here, it now welcomes you to...*

⓲ Paternoster Square

This gate originally stood a half-mile west of here. It marked "Temple Bar," the boundary between the City of London and Westminster, where the griffin monument now stands (see page 246). The original Temple Bar gate was built of stone by St. Paul's architect, Christopher Wren, in 1672. But given the increase in traffic and new construction around it, the gate didn't "fit" at Temple Bar anymore. It was disassembled in 1878 and carted off to ornament the rural estate of a brewery owner. Finally, in 2004, the 2,700 stones were brought back to The City and painstakingly rebuilt here in Paternoster Square.

Go through the arch into the fine square and enjoy a view of the dome from behind the church's red-brick Chapter House (a good example of Wren's Neoclassicism). This square was designed in the early 21st century to save views of the church, while allowing maximum modern development here in the city center.

• *Stride right past the* Shepherd and Sheep *statue and head up the pedestrian street, then bear right onto the busy, noisy street called...*

⓳ Cheapside—Shakespeare's London

This was the main east-west street of Shakespeare's London, which had a population of about 200,000 back then. The wide street host-

ed The City's marketplace ("cheap" meant market), seen today in the names of the streets that branch off from it: Bread, Milk, Honey. Rebuilt cheaply after the war, more recently it has been upgraded with brand-new glassy facades—leaving Cheapside anything but.

At busy New Change Street turn right and walk half a block directly behind St. Paul's. On the left (marked by a 30-foot-tall statue of a rusty nail) is the huge, glassy ❷❶ **One New Change** shopping mall with a glass elevator at its center. Ride it to the rooftop terrace for a free, fantastic view of the city skyline, including St. Paul's Cathedral.

Return to Cheapside Street, turn right, and continue walking away from St. Paul's. If you were to detour two blocks south on Bread Street, you would not see even a trace of the ❷❷ **Mermaid Tavern,** Shakespeare's favorite haunt—but that's where it stood. In the early 1600s, "Sweet Will" would meet Ben Jonson, Sir Walter Raleigh, and John Donne at the Mermaid for food, ale, and literary conversation. Francis Beaumont, one of the group, wrote: "What things have we seen / Done at the Mermaid! heard words that have been / So nimble, and so full of subtle flame..."

• *Head straight toward the pointy steeple just past One New Change on the right. This marks...*

❷❸ St. Mary-le-Bow

From London's earliest Christian times, a church has stood here. The steeple of St. Mary-le-Bow, rebuilt after the Fire, is one of Wren's most impressive. He incorporated the ribbed-arch design of the former church (a "bow" is an arch) in the steeple's midsection. In the courtyard is a statue of a smiling Captain John Smith, who in 1607 established an English colony in Jamestown, Virginia, USA, before retiring here near the church. Inside the church, see not one but two pulpits, used today for point-counterpoint debates of moral issues. The church was rebuilt after being hit by WWII bombs. The crucifix hanging from the ceiling is a gift of atonement from the people of Bavaria.

This is the very center of old London, where, in medieval times, the church's bells rang each evening, calling Londoners safely back in to the walled town before the gates were locked. To be born "within the sound of Bow bells" long defined a true local, or "Cockney."

This is also the "Cockney" neighborhood of plucky street-wise urchins, where a distinctive Eliza Doolittle dialect is sometimes still spoken. Today's Cockney is the hard accent of rough-and-tumble, working-class Londoners—and the GEICO gecko on American TV ads. There are no Hs. "Are you 'appy, 'arry?" "Where's your 'orse? ...'urry up now." (Another fun element of the Cockney dialect—its creative rhyming slang—is described in the sidebar.) Nineteenth-century social climbers added extra H's in order not to sound Cockney. "I hunderstand you are hinterested in renting my hattic."

These days, few people actually live within the sound of Bow bells. The City's population, while 400,000 during working hours, falls to about 10,000 at night.

Cockney Rhyming Slang

The East End (specifically, the area around the Church of St. Mary-le-Bow) is known as the traditional home of the Cockneys. This colorful, working-class group spoke in a quirky pastiche that was the opposite of the Queen's English...think Audrey Hepburn as Eliza Doolittle in *My Fair Lady,* Dick van Dyke as the chimneysweep in *Mary Poppins,* or Don Cheadle in *Ocean's Eleven.*

One colorful Cockney invention that survives from the mid-19th century is the neighborhood's unique rhyming slang. According to urban legend, the Cockneys devised this secret way of talking to confuse policemen who might be listening. Another theory suggests that it was used between market vendors in order to rip off customers. Either way, Cockney rhyming slang helped create a sort of neighborhood pride for this downtrodden community.

Here's how it works: Simply replace an everyday word with a nonsensical phrase that rhymes with it. Instead of stairs, it's "apples and pears"—often shortened to simply "apples," as in, "I'm walking up the apples." For teeth, it's "Hampstead Heath" (or just "hampstead": "The dentist took a bloody good whack at me hampsteads").

Some Cockney rhyming slang words have become integrated into everyday American speech. For example, "blow a raspberry" comes from the slang "raspberry tart" for fart. And did you ever notice that "getting down to brass tacks" rhymes with "facts"? Many others—including several on the list on the next page—remain widely used as slang throughout the UK (if not in the US).

The tradition has continued into the 21st century—though these days it's done as a fun bit of irony, rather than as an actual secret language. For curry, they might say "Ruby Murray"—also

• *Just around and behind St. Mary-le-Bow is...*

❷ Bow Lane

Today, pedestrian-only Bow Lane features smart clothing shops, sandwich bars, and pubs. The entire City once had narrow lanes like Bow, Watling, and Bread Streets. Explore this area between Cheapside and Cannon Street.

When Shakespeare bought his tights and pointy shoes in Bow Lane, the shops were wooden, the streets were dirt, and the toilet was a ditch down the middle of the road. (The garbage brought rats, and rats brought plagues, like the one in 1665.) You bought your water in buckets carted up from the Thames. And at night, the bellman walked the streets, ringing the hour.

(For more Shakespearean ambience, it's a three-block walk south from St. Paul's to the river, where the Millennium Bridge crosses the Thames to Shakespeare's Globe, a reconstruction of the

the name of an Irish pop singer from the 1950s. Someone might suggest, "After work, let's head to the pub for some Britneys" (Britney Spears = beers), or "Go wash yer Chevy" (Chevy Chase = face).

Cockney Rhyming Slang	Translation
a la mode	code
Adam and Eve	believe
Barnet Fair (barnet)	hair (hairstyle)
bubble and squeak (bubble)	Greek
butcher's hook (butcher's)	look
china plate (china)	mate (friend)
deep sea diver	fiver (£5 note)
loaf of bread (loaf)	head
Mutt and Jeff (mutton)	deaf
plates of meat (plates)	feet
porkpies (porkies)	lies
rabbit and pork (rabbit)	talk
Scapa Flow (scarper)	go
septic tank (septic, seppo)	Yank (American)
tea leaf	thief
trouble and strife	wife
whistle and flute	suit

So the next time you find yourself 'avin' a rabbit with a Cockney, slip the bartender a deep sea diver to buy him a Britney and ask him about his trouble and strife's new barnet. Or take a butcher's at his fancy whistle and flute, and try out the local a la mode. Maybe he'll tap his loaf and say, "Not bad fer a seppo."

theater where many of Shakespeare's plays premiered. See page 90.)

• *Turn left on Bow Lane and then right on Cheapside. After a block, you can side-trip left on King Street to the fanciful facade of* **The Guildhall**, *a free art gallery and a fine medieval meeting hall, described on page 73. Continue east on Cheapside a few blocks to the long, wide intersection where nine streets meet, called Bank Junction (Tube: Bank). In the middle of all the traffic is a tiny park with a Wellington statue. Walk there and find the pyramid-shaped metal info post showing "The Heart of the City." From here, survey...*

⑳ Bank Junction

You're at the center of financial London. The Square Mile hosts 500 foreign and British banks. London, centrally located amid the globe's time zones, can find someone around the world to trade with 24 hours a day. In 2009, thousands of protesters packed this square, smashing bank windows in anger over the government's response to Britain's severe financial downturn. (Banks got the same "too big to fail" treatment they enjoyed in the USA.)

• *Look across the square at the eight-columned entrance to the...*

㉖ Royal Exchange: When London's original stock exchange opened, "stock" meant whatever could be loaded and unloaded onto a boat in the Thames. Remember, London got its start as a river-trading town. Soon, Londoners were gathering here, trading slips of paper and "futures" in place of live goats and chickens. Traders needed money changers, who needed bankers...and London's financial district boomed. Today, you can step inside to a skylight-covered courtyard lined with traders of retail goods and cappuccinos.

• *To the left of the Royal Exchange is the city-block-sized Bank of England (main entrance just across Threadneedle Street from the Royal Exchange entrance).*

㉗ Bank of England: This 3.5-acre, two-story complex houses the country's national bank. In 1694, it loaned £1.2 million to King William III at 8 percent interest to finance a war with France; it's managed the national debt ever since. It's an investment bank (a banker's bank), loaning money to other financial institutions. Working in tandem with the government (nationalized 1946, independent 1997), "The Old Lady of Threadneedle Street" sets interest rates, prints pound notes, and serves as the country's Fort Knox, housing stacks of gold bars.

The complex has a good **Bank Museum** inside (enter from far side, on Bartholomew Lane). See banknotes from 1699, an old safe, and account books. Also see current pound notes—with a foil hologram and numbers visible under UV light (to stay one step ahead of counterfeiters). The museum's highlight is under the rotunda, displaying a real gold bar that's worth more than $500,000 (check today's rates at the entrance) and weighs 28 pounds. Try lifting it.

• *Opposite the Royal Exchange is Mansion House, marked by its six (not eight) columns.*

㉘ Mansion House: This is the official residence of The City's Lord Mayor. The Lord Mayor governs not all of London but just this neighborhood. In the year 2000, a new post was created— "Mayor of London"—overseeing all of London. But the "Lord Mayor of the City" still carries out the old traditions, presiding from this palatial building. Once a year, he rides the streets in the Lord Mayor's Coach, a gilded carriage pulled by six white horses that looks like something out of *Cinderella* (the rest of the year, you can see the coach in the Museum of London).

• *Walk a block down Cornhill, with the Royal Exchange on your left, and a monument to James Henry Greathead (the 19th-century engineer who made constructing the Tube possible by inventing the "traveling shield"). On the right, at Cornhill #50, pop into The Counting House pub, built as a bank in 1893 (and my favorite lunch stop in this area). Cross over Gracechurch Street and continue straight on Leadenhall Street. At the first corner, look right at the ornate entry to the Leadenhall Market (with the giant "Walkie-Talkie" skyscraper towering above it). We'll return here after a quick side-trip—zip ahead to the next corner to see a towering modern forest of skyscrapers, the new face of The City. Also called "One Square Mile," this is the richest square mile on earth. When there's bad economic news, TV reporters declare, "The Square Mile won't like this." Backtrack half a block, turn left on Whittington Avenue and enter...*

㉙ Leadenhall Market

Site of Londinium's Roman Forum, this spot has hosted 2,000 years of commerce. It was named for the new-fangled lead roof of the medieval market hall. Today's hall—a classic 19th-century Victorian structure, still sporting its evocative iron meat hooks—is a getaway for office workers. Given the value of land in this 21st-century environment of skyscrapers, this survives only because it's protected by the government.

• *At the center of the market, turn right and head out to big and busy Gracechurch Street, then turn left and go three blocks to...*

㉚ The Monument to the Great Fire of 1666

The 202-foot hollow column is Wren's tribute to the Great Fire that gave him a blank canvas upon which to create modern London. At 2:00 in the morning of September 2, 1666, a small fire broke out in a baker's oven in nearby Pudding Lane. Supposedly, if you tipped the Monument over (to the east), its top would fall on the exact spot. Fanned by hot, blustery weather, the fire swept westward, leaping from house to house until The City was a square mile of flame.

You can climb the Monument's 311 steps for a view that's still pretty good, despite modern buildings.

• *From here, go uphill a short block on Monument Street, then turn left to hike out over the river on...*

❸ London Bridge

End our walk at The City's beginning. (For the history of London Bridge, see page 294.)

The City was born as a river-trading town. The Thames flows west to east, from the interior of England to the open sea. It's a tidal river from here to the sea, so ancient and medieval boats hitched rides on the tide in both directions. London Bridge, first built by the ancient Romans, established a north-south axis through the city. Soon, goods from every corner of the world were pouring into this, one of the modern world's first great urban centers. Surviving plagues, fires, blitzes, economic changes, and even great recessions, with its worldwide financial network and cultural heritage, The City still thrives.

Today's London, represented by the Shard and the Walkie-Talkie, flanks the river as you look downstream to the rest of the world.

• From here, the **Tower of London** (📖 see the Tower of London Tour chapter) is a 10-minute walk east, down the park-like riverside path. The **Bankside Walk** (📖 see the Bankside Walk chapter) begins across London Bridge. The start of the **East End Walk** (see page 79 in the Sights in London chapter) is a 20-minute walk (up Gracechurch/Bishopsgate) or one Tube stop to the north, at Liverpool Street Station. Or you can return to **Trafalgar Square** on the Tube (Monument stop nearby) or bus #15 (from Cannon Street).

THE CITY

ST. PAUL'S CATHEDRAL TOUR

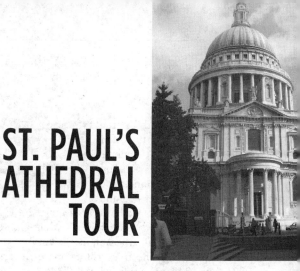

No sooner was Sir Christopher Wren selected to refurbish Old St. Paul's Cathedral than the Great Fire of 1666 incinerated it. Within a week, Wren had a plan for a whole new building...and for the city around it, complete with some 50 new churches. For the next four decades he worked to achieve his vision—a spacious church, topped by a dome, surrounded by a flock of Wrens.

St. Paul's is England's national church. There's been a church on this spot since 604. It was the symbol of London's rise from the Great Fire of 1666 and of the city's survival of the Blitz of 1940. It's been the site of important weddings (Prince Charles and Lady Diana) and state funerals (Prime Ministers Churchill and Thatcher). Architecturally, it's the masterpiece of England's greatest Neoclassical architect. Today, it's the center of the Anglican faith. Military buffs will find memorials to many great wars and their war heroes. Dome climbers will be rewarded with expansive views over London's skyline.

Orientation

Cost: £18, £15.50 in advance on website (includes church entry, dome climb, crypt, tour, and audioguide). Free on Sun but officially open only to worshippers.

Hours: Mon-Sat 8:30-16:30 (dome opens at 9:30), closed Sun except for worship. Sometimes closed for special events—check online. The church is also open Mon-Sat 16:15-18:00 for evening worship. It's always free to enter the church to worship, but your visit is restricted to the back of the nave.

Avoiding Lines: Purchasing online tickets in advance saves time (and a little money), allowing you to skip the line; otherwise the wait can be 15-30 minutes in summer and on weekends.

To avoid the crowds in general, arrive first thing in the morning or late in the afternoon.

Getting There: Located in The City; Tube: St. Paul's (other nearby Tube stops include Mansion House, Cannon Street, and Blackfriars). You can take handy buses #15 and #11 (see page 28), as well as #4, #23, or #26. Careful: Don't head for tiny St. Paul's Church near Covent Garden; your destination is St. Paul's Cathedral, in The City.

Information: Pick up the free visitor's map. Recorded info tel. 020/7246-8348, reception tel. 020/7246-8350, www.stpauls. co.uk.

Music and Church Services: If interested, check the website for worship times the day of your visit. Communion is generally Mon-Sat at 8:00 and 12:30. On Sunday, services are held at 8:00, 10:15 (Matins), 11:30 (sung Eucharist), 15:15 (evensong), and 18:00. The rest of the week, evensong is at 17:00 Tue-Sat (not Mon). If you come 20 minutes early for evensong worship (under the dome), you may be able to grab a big wooden stall in the choir, next to the singers. On some Sundays, there's a free organ recital at 16:45.

Tours: Guided 1.5-hour **tours** are offered Mon-Sat at 10:00, 11:00, 13:00, and 14:00 (call to confirm or ask at church). Free 20-minute **introductory talks** are offered throughout the day. The **audioguide** (included in admission) contains video clips that show the church in action.

🎧 Download my free St. Paul's Cathedral **audio tour.**

Climbing the Dome: It's 528 steps to the top and a mere 257 to the first viewing level. (While there's an elevator for people with disabilities, it does not go up into the dome's galleries—only down to the crypt.) Allow an hour to go up and down. The tower has three levels, called galleries. The climb gets steeper, narrower, and more claustrophobic as you go higher. It's a one-way system, so you can't come back down until you reach the next level.

Length of This Tour: Allow one hour, two if you climb the dome. If you're in a rush, skip the crypt and the dome.

Photography: No photography allowed.

Eating: There's a good café (£5 soups and sandwiches, £8 main dishes) and a pricier restaurant (£16 "express lunch," £22-26 meals, afternoon tea) in the crypt; free access from north side of church. There are several places to get a quick bite in Paternoster Square; for another choice, see page 413.

Nearby: A helpful TI is located to the right of the church. Just behind the church, to the east, is the One New Change modern shopping mall topped by a terrace with great views of the church—not a bad substitute for the dome climb for those disinclined to pay the entry fee and/or climb so many steps (free elevator to top floor). Millennium Bridge is a five-minute walk south, leading to the South Bank (Tate Modern and Shakespeare's Globe).

Starring: Sir Christopher Wren, his dome, and World War II.

The Tour Begins

Even now, as skyscrapers encroach, the 365-foot-high dome of St. Paul's rises majestically above the rooftops of the neighborhood. The tall dome is set on classical columns, capped with a lantern, topped by a six-foot ball, and iced with a cross. As the first Anglican cathedral built in London after the Reformation, it is Baroque: St. Peter's in Rome filtered through clear-eyed English reason.

Viewing St. Paul's facade from in front of the church, you can see the story of Paul's conversion told in the stone pediment. A blinding flash of light leaves Saul sightless on the road to Damascus (see cityscape, lower left). When his sight is restored he becomes Paul, the Christian. This was the pivotal moment in the life of the man who established Christianity as a world religion through his travels, writing, and evangelizing.

While Paul stands on the top, Peter (with the annoying cock that crowed three times, symbolizing his betrayal of Jesus) is to the left, and James is on the right. The four evangelists at the towers' bases each carry the gospel they wrote. As Queen Anne was on the

throne when the church was finished in 1710, the statue in front portrays her.

• *Enter, buy your ticket, pick up the free visitor's map, and stand at the far back of the nave, behind the font.*

ST. PAUL'S CATHEDRAL

St. Paul's Cathedral

1. Nave
2. Wellington Monument
3. Dome
4. Choir & High Altar
5. HUNT—The Light of the World
6. MOORE—Mother and Child
7. American Memorial (Jesus Chapel)
8. John Donne Statue
9. Nelson & Cornwallis Monuments
10. Climb the Dome (2 entrances)
11. Crypt Entrance (2 entrances)

ST. PAUL'S CATHEDRAL

❶ Nave

Look down the nave through the choir stalls to the stained glass at the far end. This big church feels big. At 515 feet long and 250 feet wide, it's Europe's fourth largest, after those in Rome (St. Peter's), Sevilla, and Milan. The spaciousness is accentuated by the relative lack of decoration. The simple, cream-colored ceiling and the clear glass in the windows light everything evenly. Wren wanted this: a simple, open church with nothing to hide. Unfortunately, only this entrance area keeps his original vision—the rest was encrusted with 19th-century Victorian ornamentation.

A diamond-shaped plaque on the floor honors the guards ("St. Paul's Watch") who worked so valiantly from 1939 until 1945 to save the church from WWII destruction. On the wall next to the door a dirty panel of stone remains, reminding visitors how dark the entire church was before undergoing a huge cleaning in preparation for the 300th anniversary of the first service held here. Remarkably, this is the first great church completed in the lifetime of its architect (built 1675-1710).

• *Glance up and behind. The organ trumpets say, "Come to the evensong and hear us play." Ahead and on the left is the towering, black-and-white...*

❷ Wellington Monument

It's so tall that even Wellington's horse has to duck to avoid bumping its head. Wren would have been appalled, but his church has become so central to England's soul that many national heroes are buried here (in the basement crypt). General Wellington, Napoleon's conqueror at Waterloo (1815) and the embodiment of British stiff-upper-lippedness, was honored here in a funeral packed with 13,000 fans. The church is littered with memorials. While all the monuments are upstairs, all the tombs are downstairs.

• *Stroll up the same nave Prince Charles and Lady Diana walked on their 1981 wedding day. Imagine how they felt making the hike to the altar with the world watching. Grab a chair underneath the impressive...*

❸ Dome

The dome you see from here, painted with scenes from the life of St. Paul, is only the innermost of three. From the painted interior

of the first dome, look up through the opening to see the light-filled lantern of the second dome. Finally, the whole thing is covered on the outside by the third and final dome, the shell of lead-covered wood that you see from the street. Wren's ingenious three-in-one design was psychological as well as functional—he wanted a low, shallow inner dome so worshippers wouldn't feel diminished.

You'll see tourists walking around the base of the dome in the Whispering Gallery. The dome is constructed with such acoustic precision that secrets whispered from one side of it are heard on the opposite side, 170 feet away.

Christopher Wren (1632-1723) was the right man at the right time. Though the 31-year-old astronomy professor had never built a major building in his life when he got the commission for St. Paul's, his reputation for brilliance and his unique ability to work with others carried him through. The church has the clean lines and geometric simplicity of the age of Newton, when reason was holy and God set the planets spinning in perfect geometrical motion.

For more than 40 years, Wren worked on this site, overseeing every detail of St. Paul's and the 65,000-ton dome. It's estimated that the dome cost $850 million (in today's dollars). At age 75, Wren got to look up and see his son place the cross on top of the dome, completing the masterpiece.

On the floor directly beneath the dome is a brass grate—part of a 19th-century attempt to heat the church. Encircling it is

Christopher Wren's name and epitaph, written in Latin: *Lector, si monumentum requiris circumspice (Reader, if you seek his monument, look around you).*

Now review the ceiling: Behind is Wren simplicity and ahead is Victorian ornateness.

• *The choir area blocks your way, but you can see the altar at the far end under a golden canopy.*

❹ Choir and High Altar

English churches, unlike most in Europe, often have a central choir area (a.k.a. a "quire" or "chancel"), where church officials and the

singers sit. (You can see St. Paul's well-known choir of 30 boys and 12 men in action, singing psalms, at the evensong service, held daily except Monday.) St. Paul's—a cathedral since 604—is home to the local Anglican bishop, who presides in the chair nearest the altar on the south, or right, side (the carved bishop's hat hangs over the chair).

The ceiling above the choir is a riot of glass mosaics, representing God (above the altar) and his creation. The mosaics are very Victorian. In fact, Queen Victoria complained that the earlier ceiling was "dreary and undevotional." The Dean and chapter wisely took note and had it spiffed up with this brilliant mosaic work... textbook late Victorian. In separate spheres, eight "Angels of the Morning" hold up creatures of the earth, sea, and sky.

The high altar (the marble slab with crucifix and candlesticks—you'll get a close look later) sits under a huge canopy with corkscrew columns. The canopy looks ancient, but it only dates from 1958, when it was rebuilt after being heavily damaged in October of 1940 by the bombs of Hitler's Luftwaffe. For regular services, the priest stands beneath the dome on the low wooden platform.

• *In the north transept (to your left as you face the altar), find the big painting of Christ, in a golden wood altarpiece. Glare? Try walking side-to-side to find the best viewing angle.*

❺ The Light of the World (1904)

In the dark of night, Jesus—with a lantern, halo, jeweled cape, and crown of thorns—approaches an out-of-the-way home in the woods, knocks on the door, and listens for an invitation to come in. A Bible passage on the picture frame says: "Behold, I stand at the door and knock..." (Revelation 3:20).

In his early twenties, William Holman Hunt (1827-1910) was

The Anglican Communion

St. Paul's Cathedral is the symbolic (but not official) nucleus of earth's 70 million Anglicans. The Anglican Communion is a loose association of churches—including the Church of England and the Episcopal Church in the US—with common beliefs. The rallying point is *The Book of Common Prayer,* their handbook for worship services.

Forged in the fires of Europe's Reformation, Anglicans see themselves as a "middle way" between Catholics and Protestants. They retain much of the pomp and ceremony of traditional Catholic worship but with Protestant elements such as married priests (and, recently, female priests); attention to Scripture; and a less hierarchical, more consensus-oriented approach to decision making. Among Anglicans there are divisions, from Low Church congregations (more evangelical and "Protestant") to High Church (more traditional and "Catholic").

The Church of England, the largest single body, is still the official religion of the state, headed by the Archbishop of Canterbury (who presides in Canterbury but lives in London). In 1982, Pope John Paul II and the then Archbishop of Canterbury met face-to-face. In 2010, Pope Benedict XVI visited London and joined the Archbishop in prayer. Pope Francis has indicated that he wants to continue bridging the gap that has existed since the Reformation. These symbolic gestures signal a new ecumenical spirit.

in the dark night of a spiritual crisis when he heard this verse knocking in his head. He opened his soul to Christ, his life changed forever, and he tried to capture the experience in paint. As one of the Pre-Raphaelites who adored medieval art (see page 341), he used symbolism, but only images the average Brit-on-the-street could understand. The door is the closed mind, the weeds the neglected

soul, the darkness is malaise, while Christ carries the lantern of spiritual enlightenment.

In 1854, Hunt debuted *The Light of the World* (not this version, but a smaller one now at Oxford). The critics savaged it—"syrupy," "too Catholic," "simple"—but the masses lapped it up. It became the most famous painting in Victorian England—in fact, in the whole world. It was taken on tour through the vast British Empire, and was reproduced in countless engravings. It became a pop icon that inspired sermons, poems, hymns, and countless Christ-at-the-door paintings in churches and homes. Hunt's humble-hippie image of Christ was stamped forever on the minds of generations of schoolkids. It was so popular that late in life Hunt was asked to do this larger version specifically for St. Paul's. Nearly blind, he needed an assistant. (*The Guardian* newspaper once published a list of "Britain's Ten Worst Paintings." They honored *The Light of the World* as number seven, comparing it to a plastic crucifix.)

• *Return to the area underneath the dome and walk toward the altar, along the left side of the choir, pausing at a modern statue.*

❻ *Mother and Child* (1983)

Britain's (and perhaps the world's?) greatest modern sculptor, Henry Moore, rendered a traditional subject in marble in an abstract, minimalist way. This Mary-and-Baby-Jesus was inspired by the sight of British moms nursing babies in WWII bomb shelters. Moore intended the viewer to touch and interact with the art. It's OK.

• *Continue to the altar at the far end of the church. The area behind it has three bright and modern stained-glass windows.*

❼ American Memorial Chapel (Jesus Chapel)

This special spot in St. Paul's honors the Americans who sacrificed their lives to save Britain in World War II. An inscription on the floor reads: "To the American Dead of the Second World War, From the People of Britain."

Each of the three windows has a central core of religious scenes, but the brightly colored panes that arch around them have some unusual iconography: American. Spot the American eagle (center window, to the left of Christ), George Washington (right window, upper-right corner), and symbols of all 50 states (find your state seal). In the carved wood beneath the windows, you'll see birds and foliage native to the US. And at the very far right of the paneling, check out the tiny tree "trunk" (amid foliage, below the bird)—it's a US rocket ship circa 1958, shooting up to the stars.

Britain is very grateful to its WWII saviors, the Yanks, and remembers them religiously with the Roll of Honor (immediately behind the altar). This 500-page book under glass lists the names of 28,000 US servicemen and women based in Britain who gave their lives during the war.

• *Take a close look at the high altar and the view back to the entrance from here. Look up and enjoy the Victorian mosaic ceiling above the choir.*

Then continue around the altar and head back toward the entrance. On the left wall of the aisle, standing white in a black niche, is a statue of...

❽ John Donne

John Donne (1573-1631), shown here wrapped in a burial shroud, was not only a great poet, but also a passionate preacher. He spent

the last decade of his life working in old St. Paul's. Donne personally chose to be portrayed here in a shroud to capture the melancholy he felt after his wife's death. The statue is one of the few treasures to survive the Great Fire of 1666. You can still see the dark scorch marks on the urn beneath Donne's feet.

Imagine hearing Donne deliver a funeral sermon here, with the huge church bell tolling in the background: "No man is an island... Any man's death diminishes me, because I am involved in Mankind. Therefore, never wonder for whom the bell tolls—it tolls for thee."

• *And also for dozens of people who lie buried beneath your feet, in the crypt where you'll end your tour. But first, in the south transept, find the...*

❾ Horatio Nelson Monument and Charles Cornwallis Monument

Admiral Horatio Nelson (1758-1805) leans on an anchor, his coat draped discreetly over the arm he lost in battle.

In October of 1805, England trembled in fear as Napoleon—bent on world conquest—prepared to invade from across the Channel. Meanwhile, hundreds of miles away, off the coast of Spain, the daring Lord Nelson sailed the HMS *Victory* into battle against the French and Spanish navies. His motto: England expects that every man shall do his duty.

Nelson's fleet smashed the enemy at Trafalgar, and Napoleon's hopes for a naval invasion of Britain sank. Unfortunately, Nelson took a sniper's bullet in the spine and died. The lion at Nelson's feet groans sadly, and two little boys gaze up—one at Nelson, one at Wren's dome. You'll find Nelson's tomb directly beneath the dome, downstairs in the crypt.

Opposite Nelson is a monument to another great military man, Charles Cornwallis (1738-1805), honored here for his service as Governor General of Bengal (India). Yanks know him better as

St. Paul's, the Blitz, and the Battle of Britain

Nazi planes mercilessly firebombed London in 1940. Even though The City around it burned to the ground, St. Paul's survived, giving hope to the citizens. The church took two direct hits, crumbling the altar and collapsing the north transept. On December 29, 1940, some 28 bombs fell on the church. The surrounding neighborhood was absolutely flattened, while the church rose above it, nearly intact. Some swear that many bombs bounced miraculously off Wren's dome, while others credit the heroic work

of local firefighters. (There's a memorial chapel to the firefighters who kept watch over St. Paul's with hoses cocked.) Still, it's clear from the damage that St. Paul's was not fully Blitz-proof.

Often used synonymously, the Blitz and the Battle of Britain are actually two different phases of the Nazi air raids of 1940-1941. The Battle of Britain (June-Sept 1940) pitted Britain's Royal Air Force against German planes trying to soften up Britain for a land-and-sea invasion. The Blitz (Sept 1940-May 1941) was Hitler's punitive terror campaign against civilian London.

In the early days of World War II, the powerful, technologically superior Nazi army quickly overran Poland, Belgium, and France. The British army hightailed it out of France, crossing the English Channel from Dunkirk, and Britain hunkered down, waiting to be invaded. Hitler bombed R.A.F. airfields while his ground troops massed along the Channel. Britain was hopelessly

the general who lost the American Revolutionary War (or "American War," as it's known here) when George Washington—aided by French ships—forced his surrender at Yorktown in 1780.

• *There are several entrances to the dome and its galleries, but only one is open to the public at any given time, so check the free visitor's map.*

❿ Climb the Dome

The 528-step climb is worthwhile, and each level (or gallery) offers something different.

First you get to the Whispering Gallery (257 steps, with views of the church interior). Whisper sweet nothings into the wall, and your partner (and anyone else) standing far away can hear you. Exactly how it works is debated outmatched, but Prime Minister Winston Churchill vowed, "We shall fight on the beaches...We shall fight in the fields and in the streets...We shall never surrender."

Britain fought back. Though greatly outgunned, they had a new and secret weapon—radar—that allowed them to get the jump on puzzled Nazi pilots. Speedy Spitfires flown by a new breed of young pilots shot down 1,700 German planes. By September of 1940, the German land invasion was called off, Britain counterattacked with a daring raid on Berlin...and the Battle of Britain was won.

A frustrated Hitler retaliated with a series of punishing air raids on London itself, known as the Blitz. All through the fall, winter, and spring of 1940-1941, including 57 consecutive nights, Hermann Göring's Luftwaffe pummeled a defenseless London, killing 20,000 and leveling half the city (mostly from St. Paul's eastward). Residents took refuge deep in the Tube stations. From his Whitehall bunker, Churchill made radio broadcasts exhorting his people to give their all, their "blood, toil, sweat, and tears."

Late in the war (1944-1945), Hitler ordered another round of terror-inducing attacks on London (sometimes called the "second Blitz") using car-sized V-1 and V-2 bombs, an early type of cruise missile. But Britain's resolve had returned, the United States had entered the fight, and the pendulum shifted. Churchill could say that even if the empire lasted a thousand years, Britons would look back and say, "This was their finest hour."

Churchill's state funeral was held in 1965 at St. Paul's in a bittersweet remembrance of Britain's victory.

(some even question *if* it works). Most likely, the sound does not travel up and over the dome to the diametrically opposite side (as it would in a perfect sphere). Rather, it goes around the curved wall horizontally, so you don't have to stand in any particular spot. For best effects, try whispering (not talking) with your mouth close to the wall, while your partner stands a few dozen yards away with his or her ear to the wall.

After another set of stairs, you're at the Stone Gallery, with views of London. If you're exhausted, claustrophobic, or wary of heights, this middle level might be high enough. (The top level has very little standing room for tourists.)

Finally a long, tight, metal staircase takes you to the very top of the cupola, the Golden

Gallery. (Just before the final dozen stairs to the top, there's a tiny window at your feet that allows you to peek directly down—350 feet—to the church floor.) Once at the top, you emerge to stunning unobstructed views of the city. Looking west, you'll see the London Eye and Big Ben. To the south, across the Thames, is the rectangular smokestack of the Tate Modern, with Shakespeare's Globe nestled nearby. To the east sprouts a glassy garden of new skyscrapers, including the 600-foot-tall, black-topped Tower 42 and the bullet-shaped 30 St. Mary Axe building (nicknamed "The Gherkin"). Newer still are two buildings easily ID'd by their nicknames—"The Cheese Grater" and "The Walkie-Talkie." Looking farther into the distance, the cluster of skyscrapers marks Canary Wharf. Just north of that was the site of the 2012 Olympic Games, now a pleasant park. Demographers speculate that the rapidly growing East End and Docklands may eventually replace the West End and The City as the center of London. So as you look to the east, you're gazing into London's future.

• *Descend the dome to church level, then follow signs directing you downstairs to the...*

⓫ Crypt

Many famous people are buried here. Start by locating the central tomb of **Horatio Nelson,** who wore down Napoleon. It's a big coffin-on-a-pedestal in a round alcove at the center of the crypt, directly beneath the dome. Nearby (toward the altar) is the granite tomb of the Duke of Wellington (who finished Napoleon off). The flags near the tomb were carried at his funeral procession.

Continuing up the central axis of the crypt, you enter a chapel. At the chapel's altar, turn right to reach **Christopher Wren's** tomb—a simple black slab with no statue. Next to it is a hunk of rough Portland stone quarried but unused by Wren while building St. Paul's; see his triangle brand on the left end. These few stones are not much of an honor for the man who built this great church. "If you seek his monument..." you'll be disappointed.

Use your visitor's map to find other **tombs and memorials:** of painters Turner and Reynolds (located near Wren); of Florence Nightingale (near Wellington); and a memorial to George Washington, who lies buried back in old Virginny.

Back near Nelson's tomb you'll find **temporary exhibits** (they change frequently) that chronicle important events in the church's long history, and models of previous churches that stood on this spot.

The crypt contains a fine gift shop, a WC, a restaurant, and the grim-sounding **Crypt Café,** which nevertheless serves tasty food.

TOWER OF LONDON TOUR

William I, still getting used to his new title of "the Conqueror," built the stone "White Tower" (1077-1097) to keep the Londoners in line. The Tower also served as an effective lookout for seeing invaders coming up the Thames. His successors enlarged it to its present 18-acre size. Because of the security it provided, the Tower served over the centuries as a royal residence, the Royal Mint, the Royal Jewel House, and, most famously, as the prison and execution site of those who dared oppose the Crown.

The Tower's hard stone and glittering jewels represent the ultimate power of the monarch. So does the executioner's block. You'll find more bloody history per square inch in this original tower of power than anywhere else in Britain. Today, though its military purpose is history, it's still home to the Yeoman Warders, a.k.a. the "Beefeaters," who host three million visitors a year.

Your visit has four parts: the lively Beefeater tour (included in admission price, 1 hour), the White Tower (a serious museum and armory, which many rush through and underappreciate), the crown jewels (best in Europe, generally with a bit of a wait), and the grounds and walls (a simple and enjoyable stroll).

Orientation

Cost: £24.50, family-£61 (for 2 adults plus up to 3 kids age 5-15).

Hours: March-Oct Tue-Sat 9:00-17:30, Sun-Mon 10:00-17:30; Nov-Feb closes one hour earlier.

Advance Tickets: To avoid the long ticket-buying lines at the Tower, the easiest option is to buy your ticket at the Trader's Gate gift shop, located down the steps from the Tower Hill Tube stop (tickets here are slightly cheaper than at the gate— they don't include the voluntary donation—and can be used any day). Tickets are also sold at various locations (such as travel agencies) throughout London. You can also try buying tickets, with credit card only, at the Tower Welcome Centre to the left of the normal ticket lines—though on busy days they may turn you away. It's easy to book online, but you must use your ticket within seven days of purchase (www.hrp.org.uk, 10 percent discount). You can also book by phone (tel. 0844-482-7799 within UK or tel. 011-44-20-3166-6000 from the US; £2 fee), then pick up your tickets at the Tower's group ticket office.

More Crowd-Beating Tips: It's most crowded in summer, on weekends (especially Sundays), and during school holidays. Any time of year, the line for the crown jewels—the best on earth—can be just as long as the line for tickets. For fewer crowds, arrive before 10:00 and go straight for the jewels. Alternatively, arrive in the afternoon, tour the rest of the Tower first, and see the jewels an hour before closing time, when crowds die down.

Getting There: The Tower is located in East London (Tube: Tower Hill). For speed, take the Tube there (about 10-12 minutes from central London); for romance, take the boat. Thames Clippers boats make the trip between the Tower of London and Westminster Pier near Big Ben in 30 minutes; the boat continues on to Greenwich from the Tower Pier. For details about these cruises, see page 41. Buses #15 and #RV1 make the trip from Trafalgar Square (see map on page 28).

Information: Upon arrival, pick up the free map/guide, and printed schedule of the day's events and special demonstrations (such as knights in armor explaining medieval fighting techniques; these are most common on particularly busy days such as school holidays). Everything inside is well described, so skip the £5 Tower guidebook. Switchboard tel. 0844-482-7788, www.hrp.org.uk.

Sunday Worship: On Sunday morning, visitors are welcome on the grounds for free to worship in the Chapel Royal of St. Peter ad Vincula. You get in without the lines, but you can only see the chapel—no sightseeing (9:15 Communion or 11:00 service with fine choral music, meet at west gate 30 minutes early, dress for church, may be closed for ceremonies—call ahead; phone number listed above).

Yeoman Warder (Beefeater) Tours: Free, worthwhile, one-hour Beefeater tours leave every 30 minutes from just inside the entrance gate (first tour Tue-Sat at 10:00, Sun-Mon at 10:30, last one at 15:30—or 14:30 in Nov-Feb). The boisterous Beefeaters are great entertainers, whose historical talks include lots of bloody anecdotes and corny jokes. Check the clock inside the entrance gate. If you just miss the start of a tour, you can join it in progress (just catch up to the group a bit ahead). You won't need the £4 audioguide.

Length of This Tour: Allow two hours. If you have less time, see the crown jewels, and try to squeeze in a Beefeater tour to get an overview. If time allows, also tour the White Tower Museum.

Photography: Photos allowed, except of the jewels and in chapels.

Eating: The New Armouries Café, inside the Tower, is a big, efficient, inviting cafeteria (large, splittable meals for £8-10). Outside the Tower, there's an Apostrophe food shop along the river; the big, modern Eat, uphill from the ticket lines; a row of familiar fast-food joints just behind the Welcome Centre; and various takeout stands all around. Picnicking is allowed on Tower grounds but not inside the buildings.

Nearby: Adjacent to the Tower is **Tower Hill,** with two memorials (WWI and WWII) and part of the old **Roman Wall.**

The Tower is also close to three of my self-guided walks: You could walk from Trafalgar Square to the Tower following ▢ The City Walk (which is also available as a ∩ free audio tour). Across the river is the start of the ▢ Bankside Walk (begins at London Bridge, upstream). And just to the north, near Liverpool Street Station, is the start of the ▢ East End Walk (see page 79). Also, the Tower is a short Thames cruise away from Greenwich (see page 39).

Starring: The crown jewels, Beefeaters, William the Conqueror, and Henry VIII.

The Tour Begins

❶ Entrance Gate

Even an army the size of the ticket line couldn't storm this castle. After the drawbridge was pulled up and the iron portcullis slammed down, you'd have to swim a 120-foot moat; cross an island prowled by wild animals; then toss a grappling hook onto a wall and climb up while the enemy poured boiling oil on you. If you made it this far, you'd only be halfway there. You'd still have to swim a second moat (eventually drained to make the grassy parade ground we see today), then, finally, scale a second, higher wall. In all, the central keep (tower) was surrounded by two concentric rings of complete defenses. Yes, it was difficult to get

TOWER OF LONDON

Tower of London Tour

Tour

1. Entrance Gate
2. Traitors' Gate
3. White Tower
4. White Tower Museum
5. Tower Green
6. Scaffold Site
7. Beauchamp Tower
8. Crown Jewels
9. Bloody Tower
10. Medieval Palace
11. Walk the Wall
12. Ravens

Other

- A. Chapel Royal of St. Peter ad Vincula
- B. Salt Tower
- C. Royal Fusiliers Museum
- D. Café
- E. Trader's Gate Gift Shop (Tower Tickets)

into the Tower (if you were a foreign enemy)...but it was almost as impossible to get out (if you were an enemy of the state).

• *Show your ticket, enter, consult the daily event schedule, and consider catching a one-hour Beefeater tour. If you didn't get a free map on the way in, pick one up at the bookstore up ahead (you may have to ask for it). WCs are 100 yards ahead.*

When you're all set, go 50 yards straight ahead to the...

❷ Traitor's Gate

This was the boat entrance to the Tower from the Thames. Princess Elizabeth, who was a prisoner here before she became Queen

Elizabeth I, was carried down the Thames and through this gate on a barge, thinking about her mom, Anne Boleyn, who had been decapitated inside just a few years earlier. Many English leaders who fell from grace entered through here—Elizabeth was one of the lucky few to walk out.

• *Turn left to pass underneath the "Bloody Tower" into the inner courtyard. The big, white tower in the middle is the...*

❸ White Tower

This square, 90-foot-tall tower was the original structure that gave this castle complex of 20 towers its name. William the Conqueror built it more than 900 years ago to put 15 feet

of stone between himself and those he conquered. Over the centuries, the other walls and towers were built around it.

The keep was a last line of defense. The original entry (on the south side) is above ground level so that the wooden approach (you'll climb its modern successor to get in, and lots more stairs once you're inside) could be removed, turning the tower into a safe refuge. Originally, there were even fewer windows—the lower windows were added during a Christopher Wren-ovation in 1660. In the 13th century, the tower was painted white (hence the name).

Standing high above the rest of old London, the White Tower provided a gleaming reminder of the monarchs' absolute power over their subjects. If you made the wrong move here, you could be feasting on roast boar in the Banqueting Hall one night and chained to the walls of the prison the next. Torture ranged from stretching on the rack to the full monty: hanging by the neck until nearly dead, then "drawing" (cut open to be gutted), and finally quartering, with your giblets displayed on the walls as a warning. (Guy Fawkes, who tried to blow up Parliament with 36 barrels of gunpowder, received this treatment after being tortured here.) Any cries for help were muffled by the thick stone walls—15 feet at the base, a mere 11 feet at the top.

• *Either now or later, find time to go inside the White Tower for its excellent museum.*

❹ White Tower Museum

Inside the White Tower, a one-way route winds through exhibits recreating medieval life and the Tower's bloody history of torture and executions.

The **Line of Kings,** greeting you at the doorway and spread throughout this level, includes an array of painted wooden horses,

some carved in the 17th century by revered sculptor Grinling Gibbons, the "King's Carver." For centuries, these horses held the royal suits of armor in the Tower's original exhibits.

In the **Royal Armory,** you'll see some suits of armor of Henry VIII—on a horse, slender in his youth (c. 1515), then more heavy-set by 1540 (with his bigger-is-better codpiece). Next to Henry is the child-size armor once thought to be for his long-awaited male heir, Edward VI, who died young. But the armor actually belonged to Henry, Prince of Wales (1594-1612), the popular son of James I. Get up close to see the incredibly detailed battle scenes. Continuing along, other suits of armor, including those of a 6'8" giant and a 3'1" midget (more likely a child), and swords are identified by king. End this section by finding some memorabilia of Princes William and Harry.

Upstairs, pass through the long hall to reach the rare and lovely **St. John's Chapel** (1080). This is where Lady Jane Grey (described later) offered up a last unanswered prayer. The oldest surviving part of the original Tower—and the oldest church in London—the chapel's round Norman (Romanesque) arches and column capitals decorated with the T-shaped Tau cross evoke the age of William the Conqueror.

Moving on, the **Arsenal** displays the heaviest suit of armor in the world (130 pounds!), as well as various weapons used through the ages, including machine guns and the jeweled "Tiffany Revolver."

On the top floor, ogle the giant dragon made out of old weapons. In the case at the end of this hall, see the Tower's actual **execution ax** and chopping block. In 1747, this seven-pound ax sliced through the neck of Lord Lovat, a Scottish supporter of

The Beefeaters

The original duty of the Yeoman Warders (called "Beefeaters") was to guard the Tower, its prisoners, and the jewels.

Their nickname may come from an original perk of the job—large rations of the king's beef. The Beefeaters dress in blue knee-length coats with red trim and a top hat. The "ER" on the chest stands for the monarch they serve—Queen Elizabeth II (Elizabetha Regina in Latin). On special occasions, they wear red. All are retired noncommissioned officers from the armed forces with distinguished service records.

These days, the Yeoman Warders are no longer expected to protect the Tower. Instead, they've evolved into great entertainers, leading groups of tourists through the Tower. At night, they ritually lock up the Tower in the Ceremony of the Keys (possible to watch if you book upwards of four months in advance). There are 35 Yeoman Warders, including one woman. They and their families make for a Beefeating community of 120 that live inside the Tower.

Bonnie Prince Charlie's claim to the throne. With his death, the ax was retired.

In the next room, kid-oriented, hands-on exhibits bring the history engagingly to life. I learned how hard it is to nock an arrow (to properly align the arrow on the bow prior to release).

• *Back outside, find the courtyard to the left of the White Tower, called...*

❺ Tower Green

In medieval times, this spacious courtyard within the walls was the "town square" for those who lived in the castle. Knights exercised and jousted here, and it was the last place of refuge in troubled times. The Tower is still officially a royal residence, and the Queen's lodgings are on the south side of the green, in the white half-timbered buildings where a bearskin-hatted soldier stands guard.

The north side of the Green is bordered by the stone **Chapel Royal of St. Peter ad Vincula** ("in Chains"). The current structure was built by Henry VIII, and his most famous victims are buried here (among them his wives Anne Boleyn and Catherine Howard). The chapel's interior is open only on the Beefeater tour, except during the last hour of the day, when anyone can go inside to see it. If you aren't on a tour, wait for one to come around, discreetly squeeze into the group while the Beefeater is talking outside the chapel, and go in with the group.

• *Near the middle of Tower Green is a granite-paved square marked* Site of Scaffold.

⑥ Scaffold Site

The actual execution site looks pleasant enough today; the chopping block has been moved to inside the White Tower, and a modern sculpture encourages visitors to ponder those who died.

It was here that enemies of the Crown would kneel before the king for the final time. With their hands tied behind their backs, they would say a final prayer, then lay their heads on a block, and—*shlit*—the blade would slice through their necks, their heads tumbling to the ground. The headless corpses were buried in unmarked graves in Tower Green or under the floor of the Chapel Royal of St. Peter ad Vincula. The heads were stuck on a stick and displayed at London Bridge. Passersby did not really see the heads—they saw spheres of insects and parasites.

Tower Green was the most prestigious execution site at the Tower. Common criminals were hanged outside the Tower. More prominent evil-doers were decapitated before jeering crowds atop Tower Hill (near today's Tube station). Inside the Tower walls was reserved for the most heinous traitors.

Henry VIII axed a couple of his ex-wives here (divorced readers can insert their own cynical joke). Anne Boleyn was the appealing young woman Henry had fallen so hard for that he broke with the Catholic Church in order to divorce his first wife and marry her. But when Anne failed to produce a male heir, the court turned against her. She was locked up in the Tower, tried in a kangaroo court, branded an adulteress and traitor, and decapitated.

Henry's fifth wife, teenage Catherine Howard, was beheaded and her body laid near Anne's in the church. Jane Boleyn (Anne's sister-in-law) was also executed here for arranging Catherine's adulterous affair behind Henry's back. Next.

Henry even beheaded his friend Thomas More (a Catholic) because he refused to recognize (Protestant) Henry as head of the Church of England. (Thomas died at the less-prestigious Tower Hill site near the Tube stop.)

The most tragic victim was 17-year-old Lady Jane Grey, who was manipulated into claiming the Crown for nine days during the scramble for power after Henry's death and the six-year reign and death of his sickly young son, Edward VI. When Bloody Mary (Mary I, Henry's daughter) took control, she forced her Protestant cousin Jane to kneel before the executioner. Young Jane bravely blindfolded herself, but then couldn't find the block. She crawled around the scaffolding pleading, "Where is it?!" (The scene is depicted, beautifully if not entirely accurately, in sharp Pre-Raphaelite detail in one of the National Gallery's most popular paintings; see page 164.)

Years ago, a Beefeater, tired of what he called "Hollywood coverage" of the Tower, grabbed my manuscript, read it, and told me that in more than 900 years as a fortress, palace, and prison, the place held 8,500 prisoners. But only 120 were executed, and, of those, only six were executed inside it. Stressing the hospitality of the Tower, he added, "Torture was actually quite rare here."

• *Overlooking the scaffold site is the...*

❼ Beauchamp Tower—Prisoners

The Beauchamp Tower (pronounced "BEECH-um") was one of several places in the complex that housed Very Important Prisoners. Climb upstairs to a room where the walls are covered with dozens of final messages—graffiti carved into the stone by bored and despondent inmates.

Picture Philip Howard, the Earl of Arundel (c. 1555-1595), warming himself by this fireplace and glancing out at the execution

site during his 10-year incarceration. Having lived a devil-may-care life of pleasure in the court of Queen Elizabeth, the pro-Catholic Arundel was charged with treason by the Protestant government. He pleaded with the queen—his former friend—to at least let him see his wife and young children. She refused, unless he would renounce his faith. On June 22, 1587, he carved his family name "Arundell" into the chimney (graffiti #13) and wrote in Latin: "*Quanto plus afflictionis...*" ("The more we suffer for Christ in this world, the more glory with Christ in the next.") Arundel suffered faithfully another eight years here before he wasted away and died at age 40.

Graffiti #85 belongs to Lady Jane Grey's young husband, Lord Guilford Dudley. Locked in the Beauchamp Tower and executed the same day as his wife, Dudley vented his despair by scratching

"IANE" into the stone. Cynics claim he was actually whining for his mommy, who was also named Jane.

Read other pitiful graffiti, like the musings of James Typping (#18). Imprisoned for three years "in great disgrace," he wonders what will happen to him: "I cannot tell but be death." Consider the stoic cry of Thomas Miagh (#29), an Irish rebel, who writes: "By torture straynge my truth was tried," having suffered some form of the rack. Thomas Clarke (#28), a Catholic priest who later converted to Protestantism, wrote pathetic poetry: "Unhappy is that man whose acts doth procure/the misery of this house in prison to endure." Many held onto their sense of identity by carving their family's coats of arms.

The last enemy of the state imprisoned in the Tower complex was one of its most infamous: the renegade Nazi Rudolf Hess. In 1941, Hitler's henchman secretly flew to Britain with a peace proposal (Hitler denied any such plan). He parachuted into a field, was arrested and held for four days in the Tower, and was later given a life sentence.

• *Join the looooong line leading to the crown jewels. Pass time in line reading ahead—it's too dark inside to read.*

❽ Crown Jewels

When you finally enter the building, you'll pass through a series of rooms with instructive warm-up videos. Don't let the crowd rush you—just step aside if you want to keep watching. The videos touch on the many kings and queens who have worn the crown jewels, from William I the Conqueror (1066), to Henry VIII, to his daughter Elizabeth I, to the current Queen Elizabeth II. Film clips show you close-up highlights of coronation regalia, as well as the most recent coronation—Elizabeth II's, in 1953.

After the videos, you enter the exhibits, seeing each of the actual coronation items in the order that they're used whenever a new king or queen is crowned. First, you walk down a hallway displaying the ceremonial maces, swords, and trumpets that lead the actual coronation procession into Westminster Abbey.

Next comes a room with the royal regalia. The monarch-to-be is anointed with holy oil poured from the eagle-beak flask; handed the jeweled Sword of Offering; and dressed in the 20-pound gold robe and other gear. (Other items in the first case are simply standing by. The 12th-century coronation spoon, last used in 1953 to anoint the head of Queen Elizabeth, is the most ancient object here.) Most of the original crown jewels from medieval times were lost during Cromwell's 1648 revolution.

After being dressed and anointed, the new monarch prepares for the "crowning" moment.

• *Five glass cases display the various crowns, orbs, and scepters used in various royal ceremonies. Ride the moving sidewalk that takes you past them. You're welcome to circle back and glide by again (I did, several times). Or, to get away from the crowds, hang out on the elevated viewing area with the guard. Chat with the guards—they're actually here to provide information (and to keep you from taking photos, which aren't allowed). As you glide by on the walkway, you'll see the following items. (The collection rotates, so you may not see all of the crowns described here.)*

Scepter and Orb: After being crowned, the new monarch is handed these items. The **Sovereign's Scepter** is encrusted with the world's largest cut diamond—the 530-carat Star of Africa, beefy as a quarter-pounder. This was one of nine stones cut from the original 3,106-carat (1.37-pound) Cullinan diamond. The **orb** symbolizes how Christianity rules over the earth, a reminder that even a "divine monarch" is not above God's law. The coronation is a kind of marriage between the church and the state in Britain, since the king or queen is head of both, and the ceremony celebrates the monarch's power to do good for the whole of the nation.

St. Edward's Crown: This coronation crown is the one placed by the archbishop upon the head of each new monarch on coronation day in Westminster Abbey. It's worn for 20 minutes, then locked away until the next coronation. The original crown, destroyed by Cromwell, was older than the Tower itself and dated back to 1061, the time of King Edward the Confessor, "the last English king" before William the Conqueror invaded from France (1066). This 1661 remake is said to contain some of the original's gold amid its 443 precious and semiprecious stones. Because the crown weighs nearly five pounds, weak or frail monarchs have opted not to wear it.

Other Crowns: Various other crowns illustrate a bit of regalia symbolism. Kings and queens get four arches on their crowns, emperors get eight arches (e.g., the Imperial Crown of India you'll see in the case at the exit), and princes get only two (for example, see the crowns of Prince George—before he became King George V—and Prince Frederick; today's Prince Charles keeps his two-arch crown in Wales).

The Crown of the Queen Mother: This crown, last worn by Elizabeth II's famous mum (who died in 2002), has the 106-carat Koh-I-Noor diamond glittering on the front. The Koh-I-Noor diamond is considered unlucky for male rulers and, therefore, only adorns the crown of the king's wife. If Charles becomes king, Camilla might wear this. This crown was remade in 1937 and given an innovative platinum frame.

• *Continuing on from the moving walkway, but in the same room (toward the exit), you'll find...*

Queen Victoria Small Diamond Crown: It's tiny. Victoria had a normal-sized head, but this was designed to sit atop the widow's veil she insisted on wearing for decades after the death of her husband, Prince Albert. This four-ounce job was made in 1870 for £50,000—personally paid for by the queen.

• *Moving on, you'll see gilded platters and bowls used in the post-coronation banquet before you reach one final room, with one last crown.*

The **Imperial State Crown** is what the Queen wears for official functions such as the State Opening of Parliament. When

Victoria was queen, she insisted on wearing her small crown, but by law, this State Crown had to be carried next to her on a pillow, as it represents the sovereign. Among its 3,733 jewels are Queen Elizabeth I's former earrings (the hanging pearls, top center), a stunning 13th-century ruby look-alike in the center, and Edward the Confessor's ring (the blue sapphire on top, in the center of the Maltese cross of

diamonds). When Edward's tomb was exhumed—a hundred years after he was buried—his body was "incorrupted." The ring on his saintly finger featured this sapphire and ended up on the crown of all future monarchs. This is the stylized crown you see representing the royalty on Britain's coins and stamps. It's depicted on the Beefeater uniforms and on the pavement at the end of the sliding walk.

• *The final room is the epilogue of the jewels collection, with videos showing attendants putting all of these precious items back into their cases after the last coronation—emphasizing that these aren't just pretty museum pieces, but a vital part of an ongoing tradition.*

Leave the jewels by exiting through the thick vault doors and head back toward the Scaffold Site. Find the entrance to the Bloody Tower, at the far end of Tower Green.

❾ Bloody Tower

Not all prisoners died at the block. The 13-year-old King Edward V and his kid brother were kidnapped in 1483 during the Wars of the Roses by their uncle Richard III ("Now is the winter of our discontent...") and locked in the Bloody Tower, never to be seen again. End of story? Two centuries later, the skeletons of two unidentified children were found here. The 2013 discovery of the remains of Richard III (in Leicester, in central England) may allow modern forensics to solve this centuries-old mystery.

Sir Walter Raleigh—poet, explorer, and political radical—was imprisoned here for 13 years. In 1603, the English writer and adventurer was accused of plotting against King James and sentenced to death. The king commuted the sentence to life imprisonment in the Bloody Tower. While in prison, Raleigh wrote the first volume of his *History of the World*. Check out his rather cushy bedroom, study, and walkway (courtesy of the powerful tobacco lobby?). Raleigh promised the king a wealth of gold if he would release him to search for El Dorado. The expedition was a failure. Upon Raleigh's return, the displeased king had him beheaded in 1618.

• *Next door to the Bloody Tower, inside the base of the Lower Wakefield Tower, is a cellar filled with some replica torture equipment. To reach the next sight, walk under the Bloody Tower, cross the cobbled road, and bear right a few steps to find the stairs up onto the wall.*

⑩ Medieval Palace

The Tower was a royal residence as well as a fortress. These rooms were built around 1240 by Henry III, the king most responsible for the expansive Tower of London complex we see today. The well-described rooms are furnished as they might have been during the reign of his son, Edward I ("Longshanks"). You'll see his re-created bedroom, then—up a flight of stairs—his throne room, both with massive fireplaces to keep this cold stone palace cozy. After Cromwell temporarily deposed the monarchy (in the 17th century), the Tower ceased to be a royal residence except in name.

• *From the throne room, continue up the stairs to...*

⑪ Walk the Wall

The Tower was defended by state-of-the-art walls and fortifications in the 13th century. This walk offers a good look. From the walls, you also get a fine view of the famous bridge straddling the Thames, with the twin towers and blue spans. It's not London Bridge (which is the nondescript bridge just upstream), but **Tower Bridge.**

Although it looks somewhat medieval, this drawbridge was built in 1894, of steel and concrete. Sophisticated steam engines raise and lower the bridge, allowing tall-masted ships to squeeze through.

Gaze out at the bridge, the river, City Hall (the egg-shaped glass building across the river—see page 94), the Shard (London's bold new exclamation point—see page 93), and life-filled London.

• *Between the White Tower and the Bloody Tower are cages housing the...*

⑫ Ravens

According to goofy tradition, the Tower and the British throne are only safe as long as ravens are present here. These eight impressive birds—the traditionally re- quired six, plus two spares— have clipped wings to keep them close. World War II bombing raids reduced the population to one. Some years ago, with their clipped wings, the birds had trouble mating, so a slide was built to help them get a bit of lift to facilitate the process. Happily, that worked, and a baby raven was born. A children's TV show sponsored a nationwide contest to come up with a name. The winner: "Ronald Raven." Today, they mimic and answer tourists like Edgar Allan Poe's Magic 8 Ball (though I've only heard them answer German *Fraus* with something akin to "Google it") and are as much a part of the Tower as the jewels. As you leave through the riverside exit, look into the moat on the right for the tiny raven graveyard. There lie Cedric (2003), Gundolf (2005), Hardey (2006), and Jubilee and Grip (2013). RIP.

Other Sights

Get out your Tower-issued map to check out other areas you can visit. The **Salt Tower** has graffiti by Henry Walpole, a staunch Catholic who was imprisoned here by Queen Elizabeth I, tor- tured on the rack, and had a finger torn off. At the **Royal Fusiliers Regimental Museum** you can see the uniforms, swords, and fusils (flintlock rifles) of the army of Redcoats who fought Napoleon, the American War of Independence, two World Wars ("Monty"— Field Marshal Bernard Montgomery of D-Day fame—was a Fu- silier), and wars in the Persian Gulf.

Take one final look at the stern stone walls of the Tower. Be glad you can leave.

TOWER OF LONDON

BANKSIDE WALK

*Along the South Bank
of the Thames*

Bankside—the neighborhood between London Bridge and Black-friars Bridge—is the historic heart of the revamped southern bank of the Thames. In ancient times "greater London" consisted of two Roman settlements straddling the easiest place to ford the river: One settlement was here, and the other was across the river—in the financial district known today as "The City."

From the Roman era until recently, the south side of the river was the wrong side of the tracks. For centuries, it was London's red light district. In the 20th century, it became an industrial wasteland of empty warehouses and street crime. Today, the prostitutes and pickpockets are gone, replaced by a riverside promenade dotted with trendy pubs, cutesy shops, and historic tourist sights.

This half-mile Bankside Walk gives you plenty of history and sights to choose from—you can see it all, design your own plan, or just enjoy the view of London's skyline across the river.

Orientation

Length of This Walk: One hour (or up to a half-day if you tour Shakespeare's Globe and the Tate Modern).

Getting There: Take the Tube to the London Bridge stop to begin the walk. (The Monument stop, on the Circle Line, is also nearby.)

Old Operating Theatre Museum and Herb Garret: £6.50, daily 10:30-17:00, closed Dec 15-Jan 5.

Southwark Cathedral: Free, but £4 donation requested (be prepared with at least £1 or a simple "No"); Mon-Fri 8:00-18:00, Sat-Sun 8:30-18:00 (but partially closed during frequent services—schedule posted out front).

Borough Market: Retail food market open Wed-Thu 10:00-17:00,

Fri 10:00-18:00, Sat 8:00-17:00, closed Sun-Tue; surrounding eatery stalls open daily 10:00-17:00.

Golden Hinde Replica: £6, daily 10:00-17:00, sometimes closed for private events.

The Clink Prison Museum: Overpriced at £7.50; July-Sept daily 10:00-21:00; Oct-June Mon-Fri 10:00-18:00, Sat-Sun until 19:30.

Shakespeare's Globe: £13.50, includes museum, audioguide, and 40-minute guided tour; open daily 9:00-17:30, late April-mid-Oct last tour Mon at 17:00, Tue-Sat at 12:30, Sun at 11:30 (see page 90 or the Entertainment in London chapter for how to buy tickets to a performance).

Tate Modern: Free, but £4 donation appreciated (fee for special exhibits), daily 10:00-18:00, Fri-Sat until 22:00, last entry to temporary exhibits 45 minutes before closing, view restaurant on top floor.

Starring: Shakespeare's world, London Bridge, historic pubs, and views of the London skyline.

The Walk Begins

• *Start at the south end of London Bridge (where "The City Walk" ends; see page 262). From the London Bridge Tube stop, take the "Borough High Street east" exit and turn right (north), pass the One London Bridge complex, and walk out on the bridge about 100 yards*

❶ London Bridge

The City (across the river) is to the north, Tower Bridge is east, and the Thames flows from west to east (left to right). Looking to the east (downstream) and turning counterclockwise, you'll see the following:

Downstream

• Tower Bridge, the Neo-Gothic towered drawbridge that many Americans mistakenly call London Bridge.
• The HMS *Belfast* (in the foreground, docked on the southern bank), a WWII cruiser that's open to tourists.
• Canary Wharf Tower (the distant 800-foot skyscraper with pyramid top and blinking light), built in 1990 on the Isle of Dogs. It recently lost its standing as the UK's tallest building to The Shard. This marks the Docklands, London's "new Manhattan" and a thriving business district. Once the biggest port in the world, serving the empire upon which

BANKSIDE

Legend:
1. London Bridge
2. View of London Bridge
3. Southwark Cathedral
4. Old Operating Theatre Museum & Herb Garret
5. The George Inn
6. Borough Market
7. Golden Hinde Replica
8. Winchester Palace

Ⓑ #RV1 Bus Stop

"the sun never set," today the wharves have moved farther out to accommodate bigger ships.

- The "Pool of London." This is the stretch of river between Tower Bridge (a drawbridge) and London Bridge, which marks the farthest point seagoing vessels can sail inland. In the 18th century this was the busiest port in the world.

North Bank

- The Tower of London (four domed spires and a flag rising above the trees).
- The 20 Fenchurch Street skyscraper (a.k.a. "The Walkie-

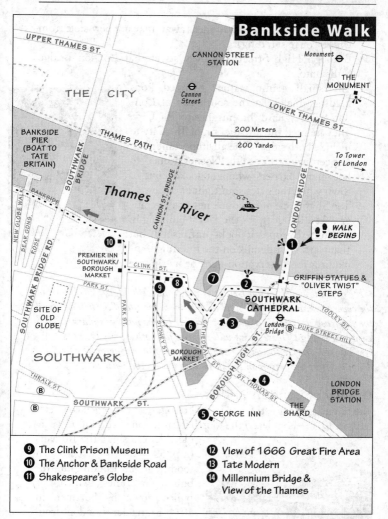

Bankside Walk

9 The Clink Prison Museum
10 The Anchor & Bankside Road
11 Shakespeare's Globe

12 View of 1666 Great Fire Area
13 Tate Modern
14 Millennium Bridge &
   View of the Thames

Talkie") and, behind it, the Leadenhall Building (a.k.a. "The Cheese Grater").

- St. Paul's Cathedral (to the northwest, with a dome like a state capitol and twin spires).
- St. Bride's Church, the pointed, stacked steeple (nestled among office buildings) that supposedly inspired the wedding cake.
- BT Tower, a communications tower.

South Bank

- The Tate Modern art museum (square brick smokestack tower, barely visible).

- Southwark Cathedral (100 yards away, may not be visible from where you're standing).
- Borough High Street, the busy street that London Bridge spills onto.
- The small griffin statues (winged lions holding shields) at the south end of London Bridge guard the entrance to The City. They marked the jurisdiction of The City to include both sides of the all-important river. For centuries, they said, "Neener neener" to late-night partiers who got locked out of town when the gates shut tight at curfew.

- The Shard, one of London's newer skyscrapers. At 1,020 feet, it's the tallest building in Western Europe. It looks unfinished, but that's art. (For details on the building—including the observation deck at its tip, see page 93.)

• The best view of London Bridge is not from the bridge itself, but from the riverbank. Retrace your steps back to the south end of the bridge. Find the staircase next to the southwest griffin, by the building marked Two London Bridge. *These stairs will impress fans of Charles Dickens'* Oliver Twist—*they're the setting of the infamous "Meeting on the Bridge." Turn right at the bottom of the stairs and follow the river to a...*

❷ View of London Bridge

The bridge of today—three spans of boring, traffic-clogged concrete, built in 1972—is (at least) the fourth incarnation of this 2,000-year-

old river crossing. The Romans (A.D. 50) built the first wooden footbridge to Londinium (rebuilt many times), which was pulled down by boatmen in 1014 to retake London from Danish invaders. (They celebrated with a song passed down to us as "London Bridge is falling down, my fair lady.")

The most famous version—crossed by everyone from Richard the Lionheart, to Henry VIII, to Shakespeare, to Newton, to Darwin—was built around 1200 and stood for more than six centuries, the only crossing point into this major city. Built of stone on many thick pilings, stacked with houses and shops that arched over the roadway and bulged out over the river, with its own chapel and a fortified gate at each end, it was a neighborhood unto itself (pop. 300). Picture Mel Gibson's head boiled in tar and stuck on a spike along the bridge (like the Scots rebel William Wallace in 1305, depicted in Gibson's movie *Braveheart*), and you'll capture the local color of that time.

In 1823, the famous bridge was replaced with a more modern (but less impressive) brick one. In 1967, that brick bridge was sold to an American, dismantled, shipped to Arizona, and reassembled (all 10,000 bricks) in Lake Havasu City. (Humor today's Brits, who'd like to believe the Yank thought he was buying Tower Bridge.) It was only then that today's bridge was built.

• *Circle around the cathedral and find the entrance on the opposite side.*

❸ Southwark Cathedral

This neighborhood parish church is where Shakespeare prayed while his brother Edmund rang the bells. The Southwark (SUTH-

uck) church dates back to 1207, though the site has had a church for at least a thousand years, and inhabitants for 2,000. The church is simply filled with history (pick up the info flier).

❹ **View down the Nave:** Clean and sparse, with warm golden stone, the church is a symbol of the urban renewal of the whole Bankside/Southwark area. Its WWII damage has been repaired, with replacement windows of unstained glass on the right side. The nave bends slightly to the left (the chandelier, ceiling arches, and altar don't line up until you take two baby steps left) as a medieval tribute to Christ's bent body on the cross.

• *Work your way counterclockwise around the church.*

❺ **Shakespeare Monument:** William reclines in front of a backdrop of the 16th-century Bankside skyline (view looking

north). Find (left to right) the original Globe Theatre, Winchester Palace, Southwark Cathedral, and the old London Bridge with its arched gate—complete with heads on pikes, ISIS-style. Shakespeare seems to be dreaming about the many characters of his plays, depicted in the stained-glass window

above (see Hamlet addressing a skull, right window). To the right is a plaque to the American actor Sam Wanamaker, who spearheaded the building of a replica of Shakespeare's Globe Theatre (explained later in this chapter). Shakespeare's brother Edmund is buried in

BANKSIDE

the church, possibly under a marked slab on the floor of the choir area, near the very center of the church. (The Bard lies buried in his hometown of Stratford-upon-Avon.)

C Retro-Choir: The 800-year-old crisscross arches and stone tracery in the windows are some of the oldest parts of this historic church. Located in the heart of the industrial district, the church was heavily bombed during World War II and then rebuilt.

D Model of Church: Tucked in behind the choir, find a model (marked *Church and Priory of St. Mary Overy*) of the church and old Winchester Palace complex—a helpful reconstruction before we visit the paltry Winchester Palace ruins.

E John Harvard Chapel: The Southwark-born son of an innkeeper (see the record of baptism at the bottom of the window) inherited money from the sale of The Queen's Head tavern, got married, and sailed to Boston (1637), where he soon died. The money and his 400-book library funded the start of Harvard University.

F Tomb of John Gower: The poet and friend of Chaucer (c. 1400) rests his head on his three books, one written in Middle English, one in French, and one in Latin—the three languages from which modern English soon emerged.

• *This walk is a pick-and-choose collection of sights. If you're interested in visiting the Old Operating Theatre Museum and Borough High Street inns, described next, see them first before heading west (use the map to locate these nearby sights).*

O Old Operating Theatre Museum and Herb Garret

Back when the common cold was treated with a refreshing blood-letting, the Old Operating Theatre—a surgical operating room from the 1800s—was a shining example of "modern" medicine. Today a museum, this is a quirky, sometimes gross look at that painful transition from folk remedy to clinical health care. Originally part of a larger hospital complex, the Old Operating Theatre was boarded up when the hospital relocated, lying untouched for 100 years until its chance discovery in 1956. The location alone—in a long-forgotten attic above a church, reached by a steep spiral staircase—makes this odd place worth a visit.

After buying your ticket, climb a few more stairs into a big room under heavy timbers—the Herb Garret, which was used to dry herbs for the former hospital. Today, it displays healing plants used for millennia—different ones for each of the traditional four ailments (melancholic, choleric, sanguine, phlegmatic), supposedly caused by an imbalance in the body's traditional four substances, or "humours" (black bile, yellow bile, blood, and phlegm), corresponding to the earth's traditional four elements (earth, wind, fire, and Ringo). Florence Nightingale, the nurse famed for saving so many Crimean War soldiers wounded in Russia, worked here to improve sanitation and to turn nurses from low-paid domestics into trained doctors' assistants.

The small hallway leading to the theater displays crude anesthetics (ether, chloroform, three pints of ale), surgical instruments by Black & Decker (knives, saws, drills), and a glaring lack of antiseptics—that is, until young Dr. Joseph Lister discovered carbolic acid, which reduced the high rates of mortality (and halitosis).

Up the stairs, the Old Operating Theatre is the highlight—a semicircular room surrounded by railings for 150 spectators (truly a "theater"), where doctors operated on patients while med students observed.

The patients were often poor women, blindfolded for their own modesty. The doctors donated their time to help, practice, and teach (see the motto *Miseratione non Mercede:* "Out of compassion, not for profit"). The surgeries, usually amputations, were performed under very crude working conditions—under the skylight or by gaslight, with no sink, and only sawdust to sop up blood. (A false floor held another layer of sawdust to stop the blood before it dripped through to the ceiling of the church below.) The wood still bears bloodstains. Nearly one in three patients died. There was a fine line between Victorian-era surgeons and Jack the Ripper.

• *Farther down Borough High Street (on the left-hand side), you'll find...*

❺ The George Inn and (Faint Echoes of) Other Historic Taverns

The George is the last of many "coaching inns" that lined the main highway from London to all points south. Like Greyhound bus stations, each inn was a terminal for far-flung journeys, since coaches were forbidden inside The City. They offered food, drink, beds, and entertainment for travelers—Shakespeare, as a young actor, likely performed in The George's courtyard. On a sunny day, the courtyard is a fine place for a break from the Borough High Street bustle (food served all day long, five ales on tap including their own brew).

• *Walk back to Southwark Cathedral. On your way, you'll find the...*

❻ Borough Market

Historically, the first trading started at 2:00 in the morning at this open-air wholesale produce market. Workers could knock off by sunrise for a pint at the specially licensed Market Porter tavern (on Park Street—and still popular). From Wednesday through Saturday, the colorful market opens for retail sales to Londoners seeking trendy specialty and organic foods. It's great for gathering a picnic on a sunny day. Of the many market stalls, the Ginger Pig is *the* place

for serious English sausage and bacon (west end of market, across from Park Street), while Maria's Market Café is a colorful eatery popular with market workers (the red stall in the middle of the market).

First started a thousand years ago on London Bridge, where country farmers brought fresh goods to the city gates, the market now sits here under a Victorian arcade. The railroad rumbling overhead, knifing right through dingy apartment houses (and the Globe Tavern), only adds to the color of London's oldest vegetable market and public gathering spot.

A detour westward through the market leads to Park Street, with an old 19th-century ambience that makes it popular as a filming location. Check out the colorful pub and the fragrant cheese shop at Neal's Yard Dairy.

If you're hungry, food stalls are plentiful here (and open daily), but seating is scarce. A new glassed-in section by High Street has lots of benches for munching.

• *Walk to the river along Cathedral Street, veering left at the Y. (Alternatively, from the far end of the market, turn right down Stoney Street, then right again on Clink Street.)*

❼ *Golden Hinde* Replica

As we all learned in school, "Sir Francis Drake circumcised the globe with a hundred-foot clipper." Or something like that...

Imagine a hundred men on a boat this size (yes, this replica is full-size) circling the globe on a three-year voyage, sleeping on the wave-swept decks, suffering bad food, floggings, doldrums, B.O., and attacks from foreigners. They explored unknown waters and were paid only from whatever riches they could find or steal along the way. (I took a bus tour like that once.)

The *Golden Hinde* (see the female deer, or hind, on the prow and stern) was Sir Francis Drake's flagship as he circumnavigated the globe (1577-1580). Drake, a farmer's son who followed the lure of the sea, hated Spaniards. So did Queen Elizabeth I, who hired him to plunder rich Spanish vessels and New World colonies in England's name.

With 164 men on five small ships (the *Hinde* was the largest, at 100 tons and 18 cannons), he sailed southwest, dipping

around South America, raiding Spanish ships and towns in Chile, and inching up the coast perhaps as far as Canada. By the time it continued across the Pacific to Asia and beyond, the *Hinde* was so full of booty that its crew replaced the rock ballast with gold ingots and silver coins. Three years later, Drake—with only one remaining ship and 56 men—sailed the *Hinde* up the Thames, unloading a fabulously valuable hoard of gold, silver, emeralds, diamonds, pearls, silks, cloves, and spices before the queen. A grateful Elizabeth knighted Drake on the main deck and kissed him on his *Golden Hinde.*

The *Hinde* was retired gloriously, but rotted away from neglect. Drake received a large share of the wealth, became enormously famous, and later gained more glory defeating the Spanish Armada

BANKSIDE

(aided by "the winds of God") in the decisive battle in the English Channel, off Plymouth (1588), making England ruler of the waves.

The galleon replica, a working ship that has itself circled the globe, is berthed at St. Mary Overie Dock ("St. Mary's over the river"), a public dock available for free to all Southwark residents. A victim of WWII bombing and container ships that require big berths and deep water, the Thames river trade that used to thrive even this far upstream is now concentrated east of Tower Bridge. Only a few brick warehouses remain (just west of here), waiting to be leveled or yuppified. Although you can pay to enter the ship, it's not worth the cost of admission.

• *There's a fine view (with a handy chart to identify things) from the riverside. The beach below is fun for beachcombing—old red roof tiles and little chunks of disposable clay tobacco pipes litter the rocks at low tide. From here, the Monument is visible across London Bridge, poking its bristly bronze head above the ugly postwar buildings. Londoners have fun nicknaming their new skyscrapers. See if you can pick out The Gherkin, The Cheese Grater, and The Walkie-Talkie. Now go up the street across from the* Golden Hinde's *gangplank (Pickfords Wharf) and head west. About 25 yards ahead on the left are the excavated ruins of...*

❽ Winchester Palace

All that remains today is a wall with a medieval rose window, but this was once a lavish 80-acre estate stretching along 200 feet of waterfront. It had a palace, gardens, fountains, stables, tennis courts, a working farm, and a fish-stocked lake. The wall marks the west end of the Great Hall (134 feet by 29 feet), the banquet room for receptions held by the palace's owner, the Bishop of Winchester.

Bishops from 1106 to 1626 lived here as wealthy, worldly rulers of the Bankside area, outside the jurisdiction of The City. They profited from activities that were illegal across the river, such as prostitution and gambling. They were a law unto themselves, with their own courts and prisons. One famous prison—the Clink—built by the bishops remained, even after its creators were ousted by a Puritan Parliament.

• *Fifty yards farther west (along what is now called Clink Street) is...*

❾ The Clink Prison Museum

Now an overpriced and disappointing museum that feels like a Disney ride with a few historic artifacts tossed in, this prison gave us our expression "thrown in the Clink," from the sound of prison-

BANKSIDE

ers' chains. It burned down in 1780, but the underground cells remain, featuring historical information on wall plaques, many torture devices, and a generally creepy, claustrophobic atmosphere.

Originally part of Winchester Palace, it housed troublemakers who upset the smooth running of the bishop's 22 licensed brothels (called "the stews"), gambling dens, and taverns. Bouncers delivered drunks who were out of control, johns who couldn't pay, and prostitutes ("women living by their bodies") who tried to go freelance or cheated loyal customers. Offending prostitutes had their heads shaved and breasts bared, and were carted through the streets and whipped while people jeered. They might share cells side by side with "heretics"—namely, priests who'd crossed their bishops.

In 1352, debtors (who'd maxed out their VISA cards) became criminals, housed here among harder criminals in harsh conditions. Prisoners were not fed. They had to bribe guards to get food, to avoid torture, or even to gain their release. (The idea was that you'd brought this on yourself.) Prisoners relied on their families for money, prostituted themselves to guards and other inmates, or reached through the bars at street level, begging from passersby. Murderers, debtors, Protestants, priests, and many innocent people experienced this strange brand of justice...all part of the rough crowd that gave Bankside such a seedy reputation.

• *Continuing west and crossing under the Cannon Street Bridge, just ahead and across the street is...*

⑩ The Anchor and Bankside Road

The Anchor is the last of the original 22 licensed "inns" (tavern/brothel/restaurant/nightclub/casino) of Bankside's red light district heyday in the 1600s. A tavern has stood here for 800 years. The big brick buildings behind the inn were once part of the mass-producing Anchor brewery, with the inn as its brew pub. (Even back in the 1300s, Chaucer wrote, "If the words get muddled in my tale/Just put it down to too much Southwark ale.")

In the cozy, maze-like interior are memories of greats who've drunk here (I have) or indulged in a new drug that hit London in the 1560s—tobacco. Shake-

ANCHOR TAP

speare, who may have lived along Clink Street, may have tippled here, especially because the original Globe Theatre was right behind The Anchor (see map on page 293). Dr. Samuel Johnson also worked here while writing the famous dictionary that helped codify the English language and spelling (for more on Dr. Johnson, see page 249).

The Anchor marks the start of the once-notorious Bankside Road that runs along a river retaining wall. In Elizabethan times (16th century), the street was lined with "inns" offering one-stop shopping for addictive personalities. The streets were jammed with sword-carrying punks in tights looking for a fight, prostitutes, gaping tourists from the Borough High Street coaching inns, pickpockets, river pirates, highwaymen, navy recruiters kidnapping drunks, and many proper ladies and gentlemen who ferried across from The City for an evening's entertainment. And then there were the really seedy people—yes, actors.

• *Crossing under the green-and-yellow Southwark Bridge, notice the metal reliefs depicting London's "Frost Fair" of 1564. Because the old London Bridge was such a wall of stone, the swift-flowing Thames would back up and even freeze over during cold winters. Emerging from under the bridge, head farther west on Bankside to . . .*

⑪ Shakespeare's Globe

All the world's a stage,
And all the men and women merely players.
They have their exits and their entrances,
And one man, in his time, plays many parts.
—As You Like It

By 1599, 35-year-old William Shakespeare was a well-known actor, playwright, and businessman in the booming theater trade (see sidebar on page 236). His acting company, the Lord Chamberlain's Men, built the 3,000-seat Globe Theatre, by far the largest of its day (200 yards from today's replica, where only a plaque stands now). The Globe premiered Shakespeare's greatest works—*Hamlet, Othello, King Lear, Macbeth*—in open-air summer afternoon performances, though occasionally at night by the light of torches and buckets of tar-soaked ropes.

In 1612, it featured Shakespeare's *All Is True (Henry VIII).* During Scene 4, a stage cannon boomed, announcing the arrival of King Henry, who started flirting with Anne Boleyn. As the two

BANKSIDE

actors generated sparks onstage, play-watchers smelled fire. Some stray cannon wadding had sparked a real fire offstage. Within an hour, the wood-and-thatch building had burned completely to the ground, but with only one injury: A man's pants caught fire and were quickly doused with a tankard of ale.

Built in 1997, the new Globe—round, half-timbered, thatched, with wooden pegs for nails—is a quite realistic replica, though slightly smaller (seating 1,500 spectators), located a block away from the original site, and constructed with fire-repellent materials. Performances are staged almost nightly in summer—check at the box office (at the east end of the complex). A recent addition is the indoor Sam Wanamaker Playhouse, behind the Globe complex, around the left side. For more on touring the Globe, see page 90.

Bankside's theater scene vanished in the 1640s, closed by a Parliament dominated by hard-line Puritans. Drama seemed to portray and promote immoral behavior, and actors—men who also played women's roles—parodied and besmirched fair womanhood. Bearbaiting was also outlawed by the outraged moralists (to paraphrase the historian Thomas Macaulay)—not because it caused bears pain, but because it gave people pleasure.

• *From the Globe, belly up to the railing overlooking the Thames and imagine the view on September 2, 1666.*

ⓘ View of 1666 Great Fire Area

On Sunday, September 2, 1666, stunned Londoners quietly sipped beers in Bankside pubs and watched The City across the river go up in flames. ("When we could endure no more upon the water," wrote Samuel Pepys in his diary, "we went to a little alehouse on the Bankside.") Started in a bakery shop near the Monument (north end of London Bridge) and fanned by strong winds, the fire swept westward, engulfing the mostly wooden city, devouring Old St. Paul's, and moving past what is now Blackfriars Bridge and St. Bride's to Temple Church (near the pointy, black, gold-tipped steeple of the Royal Courts of Justice).

In four days, 80 percent of The City was incinerated, including 13,000 houses and 89 churches. The good news? Incredibly, only nine people died, the fire cleansed a plague-infested city, and Christopher Wren was around to rebuild London's skyline.

The fire also marked the end of Bankside's era as London's naughty playground. Having recently been cleaned up by the Puritans, it now served as a temporary refugee camp for those displaced by the fire. And, with the coming Industrial Age, businessmen demolished the inns and replaced them with brick warehouses, docks, and factories to fuel the economy of a world power.

• At the pedestrian bridge is a towering former power plant, now turned into a huge modern art museum.

⓭ Tate Modern

London's large, impressive modern art collection is housed in a former power station—typical of the move to renovate empty, ugly Industrial Age hulks on the South Bank. Even if you don't tour the collection, pop inside the north entrance (free) to view the spacious interior, decorated each year with a new industrial-sized installation by one of the world's top contemporary artists. As the Tate is in the process of adding a new annex (behind the building), it's interesting to see what new spaces they've opened up to the public.

📖 See the Tate Modern Tour chapter.

• End this walk on the Millennium Bridge, enjoying a view of the Thames.

⓮ Millennium Bridge and View of the Thames

This pedestrian bridge was built in 2000 to connect the Tate Modern with St. Paul's Cathedral and The City. For its first two glori-

ous days, Londoners made the pleasant seven-minute walk across...before the $25 million "bridge to the next millennium" started wobbling dangerously (insert your own ironic joke here) and was closed for rethinking. After much work, 20 months, and $8 million in retrofits, the bridge reopened. Nicknamed the "blade of light," it was designed (partly by Lord Norman Foster, who also did The Gherkin and City Hall downstream) to allow a wide-open view of St. Paul's. Now stabilized, it links two revitalized sections of London.

From the Cotswolds to the North Sea, the Thames winds eastward a total of 210 miles. London is close enough to the estuary to be affected by the North Sea's tides, so the river level does indeed rise and fall twice a day. In fact, one of the reasons Romans found this a practical location—even though it was about 40 miles inland—was that their boats could hitch a free ride with the tides between the sea and the town twice a day. But tides also mean floods. After centuries of periodic flooding (spring rains plus high tides), barriers to regulate the tides were built in 1982, east of Tower Bridge. The barriers also slow down the once fast-moving river.

The Thames is still a major commercial artery (east of Tower Bridge). In the previous two centuries, it ran brown with Industrial Revolution pollution. Today it's brown because of estuary silt—the Thames is now one of the cleanest rivers in the industrialized world.

• *Your tour is over. From here you can enjoy the Tate Modern or continue strolling the South Bank (follow the Jubilee Walkway 20 minutes or so to the London Eye and Big Ben—particularly enjoyable in the evening). Or cross the Thames on the Millennium Bridge to a pedestrian mall that leads past the glassy Salvation Army headquarters (good café and small, free Salvation Army history display in daylight basement) to St. Paul's Cathedral and Tube station.*

TATE MODERN TOUR

Remember the 20th century? Accelerated by technology and fragmented by war, it was an exciting and chaotic time, with art as turbulent as the world that created it. The Tate Modern lets you walk through the explosive last century with a glimpse at its brave new art.

This Is Not a "Tour": The Tate Modern is (controversially) displayed by concept—"Poetry and Dream," for example—rather than by artist and chronology. But unlike the museum, this chapter is neatly chronological. It's not intended as a painting-by-painting guide, but to give context to the various cultural periods that produced the art of the Tate Modern.

Read through this chapter for a general introduction, use it as a reference, then take advantage of the Tate's excellent multimedia guide to focus on specific works. With this background in 20th-century art, you'll appreciate the Tate's even greater strength: art of the 21st century.

Tate Modern Expansion: The Tate Modern opened in 2000 anticipating two million visitors a year. More than twice that number visit, mostly on Saturdays. To meet the growing demand, the Tate is opening a new wing to the south, which will double the museum's exhibition space. The twisted-rectangle building is essentially done, and its official opening is scheduled for late 2016. In addition to showing off more of the Tate's impressive collection, it will host performances and large-scale installations. An 11th-floor restaurant promises grand views over London.

Even before its official debut, the new wing is opening bit by bit, so check out its progress during your visit.

Orientation

Cost: Free (but £4 donations appreciated); fee for special exhibits.

Hours: Daily 10:00-18:00, Fri-Sat until 22:00, last entry to special exhibits 45 minutes before closing.

When to Go: This popular place is especially crowded on weekends (crowds thin out on Fri and Sat evenings).

Getting There: Located on the South Bank of the Thames, across from St. Paul's and near the Globe Theatre. You can get here by Tube, ferry, or foot:

> **By Tube:** Take the Tube to Southwark, London Bridge, St. Paul's, Mansion House, or Blackfriars, then follow signs to the museum (10- to 15-minute walk).

> **By Ferry:** Catch Thames Clippers' Tate Boat ferry from the Tate Britain for a 15-minute crossing (£7.15 one-way, £17.35 day ticket, discount with Travelcard or Oyster card, buy ticket at self-serve machines before boarding or use Oyster Card, departs every 40 minutes Mon-Fri from 10:00 to 16:30, Sat-Sun from 9:15 to 18:40, www.tate.org.uk/visit/tate-boat).

> **On Foot:** Walk across the Millennium Bridge from St. Paul's Cathedral.

Information: The two lowest floors (levels 0 and 1) have the basic services: info desks, baggage check, bookstores, multimedia guide rentals, and tickets for temporary exhibits. The helpful staff at the info desk (level 1) can tell you the location of specific works. The floor plan (suggested £1 donation) is also useful. In addition, **touch-screen computers** are scattered throughout the museum. Tel. 020/7887-8888, www.tate.org.uk.

Tours: The £4.50 **multimedia guide** covers the entire permanent collection, and includes a tour geared for kids ages 8-12. Free 45-minute **guided tours** are offered at 11:00, 12:00, 14:00, and 15:00 (see info desk for details).

Length of This Tour: Allow at least an hour. Read this chapter ahead of time, then browse according to your tastes.

Cloakroom: Level 0 (free, £2 suggested donation).

Photography: Photos allowed without flash.

Cuisine Art: View coffee shops are on levels 1 and 3. On level 6, there's a table-service restaurant (£25 for two courses, £30 for three courses, £15 afternoon tea served 15:00-17:30, until 17:00 Fri-Sun); even better, you can sit at one of the many stools at the casual bar, with the best views of all and lower prices (£3-10 drinks and snacks). This perch provides stunning panoramas of St. Paul's and The City. Some trendy restaurants are several blocks southwest of the Tate, along the street named "the Cut" (near Southwark Tube stop).

Starring: Picasso, Matisse, Dalí, and all the "classic" modern artists, plus the Tate Modern's specialty—British and American artists of the last half of the 20th century.

Know Your Tates: Don't confuse the Tate Modern with the Tate Britain (south of Big Ben), which features British art.

OVERVIEW

Even though the layout of the Tate Modern changes constantly, the collection's focus is the same: the 20th-century postwar period.

Don't just come to see the Old Masters of modernism (Matisse, Picasso, Kandinsky, and so on). Push your mental envelope with works by Pollock, Miró, Bacon, Picabia, Beuys, Twombly, and others.

More modern art from British artists is on display at the Tate Britain museum (☐ see the Tate Britain Tour chapter).

Reminder: The following is not a painting-by-painting tour but rather a chronological overview of the modern art movement as a whole.

The Tour Begins

• *Start at the main entrance (on the west side of the building). To reach it from the river: With the Thames at your back, walk to the right around the corner of the building, down the slope and into the massive empty space of the former electricity-generating powerhouse.*

This huge, grand entrance usually dwarfs the art it houses (a metaphor for the triumph of 20th-century technology, perhaps?). The Turbine Hall displays major art installations by contemporary artists—always one of the highlights of the art world.

You're on underground level 0 (the riverfront entrance leads to level 1). To see the core of the permanent collection—and the artwork described in this chapter—head upstairs (via the escalator near the ground-floor cloakroom) to levels 2 through 4.

Paintings are arranged according to theme, not artist. Paintings by Picasso, for example, are scattered all over the building. Special exhibits are often on levels 2 and 3.

Overview of Modern Art

1900—VICTORIA'S LEGACY

Anno Domini 1900, a new century dawns. Europe is at peace, Britannia rules the world. Technology is about to usher in a golden age.

Claude Monet

Monet (1840-1926) captures the relaxed, civilized spirit of belle époque France and Victorian England with Impressionist snapshots of peaceful landscapes and middle-class family picnics. But the true subject is the shimmering effect of reflected light, rendered with rough brushstrokes and bright paints that look messy up close but blend at a distance. The newfangled camera made camera-eye realism obsolete. Artists began placing more importance on *how* something was painted rather than on *what* was painted.

1905—COLONIAL EUROPE

Europe ruled a global empire, tapping its dark-skinned colonies for raw materials, cheap labor, and bold new ways to look at the world. The cozy Victorian world was shattering. Nietzsche murdered God. Darwin stripped off Man's robe of culture and found a naked ape. Primitivism was modern. Ooga-booga.

Henri Matisse

Matisse (1869-1954) was one of the Fauves, or "wild beasts," who tried to inject a bit of the jungle into civilized European society. Inspired by "primitive" African and Oceanic masks and voodoo dolls, the Fauves made modern art that looked primitive: long, mask-like faces with almond eyes; bright, clashing colors; simple figures; and "flat," two-dimensional scenes.

Matisse simplifies. A man is a few black lines and blocks of paint. A snail is a spiral of colored paper. A woman's back is an outline. Matisse's colors are unnaturally bright. The "distant" landscape is as crisp and clear as close objects, and the slanted lines meant to suggest depth are crudely done.

Traditionally, the canvas was like a window that you looked "through" to see a slice of the real world stretching off into the horizon. With Matisse, you look "at" the canvas, like wallpaper, to appreciate the decorative pattern of colors and shapes.

Though his style is modern, Matisse builds on 19th-century art—the bright colors of Van Gogh, the primitive figures of Gauguin, the colorful designs of Japanese wood-block prints, and the Impressionist patches of paint that blend together only at a distance.

Paul Cézanne

Cézanne (1839-1906) brings Impressionism into the 20th century. Whereas Monet uses separate dabs of different-colored paint to "build" a figure, Cézanne "builds" a man with somewhat larger slabs of paint, giving him a kind of 3-D chunkiness. It's not hard to see the progression from Monet's dabs to Cézanne's slabs to Picasso's cubes—Cubism.

1910—THE MODERNS

The modern world was moving fast, with automobiles, factories, and mass communication. Motion pictures captured the fast-moving world, while Einstein explored the fourth dimension: time.

Cubism and Pablo Picasso

Born in Spain, Picasso (1881-1973) moved to Paris as a young man. He worked with painter and sculptor Georges Braque in poverty so dire they often didn't know where their next bottle of wine was coming from.

Picasso's Cubist works show the old European world shattering to bits. He pieces the fragments back together in a whole new way, showing several perspectives at once (for example, looking up the left side of a woman's body and, at the same time, down at her right).

Whereas newfangled motion pictures capture several perspectives in succession, Picasso achieves it on a canvas with overlapping

images. A single "cube" might contain an arm (in the foreground) and the window behind (in the background), both painted the same color. The foreground and background are woven together so that the subject dissolves into a pattern.

Picasso, the most famous and—OK, I'll say it—the greatest artist of the 20th century, constantly explored and adapted his style to new trends. He made collages, tried his hand at "statues" out of wood, wire, or whatever, and even made art out of everyday household objects.

These multimedia works, so revolutionary at the time, have become stock-in-trade today. Scattered throughout the museum are works from the many periods of Picasso's life.

Futurism

The Machine Age is approaching, and the whole world gleams with promise in cylindrical shapes ("Tubism"), like an internal-combustion engine. Or is it the gleaming barrel of a cannon?

1914—WORLD WAR I

A soldier—shivering in a trench, ankle-deep in mud, waiting to be ordered "over the top," to run through barbed wire, over fallen comrades, and into a hail of machine-gun fire, only to capture a few hundred yards of meaningless territory that would be lost the next day. This soldier was not thinking about art.

World War I left nine million dead. (At times, England lost more men per month than America lost during the entire Vietnam War.) The war also killed the optimism and faith in humankind that had guided Europe since the Renaissance.

Expressionism

Cynicism and decadence settled over postwar Europe. Artists such as Grosz, Beckmann, and Kokoschka "expressed" their disgust by showing a distorted reality that emphasized the ugly. Using the lurid colors and simplified figures of the Fauves, they slapped paint on in thick brushstrokes, depicting a hypocritical, hard-edged, dog-eat-dog world—a civilization watching its Victorian moral foundations collapse.

Dada

When they could grieve no longer, artists turned to grief's giddy twin, laughter. The war made all old values a joke, including artistic ones. The Dada movement, choosing a purposely childish name, made art that was intentionally outrageous: a moustache on the *Mona Lisa,* a shovel hung on the wall, or a modern version of a Renaissance "fountain"—a urinal (by Marcel Duchamp...or was it I. P. Freeley?).

It was a dig at all the pompous prewar artistic theories based on the noble intellect of Rational Women and Men. While the experts ranted on, Dadaists sat in the back of the class and made cultural fart noises.

Hey, I love this stuff. My mind says it's sophomoric, but my heart belongs to Dada.

1920s—ANYTHING GOES

In the Jazz Age, the world turned upside down. Genteel ladies smoked cigarettes. Gangsters laid down the law. You could make a fortune in the stock market one day and lose it the next. You could dance the Charleston with the opposite sex, and even say the word "sex" while talking about Freud over cocktails. It was almost...surreal.

Abstract Art

Abstract art simplifies. A man becomes a stick figure. A squiggle is a wave. A streak of red expresses anger. Arches make you want a cheeseburger. These are universal symbols that everyone from a caveman to a banker understands. Abstract artists capture the essence of reality in a few lines and colors, boldly capturing objects and ideas that even a camera can't—emotions, abstract concepts, musical rhythms, and spiritual states of mind.

With abstract art, you don't look "through" the canvas to see the visual world, but "at" it to read the symbolism of lines, shapes, and colors. Most 20th-century paintings are a mix of the real world (representation) and colorful patterns (abstraction).

Surrealism

Artists caught the jumble of images on a canvas. A telephone made from a lobster, an elephant with a heating-duct trunk, Venus sleepwalking among skeletons. Take one mixed bag of reality, jumble it in a blender, and serve on a canvas—Surrealism.

The artist scatters seemingly unrelated things on the canvas, leaving us to trace the connections in a kind of connect-the-dots without numbers.

Further complicating the modern world was Freud's discovery of the "unconscious" mind, which thinks dirty thoughts while we sleep. Surrealists let the id speak. The canvas is an uncensored, stream-of-consciousness "landscape" of these deep urges, revealed in the bizarre images of dreams. Salvador Dalí, the most famous Surrealist, combined an extraordinarily realistic technique with an extraordinarily twisted mind. He painted "unreal" scenes with photographic realism, making us believe they could really happen. Dalí's images—crucifixes, political and religious figures, and naked bodies—pack an emotional punch.

1930s—DEPRESSION

As capitalism failed around the world, governments propped up their economies with vast building projects. The architecture style was modern, stripped-down (i.e., cheap), and functional. Propagandist campaigns championed noble workers in the heroic Social Realist style.

Piet Mondrian
Like blueprints for modernism, Mondrian's T-square style boils painting down to its basic building blocks: a white canvas, black lines, and the three primary colors—red, yellow, and blue—arranged in orderly patterns. (When you come right down to it, that's all painting ever has been. A schematic drawing of, say, the *Mona Lisa* shows that it's less about a woman than about the triangles and rectangles she's composed of.)

Mondrian (1872-1944) started out painting realistic landscapes of the orderly fields in his native homeland of Holland. Increasingly, he simplified his style into horizontal and vertical patterns. For Mondrian, who was heavily into Eastern mysticism, "up versus down" and "left versus right" were the perfect metaphors for life's dualities: good versus evil, body versus spirit, fascism versus communism, man versus woman. The canvas is a bird's-eye view of Mondrian's personal landscape.

1940s—WORLD WAR II
World War II was a global war (involving Europe, the Americas, Australia, Africa, and Asia) and a total war (saturation bombing of civilians and ethnic cleansing). It left Europe in ruins.

Alberto Giacometti's skinny statues have the emaciated, haunted, and faceless look of concentration-camp survivors. In the sweep of world war and overpowering technology, man is frail and fragile. All he can do is stand at attention and take it like a man.

Meanwhile, Francis Bacon's caged creatures speak for all of war-torn Europe when they scream, "Enough!" (For more on Bacon, see page 347.)

1950s—AMERICA, THE GLOBAL SUPERPOWER
As converted war factories turned swords into kitchen appliances, America helped rebuild Europe while pumping out consumer goods for its own booming population. Prosperity, a stable government, national television broadcasts, and a common fear of Soviet communism threatened to turn America into a completely homogeneous society.

Some artists, centered in New York, rebelled against conformity and superficial consumerism. (They'd served under Eisenhower in war and now had to in peace, as well.) They created art that was the very opposite of the functional, mass-produced goods of the American marketplace.

Art was a way of asserting your individuality by creating a completely original and personal vision. The trend was toward bigger canvases, abstract designs, and experimentation with new materials and techniques. It was called "Abstract Expressionism"—expressing emotions and ideas using color and form alone.

Jackson Pollock

"Jack the Dripper" attacks convention with a can of paint, dripping and splashing a dense web onto the canvas. Picture Pollock (1912-1956) in his studio, jiving to the hi-fi, bouncing off the walls, throwing paint in a moment of enlightenment. Of course, the artist loses some control this way—over the paint flying in midair and over himself in an ecstatic trance. Painting becomes a whole-body activity, a "dance" between the artist and his materials.

The intuitive act of creating is what's important, not the final product. The canvas is only a record of that moment of ecstasy.

Big, Empty Canvases

With all the postwar prosperity, artists could afford bigger canvases. But what reality are they trying to show?

In the modern world, we find ourselves insignificant specks in a vast and indifferent universe. Every morning, each of us must confront that big, blank, existential canvas, and decide how we're going to make our mark on it.

Another influence was the simplicity of Japanese landscape painting. A Zen master studies and meditates for years to achieve the state of mind in which he can draw one pure line. These canvases, again, are only a record of that state of enlightenment. (What is the sound of one brush painting?)

On more familiar ground, postwar painters were following in the footsteps of artists such as Mondrian. The geometrical forms here reflect the same search for order, but these artists painted to the musical 5/4 asymmetry of the Dave Brubeck Quartet's jazzy *Take Five*.

Patterns and Textures

Enjoy the lines and colors, but also a new element: texture. Some works have very thick paint piled on, where you can see the brushstrokes clearly. Some have substances besides paint applied to the canvas, or the canvas is punctured so the fabric itself (and the hole) becomes the subject. Artists show their skill by mastering new materials. The canvas is a tray, serving up a delightful buffet of different substances with interesting colors, patterns, shapes, and textures.

Mark Rothko

Rothko (1903-1970) makes two-toned rectangles, laid on their sides, that seem to float in a big, vertical canvas. The edges are blurred, so if you get close enough to let the canvas fill your field of vision (as Rothko intended), the rectangles appear to rise and sink from the cloudy depths like answers in a Magic 8 Ball.

Serious students appreciate the subtle differences in color between the rectangles. Rothko experimented with different bases

20th-Century British Artists

Since 1960, London has rivaled New York as a center for the visual arts. You'll find British artists displayed in both the Tate Modern and the Tate Britain. Check out the Tate Britain Tour chapter for more on the following artists: David Hockney, Stanley Spencer, Jacob Epstein, Gilbert and George, Henry Moore, Francis Bacon, and Barbara Hepworth.

for the same color and used a single undercoat (a "wash") to unify them. His early works are warmer, with brighter reds, yellows, and oranges; his later works are maroon and brown, approaching black.

Still, these are not intended to be formal studies in color and form. Rothko was trying to express the most basic human emotions in a pure language. (A "realistic" painting of a person is inherently fake because it's only an illusion of the person.) Staring into these windows onto the soul, you can laugh, cry, or ponder, just as Rothko did when he painted them.

Rothko, the previous century's "last serious artist," believed in the power of art to express the human spirit. When he found out that his nine large Seagram canvases were to be hung in a corporate restaurant, he refused to sell them, and they ended up in the Tate. (A 2010 Tony Award-winning play called *Red* dealt with Rothko's anguished decision.)

In his last years, Rothko's canvases—always rectangles—got bigger, simpler, and darker. When Rothko finally slashed his wrists in his studio, one nasty critic joked that what killed him was the repetition. Minimalism was painting itself into a blank corner.

1960s—POP AND POLITICS

The decade began united in idealism—young John F. Kennedy pledged to put a man on the moon, newly launched satellites signaled a united world, the Beatles sang exuberantly, peaceful race demonstrations championed equality, and the Vatican II Council preached liberation. By decade's end, there were race riots, assassinations, student protests, and America's floundering war in distant Vietnam. In households around the world, parents screamed, "Turn that down...and get a haircut!"

Culturally, every postwar value was questioned by a rising, wealthy, and populous baby-boom generation. London—producer of rock-and-roll music, film actors, mod fashions, and Austin Powers joie de vivre—once again became a world cultural center.

Though government-sponsored public art was dominated by big, abstract canvases and sculptures, other artists pooh-poohed the highbrow seriousness of abstract art. Instead, they mocked lowbrow, popular culture by embracing it in a tongue-in-cheek way (Pop Art), or they attacked authority with absurd performances to make a political statement (conceptual art).

Pop Art
America's postwar wealth made the consumer king. Pop Art is created from the popular objects of that throwaway society—soup cans, car fenders, tacky plastic statues, movie icons. Take a Sears product, hang it in a museum, and you have to ask: Is this art? Are mass-produced objects beautiful? Or crap? Why do we work so hard to acquire them? Pop Art, like Dadaism before it, questions our society's values.

Andy Warhol (who coined "15 minutes of fame") concentrated on another mass-produced phenomenon: celebrities. He took publicity photos of famous people and reproduced them. The repetition—like the constant bombardment we get from recurring images on TV—cheapens even the most beautiful things.

Roy Lichtenstein took a comic strip, blew it up, hung it on a wall, and charged a million bucks—whaam, Pop Art. Lichtenstein supposedly was inspired by his young son, who challenged him to do something as good as Mickey Mouse. The huge newsprint dots never let us forget that the painting—like all commercial art—is an illusionistic fake. The work's humor comes from portraying a lowbrow subject (comics and ads) on the epic scale of a masterpiece.

Op Art
Optical illusions play tricks with your eyes, the way a spiral starts to spin when you stare at it. These obscure scientific experiments in color, line, and optics suddenly became trendy in the psychedelic '60s.

1970s—THE "ME DECADE"
All forms of authority—"The Establishment"—seemed bankrupt. America's president resigned in the Watergate scandal, corporations were polluting the earth, and capitalism nearly ground to a halt when Arabs withheld oil.

Artists attacked authority and institutions, trying to free individuals to discover their full human potential. Even the concept of "modernism"—that art wasn't good unless it was totally original and progressive—was questioned. No single style could dictate in this postmodern period.

Earth Art

Fearing for the health of the earth's ecology, artists rediscovered the beauty of rocks, dirt, trees, even the sound of the wind, using them to create natural art. A rock placed in a museum or urban square is certainly a strange sight.

Performance Art

The Tate Modern's collection of "sculptures" by Joseph Beuys—assemblages of steel, junk, wood, and, especially, felt and animal fat—only hint at his greatest artwork: Beuys himself.

Imagine Beuys walking through the museum, carrying a dead rabbit, while he explains the paintings to it. Or taking off his clothes, shaving his head, and smearing his body with fat.

This charismatic, ex-Luftwaffe art shaman did ridiculous things to inspire others to break with convention and be free. He choreographed "Happenings"—spectacles where people did absurd things while others watched—and pioneered performance art, in which the artist presents himself as the work of art. Beuys inspired a whole generation of artists to walk on stage, cluck like a chicken, and stick a yam up themselves. Beuys will be Beuys.

New Media

Minimalist painting and abstract sculpture were old hat, and there was an explosion of new art forms. Performance art was the most controversial, combining music, theater, dance, poetry, and the visual arts. New technologies brought video, assemblages, installations, artists' books (paintings in book form), and even (gasp!) realistic painting.

Conceptual Art

Increasingly, artists are not creating an original work (painting a canvas or sculpting a stone) but assembling one from premade objects. The *concept* of which object to pair with another to produce maximum effect ("Let's stick a crucifix in a jar of urine," to cite one notorious example) is the key.

1980s—MATERIAL GIRL

Ronald Reagan in America, Margaret Thatcher in Britain, and corporate executives around the world ruled over a conservative and materialistic society. On the other side were starving Ethiopians, gay men with the new disease AIDS, people of color, and women—all demanding power. Intelligent, peaceful, straight white males assumed a low profile.

The art world became big business, with a Van Gogh painting fetching $54 million. Corporations paid big bucks for large, colorful, semi-abstract canvases. Marketing became an art form. Gender and sexual orientation were popular themes. Many women picked up paintbrushes, creating bright-colored abstract forms hinting at vulva and penis shapes. Visual art fused with popular music, bringing us installations in dance clubs and fast-edit music videos. The crude style of graffiti art demanded to be included in corporate society.

1990s—MULTICULTURAL DIVERSITY

The communist-built Berlin Wall was torn down, ending four decades of a global Cold War between capitalism and communism. The new battleground was the "Culture Wars," the struggle to include all races, genders, and lifestyles within an increasingly corporate-dominated, global society.

Artists looked to Third World countries for inspiration and championed society's outsiders against government censorship and economic exclusion. A new medium, the Internet, arose, allowing instantaneous multimedia communication around the world through electronic signals carried by satellites and telephone lines.

2000—?

A new millennium dawned. Thanks to the Internet, art has taken on a new sense of connectivity. A work of art can mean strangers meeting for intricate "Flashmob" street performances; graffiti artists like Banksy reaching the masses by tagging public spaces; and people everywhere "sharing" moments through social networking sites. "Selfies" have become the modern Gainsborough portrait, presenting an idealized image to the world of how we wish to be seen. Technology has empowered everyone to make art...only instead of a paintbrush, we use selfie-sticks.

VICTORIA AND ALBERT MUSEUM TOUR

With one of the biggest, most eclectic collections of objects anywhere, the Victoria and Albert (V&A) has something for everyone. It bills itself as a museum for the decorative arts, and Martha Stewart types will be in hog heaven. You'll see furniture, glassware, clothing, jewelry, and carpets from every corner of the world. Throw in historical artifacts, a few fine-arts masterpieces (painting and sculpture), and a bed that sleeps seven, and you have a museum built for browsing.

The V&A grew out of the Great Exhibition of 1851, that ultimate celebration of the Industrial Revolution. Now "art" could be brought to the masses through modern technology and mass production. The museum was founded on the idealistic Victorian notion that anyone can be continually improved by education and example. After much support from Queen Victoria and Prince Albert, the museum was renamed for the royal couple, and its present building was opened in 1909.

You could spend days in this place. The museum is large and gangly, with 150 rooms and more than 12 miles of corridors. My quick tour gives you a sample of the V&A's range, covering fine art, historical objects, interior design, fashion, and beautiful objects from around the globe. Use this tour to get your bearings, then use the museum's map to wander at will.

The V&A is in the midst of a long-term update and expansion. During this time, exhibits may be rearranged, so check with the information desk for current room closures, carry a copy of the museum's detailed map, and ask a nearby guard if you can't find one of the objects in this tour.

Orientation

Cost: Free (£4 donation requested); fee for some special exhibits.

Hours: Daily 10:00-17:45. Some galleries—including most on this tour—stay open Fri until 22:00.

Getting There: The Grand Entrance—where our tour begins—is on Cromwell Road in the South Kensington neighborhood (Tube: South Kensington). You can also reach the Grand Entrance via a tunnel that leads directly from the Tube station: Once inside the museum (on level 1), continue straight down the long sculpture gallery. After about 100 yards, turn right through the gift shop, which takes you to the Grand Entrance lobby (Tube tunnel closed Fri eve).

Information: Pick up the much-needed museum map (£1 suggested donation). Check the V&A's helpful website for a list of current exhibitions. Once at the museum, strategically located computer terminals tell you more about the collection. Tel. 020/7942-2000, www.vam.ac.uk.

Tours: Free one-hour tours (general orientation and other, more specific topics) leave from the Grand Entrance lobby daily on the half-hour from 10:30 to 15:30. Additional tours and lectures are offered sporadically; check the website for details.

Length of This Tour: Allow 1.5 hours (not counting the British Galleries). With limited time, don't miss the Cast, the Fashion Galleries, and the Raphael Cartoons.

Cloakroom: Free, mandatory for large bags.

Photography: Permitted in most of the galleries without flash or tripod, but not allowed for the Jewelry gallery, special exhibits, and works loaned by other museums.

Cuisine Art: The V&A Café offers self-service lunch and tea in the elegant Morris, Gamble, and Poynter rooms. These three

rooms formed the world's first museum restaurant (£10-13 meals, £7-10 sandwiches and salads). In summer, a self-service café (£4-6 sandwiches) sets up in the Madejski Garden—grab a bite there or bring a picnic. For a list of recommended eateries in the neighborhood, see page 410.

Starring: A little of everything—and all of it beautiful.

The Tour Begins

• *Start at the Grand Entrance lobby, on level 1. Look up into the rotunda.*

❶ Dale Chihuly Chandelier

This modern chandelier/sculpture by the American glass artist epitomizes the spirit of the V&A's collection—beautiful manufactured objects that demonstrate technical skill and innovation, wedding the old with the new, and blurring the line between arts and crafts.

V&A MUSEUM

Each blue-and-yellow strand of the chandelier is tied with a wire to a central spine. When the chandelier first went up in 2001, Chihuly said, "Too small," had it disassembled, and fired up still more glass bubbles.

Dale Chihuly (b. 1941)—face-famous for the eye-patch he's worn since a car accident—studied glassmaking in Venice, then set up his own studio/factory in Seattle, making art as the director of a creative team. He makes an old medium seem fresh and modern...and the V&A keeps his chandelier looking fresh with a long feather duster.

• *From the lobby, look up to the balcony and see the pointed arches of the...*

❷ Hereford Screen (1862)

In the 1800s, just as Britain was steaming into the future on the cutting edge of the Industrial Revolution, the public's taste went

retro. This 35-by-35-foot, eight-ton rood screen (built for the Hereford Cathedral's sacred altar area) looks medieval, but it was created with the most modern materials the Industrial Revolution could produce. The metal parts were not hammered and hand-worked as in olden days, but are made of electroformed copper. The parts were first cast in plaster, then bathed in molten copper with an electric current running through it, leaving a metal skin around the plaster. The entire project—which might have taken years in medieval times—was completed in five months.

George Gilbert Scott (1811-1878), who built the screen, redesigned much of London in the Neo-Gothic style, restoring old churches such as Westminster Abbey, renovating the Houses of

Parliament, and building new structures like St. Pancras Station and the Albert Memorial—some 700 buildings in all.

The world turns, and a century later (1960s), the Gothic style was "out" again, modernism was in, and this screen was neglected and ridiculed. Considering that the V&A was originally called the Museum of Manufactures (1857), it's appropriate that the screen was brought here, where it shows off the technical advances of the Industrial Revolution.

• To the right of the Grand Entrance lobby, look into a large hall of statues (Room 50a), including a spiraling statue of two battling men.

❸ Samson Slaying a Philistine, by Giambologna (c. 1562)

Carved from a single block of marble, the statue shows the testy Israelite warrior rearing back, brandishing the jawbone of an ass, preparing to decapitate a man who'd insulted him. Samson pauses to make sure the Philistine looks him in the eye so he can see what's coming. Circle the statue and watch it spiral around its axis. Giambologna was clearly influenced by Michelangelo, who pioneered both the theme of the fallen enemy and the spiral-shaped

Victoria & Albert Museum Tour

❶ Dale Chihuly Chandelier
❷ Hereford Screen (above lobby)
❸ GIAMBOLOGNA – Samson Slaying a Philistine
❹ Medieval & Renaissance Galleries
❺ Becket Casket
❻ Boar & Bear Hunt Tapestry
❼ Stairs up to Leonardo Notebook
❽ Michelangelo Casts
❾ Trajan's Column Casts
❿ Henry II Tomb Effigies
⓫ Islamic Art
⓬ Shiva Nataraja Statue
⓭ Possessions of Emperor Shah Jahan
⓮ Tippoo's Tiger
⓯ Fashion Galleries
⓰ RAPHAEL – Tapestry Cartoons
⓱ British Galleries
⓲ Stairs up to Jewelry, Theater & British Silver
⓳ Stairs up to view of Cast Courts

V&A MUSEUM

pose that many artists imitated. The V&A has (arguably) the best collection of Italian Renaissance sculpture outside Italy.

• *From the Grand Entrance lobby (near the main doorway), find the entrance to the rooms labeled* Medieval & Renaissance, 300-1500. *It's down a few steps, on level 0 (Rooms 8-10).*

❹ Medieval and Renaissance Galleries, A.D. 300-1500

Walk through 1,200 years of decorative arts, seeing how the mix of pagan-Roman and medieval-Christian elements created modern Europe.

It's A.D. 300, and Rome's Europe-wide empire is beginning to unravel. Within two centuries, its political dominance would be over, but Rome's culture lived on in the Christian faith. Rooms 8-10 show how traditional Roman media (mosaics, carved ivory, column-and-arch building techniques) were adapted to make Christian-themed art and churches.

• *About three-fourths of the way down the long Room 8 is a glass case displaying the shoebox-sized...*

❺ Becket Casket (c. 1180)

The blue-and-gold box contains the mortal remains (or relics) of St. Thomas Becket, who was brutally murdered. Look at the scene depicted along the side—the Archbishop of Canterbury is about to grab a chalice from the altar, when knights tiptoe up, draw their swords, and slice off his head. Two shocked priests throw up their hands.

Becket's soul (upper right) is borne aloft on a sling by two angels. His body is laid to rest (upper left) and blessed by the new bishop. Mourners kneel at the tomb, just as the man behind Becket's murder—King Henry II—is said to have done, out of remorse.

Henry II had handpicked his good friend Thomas Becket (1118-1170) for the job of archbishop, assuming he'd follow the king's orders. In two days, Thomas was made a priest, a bishop, then archbishop—the head of all England's Christians. But when Becket proved loyal to the Church and opposed Henry's policies, the king, in a rash fit of anger, said he wanted Becket dead. Remorseful after his knights murdered the archbishop, Henry had 80 monks whip him, and then he spent all night at the foot of the tomb.

Just three years after his death, Becket was made a saint. Pieces of Becket's DNA—valuable relics—were conserved in this enamel-and-metal work box, a specialty of Limoges, France.

• *Continue straight to the far end of this long set of rooms. In Room 10a, you'll run right into...*

❻ Boar and Bear Hunt Tapestry (c. 1425-1430)

Though most medieval art depicted the Madonna and saints, this colorful wool tapestry—woven in Belgium—provides a secular slice of life.

"Read" it from right to left: The nobles want to go hunting, so they hire some professional guides. One pro (in red) enters with his dogs and hunting horn, leading two nobles. His colleague (above) rousts bear cubs from their den, so the mama and papa bears can be flushed out into the open. Men and dogs (in the center) surround a bear, while another is lanced by a nobleman on horseback. Below, well-dressed ladies look on.

Continuing to the left, the hunt turns to wild boar, as two dogs flush one out of hiding. Finally (far left, bottom corner), the boar has been caught, and they begin to skin him for dinner.

In the nearby Room 10c, you'll find a **world map** (c. 1300) showing Christ sitting at the center of the known universe: Jerusalem. Try a little **brass rubbing** at the hands-on station.

• *Backtrack 20 paces and find the nearby staircase (or use the elevator). Head upstairs two flights to level 2 to see how the foundation of civilization laid in medieval times would launch the Renaissance. You'll spill out into Rooms 62-64b, labeled* Medieval & Renaissance, 1400-1600. *In Room 64 (hiding behind a partition on the left), find the tiny, pocket-size...*

❼ Notebook by Leonardo da Vinci *(Codex Forster III)*, 1490-1493

Leonardo da Vinci—painter, sculptor, engineer, musician, and scientist—epitomized the merging of art, knowledge, and science

we call the Renaissance. He recorded his observations and inventions in tiny notebooks like this. This particular codex (or bound manuscript) dates from years when he was living in Milan, shortly before undertaking his famous *Last Supper* fresco. He was always busy, but completed little from this time.

The book's contents are all over the map: meticulous sketches of the human head, diagrams illustrating nature's geometrical perfection, a horse's leg for a huge equestrian statue, and even drawings of the latest ballroom fashions. The adjacent computer lets you flip his backwards handwriting to make it readable.

In Room 64a (off to the left), an exhibit shows works by the sculptor Donatello, who blazed the artistic path followed by his fellow Florentine Michelangelo. This all leads (in Room 63, at the opposite end of Room 64) to works showing the new wealth of Europe as it enters the modern age.

• *Get out your V&A map to help you find our next destination, in Rooms 46a and 46b. To get there, go back down the stairs one flight to the ground floor (level 1). Cross the big sculpture hall and find Rooms 46a and 46b, labeled* The Cast Courts—*filled with replicas of famous statues.*

These two rooms are taking turns being renovated. Room 46b recently reopened; next door, Room 46a will likely close soon. Because these plaster casts are gigantic and hard to move, they're being rehabbed right here where they stand. If you'd like to see the conservation work in action, go up the ❿ stairs at the Cast Courts entryway to a gallery overlooking both rooms.

But first, visit whichever of the next two rooms you find open.

❽ Michelangelo Casts and Other Replica Statues

These plaster-cast versions of famous Renaissance statues by Michelangelo and others allowed 19th-century art students who

couldn't afford a rail pass to go study the classics.

The statues were made by coating the original with a non-stick substance, then laying wet plaster strips over it that dried to form a mold, from which a plaster cast was made. They look solid but are very fragile. In a single glance, you can follow Michelangelo's career, from youthful optimism *(David)*, to his never-finished masterpiece (statues from the tomb of Julius II, including *Moses* and two *Slaves*), to full-blown midlife crisis (while sculpting the brooding Medici Tomb statues of Lorenzo and Giuliano). Compare Michelangelo's monumental *David* with Donatello's girlish *David* (in the other room), and see Ghiberti's bronze Baptistery doors, which inspired the Florentine Renaissance.

David was a gift from Tuscany to Queen Victoria, who immediately donated it to the museum. Circle behind *David* to see the clip-on fig leaf that was hung on him when modest aristocrats visited (this was "the Victorian Age," after all). On the wall above David's right shoulder, you might recognize a copy of Raphael's *School of Athens* painting, pairing the biggest players of the Renaissance with the stars of antiquity (the original is in Rome's Vatican Museums). With Michelangelo front and center, it hangs appropriately over his most famous statue.

• *Across the hall, in Room 46a, you can't miss the two halves of...*

❾ Trajan's Column Casts

Rising 140 feet and decorated with a spiral relief of 2,500 figures trumpeting the exploits of the Roman Emperor Trajan (c. A.D. 100), this is a copy of the world's grandest column from antiquity. The original column still stands in Rome, but the V&A's version was cast from a copy in Paris. In fact, they had to cut it in half to fit it here.

The column's relief unfolds like a scroll, telling the story of Trajan's conquest of Dacia (modern-day Romania). It starts at the bottom (the half with the pedestal) with a trickle of water that becomes a river and soon picks up boats full of supplies. Then come the soldiers themselves, who spill out from the gates of the city. A river god surfaces to bless the journey. Along the way (second band), they build roads and forts to sustain the vast enterprise. Trajan himself (fourth band, in military skirt with toga over his arm) mounts a podium to fire up the troops. They hop into a Roman galley (fifth band) and head off to fight the valiant Dacians in the middle of a forest (eighth band). Finally, at the very top, the Romans hold a sacrifice to give thanks for the victory, while the captured armor is displayed on the pedestal.

Originally, the entire story was painted in bright colors. If you unwound the scroll, it would stretch the length of two football fields—it's far longer than the frieze around Athens' Parthenon.

• *Near Trajan's column, find several casts of knights and ladies on their backs, staring at the ceiling (in faded hues of red, gold, and blue). Some of these (near where you entered, top row, far end) are the...*

❿ Plaster Casts of Tomb Effigies of Henry II and Family

This was a remarkable and dysfunctional royal family. England's King Henry II (1133-1189)—Becket's murderer—lies alongside his

wife and their children. Henry's wife, Eleanor of Aquitaine, the ex-wife of the King of France, was renowned as Europe's most sophisticated lady. The wedding of Henry and Eleanor united their families' large land holdings, creating an "England" that stretched as far down as southern France. It would eventually take the Hundred Years' War (1336-1453) to sort out the current border between England and France.

As king, Henry placed church courts under secular control, causing the rift that led to Becket's bloody murder. In Henry's old age, his children rebelled, taking arms against him for their slice of the royal pie. Henry's heir, Richard the Lionheart, famous as the good guy in the Robin Hood legend, was actually an absentee monarch—a French-speaking dandy allied with the King of France. Younger son John, the "evil" King John of the Robin Hood legend, became a tyrant, prompting English nobles to make him sign the document called the Magna Carta, which established the principle that even kings must follow the law. (The British Library

V&A MUSEUM

has a copy of the Magna Carta—📖 see the British Library Tour chapter or 🎧 download my free audio tour.)

• *From the Cast Court entryway, head down the long hallway, past the shop, then turn right into Room 42, which contains art of the Islamic Middle East.*

⓫ Islamic Art

While owing much to Islam as a religion, Islamic art also reflected a sophisticated secular culture. Many Islamic artists expressed themselves with beautiful but functional objects.

In the center of the room is the 630-square-foot Ardabil Carpet (1539-1540). Its silk-thread underpinnings are topped by a dense wool pile made of 304 knots per square inch. (Carpet connoisseurs will nod approvingly at this impressively high KPI number.) Woven on a huge standing loom, it likely took a dozen workers years to make. In the center of the design is a yellow medallion ringed with ovals, supporting two hanging lamps. If you sat on the carpet near the smaller of the two lamps, you'd have the illusion of a symmetrical pattern. The carpet is illuminated on the hour and half-hour.

Also in the room are more carpets, ceramics (mostly blue-and-white or red-and-white), and glazed tile—all covered top to bottom in similarly complex patterns. The intricate interweaving, repetition, and unending lines suggest the complex, infinite nature of God (Allah).

You'll likely see only a few pictures of humans or animals—the Islamic religion reserves the creation of living beings to God alone. However, secular art for homes and palaces was not bound by this, and you may see realistic depictions of men and women enjoying a garden paradise, a symbol of the Muslim heaven.

Notice floral patterns (twining vines, flowers, arabesques) and geometric designs (stars, diamonds). But the most common pattern is calligraphy—elaborate lettering of an inscription in Arabic, the language of the Quran (and the lettering used even in non-Arabic languages). A quote from the Quran on a vase or lamp combines the power of the message with the beauty of the calligraphy.

• *Return to the hall and continue on. In the hallway (technically "Room 47b) is a glass case with a statue of...*

⓬ Shiva Nataraja (12th Century)

The Hindu god Shiva—one of the hundreds, if not thousands, of godlike incarnations of Hinduism's eternal being, Brahma—steps lively and creates the world by dancing. His four arms are busy creating, and he treads on the sleepy dwarf of ignorance.

This bronze statue, one of Hindu-ism's most popular, is loaded with sym-bolism, summing up where humans came from and where we're going. Sur-rounded by a ring of fire, Shiva crosses a leg in time to the music. Smiling se-renely, he blesses with one hand, while another beats out the rhythm of life with a hand drum. The cobra draped over his arm symbolizes the *Kundalini Sakti*, the cosmic energy inside each of us that can, with the right training, uncoil and bring us to enlightenment.

As long as Shiva keeps dancing, the universe will continue. But Shiva also holds a flame, a reminder that, at the end of time, he will transform into his female alter ego, Kali, and destroy the world by fire, clearing the slate for another round of existence.

• *Head through the doorway into the adjoining Room 41 (labeled South Asia). You'll run right into a glass case in the center of the room contain-ing small items that were the...*

⓭ Possessions of Emperor Shah Jahan (r. 1628-1658)

Look at the cameo portrait, thumb ring, and wine cup (made of white nephrite jade, 1657) that belonged to one of the world's most

powerful men.

Shah Jahan—or "King of the World"—ruled the largest em-pire of the day, covering northern India, Pakistan, and Afghanistan. His Mughal Empire was descended from Genghis Khan and the Mon-gol horde, who conquered and then settled in central Asia and converted to Islam.

Shah Jahan was known for his building projects, especially the Taj Mahal (see a picture of it nearby), built as a mausoleum for his favorite wife, Mumtaz, who bore him 14 children before dying in childbirth.

His unsuccessful attempts to expand the empire drained the treasury. In his old age, his sons quarreled over the inheritance. Imprisoned by his sons in the Agra fort, Shah Jahan died gazing across the river at the Taj Mahal, where he, too, would be buried. India's glory days were ending.

Then came the British.

• *At the far end of Room 41 (facing the door) is the huge wood-carved...*

The British in India

December 31, 1600: The British East India Company—a multi-national trading company owned by stockholders—is founded with a charter from Queen Elizabeth I. They're given a virtual monopoly on trade with India.

1600s: The British trade peacefully with Indian locals on the coast, competing with France, Holland, and Portugal for access to spices, cotton, tea, indigo, and jute (for rope-making).

1700s: As the Mughal (Islamic) Empire breaks down, Britain and France vie for trade ports and inland territory. By the 1750s, Britain is winning. Britain establishes itself in Bombay, Madras, and Calcutta. First they rule through puppet Mughal leaders, then dump local leaders altogether.

1800s: By midcentury, two-thirds of the subcontinent is under British rule, exporting opium and tea (transplanted from its native China) and importing British-made cloth. Britain tries to reform Indian social customs (such as outlawing widow suicides) with little long-lasting effect. They build railways, roads, and irrigation systems.

1857-1858: The "Indian Mutiny"—sparked by high taxes, British monopoly of trade, and a chafing against foreign rule—is the first of many uprisings that slowly erode British power.

1900s: Two world wars drain and distract Britain while Indians lobby for self-rule.

August 15, 1947: After a decade of peaceful protests led by Mahatma Gandhi, India gains its independence.

⑭ Tippoo's Tiger (1790s)

This life-size robotic toy, once owned by an oppressed Indian sultan (see Tipu's portrait and belongings nearby), is perhaps better called

"India's revenge." The Bengal tiger has a British redcoat down, sinking its teeth into his neck. When you turned the crank, the Brit's left arm would flail, and both he and the tiger would roar through organ pipes. (The mechanism still works.)

Tipu, the Sultan of Mysore (1750-1799), called himself the "Tiger of Mysore." He was well-educated in several languages and collected a library of 2,000 books. An enlightened ruler, he built roads and dams and promoted new technology. Tipu could see that India was being swallowed up by the all-powerful British East India Company. He allied himself with France and fought several successful wars against the British, but he was eventually defeated and forced to give up half his kingdom to them. Tipu was later killed by the Brits in battle (1799), his palace ransacked, and his possessions—including this toy—were taken, like much of India, by the British East India Company.

• *Backtrack out of Room 41 and turn right, then right again into Room 40. Here you'll find the...*

⓯ Fashion Galleries

Centuries of English fashion are corseted into 40 display cases. The cases around the perimeter show the evolution of a particular article of clothing. You'll see ladies' underwear through the ages, formal wear, men's suits, and so on. Temporary exhibits here usually enliven the displays. For more on old English fashion, visit the British Galleries (described later).

• *Directly across the hall from Room 40 is the cavernous Room 48a, filled with...*

⓰ Raphael's Tapestry Cartoons

For Christmas in 1519, Pope Leo X unveiled 10 new tapestries in the Sistine Chapel, designed by the famous artist Raphael. The project was one of the largest ever undertaken by a painter—it cost far more than Michelangelo's Sistine ceiling—and when it was done, the tapestries were a hit, inspiring princes across Europe to decorate their palaces in masterpieces of cloth.

The V&A owns seven of the full-size designs by Raphael that were used to produce the tapestries (approximately 13 by 17 feet, done in tempera on paper, now mounted on canvas). The cartoons were sent to factories in Brussels, cut into strips (see the lines), and placed on the looms. The scenes are the reverse of the final product—lots of left-handed saints.

Raphael (1483-1520) chose scenes from the Acts of the Apostles—particularly of Peter and Paul, the two early saints most as-

sociated with Rome, the seat of the popes. Knowing where the tapestries were to be hung, Raphael was determined to top Michelangelo's famous Sistine ceiling, with its huge, dramatic figures and subtle color effects. He matched Michelangelo's body-builder muscles (for example, the fishermen in *The Miraculous Draught of Fishes*), dramatic gestures, and reaction shots (as in the busy crowd scenes in *St. Paul Preaching in Athens*), and he exceeded Michelangelo in the subtleties of color.

Unfortunately, it was difficult to reproduce Raphael's painted nuances in the tapestry workshop. Traditional tapestries were simple, depicting either set patterns or block figures on a neutral background. Raphael challenged the Flemish weavers. Each brushstroke had to be reproduced by a colored thread woven horizontally. The finished tapestries (which are still in the Vatican) were glorious, but these cartoons capture Raphael's original vision.

• *From the Raphael room (48a), go up the staircase. At the top of the stairs (on level 2), turn left into Room 57. This is the heart of the British Galleries, featuring the Great Bed of Ware and Elizabethan miniatures.*

⑰ British Galleries

Room 57 covers the era of Queen Elizabeth I. Find rare miniature portraits—a popular item of the day—including Hilliard's oft-reproduced *Young Man Among Roses* miniature, capturing the romance of a Shakespeare sonnet. Also in the room are musical instruments and suits of armor—a love-and-war combination appropriate to the Elizabethan Age. Finally, there's the Great Bed of Ware. Built as a tourist-attracting gimmick by an English inn around 1600, this four-poster bed still wows. You and six of your favorite friends could bed down here, taking a well-earned rest after this eclectic tour.

Continue into the next room (Room 58), dedicated to *Birth, Marriage, and Death*, and displaying swaddling clothes, a wedding portrait, and a casket pall. Continuing on, you'll pass through a couple of alcoves with Tudor-era tapestries. The far end of Room 58, devoted to Henry VIII, has a portrait of him; his writing box (with quill pens, ink, and sealing wax); and a whole roomful of the fancy furniture, tapestries, jewelry, and dinnerware that may have decorated his palaces.

If you're interested, there's much more to the British Galleries, which sweep chronologically through 400 years of British high-class living (1500-1900)—all laid out over two floors and beautifully described.

• *For now, pop out the doorway of Room 58. You'll notice we've come full circle: You're overlooking the Grand Entrance lobby. This tour is officially over. But if you'd like more suggestions, there's great stuff upstairs.*

⓲ Jewelry, Theater, Silver, and More

• *From the Grand Entrance lobby, pass through the shop, turn right into Room 24, and climb the staircase to level 3.*

Jewelry (Rooms 90-93): This collection is understandably popular. In one long glittering gallery, you can trace the evolution of jewelry from ancient Egyptian, Greek, and Roman to the 20th century. The Art Nouveau style of Parisian jeweler Rene Lalique is hard not to love.

• *Exit the jewelry rooms at the far end and turn right to find...*

Theater and Performance (Rooms 103-106): With artifacts from Hamlet skulls to rock-and-roll tour posters, this exhibit re-

cords the history of live performance in the UK. Kids will enjoy the costumes from *The Lion King* and the dress-up costume box. Nearby, aging boomers will see Mick Jagger's jumpsuit...and marvel that he used to fit into it.

• *Exit the collection where you entered, turn right (into "Prints & Drawings"), then left to find...*

British Silver (Rooms 65-68): The displays in these galleries are bursting with flamboyant silver treasures dating from the 1600s to modern times, including teething rattles, gambling counters, punch bowls, and pitchers.

• *I'll leave you here (find exit stairs at the far-right end of Room 74), but there's plenty left to see. If you have stamina, use your V&A map to plot the rest of your Grand Tour of this museum.*

V&A MUSEUM

TATE BRITAIN TOUR

The National Gallery of British Art, otherwise known as the Tate Britain, features the world's best collection of British art—sweeping you from 1500 until today. This is people's art, with realistic paintings rooted in the people, landscape, and stories of the British Isles. The recently renovated Tate shows off Hogarth's stage sets, Gainsborough's ladies, Blake's angels, Constable's clouds, Turner's tempests, the naturalistic realism of the Pre-Raphaelites, and the camera-eye portraits of Hockney and Freud. Even if these names are new to you, don't worry. You'll likely see a few "famous" works you didn't know were British and exit the Tate Britain with at least one new favorite artist.

Orientation

Cost: Free (£4 donation requested); fee for special exhibits.

Hours: Daily 10:00-18:00, last entry 45 minutes before closing.

Getting There: It's on the Thames River, south of Big Ben and north of Vauxhall Bridge. The museum has two entrances: the main entrance on Millbank, facing the Thames, and the Manton entrance on Atterbury Street.

You can reach the museum by Tube, ferry, bus, or on foot:

By Tube: Tube: Pimlico plus seven-minute walk, or Tube: Westminster plus 15-minute walk.

By Ferry: Hop on Thames Clippers' Tate Boat ferry from the Tate Modern for a 15-minute crossing (roughly £7 one-way, £17 day ticket, discount with Travelcard or Oyster card, buy ticket at self-serve machines or use Oyster Card, departs every 40 minutes Mon-Fri from 10:15 to 16:30, Sat-Sun from 9:40 to 18:30, www.tate.org.uk/visit/tate-boat).

By Bus: Bus #87 leaves from the National Gallery, and

drops off in front of the Tate. Bus #88 leaves from Oxford Circus, and drops off behind the museum. Both connect the museum to Westminster.

   On Foot: Walk 15 minutes south along the Thames from Big Ben.

Information: Pick up a map (£1 suggested donation) at the information desk. The spacious reading room downstairs is designed as a creative thinking space for the public. The museum's shops are great for books, magazines, and trinkets. Tel. 020/7887-8888, www.tate.org.uk.

Tours: Free **guided tours** are generally offered daily at 11:00, 12:00, 14:00, and 15:00, but call to confirm schedule. Use the Tate's Wi-Fi and download their handy room-by-room **audio tour** or **app.** The museum also hosts games, activities, and art projects for children (Sat-Sun 11:00-15:00 plus other times as scheduled).

Length of This Tour: Allow one hour. If you have less time, focus on the Pre-Raphaelites and Turner.

Cloakroom: Bag and coat check are free (£2 suggested donation).

Photography: Photos are allowed without a flash or tripod.

Cuisine Art: Your options are a café with an affordable gourmet buffet line (daily 10:00-18:00) or a pricey-but-delightful restaurant (daily 12:00-15:00; £18 afternoon tea served Sat-Sun and sometimes weekdays, 15:30-17:00).

Starring: Hogarth, Gainsborough, Reynolds, Blake, Constable, Pre-Raphaelites, and Turner.

Know Your Tates: Don't confuse the Tate Britain (British art) with the Tate Modern (at Bankside, on the South Bank of the Thames across from St. Paul's Cathedral), which features modern art.

ORIEN-TATE: GALLERY IN MOTION

This tour covers, in roughly chronological order, British paintings from 1500 to today. Works from the early centuries are located in the west half of the building, 20th-century art is in the east half, and the works of J. M. W. Turner are in an adjacent wing (the Clore Gallery). Temporary exhibits (some free, some requiring an entrance fee) are in the east wing and in the basement.

   Though the Tate's layout is roughly chronological, the emphasis here is on *rough*. Certain artists' works (such as Blake's and Henry Moore's) are placed in special rooms outside the chronological flow. Other rooms focus on a particular aspect of British art. In addition, the Tate rotates its vast collection of paintings, so it's difficult to predict exactly which works will be on display. Pick up the latest map as you enter, or download their handy audio tour or app. Consider reading this chapter ahead of time as an overview of

British art, then let the Tate surprise you with its current array of masterpieces.

The Tour Begins

British artists painted people, countrysides, and scenes from daily life, realistically and without the artist passing judgment (substance over style). What you won't see here are the fleshy goddesses, naked baby angels, and Madonna-and-child altarpieces so popular elsewhere in Europe. The largely Protestant English abhorred the "graven images" of the wealthy Catholic world; many such images were destroyed during the 16th-century Reformation. They preferred portraits of flesh-and-blood English folk.

• *From the main Millbank entrance, walk through the bright, white rotunda and down the long central hall, usually adorned with sculpture or temporary installations. Near the far end, enter the rooms on the left, where you'll find the beginnings of British painting (as you enter each room, you'll find the year etched into the floor).*

1500-1700—Portraits of Lord and Lady Whoevertheyare

Stuffy portraits of a beef-fed society try to turn crude country nobles into refined men and delicate women. Men in ruffled collars clutch symbols of power. Women in ruffled collars, puffy sleeves, and elaborately patterned dresses display their lily-white complexions, turning their pinkies out.

English country houses often had a long hall built specially to hang family portraits. You could stroll along and see your noble forebears looking down their noses at you. Britain's upper crust had little interest in art other than as a record of themselves along with their possessions—their wives, children, jewels, furs, ruffled collars, swords, and guns.

You'll see many more portraits in the Tate Britain, right up to modern times. Each era had its own style. Portraits from the 1500s are stern and dignified. The 1600s brought a more relaxed and elegant style and more décolletage.

1700s—ART BLOSSOMS

With peace at home (under three King Georges), a strong overseas economy, and a growing urban center in London, England's artistic life began to bloom. As the English grew more sophisticated, so did their portraits. Painters branched out into other subjects, capturing slices of everyday life. The Royal Academy added a veneer of classical Greece to even the simplest subjects.

William Hogarth (1697-1764)

Hogarth loved the theater. "My picture is my stage," he said, "and my men and women my players." The curtain goes up, and we see

Tate Britain Overview

1500-1700
PORTRAITS

1700-1800
HOGARTH
REYNOLDS
STUBBS
GAINSBOROUGH

1800-1850
BLAKE &
ROMANTIC
LANDSCAPES

1837-1901
VICTORIAN
PRE-RAPHAELITES
BRITISH
IMPRESSIONISM

MANTON ENTRANCE

OCTAGON

TEMPORARY EXHIBITIONS

ROTUNDA

1950-2000
HOCKNEY
FREUD
RILEY
GILBERT & GEORGE

1900-1950
WORLD WARS
CUBIST, ABSTRACT
EPSTEIN
MOORE
HEPWORTH
BACON

Not to Scale

CONSTABLE

**THE
TURNER
COLLECTION**
(CLORE GALLERY)

CLORE
ENTRANCE

RESTAURANT
(DOWNSTAIRS)
SHOP

CAFÉ
(DOWNSTAIRS)

**MAIN
ENTRANCE**
MILLBANK
ENTRANCE

← To Pimlico ⊖
(5 min. walk)

To Westminster ⊖
& Big Ben →
(15 min. walk)
#87
Ⓑ

TATE BRITAIN

MILLBANK

MILLBANK PIER
(BOAT TO
TATE MODERN)

Thames River

one scene that tells a whole story, often satirizing English high society. The London theater scene came into its own (after post-Shakespeare censorship) during Hogarth's generation. He often painted series based on popular plays of the time.

A born Londoner, Hogarth loved every gritty aspect of the big city. You'd find him in seedy pubs and brothels, at the half-price ticket booth in Leicester Square, at prizefights, cockfights, duels, and public executions—all with sketchbook in hand. An 18th-century Charles Dickens, he exposed the hypocrisy of fat-bellied squires, vain ladies, and gluttonous priests. He also gave the upper classes a glimpse into the hidden poverty of "merry olde England"—poor soldiers with holes in their stockings, overworked servants, and unwed mothers.

Hogarth's portraits (and self-portraits) are unflinchingly honest, quite different from the powdered-wig fantasies of his contemporaries. Hogarth was an accomplished engraver; his works were mass-produced, giving Londoners a sense of their city and themselves.

Sir Joshua Reynolds (1723-1792) and the "Grand Manner"

Real life wasn't worthy of a painting. So said Sir Joshua Reynolds, the pillar of Britain's Royal Academy. Instead, people, places, and things had to be gussied up with Greek columns, symbolism, and great historic moments, ideally from classical Greece.

In his portraits, he'd pose Lady Bagbody like the Medici Venus, or Lord Milquetoast like Apollo Belvedere. In landscapes you get Versailles-type settings of classical monuments amid perfectly manicured greenery. Inspired by Rembrandt, Reynolds sometimes used dense, clotted paint to capture the look of the Old Masters.

This art was meant to elevate the viewer, to appeal to his rational nature and fill him with noble sentiment. Sir Joshua Reynolds, the pillar of England's art establishment, stood for all that was upright, tasteful, rational, brave, clean, reverent, and...zzzzzzz....

George Stubbs (1724-1806)

Stubbs was the Michelangelo of horse painters. He understood these creatures from the inside out, having dissected them in his studio. He even used machinery to prop the corpses up into lifelike poses. He painted the horses first on a blank canvas, then filled in the background landscape around them (notice the heavy outlines that make them stand out clearly from the countryside). The result is both incredibly natural—from the veins in their noses to their freshly brushed coats—and geometrically posed.

Thomas Gainsborough (1727-1788)

Gainsborough showcased the elegant, educated women of his generation. He portrayed them as they wished to see themselves: a feminine ideal, patterned after fashion magazines. The cheeks are rosy, the poses relaxed and S-shaped, the colors brighter and more pastel, showing the influence of the refined French culture of the court at Versailles. His ladies tiptoe gracefully toward us, with clear, Ivory-soap complexions that stand out from the swirling greenery of English gardens. (Though he painted portraits, he longed to do landscapes.) Gainsborough worked hard to prettify his subjects, but the results were always natural and never stuffy.

1800-1850—THE INDUSTRIAL REVOLUTION

Newfangled inventions were everywhere. Railroads laced the land. You could fall asleep in Edinburgh and wake up in London, a trip that used to take days or weeks. But along with technology came factories coating towns with soot, urban poverty, regimentation, and clock-punching. Machines replaced honest laborers, and once-noble Man was viewed as a naked ape.

Strangely, you'll see little of the modern world in paintings of the time—except in reaction to it. Many artists rebelled against "progress" and the modern world. They escaped the dirty cities to commune with nature (Constable and the Romantics). Or they found a new spirituality in intense human emotions (dramatic scenes from history or literature). Or they left the modern world altogether.

• *The work of William Blake is displayed in a dedicated room on the other side of the central sculpture hall.*

William Blake (1757-1827)

At the age of four, Blake saw the face of God. A few years later, he ran across a flock of angels swinging in a tree. Twenty years later, he was living in a run-down London flat with an illiterate wife, scratching out a thin existence as an engraver. But even in this squalor, ignored by all but a few fellow artists, he still had his heavenly visions, and he described them in poems, paintings, drawings, and prints.

One of the original space cowboys, Blake also was a unique artist, often classed with the Romantics because he painted in a fit of ecstatic inspiration rather than by studied technique. He painted angels, not the dull material world. While Britain was conquering the world with guns and nature with machines, and while his fellow Londoners were growing rich, fat, and self-important, Blake turned his gaze inward, illustrating the glorious visions of the soul.

Blake's work hangs in a darkened room to protect his watercolors from deterioration. Enter his mysterious world and let your pupils dilate opium-wide.

His pen and watercolor sketches glow with an unearthly aura. In visions of the Christian heaven or Dante's hell, his figures have superhero musculature. The colors are almost translucent.

Blake saw the material world as bad, trapping the divine spark inside each of our bodies and keeping us from true communion with God. Blake's prints illustrate his views on the ultimate weakness of material, scientific man. Despite their Greek-god anatomy, his men look noble but tragically lost.

A famous poet as well as painter, Blake summed up his distrust of the material world in a poem addressed to "The God of this World"—that is, Satan:

Tho' thou art Worship'd by the Names Divine
Of Jesus and Jehovah, thou art still
The Son of Morn in weary Night's decline,
The lost Traveller's Dream under the Hill.

"Romantic" Landscapes—Art and the Sublime

Artists in the Romantic style saw the most intense human emotions reflected in the drama and mystery of nature. Some of them mixed landscapes with intense human emotion to produce huge, colorful canvases depicting storms, burning sunsets, towering clouds, and crashing waves, all dwarfing puny humans.

History paintings reflected great moments from the past, from ancient Greece to medieval knights, Napoleon to Britain's battles abroad. These were seen as the classiest form of art, combining the high drama of heroic acts with refined technique.

Other artists made supernatural, religious fantasy-scapes. God is found within nature, and nature is charged with the grandeur and power of God.

1837-1901—THE VICTORIAN ERA

In the world's wealthiest nation, the prosperous middle class dictated taste in art. They admired paintings that were realistic

(showcasing the artist's talent and work ethic), depicting Norman Rockwell-style slices of everyday life.

We see families and ordinary people eating, working, and relaxing. Some paintings tug at the heartstrings, with scenes of parting couples, the grief of death, or the joy of families reuniting. Dramatic scenes from classical (Chaucer and Shakespeare) and popular literature get the heart beating. There's the occasional touching look at the plight of the honest poor, reminiscent of Dickens. Many paintings warn us to be good little boys and girls by showing the consequences of a life of sin. And then there are the puppy dogs with sad eyes.

The Pre-Raphaelites

You'll see medieval damsels in dresses and knights in tights, legendary lovers from poetry, and even a very human Virgin Mary as a delicate young woman. The women wear flowing dresses and have long, wavy hair and delicate, elongated, curving bodies. Beautiful.

Overdosed with the gushy sentimentality of their day, a band of 20-year-old artists—including Sir John Everett Millais, Dante Gabriel Rossetti, and William Holman Hunt—said "Enough!" and dedicated themselves to creating less saccharine art. Their "Pre-Raphaelite Brotherhood" (you may see the initials P. R. B. by the artist's signature) returned to a style "pre-Raphael"—that is, "medieval" in its simple style, in its melancholy mood, and often in its subject matter.

"Truth to Nature" was their slogan. Like the Impressionists who followed them, they donned their scarves, barged out of the stuffy studio, and set up outdoors, painting trees, streams, and people, like scientists on a field trip. Still, they often captured nature

with such a close-up clarity that it's downright unnatural. And despite the Pre-Raphaelite claim to paint life just as it is, this is so beautiful it hurts.

This is art from the cult of femininity, worshipping Woman's haunting beauty, compassion, and depth of soul (proto-feminism or nouveau-chauvinism?). The artists' wives and lovers were their models and muses, and the art echoed their love lives. The people are surrounded by nature at its most beautiful, with every detail painted crystal clear. Even without the people, there is a mood of melancholy.

The Pre-Raphaelites hated overacting. Their subjects—even in the face of great tragedy, high passions, and moral dilemmas—barely raise an eyebrow. Outwardly, they're reflective, accepting their fate. But sinuous postures—with lovers swooning into each other, and parting lovers swooning apart—speak volumes. These volumes are footnoted by the small objects with symbolic importance placed around them: red flowers denoting passion, lilies for purity, pets for fidelity, and so on.

The colors—greens, blues, and reds—are bright and clear, with everything evenly lit, so that we see every detail. To get the luminous color, some painted a thin layer of bright paint over a pure white, still-wet undercoat, which subtly "shines" through. These canvases radiate a pure spirituality, like stained-glass windows.

Stand for a while and enjoy the exquisite realism and human emotions of these Victorian-era works...flesh-and-blood people painted realistically. Get your fill, because beloved Queen Victoria is about to check out, the modern world is coming, and, with it, new art to express modern attitudes.

BRITISH IMPRESSIONISM

Realistic British art stood apart from the modernist trends in France, but some influences drifted across the Channel. John

Singer Sargent (American-born) studied with Parisian Impressionists, learning the thick, messy brushwork and play of light at twilight. James Tissot used Degas' snapshot technique to capture a crowded scene from an odd angle. And James McNeill Whistler (born in America, trained in Paris, lived in London) composed his paintings like music—see some of his paintings' titles. These collages of shapes and colors please the eye like a song tickles the ear. Whistler signed his paintings with his initials in the shape of a butterfly. You may also see sophisticated works by London's own "Bloomsbury Group," who put a British spin on French Post-Impressionism.

• *Before moving on to 20th-century art, first visit the Turner Collection. You'll find it in a wing adjacent to the main building: Pass through the rotunda to the east side of the gallery and just keep going through a few rooms till you enter The Turner Collection, housed in the Clore Gallery.*

THE TURNER COLLECTION

The Tate Britain has the world's best collection of works by J. M. W. Turner (1775-1851). Walking through his life's work, you can trace his progression from a painter of realistic historical scenes, through his wandering years, to Impressionist paintings of color-and-light patterns.

• *As you explore the collection, you'll watch Turner's style evolve from clear-eyed realism to hazy proto-Impressionism. You'll also see how Turner dabbled in different subjects: landscapes, seascapes, Roman ruins, snapshots of Venice, and so on.*

Self-Portrait as a Young Man

At 24, Turner has just been elected the youngest Associate of the Royal Academy. The son of a Covent Garden barber now dresses like a gentleman. His clear, realistic painting style caught the public's fancy. The full-frontal pose and intense gaze of this portrait show a young man ready to take on the world.

The Royal Academy Years

Trained in the Reynolds school of grandiose epics, Turner painted the obligatory big canvases of great moments in history—*The Destruction of Sodom, Hannibal and His Army Crossing the Alps, The Lost ATM Card, Jason and the Argonauts,* and various shipwrecks. Not content to crank them out in the traditional staid manner, he sets them in expansive landscapes. Nature's stormy mood mirrors the human events, but is so grandiose it dwarfs them.

This is a theme we'll see throughout his works: The forces of nature—the burning sun, swirling clouds, churning waves, gathering storms, and the weathering of time—overwhelm men and wear down the civilizations they build.

Travels with Turner

Turner's true love was nature—he was a born hobo. Oblivious to the wealth and fame that his early paintings gave him, he set out traveling—mostly on foot—throughout England and the Continent, with a rucksack full of sketch pads and painting gear. He sketched the English countryside—not green, leafy, and placid as so many others had done, but churning in motion, hazed over by a burning sunset.

He found the "sublime" not in the studio or in church, but in the overwhelming power of nature. The landscapes throb with life and motion. He sets Constable's clouds on fire.

Italy's Landscape and Ruins

With a Rick Steves guidebook in hand, Turner visited the great museums of Italy, drawing inspiration from the Renaissance masters. He painted the classical monuments and Renaissance architecture. He copied masterpieces, admired the works of the French classicist Claude Lorrain, and fused a great variety of styles—a true pan-European vision. Turner's Roman ruins are not grand; they're dwarfed by the landscape around them and eroded by swirling, misty, luminous clouds.

Stand close to a big canvas of Roman ruins, close enough so that it fills your whole field of vision. Notice how the buildings seem to wrap around you. Turner was a master of using multiple perspectives to draw the viewer in. On the one hand, you're right in the thick of things, looking "up" at the tall buildings. Then again, you're looking "down" on the distant horizon, as though standing on a mountaintop.

Venice

I know what color the palazzo is. But what color is it at sunset? Or through the filter of the watery haze that hangs over Venice? Can

I paint the glowing haze itself? Maybe if I combine two different colors and smudge the paint on....

Venice stoked Turner's lust for reflected, golden sunlight. You'll see both finished works and unfinished sketches...uh, which is which?

Seascapes

The ever-changing sea was his specialty, with waves, clouds, mist, and sky churning and mixing together, all driven by the same forces.

Turner used oils like many painters use watercolors. First, he'd lay down a background (a "wash") of large patches of color, then he'd add a few dabs of paint to suggest a figure. (Some artists might use pencil lines to sketch out their figures, but Turner avoided that.) The final product lacked photographic clarity but showed the power and constant change in the forces of nature. He was perhaps the most prolific painter ever, with some 2,000 finished paintings and 20,000 sketches and watercolors.

Late Works

The older Turner got, the messier both he and his paintings became. He was wealthy, but he died in a run-down dive, where

he'd set up house with a prostitute. Yet the colors are brighter and the subjects less pessimistic than in the dark and brooding early canvases. His last works—whether landscape, religious, or classical scenes—are a blur and swirl of colors in motion, lit by the sun or a lamp burning through the mist. Even Turner's own creations were finally dissolved by the swirling forces of nature.

These paintings are "modern" in that the subject is less important than the style. You'll have to read the title to "get" it. You could argue that an Englishman helped invent Impressionism a generation before Monet and his ilk boxed the artistic ears of Paris in the 1880s. Turner's messy use of paint to portray reflected light "Chunneled" its way to France to inspire the Impressionists.

• *Now, head for the corner room of the Clore Gallery that's dedicated to Turner's great rival and contemporary...*

John Constable (1776-1837)

Constable brought painting back into the real world. Although the Royal Academy thought Nature needed makeup, Constable thought she was just fine. He

painted the English landscape as it was—realistically, without idealizing it. With simple earth tones he caught leafy green trees, gathering gray skies, brown country lanes, and rivers the color of the clouds reflected in them. Many details came from actual landscapes and villages from his childhood roots in Suffolk.

Clouds are Constable's trademark. Appreciate the effort involved in sketching ever-changing cloud patterns for hours on end—the mix of dark clouds and white clouds, cumulus and stratus, the colors of sunset. A generation before the Impressionists, he actually set up his easel outdoors and painted on the spot, a painstaking process before the invention of ready-made paints-in-a-tube (about 1850).

It's rare to find a Constable (or any British) landscape that doesn't have the mark of man in it—a cottage, hay cart, field hand, or a country road running through the scene. For him, the English countryside and its people were one.

In his later years, Constable's canvases became bigger, the style more "Impressionistic" (messier brushwork), and he worked more from memory than observation.

Constable's commitment to unvarnished nature wasn't fully recognized in his lifetime, and he was forced to paint portraits for his keep. The neglect caused him to ask a friend, "Can it therefore be wondered at that I paint continual storms?"

• *Now, back to where we left off: the beginning of the 20th century. Retrace your steps to the main building, where you'll find 20th-century art in the east half of the building.*

1900-1950—WORLD WARS

As two world wars whittled down the powerful British Empire, it still remained a major cultural force.

British art mirrored many of the trends and "-isms" pioneered in Paris. You'll see Cubism like Picasso's, abstract art like Mondrian's, and so on. But British artists also continued the British tradition of realistic paintings of people and landscapes. (Note: You'll find 20th-century artists' work both here in the Tate Britain and in the Tate Modern—◫ see also the Tate Modern Tour chapter.)

World War I, in which Britain lost a million men, cast a long shadow over the land. Artists expressed the horror of war, particularly of dehumanizing battles pitting powerful machines against puny human pawns. Jacob Epstein's (1880-1959) gleaming, abstract statues suggest mangled half-human/half-machine forms.

Henry Moore (1898-1986)

Twice a week, young Henry Moore went to the British Museum to sketch ancient statues, especially reclining ones (as in the Parthenon pediment or the Mayan god, Chac Mool, which he saw in a photo). His statues—mostly female, mostly reclining—catch the primitive power of carved stone. Moore almost always carved with his own hands (unlike, say, Rodin, who modeled a small clay figure and let assistants chisel the real thing), capturing the human body in a few simple curves, with minimal changes to the rock itself.

The statues do look vaguely like what their titles say, but it's the stones themselves that are really interesting. Notice the texture and graininess of these mini-Stonehenges; feel the weight, the space they take up, and how the rock forms intermingle.

During World War II, Moore passed time in the bomb shelters sketching mothers with babes in arms, a theme found in later works.

Moore carves the human body with the epic scale and restless poses of Michelangelo but with the crude rocks and simple lines of the primitives.

Barbara Hepworth (1903-1975)

Hepworth's small-scale carvings in stone and wood—like "mini-Moores"—make even holes look interesting. Though they're not exactly realistic, it isn't hard to imagine them being inspired by, say, a man embracing a woman (she called it "sex harmony"), or the shoreline encircling a bay near her Cornwall-coast home, or a cliff penetrated by a cave—that is, two forms intermingling.

Francis Bacon (1909-1992)

With a stiff upper lip, Britain survived the Blitz, World War II, and the loss of hundreds of thousands of men—but at war's end, the bottled-up horror came rushing out. Bacon's 1945 exhibition, opening just after Holocaust details began surfacing, stunned London with its unmitigated ugliness.

His deformed half-humans/half-animals—caged in a claustrophobic room, with twisted hunk-of-meat bodies and quadriplegic, smudged-mouth helplessness—can do nothing but scream in anguish and frustration. The scream becomes a blur, as though it goes on forever.

Bacon, largely self-taught, uses "traditional" figurativism, painting somewhat recognizable people and things. His subjects express the existential human predicament of being caught in a world not of your making, isolated and helpless to change it.

1950-2000—MODERN WORLD

No longer a world power, Britain in the Swinging '60s became a major exporter of pop culture. British art's traditional strengths—realism, portraits, landscapes, and slice-of-life scenes—were redone in the modern style.

David Hockney (b. 1937)

The "British Andy Warhol"—who is bleach-blonde, horn-rimmed, gay, and famous—paints "pop"-ular culture with photographic re-

alism. Large, airy canvases of L.A. swimming pools, double portraits of his friends in their stylish homes, or mundane scenes from the artist's own life capture the superficial materialism of the 1970s and 1980s. (Is he satirizing or glorifying it by painting it on a monumental scale with painstaking detail?)

Hockney saturates the canvas with bright (acrylic) paint, eliminating any haze, making distant objects as clear and bright as close ones. This technique, combined with his slightly simplified "cut-out" figures, gives the painting the flat look of a billboard.

Lucian Freud (1922-2011)

Sigmund's grandson (who emigrated from Nazi Germany as a boy) puts every detail on the couch for analysis, then reassembles them

into works that are still surprisingly realistic. His subjects look you right in the eye, slightly on edge. Even the plants create an ominous mood. Everything is in sharp focus (unlike in real life, where you concentrate on one thing while your peripheral vision is blurred). Thick brushwork is especially good at capturing the pallor of British flesh.

In the great tradition of British portrait painting, Freud recently did an unflinching (and controversial) portrait of Queen Elizabeth.

Bridget Riley (b. 1931)

The pioneer of Op Art paints patterns of lines and alternating colors that make the eye vibrate (the way a spiral will "spin") when you stare at them. These obscure, scientific experiments in human optics suddenly became trendy in the psychedelic, cannabis-fueled 1960s. Like, wow.

Gilbert (b. 1943) and George (b. 1942)

The Siegfried and Roy of art satirize the "Me Generation" and its shameless self-marketing by portraying their nerdy, three-piece-suited selves on the monumental scale normally dedicated to kings, popes, and saints.

THE REST OF THE MUSEUM

We've covered 500 years, with social satire from Hogarth to Hockney, from Constable's placid landscapes to Turner's churning scenes, from Blake's inner visions to Pre-Raphaelite fantasies, from realistic portraits to...realistic portraits.

But the Tate's great strength is championing contemporary British art in special exhibitions. There are generally two exhibition spaces: one in the east half of the main floor (often free), and another downstairs (usually requiring separate admission). Explore the cutting-edge art from one of the world's thriving cultural capitals: London.

Enough Tate? Great. It's late.

GREENWICH TOUR

Still well within the city limits of London, the Royal Borough of Greenwich (GREN-ich)—England's maritime capital—feels like a small town all its own. Visitors come here for all things salty, including the *Cutty Sark* clipper, the area's premier attraction. Greenwich is synonymous with timekeeping and astronomy, and at the Royal Observatory Greenwich, you can learn how those pursuits relate to seafaring. Greenwich also has stately Baroque architecture, appealing markets, a fleet of nautical shops, plenty of parks, kid-friendly museums, and hordes of tourists. Since many of the major sights here are free to enter, and you can travel between central London and Greenwich on a cheap Tube ticket, it's a wonderfully inexpensive day out. And where else can you set your watch with such accuracy?

Note that Greenwich pairs perfectly with a quick visit to the Docklands, London's glittering skyscraper zone (just across the river from Greenwich, and covered in the next chapter).

GETTING TO GREENWICH

It's a joy by boat or a snap by Docklands Light Railway (DLR). I enjoy a mix-and-match approach: Ride the boat to Greenwich for the scenery and commentary, and take the DLR back—especially if you want to stop at the Docklands on the way home. On pleasant weekends, the early evening London-bound boats fill up quickly as everyone leaves around the same time (17:00-18:00)—another reason to boat here and take the DLR back to central London.

By Boat: From central London, you can cruise scenically down the Thames to Greenwich. Various tour boats—with commentary and open-deck seating up top—leave from the piers at Westminster, Waterloo, and the Tower of London (2/hour, 30-75 minutes). Most boats have commentary only on the way to Greenwich, but if you really want it on the way back, you can ask the boat staff to provide it.

Thames Clippers offers faster trips, with no commentary and only a small deck at the stern (departs every 20-30 minutes from several piers in central London, 20-45 minutes). Thames Clippers also connects Greenwich to the Docklands' Canary Wharf Pier (2-3/hour, 10 minutes).

For cruising details, see page 39.

By Docklands Light Railway (DLR): From Bank Station in central London (also accessible from the Monument Tube station), take the DLR to Cutty Sark Station in central Greenwich; it's one stop before the main—but less central—Greenwich Station (departs at least every 10 minutes, 20 minutes, all in Zone 2, covered by any Tube pass). The DLR works like the Tube; be sure to touch your card to the reader on the platform before and after your journey, or risk being fined.

Many DLR trains terminate at Canary Wharf, so make sure you get on one that continues to Lewisham or Greenwich. Some DLR trains terminate at Island Gardens, from where you can generally catch another train to Greenwich's Cutty Sark Station within a few minutes. Or, disembark at Island Gardens for the unique experience of walking under the Thames into Greenwich: To reach the pedestrian tunnel, exit the station, cross the street, and follow signs to *Island Gardens* for a good photo op. Then enter the red-brick Greenwich Foot Tunnel (opened in 1902), descend 86 spiral stairs (or ride the lift), hold your breath, and re-emerge on dry land at the bow of the *Cutty Sark*.

By Bus: Catch bus #188 from Russell Square near the British Museum (about 45 minutes to Greenwich).

Orientation to Greenwich

When to Go: To allow enough time to see everything—and to fit in a Docklands visit on your way back—head to Greenwich in the morning. Some of the sights can get crowded with families and school groups, especially in summer and on weekends. You can save a little time by reserving your *Cutty Sark* visit in advance (explained on page 352).

Opening Times: Greenwich's main sights are open daily from 10:00 to 17:00; some stay open later (complete hours are listed later for each individual sight). On Mondays, stalls at the town's popular market are closed.

Information: The TI is within the **Discover Greenwich visitors center,** inside the Old Royal Naval College gates (daily 10:00-17:00, Pepys House, 2 Cutty Sark Gardens, tel. 0870-608-2000, www.visitgreenwich.org.uk). For more on Discover Greenwich, see the listing later in this chapter.

Tours: Guided city walks, which depart from the TI within Discover Greenwich, offer an overview and go past most of the big sights (£8, daily at 12:15 and 14:15, 1.5 hours; the only sights you enter are the Painted Hall and Chapel of Sts. Peter and Paul, and only on the 14:15 tour; the 12:15 tour leaves you at the door of the Royal Observatory).

Services: Free WCs are located inside the Discover Greenwich visitors center. For eating recommendations, see the sidebar on page 355.

Markets: Thanks to its markets, Greenwich throbs with browsing Londoners on weekends. The **Greenwich Market** is an entertaining mini-Covent Garden, located in the middle of the block between the Cutty Sark DLR station and the Old Royal Naval College—right on your way to the sights (farmers market, arts and crafts, and food stands; Tue-Sun 10:00-17:30; antiques on Tue, Thu, and Fri, www.greenwichmarketlondon.com).

The **Clocktower Market** sells old odds and ends at high prices on Greenwich High Road, near the post office (Sat-Sun and bank holidays only 10:00-17:00, www.clocktowermarket.co.uk).

Exploring Back Streets: Allow time to browse the town. Greenwich has two sides: prim and proper (east of Church Street) and lived-in local (west of Church Street). Wander beyond touristy Church Street and Greenwich High Road to where flower stands spill onto the side streets, antique shops sell brass nautical knickknacks, and salty pubs occupy more than just the corner. King William Walk, College Approach, and Nelson Road (all in the vicinity of Greenwich Market) are all worth a look.

Length of This Tour: Allow about two hours simply to stroll the area and enjoy the parks, but add several hours more to enter the sights (figure about an hour for the *Cutty Sark,* 30 minutes for the Royal Naval College, and an hour or two apiece for the National Maritime Museum and the Royal Observatory).

Starring: Glorious parks and stately buildings, maritime history, and the prime meridian.

BACKGROUND

Tudor kings favored the palace at Greenwich. Henry VIII was born here. Later kings commissioned architects Inigo Jones and Christopher Wren to beautify the town and palace, and William and Mary built a grand hospital to care for retired seamen (which later became a college for training naval officers). Today, Greenwich is a pincushion of royal, maritime, and scientific sights from Britain's illustrious past.

The Tour Begins

I've linked Greenwich's major sights with handy walking directions. Each attraction is described in full and rated; you can pick and choose which ones to enter. If you're in a rush, make a beeline to only the sights that interest you.

• Our first stop is the Cutty Sark. If you're arriving by boat, it's right in front of you. If you're coming by DLR, you'll get off at the Cutty Sark stop, exit the station to the left, pass under the brick archway, and turn left. The Cutty Sark is just ahead on the right.

▲▲Cutty Sark

The Scottish-built *Cutty Sark* was the last of the great China tea clippers and the queen of the seas when first launched in 1869.

She was among the fastest clippers ever built, the culmination of centuries of ship design. With 32,000 square feet of sail—and favorable winds—she could travel 300 miles in a day. But as a new century dawned, steamers began to outmatch sailing ships for speed, and by the mid-1920s the *Cutty Sark* was the world's last operating clipper ship. After a stint as a training ship, she was retired and turned into a museum in the 1950s.

Following a five-year-long restoration, interrupted by a devastating fire, the ship reopened to the public in the spring of 2012. The spectacular new display space has one major drawback: The glass building obscures the elegant lines of the hull that gave the *Cutty Sark* her record-breaking speed (one critic groused that the ship now "looks like it has run aground in a giant greenhouse"). On the plus side, the building allows visitors to walk directly below the ship, which has been raised 11 feet above her dry dock. Above deck, the ship's rigging has been restored to original specifications, while below deck, displays explore the *Cutty Sark*'s 140-year history and the cargo she carried—everything from tea to wool to

GREENWICH

Greenwich

To Canary Wharf
& The Docklands

Recommended
Walking Route

ISLE OF DOGS

WEST FERRY ROAD

Island Gardens (DLR)

Island Gardens

PRIME MERIDIAN

200 Meters

200 Yards

Thames River

To London

PEDESTRIAN TUNNEL

Riverside Stroll

Crane St.

TRINITY HOSPITAL

OLD WOOLWICH RD.

To O2 Arena

GREENWICH PIER

FIVE FOOT WALK

TUNNEL ENTRANCE

DISCOVER GREENWICH

OLD ROYAL NAVAL COLLEGE

PARK ROW

TRAFALGAR ROAD

CUTTY SARK

TOUR BEGINS

CREEK RD.

COLLEGE APPROACH

CHURCH ST.

PAINTED HALL

CHAPEL

WC

GREENWICH UNIVERSITY

ROMNEY ROAD

GREENWICH

Cutty Sark (DLR)

KING WILLIAM WALK

NELSON

ST. ALFEGE'S CHURCH

ROAN ST.

GREENWICH STATION

GREENWICH HIGH RD.

STOCKWELL

BURNEY ST.

To London

CROOM'S HILL

COLONNADES

NATIONAL MARITIME MUSEUM

QUEEN'S HOUSE

Greenwich Park

PRIME MERIDIAN

TOUR ENDS

FLAMSTEED HOUSE

ROYAL OBSERVATORY GREENWICH

To BLACKHEATH

PETER HARRISON PLANETARIUM

WELLER ASTRONOMY GALLERIES

Eateries

1 Greenwich Market
2 Clocktower Market
3 Trafalgar Tavern
4 Marks & Spencer Simply Food

5 Meantime The Old Brewery
6 Pavilion Tea House
7 Even Keel Café

gunpowder—as she raced between London and ports all around the world.

Cost and Hours: £13.50, kids aged 5-15-£7, free for kids under age 5, family tickets available, combo-ticket with Royal Observatory-£18.50, kids combo-ticket-£8.50; daily 10:00-17:00, may stay open until 18:00 during school holidays; last entry 45 minutes before closing; £5 guidebook available but hardly necessary, reservation tel. 020/8312-6608, www.rmg.co.uk.

Crowd-Beating Tips: The ship can get busy on school holidays and on weekends. To skip the ticket-purchasing line, you can reserve ahead online or by phone, or just try showing up around 13:00, when there's often a lull in visitors.

Visiting the *Cutty Sark*: The first deck you'll visit harkens back to the ship's days in the Chinese tea trade...which didn't last long, as the Suez Canal soon opened, allowing steam-powered ships to reach China much faster than sailboats. The *Cutty Sark* turned to trading wool with Australia, as explored on the next deck up. This "Tween Deck" is full of not-quite-gimmicky displays that mostly succeed in making the ship's history come alive, even for adults. Find the fun video game that lets you attempt to beat Captain Woodget's record voyage sailing a wool-laden *Sark* from Sydney to London. Sit on the tilting benches of tea crates for a seaborne feel, enjoy the oddly mesmerizing video at the stern, and get the figurehead's take on *Sark* history in the bow.

Sailing fans will like the gorgeously restored top deck best. Notice how pathetic the crew's mattresses were—then go check out the captain's cabin. Don't miss the video showing the rigger's-eye-view as he climbs high above the deck. Your visit ends down below, where you can take a coffee break directly under the shiny hull (it may gleam like gold, but the hull's covering is actually an alloy of copper and zinc). Videos describe how the mighty vessel was designed and then preserved. Near the bow is a colorful collection of figureheads from other ships. On the floor directly under the front of the hull, note the compass rose that shows how many days at sea it'd take to reach major ports from here.

• *Leaving the museum, head left, and find the visitors center called...*

Discover Greenwich

While it's hardly a museum, this center offers a decent introduction to Greenwich and some fun exhibits for kids. In the middle, a model of the town lights up to tell its history. Surrounding the model are displays and artifacts from various people who have left their mark on the town, along with exhibits about the architecture and construction of Greenwich's fine buildings. Tours of the Royal Naval College leave from the reception desk. Adjoining Discover

Eating in Greenwich

Picnicking: Greenwich's parks are picnic-perfect. Gather picnic supplies before heading up the hill to the National Maritime Museum and Royal Observatory. **Marks & Spencer Simply Food** sells ready-made lunches (between the DLR station and the *Cutty Sark* at 55 Greenwich Church Street).

Pub Grub: Greenwich has almost 100 pubs, with some boasting that they're mere milliseconds from the prime meridian. **Meantime The Old Brewery,** in the Discover Greenwich center, is a gastropub decorated with all things beer. An adjacent café serves cheap lunches. A brewery on this site once provided the daily ration of four pints of beer for pensioners at the hospital. Today it's a microbrewery offering 50 different beers, while a beer sommelier suggests the right food pairings (£5-7 snacks, soups, salads, and sandwiches; at night part of the pub becomes a fancier restaurant with £12-16 main courses; daily 10:00-23:00, tel. 020/3327-1280). **The Trafalgar Tavern,** with a casual pub and elegant ground-floor dining room, is a historical place for an overpriced meal (£15-26 main courses in restaurant, food served Mon-Sat 12:00-22:00, Sun until 19:00, Park Row, tel. 020/8858-2909).

Greenwich Market: From Yorkshire pudding to paella to Thai cuisine, the food stalls at the Greenwich Market offer an international variety of tasty options.

Tea and Coffee: For a coffee or afternoon tea break, consider the elegant 1906 **Pavilion Tea House** behind the planetarium in Greenwich Park or the **Even Keel Café** located directly beneath the shining copper hull of the *Cutty Sark*.

Greenwich are the TI and a recommended pub, Meantime The Old Brewery.

Cost and Hours: Free, daily 10:00-17:00, tel. 020/8269-4747, www.ornc.org.

• *Leave through the far exits (away from the* Cutty Sark*), turn right at the brewery, and continue through the manicured park to the open quad, where dramatic identical-twin buildings make up the heart of the...*

▲Old Royal Naval College

The college was originally a hospital founded by Queen Mary II and King William III in 1692 as a charity to care for retired or injured naval officers (called pensioners). William and Mary spared no expense, hiring the great Christopher Wren to design the complex (though other architects completed it). Its days as a hospital ended in 1869, and it served as a college for training naval officers from 1873 to 1998. Now that the Royal Navy has moved out, the public is invited to view the college's elaborate Painted Hall and

Chapel of Sts. Peter and Paul, which are in symmetrical buildings that face each other overlooking a broad riverfront park.

Cost and Hours: Free, daily 10:00-17:00, sometimes closed for private events, service Sun at 11:00 in chapel—all are welcome, www.ornc.org.

Visiting the College: Each building sells a descriptive guide (50p-£1), or you can buy the fun *Nasty Naval College* brochure (made for children, but with entertaining offbeat facts about the place; £1). Volunteers are often standing by to answer questions. Visit the highlight—the Painted Hall—first, before touring the chapel.

Painted Hall: Originally intended as a dining hall for pensioners, this sumptuously painted room was deemed too glorious (and, in the winter, too cold) for that purpose. So almost as soon as it was completed, it became simply a place to impress visitors.

Enter the hall, climb the stairs, and gape up at one of the largest painted ceilings in Europe—112 feet long. It's a big propaganda scene, glorifying the building's founders, Queen Mary II and King William III (who, as a Protestant monarch, had recently trounced the Catholic French King Louis XIV in a pivotal battle). Crane your neck—or use the clever wheeled mirrors—to examine the scene. In the center are William and Mary. Under his foot, William is crushing a

dark figure with a broken sword... Louis XIV. William is handing a red cap (representing liberty) to the woman on the right, who holds the reins of a white horse (symbolizing Europe). On the left, a white-robed woman hands him an olive branch, a sign of peace. The message: William has granted Europe liberty by saving it from the tyranny of Louis XIV. Below the royal couple, the Spirit of Architecture shows them the plans for this very building (commemorating the sad fact that Mary died before its completion). Ringing the central image are the four seasons (represented by Zodiac signs), the four virtues, and—at the top and bottom—a captured Spanish galleon and a British man-of-war battleship.

Up the steps at the end of the room, along the wall of the upper hall, is a portrait of the family of King George I. On the right is the artist who spent 19 years of his life painting this hall, James Thornhill (he finally finished it in 1727). He's holding out his hand—reportedly, he didn't feel he was paid enough for this Sistine-sized undertaking.

• *Exit the hall, and cross the field to enter the...*

Chapel of Sts. Peter and Paul: Not surprisingly, you'll sense a nautical air in this fine chapel. Notice the rope motif in the floor tiles down the aisle. The painting above the altar, by American Benjamin West, depicts the shipwreck of St. Paul on the island of Malta. According to the Bible, Paul disturbed a poisonous viper but managed to throw it in a fire, miraculously without being

harmed. Soon after the chapel was completed, it was gutted by a fire and had to be redecorated all over again. The plans were too ambitious, so the designers cut corners. Some of the columns and capitals are fake, and the "sculptures" lining the nave high above are actually trompe l'oeil—3-D paintings meant to look real. But some items, such as the marble frame around the main door, are finely crafted from expensive materials.

• *Leave the chapel, and walk straight down to the water—enjoying the sweeping views across to the Docklands. When you hit the river, turn right for a quick...*

Riverside Stroll

Looking back toward the Old Royal Naval College, notice how it's split into two parts; reportedly, Queen Mary didn't want the view from the Queen's House blocked. The college's twin-domed towers (one giving the time, the other the direction of the wind) frame the Queen's House, and the Royal Observatory Greenwich crowns the hill beyond.

Wander east along the Thames on Five Foot Walk (named for the width of the path). From here you can see the big, white, spiky **O2** dome a mile downstream. This stadium languished for nearly a decade after its controversial construction and brief life as the Millennium Dome. Intended to

GREENWICH

be a world's fair-type site and the center of London's year 2000 celebration, it ended up as the topic of heated debates about cost overruns and its controversial looks. The site was finally bought by a developer a few years ago and rechristened "The O2" (a telecommunications company paid for the naming rights). Today it hosts sporting events and concerts. Next to the O2 are the towers of the Emirates Air Line cable car, which ferries passengers from the O2 across the Thames to, essentially, nowhere.

Continuing downstream, just outside the fenced college grounds, you'll find the recommended **Trafalgar Tavern.** Dick-

ens knew the pub well, and he used it as the setting for the wedding breakfast in *Our Mutual Friend.* Built in 1837 in the Regency style to attract Londoners downriver, the upstairs Nelson Room is still used for weddings. Its formal moldings and elegant windows with balconies over the Thames are a step back in time and worth a peek.

• *From the Trafalgar Tavern, walk two long blocks up Park Row. After crossing busy Romney Road, turn right (through the gate near the corner) into the park. The palatial buildings in the middle of the park are the Queen's House and the National Maritime Museum; the Royal Observatory Greenwich is on the hilltop beyond. This trio, paired with the Cutty Sark, form the Royal Museums of Greenwich.*

Queen's House

In 1616 Inigo Jones designed the first Palladian-style villa in Britain for James I's wife, Anne of Denmark. All traces of the queen are long gone, and the Great Hall and Royal Apartments now serve as an art gallery for the National Maritime Museum. Predictably, most of the art is nautical-themed, with plenty of paintings of ships and sea battles, and portraits of admirals and captains.

Cost and Hours: Free, although closed for renovation for much of 2016, call or check website for updates, tel. 020/8858-4422, www.rmg.co.uk.

• *From the Queen's House, walk toward the hill, pass through a colonnade, and turn right. About 300 yards farther on, you'll see a giant ship in a bottle and the...*

▲National Maritime Museum

Great for anyone interested in the sea, this museum holds everything from a giant working paddlewheel to the uniform Admiral Horatio Nelson wore when he was killed at Trafalgar (look for the bullet hole, in the left shoulder). A big glass roof tops three levels of slick, modern, kid-friendly exhibits about all things seafaring.

The Explorers exhibit covers early expeditions and an ill-fated Arctic trip, complete with a soundtrack of creaking wooden ships and crashing waves. One room displays stained-glass windows honoring members of London's Baltic Exchange (an important shipping consortium) killed in World War I, while the somber Atlantic Worlds hall thoughtfully describes how the movements of goods, ideas, and enslaved people shaped the 17th to 19th centuries. Kids like the All Hands and Bridge galleries, where they can send secret messages by Morse code and operate a miniature dockside crane. Along with displays of lighthouse technology and a whaling cannon, you'll see model ships, nautical paintings, and various salty odds and ends.

Cost and Hours: Free, daily 10:00-17:00, tel. 020/8858-4422, www.rmg.co.uk. The museum hosts frequent family-oriented events—singing, treasure hunts, and storytelling—particularly on weekends; ask at the desk. Inside, listen for announcements alerting visitors to free tours on various topics.

• *The final sight in town—the Royal Observatory Greenwich—is at the top of the hill just behind the National Maritime Museum. To reach it, exit the Maritime Museum and follow signs leading you to a tree-lined uphill path, then follow the crowds as they huff up the steep hill (allow 10-15 minutes).*

As you hike up, look along the observatory's roof for the red **Time Ball** *(also visible from the Thames), which drops daily at 13:00.*

▲▲Royal Observatory Greenwich

Located on the prime meridian (0° longitude), the observatory is famous as the point from which all time is measured. The observatory's early work, however, had nothing to do with coordinating the world's clocks to Greenwich Mean Time (GMT). The observatory was founded in 1675 by King Charles II for the purpose of improving navigation by more accurately charting the night sky. Today, the Greenwich time signal is linked with the BBC (which broadcasts the famous "pips" worldwide at the top of the hour). A visit here gives you a taste of the sciences of astronomy, timekeeping, and seafaring—and how they all meld together—along with great views over Greenwich and the distant London skyline. The Royal Observatory grounds are made up of the observatory (with

The Longitude Problem

Around 1700, as the ships of seafaring nations began to venture farther from their home bases, the alarming increase in the number of shipwrecks made it clear that navigational tools had to be improved. Determining latitude—the relative position between the equator and the North or South Pole—was straightforward; sailors needed only to measure the angle of the sun at noon. But figuring out longitude, or their east-west position, was not as easy without a fixed point (such as the equator) from which to measure.

In 1714, the British government offered the £20,000 Longitude Prize. Two successful solutions emerged, and both are tied to Greenwich.

The first approach was to observe the position of the moon, which moves in relation to the stars. Sailors would compare the night sky they saw with the sky over Greenwich by consulting a book of tables prepared by Greenwich astronomers. This told them how far they were from Greenwich—their longitude. Visitors to the Royal Observatory can still see the giant telescopes—under retractable roofs—that were used to carefully chart the heavens to create these meticulous tables.

The second approach was to create a clock that would remain completely accurate on voyages—no easy feat back then, when turbulence and changes in weather and humidity made timepieces notoriously unreliable at sea. John Harrison spent 45 years working on this problem, finally succeeding in 1760 with his fourth effort, the H4 (which won him the Longitude Prize). All four of his attempts are on display at the Royal Observatory.

So, how can a clock determine longitude? Every 15° of longitude equals an hour when comparing the difference in sunrise or sunset times between two places. For example, the time gap between Greenwich and New York City is five hours, which translates into a longitudinal difference of 75°. Equipped with an accurate timepiece set to Greenwich Mean Time, sailors could figure out their longitude by comparing sunset time at their current position with sunset time back in Greenwich.

Notice that both approaches use Greenwich as a baseline—either on an astral map or on a clock. That's why, to this day, the prime meridian and official world time are both centered in this unassuming London suburb.

the prime meridian and three worthy exhibits), the Weller Astronomy Galleries, and the Peter Harrison Planetarium.

If your only interest in the Royal Observatory is the famous prime meridian line, you can go through an unassuming iron gate just below the entrance for a free, more simplistic (and significantly less crowded) display of the prime meridian. Under the analog clock just outside the courtyard, see how your foot measures up to the foot where the public standards of length are cast in bronze.

Observatory: £9.50, includes free audioguide, combo-ticket with *Cutty Sark*-£18.50, combo-ticket with planetarium-£12.50, saves money for either pair of sights; daily 10:00-17:00, later in summer.

Weller Astronomy Galleries: Free, daily 10:00-17:00.

Peter Harrison Planetarium: £7.50, combo-ticket with observatory-£12.50; 30-minute shows generally run every hour

(usually Mon-Fri 13:00-16:00, Sat-Sun 11:00-16:00, fewer in winter). Confirm times in advance by phone or online, or by picking up a flier at the observatory. As these shows can sell out, consider calling ahead to order tickets. Most shows are family-oriented, with early shows intended for young children.

Information: Tel. 020/8858-4422, www.rmg.co.uk.

◌ Self-Guided Tour: At the top of the hill, you can buy tickets for the observatory or head to the Weller Astronomy Galleries. Since the observatory is more interesting, do that first (but note that the Weller Galleries won't let you in after 16:30).

• *After purchasing your ticket, enter the courtyard.*

Running through the middle of this space is The Line—the **prime meridian.** Visitors wait patiently to have their photographs taken as they straddle the line in front of the monument, with one foot in each hemisphere. While watching all this fuss over a little line, consider that—unlike the equator—the placement of the prime meridian is totally arbitrary. It could just as well have been at my house, in Timbuktu, or even a few feet over—as, for a time, it was (the trough along the building's roofline shows where one astronomer had placed it).

Three different attractions are scattered around this courtyard. First, hiding in a corner is a **camera obscura.** This thrillingly low-tech device projects a live image from Greenwich onto a flat disc in a darkened room simply by manipulating light, without electricity or machinery (although the image can be pretty dim on cloudy days). Imagine how astonishing it was in the days before television.

The smaller building is the **Flamsteed House,** named for John Flamsteed, the first king-appointed Astronomer Royal (in 1675).

GREENWICH

It contains the apartments that he lived in and the Wren-designed Octagon Room, where he carried out some of his work. Downstairs is a fascinating exhibit on the "Longitude Problem" and how it was solved (see sidebar). Also on display are all four of John Harrison's sea clocks. Compared to his other contraptions, the fourth and final attempt looks like an oversized pocket watch. But, in terms of its impact, this little timepiece is right up there with the printing press, the cotton gin, the telegraph, and the money belt on the scale of human achievement.

The **Meridian Observatory Building,** in the larger house, has a wide assortment of historical telescopes, including a room-sized one designed by George Airy that was used to define the prime meridian. Watch the video (in the back corner of this room) of the telescope in action. If the meridian was too crowded outside, you can straddle it when you walk around this telescope. Upstairs from the gift shop, a skippable exhibit explores the role of timekeeping in our society.

• *Now head out back.*

Walk past the giant rusted-copper cone top of the planetarium. The building beyond houses the **Weller Astronomy Galleries,** where interactive, kid-pleasing displays allow you to guide a space mission and touch a 4.5-billion-year-old meteorite. You can also buy tickets for and enter the state-of-the-art, 120-seat **Peter Harrison Planetarium** from here.

Before you leave the observatory grounds, enjoy the **view** from the overlook—the symmetrical royal buildings, the Thames, and the Docklands and its busy cranes (including the prominent Canary Wharf Tower, with its pyramid cap). You may be able to see—poking up between buildings—the white stadium and red

Orbit tower in Queen Elizabeth Olympic Park. To the right is the huge O2 dome and the towers of the Emirates Air Line cable car. To the left lies the square-mile City of London, with skyscrapers and the dome of St. Paul's Cathedral. The Shard is to the far left. At night (17:00-24:00), look for the green laser beam the observatory projects into the sky (best viewed in winter), which extends along the prime meridian for 15 miles.

• *Our tour through Greenwich is finished. Enjoy the views from this hill-top perch, then head back down The Avenue into town. The road becomes* King William Walk *and ends at the* Cutty Sark *and Greenwich Pier, where you can catch a boat or DLR train back to downtown London. If you have time, on your way back, remember that it's easy to hop off the DLR for a quick visit to the Docklands; for details, just turn the page.*

THE DOCKLANDS WALK

Survey London's skyline (or a Tube map), and it becomes clear that London is shifting east. The thundering heart of this new London is the Docklands. Nestled around a hairpin bend in the Thames, this area was London's harbor and warehouse district back in the 19th century, when Britannia ruled the waves. Today it's been gentrified into a futuristic, skyscraper-filled landscape rising from the canals and docks.

The heart of the Docklands is the Isle of Dogs, a marshy peninsula in the river's curve. From the Isle rises the 800-foot-tall Canary Wharf Tower (officially the "One Canada Square" building), which is surrounded by a cluster of other office buildings.

Don't expect Jolly Olde England here. The Docklands is more about businessmen in suits, creatively planned parks, art-filled plazas, and trendy cafés. But there are also traces of its rugged dockworker past. You'll see canals, former docks, brick warehouses, and a fine history museum. Most impressive of all, there's not a tourist in sight.

If your London visit is brief and focused on the big, famous sights, the Docklands is not worth a special trip. But if you're visiting nearby Greenwich, it's very easy to add on a quick peek at the Docklands (which you'll pass by—or under—as you travel to Greenwich anyway). You can also combine the Docklands with a quick look at London's newest park, Queen Elizabeth Olympic Park, to the north.

If you want to say you've seen today's London, visit the Docklands.

Orientation

Length of This Walk: 1.5 hours, including museum tour.

When to Go: As it's now a financial district, the Docklands bustles only on weekdays. (On weekends, it can either be laid-back and festive if it's sunny, or empty and dead if rainy.)

Ideally time your visit here for late afternoon on a weekday, when the area is enlivened by business workers headed for happy hour. But don't wait too long—the fine museum at the end of this walk closes at 18:00. To catch the *après*-work bustle and still make it to the museum, I'd aim to begin this walk by 16:00.

Getting There: This walk starts at the South Quay canal footbridge bridge near the South Quay Docklands Light Railway (DLR) stop. If you're coming from central London, take the Tube to a DLR stop (the Bank/Monument stops are the most central), then take the Lewisham line to South Quay. If you're coming from Greenwich, take any northbound DLR line to South Quay.

Combining the Docklands with Greenwich or Queen Elizabeth Olympic Park: All three places lie a few minutes apart along the north-south DLR train line. You could sightsee Greenwich in the morning and early afternoon, then make a brief stop at the Docklands on your way back to central London. Or, to reach Greenwich from the Docklands, hop a DLR train bound for Greenwich or Lewisham, then get off at the Cutty Sark station (for Greenwich coverage, see the previous chapter).

To reach Queen Elizabeth Olympic Park (described on page 106), catch a DLR train heading north toward Stratford and get off at the Pudding Mill Lane DLR stop (about 10 minutes).

Shopping and Eating: Three different subterranean shopping malls all flow into each other via underground corridors. There's Cabot Place shopping mall (enter at Cabot Square), the mall beneath Canary Wharf Tower, and Jubilee Place (enter from Jubilee Place Park).

Waterside restaurants abound—at the West India Dock, along Mackenzie Walk, and elsewhere. Or enjoy a picnic in Jubilee Place Park (delis and sandwich shops abound).

OVERVIEW

Centuries ago, this end of town was notorious for its smelly industries (bone boiling, glue making, chemical works). It was conveniently downwind from the rest of London. By the late 1700s, 13,000 ships a year were loaded and unloaded in central London,

DOCKLANDS

Docklands Area

DOCKLANDS

congesting the Thames. So in 1802, the world's largest-of-its-kind harbor was built in the Docklands, organizing shipping for the capital of the empire upon which the sun never set. When Britannia ruled the waves, the Isle of Dogs hosted the world's leading harbor, with direct connections to the North Sea.

After being destroyed by Nazi bombers during World War II, the Docklands struggled for several decades and never regained its status as a port. With the advent of container shipping in the 1960s, London's shipping industry moved farther east, to deep-

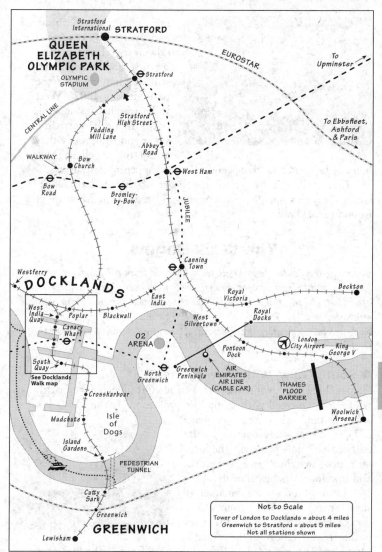

STRATFORD

Stratford International

QUEEN ELIZABETH OLYMPIC PARK

OLYMPIC STADIUM

Stratford

EUROSTAR

To Upminster

CENTRAL LINE

Pudding Mill Lane

Stratford High Street

Abbey Road

To Ebbsfleet, Ashford & Paris

WALKWAY

Bow Church

West Ham

Bow Road

Bromley-by-Bow

JUBILEE

Westferry

DOCKLANDS

Canning Town

East India

Royal Victoria

Beckton

West India Quay

Poplar

Blackwall

West Silvertown

Royal Docks

Canary Wharf

O2 ARENA

Pontoon Dock

London City Airport

King George V

South Quay

North Greenwich

Greenwich Peninsula

AIR EMIRATES AIR LINE (CABLE CAR)

THAMES FLOOD BARRIER

See Docklands Walk map

Crossharbour

Woolwich Arsenal

Mudchute

Isle of Dogs

Island Gardens

PEDESTRIAN TUNNEL

Cutty Sark

Greenwich

GREENWICH

Lewisham

Not to Scale
Tower of London to Docklands = about 4 miles
Greenwich to Stratford = about 5 miles
Not all stations shown

DOCKLANDS

water docks. The old Docklands became a derelict and dangerous wasteland. Until a generation ago, local surveys ranked it as one of the least desirable places to call home. It was said that for every Tube stop you lived east of central London, your life expectancy dropped one year.

But all of this misfortune paid off in the 1980s, when investors realized that the Docklands was ripe for redevelopment...the perfect place to host a new and vibrant economic center. Over the past few decades, Britain's new Information Age industries—banking, finance, publishing, and media—have vacated downtown London and set up shop here. You'll still see remnants of the past—those 1802 West India warehouses survive, but rather than trading sugar and rum, today they house the excellent Museum of London Docklands and a row of happening restaurants.

Our walk takes us from the heart of the modern Docklands, through some pleasant squares, and ends at the Museum of London Docklands.

The Walk Begins

• *Start at the South Quay DLR stop. Descend from the platform, cross busy Marshall Street and cut through the South Quay plaza, turning left after Pret a Manger and Tesco. Follow the walkway through a courtyard and when you reach water (the South Dock canal), turn left. Continue on to the curvy, modernistic footbridge, pausing before you cross to take in the full skyline.*

❶ South Quay, with View of the O2

Across the water, in the distance, you see Greenwich. The prickly white dome pierced with crane-like projections is the O2 (a.k.a. "the Dome," described on page 357), a costly and long-unpopular edifice that's now primarily the locus of sports matches, arena concerts, and Londoners' habitual disdain.

In front of you, a bouquet of skyscrapers blossoms from London's former wasteland. Of the many buildings, the tallest, in the center, is One Canada Square (a.k.a. Canary Wharf Tower). The 800-foot, 50-story building is known throughout London for its distinctive pyramid cap. Once the tallest building in the UK, and, for a time, in Europe, it was surpassed by The Shard in 2012.

• *Cross the bridge, walk through the office building, and continue straight into...*

❷ Canada Square

Stand in the square and take it all in. You're surrounded by soaring

Docklands Walk

To Central London

100 Meters
100 Yards

To Stratford (Olympic Park) & London City Airport

Poplar

MUSEUM OF LONDON DOCKLANDS

MARRIOTT

West India Quay

BILLINGSGATE FISH MARKET

7

6 WEST INDIA DOCK

CANARY WHARF TOWER

Westferry Cross

Cabot Square

WEST INDIA AVE.

5

Canary Wharf DLR

THAMES CLIPPERS BOAT DOCK

STAIRS

To London

MIDDLE DOCK

4

2

Canary Wharf Tube (Jubilee Line)

To Greenwich

WESTFERRY RD.

Heron Quays

3

Jubilee Place Park

Thames River

WALK BEGINS

1 SOUTH DOCK

South Quay

To Greenwich

1 South Quay, with View of the O2
2 Canada Square
3 Jubilee Place Park
4 Mackenzie Walk
5 Cabot Square
6 West India Quay
7 Museum of London Docklands

Docklands Light Railway (DLR)

DOCKLANDS

skyscrapers, three glitzy shopping malls, lively cafés, and hurried businesspeople.

Standing in this busy square, it can seem like continual rush hour—with the young high-tech workforce coursing through the battery of turnstiles. Flash back 200 years, to this area's heyday as a shipping harbor. "Canary Wharf"—the name for the whole neighborhood—is a reminder of the trading connection London had with distant ports such as the Canary Islands, off the western coast of Africa. Where sailors once drank grog while stevedores unloaded cargo, today thousands of office workers (the stevedores of the Information Age) populate a forest of skyscrapers, towering high above the remnants of the Industrial Age.

Canary Wharf Tower is filled with big banks and financial

and media companies. The plaza under it has a playful display of clocks on lampposts. If you like modern art, enter the lobby from street level and poke around to see what's on display.

• *Behind the Canary Wharf Tube station is a grassy park. You can reach it by a path to the right of the Tube entrance.*

❸ Jubilee Place Park

Opened in 2002 on the 50th anniversary ("Golden Jubilee") of Queen Elizabeth's rule, this delightful little park is an example

of how the new Canary Wharf was designed with a futuristic people-friendliness. Workers and residents enjoy plenty of green spaces, waterways, public art, and good public-transit service. The entire ensemble sits upon an underground shopping mall. (The entrance to the mall is in the middle of the park.) Stroll through the park past meandering fountains and outdoor art.

• *Return to Canada Square. Head north (directly toward Canary Wharf Tower), turning left along the canalside promenade called...*

❹ Mackenzie Walk

Stroll along the canal, called Middle Dock, past All Bar One and other inviting eateries, and under the train bridge. The canal is

a surviving remnant of the many artificial harbors and canals from the Docklands' 19th-century shipping heyday. The land here on the Isle of Dogs was marshy, flooded by the Thames, and unsuitable for farming or habitation. But it was perfect for accommodating large

seagoing vessels. Beginning around 1800, industrious Londoners channeled the water into canals and lined them with docks. Picture the lively scene: burly men off-loading goods from ships at anchor, while an army of poor laborers bustled between storage warehouses, dry docks for ship repair, and various ship-building enterprises. Each dock specialized in a particular product—spices, coal, whatever. By the mid-1800s, the Docklands had siphoned away shipping from London's traditional port (near London Bridge) and was the world's busiest port.

• *Cross under the DLR bridge and keep going. When you reach the*

DOCKLANDS

arched footbridge, turn right, passing a sculpture of two figures sitting on a bench, and hike up Cubitt Steps, into...

❺ Cabot Square

Enjoy the square's big fountain and views of domineering skyscrapers. From the west (left) end of the square, you have the iconic photo-op of Canary Wharf Tower with the fountain in the foreground. Many newlyweds come here for their wedding photos.

• *Exit the square at the north side (near another sculpture couple), where steps lead down to a footbridge that crosses another canal to the...*

❻ West India Quay

This row of 19th-century brown-brick warehouses typifies today's Docklands. Standing side by side are elements of the old Docklands

(the warehouses, canal, a few barges) and the new (the esplanade of umbrella-shaded restaurants, the futuristic Marriott skyscraper). Back in the 19th century, the water originally lapped up right against those buildings. You can still see the rustic gates to the lofts. Imagine heavily laden cargo boats off-loading there.

The Docklands thrived as a shipping port until the mid-20th century; two big gray cranes-on-tracks are reminders of the two events that eventually doomed the area. First, the Blitz of World War II obliterated the Docklands—it was hit by more than 2,000 bombs. Hitler's aim was to wipe out this vital industrial area.

Though it survived the Blitz, the Docklands couldn't survive the next hit—when the shipping industry converted to containers. The large container ships couldn't make it this far up the shallow Thames, and almost overnight, the industry rapidly shifted to seaports. In the 1970s, the Docklands became London's poorest area.

• *In the left part of the row of warehouses you'll find the...*

❼ Museum of London Docklands

This modern and interesting museum, which fills an old sugar warehouse, gives the Docklands historic context. In telling the story of the world's leading 19th-century port, it also conveys the story of London. It has a nice café, a hip bar, and a great kids' play area. Ride the elevator up to the third floor, then work your

DOCKLANDS

way down, going on a 2,000-year walk through the story of commerce on the Thames.

Cost and Hours: Free, daily 10:00-18:00, last entry one hour before closing, www.museumoflondon.org.uk/docklands.

Visiting the Museum: Start on the **third floor,** in old London, back when London's port was at London Bridge, and the Docklands was a barely inhabited swamp far to the east. You'll see fascinating models of Old London Bridge, crammed with little houses and shops.

Exhibits show how the Docklands rapidly developed in the 1800s. A reconstruction of a "Legal Quay," where cargo was processed, has a life-size mannequin in a hamster-wheel contraption used for lifting cargo from ships. Displays show the brutality of punishment in those days: Executed pirates were displayed publicly, suspended in metal cages called "gibbets." The next, thought-provoking section traces the ramifications of transatlantic trade, sugar, and slavery.

The **second floor** explores London's growth after 1800—its population was more than one million by 1810. Stroll through a gritty reconstruction of "Sailortown," listening to the salty voices of those who lived and worked in quarters like this. A painted *Stevedores* banner from the 1889 Dock Strike is a reminder that while the Industrial Revolution first exploited workers, it later provoked them to rise up. During World War II, the Docklands was a prime target for Nazi bombers bent on crippling British shipping. Find the claustrophobic, dome-shaped "consul shelter," where dockworkers could take cover in case of attack. There's also a re-creation of the top-secret fuel pipeline that was laid under the English Channel after D-Day to supply the Allies on the Continent. The final section, "New Port, New City," traces the Docklands' post-WWII rebuilding.

When you're finished, step out into today's Docklands and take in this combination of old and new.

• *Our walk is over. You have several options from here:*

Return to Central London: The Tube is your fastest way back into the city—retrace your steps to the Canary Wharf Tube station and catch the Jubilee line. Depending on where you're going in London, it may be more convenient to head to the other end of the West India Quay to catch the DLR there (stop: West India Quay), and get off at Bank, where you can transfer to the Tube's Central line.

To catch a boat (slower but very scenic), return to Cabot

Square, turn right, and walk five minutes along West India Avenue to the round Westferry Circus park; the Thames Clippers dock is just beyond (£7.15 one-way, £17.35 all-day pass, discounts with Travelcard or Oyster Card; boats leave every 20-30 minutes, 10- to 30-minute trip to major London docks).

Visiting Greenwich or Queen Elizabeth Olympic Park: *Catch a DLR train south to Greenwich or north to the Olympic Park.*

Riding the Emirates Air Line Cable Car: *The much-hyped aerial gondola makes a pointless trip across the Thames between the O2 dome and what has to be London's least-interesting district. There's not much to see from here, but the ride itself is a thrill, reasonably priced, and easily tacked on to a day of Docklands sightseeing.*

To reach the gondola, take the Jubilee Line from Canary Wharf one stop to North Greenwich Pier. Above ground, follow signs to Air Emirates (about 5 minutes away). The ride costs £3.40 with an Oyster card (otherwise £4.50); you can head right to the turnstiles if you have enough credit on your Oyster card. The gondola ride itself is a 10-minute dangle 300 feet above the Thames that lands you at the Royal Docks station.

From there it's a two-minute walk to the Royal Victoria DLR station; ride one stop (on either line) to Canning Town. From Canning Town, you can hop a Bank-bound train back to central London.

SLEEPING IN LONDON

Victoria Station Neighborhood 375
South Kensington Neighborhood 380
North of Kensington Gardens 382
Elsewhere in Central London 388
Other Sleeping Options 390

Choosing the right neighborhood in London is as important as choosing the right hotel. I've focused on several favorite neighborhoods (Victoria Station, South Kensington, Bayswater, Notting Hill, and Paddington Station, among others) and recommend the best accommodations values for each, from £20 bunks to deluxe £300 doubles with all the comforts. I've also listed big, good-value, modern chain hotels scattered throughout London, along with hostels, dorms, and apartment rental information. For accommodations in Windsor and Cambridge, see the Day Trips from London chapter.

London is an expensive city for lodging. Cheaper rooms are relatively dumpy. Don't expect £160 cheeriness in an £80 room. For £80, you'll get a double with breakfast in a safe, cramped, and dreary place with minimal service and the bathroom down the hall. For £100, you'll get a basic, reasonably cheery double with worn carpet and a private bath in a usually cramped, somewhat outdated, cracked-plaster building, or a soulless but comfortable room without breakfast in a huge Motel 6-type place. My London splurges, at £160-300, are spacious, thoughtfully appointed places good for entertaining or romancing.

Given London's high hotel prices, it's worth searching online for a deal. Various websites list rooms in London in high-rise, three- and four-star business hotels. You'll give up the charm and warmth of a family-run establishment, and breakfast probably won't be in-

Sleep Code

Abbreviations (£1=about $1.60, country code: 44)
S=Single, **D**=Double/Twin, **T**=Triple, **Q**=Quad, **b**=bathroom
Price Rankings
$$$ **Higher Priced**—Most rooms £125 or more
 $$ **Moderately Priced**—Most rooms £75-125
  $ **Lower Priced**—Most rooms £75 or less

Unless otherwise noted, breakfast is included, credit cards are accepted, and free Wi-Fi and/or a guest computer is generally available. For most places, the rates I list include the 20 percent VAT tax—but it's smart to ask when you book your room. Prices change; verify current rates online or by email. For the best prices, always book directly with the hotel.

cluded, but you might find that the price is right. Start by browsing the websites of several chains to get a sense of typical rates and online deals (I've described some budget chains on page 390). Pricier London hotel chains include Millennium/Copthorne, Thistle, InterContinental/Holiday Inn, Radisson, Hilton, and Red Carnation. Auction-type sites (such as Priceline and Hotwire) match flexible travelers with empty hotel rooms, often at prices well below the hotel's normal rates. You can also browse these accommodation discount sites: www.londontown.com (an informative site with a discount booking service), athomeinlondon.co.uk and www.londonbb.com (both list central B&Bs), www.lastminute.com, www.visitlondon.com, and www.eurocheapo.com.

Book your accommodations well in advance if you'll be traveling during peak season or if your trip coincides with a major holiday or festival (see page 576). For information and tips on pricing, getting deals, making reservations, and much more, see page 550.

VICTORIA STATION NEIGHBORHOOD

The streets behind Victoria Station teem with little, moderately-priced-for-London B&Bs. It's a safe, surprisingly tidy, and decent area without a hint of the trashy, touristy glitz of the streets in front of the station. I've divided these accommodations into two broad categories: Belgravia, west of the station, feels particularly posh, while Pimlico, to the east, is still upscale and dotted with colorful eateries. While I wouldn't go out of my way just to dine here, each area has plenty of good restaurants (see the Eating in London chapter). All of my recommended hotels are with-

SLEEPING

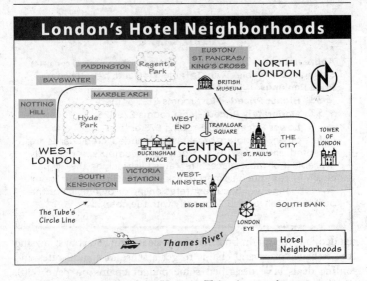

London's Hotel Neighborhoods

in a five-minute walk of the Victoria Tube, bus, and train stations. On hot summer nights, request a quiet back room; most of these B&Bs lack air-conditioning and may front busy streets.

Laundry: The nearest laundry option is **Pimlico Launderette,** on the east—Pimlico—side about five blocks southwest of Warwick Square. Low prices and friendly George brighten your chore (£7.40 for small-load, same-day full service, £5-6 self-service, daily 8:00-19:00, last wash at 17:30; 3 Westmoreland Terrace—go down Clarendon Street, turn right on Sutherland, and look for the launderette on the left at the end of the street; tel. 020/7821-8692).

Parking: The 400-space Semley Place **NCP parking garage** is near the hotels on the west/Belgravia side (£42/day, possible discounts with hotel voucher, just west of Victoria Coach Station at Buckingham Palace Road and Semley Place, tel. 0845-050-7080, www.ncp.co.uk). **Victoria Station car park** is about half the price and a quarter of the size, making it hard to find a spot here; check here first, but don't hold your breath (£24/day on weekdays, £12/day on weekends, entrance on Eccleston Bridge between Buckingham Palace Road and Bridge Place, tel. 0345-222-4224, www.apcoa.co.uk).

West of Victoria Station (Belgravia)

In Belgravia, the prices are a bit higher and your neighbors include some of the world's wealthiest people. These two places sit on tranquil Ebury Street, two blocks over from Victoria Station (or a slightly shorter walk from the Sloane Square Tube stop). You can cut the walk from Victoria Station to nearly nothing by taking a short ride on frequent bus #C1 (leaves from Buckingham Palace

Road side of Victoria Station and drops you off on corner of Ebury and Elizabeth streets).

$$$ Lime Tree Hotel, enthusiastically run by Charlotte and Matt, is a gem, with 25 spacious, stylish, comfortable, thoughtfully decorated rooms, a helpful staff, and a fun-loving breakfast room (Sb-£115, Db-£175, larger superior Db-£205, Tb-£220, usually cheaper Jan-Feb, small lounge opens onto quiet garden, 135 Ebury Street, tel. 020/7730-8191, www.limetreehotel.co.uk, info@limetreehotel.co.uk, Laura manages the office).

$$$ B&B Belgravia, with its bright, airy rooms and traveler-chic style, feels more boutique but less like you've found your home—and family—away from home. Most of its 28 rooms come with closets, high ceilings, and larger-than-average space. If you're a light sleeper, ask for a room in the back (Sb-£140, Db-£160, family rooms-£179, 64 Ebury Street, tel. 020/7259-8570, www.bb-belgravia.com, info@bb-belgravia.com).

East of Victoria Station (Pimlico)

This area feels a bit less genteel than Belgravia, but it's still plenty inviting, with eateries and grocery stores. Most of these hotels are on or near Warwick Way, the main drag through this area. Generally the best Tube stop for this neighborhood is Victoria (though the Pimlico stop works equally well for the Luna Simone). Bus #24 runs right through the middle of Pimlico, connecting the Tate Britain to the south with Victoria Station, the Houses of Parliament, Trafalgar Square, the British Museum, and much more to the north.

$$ Luna Simone Hotel rents 36 fresh, spacious, remodeled rooms with modern bathrooms. It's a smartly managed place, run for more than 40 years by twins Peter and Bernard—and Bernard's son Mark—and they still seem to enjoy their work (Sb-£85-90, Db-£115-140, Tb-£165-185, Qb-£180-210, prices vary with season, 10 percent discount when you book direct in 2016, at 47 Belgrave Road near the corner of Charlwood Street, handy bus #24 stops out front, tel. 020/7834-5897, www.lunasimonehotel.com, stay@lunasimonehotel.com).

$$ Bakers Hotel shoehorns 11 brightly painted rooms into a small building, but it's conveniently located and offers modest prices and a small breakfast (S-£50-60, Sb-£80-95, D-£85-95, Db-£85-105, T-£85-105, Tb-£105-120, family room with bath-£135, can be about £5-8 cheaper per person off-season, discounts for stays of at least a week, ask for Rick Steves discount when booking directly with hotel, 126 Warwick Way, tel. 020/7834-0729, www.bakershotel.co.uk, reservations@bakershotel.co.uk, Amin Jamani).

$$ New England Hotel, run by Jay and the Patel family, has very worn public spaces but well-priced rooms in a tight, old corner

Victoria Station Neighborhood

1 Lime Tree Hotel
2 B&B Belgravia
3 Luna Simone Hotel
4 Bakers Hotel
5 New England Hotel
6 Best Western Victoria Palace
7 Jubilee Hotel
8 Cherry Court Hotel
9 easyHotel Victoria
10 Ebury Wine Bar
11 La Bottega Deli
12 The Thomas Cubitt Pub
13 To The Duke of Wellington Pub
14 The Orange Pub
15 Daylesford Deli
16 Grumbles Restaurant
17 Pimlico Fresh
18 Seafresh Fish Restaurant
19 The Jugged Hare Pub
20 St. George's Tavern
21 Yo! Sushi
22 Wagamama
23 Wasabi (2)
24 Itsu
25 Grocery Stores (3)
26 To Launderette
27 Bus Tours – Day (2)
28 Bus Tours – Night
29 Tube, Taxis, City Buses
30 Green Line Coach Terminal
31 Buses to Luton & Stansted Airports

building. The family is working on a major facelift to the place (small Sb-£69-89, Db-£79-109, Tb-£119-149, Qb-£129-169, prices soft during slow times, breakfast is very basic, free Wi-Fi with this book, 20 Saint George's Drive, tel. 020/7834-8351, www.newenglandhotel.com, mystay@newenglandhotel.com).

$$ **Best Western Victoria Palace** offers modern business-class comfort compared with some of the other creaky old hotels listed here. Choose from the 43 rooms in the main building (Db-£120, Tb-£200, prices flex with demand—often around Db-£90/

Tb-£160 off-season, sometimes includes breakfast, elevator, at 60 Warwick Way), or pay about 20 percent less by booking a nearly identical room in one of the annexes, each a half-block away—an excellent value for this neighborhood if you skip breakfast (Db-£85-90, breakfast-£12.50, air-con, no elevator, 17 Belgrave Road and 1 Warwick Way, reception at main building). Book in advance for the best rates (tel. 020/7821-7113, www.bestwesternvictoriapalace. co.uk, info@bestwesternvictoriapalace.co.uk).

$$ Jubilee Hotel is a well-run but slightly shabby slumbermill with 24 simple rooms, high ceilings, and neat beds. The cheapest rooms, which share bathrooms, are just below street level (S-£45, Sb-£65, tiny twin D-£65, Db-£89, Tb-£95, Qb-£119, rates depend on season and length of stay, 5 percent discount for Rick Steves readers if you book direct and pay cash, 31 Eccleston Square, tel. 020/7834-0845, www.jubileehotel.co.uk, stay@jubileehotel.co.uk, Bob Patel).

   $ Cherry Court Hotel, run by the friendly and industrious Patel family, rents 12 very small but bright and well-designed rooms with firm mattresses in a central location. Considering London's sky-high prices, this is a fine budget choice (Sb-£65, Db-£75, Tb-£110, Quint/b family room-£135, these prices with this book in 2016, 5 percent credit-card fee, fruit-basket breakfast in room, air-con, laundry, 23 Hugh Street, tel. 020/7828-2840, www.cherrycourthotel.co.uk, info@cherrycourthotel.co.uk, daughter Neha answers emails and offers informed restaurant advice).

   $ easyHotel Victoria, at 36 Belgrave Road, is part of the budget chain described on page 391.

"SOUTH KENSINGTON," SHE SAID, LOOSENING HIS CUMMERBUND

To stay on a quiet street so classy it doesn't allow hotel signs, make "South Ken" your London home. The area has plenty of colorful restaurants, and shoppers like being a short walk from Harrods and the designer shops of King's Road and Chelsea. When I splurge, I splurge here. Sumner Place (where my first two listings are located) is just off Old Brompton Road, 200 yards from the handy South Kensington Tube station (on Circle Line, two stops from Victoria Station; and on Piccadilly Line, direct from Heathrow).

   $$$ Aster House, well-run by friendly and accommodating Simon and Leonie Tan, has a cheerful lobby, lounge, and breakfast room. Its 13 rooms are comfy and quiet, with TV, phone, and air-conditioning. Enjoy breakfast or just lounging in the whisper-elegant Orangery, a glassy greenhouse. Simon and Leonie offer free loaner mobile phones to their guests (Sb-£180, Db-£240, bigger Db-from £270, more for garden room or superior twin; significant discount offered to readers of this book in 2016—up to 20 percent if you book three or more nights, up to 25 percent for five or more nights; additional 5 percent off when you pay with cash, check website for specials, 3 Sumner Place, tel. 020/7581-5888, www.asterhouse.com, asterhouse@gmail.com).

   $$$ Number Sixteen, for well-heeled travelers, packs over-the-top class into its 41 artfully imagined rooms, plush designer-chic lounges, and tranquil garden. It's in a labyrinthine building, with boldly modern decor—perfect for an urban honeymoon (Sb-from £180, "superior" Db-from £276—but soft, ask for discounted

South Kensington Neighborhood

1. Aster House
2. Number Sixteen Hotel
3. The Pelham Hotel
4. Exhibition Road Eateries
5. Moti Mahal Indian Rest.
6. Bosphorus Kebabs & Beirut Express
7. Franco Manca, La Bottega & Byron Hamburgers
8. The Anglesea Arms Pub
9. Rocca
10. Wasabi
11. Itsu
12. Groceries (2)

"seasonal rates," especially on weekends and in Aug—subject to availability, larger "luxury" Db-£330, breakfast buffet in the conservatory-£19 continental or £24 full English, elevator, 16 Sumner Place, tel. 020/7589-5232, US tel. 1-888-559-5508, www.numbersixteenhotel.co.uk, sixteen@firmdale.com).

$$$ **The Pelham Hotel,** a 51-room business-class hotel with crisp service and a pricey mix of pretense and style, is genteel, with low lighting and a pleasant drawing room among the many perks (Db-£210-320, rate depends on room size and season, breakfast-£15 continental or £19.50 full English, slightly lower prices on weekends and in Aug, Web specials can include free breakfast; aircon, elevator, fitness room, 15 Cromwell Place, tel. 020/7589-8288, US tel. 1-888-757-5587, www.pelhamhotel.co.uk, reservations.thepelham@starhotels.co.uk, Jamie will take good care of you).

NORTH OF KENSINGTON GARDENS

From the core of the tourist's London, the vast Hyde Park spreads west, eventually becoming Kensington Gardens. Three good accommodations neighborhoods line up side by side along the northern edge of the park: Bayswater (with the highest concentration of good hotels) anchors the area; it's bordered by Notting Hill to the west and Paddington to the east. This area has quick bus and Tube access to downtown and, for London, is very "homely" (Brit-speak for cozy).

Bayswater

Most of my Bayswater accommodations flank a tranquil, tidy park called Kensington Gardens Square (not to be confused with the much bigger Kensington Gardens adjacent to Hyde Park), a block west of bustling Queensway, north of Bayswater Tube station. These hotels are quiet for central London, but the area feels a bit sterile, and the hotels here tend to be impersonal. Popular with young international travelers, the Bayswater street called Queensway is a multicultural festival of commerce and eateries (see page 413 in the Eating in London chapter).

$$$ **Vancouver Studios** offers one of the best values in this neighborhood. Its 45 modern, tastefully furnished rooms come with fully equipped kitchenettes (utensils, stove, microwave, and fridge) rather than breakfast. It's nestled between Kensington Gardens Square and Princes Square and has its own tranquil garden patio out back, which is refreshing if you land a somewhat-smoky room (Sb-£97, Db-£149, Tb-£189, extra bed-£20, 10 percent discount for seven or more nights, welcoming lounge, 30 Princes Square, tel. 020/7243-1270, www.vancouverstudios.co.uk, info@vancouverstudios.co.uk).

$$$ **Garden Court Hotel** is understated, with 40 simple,

homey-but-tasteful rooms (prices vary seasonally with demand—these are normal/low-demand rates: Sb-£74, Db-£129, Tb-£149, Qb-£179, all rooms can be £20 more when demand is especially high, continental breakfast included or English breakfast-£3.50, elevator, 30 Kensington Gardens Square, tel. 020/7229-2553, www.gardencourthotel.co.uk, info@gardencourthotel.co.uk).

$$$ **London House Hotel** has 103 spiffy, modern, cookie-cutter rooms on Kensington Gardens Square. Its rates are great considering the quality and fine location (rates fluctuate, but generally Db-£105 weekdays and £130 on weekends, expect to pay more during busiest times and less in winter, smaller rooms not facing the square are about £10-20 cheaper, basement family rooms-£140, check online for specific rates and last-minute deals, continental breakfast-£7, elevator, 81 Kensington Gardens Square, tel. 020/7243-1810, www.londonhousehotels.com, reservations@londonhousehotels.com).

$$$ **Phoenix Hotel** offers spacious public spaces and 125 modern-feeling rooms. Its prices—which range from fine-value to rip-off—are determined by a greedy computer program, with huge variations according to expected demand. Book online to save money (Sb-£80-110, Db-£110-140, Tb-£150-180, elevator, 1 Kensington Gardens Square, tel. 020/7229-2494, www.phoenixhotel.co.uk, info@phoenixhotel.co.uk).

$$ **Princes Square Guest Accommodation** is a crisp (if impersonal) place renting 50 businesslike rooms with pleasant, modern decor. It's well-located, practical, and a very good value, especially if you can score a good rate (prices fluctuate with demand, but generally Db-£100-160, £20 less for a single, £40 more for a triple; email to ask for best price, elevator, 23 Princes Square, tel. 020/7229-9876, www.princessquarehotel.co.uk, info@princessquarehotel.co.uk).

$$ **Kensington Gardens Hotel** laces 17 pleasant, slightly scuffed rooms together in a tall, skinny building (S with shower only and toilet down the hall-£68, Sb-£85, Db-£120, Tb-£145; continental breakfast served at Phoenix Hotel, 9 Kensington Gardens Square, tel. 020/7243-7600, www.kensingtongardenshotel.co.uk, info@kensingtongardenshotel.co.uk, Rowshanak).

$$ **Bayswater Inn Hotel**'s 140 tidy, perfectly adequate rooms come with dated style, an impersonal feel, and outrageously high official rack rates. But rooms commonly go for much lower prices, making this a decent—sometimes great—budget option (if you book direct with hotel in advance prices are roughly Sb-£60, Db-£90, Tb-£125, Qb-£150, stay for free on fifth consecutive night, elevator, 8 Princes Square, tel. 020/7727-8621, www.bayswaterinnhotel.com, reservations@bayswaterinnhotel.com).

North of Kensington Gardens

1. Vancouver Studios
2. Garden Court Hotel
3. London House Hotel
4. Phoenix & Kensington Gardens Hotels
5. Princes Square Guest Accommodation
6. Bayswater Inn Hotel
7. Portobello Hotel
8. To Norwegian YWCA
9. Tudor Court Hotel
10. St. David's Hotels
11. Falcon Hotel
12. easyHotel
13. Stylotel
14. Olympic House Hotel
15. Maggie Jones Restaurant
16. Geales Restaurant
17. The Churchill Arms Pub & Thai Kitchen
18. Hereford Road Restaurant
19. The Prince Edward Pub
20. Café Diana
21. Royal China Restaurant
22. Byron Hamburgers & Côte
23. Masala Zone
24. Itsu
25. Wagamama
26. Yo! Sushi
27. Groceries (4)
28. The Orangery (Afternoon Tea)

SLEEPING

Notting Hill and Nearby

The Notting Hill neighborhood, just west of Bayswater (spreading out from the northwest tip of Kensington Gardens) is famous for two things: It's the site of the colorful Portobello Road Market (see page 431) and the setting of the 1999 Hugh Grant/Julia Roberts film of the same name. While the neighborhood is now a bit more upscale and less funky than the one shown in that film, it's still a pleasant place to stay.

$$$ Portobello Hotel is on a quiet residential street in the heart of Notting Hill. Its 21 freshly refurbished rooms are funky yet elegant. Prices vary greatly with the season and size of the room (Sb-£140-175, "Good" Db-£175-240, "Better" Db-£195-245, "Great" Db-£225-315, elevator, 22 Stanley Gardens, tel. 020/7727-2777, www.portobellohotel.com, stay@portobellohotel.com, Hannah).

Near Holland Park: **$ Norwegian YWCA (Norsk K.F.U.K.)**—where English is definitely a second language—is open to any Norwegian woman and to non-Norwegian women under 30. (Men must be under 30 with a Norwegian passport.) Located on a quiet, stately street, it offers a study, TV room, piano lounge, and an open-face Norwegian ambience (goat cheese on Sundays!). They have mostly quads, so those willing to share with strangers are most likely to get a bed (S with shower only and toilet down the hall-£54, shared double-£46/bed, shared triple-£44/bed, shared quad-£42/bed, includes sheets and towels, includes breakfast year-round plus sack lunch and dinner Sept-June, £20 key deposit and £3 membership fee required, 52 Holland Park, Tube: Holland Park, tel. 020/7727-9346, www.kfukhjemmet.org.uk, kontor@kfukhjemmet.org.uk). With each visit, I wonder which is easier to get—a sex change or a Norwegian passport?

Paddington Station Neighborhood

Just to the east of Bayswater, the neighborhood around Paddington Station—while much less charming than the other areas I've recommended—is pleasant enough and very convenient to the Heathrow Express airport train. The area is flanked by the Paddington and Lancaster Gate Tube stops. Most of my recommendations circle Norfolk Square, just two blocks in front of Paddington Station, but are still quiet and comfortable. The main drag, London Street, is lined with handy eateries—pubs, Indian, Italian, Moroccan, Greek, Lebanese—plus convenience stores and more. (Better restaurants are a short stroll to the west, near Bayswater and Notting Hill—see page 411.)

To reach this area, exit the station toward Praed Street (with your back to the tracks, it's to the left). Once outside, continue straight across Praed Street and down London Street; Norfolk Square is a block ahead on the left.

On Norfolk Square

These places (and many more on the same street) all offer small rooms at a reasonable price in tall buildings with lots of stairs and no elevator. I've chosen the ones that offer the most reasonable prices and the warmest welcome.

$$ Tudor Court Hotel has 38 colorful rooms and is conscientiously run by Connan and the Gupta family. While the tiny rooms are tight (with prefab plastic bathrooms and creaky plumbing) and the rates are a bit high, this place distinguishes itself with its warm welcome. If you smell a big batch of curry rice cooking, the Guptas are getting ready to take it to the homeless shelter, where they volunteer each week (S-£54-63, Sb-£95-108, "compact" Db-£99-129, larger "standard" Db-£135-165, Tb-£155-185, family room-£180-225, higher rates are for Fri-Sat and other busy times, 10 Norfolk Square, tel. 020/7723-5157, www.tudorcourtpaddington.co.uk, reservations@tudorcourtpaddington.co.uk).

$$ St. David's Hotels, run by the Neokleous family, has 60 rooms in several adjacent buildings. The rooms are small—as is typical for less-expensive hotels in London with minimal amenities—but the staff is friendly, and their non-en-suite rooms are a workable budget option (S-£50-60, Sb-£70-85, Db-£90-120, Tb-£100-130, pay Wi-Fi in rooms, 14 Norfolk Square, tel. 020/7723-3856, www.stdavidshotels.com, info@stdavidshotels.com).

$$ Falcon Hotel, a lesser value, has less personality and 19 simple, old-school, slightly dingy rooms (S-£64, Sb-£74, D-£94, Db-£99, Tb-£145, Qb-£155, rates flex with demand, free Wi-Fi if you book direct, 11 Norfolk Square, tel. 020/7723-8603, www.falcon-hotel.com, info@falcon-hotel.com).

$ easyHotel, the budget chain described on page 391, has a branch at 10 Norfolk Place.

On Sussex Gardens

To reach these hotels, follow the directions to Norfolk Square (described earlier), but continue away from the station past the square to the big intersection with Sussex Gardens; you'll find them immediately to the left.

$$ Stylotel feels like the stylish, super-modern, aluminum-clad big sister of the easyHotel chain. Their tidy 39 rooms come with hard surfaces—hardwood floors, prefab plastic bathrooms, and metallic walls. While rooms can be a little cramped, the beds have space for luggage underneath. You may feel like an astronaut in a retro science-fiction film, but if you don't need ye olde doilies, this place offers a good value (Sb-£65, Db-£95, Tb-£115, Qb-£135, prices go up with demand—book early and direct to get these

SLEEPING

North London Accommodations

1. The Sumner Hotel
2. The 22 York Street B&B
3. Premier Inn London King's Cross St. Pancras
4. Premier Inn London Euston
5. Travelodge London King's Cross
6. Travelodge London Euston
7. Ibis London Euston St. Pancras
8. London Central Youth Hostel
9. Oxford Street Youth Hostel
10. Generator Hostel
11. Salumeria Dino Italian Deli & Lantana OUT Takeaway
12. Wagamama
13. Côte Brasserie
14. Byron Hamburgers (2)
15. Itsu (2)
16. Wasabi (2)
17. Bi Bim Bap
18. Drummond Street Eateries

400 Meters

400 Yards

rates, elevator, pay Wi-Fi, 160 Sussex Gardens, tel. 020/7723-1026, www.stylotel.com, info@stylotel.com, well-run by Andreas). They also have eight fancier, pricier, air-conditioned suites across the street (£180-220 for 2-4 people, kitchenettes, no breakfast).

$$ Olympic House Hotel has clean public spaces and a no-nonsense welcome, but its 38 business-class rooms offer predictable comfort and fewer old-timey quirks than many hotels in this price range (Sb-£75, Db-£105, Tb-£135, rates vary with demand, air-con in most rooms costs extra, elevator, pay Wi-Fi, 138 Sussex Gardens, tel. 020/7723-5935, www.olympichousehotel.co.uk, olympichousehotel@btinternet.com).

ELSEWHERE IN CENTRAL LONDON

$$$ The Sumner Hotel rents 19 rooms in a 19th-century Georgian townhouse sporting a lounge decorated with fancy modern Italian furniture and large contemporary rooms. This swanky place packs in all the amenities and is conveniently located north of Hyde Park and near Oxford Street, a busy shopping destination—close to Selfridges and a Marks & Spencer (queen Db-£193, king Db-£213, "deluxe" Db-£229, mention this book to get these Rick Steves rates, can be cheaper off-season, extra bed-£60, air-con, elevator, 54 Upper Berkeley Street, a block and a half off Edgware Road, Tube: Marble Arch, tel. 020/7723-2244, www.thesumner.com, reservations@thesumner.com).

$$$ The 22 York Street B&B offers a casual alternative in the city center, renting 10 traditional, hardwood, comfortable rooms, each named for a notable London landmark (Sb-£120, Db-£150, Tb-£180, inviting lounge; near Marylebone/Baker Street: from Baker Street Tube station, walk 2 blocks down Baker Street and take a right to 22 York Street—no sign, just look for #22; tel. 020/7224-2990, www.22yorkstreet.co.uk, mc@22yorkstreet.co.uk, energetically run by Liz and Michael Callis).

$$$ The Fielding Hotel is a simple and affordable little place lodged in the center of all the action—just steps from Covent Garden—on a quiet lane. They rent 25 basic rooms, serve no breakfast, and have almost no public spaces. Grace Langley, the manager, sticks with straight pricing (Sb-£108, Db-£168, family rooms for 3 or 4-£216, 12 percent more on Fri-Sat, air-con, 4 Broad Court off Bow Street, Tube: Covent Garden—for location see map on page 396, tel. 020/7836-8305, www.thefieldinghotel.co.uk, reservations@thefieldinghotel.co.uk).

$$ **Seven Dials Hotel**'s 18 no-nonsense rooms are plain and fairly tight, but they're also clean, reasonably priced, and incredibly well-located. Since doubles here all cost the same, request one of their larger rooms when you book (Sb-£90, Db-£110 but £10 more for twin beds, Tb-£135, Qb-£150, 7 Monmouth Street, Tube: Leicester Square or Covent Garden—for location see map on page 396, tel. 020/7681-0791, www.sevendialshotel.co.uk, info@sevendialshotel.co.uk, run by friendly and hardworking Hanna).

OTHER SLEEPING OPTIONS
Big, Good-Value, Modern Hotels

These chain hotels—popular with budget tour groups—offer all the modern comforts in a no-frills, practical package. If you can score a double for £90-100 (or less—often possible with promotional rates) and don't mind a modern, impersonal, American-style hotel, one of these can be a decent value in pricey London. This option is especially worth considering for families, as kids often stay for free. While most of these hotels have 24-hour reception and elevators, breakfast and Wi-Fi generally cost extra, and the service lacks a personal touch (at some, you'll check in at an automated kiosk). When comparing your options, keep in mind that for about the same price, you can get a basic room at a budget hotel or B&B that has less predictable comfort but more funkiness and friendliness in a more enjoyable neighborhood.

On each chain's website, you can see information about individual branches and book a stay. The rate you'll pay changes from day to day and varies depending on how far ahead you book. Midweek prices are generally higher than weekend rates, and Sunday nights can be shockingly cheap. To compare prices, visit several sites to find the going rate for your travel dates. The best deals generally must be prepaid a few weeks ahead and may not be refundable—read the fine print carefully.

I've listed a few of the dominant chains, along with a quick rundown on their more convenient London locations. Many of these hotels sit on busy streets in dreary train-station neighborhoods, so use common sense after dark and wear a money belt.

Premier Inn's locations include a branch inside **London County Hall** (next door to the London Eye), at **Southwark/Borough Market** (near Shakespeare's Globe on the South Bank, 34 Park Street, Tube: London Bridge), **Southwark/Tate Modern** (on Great Suffolk Street), **London King's Cross St. Pancras** (across the street from the east end of King's Cross Station and near the Eurostar terminus at St. Pancras), **London Euston** (handy but noisy location at corner of Euston Road and Dukes Road), **Kensington/Earl's Court** (11 Knaresborough Place, Tube: Earl's Court or Gloucester Road), **Victoria** (82 Eccleston Square, Tube: Victoria), **Leicester Square** (1 Leicester Place), and **Putney Bridge** (farther out, 3 Putney Bridge Approach). Avoid the **Tower Bridge** location, which is an inconvenient 15-minute walk from the nearest Tube stop. Book online at www.premierinn.com or call 0871-527-9222; from North America, dial 011-44-1582-567-890.

Travelodge has quite a few locations in London, including at **King's Cross** (200 yards in front of King's Cross Station, Grays Inn Road, Tube: King's Cross St. Pancras), **Kings Cross Royal Scot, Euston, Marylebone, Covent Garden, Liverpool Street,** and **Farringdon** (www.travelodge.co.uk).

Ibis has only two locations that are convenient to London's center: **Euston St. Pancras** (on a quiet street a block west of Euston Station, 3 Cardington Street, Tube: Euston) and **The City** (5 Commercial Street, Tube: Aldgate East); book at www.ibishotel.com.

easyHotel, with several branches in good neighborhoods around London, has a unique business model inspired by its parent company, the easyJet budget airline. The generally tiny, super-efficient, no-frills rooms feel popped out of a plastic mold, down to the prefab ship's head-type "bathroom pod." Rates can be surprisingly low (with doubles as cheap as £30 if you book early enough)—but you'll be charged à la carte for expensive add-ons, such as TV use, Wi-Fi, luggage storage, fresh towels, and daily cleaning (breakfast, if available, comes from a vending machine). If you go with the base rate, it's like hosteling with privacy—a hard-to-beat value. But you get what you pay for (like thin walls, flimsy construction, noisy fellow guests, and so on). They're only a good deal if you book far enough ahead to get a good price and skip the many extras. Locations include **Victoria** (34 Belgrave Road—see map on page 378, Tube: Victoria), **South Kensington** (14 Lexham Gardens, Tube: Earl's Court or Gloucester Road), **Earl's Court** (44 West Cromwell Road, Tube: Earl's Court), and **Paddington** (10 Norfolk Place, Tube: Paddington); www.easyhotel.com.

Hostels

Hostels can slash accommodation costs while meeting your basic needs. Prices listed here include sheets and lockers (bring your own lock), but you'll likely have to rent towels and pay a bit extra for breakfast. All of these places are open 24 hours, give members a £3 discount, and have guest computers and Wi-Fi (usually free in the common areas).

$ London Central Youth Hostel is the flagship of London's hostels, with 300 beds and all the latest in security and comfortable efficiency. Families and travelers of any age will feel welcome in this wonderful facility. You'll pay the same price for any bed in a four- to eight-bed single-sex dorm—with or without private bathroom—so try to grab one with a bathroom (£18-34/bunk depending on demand, twin D-£50-70, families welcome to book an entire room, members' kitchen, book long in advance, between Oxford Circus and Great Portland Street Tube stations at 104 Bolsover Street—see map on page 388, tel. 0845-371-9154, www.yha.org.uk, londoncentral@yha.org.uk).

$ Oxford Street Youth Hostel is right in the shopping and clubbing zone in Soho, with 90 beds (£20-30/bunk, twin D-£50-70, members' kitchen, 14 Noel Street, Tube: Oxford Street, tel. 0845-371-9133, www.yha.org.uk, oxfordst@yha.org.uk).

$ St. Paul's Youth Hostel, near St. Paul's Cathedral, is modern, friendly, well-run, and a bit scruffy. Most of the 213 beds are in shared, single-sex, 3- to 11-bunk rooms (£16-30/bunk depending on demand, twin D-£45-70, cheap meals, 36 Carter Lane, Tube: St. Paul's, tel. 020/7236-4965 or 0845-371-9012, www.yha.org.uk, stpauls@yha.org.uk).

$ Generator Hostel is a brightly colored, hip hostel with a café, a DJ spinning the hits, and 870 beds in 220 rooms, including doubles. It's in a renovated building tucked behind a busy street halfway between Kings Cross and the British Museum (£18-34/bunk depending on demand, twin Db-£70-120, breakfast-£5, 37 Tavistock Place, Tube: Russell Square, tel. 020/7388-7666, www.generatorhostels.com, london@generatorhostels.com).

$ A cluster of three **St. Christopher's Inn** hostels, south of the Thames near London Bridge, have cheap dorm beds; one branch (the Oasis) is for women only. All have loud and friendly bars attached (£22-36, higher price is for weekends, less in off-season, D-£70-80 or thereabouts, includes small breakfast, must be over 18 years old, 161 Borough High Street, Tube: Borough or London Bridge, reservations tel. 020/8600-7500, www.st-christophers.co.uk, bookings@st-christophers.co.uk).

Dorms

$$ The **University of Westminster** opens its dorm rooms to travelers during summer break, from June through mid-September. Located in several high-rise buildings scattered around central London, the most convenient are Marylebone Hall and Wigram House—which have the higher rates. Some rooms have private bathrooms; others have shared bathrooms nearby. They all come with access to well-equipped kitchens and big lounges (S-£37-43, Sb-£61-73, D-£56-65, Db-£70-95, discounts for long stays, tel.

020/7911-5181, www.westminster.ac.uk/summeraccommodation, summeraccommodation@westminster.ac.uk).

$$ The **London School of Economics** has openings in its dorms from July through September (S-£45, Sb-£55-76, Db-£66-110, prices vary according to location and length of stay, may include breakfast, tel. 020/7955-7676, www.lsevacations.co.uk, vacations@lse.ac.uk).

$ **University College London** has rooms for travelers from late June until mid-September (S-£36-41, Sb-£53, 2-night minimum, linens and towels provided, cable Internet access in rooms, Wi-Fi available in some common areas, tel. 020/7387-4537, www.ucl.ac.uk/residences, accommodation@ucl.ac.uk@ucl.ac.uk).

Apartment Rentals

Consider this option if you're traveling as a family, in a group, or staying five days or longer. Websites such as Airbnb and VRBO let you correspond directly with European property owners or managers, or consider one of the sites listed below. Some specialize in London, while others also cover areas outside of London. For more information on renting apartments, see page 551 in the Practicalities chapter.

LondonConnection.com is a Utah-based company that owns and rents several properties around London. The owner, Thomas, prides himself on providing personal service.

OneFineStay.com focuses on finding stylish, contemporary flats (most of them part-time residences) in desirable London neighborhoods. While pricey, it can be a good choice if you're seeking a hip, nicely decorated home away from home.

Other options include **Cross-Pollinate.com, Coach House Rentals** (rentals.chslondon.com), **APlaceLikeHome.co.uk, HomeFromHome.co.uk, London-House.com,** and **GoWithIt.co.uk**.

Staying near the Airports

It's so easy to get to Heathrow and Gatwick from central London, I see no reason to sleep at either one. But if you do, here are some options.

Heathrow: A **Yotel** is inside the airport (Terminal 4), while **easyHotel** and **Hotel Ibis London Heathrow** are a short bus or taxi ride away.

Gatwick: The South Terminal has a **Yotel,** while **Gatwick Airport Central Premier Inn** rents cheap rooms 350 yards away, and **Gatwick Airport Travelodge** has budget rooms about two miles from the airport.

SLEEPING

EATING IN LONDON

Eating Tips 394
Central London 395
West London 408
Elsewhere in London 413
Taking Tea in London 414

Whether it's dining well with the upper crust, sharing hearty pub fare with the blokes, or joining young professionals at the sushi bar, eating out has become an essential part of the London experience. You could try a different cuisine for each meal and never eat "local" English food, even on a lengthy stay in London. The sheer variety of foods—from every corner of Britain's former empire and beyond—is astonishing.

But the thought of a £50 meal in Britain generally ruins my appetite, so my London dining is limited mostly to easygoing, fun, moderately priced alternatives. I've listed places by neighborhood—handy to your sightseeing or hotel. Considering how expensive London can be, if there's any good place to cut corners to stretch your budget, it's by eating cheaply (see page 553 for tips).

EATING TIPS

For advice on eating in London, including information on pubs, beer, ethnic eats, and good chain restaurants, plus details on tipping, eating on a budget, English breakfasts, and afternoon tea, see page 552. Most London restaurants generally open daily no later than noon and close sometime between 22:00 and midnight.

Finding Restaurants: If you want to dine (as opposed to eat), drop by a newsstand to get a weekly entertainment guide or an annual restaurant guide (both have extensive restaurant listings). Or you can visit www.london-eating.co.uk, www.squaremeal.co.uk, or www.timeout.com.

Pubs: Many of London's 7,000 pubs serve reasonably priced, traditional British classics (around £8-12). You can get beer almost any time of day (about 11:00-23:00, and later on Fridays and Saturdays). You can usually get pub grub around 12:00-14:00 and 18:00-20:00. For more on pubs and pub grub, see page 554. For tips on ordering beer, see page 559. I list several historic pubs in London on page 400.

Chain Restaurants: The big news for budget eating in London is the modern, super-efficient chain restaurant—which comes in countless varieties, from burgers (Byron) and sushi (Yo!) to Indian (Masala Zone) and Thai (Thai Square). For a description of some of my favorite chains, see page 555. I've listed some conveniently located branches in this chapter.

Picnicking: London has an array of carry-out options, from Pret, selling fresh salads and sandwiches, to Marks & Spencer department stores (with a good deli) and their offshoot M&S Simply Food. I've listed several well-located supermarkets in this chapter.

CENTRAL LONDON

I've arranged these options by neighborhood, but they're all within about a 20-minute walk of each other. Survey your options before settling on a place.

Near Soho and Chinatown

London has a trendy scene that many Beefeater seekers miss. Foodies who want to eat well skip the more staid and touristy zones near Piccadilly and Trafalgar Square, and head to Soho instead. Make it a point to dine in Soho at least once, to feel the pulse of London's eclectic urban melting pot of international flavors. These restaurants are scattered throughout a chic, creative, and borderline-seedy zone that teems with hipsters, theatergoers, and London's gay community. Even if you plan to have dinner elsewhere, it's a treat just to wander around Soho (see my ▢ West End Walk, which takes you through Soho).

Note: While gentrification has mostly stripped this area of its former "red light district" vibe, a few pockets of sex for sale survive. Beware of the extremely welcoming women standing outside the strip clubs (especially on Great Windmill Street). Enjoy the sales pitch—but know that only fools fall for the "£5 drink and show" lure.

EATING

Central London Eateries

1 The Fielding Hotel	**11** Jen Café
2 Seven Dials Hotel	**12** Wong Kei
3 Princi Italian Deli	**13** Andrew Edmunds Restaurant
4 Bi Bim Bap	**14** Mildred's Vegetarian Rest.; Bao; Fernandez & Wells
5 The Gay Hussar	**15** St. Martin-in-the-Fields
6 Bocca di Lupo	**16** The Chandos Pub
7 Gelupo Gelato	**17** Gordon's Wine Bar
8 Yalla Yalla	**18** The Harp Pub
9 Ducksoup	**19** The Wolseley
10 Y Ming Chinese Restaurant	

EATING

20 Criterion Restaurant

21 Rules Restaurant

22 Joe Allen

23 Dishoom

24 Sitar Indian Restaurant

25 Belgo Centraal

26 Union Jacks

27 Lamb & Flag Pub

28 Byron (7)

29 Thai Square (5)

30 Wagamama (4)

31 Masala Zone (2)

32 Yo! Sushi (3)

33 Côte (4)

34 Itsu (2)

35 Wasabi (2)

36 Loch Fyne Fish Restaurant

37 The Princess Louise Pub

On and near Wardour Street, in the Heart of Soho

Running through the middle of Soho, rumbling past what's left of the strip-club zone, Wardour Street is ground zero for creative restaurateurs hoping to break into the big leagues. Strolling up this street—particularly from Brewer Street northward—you can take your pick from a world of options: Thai, Indonesian, Vietnamese, Italian, French, and even...English. Not yet tarnished by the corporatization creeping in from areas to the south, this drag still seems to hit the right balance between trendy and accessible. While I've listed several choices below (including some that are a block or two off Wardour Street), simply strolling the length of the street and following your appetite to the place that looks best is a great plan.

Princi is a vast, bright, efficient, wildly popular Italian deli/bakery with Milanese flair. Along one wall is a long counter with display cases offering a tempting array of *pizza rustica, panini* sandwiches, focaccia, a few pasta dishes, and desserts (look in the window from the street to see their wood-fired oven in action). Order your food at the counter, then find a space at a long shared table; or get it to go for an affordable and fast meal (£7-13 meals, daily 8:00-24:00, 135 Wardour Street, tel. 020/7478-8888).

Bi Bim Bap is a popular and muggy little diner named for what it sells: *bibimbap* (literally "mixed rice"), a scalding stone bowl of rice and thinly sliced veggies, topped with a fried egg. Flavor it to taste with the two sauces, then mix it up. You can pay a few pounds extra to add other toppings—including chicken, *bulgogi* (marinated beef strips), and mushrooms. Though the food is traditional Korean, the stylish, colorful interior reminds you you're in Soho (£7-10 meals, Mon-Sat 12:00-15:00 & 18:00-23:00, closed Sun, 11 Greek Street, second location near British Museum at 8 Charlotte Street, tel. 020/7287-3434).

The Gay Hussar, dressy and tight, squeezes several elegant tables into what the owners say is the only Hungarian restaurant in England. It's traditional fare: cabbage, sauerkraut, sausage, paprika, and pork, as well as duck and chicken. Wash down this Hungarian comfort food with a Hungarian wine (£15-18 meals, Mon-Sat 12:15-14:30 & 17:30-22:45, closed Sun, 2 Greek Street, tel. 020/7437-0973).

Bocca di Lupo, a stylish and popular option, serves half and full portions of classic regional Italian food. Dressy but with a fun energy, it's a place where you're glad you made a reservation. The counter seating, on cushy stools with a view into the open kitchen, is particularly memorable, or you can take a table in the snug, casual back end (£12-20 dishes, daily 12:30-15:00 & 17:30-23:00, 12 Archer Street, tel. 020/7734-2223, www.boccadilupo.com).

Gelupo, Bocca di Lupo's sister *gelateria* across the street, has a wide array of ever-changing but always creative and delicious dessert favorites—including popular standbys like the incredibly rich chocolate sorbet and fresh-mint *stracciatella*. A £4 sampler cup or cone gets you two flavors (and little taster spoons are generously offered to help you choose). Everything is homemade, and the interior feels clean and bright. They also have espresso drinks (daily 11:00-23:00, 7 Archer Street, tel. 020/7287-5555).

Yalla Yalla is a hole-in-the-wall serving up high-quality Beirut street food—hummus, baba ghanoush, tabbouleh, and *shawarmas*. Stylish as you'd expect for Soho, it's tucked down a seedy alley across from a sex shop. Eat in the cramped and cozy interior or at one of the few outdoor tables, or get your food to go (£3-4 sandwiches, £4-6 *meze*, £8 *mezes* platter available until 17:00, £10-15 bigger dishes, daily 10:00-23:00, 1 Green's Court—just north of Brewer Street, tel. 020/7287-7663).

Ducksoup, a short block over from Wardour Street, is an upscale-feeling yet cool and relaxed little bar, with a small but thoughtful menu of well-executed international and modern British dishes (£7 small plates, £14 big plates—sharing several items can add up). The menu is handwritten, the music is on vinyl, and the rough woodwork and cramped-but-convivial atmosphere give it the feeling of a well-loved wine bar. While a bit overpriced, the atmosphere is memorable (Mon-Sat 12:00-22:30, Sun 13:00-17:00, 41 Dean Street, tel. 020/7287-4599, reservations smart, www.ducksoupsoho.co.uk).

And for Dessert: In addition to the outstanding gelato at **Gelupo** and the treats at **Princi** (both described earlier), several other places along Wardour Street boast window displays that tickle the sweet tooth. In just a couple of blocks, you'll see pastry shops, a *crêperie*, and a Hummingbird cupcake shop.

Chain Restaurants in Soho: Some of Britain's most popular chain restaurants started out here in Soho, but in this fast-evolving neighborhood, they're now a little like stale sushi. While I wouldn't waste a Soho meal on one of these places, they're a convenient fallback. You'll find **Byron Hamburgers** (particularly appealing industrial-mod branch at 97 Wardour Street, also near Golden Square at 16 Beak Street and at 1A St. Giles High Street), **Thai Square** (27 St. Anne's Court, also at 5 Princes Street on Hanover Square), **Wagamama** (42 Great Marlborough Street), **Masala Zone** (9 Marshall Street), **Yo! Sushi** (52 Poland Street), and **Côte** (124 Wardour Street and near Oxford Circus at 4 Great Portland Street). For descriptions, see page 555 of the Practicalities chapter.

EATING

Pub Appreciation

The pub is the heart of the people's England, where all manner of folks have, for generations, found their respite from work and a home away from home. England's classic pubs are national treasures, with great cultural value and rich history, not to mention good beer and grub (you'll find details on beer and pub food in the Practicalities chapter on pages 559 and 554).

Their odd names can go back hundreds of years. Because so many medieval pub-goers were illiterate, pubs were simply named for the picture hung outside (e.g., The Crooked Stick, The Queen's Arms—meaning her coat of arms).

The Golden Age for pub-building was in the late Victorian era (c. 1880-1905), when pubs were independently owned and land prices were high enough to make it worthwhile to invest in fixing them up. The politics were pro-pub as well: Conservatives, backed by Big Beer, were in, and temperance-minded Liberals were out.

Especially in class-conscious Victorian times, traditional pubs were divided into sections by elaborate screens (now mostly gone), allowing the wealthy to drink in a more refined setting, while commoners congregated on the pub's rougher side. These were really "public houses," featuring nooks (snugs) for groups and clubs to meet, friends and lovers to rendezvous, and families to get out of the house at night.

Historic pubs still dot the London cityscape. The only place to see the very oldest-style tavern in the "domestic tradition" is at **Ye Olde Cheshire Cheese,** which was rebuilt in 1667 (after the Great Fire) from a 16th-century tavern (see description on page 252; £6-12 pub grub, £11-16 meals in the restaurant, open daily, 145 Fleet Street, Tube: Blackfriars, tel. 020/7353-6170). Imagine this mazelike place, with three separate bars, in the pre-Victorian era: With no bar, drinkers gathered around the fireplaces, while tap boys shuttled tankards up from the cellar. (This was long before barroom taps were connected to casks in the cellar. Oh, and don't say "keg"—that's a gassy modern thing.)

Late-Victorian pubs are more common, such as the lovingly restored 1897 **Princess Louise** (daily midday until 23:00, lunch and dinner served Mon-Sat 12:00-21:00 in less atmospheric upstairs lounge, no food Sun, 208 High Holborn, see map on page 396, Tube: Holborn, tel. 020/7405-8816). These places are fancy, often with heavily embossed wallpaper ceilings, decorative tile work, fine-etched glass, ornate carved stillions (the big central hutch for storing bottles and glass), and even urinals equipped with a place to set your glass.

London's best Art Nouveau pub is **The Black Friar** (c. 1900-1915), with fine carved capitals, lamp holders, and quirky phrases worked into the decor (£9-15 meals, Mon-Sat 9:00-23:00, Sun

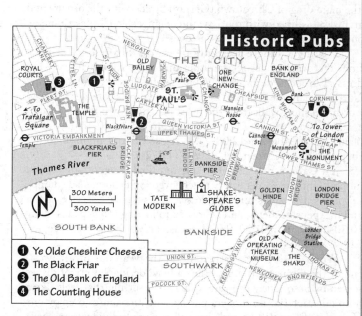

Historic Pubs

1 Ye Olde Cheshire Cheese
2 The Black Friar
3 The Old Bank of England
4 The Counting House

12:00-22:30, food daily until 22:00, outdoor seating, 174 Queen Victoria Street, Tube: Blackfriars, tel. 020/7236-5474).

The "former-bank pubs" represent a more modern trend in pub-building. As banks increasingly go electronic, they're moving out of lavish, high-rent old buildings. Many of these former banks are being re-fitted as pubs with elegant bars and freestanding stillions, which provide a fine centerpiece. Three such pubs are **The Old Bank of England** (£10-13 meals, Mon-Fri 11:00-23:00, food served 12:00-21:00, closed Sat-Sun, 194 Fleet Street, Tube: Temple, tel. 020/7430-2255), **The Jugged Hare** (open daily, 172 Vauxhall Bridge Road—see map on page 378, Tube: Victoria, tel. 020/7614-0134, also see listing on page 410), and **The Counting House** (Mon-Fri 11:00-23:00, closed Sat-Sun, 50 Cornhill, Tube: Bank, tel. 020/7283-7123, see listing on page 413).

Go pubbing in the evening for a lively time, or drop by during the quiet late morning (from 11:00), when the pub is empty and filled with memories.

EATING

Authentic Chinese Food in and near Chinatown

The main drag of Chinatown (Gerrard Street, with the ornamental archways) is lined with touristy, interchangeable Chinese joints—but these places seem to have an edge.

Y Ming Chinese Restaurant—across Shaftesbury Avenue from the ornate gates, clatter, and dim sum of Chinatown—has dressy European decor, serious but helpful service, and authentic Northern Chinese cooking. London's food critics consider this well worth the short walk from the heart of Chinatown for food that's a notch above (good £12 meal deal offered 12:00-18:00, £8-12 plates, open Mon-Sat 12:00-23:45, closed Sun, turquoise corner shop at 35 Greek Street, tel. 020/7734-2721).

Jen Café, across the little square called Newport Place, is a humble Chinese corner eatery much loved for its homemade dumplings. It's just stools and simple seating, with fast service, a fun and inexpensive menu, and a devoted following (£6-8 plates, daily 10:30-20:30, until 21:30 Thu-Sun, cash only, 4 Newport Place, tel. 020/7287-9708).

Wong Kei Chinese restaurant, at the Wardour Street (west) end of the Chinatown drag, offers a bewildering variety of dishes served by notoriously brusque waiters in a setting that feels like a hospital cafeteria. Londoners put up with the abuse to enjoy one of the satisfying BBQ rice dishes or hot pots. Individuals and couples are usually seated at communal tables, while larger parties are briskly shuffled up or down stairs (£7-12 main dishes, £10-15 chef special combos, daily 11:30-23:30, cash only, 41 Wardour Street, tel. 020/7437-8408).

Sedate and Upscale Options on Lexington Street, in the Heart of Soho

Andrew Edmunds Restaurant is a tiny, candlelit space where you'll want to hide your camera and guidebook and not act like a tourist. This little place—with a jealous and loyal clientele—is the closest I've found to Parisian quality in a cozy restaurant in London. The extensive wine list, modern European cooking, and creative seasonal menu are worth the splurge (£5-8 starters, £12-20 main dishes, Mon-Sat 12:00-15:30 & 17:30-22:45, Sun 13:00-16:00 & 18:00-22:30, these are last-order times, come early or call ahead, request ground floor rather than basement, 46 Lexington Street, tel. 020/7437-5708, www.andrewedmunds.com).

Mildred's Vegetarian Restaurant, across from Andrew Edmunds, has an enjoyable menu and a pleasant interior filled with happy eaters (£8-11 meals, £6-7 dishes from small takeaway menu, Mon-Sat 12:00-23:00, closed Sun, vegan options, 45 Lexington Street, tel. 020/7494-1634).

Bao is a tight, minimalist eatery selling top-quality Taiwanese cuisine, specializing in delicate and delectable steamed-bun sandwiches. The menu may resemble some in old Chinatown haunts, but the quality is peerless. Because they only have a few tables, try to arrive early or late (those on the wait list are directed to line up across the street; no reservations). While it's not cheap (dishes are £3-6, but portions are small, so your bill can add up), it's worth the splurge (Mon-Sat 12:00-15:00 & 17:30-22:00, closed Sun, 53 Lexington Street, www.baolondon.com).

Fernandez & Wells is a cozy, convivial, delightfully simple little wine, cheese, and ham bar. Drop in and grab a stool as you belly up to the big wooden bar. Share a plate of top-quality cheeses and/or Spanish, Italian, or French hams with fine bread and oil, all while sipping a nice glass of wine (daily 11:00-23:00, shorter hours Sat-Sun, quality sandwiches at lunch, 43 Lexington Street, tel. 020/7734-1546).

Traditional Choices near Trafalgar Square

These places, all of which provide a more "jolly olde" experience than high cuisine, are within about 100 yards of Trafalgar Square.

St. Martin-in-the-Fields Café in the Crypt is just right for a tasty meal on a monk's budget—maybe even on a monk's tomb. You'll dine sitting on somebody's gravestone in an ancient crypt. Their enticing buffet line is kept stocked all day, serving breakfast, lunch, and dinner (£7-10 cafeteria plates, hearty traditional desserts, free jugs of water). They also serve a restful cream tea (£6.50, daily 14:00-18:00). You'll find the café directly under the St. Martin-in-the-Fields Church, facing Trafalgar Square—enter through the glass pavilion next to the church (generally about 8:00-20:00 daily, profits go to the church, Tube: Charing Cross, tel. 020/7766-1158 or 020/7766-1100). On Wednesday evenings you can dine to the music of a live jazz band at 20:00 (£5.50-12 tickets). While here, check out the concert schedule for the busy church upstairs (or visit www.smitf.org).

The Chandos Pub's Opera Room floats amazingly apart from the tacky crush of tourism around Trafalgar Square. Look for it opposite the National Portrait Gallery (corner of William IV Street and St. Martin's Lane) and climb the stairs—to the left or right of the pub entrance—to the Opera Room. This is a fine Trafalgar rendezvous point and wonderfully local pub. They serve £6 sandwiches and a better-than-average range of traditional pub meals for under £10—meat pies and fish-and-chips are their specialty. The ground-floor pub is stuffed with regulars and offers snugs (private booths) and more serious beer drinking. To eat on that level, you have to order upstairs and carry it down. Chandos proudly serves the local Samuel Smith beer at £3 a pint (kitchen open daily 11:30-21:00,

Fri until 18:00, order and pay at the bar, 29 St. Martin's Lane, Tube: Leicester Square, tel. 020/7836-1401).

Gordon's Wine Bar is really a Back Door eatery—you have to enter through its leafy patio just past its locked street entrance. The candlelit 15th-century wine cellar is filled with dusty old bottles, faded British memorabilia, and nine-to-fivers. At the "English rustic" buffet, choose a hot meal or cold meat dish with a salad (figure around £7-10/dish); the £11 cheese plate comes with two cheeses, bread, and a pickle. Then step up to the wine bar and consider the many varieties of wine and port available by the glass (this place is passionate about port). The low carbon-crusted vaulting deeper in the back seems to intensify the Hogarth-painting atmosphere. Although it's crowded—downright packed on nice days—you can normally corral two chairs and grab the corner of a table. The crowd often spills out onto the tight, parkside patio, where on hot days a chef cooks at an outdoor cooktop for a long line of happy customers (arrive before 17:00 to get a seat, Mon-Sat 11:00-23:00, Sun 12:00-22:00, 2 blocks from Trafalgar Square, bottom of Villiers Street at #47, Tube: Embankment, tel. 020/7930-1408, manager Gerard Menan).

Ales: **The Harp,** clearly a local favorite, is a crowded and cluttered little pub just a block above Trafalgar Square. While they serve no food, this is a good, central spot to nurse a fine ale and befriend one of the Londoners crowded around the coaster-coated bar. This is a top choice for an après-work pint among nine-to-fivers, who stand in the dozens out front after the workday, sipping their beers (Mon-Sat 10:30-23:30, Sun 12:00-22:30, 47 Chandos Place, tel. 020/7836-0291).

Near Piccadilly

The first few listings are upscale and snooty—but if you want something cheaper in this area, you'll find plenty of other options.

Swanky Splurges

The Wolseley is the grand 1920s showroom of a long-defunct British car. The last Wolseley drove out with the Great Depression, but today this old-time bistro bustles with formal waiters serving traditional Austrian and French dishes in an elegant black-marble-and-chandeliers setting fit for its location next to the Ritz. Although the food can be unexceptional, prices are reasonable, and the presentation and setting are grand. Reservations are a must (£13-30 main courses; cheaper soup, salad, and sandwich "café menu" available; both menus available in all areas of restaurant, daily 7:00-24:00, 160 Piccadilly, tel. 020/7499-6996, www.thewolseley.com). They're popular for their fancy cream or afternoon tea (for details, see page 414).

The Criterion is a palatial dining hall offering grand-piano ambience beneath gilded tiles and chandeliers in a dreamy Byzantine church setting from 1880. It's right on Piccadilly Circus but a world away from the punk junk. It's a deal for the visual experience during lunch and if you order the £20-25 fixed-price meal (except on Sun, when you must order from the expensive à la carte menu). At any hour, the service couldn't care less. Anyone can drop in for coffee or a drink (daily 12:00-14:30 & 17:30-23:30, 224 Piccadilly, tel. 020/7930-0488, www.criterionrestaurant.com).

Rules Restaurant, established in 1798, is as traditional as can be—extremely British, classy yet comfortable. It's a big place where you'll eat in a plush Edwardian atmosphere with formal service and plenty of game on the menu. (A warning reads "Game birds may contain lead shot.") This is the place to splurge for classic English dishes (£15 starters, £30 main courses, daily 12:00-24:00, between the Strand and Covent Garden at 34 Maiden Lane, tel. 020/7836-5314, www.rules.co.uk).

Cheaper Options near Piccadilly

Hungry and broke in the theater district? Head for Panton Street (off Haymarket, two blocks southeast of Piccadilly Circus), where several hardworking little places compete, all seeming to offer a pretheater menu. Peruse the entire block (vegetarian, Pizza Express, Moroccan, Chinese, noodle houses, and diners) before making your choice.

Chain Restaurants near Piccadilly: **Wagamama** (in Leicester Square at 14 Irving Street), **Byron Hamburgers** (11 Haymarket, also at 24 Charing Cross near Leicester Square), **Thai Square** (near Trafalgar Square at 21 Cockspur Street), **Yo! Sushi** (57 Haymarket, also at Trocadero Center on Rupert Street), **Côte** (beyond Leicester Square at 50 St. Martin's Lane), **Itsu** (west of Regent Street at 27 Sackville Street), and **Wasabi** (also west of Regent at 42 Piccadilly).

Near Covent Garden

Covent Garden bustles with people and touristy eateries. The area feels overrun, but if you must eat around here, you have some good choices.

Joe Allen, tucked in a brick cellar a block away from the market, serves modern international and American cuisine with both style and hubbub. Downstairs off a quiet street with candles and white tablecloths, it's comfortably spacious and popular with the theater crowd. It feels a bit old-fashioned and cluttered, but in a welcoming way (£7 starters, £11-30 main courses, £15 two-course specials and £18 three-course specials available at lunch and 17:00-

18:45, open daily 12:00-24:00, piano music after 19:00, 13 Exeter Street, tel. 020/7836-0651).

Dishoom is London's hotspot for upscale Indian cuisine, with top-quality ingredients and carefully executed recipes. The dishes seem familiar, but the flavors are a revelation. People line up early (starting around 17:30) for a seat, either in the bright, rollicking, brasserie-like ground floor or in the less appealing basement. If the line is long, you'll have to queue outside while waiting for a chance to head down to the bar to kill your remaining wait time—not a bad thing, as they offer a wide range of creative cocktails (£4-6 small plates, £8-12 main courses, daily 8:00-23:00, 12 Upper St. Martin's Lane, tel. 020/7420-9320, www.dishoom.com). They also have locations near King's Cross Station and in trendy Shoreditch.

Sitar Indian Restaurant is a well-respected Indian/Bangladeshi place serving dishes from many regions, fine fish, and a tasty £15 vegetarian *thali* (combo platter). It's small and dressy, with snappy service (£10-18 main dishes, Mon-Fri 12:00-14:30 & 17:30-23:30, Sat 15:00-23:30, closed Sun, next to Somerset House at 149 Strand, tel. 020/7836-3730, www.sitarstrand.co.uk).

Belgo Centraal serves hearty Belgian specialties in a vast 400-seat underground lair. It's a mussels, chips, and beer emporium dressed up as a mod-monastic refectory—with noisy acoustics and vibrant diners. The classy restaurant section is more comfortable and less rowdy, but it usually requires reservations. It's often more fun just to grab a spot in the boisterous beer hall, with its tight, communal benches (no reservations accepted). Both sides have the same menu and specials. Belgians claim they eat as well as the French and as heartily as the Germans. This place, which offers a stunning array of dark, blonde, and fruity Belgian beers, actually makes Belgian things trendy—a formidable feat (£10-14 main dishes, open daily 12:00-23:00; 1 kid eats free for each parent ordering a regular entrée; 1 block north of Covent Garden Tube station at 50 Earlham Street, tel. 020/7813-2233).

Union Jacks, a venture of British celebrity chef Jamie Oliver, fuses traditional British ingredients to make inventive modern dishes. Jamie's wood-fired pizzas are topped not with cheese and tomatoes, but roast pig shoulder or oxtail and brisket. While this sounds risky, he pulls it off with great flavors, plus fun "fizzy drinks" (£6-8 small plates are very small, £12-14 pizzas, £15 classic British dishes, daily 12:00-23:00, right inside Covent Garden market hall, tel. 020/3640-7086).

Lamb and Flag Pub is a survivor—a spit-and-sawdust pub serving traditional grub two blocks off Covent Garden, yet seemingly a world away. Here since 1772, this pub was a favorite of Charles Dickens. Once known for fights, it's now peaceful and a hit with local workers (long hours daily, 33 Rose Street, across from Stanfords bookstore entrance on Floral Street—find Lazenby Court, then duck and enter, tel. 020/7497-9504).

Chain Restaurants near Covent Garden: **Masala Zone** (particularly fun branch at top end of market with giant, colorful marionettes suspended from the ceiling, 48 Floral Street), **Côte** (17 Tavistock Street), **Thai Square** (166 Shaftesbury Avenue, plus one next to Sitar Indian Restaurant at 148 The Strand), **Wagamama** (1 Tavistock Street), **Byron Hamburgers** (behind the London Transport Museum at 33 Wellington Street), **Wasabi** (two blocks down Southampton Street at 388 The Strand), **Itsu** (past Wasabi and across the street at 82 The Strand), and **Loch Fyne** (a couple of blocks behind the square at 2 Catherine Street). A **Marks & Spencer** with a good deli section is across from the Covent Garden Tube station.

Near the British Museum, in Fitzrovia

To avoid the touristy crush right around the museum (and just southwest, in Soho), Londoners head a few blocks west, to the Fitzrovia area. Here, tiny Charlotte Place is lined with small eateries (including the first two listed below); nearby, the much bigger Charlotte Street has several more good options. The higher street signs you'll notice on Charlotte Street are a holdover from a time when they needed to be visible to carriage drivers. This area is a short walk from the Goodge Street Tube station—convenient to the British Museum, and just two blocks from Pollock's Toy Museum. See the map on page 388 for locations.

Salumeria Dino serves up hearty sandwiches, pasta, and Italian coffee. Dino, a native of Naples, has run his little shop for more than 30 years and has managed to create a classic Italian deli that's so authentic you'll walk out singing "O Sole Mio" (£4-5 sandwiches, £1 takeaway cappuccinos, Mon-Fri 9:00-18:00, closed Sat-Sun, 15 Charlotte Place, tel. 020/7580-3938).

Lantana OUT, next door to Salumeria Dino, is an Australian coffee shop that sells modern soups, sandwiches, and salads at their takeaway window (£3-8 meals, pricier sit-down café—**Lantana IN**—serves £9-12 meals next door, Mon-Fri 7:30-15:00, café also open Sat-Sun 9:00-17:00, 13 Charlotte Place, tel. 020/7637-3347).

Chain Restaurants near the British Museum: **Wagamama** (4 Streatham Street; another location near Holborn Tube stop at 123 Kingsway—see map on page 388), **Côte** (5 Charlotte Street), **Byron Hamburgers** (6 Store Street, also at 6 Rathbone Place), **Itsu** (54 Tottenham Court Road, also at 74 New Oxford Street), and **Wasabi** (17 Tottenham Court Road, also at 58 Oxford Street). There's also another **Bi Bim Bap** here (8 Charlotte Street, see listing on page 398).

WEST LONDON
Near Victoria Station Accommodations

These restaurants are within a few blocks of Victoria Station—and all are places where I've enjoyed eating. As with the accommodations in this area, I've grouped them by location: east or west of the station (see the map on page 378).

Cheap Eats: For groceries, a handy **M&S Simply Food** is inside Victoria Station (daily 7:00-24:00, near the front, by the bus terminus), along with a **Sainsbury's Local** (daily 6:00-23:00, at rear entrance, on Eccleston Street). A larger Sainsbury's is on Wilton Road near Warwick Way, a couple of blocks southeast of the station (Mon-Sat 7:00-23:00, Sun 11:00-17:00). A string of good ethnic restaurants lines Wilton Road. For affordable if forgettable meals, try the row of cheap little eateries on Elizabeth Street.

Chain Restaurants near Victoria Station: **Yo! Sushi** and **Wasabi** are in the main concourse of Victoria Station (another Wasabi is at 131 Victoria Street). You'll also find **Wagamama** (at Cardinal Place off Victoria Street) and an **Itsu** (163 Victoria Street).

West of Victoria Station (Belgravia)

Ebury Wine Bar, filled with young professionals, provides a cut-above atmosphere (rumor has it that Prince William held his bachelor party here). In the delightful back room, the fancy menu features modern European cuisine with a French accent, including delicious £16-22 main dishes and a £23 two-course or £29 three-course special (available Mon-Fri at lunch and daily 18:00-20:00; three-course meal includes a glass of Prosecco that you're welcome to swap for house wine). At the wine bar, find a cheaper bar menu that's better than your average pub grub (£9-15 meals). This is emphatically a "traditional wine bar," with no beers on tap (restaurant open daily 12:00-15:00 & 18:00-22:30, wine bar open all day long, reservations smart, at intersection of Ebury and Elizabeth Streets, 139 Ebury Street, tel. 020/7730-5447, www.eburyrestaurant.co.uk).

La Bottega is an Italian delicatessen that fits its upscale Belgravia neighborhood. It offers tasty, freshly cooked pastas (£6), lasagnas, and salads (£9 lasagna-and-salad meal), along with great sandwiches (£3-5) and a good coffee bar with Italian pastries. It's fast (order at the counter), and the ingredients would please an Italian grandmother. Grab your meal to go, or enjoy the Belgravia good life with locals, either sitting inside or on the sidewalk (Mon-Fri 8:00-19:00, Sat-Sun 9:00-18:00, on corner of Ebury and Eccleston Streets, tel. 020/7730-2730; second location in South Kensington at 97 Old Brompton Road).

The Thomas Cubitt pub, named for the urban planner who designed much of Belgravia, is a trendy neighborhood gastropub packed with young professionals. It's pricey and a pinch pretentious and prides itself on using sustainable ingredients in its modern English cooking. With a bright but slightly cramped interior and fine sidewalk seating, it's great for a drink or meal (£8 small plates, £14-18 main dishes, 44 Elizabeth Street). Upstairs is a more refined restaurant with the same kitchen, but an emphasis on finer technique and presentation (£8-12 starters, £18-22 main courses, reservations recommended, food served daily 12:00-22:00, tel. 020/7730-6060, thethomascubitt.co.uk).

The Duke of Wellington pub is a classic neighborhood place with forgettable grub, sidewalk seating, and an inviting interior. A bit more lowbrow than my other Belgravia listings, this may be your best shot at meeting a local (£5-7 sandwiches, £9-10 meals, food served Mon-Sat 12:00-15:00 & 18:00-21:00, Sun lunch only, 63 Eaton Terrace, tel. 020/7730-1782).

South End of Ebury Street: A five-minute walk down Ebury Street, where it intersects with Pimlico Road, you'll find a pretty square with a few more eateries to consider—including **The Orange,** a high-priced gastropub with the same owners and a similar menu to The Thomas Cubitt (described earlier); and **Daylesford,** the deli and café of an organic farm (£3-5 light meals to go—a good picnic option).

East of Victoria Station (Pimlico)

Grumbles brags it's been serving "good food and wine at nonscary prices since 1964." Offering a delicious mix of "modern eclectic French and traditional English," this unpretentious little place with cozy booths inside (on two levels, including a cellar) and four nice sidewalk tables is the best spot to eat well in this otherwise workaday neighborhood. Their traditional dishes are their forte (£11-18 plates, early-bird specials, open daily 12:00-14:30 & 18:00-23:00, reservations wise, half a block north of Belgrave Road at 35 Churton Street, tel. 020/7834-0149, www.grumblesrestaurant.co.uk).

Pimlico Fresh's breakfasts and lunches feature fresh, organic ingredients, served up with good coffee and/or fresh-squeezed juices. Choose from the dishes listed on the wall-sized chalkboard that lines the small eating area, then order at the counter. This place is heaven if you've slept through your hotel's breakfast hour, or if you just need a break from the bacon-eggs-beans routine (£5-10 meals, takeout lunches, plenty of vegetarian options; Mon-Fri 7:30-19:30, breakfast served until 15:00; Sat-Sun 9:00-18:00; 86 Wilton Road, tel. 020/7932-0030).

Seafresh Fish Restaurant is the neighborhood place for plaice—and classic and creative fish-and-chips cuisine. You can either take out on the cheap or eat in, enjoying a white-fish ambience. Though Mario's father started this place in 1965, it feels like the

EATING

chippie of the 21st century (£5-8 meals to go, £13-17 to sit, Mon-Sat 12:00-15:00 & 17:00-22:30, closed Sun, 80 Wilton Road, tel. 020/7828-0747).

The Jugged Hare pub, a 10-minute walk from Victoria Station, sits in a lavish old bank building, with vaults replaced by tankards of beer and a kitchen. They have a traditional menu and a plush, vivid pub scene good for a meal or just a drink (£7 sandwiches, £10-12 meals, food served daily 12:00-21:30, 172 Vauxhall Bridge Road, tel. 020/7828-1543).

St. George's Tavern is the neighborhood's best pub for a full meal. They serve dinner from the same menu in three zones: on the sidewalk to catch the sun and enjoy some people-watching, in the ground-floor pub, and in a classier downstairs dining room with full table service. They're proud of their sausages. The scene is inviting for just a beer, too (£10-14 meals, food served daily 10:00-22:00, corner of Hugh Street and Belgrave Road, tel. 020/7630-1116).

South Kensington

These places are close to several recommended hotels and just a couple of blocks from the Victoria and Albert Museum and Natural History Museum (Tube: South Kensington; for locations see map on page 381).

Exhibition Road Food Circus, a one-block-long road (on the Victoria and Albert Museum side of the South Kensington Tube station), is a traffic-free pedestrian zone lined with enticing little eateries. There's a good amount of choice, including **Fernandez and Wells** (if you want wine, fine meats, and cheese), **Thai Square** (for good Thai), **Casa Brindisa** (for tapas and shared Mediterranean-style dishes), **Daquise** (a venerable Polish restaurant much loved by the local Polish community and the only nonchain mentioned here; at 20 Thurloe Street), and much more.

Moti Mahal Indian Restaurant, with minimalist-yet-upscale ambience and attentive service, serves mostly Bangladeshi cuisine that's delicious. Consider chicken *jalfrezi* if you like spicy food, and buttery chicken if you don't (£9-15 main dishes, daily 12:00-14:30 & 17:30-23:30, Sat-Sun open all day, 3 Glendower Place, tel. 020/7584-8428).

Bosphorus Kebabs is the student favorite for a quick, fast, and hearty Turkish dinner. While mostly for takeaway, they have a few tight tables indoors and on the sidewalk (£5-7 meals, Turkish kebabs, daily 10:30-24:00, 59 Old Brompton Road, tel. 020/7584-4048).

Beirut Express has fresh, well-prepared Lebanese cuisine. In the front, you'll find takeaway service as well as barstools for a quick bite (£4.50 sandwiches). In the back is a sit-down restaurant with £15-18 plates and £6-8 *mezes* (daily 12:00-24:00, 65 Old Brompton Road, tel. 020/7591-0123).

Franco Manca, a taverna-inspired pizzeria, is part of a chain serving Neapolitan-style pies using organic ingredients and boasting typical Italian charm. If you skip the pricey drinks you can feast like a king on a paisano's budget (£5-7 pizzas, daily 11:30-23:00, 97 Old Brompton Road, tel. 020/7584-9713).

La Bottega occupies a busy corner, with a similar menu to the one at its Belgravia location (daily 9:00-20:00, 97 Old Brompton Road, tel. 020/7581-6622, see listing on page 408).

The Anglesea Arms, with a great terrace surrounded by classy South Kensington buildings, is a destination pub that feels like the classic neighborhood favorite. It's a thriving and happy place, with a woody ambience and a mellow step-down back dining room a world away from any tourism. While the food is the main draw, this is also a fine place to just have a beer. Don't let the crowds here put you off. Behind all the drinkers is an elegant and more peaceful back dining room (£6-8 starters, £12-17 main dishes, meals served daily 12:00-15:00 & 18:00-22:00; from Old Brompton Road, turn left at Onslow Gardens and go down a few blocks to 15 Selwood Terrace; tel. 020/7373-7960).

Rocca is a bright and dressy Italian place with a heated terrace (£6-9 pizza, pasta, and salads; daily 11:30-23:30, 73 Old Brompton Road, tel. 020/7225-3413).

Supermarkets: **Tesco Express** (50 Old Brompton Road) and **Little Waitrose** (99 Old Brompton Road) are both open long hours daily.

Chain Restaurants in South Kensington: **Byron Hamburgers** (93 Old Brompton Road), **Wasabi** (21 Old Brompton Road), and **Itsu** (five-minute walk east of South Kensington Tube station at 118 Draycott Avenue).

Near Bayswater and Notting Hill Accommodations

For locations, see the map on page 384.

Maggie Jones's has been feeding locals for 40 years in a neighborhood where eateries come and go. Its countryside antique decor and candlelight make a visit a step back in time. It's a longer walk than most of my recommendations, but you'll get solid English cuisine. It's pricey, but the portions are huge (especially the meat-and-fish pies, their specialty). You're welcome to save lots by splitting your main course. The candlelit upstairs is the most romantic, while the basement is kept lively with the kitchen, tight seating, and lots of action. The staff is young and slightly aloof (lunch—£5 starters, £7-8 main dishes; dinner—£7-9 starters, £17-24 main dishes; daily 12:00-14:30 & 18:00-23:00, reservations recommended, 6 Old Court Place, just east of Kensington Church Street, near High Street Kensington Tube stop, tel. 020/7937-6462, www. maggie-jones.co.uk).

Geales, which opened its doors in 1939 as a fish-and-chips shop, has been serving Notting Hillbillies ever since. Today the menu is much more varied, but the emphasis is still on fish. The gingham-clad tables are casual, but the food is upscale. If you still want the crispy battered cod that put them on the map, it's the best around (lunch—£10 two-course express menu; dinner—£4-11 starters and salads, £14-23 main dishes; daily 12:00-15:00 & 18:00-22:30, reservations smart, 2 Farmer Street, just south of Notting Hill Gate Tube stop, tel. 020/7727-7528, www.geales.com).

The Churchill Arms pub and **Thai Kitchen** (same location) are local hangouts, with good beer and a thriving old-English ambience in front, and hearty £9 Thai plates in an enclosed patio in the back. You can eat the Thai food in the tropical hideaway (table service) or in the atmospheric pub section (order at the counter and they'll bring it to you). The place is festooned with Churchill memorabilia and chamber pots (including one with Hitler's mug on it—hanging from the ceiling farthest from Thai Kitchen—sure to cure the constipation of any Brit during World War II). Arrive by 18:00 or after 21:00 to avoid a line. During busy times, diners are limited to an hour at the table (food served daily 12:00-22:00, 119 Kensington Church Street, tel. 020/7727-4242 for the pub or 020/7792-1296 for restaurant reservations, www.churchillarmskensington. co.uk).

Hereford Road is a cozy, mod eatery tucked at the far end of Prince's Square. It's stylish but not pretentious, serving heavy, meaty English cuisine made with modern panache. Cozy two-person booths face the open kitchen up top; the main dining room is down below. There are also a few sidewalk tables (£7-10 starters, £14-17 main dishes, reservations smart, daily 12:00-15:00 & 18:00-22:00, 3 Hereford Road, tel. 020/7727-1144, www. herefordroad.org).

The Prince Edward serves good grub in a comfy, upscale-pub setting and at its sidewalk tables (£10-15 meals, daily 10:30-23:00, family-friendly, 2 blocks north of Bayswater Road at the corner of Dawson Place and Hereford Road, 73 Prince's Square, tel. 020/7727-2221).

Café Diana is a healthy little eatery serving sandwiches, salads, and Middle Eastern food. It's decorated—almost shrine-like—with photos of Princess Diana, who used to drop by for pita sandwiches. You can dine in the simple interior, or order some food from the counter to go (£3-5 sandwiches, £6-10 meat dishes, daily 8:00-23:00, cash only, 5 Wellington Terrace, on Bayswater Road, opposite Kensington Palace Garden Gates, where Di once lived, tel. 020/7792-9606, Abdul).

On Queensway: The road called Queensway is a multiethnic food circus, lined with lively and inexpensive eateries—browse the options along here and choose your favorite. For a cut above, head for **Royal China Restaurant**—filled with London's Chinese, who consider this one of the city's best eateries. It's dressed up in black, white, and gold, with candles and brisk waiters. While it's pricier than most neighborhood Chinese restaurants, the food is noticeably better (£9-13 dim sum menu, served until 17:00, £10-14 main dishes, £25-40 special dishes, daily 12:00-23:00, 13 Queensway, tel. 020/7221-2535). For a lowbrow alternative, **Whiteleys Shopping Centre Food Court**—at the top end of Queensway—offers fast-food chain eateries among Corinthian columns, and a multiscreen theater in a mall that dates back to 1912 (most restaurants daily 12:00-22:00, some eateries open shorter hours; options include Yo! Sushi, good salads at Café Rouge, pizza, gelato, and Starbucks; third floor, corner of Porchester Gardens and Queensway).

Supermarkets: There are a handful of options, all of which open early and close late (except on Sundays). **Tesco** is a half-block from the Notting Hill Gate Tube stop (near intersection with Pembridge Road at 114 Notting Hill Gate). Queensway is home to several supermarkets, including **Sainsbury's Local** and **Tesco Express** (both next to Bayswater Tube stop), **Spar Market** (at #18), and **Marks & Spencer** (Whiteleys Shopping Centre).

Chain Restaurants in Bayswater and Notting Hill: **Byron Hamburgers** (103 Westbourne Grove), **Masala Zone** (75 Bishop's Bridge Road), **Yo! Sushi** (Whiteleys Shopping Centre), **Itsu** (100 Notting Hill Gate), and **Côte** (98 Westbourne Grove). To the south, past Kensington Palace, is **Wagamama** (26 Kensington High Street).

ELSEWHERE IN LONDON

Between St. Paul's and the Tower: The **Counting House,** formerly an elegant old bank, offers great £10-13 meals, nice homemade £11-13 meat pies, fish, and fresh vegetables. The fun "nibbles menu," with £3-7 snacks, is available starting in the early evening until 22:00 (open Mon-Fri 11:00-23:00, closed Sat-Sun; gets really busy with the buttoned-down 9-to-5 crowd after 12:15, especially Thu-Fri; near Mansion House in The City, 50 Cornhill—see map on page 401, tel. 020/7283-7123).

Near the British Library: Drummond Street (running just west of Euston Station—see map on page 388) is famous for cheap and good Indian vegetarian food (£5-10 dishes, £7 lunch buffets). For a good *thali* (combo platter) consider **Chutneys** (124 Drummond, tel. 020/7388-0604) and **Ravi Shankar** (133 Drummond, tel. 020/7388-6458, both open long hours daily).

Near the Tower of London: In **The Medieval Banquet**'s un-

EATING

derground, brick-arched room, costumed wenches bring you a tasty four-course medieval-themed meal (includes ale and red wine, juice for kids) as minstrels, knights, jesters, and contortionists perform. If you enjoy an act, pound on the table. Reserve in advance online or by phone (adult-£50, child-£30, family deal for 2 adults and 2 kids-£110—Thu-Sun only, 15 percent discount for Rick Steves readers—can't combine with family deal, doors open Wed-Sat at 19:15, Sun at 17:15, show starts about 30 minutes later, closed Mon-Tue, veggie option possible, rentable medieval garb, The Medieval Banquet Ivory House, St. Katharine Docks, enter docks off East Smithfield Street, Tube: Tower Hill, tel. 020/7480-5353, www.medievalbanquet.com).

Near East End Street Markets: Brick Lane in "Banglatown" is where London's Bangladeshi community goes to dine at their favorite curry house. If you join them, be prepared for curbside hawkers pitching their eateries (Tube: Aldgate East, see page 79).

TAKING TEA IN LONDON

While visiting London, consider partaking in this most British of traditions. While some tearooms—such as the wallet-draining £50-a-head tea service at Claridges and the finicky Fortnum & Mason—still require a jacket and tie, most others happily welcome tourists in jeans and sneakers. Most tearooms are usually open for lunch and close about 17:00. At all the places listed below, it's perfectly acceptable for two people to order one afternoon tea and one cream tea (at about £5) and share the afternoon tea's goodies. For details on afternoon tea, see page 558.

Traditional Tea Experiences

The Wolseley serves a good afternoon tea between their meal service. Split one with your companion and enjoy two light meals at a great price in classic elegance (£11 cream tea, £24 afternoon tea, £34 champagne tea, generally served 15:00-18:30 daily, see full listing on page 404).

The Orangery at Kensington Palace serves a £26 "Orangery tea" and a £32-36 champagne tea in its bright white hall near William and Kate's residence. You can also order treats à la carte. The portions aren't huge, but who can argue with eating at a royal orangery or on the terrace? (Tea served 12:00-18:00, no reservations taken; a 10-minute walk through Kensington Gardens from either Queensway or High Street Kensington Tube stations to the orange brick building, about 100 yards from Kensington Palace—see map on page 384; tel. 020/3166-6113, www.hrp.org.uk.)

The Capital Hotel, a luxury hotel a half-block from Harrods, caters to weary shoppers with its intimate five-table,

EATING

linen-tablecloth tearoom. It's where the ladies-who-lunch meet to decide whether to buy that Versace gown they've had their eye on. Even so, casual clothes, kids, and sharing plates are all OK (£30 afternoon tea, daily 14:00-17:30, call to book ahead —especially on weekends, 22 Basil Street—see color map on page v, Tube: Knightsbridge, tel. 020/7591-1202, www. capitalhotel.co.uk).

The **Fortnum & Mason** department store offers tea at several different restaurants within its walls. You can "Take Tea in the Parlour" for £20 (including ice-cream cakes; Mon-Sat 10:00-19:30, Sun 11:30-17:00). The pièce de resistance is their Diamond Jubilee Tea Salon, named in honor of the Queen's 60th year on the throne (and, no doubt, to remind visitors of Her Majesty's visit for tea here in 2012 with Camilla and Kate). At these royal prices, consider it dinner (£40-44, daily 12:00-19:00, Sun until 18:00, dress up a bit—no shorts, "children must be behaved," 181 Piccadilly—see map on page 428, smart to reserve at least a week in advance, tel. 020/7734-8040, www. fortnumandmason.com).

Other Places to Sip Tea

Taking tea is not just for tourists and the wealthy—it's a true English tradition. If you want the teatime experience but are put off by the price, consider these options.

Teapod, a modern place near the Tower Bridge, serves cream tea for £6 and afternoon tea for £9 (daily until 18:00, 31 Shad Thames, tel. 020/7407-0000).

Museum Cafés: Many museum restaurants offer a fine, inexpensive tea service. The **National Dining Rooms,** within the National Gallery on Trafalgar Square, serves a £7 cream tea and £17.50 afternoon tea with a great view (14:30-17:00, in Sainsbury Wing of National Gallery, Tube: Charing Cross or Leicester Square, tel. 020/7747-2525). The **Victoria and Albert Museum** café serves a classic cream tea in an elegant setting that won't break your budget.

Shop Cafés: You'll find good-value teas at various cafés in shops and bookstores across London. Most department stores on Oxford Street (including those between Oxford Circus and Bond Street Tube stations) offer an afternoon tea. **John Lewis'** mod third-floor brasserie serves a nice afternoon tea from 15:30 (£10, on Oxford Street one block west of Bond Street Tube station, tel. 020/7629-7711, www.johnlewis.com).

The **Café at Sotheby's,** on the ground floor of the auction giant's headquarters, gives shoppers a break from fashionable New Bond Street (£9-25, tea served Mon-Fri 15:00-16:45, reservations smart, 34 New Bond Street—see map on page 56, Tube: Bond Street or Oxford Circus, tel. 020/7293-5077, www.sothebys.com/cafe).

At **Waterstones'** bookstore you can put together a spread for less than £10 in their fifth-floor view café (203 Piccadilly).

LONDON WITH CHILDREN

London is a great city for kids. Big parks, colorful pageantry, engaging museums, and evocative historical sights make for happy little travelers. Add to that the buses, boats, trains, and Ferris wheels ready for riding, and your newly minted Londonders might never want to go home. However, the key to a successful family trip to this big city is making everyone happy, including the parents. My family-tested recommendations are designed to do just that.

Trip Tips

PLAN AHEAD

Choose **hotels** in a kid-friendly area near a park. Bayswater and Notting Hill neighborhoods put you close to Kensington Gardens, with its imaginative playground (see Hyde Park listing later). Some of my recommended spots in North London are a stone's throw from Regent's Park. If you're staying a week or more, rent an apartment (see page 551). London's big, budget chain hotels generally allow kids to sleep for free (see page 390).

If traveling with older kids, help them **keep in touch** with friends at home with cheap texting plans or email. Hotel guest computers and Wi-Fi hotspots are a godsend. Readily available Wi-Fi (at hotels, some cafés, and all Starbucks and McDonald's) makes bringing a mobile device worthwhile. Most parents find it worth the peace of mind to buy a supplemental messaging plan for the whole family: Adults can stay connected to teenagers while allowing them maximum independence (see page 560).

EATING

Try these tips to keep your kids content throughout the day.
- Eat dinner early (around 18:00) to miss the romantic crowd.

Skip the famous places. Look instead for relaxed cafés, pubs (kids are welcome, though sometimes restricted to the restaurant section or courtyard area), or fast-food restaurants where kids can move around.

- Quality chain restaurants pop up at many of the places you're likely to visit, providing some good go-to options that are likely to please young pallets. Look for Byron Hamburgers, Wagamama Noodle Bar, and Pizza Express.

- Picnic lunches and dinners work well; stop by a grab-and-go shop, such as Pret, or a supermarket with good take-out food, such as Sainsbury's Local or M&S Simply Food (see the Eating in London chapter for more ideas). Fun places to picnic are Hyde Park's rose garden, the grounds of the Tower of London, Greenwich Park, Jubilee Place Park in the Docklands area, or on the move—aboard a boat cruising the Thames or on an open-top sightseeing bus.

- Some of London's sights offer atmospheric eating options and good deals for families. Kids under age 12 eat free at the British Museum's cafeteria-style Gallery Café. St. Martin-in-the-Fields' Café in the Crypt, underneath the church, is more cozy than creepy. Would-be knights love The Medieval Banquet near the Tower of London, where costumed servers, minstrels, jesters, and contortionists accompany the four-course meal. Aspiring royals will enjoy having high tea in the Orangery at Kensington Palace. Boat-loving littles might want to snack at the café beneath the copper hull of the *Cutty Sark* in Greenwich.

SIGHTSEEING

The key to a successful London family vacation is to slow down. Take extended breaks when needed.

- Buy your child a trip journal, and encourage him or her to write down observations, thoughts, and favorite sights and memories. This journal could end up being your child's treasured souvenir.

- Let your kids make some decisions, such as choosing lunch spots or deciding which museums or stores to visit. Deputize your child to lead you on my self-guided walks and museum tours.

- Don't overdo it. Tackle only one or two key sights a day, and mix in a healthy dose of fun activities, like exploring London's fabulous parks. If you're visiting museums with younger children, you could hit the gift shop first so you can buy postcards, then hold a scavenger hunt to find the pictured items. Museum audioguides are great for older children, and some museums even offer audioguides just for kids.

CHILDREN

- Take advantage of Time Out London's frequently updated website, which includes handy kids' calendars listing activities, shows, and museum events, all searchable by date and location (www.timeout.com/london/kids). Their annually updated guidebook, *London for Children* (£12, available in bookstores and many newsstands), is chockablock with ideas for the serious parent tour-guide in London.

- Follow this book's crowd-beating tips. Kids get antsy standing in line. At each sight, ask about a kids' guide or flier.

- Most of the big museums—such as the Tate Modern, Tate Britain, and National Gallery—schedule children's activities on weekends. Some museums also offer "backpacks" with activities to make the visit more interesting. Ask at museum information desks.

- Many museums—such as the Science Museum and Museum of London Docklands—have play areas for children under age seven. (The Army Museum will too when it reopens in the summer of 2016.)

- Give your child a money belt and an expanded allowance; you are on vacation, after all. Let your children budget their funds by comparing and contrasting the dollar and pound.

- It's good to have a "what if" procedure in place in case something goes wrong. Give your kids your hotel's business card, your phone number (if you brought a mobile phone), and emergency taxi fare. Let them know to ask to use the phone at a hotel if they are lost. And if they have mobile phones, show them how to make calls in the UK.

- If you allow kids to explore a museum or neighborhood on their own, be sure to establish a clear meeting time and place.

- Public WCs can be hard to find. Try department stores, museums, and restaurants, particularly fast-food places.

Top Kids' Activities and Sights

EAST LONDON
Tower of London

The crown jewels are awesome, the Beefeater tour plays off kids in a memorable and fun way, and the welcome center offers quizzes, badges, and activities. Avoid the long ticket lines by buying your ticket in advance at the gift shop just below the Tower Hill Tube station ticket office, London travel agencies, or online at a slight discount (tickets purchased online must be used within 7 days).

📕 See the Tower of London Tour chapter.

Books and Films for Kids

Get your kids into the spirit of London with these books and movies:

101 Dalmatians (1961). In this Disney animation set in London, two Dalmatian dogs and their owners must save a group of puppies before the evil Cruella de Vil turns their fur into a coat.

A Bear Called Paddington (Michael Bond, 1958). A bear from Peru winds up in a London train station, where he's found and adopted by a human family.

The Chronicles of Narnia (C.S. Lewis, 1949-1954). The story of four siblings and their escape from WWII London into the magical world of Narnia unfolds in this classic of children's literature (also a BBC miniseries and three feature-length films).

Harry Potter books (J.K. Rowling, 1997-2007) and films (2001-2011). After discovering he's a wizard, a young boy in England gets whisked off to a magical world of witchcraft and wizardry. There, he finds great friendships as well as grave evils.

A Little Princess (1939). In this film adaptation of the classic novel, Shirley Temple plays a girl whose fortunes fall and rise again in a Victorian London boarding school.

The London Eye Mystery (Siobhan Dowd, 2007). Ted and Kat try to solve the mystery of their missing cousin, who disappeared after boarding the London Eye.

London Through Time (Angela McAllister, 2015). A boy and girl journey through time as they walk down one London street that folds out of this inventive book to reveal the past.

Mary Poppins (1964). Though filmed on a set in California, this beloved musical starring Julie Andrews and Dick Van Dyke is set in Edwardian London.

Mission London: A Scavenger Hunt Adventure (Catherine Aragon, 2014). Young explorers will have hands-on fun undertaking spy-themed challenges while discovering the city.

This Is London (Miroslav Sasek, 1959, updated 2004). Vivid illustrations bring the English capital to life in this classic picture book.

A Walk in London (Salvatore Rubbino, 2011). A mother and daughter experience the city—from the changing of the guard to Saint Paul's Cathedral—in this charming picture book.

Wallace & Gromit TV series and films (1990-2012). Absent-minded inventor Wallace and his dog Gromit may live in northwest England, but these uniquely British characters are beloved by children around the country and the world.

Young Sherlock Holmes (1985). In this film, young Sherlock and his sidekick, Watson, work to solve the mystery of a series of nonsensical suicides (some scenes may be frightening for younger children).

CHILDREN

Museum of London
The museum has a very kid-friendly presentation that takes you from prehistoric times to the present. The events guide at the entrance details current kids' activities (see page 74).

Unicorn Theatre
This modern complex presents professional theater for children on two stages (ask about family discounts, check play's recommended ages before booking, café, on the South Bank just behind City Hall, 147 Tooley Street, Tube: London Bridge; tel. 020/7645-0560, www.unicorntheatre.com).

CENTRAL LONDON
Covent Garden
This is a great area for people-watching and candy-licking. Kids like the **London Transport Museum,** with its interactive zone (see page 55).

Trafalgar Square
The grand square is fun for kids (Tube: Charing Cross). Climb the lions, munch a meal in a crypt (at St. Martin-in-the-Fields), and tour the National Gallery.

National Gallery
Ask about their children's printed guides, audioguide programs, and events—Sunday mornings are especially kid-friendly. Look for the "Family Fun" brochure at the information desk.

   📖 See the National Gallery Tour chapter.

St. Martin-in-the-Fields
Next to the church on Trafalgar Square is a glass pavilion, with a brass-rubbing center below that's fun for kids who'd like a souvenir to show for their efforts (£4.50 and up, Mon-Wed 10:00-18:00, Thu-Sat 10:00-20:00, Sun 11:30-17:00, tel. 020/7766-1122; for church details, see page 54). The affordable Café in the Crypt has just the right spooky tables-on-gravestones ambience (see page 403).

London Eye and Nearby
The **grand observation wheel** is a delight for the whole family (for specifics, including crowd-avoidance tips, see page 84). The free playground in adjacent Jubilee Gardens has an adventurous complex of nets and logs for climbing and balancing, and the little

carousel in the London Wonderground carnival area next door delights (small fee).

Part of the London Eye complex and run by Merlin Entertainment (same company as Madame Tussauds), the small, pricey, but entertaining **Sealife Aquarium** resembles an overpriced theme park. Although there are far better aquariums elsewhere, this place packs in school groups and families looking for a break from museums (daily, check for discounts online, Tube: Waterloo or Westminster, www.visitsealife.com).

In the same complex, **Shrek's Adventure** is part walk, part 4-D ride. The crowded journey through Shrek's swamp re-creates scenes from the movie series (also run by Merlin Entertainment; timed entry daily every 15 minutes; check for discounts and combo deals online, www.shreksadventure.com).

Changing of the Guard
Kids enjoy the bands and pageantry of the Buckingham Palace Changing of the Guard, but little ones get a better view at the inspection (see page 60).

Horse Guards
The Horse Guards change daily, and most kids find them fascinating (on Whitehall, between Trafalgar Square and #10 Downing Street, Tube: Westminster, see page 49).

Piccadilly Circus
This titillating district has lots of schlocky amusements, such as the pricey Ripley's Believe It or Not. Be careful of fast-fingered riff-raff. Hamleys toy store is just two blocks up Regent Street (listed below).

Shopping
If your teenager wants to bring home a few chic and cheap London fashions, **Oxford Street** (at the intersection of Regent Street) is a good place to start. Take the Tube to the Oxford Circus stop, and you'll be surrounded by lots of shops selling inexpensive, trendy clothes for teens. Stores include Topshop, Miss Selfridge, Zara, H&M, and music stores like HMV. Sandwich shops and coffeehouses (including a half-dozen Starbucks) offer easy rest stops. Also see the Regent Street Shopping Walk (on page 435).

Hamleys is the biggest toy store in Britain, with seven floors of toys (daily, 188 Regent Street, Tube: Oxford Circus, www.hamleys.com).

Harrods in Knightsbridge, with its over-the-top toy and food departments, can be fun for kids of all ages (see page 427).

Markets, particularly the Camden Lock Market, will hit the spot for finicky teenagers in need of loud music, cool clothes, and plenty of food choices (see page 431).

CHILDREN

Theater
Long-running shows (such as *Wicked, Matilda,* and *The Lion King*) are kid- and parent-pleasers (see the Entertainment in London chapter).

Harry Potter Sights
Fans (and Muggle parents) enjoy visiting places in London where scenes from the movies were filmed (see page 110). Or, better yet, visit the actual sets at the studio where the movie magic was made (see "The Making of Harry Potter," later in this chapter).

WEST LONDON
Hyde Park
London's backyard is the perfect place for museum'd-out kids to play and run free. For older kids, the park has a tennis court, a putting green, and trails for running or biking. Young children will enjoy the Diana, Princess of Wales Memorial Playground in adjacent Kensington Gardens, with its Peter Pan-themed climbing equipment, including a huge wooden pirate ship (Tube: Queensway). Events such as music, plays, and clown acts are scheduled throughout the summer. The Serpentine Lake offers paddleboat rentals and a swimming area with a playground and a shallow kiddie pool (Easter-Oct daily 10:00-dusk, closed off-season; Tube: Knightsbridge, South Kensington, and more). The park is open daily from 5:00 in the morning until midnight (www.royalparks.org.uk).

Natural History Museum
This wonderful world of dinosaurs, volcanoes, meteors, and creepy-crawlies offers creative interactive displays (see page 104).

Science Museum
Next door to the Natural History Museum, this museum offers lots of hands-on fun and IMAX movies (see page 105). The Garden play area on Floor B entertains younger children with water, textures, sounds, and climbing areas.

Both the Natural History and Science museums are kid-friendly and can be clogged with school groups during the school year. Check for special events and exhibits (noted at each museum's entry and on their websites).

NORTH LONDON
Madame Tussauds Waxworks
Despite the lines outside and the crowds inside, the waxworks are popular with kids for gory stuff, pop and movie stars, everyone's favorite royals, and more (see page 66).

London Zoo and Regent's Park

This venerable animal habitat features more than 17,000 creatures and a fine petting zoo. Call for feeding and event times (daily, in Regent's Park, Tube: Camden Town, then bus #274, tel. 0344/225-1826, www.zsl.org).

For a scenic treat that also happens to be a good value, take the London Waterbus down Regent's Canal to the zoo. They drop you off right at the entry (ticket includes one-way trip and admission to the zoo; board at Camden Lock Market, Tube: Camden Town, or at Little Venice, Tube: Warwick Avenue; www.londonwaterbus.com).

Regent's Park also has rental rowboats.

Pollock's Toy Museum

Kids will wonder how their grandparents ever survived without Xbox as they wander through this rickety old house filled with toys that predate batteries and microchips. Be aware, though, that you must exit through a neat toy shop (see page 68).

SOUTH LONDON

The Bankside Walk (see page 290) links several sights children might enjoy: The *Golden Hinde* ship, Shakespeare's Globe Theatre, Clink Prison Museum, and Old Operating Theatre. Nearby is the...

HMS *Belfast*

Older kids might like scrambling across the decks of this WWII warship (see page 94).

GREATER LONDON

Cutty Sark

This beautifully restored sailing ship, now on dry land in Greenwich, is full of kid-friendly, hands-on displays (see page 352). The café beneath its enormous, gleaming hull is a novel place for a bite.

The Making of Harry Potter: Warner Bros. Studio Tour

A nirvana for Potterphiles, this attraction (in Leavesden, a 20-minute train ride from London) lets fans young and old see the actual sets and props that were used to create the Harry Potter films. Shuttle buses run to the studio from the Leavesden train station; for details, see page 112.

Kew Gardens

These famous 300-acre gardens include the Rhizotron and Xstrata Treetop Walkway, which lets kids explore the canopy 60 feet above the ground on a 200-yard-long scenic steel walkway. Younger children will love the Climbers and Creepers indoor play area and kid-size zip line (see page 107).

London Museum of Water and Steam

This impressive collection of steam-powered pumping engines that once powered waterworks across the UK is mesmerizing for children. The engines operate only on weekends—search the website for "What's On" to make sure they're "in steam." An outdoor water-play area is fun in nice weather (kids-£5, adults-£11.50, check online for discounts; daily 11:00-16:00, Green Dragon Lane, tel. 020/8568-4757, www.waterandsteam.org.uk).

FUN TRANSPORTATION
Thames Cruise

Young sailors delight in boats. Westminster Pier (near Big Ben) offers a lot of action, with round-trip cruises and boats to the Tower of London, Greenwich, and Kew Gardens. For details, see page 39.

Hop-On, Hop-Off London Bus Tours

These two-hour double-decker bus tours, which drive by all the biggies, are fun for kids and stress-free for parents. You can stay on the bus the entire time, or hop on and hop off at any of the nearly 30 stops (every 10-15 minutes in summer, every 10-20 minutes in winter, see page 33). The Original London Sightseeing Tour's "City Sightseeing Tour" bus (marked with a red triangle) has a kids' soundtrack on the earphones. Bus-top picnics are allowed.

DAY TRIP TO WINDSOR
Legoland Windsor

If your kids are loopy over Legos, they'll love a day trip to Legoland Windsor. While older kids will probably enjoy it, the park is really aimed at the 11-and-under crowd (see page 482 for cost, hours, and other details).

WHAT TO AVOID

The **London Dungeon**'s popularity with teenagers makes it one of London's most-visited sights. I enjoy gore and torture as much as the next boy, but this is lousy gore and torture, and I would not waste the time or money on it with my child. **The London Bridge Experience** (not to be confused with the Tower Bridge Exhibition) and **The London Tombs** are also to be avoided. They're copycat rip-offs of the London Dungeon.

SHOPPING IN LONDON

London is great for shoppers—and, thanks to the high prices, perhaps even better for window-shoppers. This chapter will tell you where to get essentials, where to get souvenirs, where to browse through colorful street markets, and where to gawk at some high-end stores in this major fashion capital.

Most stores are open Monday through Saturday from roughly 9:00 or 10:00 until 17:00 or 18:00 with a late night on Wednesday or Thursday (usually until 19:00 or 20:00). Many close on Sundays. Large department stores stay open later during the week (until about 21:00 Mon-Sat) and are open shorter hours on Sundays.

Consider these tips for shopping in London:

- If all you need are souvenirs, a surgical strike at any souvenir shop will do.
- London's museums have extraordinarily good shops. The Transport Museum's is one of the best, and stays open at least a half-hour later than the museum itself (listed on page 56). Other sights with great shops include the British Museum (page 63), the Victoria and Albert Museum (page 101), the Museum of London (page 74), the National Portrait Gallery (page 53), the Tate Modern (page 89), and the wacky selections at Pollock's Toy Museum (page 68) and the Old Operating Theatre (page 93).
- Large department stores offer relatively painless one-stop shopping. Consider the down-to-earth Marks & Spencer (Mon-Sat 9:00-21:00, Sun 12:00-18:00, 173 Oxford Street, Tube: Oxford Circus; another at 458 Oxford Street, Tube: Bond Street or Marble Arch; see www.marksandspencer.com for more locations).
- For flea-market fun and bargains, try one of the many street markets.

- Gawkers as well as serious bidders can attend high-end auctions.

For information on **VAT refunds** and **customs regulations,** see page 540. Refuse any offers to charge your credit card in dollars. This is called **dynamic currency conversion** (DCC), and it's offered by some stores (including Harrods) as a "convenience." The very bad exchange rate they use is convenient only for increasing the store's profits.

Shopping Options

SHOPPING STREETS

London is famous for its shopping. The best and most convenient shopping streets are in the West End and West London (roughly between Soho and Hyde Park). You'll find midrange shops along **Oxford Street** (running east from Tube: Marble Arch), and fancier shops along **Regent Street** (stretching south from Tube: Oxford Circus to Piccadilly Circus) and **Knightsbridge** (where you'll find Harrods and Harvey Nichols; Tube: Knightsbridge). Other streets are more specialized, such as **Jermyn Street** for old-fashioned men's clothing (just south of Piccadilly Street) and **Charing Cross Road** for books. **Floral Street,** connecting Leicester Square to Covent Garden, is lined with fashion boutiques. My **"Regent Street Shopping Walk,"** at the end of this chapter, connects several shopping areas, including Oxford, Regent, Carnaby, and Jermyn streets.

FANCY DEPARTMENT STORES IN WEST LONDON
Harrods

Harrods is London's most famous and touristy department store. With more than four acres of retail space covering seven floors, it's a place where some shoppers could spend all day. (To me, it's still just a department store.) Big yet classy, Harrods has everything from elephants to toothbrushes (Mon-Sat 10:00-21:00, Sun 11:30-18:00; baggage check outside on Basil Street—follow *left luggage* signs at back of

SHOPPING

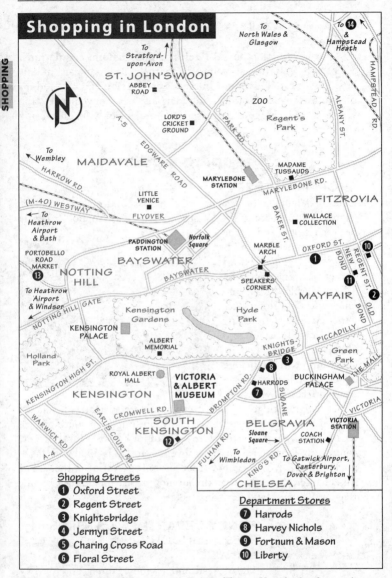

Shopping in London

To North Wales & Glasgow

To 14 & Hampstead Heath

HAMPSTEAD RD.

To Stratford-upon-Avon

ST. JOHN'S WOOD

ABBEY ROAD

ZOO

Regent's Park

ALBANY ST.

PARK RD.

LORD'S CRICKET GROUND

A-5

EDGWARE ROAD

To Wembley

MAIDAVALE

MARYLEBONE STATION

MADAME TUSSAUDS

HARROW RD.

MARYLEBONE RD.

FITZROVIA

(M-40) WESTWAY

LITTLE VENICE

BAKER ST.

WALLACE COLLECTION

To Heathrow Airport & Bath

FLYOVER

PADDINGTON STATION

Norfolk Square

MARBLE ARCH

OXFORD ST.

① ❿

NEW BOND

REGENT ST.

PORTOBELLO ROAD MARKET

BAYSWATER

BAYSWATER

SPEAKERS CORNER

⓫

MAYFAIR

② OLD BOND

❸

NOTTING HILL

To Heathrow Airport & Windsor

NOTTING HILL GATE

Kensington Gardens

Hyde Park

KENSINGTON PALACE

ALBERT MEMORIAL

KNIGHTS-BRIDGE

PICCADILLY

Green Park

THE MALL

Holland Park

ROYAL ALBERT HALL

VICTORIA & ALBERT MUSEUM

❽ ❸

BUCKINGHAM PALACE

BROMPTON RD.

HARRODS

❼

SLOANE ST.

KENSINGTON HIGH ST.

KENSINGTON

CROMWELL RD.

VICTORIA

EARLS COURT RD.

WARWICK RD.

A-4

SOUTH KENSINGTON

⓬

BELGRAVIA

Sloane Square

FULHAM RD.

To Wimbledon

KING'S RD.

COACH STATION

VICTORIA STATION

To Gatwick Airport, Canterbury, Dover & Brighton

CHELSEA

Shopping Streets
1 Oxford Street
2 Regent Street
3 Knightsbridge
4 Jermyn Street
5 Charing Cross Road
6 Floral Street

Department Stores
7 Harrods
8 Harvey Nichols
9 Fortnum & Mason
10 Liberty

the store, £10/bag; Brompton Road, Tube: Knightsbridge, tel. 020/7730-1234, www.harrods.com).

Sightseers should pick up the free *Store Guide* at any info post. Here's what I enjoy: On the ground floor, find the Food Halls, with their Edwardian tiled walls, creative and exuberant displays, and staff in period costumes—not quite like your local supermarket back home.

Descend to the lower ground floor (fewer crowds) and follow

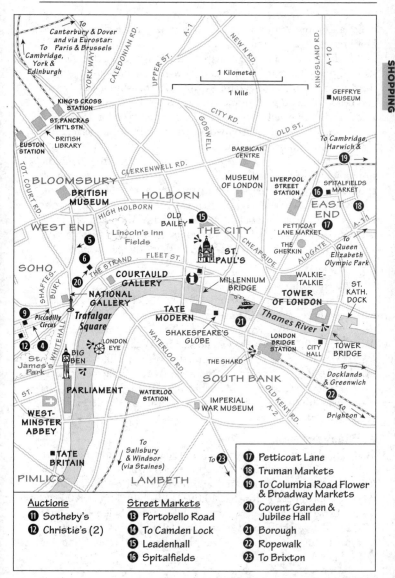

SHOPPING

signs to the Egyptian Escalator (in the center of the store). Here you'll find a memorial to Princess Diana and her boyfriend, Dodi Fayed, who both died in a car crash in Paris in 1997 (Dodi's father, Mohamed Al Fayed, was the store's former owner). Photos and flowers honor the late princess and her lover. Inside a small, clear pyramid, you can see a wine glass still dirty from their last dinner and the engagement ring that Dodi purchased the day before they died. True Di-hards can even sign the official condolence book. A huge (and more than a little creepy) bronze statue shows Di and Dodi releasing a symbolic albatross.

Ride the Egyptian Escalator—lined with pharaoh-headed sconces, papyrus-plant lamps, and hieroglyphic balconies—to the third floor. From the escalator, turn right, then immediately left, and head to the far end to find the incredible Toy Land, which includes an impressive Harry Potter section (wands go for upwards of £100), and child-size luxury pedal cars (£7,000)—the perfect gift for the child who has everything.

More than two dozen eateries are scattered throughout the store, including a sushi bar, deli, pizzeria, Ladurée *macaron* parlor, and—for the truly homesick—an American burger bar.

Many of my readers report that Harrods is overpriced, snooty, and teeming with American, Japanese, and Middle Eastern tourists with zero concept of bargain shopping. It's the only shopping mall I've seen with its own gift store. Still, it's the palace of department stores.

Harvey Nichols

Once Princess Diana's favorite, "Harvey Nick's" remains the department store *du jour* (Mon-Sat 10:00-20:00, Sun 11:30-18:00, near Harrods, 109 Knightsbridge, Tube: Knightsbridge, tel. 020/7235-5000, www.harveynichols.com). Want to pick up a £20 scarf? You won't do it here, where they're more like £200. The store's fifth floor is a veritable food fest, with a gourmet grocery store, a fancy restaurant, a Yo! Sushi bar, and a lively café. Consider a takeaway tray of sushi to eat on a bench in the Hyde Park rose garden two blocks away.

Fortnum & Mason

The official department store of the Queen, Fortnum & Mason embodies old-fashioned, British upper-class taste. While some feel it is too stuffy, you won't find another store with the same storybook atmosphere (Mon-Sat 10:00-21:00, Sun 11:30-18:00, elegant tea served in their Diamond Jubilee Tea Salon—see page 415, 181 Piccadilly, Tube: Green Park, tel. 020/7734-8040, www.fortnumandmason.com; also see the "Regent Street Shopping Walk," later).

Liberty

Designed to make well-heeled shoppers feel at home, this half-timbered, mock-Tudor emporium is a 19th-century institution that thrives today. Known for its gorgeous floral fabrics and well-stocked crafts department, it's fun to stroll through just for a look at its hip, artful displays and castle-like interior, constructed of two decommissioned battleships (Mon-Sat 10:00-20:00, Sun 12:00-18:00, Great Marlborough Street, Tube: Oxford Circus, tel.

020/7734-1234, www.liberty.co.uk, also see the "Regent Street Shopping Walk," later).

STREET MARKETS

Antiques buffs, people-watchers, and folks who brake for garage sales love London's street markets. There's good early-morning market activity somewhere any day of the week. The best markets—which combine lively stalls and a colorful neighborhood with cute and characteristic shops of their own—are Portobello Road and Camden Lock Market. Any London TI has a complete, up-to-date list. Hagglers will enjoy the no-holds-barred bargaining encouraged in London's street markets.

Warning: Markets attract two kinds of people—tourists and pickpockets.

In Notting Hill
Portobello Road Market

Arguably London's best street market, Portobello Road stretches for several blocks through the delightful, colorful, funky-yet-quaint Notting Hill neighborhood. Already charming streets lined with pastel-painted houses and offbeat antique shops are enlivened on Fridays and Saturdays with 2,000 additional stalls (9:00-19:00), plus food, live music, and more. (The best strategy is to come on Friday; most stalls are open, with half the crowds of Saturday.) If you start at Notting Hill Gate and work your way north, you'll find these general sections: antiques, new goods, produce, vintage clothing, more new goods, a flea market, and more food. While Portobello Road is best on Fridays and Saturdays, it's enjoyable to stroll this street on most other days as well, since the quirky shops are fun to explore (Tube: Notting Hill Gate, near recommended accommodations, tel. 020/7727-7684, www.portobelloroad.co.uk).

In Camden Town
Camden Lock Market

This huge, trendy arts-and-crafts festival is divided into three areas,

each with its own vibe (but all of them fresh and funky). The whole complex sprawls around an old-fashioned, still-functioning lock (used mostly for leisure boats) and its retro-chic, yellow-brick industrial buildings. The main market, set alongside the picturesque canal, features a mix of shops and stalls selling boutique crafts and artisanal foods. The market on the opposite side of Chalk Farm Road is edgier, with cheap ethnic food stalls, lots of canalside seating, and punk crafts. The Stables, a sprawling, incense-scented complex, is decorated with fun statues of horses and squeezed into tunnels under the old rail bridge just behind the main market. It's a little lowbrow and wildly creative, with cheap clothes, junk jewelry, and loud music (daily 10:00-18:00, busiest on weekends, tel. 020/3763-9999, www.camdenlockmarket.com).

To escape the crowds, stroll for a while in either direction along the tranquil canal; it's possible to walk east from here all the way to Queen Elizabeth Olympic Park in Stratford (about six miles away).

Arriving by Tube, avoid the tacky, crowded area between the market and the Camden Town Tube station (which bills itself as "The Camden Market," but lacks the real one's canalside charm) by getting off at the Chalk Farm stop. Better yet, arrive via a scenic waterbus ride from Little Venice: Consider London Waterbus Company (tel. 020/7482-2660, www.londonwaterbus.com), Jason's Trip (www.jasons.co.uk), or the *Jenny Wren* (tel. 020/7485-4433, www.walkersquay.com). Bus #24 heads from Pimlico to Victoria Station to Trafalgar Square and then straight up to Camden, before continuing on to Hampstead Heath.

In the City
Leadenhall Market
One of London's oldest, Leadenhall Market stands on the original Roman center of town. Today, cheese and flower shops nestle between pubs, restaurants, and fashion boutiques, all beneath a beautiful Victorian arcade (Harry Potter fans may recognize it as Diagon Alley). This is not a "street market" in the true sense, but more a hidden gem in the midst of London's financial grind (Mon-Fri 10:00-18:00, closed Sat-Sun, tel. 020/7332-1523, Tube: Monument or Liverpool; off Gracechurch Street near Leadenhall Street and Fenchurch).

In the East End
Most of these East End markets are busiest and most interesting on Sundays; the Broadway Market is best on Saturdays. For a walk tying together several of these markets—and a lot more in this neighborhood, which combines Cockney memories with London's biggest Bangladeshi community—see page 79.

Spitalfields Market
This huge, mod-feeling market hall (pronounced "spittle-fields") combines a shopping mall with old brick buildings and sleek modern ones, all covered by a giant glass roof. The shops, stalls, and a rainbow of restaurant options are open every day, tempting you

with ethnic eateries, crafts, trendy clothes, bags, and an antiques-and-junk market (Mon-Fri 10:00-17:00, Sat 11:00-17:00, Sun 9:00-17:00, Tube: Liverpool Street; from the Tube stop, take Bishopsgate East exit, turn left, walk to Brushfield Street, and turn right; www.spitalfields.co.uk).

Petticoat Lane Market

Just a block from Spitalfields Market, this line of stalls sits on the otherwise dull, glass-skyscraper-filled Middlesex Street; adjoining Wentworth Street is grungier and more characteristic. Expect budget clothing, leather, shoes, watches, jewelry, and crowds (Sun 9:00-14:00, sometimes later; smaller market Mon-Fri on Wentworth Street only; closed Sat; Middlesex Street and Wentworth Street, Tube: Liverpool Street).

Truman Markets

Housed in the former Truman Brewery on Brick Lane, this cluster of markets is in the heart of the "Banglatown" Bangladeshi community. Of the East End market areas, these are the grittiest and most avant-garde, selling handmade clothes and home decor as well as ethnic street food. The markets are in full swing on Sundays (roughly 10:00-17:00), though you'll see some action on Saturdays (11:00-18:00). The Boiler House Food Hall and the Backyard Market (hipster arts and crafts) go all weekend—and the Vintage Market (clothes) even operates on Thursdays and Fridays (11:00-17:30). Surrounding shops and eateries are open all week (Tube: Liverpool Street or Aldgate East, tel. 020/7770-6028, www.bricklanemarket.com).

Columbia Road Flower Market

From the Truman Brewery complex, Brick Lane is lined with Sunday market stalls all the way up to Bethnal Green Road, about a ten-minute walk. Continuing straight (north) about five more minutes takes you to Columbia Road, a colorful shopping street made even more so by the Sunday-morning commotion of shouting flower vendors. The prices are good (why not brighten up your hotel room with a bouquet?), and the sales pitches are entertaining (Sun 8:00-15:00, closed Mon-Sat, http://columbiaroad.info). Halfway up Columbia Road, be sure to loop left up little Ezra Street, with characteristic eateries, boutiques, and antiques vendors.

Broadway Market

While the other listed East End markets are best on Sundays, Saturdays are best for the festive market sprawling through this aptly named neighborhood—ground zero for London's hipsters. Several blocks are filled with foodie delights, along with a few arts and crafts (www.broadwaymarket.co.uk). On sunny days, the London Fields park just north of the market is filled with thousands of picnicking and sunbathing locals enjoying their little slice of the city. A bit farther out, this market can be trickier to reach; it's easiest to take the Overground from Liverpool Street Station three stops to London Fields, then walk through that park to the market.

In the West End
Covent Garden Market
Originally the convent garden for Westminster Abbey, the iron-and-glass market hall hosted a produce market until the 1970s (earning it the name "Apple Market"). Now it's a mix of fun shops, eateries, markets, and—thanks to Steve Jobs—a more modern-day Apple store. Mondays are for antiques, while arts and crafts dominate the rest of the week. Yesteryear's produce stalls are open daily 10:30-18:00, and on Thursdays, a food market brightens up the square (Tube: Covent Garden, tel. 020/7395-1350, www. coventgardenlondonuk.com, also see 📖 West End Walk).

Jubilee Hall Market
Located on the south side of Covent Garden, this market features antiques on Mondays; a general market Tuesday through Friday; and arts and crafts on Saturdays and Sundays (Mon 5:00-17:00, Tue-Fri 10:30-19:00, Sat-Sun 10:00-18:00, tel. 020/7379-4242, www.jubileemarket.co.uk).

In South London
Borough Market
London's oldest fruit and vegetable market has been serving the Southwark community for over 800 years. These days there are as many people taking photos as buying fruit, cheese, and beautiful breads, but it's still a fun carnival atmosphere with fantastic stall food. For maximum market and minimum crowds, join the locals on Thursdays (full market open Wed-Thu 10:00-17:00, Fri 10:00-18:00, Sat 8:00-17:00, closed Sun; surrounding food stalls open daily; south of London Bridge, where Southwark Street meets Borough High Street; Tube: London Bridge, tel. 020/7407-1002, www.boroughmarket.org.uk, also see 📖 Bankside Walk).

Ropewalk (Maltby Street Market)
This short-but-sweet, completely untouristy food bazaar bustles on weekends under a nondescript rail bridge in the shadow of the Shard. Two dozen vendors fill the narrow passage with a festival of hipster/artisan food carts, offering everything from gourmet burgers to waffles to scotch eggs to ice-cream sandwiches. Come as hungry as possible and graze your way to a satisfying lunch (Sat 9:00-16:00, Sun 11:00-16:00, www.maltby.st). This area of South London—called Bermondsey—is a lowbrow but emerging neighborhood that's fun to explore for a slice of youthful, untrampled

city. A short walk southeast of Tower Bridge, it has several rustic microbreweries tucked between self-storage shops and auto-repair garages.

Brixton Market

This seedy neighborhood south of the Thames features yet another thriving market. Here the food, clothing, records, and hair-braiding throb with an Afro-Caribbean beat (stalls open Mon-Sat 8:00-18:00, Wed until 15:00, farmers market Sun 10:00-14:00 but otherwise dead on Sun; Tube: Brixton, www.brixtonmarket.net).

In Greenwich

With several sightseeing treats just a quick DLR ride from central London, Greenwich has its share of great markets, especially lively on weekends. For details, see page 350.

FAMOUS AUCTIONS

London's famous auctioneers welcome the curious public for viewing and bidding. You can preview estate catalogs or browse auction calendars online. To ask questions or set up an appointment, contact **Sotheby's** (opening times vary, tel. 020/7293-5000, www.sothebys.com; recommended café on site, 34 New Bond Street, Tube: Oxford Circus or **Christie's** (Mon-Fri 9:00-17:00; 85 Old Brompton Road, Tube: South Kensington, tel. 020/7930-6074; second location at 8 King Street, Tube: Green Park, tel. 020/7839-9060; www.christies.com).

Regent Street Shopping Walk

This mile-long walk—along Regent Street to Piccadilly Circus, then up the street called Piccadilly and down Jermyn Street—takes you by the most typically London stores and shops. While useful for true shoppers, this walk is also a lot of fun for window-shoppers. Only you know how much time—and money—to allow for this walk.

• *Start your walk at the Oxford Circus Tube stop.*

❶ Oxford Street

Today, Oxford Street is a midrange shopping area, lined by less-distinguished chains and department stores, and a bit scruffy. But it was once one of London's great shopping streets, and is still one of the most decorative at Christmastime. The original Selfridges (250 yards west of Oxford Circus), opened in 1910, helped pioneer the modern concept of the department store.

• *From the Oxford Circus Tube stop, head south on Regent Street (heading slightly downhill, away from the steeple in the road). Stay along the left (east) side of Regent Street. Two blocks down, where Regent crosses Great Marlborough Street, look left to spot...*

❷ Liberty Department Store

The venerable Liberty is a big, stately, local-favorite department store established in 1875, now housed in this distinctive faux-Tudor building (built in the 1920s from the timbers of two Royal Navy ships). Liberty is known for its fine design and "Liberty Print" patterned cloth.

Before moving on, note the nearby Apple Store—it's behind you, a half-block up from Liberty at #235 Regent Street. The building looks more like a palace. It's popular with Londoners, who appreciate its free Wi-Fi...and are astounded by its customer service. The English are capable of good service too, but, as a Londoner put it to me, "not the obsequious butt-kissing some Americans expect, because that makes you feel like a servant."

• *Turn left on Great Marlborough Street, go past Liberty, and turn right onto...*

❸ Carnaby Street

In the Swinging '60s, when Pete Townshend needed a paisley shirt, John Lennon a Nehru jacket, or Twiggy a miniskirt, they came here—where those mod fashions were invented. If you were a "Dedicated Follower of Fashion" (as a Kinks' song put it), you were one of the trendy "Carnaby-tian army." Today, there's not a hint of hippie. For the most part, Carnaby Street looks like everything else from the '60s does now—sanitized and co-opted by upscale franchises. At least the upper end of the street retains a whiff of funkiness.

• *After exploring Carnaby Street, walk back toward Great Marlborough Street, heading left (west) on Foubert's Place (near the Shakespeare's Head Pub). Then turn left again to continue strolling downhill along...*

❹ Regent Street

You're in the heart of London's shopping neighborhood. By now, you may have noticed a sort of class divide among London shoppers.

Where the area near Oxford Circus was a bit

SHOPPING

Regent Street Shopping Walk

1. Oxford Street
2. Liberty Dep't Store
3. Carnaby Street
4. Regent Street
5. Piccadilly Circus
6. Piccadilly Street
7. Jermyn Street

WALK BEGINS

Oxford Circus

OXFORD STREET

POLAND ST.

To Marble Arch

200 Meters

200 Yards

PRINCES ST.

REGENT ST.

APPLE STORE

LIBERTY DEP'T STORE

GREAT MARLBOROUGH ST.

Hanover Square

HANOVER ST.

FOUBERT'S PLACE

CARNABY STREET

MARSHALL ST.

BROADWICK ST.

SOHO

ST. GEORGE'S

MADDOX ST.

CONDUIT ST.

HAMLEYS

HACKETT

KINGLY ST.

BEAK ST.

LEXINGTON ST.

HOPKINS ST.

TISBURY CT.

SOTHEBY'S AUCTION HOUSE

NEW BURL. PL.

REGENT STREET

MAPPIN & WEBB

Golden Square

WARWICK ST.

BRIDLE LN.

LOWER JAMES ST.

GREAT PULTENEY

BREWER ST.

SHERWOOD ST.

SHAFTESBURY AVE.

To Leicester Square

N

CLIFFORD

SAVILE ROW

OLD BURLINGTON ST.

PENHALIGON'S

BURBERRY

VIGO ST.

GLASSHOUSE ST.

REGENT ST.

DENMAN ST.

Piccadilly Circus

COVENTRY

Piccadilly Circus

OLD BOND ST.

BURLINGTON GARDENS

SACKVILLE ST.

BURLINGTON ARCADE

PICCADILLY STREET

EROS STATUE

ALBEMARLE ST.

DOVER ST.

ROYAL ACADEMY OF ARTS

ST. JAMES

WATER-STONES

JERMYN ST.

LOWER REGENT ST.

FORTNUM & MASON

DUKE OF YORK ST.

PICCADILLY ARCADE

THE WOLSLEY

WALK ENDS

St. James's Square

Green Park

RITZ HOTEL

ST. JAMES ST.

BEAU BRUMMELL STATUE

CHRISTIE'S AUCTION HOUSE

PICCADILLY

KING ST.

PALL MALL

low-rent, you've now entered London's high-class, top-dollar boulevard. This street has wide sidewalks, fine architecture, and royal-family connections. Most of its shops call the Queen their landlord, as she owns much of the land here.

Once on Regent Street, follow the giddy kids to **Hamleys** (just downhill from Foubert's Place, on the left at #188), Britain's biggest toy store. In 2010 it marked its 250th anniversary of delighting children. Seven floors buzz with 50,000 toys, managed by a staff of 200. Employees, some dressed in playful costumes, give demos of the latest gadgets. It was here at Hamleys that the world first got to know London's genteel Paddington Bear, and the less-genteel Build-a-Bear Workshop (now a fixture at malls everywhere).

On this stretch of Regent Street, fine bits of old English class dominate. **Hackett** (across from Hamleys at #193) is the place to go for preppy young English menswear. **Mappin and Webb** (on the left, at #132) is the Queen's jeweler. **Penhaligon's** (on the right, at #125) is the quintessential English perfumery, where royals shop (note the coat of arms at the door) for classic English scents like lavender and rose (fine sampler gift packs and free sniff samples). Once dowdy—it's a clothier of the royal family—**Burberry** (on the corner past Penhaligon's, at #121) is now hip.

• *Regent Street arcs seductively into the ever-vibrant...*

❺ Piccadilly Circus

Piccadilly Circus is where common tastes steamroll the elegance of Regent Street. **Lillywhites** (at the bottom of the square, near the Eros fountain) is a sports store popular as a place to buy the jersey of your favorite football (soccer) team. Farther left (at the start of Coventry Street) is **Cool Britannia,** a tacky palace of English kitsch and a Union Jack fantasy for anyone needing to buy a Brit-themed gift.

• *From Piccadilly Circus, turn right and wander down the busy...*

❻ Piccadilly Street

After a block on your left (at #203), escape from the frenzy of Piccadilly into the quiet of **Waterstones,** Europe's largest bookshop and the flagship store of its widespread chain. Page through seven orderly floors. The fifth floor offers a hip bar with minimalist furniture and great views (see sidebar on page 88).

Next you'll pass Christopher Wren's **St. James's Church** (with free lunchtime concerts several days a week at 13:10—see page 449) and a tiny all-day flea market (antiques Tue 10:00-18:30, crafts Wed-Sat 11:00-18:30, closed Sun-Mon). One block farther (on the left, at #181) is the **Fortnum & Mason** department store, which eschews the glitz of bigger stores and revels in understated, old-school elegance. At the top of the hour the fancy clock on the facade is the scene of a low-key spectacle, as the venerable store's founders—Fortnum and Mason—come out and bow to each other (best viewed from across the street). This reminds shoppers of the store's humble beginnings 300 years ago, when it was started by these two footmen of Queen Anne. With rich displays and deep red carpet, Fortnum's feels classier and more relaxed than Harrods. The Queen, Camilla, and Kate—three generations of royalty—enjoyed tea here together in 2012.

An elegant way to cap your shopping stroll (we'll finish just

a block from here) is with a traditional **afternoon tea.** While pricey, many consider this ritual an essential part of any London visit. My two favorite places in town for a traditional afternoon tea are within a block of here: Fortnum & Mason (with several restaurants and price ranges), and a block farther down Piccadilly Street, **The Wolseley,** the grand 1920s former showroom of a now defunct car manufacturer (where couples are allowed to split a £24 tea in sumptuous surroundings; on the left at #160); for details on F&M and The Wolseley, see "Taking Tea in London" on page 414. Beyond that is the original **Ritz Hotel,** where the tea is much fancier.

• *But before we part ways, we'll stroll a block south of big and busy Piccadilly Street. The Piccadilly Arcade leads to quiet...*

❼ Jermyn Street

A statue of **Beau Brummell,** the ultimate dandy, meets you as if to say, "Within a block in either direction are numerous fine gentlemen's shirtmakers and many other delightful small shops." It was Brummell (1778-1840) who popularized the understated jacket-trousers-and-tie ensemble that men still wear today. As the quote on his statue reads, "To be truly elegant, one should not be noticed."

Stand by the statue and survey the landscape of man-scaping options: **Bates Hats** (#37) still sells bowlers and top hats, as it has for a century. **Turnbull & Asser** (#71) has dressed Winston Churchill, Prince Charles, and James Bond with its "bespoke" (custom-made) shirts and suits. **John Lobb** (#88) has sold boots to Princes William and Harry. **Tricker's** (#67) has been making shoes for the gentleman since the days of Beau Brummell. **Taylor of Old Bond Street** (#74), established in the mid-19th century, specializes in gentleman's shaving and botanical products. After sauntering these few blocks, even the most weary traveler will leave Jermyn Street feeling (if not looking) more refined.

• *Our walk is finished. From here, you have several nearby options. If you're ready for **teatime,** cut back through the block to Piccadilly Street and the places I mentioned earlier.*

Or, to head back to **Piccadilly Circus** *(and its handy Tube stop), walk east down Jermyn Street, pausing at the classic perfume shop Floris (at #89) and at Paxton & Whitfields (#93), which has served exceptional cheese since 1797, with generous tastings. On the little Duke of York Street (behind St. James's Church) is an old-fashioned barbershop called Geo. F. Trumper (selling top-quality shaving gear) and the classic Red Lion Pub. If all of this is just too elegant, dip into Piccadilly Square's Cool Britannia and buy some Union Jack underwear.*

ENTERTAINMENT IN LONDON

London bubbles with top-notch entertainment seven days a week: plays, movies, concerts, exhibitions, walking tours, shopping, and children's activities. For the best list of what's happening and a look at the latest London scene, check www.timeout.com/london. The free monthly *London Planner* covers sights, events, and plays, though generally not as well as the Time Out website.

Choose from classical, jazz, rock, and far-out music, Gilbert and Sullivan, tango lessons, comedy, Baha'i meetings, poetry readings, spectator sports, theater, and the cinema. In Leicester Square, you might be able to catch a film that has yet to be released in the States—if Colin Firth (or any other A-list celebrity) is attending an opening-night premiere in London, it will likely be at one of the big movie houses here.

There are plenty of free performances, such as lunch concerts at St. Martin-in-the-Fields (at Trafalgar Square) and summertime events at The Scoop amphitheater near City Hall (see "Summer Evenings Along the South Bank," later).

Theater (a.k.a. "Theatre")

London's theater scene rivals Broadway's in quality and sometimes beats it in price. Choose from 200 offerings—Shakespeare, musicals, comedies, thrillers, sex farces, cutting-edge fringe, revivals starring movie celebs, and more. London does it all well.

Seating Terminology: Just like at home, London's theater sell seats in a range of levels—but the Brits use different ter stalls (ground floor), dress circle (first balcony), upper circle (se balcony), balcony (sky-high third balcony), and slips (cheap the fringes). Discounted tickets are called "concessions"

ENTERTAINMENT

London's Major Theaters

1 Adelphi
2 Aldwych
3 Ambassadors & St. Martin's
4 Apollo
5 Cambridge
6 Criterion
7 Dominion
8 Donmar Warehouse
9 Drury Lane
10 Duke of York's
11 Fortune
12 Garrick
13 Haymarket
14 Her Majesty's
15 Lyceum
16 Lyric
17 New London
18 Noël Coward
19 Novello
20 Palace
21 Phoenix
22 Playhouse
23 Prince Edward
24 Prince of Wales
25 Queen's & Gielgud
26 Savoy
27 Shaftesbury
28 Trafalgar Studios
29 Wyndham's

ated as "conc" or "s"). For floor plans of the various theaters, see www.theatremonkey.com.

WEST END SHOWS

...me shows are hosted in the theaters of the West ...and Soho (especially along Shaftesbury Ave-...dilly and Covent Garden. With a centuries-old ...g the masses, they present London theater at its

..., glitzy—even bombastic—musicals over serious

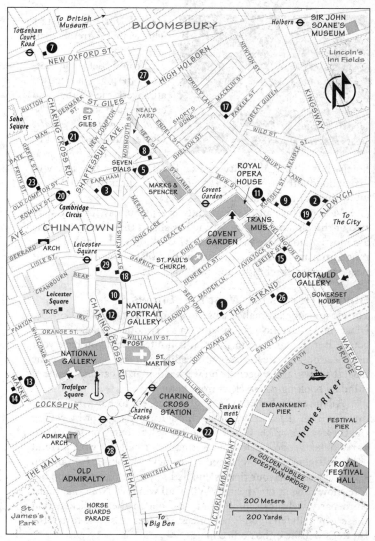

chamber dramas, simply because London can deliver the lights, booming voices, dancers, and multimedia spectacle I rarely get back home. If that's not to your taste—or you already have access to similar spectacles at home—you might prefer some of London's more low-key offerings.

Well-known musicals may draw the biggest crowds, but the West End offers plenty of other crowd-pleasers, from revivals of classics to cutting-edge works by the hottest young playwrights. These productions tend to have shorter runs than famous musicals. Many productions star huge-name celebrities—London is a magnet for movie stars who want to stretch their acting chops.

You'll see the latest offerings advertised all over the Tube and elsewhere. The free *Official London Theatre Guide,* updated weekly, is a handy tool (find it at hotels, box offices, the City of London TI, and online at www. officiallondontheatre.co.uk). If you're picky, check the reviews at www.timeout.com/london.

Most performances are nightly except Sunday, usually with two or three matinees a week. The few shows that run on Sundays are mostly family fare (*Matilda, The Lion King,* and so on). Tickets range from about £25 to £120 for the best seats at big shows. Matinees are generally cheaper and rarely sell out.

Buying Tickets for West End Shows

For most visitors, it makes sense to simply buy tickets in London. Most shows have tickets available on short notice—likely at a discount. But if your time in London is limited—and you have your heart set on a particular show that's likely to sell out (usually the newest shows, and especially on weekends)—you can buy peace of mind by booking your tickets from home.

Advance Tickets: It's generally cheapest to buy your tickets directly from the theater, either through its website or by calling the theater box office. Often, a theater will reroute you to a third-party ticket vendor such as Ticketmaster. You'll pay with a credit card, and generally be charged a per-ticket booking fee (around £3). You can have your tickets emailed to you or pick them up before show time at the theater's Will Call window. Note that many third-party websites sell all kinds of London theater tickets, but these generally charge higher prices and fees. It's best to try the theater's website or box office first.

Discount Tickets from the TKTS Booth: This famous outlet at Leicester Square sells discounted tickets (25-30 percent off) for many shows (£3/ticket service charge, open Mon-Sat 10:00-19:00, Sun 11:00-16:30). TKTS offers a wide variety of shows on any given day, though they may not have the hottest shows in town. You must buy in person at the kiosk, and the best deals are same-day only.

The list of shows and prices is posted outside the booth and updated throughout the day. The same info is available on their constantly refreshed website (www.tkts.co.uk), which is worth checking before you head to Leicester Square. For the best choice and prices, come early in the day—the line starts forming even before the booth opens (it moves quickly). Have a second-choice show in mind, in case your first choice is sold out by the time you reach the ticket window. If you're less picky, come later in the day, when lines (and choices) diminish.

TKTS also sells advance tickets for some shows (but not as cheaply) and some regular-price tickets to extremely popular shows—convenient, but no savings. If TKTS runs out of its ticket allotment for a certain show, it doesn't necessarily mean the show is sold out—you can still try the theater's box office.

Is the TKTS booth right for you? If you're not committed to a particular show and just want a decent deal, this is a great option. You might snag a top-price seat for a popular-but-not-too-popular show (say, *Billy Elliot*) for about half-price through TKTS. But if you're committed to a particular show—especially a popular one—or if you want the absolutely cheapest seats, it's better to book directly at the theater—read on.

Take note: The real TKTS booth (with its prominent sign) is a freestanding kiosk at the south edge of Leicester Square. Several dishonest outfits nearby advertise "official half-price tickets"— avoid these, where you'll rarely pay anything close to half-price.

Tickets at the Theater Box Office: Even if a show is "sold out," there's usually a way to get a seat. Many theaters offer various discounts or "concessions": same-day tickets, cheap returned tickets, standing-room, matinee, senior or student standby deals, and more. Start by checking the show's website, call the box office, or simply drop by (many theaters are right in the tourist zone).

Same-day tickets (called "day seats") are generally available only in person at the box office starting at 10:00 (people start lining up well before then). These tickets (£20 or less) tend to be either in the nosebleed rows or have a restricted view (behind a pillar or extremely far to one side).

Another strategy is to show up at the box office shortly before show time (best on weekdays) and—before paying full price—ask about any cheaper options. Last-minute return tickets are often sold at great prices as curtain time approaches.

For a helpful guide to "day seats," consult www.theatremonkey. com/dayseatfinder.htm; for tips on getting cheap and last-minute tickets, visit www.londontheatretickets.org and www.timeout. com/london/theatre.

Booking Through Other Agencies: Although booking through a middleman such as your hotel or a ticket agency is quick and easy (and may be your last resort for a sold-out show), prices are

What's On in the West End

You're likely to find these perennial favorites among the West End's evening offerings. If spending the time and money for a London play, I like a full-fledged, high-energy musical (which all of these are). Of course you could go for this year's hit, but you'll need to book long in advance and pay top price. These long-running shows are still fun, the seats are easily booked, and you're likely to find them on the discount list at the TKTS booth (see below). Generally ticket prices range from £25-120. Shows typically run Monday through Saturday at 19:30, with two or three matinees a week—confirm specifics on show websites. See the map on page 442 for locations.

Billy Elliot—This adaptation of the popular British film is part family drama, part story of a boy who just has to dance, set to a score by Elton John (Victoria Palace Theatre, Victoria Street, Tube: Victoria, tel. 0844-248-5000, www.billyelliotthemusical.com).

The Book of Mormon—Who else but the writers of *South Park* could create a snappy, irreverent, and sometimes crude musical about two Mormon missionaries and the nature of faith? (Prince of Wales Theatre, Coventry Street, Tube: Piccadilly Circus or Charing Cross, box office tel. 0844-482-5115, www.bookofmormonlondon.com).

Jersey Boys—This fast-moving, easy-to-follow show tracks the rough start and rise to stardom of Frankie Valli and the Four Seasons. It's light, but the music is so catchy that everyone leaves whistling the group's hits (Piccadilly Theatre, 16 Denman Street, Tube: Piccadilly Circus, box office tel. 0844-871-7630, www.jerseyboyslondon.com).

Les Misérables—This musical adaptation of Victor Hugo's epic follows the life of Jean Valjean as he struggles with the social and political realities of 19th-century France (Queen's Theatre, Shaft-

greatly inflated. Ticket agencies and third-party websites are often just scalpers with an address. If you do buy from an agency, choose one who is a member of the Society of Ticket Agents and Retailers (look for the STAR logo—short for "secure tickets from authorized retailers"). These legitimate resellers normally add a maximum 25 percent booking fee to tickets.

Scalpers (or "Touts"): As at any event, you'll find scalpers hawking tickets outside theaters. And, just like at home, those people may either be honest folk whose date just happened to cancel at the last minute...or they may be unscrupulous thieves selling forgeries. London has many of the latter.

THEATER BEYOND THE WEST END

Tickets for lesser-known shows tend to be cheaper (figure £15-30), in part because most of the smaller theaters are government-esbury Avenue, Tube: Piccadilly Circus, box office tel. 0844-482-5160, www.lesmis.com).

The Lion King—In this Disney extravaganza, Simba the lion learns about the delicately balanced circle of life on the savanna (Lyceum Theatre, Wellington Street, Tube: Charing Cross or Covent Garden, theater info tel. 020/7420-8100, box office tel. 0844-871-3000, www.thelionking.co.uk).

Mamma Mia!—This energetic, spandex-and-platform-boots musical weaves together a slew of ABBA hits to tell the story of a bride in search of her real dad as her promiscuous mom plans her Greek Isle wedding. The production has the audience dancing in their seats (Novello Theatre, Aldwych, Tube: Covent Garden, box office tel. 0844-482-5115, www.mamma-mia.com).

Matilda—Based on the Roald Dahl children's book, this hit is a family favorite for its tale of a precocious young girl who's unappreciated by her parents (Cambridge Theatre, Seven Dials, Tube: Covent Garden or Leicester Square, box office tel. 0844-412-4652, www.matildathemusical.com).

Phantom of the Opera—A mysterious masked man falls in love with a singer in this haunting Andrew Lloyd Webber musical about life beneath the stage of the Paris Opera (Her Majesty's Theatre, Haymarket, Tube: Piccadilly Circus or Leicester Square, US toll-free tel. 800-334-8457, box office tel. 0844-412-2707, www.thephantomoftheopera.com).

Wicked—This lively prequel to *The Wizard of Oz* examines how the Witch of the West met Glinda the Good Witch, and later became so, you know... (Apollo Victoria Theatre, just east of Victoria Station, Tube: Victoria, AGT Tickets tel. 0844-871-3001, www.wickedthemusical.co.uk).

subsidized. Remember that plays don't need a familiar title or famous actor to be a worthwhile experience—read up on the latest offerings online; Time Out's website is a great place to start.

Major Noncommercial Theaters

One particularly good venue is the **National Theatre,** which has a range of impressive options, often starring recognizable names. While the building is ugly on the outside, the acts that play out upon its stage are beautiful—as are the deeply discounted tickets it commonly offers (looming on the South Bank by Waterloo Bridge, Tube: Waterloo, www.nationaltheatre.org.uk).

The **Barbican Centre** puts on high-quality, often experimental work (right by the Museum of London, just north of The City, Tube: Barbican, www.barbican.org.uk), as does the **Royal Court Theatre,** which has £10 tickets for its Monday shows (west of the West End in Sloane Square, Tube: Sloane Square, www.royalcourttheatre.com).

Menier Chocolate Factory is a small theater in Southwark gaining popularity for its impressive productions and intimate setting. Check their website to see what's on—they tend to have a mix of plays, musicals, and even an occasional comedian (behind the Tate Modern at 56 Southwark Street, Tube: Southwark, www.menierchocolatefactory.com)

Royal Shakespeare Company: If you'll ever enjoy Shakespeare, it'll be in Britain. The RSC performs at various theaters around London and in Stratford-upon-Avon year-round. To get a schedule, contact the RSC (Royal Shakespeare Theatre, Stratford-upon-Avon, tel. 0844-800-1110, www.rsc.org.uk).

Shakespeare's Globe

To see Shakespeare in a replica of the theater for which he wrote his plays, attend a play at the Globe. In this round, thatch-roofed, open-air theater, the plays are performed much as Shakespeare intended—under the sky, with no amplification.

The play's the thing from late April through early October (usually Tue-Sat 14:00 and 19:30, Sun either 13:00 and/or 18:30, tickets can be sold out months in advance). You'll pay £5 to stand and £17-43 to sit, usually on a backless bench. Because only a few rows and the pricier Gentlemen's Rooms have seats with backs, £1 cushions and £3 add-on backrests are considered a good investment by many. Dress for the weather.

The £5 "groundling" tickets—which are open to rain—are most fun. Scurry in early to stake out a spot on the stage's edge, where the most interaction with the actors occurs. You're a crude peasant. You can lean your elbows on the stage, munch a picnic dinner (yes, you can bring in food), or walk around. I've never enjoyed Shakespeare as much as here, performed as it was meant to be in the "wooden O." If you can't get a ticket, consider waiting around. Plays can be long, and many groundlings leave before the end. Hang around outside and beg or buy a ticket from someone leaving early (groundlings are allowed to come and go). A few non-Shakespeare plays are also presented each year. If you can't attend a show, you can take a guided tour of the theater and museum by day (see page 90).

The new indoor Sam Wanamaker Playhouse allows Shakespearean-era plays and early-music concerts to be performed through the winter. Many of the productions in this intimate venue are one-offs and can be quite pricey.

To reserve tickets for plays at the Globe or Sam Wanamaker, call or drop by the box office (Mon-Sat 10:00-18:00, Sun 10:00-17:00, open one hour later on performance days, New Globe Walk entrance, no extra charge to book by phone, tel. 020/7401-9919). You can also reserve online (www.shakespearesglobe.com, £2.50 booking fee). If the tickets are sold out, don't despair; a few often free up at the last minute. Try calling around noon the day of the performance to see if the box office expects any returned tickets. If so, they'll advise you to show up a little more than an hour before the show, when these tickets are sold (first-come, first-served).

The theater is on the South Bank, directly across the Thames over the Millennium Bridge from St. Paul's Cathedral (Tube: Mansion House or London Bridge). The Globe is inconvenient for public transport, but during theater season, there's a regular supply of black cabs waiting nearby.

Outdoor and Fringe Theater

In summer, enjoy Shakespearean drama and other plays under the stars at the **Open Air Theatre,** in leafy Regent's Park in north London. You can bring your own picnic, order à la carte from the theater menu, or preorder a picnic supper from the theater at least 48 hours in advance (season runs late May-mid-Sept, tickets available beginning in mid-Jan; book at www.openairtheatre.org or—for an extra booking fee—by calling 0844-826-4242; grounds open 1.5 hours prior to evening performances, one hour prior to matinees; 10-minute walk north of Baker Street Tube, near Queen Mary's Gardens within Regent's Park; detailed directions and more info at www.openairtheatre.org).

London's rougher evening-entertainment scene is thriving. Choose from a wide range of **fringe theater** and comedy acts (generally £12).

Music, Opera, and Dance

CONCERTS AT CHURCHES

For easy, cheap, or free concerts in historic churches, attend a **lunch concert,** especially:

- St. Bride's Church, with free half-hour lunch concerts twice a week at 13:15 (usually Tue and Fri—confirm in advance, church tel. 020/7427-0133, www.stbrides.com).
- St. James's at Piccadilly, with 50-minute concerts on Mon, Wed, and Fri at 13:10 (suggested £3.50 donation, info tel. 020/7734-4511, www.sjp.org.uk).
- St. Martin-in-the-Fields, offering concerts on Mon, Tue, and Fri at 13:00 (suggested £3.50 donation, church tel. 020/7766-1100, www.smitf.org).

St. Martin-in-the-Fields also hosts fine **evening concerts** by candlelight (£8-28, several nights a week at 19:30) and live jazz in its underground Café in the Crypt (£5.50-12, Wed at 20:00).

Evensong

One of my favorite experiences in Britain is to attend evensong at a great church. Evensong is an evening worship service that is typically sung rather than said (though some parts—including scripture readings, a few prayers, and a homily—are spoken). It follows the traditional Anglican service in the Book of Common Prayer, including prayers, scripture readings, canticles (sung responses), and hymns that are appropriate for the early evening—traditionally the end of the working day and before the evening meal. In major churches with resident choirs, this service is filled with quality, professional musical elements. A singing or chanting priest leads the service, and a choir—usually made up of both men's and boys' voices (to sing the lower and higher parts, respectively)—sings the responses. The choir usually sings a cappella, or is accompanied by organ. While regular attendees follow the service from memory, visitors—who are welcome—are given an order of service or a prayer book to help them follow along. (If you're not familiar with the order of service, watch the congregation to know when to stand, sit, and kneel.)

You can attend services in many of England's grandest churches—but be aware that evensong typically takes place in the small choir area—which is far more intimate than the main nave. (To see the full church in action, a concert is a better choice.) Evensong generally occurs daily between 17:00 and 18:00 (often two hours earlier on Sun)—check with individual churches for specifics. At smaller churches, evensong is sometimes spoken, not sung.

Note that evensong is not a performance—it's a somewhat somber worship service. If you enjoy worshipping in different churches, attending evensong can be a trip-capping highlight. But if regimented church services aren't your thing, consider getting a different music fix. Most major churches also offer organ or choral concerts—look for posted schedules or ask at the information desk or gift shop.

Evensong services are held at several churches, including St. Paul's Cathedral (see details on page 263), Westminster Abbey (see page 131), Southwark Cathedral (see page 92), and St. Bride's Church (Sun at 17:30, tel. 020/7427-0133, www.stbrides.com).

Free **organ recitals** are usually held on Sunday at 17:45 in Westminster Abbey (30 minutes, tel. 020/7222-5152). Many other churches have free concerts; ask for the *London Organ Concerts Guide* at the TI.

OTHER PERFORMANCES

Prom Concerts: For a fun classical event (mid-July–mid-Sept), attend a Prom Concert (shortened from "Promenade Concert") during the annual festival at the Royal Albert Hall. Nightly concerts are offered at give-a-peasant-some-culture prices (cheap standing-room "Promming" spots sold at the door, nearly-as-cheap restricted-view seats and pricier good ones sold in advance, Tube: South Kensington, www.bbc.co.uk/proms).

Opera: Some of the world's best opera is belted out at the prestigious Royal Opera House, near Covent Garden (www.roh. org.uk), and at the London Coliseum (English National Opera, St. Martin's Lane, Tube: Leicester Square, www.eno.org). Or consider taking in an unusual opera at the King's Head pub in Islington, home of London's Little Opera House (11 Upper Street, Tube: Angel, www.kingsheadtheatre.com). In the summer, Holland Park hosts open-air opera performances (Tube: Holland Park, www. operahollandpark.com).

Dance: The critically acclaimed Royal Ballet—where Margot Fonteyn and Rudolf Nureyev forged their famous partnership—is based at the Royal Opera House (www.roh.org.uk). Sadler's Wells Theatre features both international and UK-based dance troupes (Rosebery Avenue, Islington, Tube: Angel, www.sadlerswells. com).

Evening Sightseeing

Museum Visits: Many museums are open an evening or two during the week, offering fewer crowds. See the list on page 76.

Tours: Guided **walks** are offered several times a day and vary by theme: ancient London, museums, legal London, Dickens, Beatles, Jewish quarter, Christopher Wren, and so on. In the evening, expect a more limited choice: ghosts, Jack the Ripper, pubs, or literature. See a list of walking-tour companies on page 35.

To see the city illuminated at night, consider a **bus tour.** A 1.5-hour London by Night Sightseeing Tour leaves from Victoria Station and other points (see page 34).

Cruises: In summer, boats sail as late as 19:00 between Westminster Pier (near Big Ben) and the Tower of London. (For details, see page 39.)

A handful of outfits run expensive Thames River evening cruises with four-course meals and dancing. **London Showboat** offers the best value (nightly at 19:45, 3.5 hours, departs from Westminster Pier, reservations required, tel. 020/7740-0400, www.citycruises.com). Dinner cruises are also offered by **Bateaux London** (www.bateauxlondon.com).

Summer Evenings Along the South Bank

If you're visiting London in summer, consider hitting the South Bank neighborhood after hours.

Take a trip around the **London Eye** while the sun sets over the city (the wheel spins until late—last ascent at 20:30, later in July-Aug). Then cap your night with an evening walk along the pedestrian-only **Jubilee Walkway,** which runs east-west along the river. It's where Londoners go to escape the heat. This pleasant stretch of the walkway—lined with pubs and casual eateries—goes from the London Eye past Shakespeare's Globe to Tower Bridge (you can walk in either direction).

If you're in the mood for a movie, take in a flick at the **BFI Southbank,** located just across the river, alongside Waterloo Bridge. Run by the British Film Institute, the state-of-the-art theater shows mostly classic films, as well as art cinema (Tube: Waterloo or Embankment, check www.bfi.org.uk for schedules and prices).

Farther east along the South Bank is **The Scoop**—an outdoor amphitheater next to City Hall. It's a good spot for movies, concerts, dance, and theater productions throughout the summer—with Tower Bridge as a scenic backdrop. These events are free, nearly nightly, and family-friendly. For the latest event schedule, see www.morelondon.com and click on "Events" (next to City Hall, Riverside, The Queen's Walkway, Tube: London Bridge).

Winter Diversions

London dazzles year-round, so consider visiting in winter, when airfares and hotel rates are generally cheaper and there are fewer tourists. Despite drearier weather and shorter days, London's museums, theaters, concert halls, and pubs offer a warm, cozy welcome.

London at Christmas is especially appealing, with its buildings dressed in their holiday best. Many holiday traditions have their roots in 19th-century Victorian Britain. Beginning in the 1840s, Queen Victoria's German husband, Prince Albert, popularized the decorating of Christmas trees and the sending of Christmas cards. And what could be more traditional than seeing the setting of Charles Dickens' *A Christmas Carol* come to life? God bless us, every one.

NOVEMBER TO JANUARY

Pantomimes, or "pantos," are a British holiday tradition. Though they have nothing to do with silent mimes—and they don't mention Christmas—these campy fairy-tale plays entertain with outrageous costumes, sets, and dance numbers. Verbal participation is definitely encouraged, and it doesn't take long to learn the lines. Adults will laugh at the more risqué jokes; kids will giggle at the slapstick. Two London theaters that usually stage pantos are the Hackney Empire (291 Mare Street, northeast London, Tube: Bethnal Green, then 10 minutes on bus #106 or #254, tel. 020/8985-2424, www.hackneyempire.co.uk) or the Old Vic (corner of Waterloo Road and The Cut, southeast of Waterloo Station, Tube: Waterloo, tel. 0844-871-7628, www.oldvictheatre.com). For more about the panto tradition, see www.its-behind-you.com.

Get some exercise at the **outdoor ice rinks** at the London Eye, Somerset House, Tower of London, Natural History Museum, and Hampton Court Palace, among other locations (rental skates, generally mid-Nov-mid-Jan, reservations smart).

The **Hyde Park Winter Wonderland** offers kitschy carnival fun with a Ferris wheel, carousel, and other rides, as well as an ice rink and vendors selling silly hats and plenty of food and drink (late Nov-early Jan, southeast corner of park, Tube: Hyde Park Corner, www.hydeparkwinterwonderland.com).

Stroll around and enjoy the elaborate **light displays** and store windows on major shopping streets from mid-November to early January, especially on Oxford Street, Bond Street, Regent Street, and Brompton Road. Post-holiday sales start December 26 for many stores, including the famous Harrods January sale.

The Trafalgar Square **Christmas tree** is given to London every year from the people of Oslo, Norway, in appreciation for British help during World War II (lighting ceremony first Thu in Dec, stays up until Jan 6, www.london.gov.uk). Free carol concerts are held beneath the tree in December.

The **Geffrye Museum**'s 11 historic rooms are decorated for Christmas every year, highlighting holiday customs from the 17th century to today (free, see page 83).

The grand, red-velvet-draped **Royal Albert Hall** hosts seasonal concerts; ask about "carols by candlelight" events (Tube: South Kensington, box office tel. 0845-401-5034, www.royalalberthall.com).

Instead of visiting Santa Claus at the North Pole, British children see **Father Christmas** in his grotto. In London, the poshest Santa is at Harrods, and it may be worth reserving in advance

Christmas Travel Strategies

- There is no public transit in London (Tube, train, or bus) at all on Christmas Day, and reduced services on Christmas Eve and Boxing Day (Dec 26). For specifics, see www.tfl.gov.uk. Taxis are scarce, so be prepared for a long wait (£4 holiday surcharge, tel. 0871-871-8710). Better yet, bundle up and walk.
- If arriving at Heathrow Airport on Christmas Day, research transport from the airport to your hotel in advance. There is no Tube or train service, but buses may run between Heathrow and Paddington Station, and between Gatwick Airport and Victoria Station (likely every 15-30 minutes; confirm in advance at www.heathrowexpress.com and www.nationalrail.co.uk, holiday schedules available in Nov). Or you could try a Heathrow Shuttle van (book in advance, tel. 020/309-2771, www.heathrowshuttle.com).
- Pick a central location if staying over December 25, both to save money and avoid transportation difficulties. Stay somewhere with a kitchen (such as an apartment, hostel, or hotel room with kitchenette) so you can prepare some of your own meals. Don't forget to buy groceries before stores close on Christmas Eve. For tips on finding apartment rentals, see the Sleeping in London chapter.
- If you plan to eat out December 24-26 without reservations, go ethnic: Indian, Chinese, and Middle Eastern restaurants are usually open in Soho, Chinatown, along Edgware Road, or near the East End's Brick Lane.
- Expect closures. Museums are generally closed December 24-26, and smaller shops are usually closed December 26.

to avoid long lines (early Nov-Christmas Eve, reservations available online as early as Sept, fees for reservations and photos; Tube: Knightsbridge, tel. 020/7730-1234). Father Christmas has also been known to visit the Hyde Park Winter Wonderland (described earlier), where you can see him for free.

Nibble your way through **Borough Market,** where you'll find lots of seasonal and gourmet treats (open daily the week before Christmas, closed Dec 25-26; otherwise full market open Wed-Thu 10:00-17:00, Fri-10:00-18:00, Sat 8:00-17:00, closed Sun; surrounding food stalls open daily; Tube: London Bridge, tel. 020/7407-1002, www.boroughmarket.org.uk). While at the market, be sure to sample traditional favorites such as mulled wine, mince pie, Christmas cake, and Christmas pudding (see page 298).

Don't forget to pick up some **Christmas crackers** to give your holiday meals some extra bang. Not to be confused with something you eat, these fun party favors contain a paper crown, a teeny gift, and a corny joke. Buy them at grocery or department stores, find a friend, and pull hard.

Another popular holiday food event is the German **Christmas Market,** on the South Bank between the London Eye and the Royal Festival Hall (daily late Nov-Christmas Eve, Tube: Waterloo, www.southbankcentre.co.uk).

CHRISTMAS DAY

Spending December 25 in London? While almost everything is closed, and there is no public transit (not even the Tube), you still have a few options for getting out.

Popular **church services** are held both Christmas Eve and Christmas Day at Westminster Abbey, Westminster Cathedral, St. Paul's, and St. Martin-in-the-Fields, among other places. Warning: These draw large crowds, so ask in advance about when to arrive. (For example, you may need to reserve free tickets in advance—available in Nov—and wait in line several hours for the Abbey's 16:00 service on Christmas Eve; 23:30 service is less crowded; tel. 020/7222-5152, www.westminster-abbey.org/events/christmas.)

The Peter Pan Cup **swim race,** held in Hyde Park every Christmas morning since 1864, is named in honor of *Peter Pan* playwright J. M. Barrie, who presented the first cup. Only members of the local swimming club may compete, but spectators are welcome (9:00, south side of The Serpentine—a lake in the center of the park, www.serpentineswimmingclub.com). Break the ice by asking a local where to find the nearby Peter Pan statue.

London Walks offers two guided **walking tours** on December 25, with appropriate themes such as "Christmas Morning 1660" and "Charles Dickens' *A Christmas Carol*" (meet at Trafalgar Square Christmas tree, tel. 020/7624-3978 or recorded info tel. 020/7624-9255, www.walks.com).

Watch the Queen's annual **Christmas message** on the BBC at 15:00. If you miss it, you can watch it online on Her Majesty's Royal YouTube channel (www.youtube.com/TheRoyalChannel).

If your visit extends through the **New Year,** here are two events to be aware of: New Year's Eve **fireworks** from the London Eye attract at least 500,000 revelers to Trafalgar Square and the nearby riverbank, with required £10 tickets for good viewing spots sold months in advance (www.london.gov.uk/nye). Public transport is free after the festivities (generally 23:45-04:30). The next day, a **parade** featuring 10,000 performers snakes two miles from the Ritz Hotel, past Piccadilly Circus and Trafalgar Square, to Big Ben (free to stand, or pay for grandstand seats, 11:45-15:00, tel. 020/3275-0190, http://lnydp.com).

ENTERTAINMENT

Sporting Events

London offers many sporting events. Tennis, cricket, rugby, football (soccer), and horse races all take place within an hour of the city. Each June Wimbledon draws a half-million spectators (www.wimbledon.com), while big-name English Premier League soccer clubs—including Chelsea, Arsenal, Tottenham Hotspur, and West Ham United—take the pitch in London to sell-out crowds (www.premierleague.com). The two biggest horse races of the year take place in June: the Royal Ascot Races (www.ascot.co.uk) near Windsor and the Epsom Derby (www.epsomderby.co.uk) in Surrey are both once-in-a-lifetime experiences.

Securing tickets to anything sporting-related in London can be difficult—and expensive—for travelers. Check the official team or event website several months in advance; tickets can sell out within minutes of going on sale to the general public. Third-party booking companies such as SportsEvents 365 (www.sportsevents365.com) and Ticketmaster (www.ticketmaster.co.uk) often have tickets to popular events at a premium price—a godsend for die-hard fans. Many teams also offer affordable, well-run stadium tours—check your favorite side's official website for details. Even if you can't attend a sports event in person, consider cheering on the action in a London pub.

LONDON CONNECTIONS

London is well-connected with the rest of the planet: by train, plane, bus, and cruise ship. This chapter addresses your arrival and departure from the city.

By Plane

London has six airports; I've focused my coverage on the two most widely used—Heathrow and Gatwick—with a few tips for using the others (Stansted, Luton, London City, and Southend).

For accommodations at or near the major airports, see page 390. For more on flights within Europe, see page 570.

HEATHROW AIRPORT

Heathrow Airport is one of the world's busiest airports. Think about it: 73 million passengers a year on 470,000 flights from 185

destinations traveling on 80 airlines, like some kind of global maypole dance. For Heathrow's airport, flight, and transfer information, call the switchboard at 0844-335-1801, or visit the helpful website at www.heathrowairport.com (airport code: LHR).

Heathrow's terminals are numbered T-1 through T-5. Though T-1 is now closed for arrivals and departures, it still supports other terminals with baggage, and the newly renovated T-2 ("Queen's Terminal") will likely eventually expand into the old T-1 digs. Each terminal is served by different airlines and alliances; for example, T-5 is exclusively for British

London's Airports

Luton

Luton

Stansted

Not to Scale

ST. PANCRAS

PADDINGTON

LIVERPOOL STREET

Southend

Southend

Reading

Windsor
#71 & 77t

Tube

VICTORIA

D.L.R.

London City

To Bath

Rail Air Link

Heathrow

VICTORIA COACH STN.

London

EUROSTAR

Thames

Guildford

Gatwick

Ashford

To Paris

Rail
Eurostar Rail
Tube & D.L.R.
Bus

ALL BUSES ARE NATIONAL EXPRESS
UNLESS NOTED

To Brighton

English Channel

Air and Iberia Air flights, while T-2 serves mostly Star Alliance flights, such as United and Lufthansa. Screens posted throughout the airport identify which terminal each airline uses; this information should also be printed on your ticket or boarding pass.

To navigate, read signs and ask questions. You can walk between T-2 and T-3. From this central hub (called "Heathrow Central"), T-4 and T-5 split off in opposite directions (and are not walkable). The easiest way to travel between the T-2/T-3 cluster and either T-4 or T-5 is by Heathrow Express train (free, departs every 15-20 minutes). You can also take a shuttle bus (free, serves all terminals), or the Tube (requires a ticket, serves all terminals).

If you're flying out of Heathrow, it's critical to confirm which terminal your flight will use (look carefully at your ticket/boarding pass, check online, or call your airline in advance)—if it's T-4 or T-5, allow extra time. Taxi drivers generally know which terminal you'll need based on the airline, but bus drivers may not.

Services: Each terminal has an airport information desk (open long hours daily), car-rental agencies, exchange bureaus, ATMs, a pharmacy, a VAT refund desk (tel. 0845-872-7627, you must present the VAT claim form from the retailer here to get your tax rebate on purchased items—see page 540 for details), room-booking services, and baggage storage (£5/item up to 2 hours, £10/item for

2-24 hours, daily 5:00-23:00, www.left-baggage.co.uk). Heathrow offers both Wi-Fi (first 4 hours free) and pay Internet access points (in each terminal, check map for locations). You'll find a post office on the first floor of T-3 (departures area). Each terminal also has cheap eateries.

Heathrow's small **"TI"** (tourist info shop), even though it's a for-profit business, is worth a visit if you're nearby and want to pick up free information: a simple map, the *London Planner,* and brochures (long hours daily, 5-minute walk from T-3 in Tube station, follow signs to Underground; bypass queue for transit info to reach window for London questions).

Getting Between Heathrow and Downtown London

You have five basic options for traveling the 14 miles between Heathrow Airport and downtown London: Tube (about £5-6/person), bus (£6-9/person), direct shuttle bus (£20/person), express train with connecting Tube or taxi (about £10/person for slower train, £21.50/person for faster train, price does not include connecting Tube fare), or taxi (about £75/group). The one that works best for you will depend on your arrival terminal, your destination in central London, and your budget.

By Tube (Subway): The Tube takes you from any Heathrow terminal to downtown London in 50-60 minutes on the Piccadilly Line (6/hour, buy ticket at Tube station ticket window or self-service machine). Depending on your destination in London, you may need to transfer (for example, if headed to the Victoria Station neighborhood, transfer at Hammersmith to the District line and ride six more

stops). If you plan to use the Tube for transport in London, it makes sense to buy a Travelcard or pay-as-you-go Oyster card at the airport's Tube station ticket window. (For details on these passes, see page 25.) If your Travelcard covers only Zones 1-2, you'll need to pay a small supplement for the initial trip from Heathrow (Zone 6) to downtown.

If you're taking the Tube from downtown London *to* the airport, note that Piccadilly Line trains don't stop at every terminal. Trains either stop at T-4, then T-2/T-3 (also called Heathrow Central), in that order; or T-2/T-3, then T-5. When leaving central London on the Tube, allow extra time if going to T-4 or T-5, and check the reader board in the station to make sure that the train goes to the right terminal before you board.

By Bus: Most buses depart from the outdoor common area called the Central Bus Station, a five-minute walk from the T-2/T-3 complex. To connect between T-4 or T-5 and the Central Bus Station, ride the free Heathrow Express train or the shuttle buses.

National Express has regular service from Heathrow's Central Bus Station to Victoria Coach Station in downtown London, near several of my recommended hotels. While slow, the bus is affordable and convenient for those staying near Victoria Station (£6-9, 1-2/hour, less frequent from Victoria Station to Heathrow, 45-75 minutes depending on time of day, tel. 0871-781-8181, www.nationalexpress.com). A less-frequent National Express bus goes from T-5 directly to Victoria Coach Station.

By Shuttle: Heathrow Shuttle is an economical shuttle-bus service that goes to/from your hotel and your terminal at Heathrow. You'll share a minivan with other travelers who are also being picked up or dropped off, so it's not much of a time-savings over taking the Tube (£20/person, progressive discounts for groups of two or more, 1 child under age 10 travels free with 2 adults, runs daily 4:00-18:00, book at least 24 hours in advance, office open daily 7:00-20:00, tel. 020/309-2771, www.heathrowshuttle.com, info@heathrowshuttle.com). Another option is **Just Airports,** which offers a private car service between five London airports and the city center (from £32/car; see website for price quote, tel. 020/8900-1666, www.justairports.com).

By Train: Two different trains run between Heathrow Airport and London's Paddington Station. At Paddington Station, you're in the thick of the Tube system, with easy access to any of my recommended neighborhoods—my Paddington hotels are just outside the front door, and Notting Hill Gate is just two Tube stops away. The **Heathrow Connect** train is the slightly slower, much cheaper option, serving T-2/T-3 at a single station called Heathrow Central; use free transfers to get from either T-4 or T-5 to Heathrow Central (£10.10 one-way, £20.20 round-trip, 2/hour Mon-Sat, 1-2/hour Sun, 40 minutes, tel. 0345-604-1515, www.heathrowconnect.com).

The **Heathrow Express** train is fast and runs more frequently, but it's pricey (£21.50 one-way, £35 round-trip, £5 more if you buy your ticket on board, 4/hour; 15 minutes to downtown from Heathrow Central Station serving T-2/T-3, 21 minutes from T-5; for T-4 take free transfer to Heathrow Central; covered by BritRail pass, daily 5:10-23:48, tel. 0345-600-1515, www.heathrowexpress.co.uk). At the airport, you can use the Heathrow Express as a free transfer between terminals.

By Taxi: Taxis from the airport cost £45-75 to west and central London (one hour). For four people traveling together, this can be a reasonable option. Hotels can often line up a cab back to the airport for about £40.

GATWICK AIRPORT

More and more flights land at Gatwick Airport, which is half-way between London and the south coast (airport code: LGW, tel. 0844-892-0322, www.gatwickairport.com). Gatwick has two terminals, North and South, which are easily connected by a free monorail (two-minute trip, runs 24 hours daily). Note that boarding passes say "Gatwick N" or "Gatwick S" to indicate your terminal. British Airways flights generally use Gatwick North. The Gatwick Express trains (described next) stop only at Gatwick South. Schedules in each terminal show only arrivals and departures from that terminal.

Getting Between Gatwick and Downtown London: Gatwick Express trains are the best way into London from this airport. They shuttle conveniently between Gatwick South and London's Victoria Station, with many of my recommended hotels close by (£20 one-way, £35 round-trip, at least 10 percent cheaper if purchased online, 4/hour, 30 minutes, runs 5:00-24:00 daily, a few trains as early as 3:30, tel. 0345-850-1530, www.gatwickexpress. com). If you buy your tickets at the station before boarding, ask about possible group deals. (If you see others in the ticket line, suggest buying your tickets together.) When going *to* the airport, at Victoria Station note that Gatwick Express has its own ticket windows right by the platform (tracks 13 and 14).

A train also runs between Gatwick South and **St. Pancras International Station** (£10, 3-5/hour, 45-60 minutes, www. thetrainline.com)—useful for travelers taking the Eurostar train (to Paris or Brussels) or staying in the St. Pancras/King's Cross neighborhood.

Even slower, but cheap and handy to the Victoria Station neighborhood, you can take the **bus.** National Express runs a bus from Gatwick direct to Victoria Station (£10, at least hourly, 1.5 hours, tel. 0871-781-8181, www.nationalexpress.com); easyBus has one going to near the Earls Court Tube stop (£2-10 depending on how far ahead you book, 2-3/hour, www.easybus.co.uk).

LONDON'S OTHER AIRPORTS

Stansted Airport: From Stansted (airport code: STN, tel. 0844-335-1803, www.stanstedairport.com), you have several options for getting into or out of London. Two different **buses** connect the airport and London's Victoria Station neighborhood: National Express (£10-14, every 15 minutes, 2 hours, runs 24 hours a day, picks up and stops throughout London, ends at Victoria Coach

Station or Liverpool Street Station, tel. 0871-781-8181, www. nationalexpress.com) and Terravision (£10, 2/hour, 1.5-2 hours, ends at Green Line Coach Station just south of Victoria Station). Or you can take the faster, pricier Stansted Express **train** (£19, connects to London's Tube system at Tottenham Hale or Liverpool Street, 4/hour, 45 minutes, 4:30-23:00, www.stanstedexpress. com). Stansted is expensive by **cab**; figure £100-120 one-way from central London.

Luton Airport: For Luton (airport code: LTN, airport tel. 01582/405-100, www.london-luton.co.uk), the fastest way to go into London is by **train** to St. Pancras International Station (£15.50 one-way, 1-5/hour, 25-45 minutes—check schedule to avoid slower trains, tel. 0345-712-5678, www.eastmidlandstrains.co.uk); catch the 10-minute shuttle bus (every 10 minutes, £1.60) from outside the terminal to the Luton Airport Parkway Station. The Green Line express **bus** #757 runs to Buckingham Palace Road, just south of Victoria Station, and stops en route near the Baker Street Tube station—best if you're staying near Paddington Station or in North London (£10 one-way, 2-4/hour, 1-1.5 hours, runs 24 hours, tel. 0344-800-4411, www.greenline.co.uk). If you're sleeping at Luton, consider easyHotel (see listing on page 391).

London City and Southend Airports: To get into the city center from London City Airport (airport code: LCY, tel. 020/7646-0088, www.londoncityairport.com), take the Docklands Light Railway (DLR) to the Bank Tube station, which is one stop east of St. Paul's on the Central Line (less than £5 one-way, covered by Travelcard, a bit cheaper with an Oyster card, 22 minutes, www.tfl.gov.uk/dlr). Some easyJet flights land farther out, at Southend Airport (airport code: SEN, tel. 01702/538-500, www. southendairport.com). Trains connect this airport to London's Liverpool Street Station (£16.70 one-way, 3-8/hour, 55 minutes, www.abelliogreateranglia.co.uk).

CONNECTING LONDON'S AIRPORTS BY BUS

A handy **National Express bus** runs between Heathrow, Gatwick, Stansted, and Luton airports—easier than having to cut through the center of London—although traffic can be bad and can increase travel times (tel. 0871-781-8181, www.nationalexpress.com).

From Heathrow Airport to: Gatwick Airport (1-6/hour, about 1.5 hours—but allow at least three hours between flights, £25), **Stansted Airport** (1 direct bus every 2 hours, about 1.5 hours, £27), **Luton Airport** (roughly hourly, 1-1.5 hours, £23).

By Train

London, the country's major transportation hub, has a different train station for each region. There are nine main stations (see the map):

Euston—Serves northwest England, North Wales, and Scotland.

St. Pancras International—Serves north and south England, plus the Eurostar to Paris or Brussels (see "Crossing the Channel," later).

King's Cross—Serves northeast England and Scotland, including York and Edinburgh.

Liverpool Street—Serves east England, including Essex and Harwich.

London Bridge—Serves south England, including Brighton.

Waterloo—Serves south England, including Salisbury and Southampton.

Victoria—Serves Gatwick Airport, Canterbury, Dover, and Brighton.

Paddington—Serves south and southwest England, including Heathrow Airport, Windsor, Bath, South Wales, and the Cotswolds.

Marylebone—Serves southwest and central England, including Stratford-upon-Avon.

In addition, London has several smaller train stations that you're less likely to use, such as **Charing Cross** (serves southeast England, including Dover) and **Blackfriars** (serves Brighton).

Any train station has schedule information, can make reservations, and can sell tickets for any destination. Most stations offer a baggage-storage service (£10/bag for 24 hours, look for *left luggage* signs); because of long security lines, it can take a while to check or pick up your bag (www.left-baggage.co.uk). For more details on the services available at each station, see www.nationalrail.co.uk/stations. UK train and bus info is available at www.traveline.org.uk. For information on tickets and rail passes, see page 567 of the Practicalities chapter.

TRAIN CONNECTIONS FROM LONDON
To Points West
From Paddington Station to: Windsor (Windsor & Eton Central Station, 2-3/hour, 35 minutes, easy change at Slough), **Bath** (2/hour, 1.5 hours; also consider a guided Evan Evans tour by bus—see page 465), **Oxford** (2/hour direct, 1 hour, more with transfer), **Penzance** (every 1-2 hours, 5 hours, possible change in Plymouth), and **Cardiff** (2/hour, 2 hours).

London's Major Train Stations

(map shows:)

To North Wales, Glasgow & Luton

To Cambridge, York & Edinburgh

To Harwich & Stansted

To Stratford-upon-Avon

To Canterbury & Dover and via Eurostar: Paris & Brussels

RAF MUSEUM LONDON

To Heathrow Airport, Windsor (via Slough), Bath, S. Wales, Cotswolds & Oxford

ST. PANCRAS INT'L

MARYLE-BONE

EUSTON

KING'S CROSS

STRATFORD INT'L

LONDON CITY AIRPORT

PADDINGTON

TRAF. SQ.

LIVERPOOL STREET

DOCKLANDS

LONDON

WATER-LOO

02 ARENA

VICTORIA

LONDON BRIDGE

CANARY WHARF ON ISLE OF DOGS

GREENWICH

Thames River

Kew Gardens

To Brighton

WIMBLEDON

= Central London

HAMPTON COURT PALACE

To Gatwick Airport, Canterbury, Dover & Brighton

To Salisbury & Windsor (via Staines)

5 Kilometers

5 Miles

To Points North

From King's Cross Station: Trains run at least hourly, stopping in **York** (2 hours), **Durham** (3 hours), and **Edinburgh** (4.5 hours). Trains to **Cambridge** also leave from here (2/hour, 45 minutes).

From Euston Station to: **Conwy** (nearly hourly, 3.5 hours, transfer in Chester), **Liverpool** (at least hourly, 2-3 hours, more with transfer), **Blackpool** (hourly, 3 hours, transfer at Preston), **Keswick** (hourly, 4 hours, transfer to bus at Penrith), and **Glasgow** (1-2/hour, 5 hours).

From London's Other Stations

Trains run between London and **Canterbury,** leaving from St. Pancras International Station and arriving in Canterbury West (1-2/hour, 1 hour), as well as from London's Victoria Station and arriving in Canterbury East or West (2/hour, 2 hours).

Direct trains leave for **Stratford-upon-Avon** from Marylebone Station, located near the southwest corner of Regent's Park (5/day direct, more with transfers, 2 hours).

To Other Destinations: Greenwich (from Bank or Monument Tube stop take the DLR to Cutty Sark Station, 6/hour, 20

Public Transportation near London

Rail
Bus
Boat

Area covered by
London Plus Pass

30 Kilometers

30 Miles
(approx. scale)

Note:
Bus Lines Follow
Most Rail Lines

FRANCE

minutes), **Windsor** (to Windsor & Eton Riverside Station, 2/hour, 50 minutes, from Waterloo Station), **Dover** (hourly, 1 hour, from St. Pancras International Station; also hourly, 2 hours, direct from Victoria Station or Charing Cross Station), **Brighton** (4-5/hour, 1.5 hours, direct from Victoria Station and Blackfriars Station), **Portsmouth** (3/hour, 2 hours, direct from Waterloo Station, a few with change in Clapham Junction from Victoria Station), and **Salisbury** (2/hour, 1.5 hours, from Waterloo Station). For more information on trains to **Windsor, Cambridge, or Salisbury** (connecting to Stonehenge), check the Day Trips chapter.

By Bus

Buses are slower but considerably cheaper than trains for reaching destinations around Britain and beyond. Most depart from **Victoria Coach Station,** which is one long block south of Victoria Station (near many recommended accommodations, Tube: Victoria). Inside the station, you'll find basic eateries, kiosks, and a helpful information desk stocked with schedules and staff ready to point you to your bus or answer any questions. Watch your bags carefully—luggage thieves thrive at the station.

Ideally you'll buy your tickets online (for tips on buying tickets and taking buses, see page 567 of the Practicalities chapter). But if you must buy one at the station, try to arrive an hour before the bus departs, or drop by the day before. Ticketing machines are scattered around the station (separate machines for National Express/Eurolines and Megabus; you can buy either for today or for tomorrow); there's also a ticket counter near gate 21. For UK train and bus info, check www.traveline.org.uk.

National Express buses go to: **Bath** (nearly hourly, 3-3.5 hours), **Oxford** (2/hour, 2 hours), **Cambridge** (every 60-90 minutes, 2 hours), **Canterbury** (about hourly, 2 hours), **Dover** (about hourly, 3 hours), **Brighton** (hourly, 2 hours), **Penzance** (5/day, 9-10 hours, overnight available), **Cardiff** (hourly, 3.5 hours), **Stratford-upon-Avon** (3/day, 3.5 hours), **Liverpool** (8/day direct, 5-6 hours, overnight available), **Blackpool** (4/day direct, 6.5 hours, overnight available), **York** (4/day direct, 5.5 hours), **Durham** (3/day direct, 6-8 hours, train is better), **Glasgow** (2-4/day direct, 8-9 hours, train is much better), **Edinburgh** (2/day direct, 9 hours, go by train instead).

To Dublin, Ireland: This bus/boat journey, operated by Eurolines, takes 10-12 hours (£35-40, 1/day, departs Victoria Coach Station at 18:00, check in with passport one hour before). Consider a cheap 1-hour Ryanair flight instead.

To the Continent: Especially in summer, buses run to destinations all over Europe, including Paris, Amsterdam, Brussels, and Germany (sometimes crossing the Channel by ferry, other times through the Chunnel). For any international connection, you need to check in with your passport one hour before departure. For details, call 0871-781-8181 or visit www.eurolines.co.uk. For information on crossing the Channel by bus, see page 469.

Crossing the Channel

BY EUROSTAR TRAIN

The Eurostar zips you (and up to 800 others in 18 sleek cars) from downtown London to downtown Paris or Brussels at 190 mph in 2.5 hours (1-2/hour). The tunnel crossing is a 20-minute, silent, 100 mph nonevent. Your ears won't even pop.

More high-speed connections are coming: Eurostar already runs direct service to Lyon, Avignon, and Marseille (5/week in summer, less frequent off-season). Germany's national railroad is looking to run bullet trains between Frankfurt, Amsterdam, and London, while Eurostar is hoping to expand into Amsterdam (with stops in Antwerp and at Amsterdam's airport) sometime in 2017.

Eurostar Tickets and Fares: The Eurostar is not covered by rail passes and requires a separate, reserved, nonrefundable train ticket. A one-way ticket between London and Paris or Brussels runs about $60-200 (Standard), $160-310 (Standard Premier), and $400 (Business Premier). Fares depend on how far ahead you reserve and whether you're eligible for any discounts—avail-

able for children (under age 12), youths (under 26), seniors (60 or older), round-trip travelers, and rail-pass holders. You can book tickets 4-9 months in advance. Tickets can be exchanged before the scheduled departure for a fee (about $45 plus the cost of any price increase), but only Business Premier class allows any refund.

You can buy tickets online using the print-at-home eticket option (see www.ricksteves.com/eurostar or www.eurostar.com). You can also order by phone through Rail Europe (US tel. 800-387-6782) for home delivery before you go, or through Eurostar (tel. 0843-218-6186, priced in euros) to pick up at the station. In Britain, tickets are issued only at the Eurostar office in St. Pancras International Station. In continental Europe, you can buy Eurostar tickets at any major train station in any country or at any travel agency that handles train tickets (expect a booking fee). Discount tickets for rail-pass holders (which can sell out) are available at Eurostar departure stations, through US agents, or by phone with Eurostar, but they may be harder to get at other train stations and travel agencies.

Those traveling on short notice—when only the costliest Eurostar tickets are available—can consider an "unescorted tour" to Paris, Brussels, or Bruges that includes Eurostar fare (sold by a tour company called BritainShrinkers, about £129 for one-day Paris "tour," Mon-Sat, includes one-day Paris Visite travel card; tel. 020/7713-1311, www.britainshrinkers.com).

Taking the Eurostar: Eurostar trains depart from and arrive at London's St. Pancras International Station. Check in at least 30 minutes in advance (remember that times listed on tickets are local

Building the Chunnel

The toughest obstacle to building a tunnel under the English Channel was overcome in 1986, when longtime rivals Britain and France reached an agreement to build it together. Britain began in Folkestone, France in Calais, planning a rendezvous in the middle.

By 1988, specially made machines three football fields long were boring 26-foot-wide holes under the ground. The dirt they hauled out became landfill in Britain and a hill in France. Crews crept forward 100 feet a day until June of 1991, when French and English workers broke through and shook hands midway across the Channel—the tunnel was complete. Rail service began in 1994.

The Chunnel is 31 miles long (24 miles of it underwater) and 26 feet wide. It sits 130 feet below the seabed in a chalky layer of sediment. It's segmented into three separate tunnels—two for trains (one in each direction) and one for service and ventilation. The walls are concrete panels and rebar fixed to the rock around it. Sixteen-thousand-horsepower engines pull 850 tons of railcars and passengers at speeds up to 100 mph through the tunnel.

The ambitious project—the world's longest undersea tunnel—helped to show the European community that cooperation between nations could benefit everyone.

times; Britain's time zone is one hour earlier than France and Belgium's). Pass through airport-like security, show your passport to customs officials, and locate your departure gate (shown on a TV monitor). The waiting area has shops, newsstands, horrible snack bars, and cafés (bring food for the trip from elsewhere), free Wi-Fi, and a currency-exchange booth.

CROSSING THE CHANNEL WITHOUT EUROSTAR

For speed and affordability, look into **cheap flights** (see page 570). Or consider the following old-fashioned ways of crossing the Channel (cheaper but more complicated and time-consuming than the Eurostar).

By Train and Boat: To reach **Paris,** take a train from London's St. Pancras International Station to Dover's Priory Station (hourly, 1 hour), then catch a P&O ferry to Calais, France (1/hour, 1.5 hours, www.poferries.com). From Calais, take the TGV train to Paris.

For **Amsterdam,** consider Stena Line's Dutchflyer service, which combines train and ferry tickets. Trains go from London's Liverpool Street Station to the port of Harwich (hourly, 2 hours, most transfer in Manningtree). From Harwich, Stena Line ferries sail to Hoek van Holland (8 hours), where you can catch a train to Amsterdam (book ahead for best price, 13 hours total, www. stenaline.co.uk, Dutch train info at www.ns.nl). For additional European ferry info, visit www.aferry.to.

By Bus and Boat: The bus from London's Victoria Coach Station goes direct to **Paris** (4-5/day, 8-10 hours), **Brussels** (4/day, 9 hours), or **Amsterdam** (4/day, 12 hours) via ferry or Chunnel (day or overnight; around £60-70 one-way, cheaper in advance, tel. 0870-514-3219, www.eurolines.co.uk).

By Cruise Ship

Many cruises begin, end, or call at one of several English ports offering easy access to London. Cruise lines favor two ports: Southampton, 80 miles southwest of London; and Dover, 80 miles southeast of London. If you don't want to bother with public transportation, most cruise lines offer transit-only excursion packages into London. For more details, see my *Rick Steves Northern European Cruise Ports* guidebook.

SOUTHAMPTON CRUISE PORT

Within Southampton's sprawling port (www.cruisesouthampton. com), cruises use two separate dock areas, each with two terminals.

To reach London, it's about a 1.5-hour train ride. To get to Southampton Central Station from the cruise port, you can take a taxi or walk 10-15 minutes to the public ferry dock (Town Quay), where you can ride the Citylink bus to the train station. From there, trains depart at least every 30 minutes for London's Waterloo Station.

If you have time to kill in port, consider taking the train to Portsmouth (50 minutes), best known for its Historic Dockyard and many nautical sights, or stick around Southampton and visit the excellent SeaCity Museum, with a beautifully presented exhibit about the *Titanic*, which set sail from here on April 10, 1912.

DOVER CRUISE PORT

Little Dover has a huge port. Cruises put in at the Western Docks, with two terminals.

Trains go from Dover Priory Station to London in 1-2 hours. From either cruise terminal, the best way into town (or to the train station) is by taxi or shuttle bus (take it to Market Square, then walk 15 minutes to the train station). From Dover's station, a fast train leaves for London's St. Pancras International Station (2/hour, 1 hour); slower trains go to either

Victoria Station or Charing Cross Station (each 1-2/hour, 2 hours).

If you have extra time in port, Dover Castle, perched upon chalk cliffs, is well worth a visit for its WWII-era Secret Wartime Tunnels. Or take the train to Canterbury (2/hour, less than 30 minutes), notable for its important cathedral and fine historic core.

DAY TRIPS FROM LONDON

Windsor • Cambridge • Stonehenge

Windsor, Cambridge, and Stonehenge are three great day-trip possibilities near London. Any one of these very different but equally enjoyable destinations makes for an entertaining visit from London.

The primary residence of Her Majesty the Queen, **Windsor** hosts a castle that's regally lived-in, yet open to the public. This is simply a charming town to relax in—and its proximity to Heathrow Airport (60 minutes by train west of London) makes Windsor easy to combine with a flight into or out of London. Nearby is an oddball collection of intriguing sights, including Legoland Windsor, Eton College (Britain's most elite high school), Ascot

Racecourse (for horse racing), and Highclere Castle, where the TV series *Downton Abbey* is filmed.

Britain's venerable Cambridge University is mixed into the delightful town of **Cambridge,** offering a mellow, fun-to-explore townscape with a big-league university.

Stonehenge, the world's most famous rock group, sits lonesome yet adored in a mysterious field 90 miles southwest of London.

Although I only cover these three destinations in this book, London's convenient public transit can easily whisk you to a wealth of other day-trip destinations: Bath (Roman ruins and Georgian townhouses), Canterbury (cathedral), Dover (castle-crowned chalk cliffs), Portsmouth (treasure trove of maritime history), Stratford-upon-Avon (all things Shakespeare), Warwick (fine medieval castle), Oxford (another classic university town), and Brighton (beach and pier). For details, see *Rick Steves England*.

GETTING AROUND

By Train: Take advantage of British Rail's discounts for day-trippers from London. The "off-peak day return" ticket is a round-trip fare that costs virtually the same as one-way, provided you depart London outside rush hour (usually after 9:30 on weekdays and anytime Sat-Sun). Be sure to specifically ask for the "day return" ticket (round-trip within a single day) rather than the more expensive standard "return." You can also save a little money if you purchase tickets before 18:00 the day before your trip.

By Train Tour: London Walks offers a variety of "Daytrips from London" tours year-round by train, including a Salisbury and Stonehenge tour (see page 506), as well as a Cambridge itinerary (see page 36 for more on London Walks).

Windsor

Windsor, a compact and easy walking town of about 30,000 people, originally grew up around the royal residence. In 1070, William the Conqueror continued his habit of kicking Saxons out of their various settlements, taking over what the locals called "Windlesora" (meaning "riverbank with a hoisting winch")—which eventually became "Windsor." William built the first fortified castle on a chalk hill above the Thames; later kings added on to his early designs, rebuilding and expanding the castle and surrounding gardens.

By setting up their primary residence here, modern monarchs increased Windsor's popularity and prosperity—most notably, Queen Victoria, whose stern statue glares at you as you approach the castle. After her death, Victoria rejoined her beloved husband, Albert, in the Royal Mausoleum at Frogmore House, a mile south of the castle in a private section of the Home Park (house and mausoleum rarely open). The current Queen considers Windsor her primary residence, and the one where she feels most at home. She generally hangs her crown here on weekends, using it as an escape from her workaday grind at Buckingham Palace

in the city. You can tell if Her Majesty is in residence by checking to see which flag is flying above the round tower: If it's the royal standard (a red, yellow, and blue flag) instead of the Union Jack, the Queen is at home.

While 99 percent of visitors just come to tour the castle and go, some enjoy spending the night. Daytime crowds trample Windsor's charm, which is most evident when the tourists are gone. Consider overnighting here—parking and access to Heathrow Airport are easy, and an evening at the horse races (on Mondays) is hoof-pounding, heart-thumping fun.

GETTING TO WINDSOR

By Train: Windsor has two train stations—Windsor & Eton Central and Windsor & Eton Riverside. London's Paddington Station connects with Windsor & Eton Central (2-3/hour, 35 minutes, easy change at Slough; £9.90 one-way standard class, £10-13 same-day return, www.firstgreatwestern.co.uk). London's Waterloo Station connects with Windsor & Eton Riverside (2/hour, no changes but slower—50 minutes; £10-13 one-way standard class, £16-20 same-day return, info tel. 0345-748-4950, www.nationalrail.co.uk).

If you're day-tripping into London *from* Windsor, ask at the train station about combining a same-day return train ticket with a Travelcard transit pass (£13-22, lower price for travel after 9:30, includes some London sightseeing discounts—ask or look for brochure at station, www.daysoutguide.co.uk).

By Bus: Green Line buses #701 and #702 run from London's Victoria Colonnades (between the Victoria train and coach stations) to the Parish Church stop on Windsor's High Street, before continuing on to Legoland (1-2/hour, 1.5 hours to Windsor, £5.50-9.50 one-way, £9-16 round-trip, prices vary depending on time of day, tel. 0871-200-2233, www.firstgroup.com).

By Car: Windsor is about 20 miles from London and just off Heathrow Airport's landing path. The town (and then the castle and Legoland) is well-signposted from the M-4 motorway. It's a convenient first stop if you're arriving at Heathrow and renting a car there and saving London until the end of your trip.

From Heathrow Airport: First Bus Company's buses #71 and #77 run between Terminal 5 and Windsor, dropping you in the center of town at the Parish Church stop on High Street (about £8, 1-3/hour, 50 minutes, tel. 01753/524-144, www.firstgroup.com). London black cabs can (and do) charge whatever they like from Heathrow to Windsor; avoid them by calling a local cab company, such as Windsor Radio Cars (£26, includes 40 minutes waiting time—handy if you checked your luggage, tel. 01753/677-677, www.windsorcars.com).

Orientation to Windsor

Windsor's pleasant pedestrian shopping zone litters the approach to its famous palace with fun temptations. You'll find most shops and restaurants around the castle on High and Thames Streets, and down the pedestrian Peascod Street (PESS-cot), which runs perpendicular to High Street.

TOURIST INFORMATION

The TI is immediately adjacent to Windsor & Eton Central Station, in the Windsor Royal Shopping Centre's Old Booking Hall (June-Sept Mon-Sat 9:30-17:00, Sun 10:00-16:00; Oct-May Sun-Fri 10:00-16:00, Sat 10:00-17:00; tel. 01753/743-900, www.windsor.gov.uk). The TI sells discount tickets to Legoland and is extremely enthusiastic about their Royal Windsor Historical Tour.

ARRIVAL IN WINDSOR

By Train: Whichever train station you arrive at, you're only a five-minute walk to the castle. From Windsor & Eton Central, walk through the Windsor Royal Shopping Centre (which houses the TI), and up the hill to the castle. From Windsor & Eton Riverside, you'll see the castle as you exit—just follow the wall to the ticket office.

By Car: To get into town, follow signs from the M-4 motorway for pay-and-display parking in the center. River Street Car Park is closest to the castle, but it's pricey and often full. The cheaper, bigger Alexandra Car Park (near the riverside Alexandra Gardens) is farther west. To walk to the town center from the Alexandra Car Park, head east through the tour-bus parking lot toward the castle. At the souvenir shop, walk up the stairs (or take the elevator) and cross the overpass to Windsor & Eton Central Station. Just beyond the station, you'll find the TI in the Windsor Royal Shopping Centre.

The cheapest parking option is the King Edward VII Avenue car-park-and-ride, east of the castle on B-470 (£5 for 5 or more hours; includes shuttle bus into town).

HELPFUL HINTS

Internet Access: You'll find free Wi-Fi at the **library,** located on Bachelors' Acre, between Peascod and Victoria Streets (public computer-£1.50/hour, daily, tel. 01753/743-940, www.rbwm. gov.uk).

Supermarkets: Pick up picnic supplies at **Marks & Spencer** (Mon-Sat 8:00-19:00, Sun 11:00-17:00, 130 Peascod Street, tel. 01753/852-266) or at **Waitrose** (Mon-Fri 8:00-21:00, Sat 8:00-20:00, Sun 11:00-17:00, King Edward Court Shopping Centre, just south of Windsor & Eton Central Station, tel. 01753/860-565). Just outside the castle, you'll find long benches near the statue of Queen Victoria—great for people-watching while you munch.

Bike Rental: Extreme Motion, near the river in Alexandra Gardens, rents 21-speed mountain bikes (£12.50/4 hours, £18/day, includes helmet, £150 credit-card deposit required, bring passport as ID, summer daily 10:00-18:00, Sat-Sun only off-season, tel. 01753/830-220).

Sights in Windsor

▲▲WINDSOR CASTLE

Windsor Castle, the official home of England's royal family for 900 years, claims to be the largest and oldest occupied castle in

the world. Thankfully, touring it is simple. You'll see sprawling grounds, lavish staterooms, a crowd-pleasing dollhouse, a gallery of Michelangelo and Leonardo da Vinci drawings, and an exquisite Perpendicular Gothic chapel.

Cost: £19.20, includes entry to castle grounds and all exhibits inside.

Tickets are valid for one year of reentry (get it stamped at the exit).

Crowd Control: Ticket lines can be long in summer. You can expect the worst crowds between 11:00-13:00 any time of year. Avoid the wait by purchasing tickets in advance online at www. royalcollection.org.uk (collect them at the prepaid ticket window),

DAY TRIPS

Windsor

To Heathrow Airport & London via M-4

- - - Changing of the Guard Route

To Slough & London (Paddington Station)

ETONWICK RD.

KEATS LN.

ETON COLLEGE

To London (Waterloo Station)

HIGH STREET

SOUTH MEADOW LN.

POST

Home Park (Public)

ROMNEY LOCK RD.

KING EDWARD VII AVE

MEADOW LN.

ETON CT.   ETON SQ.

N

WINDSOR BRIDGE (PEDESTRIAN)

Thames River

BARRY AVE.

BIKE RENTAL
Alexandra Gardens

DUKE ST.

ALMA RD.

BOSWELL RD.

BOAT TRIPS

RIVER ST.

THAMES AVE.

RIVERSIDE STATION

NORMAN GATE

ST. GEORGE'S CHAPEL

STATE APARTMENTS

CENTRAL STATION

THAMES ST.

B

Middle Ward

ROUND TOWER

Upper Ward

WINDSOR CASTLE

To Royal Windsor Racecourse

ARTHUR RD.

GOSWELL HILL

Lower Ward

CASTLE HILL

CASTLE TICKETS

OXFORD RD.

SHOPPING CENTER

GUILDHALL & MUSEUM

BEXLEY ST.

CLARENCE CRES.

CHARLES ST.

PEASCOD STREET

QUEEN VICTORIA STATUE

ST. JOHN

HIGH STREET

PARK ST.

POST

BACH ACRE

B

CLARENCE RD.

VICTORIA ST.

SHEET ST.

Home Park (Private)

DORSET RD.

ROAD

RUSSELL ST.

ALBANY RD.

200 Meters

CLAREMONT

ALEXANDRA RD.

GUARD BARRACKS

KING'S RD.

200 Yards

ALMA

ST. MARK'S RD.

ST. LEONARDS RD.

GROVE RD.

HELENA RD.

LONG WALK (PUBLIC)

QUEENS RD.

OSBORNE RD.

ALMA RD.

To Legoland

FRANCES RD.

ADELAIDE SQ.

To Ascot via A-332

1. MGallery Windsor Castle Hotel
2. Langton House B&B
3. To Park Farm B&B
4. 76 Duke Street B&B
5. Dee & Steve's B&B
6. Crown & Cushion Rooms
7. Bel & The Dragon
8. Cornucopia Bistro
9. The Duchess of Cambridge Pub
10. Meimo Restaurant
11. Saffron Restaurant
12. Grocery Stores (2)
13. Library (Internet Access)

or in person at the Buckingham Palace ticket office in London. There's nowhere in Windsor to buy advance tickets.

Hours: Grounds and most interiors open daily March-Oct 9:30-17:15, Nov-Feb 9:45-16:15, except St. George's Chapel, which is closed Sun to tourists (but open to worshippers; wait at the exit gate to be escorted in). Last entry to grounds and St. George's Chapel 75 minutes before closing. Last entry to State Apartments and Queen Mary's Dolls' House 45 minutes before closing.

Possible Closures: On rare occasions when the Queen is entertaining guests, the State Apartments close (and tickets are reduced to £10.40). Sometimes the entire castle closes. It's smart to call ahead or check the website (especially in mid-June) to make sure everything is open when you want to go. While you're at it, confirm the Changing of the Guard schedule.

Tours: An included audioguide (dry, reverent, informative) covers both the grounds and interiors. For a good overview—and an opportunity to ask questions—consider the free 30-minute guided walk around the grounds (usually 2/hour, schedule posted next to audioguide desk). The official £5 guidebook is full of gorgeous images and makes a fine souvenir, but the information within is covered by the audioguide and tour.

Photography: Taking photographs inside any of the buildings is strictly forbidden.

Information: Tel. 020/7766-7324, www.royalcollection.org.uk.

Changing of the Guard: The Changing of the Guard takes

place Monday through Saturday at 11:00 (April-July) and on alternating days the rest of the year (check website to confirm schedule; get there by 10:30 or earlier if you expect a line for tickets). There is no Changing of the Guard on Sundays or in very wet weather. The fresh guards, led by a marching band, leave their barracks on Sheet Street and march up High Street, hanging a right at Victoria, then a left into the castle's Lower Ward, arriving at about 11:00. After about a half-hour, the tired guards march back the way the new ones came. To watch the actual ceremony inside the castle, you'll need to have already bought your ticket, entered the grounds, and staked out a spot. Alternatively, you could wait for them to march by on High Street or on the lower half of Castle Hill.

Evensong: An evensong takes place in the chapel nightly at 17:15 (free for worshippers, line up at exit gate to be admitted).

The Order of the Garter

In addition to being the royal residence, Windsor is the home of the Most Noble Order of the Garter—Britain's most prestigious chivalrous order. The castle's history is inexorably tied to this order.

Founded in 1348 by King Edward III and his son (the "Black Prince"), the Order of the Garter was designed to honor returning Crusaders. This was a time when the legends of King Arthur and the Knights of the Round Table were sweeping England, and Edward III fantasized that Windsor could be a real-life Camelot. (He even built the Round Tower as an homage to the Round Table.)

The order's seal illustrates the story of the order's founding and unusual name: a cross of St. George encircled with a belt and a French motto loosely translated as "Shame be upon he who thinks evil of it." Supposedly while the king was dancing with a fair maiden, her garter slipped off onto the floor; in an act of great chivalry, he rescued her from embarrassment by picking it up and uttering those words.

The Order of the Garter continues to the present day as the single most prestigious honor in the United Kingdom. There can be only 24 knights at one time (perfect numbers for splitting into two 12-man jousting teams), plus the sitting monarch and the Prince of Wales. Aside from royals and the nobility, past Knights of the Garter have included Winston Churchill, Bernard "Monty" Montgomery, and Ethiopian Emperor Haile Selassie. In 2008, Prince William became only the 1,000th knight in the order's 660-year history. Other current members include various ex-military officers, former British Prime Minister John Major, and a member of the Colman's Mustard family.

The patron of the order is St. George—the namesake of the State Apartments' most sumptuous hall and of the castle's own chapel. Both of these spaces—the grandest in all of Windsor—are designed to celebrate and to honor the Order of the Garter.

Best View: While you can get great views of the castle from any direction, the classic views are from the long, wooded walkway called the Long Walk, which stretches south of the palace and is open to the public.

Eating: There are no real eateries inside (other than shops selling gifty boxes of chocolates and bottled water), so consider bringing a snack with you.

● Self-Guided Tour

After buying your ticket and going through the security check-point, pick up your audioguide and start strolling along the path through...

The Grounds: Head up the hill, enjoying the first of many fine castle views you'll see today. The tower-topped, conical hill on your left represents the historical core of the castle. William the Conqueror built this motte (artificial mound) and bailey (fortified stockade around it) in 1080—his first castle in England. Among the later monarchs who spiffed up Windsor were Edward III (flush with French war booty, he made it a palace fit for a 14th-century king), Charles II (determined to restore the monarchy properly in the 1660s), and George IV (Britain's "Bling King," who financed many such vanity projects in the 1820s). On your right, the circular bandstand platform has a seal of the Order of the Garter, which has important ties to Windsor (see sidebar).

Passing through the small gate, you approach the stately St. George's Gate. Peek through here to the Upper Ward's **Quadrangle,** which is surrounded by the State Apartments (across the field) and the Queen's private apartments (to the right).

Turn left and follow the wall. On your right-hand side, you enjoy great views of the **Round Tower** atop that original motte;

running around the base of this artificial hill is the delightful, peaceful garden of the castle governor. The unusual design of this castle has not one "bailey" (castle yard), but three, which today make up Windsor's Upper Ward (where the Queen lives, which we just saw), Middle Ward (the ecclesiastical heart of the complex, with St. George's Chapel, which you'll soon pass on the left), and Lower Ward (residences for castle workers).

Continue all the way around this mini-moat to the **Norman Gate,** which once held a prison. Walking under the gate, look up to see the bottom of the portcullis that could be dropped to seal off the inner courtyard. Three big holes are strategically situated for dumping boiling goo or worse on whoever was outside the gate. Past the gate are even finer views of the Quadrangle we just saw from the other side.

Do a 180 and head back toward the Norman Gate, but before you reach it, go down the staircase on the right. You'll emerge onto a fine **terrace** overlooking the flat lands all around. It's easy to understand why this was a strategic place to build a castle. That's Eton College across the Thames. Imagine how handy it's been for royals to be able to ship off their teenagers to an elite prep school so close that they could easily keep an eye on them...literally. The power-plant cooling towers in the distance mark the workaday burg of Slough (rhymes with "plow," immortalized as the setting for Britain's original version of *The Office*).

• *Turn right and wander along the terrace. You'll likely see two lines. The long one leads to Queen Mary's Dolls' House, then to the State Apartments. The short line skips the dollhouse and heads directly to the apartments. Read the following descriptions and decide if the dollhouse is worth waiting for (or try again later in the day, when the line sometimes eases up). You can see the Drawings Gallery and the China Museum either way.*

Queen Mary's Dolls' House: This palace in miniature (1:12 scale, from 1924) is "the most famous dollhouse in the world." It was a gift for Queen Mary (the wife of King George V, and the current Queen's grandmother), who greatly enjoyed miniatures, when she was already a fully grown adult. It's basically one big, dimly lit room with the large dollhouse in the middle, executed with an astonishing level of detail. Each fork, knife, and spoon on the expertly set banquet table is perfect and made of real silver—and the tiny pipes of its plumbing system actually have running water. But you're kept a few feet away by a glass wall, and are constantly jostled by fellow sightseers in this crowded space, making it difficult to fully appreciate. Unless you're a dollhouse devotee, it's probably not worth waiting half an hour for a five-minute peek at this, but if the line is short it's definitely worth a look.

Drawings Gallery and China Museum: Positioned at the exit of Queen Mary's Dolls' House, this gallery displays a changing array of pieces from the Queen's collection—usually including some big names, such as Michelangelo and Leonardo. The China Museum features items from the Queen's many exquisite settings for royal shindigs.

State Apartments: Dripping with chandeliers, finely furnished, and strewn with history and the art of a long line of kings and queens, they're the best I've seen in Britain. This is where Henry VIII and Charles I once lived, and where the current Queen wows visiting dignitaries. Take advantage of the talkative docents in each room, who are happy to answer your questions.

You'll climb the Grand Staircase up to the **Grand Vestibule,** decorated with exotic items seized by British troops during their missions to colonize various corners of the world. Ask a docent to help you find the bullet that killed Lord Nelson at Trafalgar (in one of the many glass cases). In the next room, the magnificent wood-ceilinged **Waterloo Chamber** is wallpapered with portraits of figures from the pan-European alliance that defeated Napoleon. Find General Wellington (high on the far wall, in red) who outmaneuvered him at Waterloo, and Pope Pius VII (right wall, in red and white) whom Napoleon befriended...then imprisoned. Next, you'll pass through a **series of living rooms**—bedchambers, dressing rooms, and drawing rooms of the king and queen (who traditionally maintained separate quarters). Many rooms are decorated with canvases by Rubens, Van Dyck, and Holbein. Finally you emerge into **St. George's Hall,** decorated with emblems representing the knights of the prestigious Order of the Garter (see sidebar). This is the site of some of the most elaborate royal banquets—imagine one long table stretching from one end of the hall to the other, seating 160 VIPs. From here, you'll proceed into the rooms that were restored after a fire in 1992, including the "Semi-State Apartments." The **Garter Throne Room** is where new members of the Order of the Garter are invested (ceremonially granted their titles).

• *Exiting the State Apartments, you have one more major sight to see. Get out your castle-issued map or follow signs to find...*

St. George's Chapel: This church is known for housing numerous royal tombs, and is an exquisite example of the Perpendicular Gothic style (dating from about 1500). Pick up a free map and circle the interior clockwise, finding these highlights:

Stand at the back and look down the **nave,** with its classic fan-vaulting spreading out from each slender pillar and nearly every joint capped with an elaborate and colorful roof boss. Most of these emblems are associated with the Knights of the Garter, who consider St. George's their "mother church." Under the upper stained-glass windows, notice the continuous frieze of 250 angels, lovingly carved with great detail, ringing the church.

In the corner (#4 on your church-issued map), take in the melodramatic monument to **Princess Charlotte of Wales,** the only child of King George IV. Heir to the throne, her death in 1817 (at 21, in childbirth) devastated the nation. Head up the left side of the nave and find the simple chapel (#6) containing the tombs of the current Queen's parents, **King George VI and "Queen Mum" Elizabeth;** the ashes of her younger sister, Princess Margaret, are also kept here (see the marble slab against the wall). It's speculated that the current Queen may choose this chapel for her final resting place. Farther up the aisle is the tomb of **Edward IV** (#8), who expanded St. George's Chapel.

Stepping into the **choir area** (#12), you're immediately aware that you are in the inner sanctum of the Order of the Garter. The banners lining the nave represent the knights, as do the fancy helmets and half-drawn swords at the top of each wood-carved seat. These symbols honor only living knights; on the seats are some 800 golden panels memorializing departed knights. Under your feet lies the **Royal Vault** (#13), burial spot of Mad King George III (nemesis of American revolutionaries). Strolling farther up the aisle, notice the marker in the floor: You're walking over the burial site of **King Henry VIII** (#14) and Jane Seymour, Henry's favorite wife (perhaps because she was the only one who died before he could behead her). The body of King Charles I, who was beheaded by Oliver Cromwell's forces at the Banqueting House (see page 124), was also discovered here...with its head sewn back on.

On your way out, you can pause at the door of the sumptuous 13th-century **Albert Memorial Chapel** (#28), redecorated in 1861 after the death of Queen Victoria's husband, Prince Albert, and dedicated to his memory.

• *On exiting the chapel, you come into the castle's...*

Lower Ward: This area is a living town where some 160 people who work for the Queen reside; they include clergy, military, and castle administrators. Just below the chapel, you may be able to enter a tranquil little horseshoe-shaped courtyard ringed with residential doorways—all of them with a spectacular view of the chapel's grand entrance.

Back out in the yard, look for the guard posted at his pillbox. Like those at Buckingham Palace, he's been trained to be a ruthless killing machine...just so he can wind up as somebody's photo op. Click!

MORE SIGHTS IN WINDSOR
Legoland Windsor

Paradise for Legomaniacs under age 12, this huge, kid-pleasing park has dozens of tame but fun rides (often with very long lines) scattered throughout its 150 acres. The impressive Miniland has 40 million Lego pieces glued together to create 800 tiny buildings and a minitour of Europe; the Creation Centre boasts an 80 percent scale-model Boeing 747 cockpit, made of two million bricks. Several of the more exciting rides involve getting wet, so dress accordingly or buy a cheap disposable poncho in the gift shop. While you may be tempted to hop on the Hill Train at the entrance, it's faster and more convenient to walk down into the park. Food is available in the park, but you can save money by bringing a picnic.

Cost: Adults-£48, children-£43, 25 percent cheaper booked online at least seven days in advance, 10 percent discount at Windsor TI, free for ages 3 and under; optional Q-Bot ride-reservation gadget allows you to bypass lines (£15-75 depending on when you go and how much time you want to save).

Hours: Convoluted schedule, but generally late July-Aug daily 10:00-19:00; mid-March-late July and Sept-Oct Mon-Fri 10:00-17:00, Sat-Sun 10:00-18:00, often closed Tue-Wed; closed Nov-mid-March. Call or check website for exact schedule, tel. 0871-222-2001, www.legoland.co.uk.

Getting There: A £5 round-trip shuttle bus runs from opposite Windsor's Theatre Royal on Thames Street, and from the Parish Church stop on High Street (2/hour). If day-tripping from London, ask about rail/shuttle/park admission deals from Paddington or Waterloo train stations. For drivers, the park is on B-3022 Windsor/Ascot road, two miles southwest of Windsor and 25 miles west of London. Legoland is clearly signposted from the M-3, M-4, and M-25 motorways. Parking is easy (£4).

Eton College

Across the bridge from Windsor Castle is the most famous "public" (the equivalent of our "private") high school in Britain. Eton was founded in 1440 by King Henry VI; today it educates about 1,300 boys (ages 13-18), who live on campus. Eton has molded the characters of 19 prime ministers as well as members of the royal family, most recently princes William and Harry. Sparse on actual sights, the college is closed to visitors except via guided tour, where you may get a glimpse of the schoolyard, chapel, cloisters, and the Museum of Eton Life. For more information visit www.etoncollege.com or call 01753/671-000.

Eton High Street

Even if you're not touring the college, it's worth the few minutes it takes to cross the pedestrian bridge and wander straight up Eton's High Street. A bit more cutesy and authentic-feeling than Windsor (which is given over to shopping malls and chain stores), Eton has a charm that's fun to sample.

Windsor and Royal Borough Museum

Tucked into a small space beneath the Guildhall (where Prince Charles remarried), this little museum does its best to give some insight into the history of Windsor and the surrounding area. They also have lots of special activities for kids. Ask at the desk whether tours are running to the Guildhall itself (visits only possible with a guide); if not, it's probably not worth the admission.

Cost and Hours: £2, includes audioguide, Tue-Sat 10:00-16:00, Sun 12:00-16:00, closed Mon, located in the Guildhall on High Street, tel. 01628/685-686, www.rbwm.gov.uk.

Boat Trips

Cruise up and down the Thames River for classic views of the castle, the village of Eton, Eton College, and the Royal Windsor Racecourse. Choose from a 40-minute or two-hour tour, then relax onboard and nibble a picnic. Boats leave from the riverside promenade adjacent to Barry Avenue.

Cost and Hours: 40-minute tour-£7, family pass-about £19, mid-Feb-Oct 1-2/hour daily 10:00-17:00, fewer and Sat-Sun only in Nov; 2-hour tour—£11, family pass-about £30, late March-Oct only, 1-2/day; closed Dec-mid-Feb; online discounts, tel. 01753/851-900, www.frenchbrothers.co.uk.

Horse Racing

The horses race near Windsor every Monday at the Royal Windsor Racecourse (£21-25 entry, online discounts, under age 18 free with an adult, April-Aug and Oct, no races in Sept, sporadic in Aug, off A-308 between Windsor and Maidenhead, tel. 01753/498-400, www.windsor-racecourse.co.uk). The romantic way to get there from Windsor is by a 10-minute shuttle boat (£6.50 round-trip, www.frenchbrothers.co.uk). The famous Ascot Racecourse (described next) is also nearby.

NEAR WINDSOR
Ascot Racecourse

Located seven miles southwest of Windsor and just north of the town of Ascot, this royally owned track is one of the most famous horse-racing venues in the world. The horses first ran here in 1711, and the course is best known for June's five-day Royal Ascot race meeting, attended by the Queen and 299,999 of her loyal subjects. For many, the outlandish hats worn on Ladies Day (Thu) are more interesting than the horses. Royal Ascot is usually the third week in June (June 14-18 in 2016). The pricey tickets go on sale the preceding November; while the Friday and Saturday races tend to sell out far ahead, tickets for the other days are often available close to the date (check website). In addition to Royal Ascot, the racecourse runs the ponies year-round—funny hats strictly optional.

Cost: Regular tickets generally £18-40—may be available at a discount at TI; Royal Ascot £25-75, online discounts, kids ages 17 and under free; parking-free-£20, depending on event; dress code

Visiting Highclere Castle

If you're a fan of *Downton Abbey,* consider a day trip from London to Highclere Castle, the stately house where much of the show is filmed. Though the hugely popular TV series is set in Yorkshire, the actual house is located in Hampshire, about an hour's train ride west of London. Highclere has been home to the Earls of Carnarvon since 1679 (and the current residents enjoy watching the TV show), but the present, Jacobean-style house was rebuilt in the 1840s by Sir Charles Berry, who also designed London's Houses of Parliament. Noted landscape architect Capability Brown laid out the traditional gardens in the mid-18th century. The castle's Egyptian exhibit features artifacts collected by Highclere's fifth Earl, George Herbert, a keen amateur archaeologist. When Howard Carter discovered King Tut's tomb in 1922, he waited three weeks for his friend and patron Herbert to join him before looking inside. The Earl died unexpectedly a few months later, giving birth to the legend of a "mummy's curse."

Cost and Hours: Entrance is by timed entry, reserve well in advance online; £20 for castle, garden, and Egyptian exhibit; £13 for castle and garden only, or Egyptian exhibit and garden only; garden only-£5; open days sporadic but generally mid-April-Sept daily 10:30-17:30, last entry at 16:00; tickets available online several months ahead, sales begin as early as Feb for following summer, last-minute afternoon-entry tickets sometimes available—call ahead; no photos inside, 24-hour info tel. 01635/253-204, www.highclerecastle.co.uk.

Getting There: Highclere is six miles south of Newbury, about 70 miles west of London, off A-34.

By Train and Taxi: First Great Western trains run from London's Paddington Station to Newbury (1-2/hour, 50-70 minutes, £24-54 same-day return, tel. 0345-026-5430, www.firstgreatwestern.co.uk). From Newbury train station, you can take a taxi (£15-22 one-way, higher price is for Sun, taxis wait outside station) or reserve a car and driver (must arrange in advance, £12.50/person round-trip; £25 minimum, WebAir, tel. 07818/430-095, mapeng@msn.com).

By Tour: Brit Movie Tours offers an all-day bus tour of *Downton Abbey* filming locations, including Highclere Castle and the fictional village of Downton (sells out early, £95, includes transport and castle/garden entry, £5 extra for Egyptian exhibit, 9 hours, depart London from outside Gloucester Road Tube Station, reservations required, tel. 0844-247-1007, from the US or Canada call 011-44-20-7118-1007, www.britmovietours.com).

Sleep Code

Abbreviations   **(£1=about $1.60, country code: 44)**
S=Single, D=Double/Twin, T=Triple, Q=Quad, b=bathroom
Price Rankings
  $$$ **Higher Priced**—Most rooms £105 or more
   $$ **Moderately Priced**—Most rooms £60-105
    $ **Lower Priced**—Most rooms £60 or less
Unless otherwise noted, credit cards are accepted, breakfast is included, and free Wi-Fi and/or a guest computer is generally available. Prices change; verify the hotel's current rates online or by email. For the best prices, always book directly with the hotel.

---

enforced in some areas and on certain days, tel. 0844-346-3000, www.ascot.co.uk.

Sleeping in Windsor

Most visitors stay in London and do Windsor as a day trip. But here are a few suggestions for those staying the night.

$$$ MGallery Windsor Castle Hotel, part of the boutique division of Accor Hotels, offers 108 rooms and elegant public spaces in a location that's as central as can be, just down the street from Her Majesty's weekend retreat (Db-from £189, breakfast-£17, check for online deals, air-con, parking-£10/day, 18 High Street, tel. 01753/851-577, www.mercure.com, h6618@accor.com).

$$ Langton House B&B is a stately Victorian home with five spacious, well-appointed rooms lovingly maintained by Paul and Sonja Fogg (S-£71, Sb-£83, D/Db-£101, huge four-poster Db-£113, Tb-£129, Qb-£149, 5 percent extra if paying by credit card, includes continental breakfast, full English breakfast-£6, prices can be soft—especially off-season, family-friendly, guest kitchen, 46 Alma Road, tel. 01753/858-299, www.langtonhouse.co.uk, bookings@langtonhouse.co.uk).

$$ Park Farm B&B, bright and cheery, is most convenient for drivers. But even if you're not driving, this beautiful place is such a good value, and the welcome is so warm, that you're unlikely to mind the bus ride into town (Sb-£70, Db-£89-95, Tb-£115, Qb-£130, family room with bunk beds, cash only—credit card solely for reservations, shared fridge and microwave, free off-street parking, 1 mile from Legoland on St. Leonards Road near Imperial Road, 5-minute bus ride or 1-mile walk to castle, £5 taxi ride from station, tel. 01753/866-823, www.parkfarm.com, stay@parkfarm.com, Caroline and Drew Youds).

$$ 76 Duke Street has two nice rooms, but only hosts one set of guests at a time. While the bathroom is (just) outside your bed-room, you have it to yourself (Db-£85-90, rent both rooms for £170-180, 15-minute walk from station at—you guessed it—76 Duke Street, tel. 01753/620-636 or 07884/222-225, www.76dukestreet. co.uk, bandb@76dukestreet.co.uk, Julia).

$$ Dee and Steve's B&B is a friendly four-room place above a window shop on a quiet residential street about a 10-minute walk from the castle and station. The rooms are cozy, Dee and Steve are pleasant hosts, and breakfast is served in the contemporary kitch-en/lounge (S-£50, Sb-£60-65, Db-£80, 169 Oxford Road, tel. 01753/854-489, www.deeandsteve.com, dee@deeandsteve.com).

$$ Crown and Cushion is a good option on Eton's High Street, just across the pedestrian bridge from Windsor's waterfront (a short uphill walk to the castle). While the pub it's situated over is worn and drab, you're right in the heart of charming Eton, and the eight creaky rooms—with uneven floors and old-beam ceilings—are nicely furnished (Sb-£70, Db-£80, free parking, 84 High Street in Eton, tel. 01753/861-531, www.thecrownandcushioneton.co.uk, info@thecrownandcushioneton.com).

Eating in Windsor

Elegant Spots with River Views: Several places flank Windsor Bridge, offering romantic dining after dark. The riverside prom-enade, with cheap takeaway stands scattered about, is a delightful place for a picnic lunch or dinner with the swans. If you don't see anything that appeals, continue up Eton's High Street, which is also lined with characteristic eateries.

In the Tourist Zone Around the Palace: Strolling the streets and lanes around the palace entrance—especially in the shopping zone near Windsor & Eton Station—you'll find countless trendy and inviting eateries. The central area also has a sampling of dependable British chains (including a Wagamama, Gourmet Burger Kitchen, and Thai Square). Residents enjoy a wide selection of unpretentious little eateries (including a fire station turned pub-and-cultural cen-ter) just past the end of pedestrian Peascod Street.

Bel & The Dragon is the place to splurge on high-quality, classic British food in a charming half-timbered building with an upscale-rustic dining space (£6-9 starters, £14-21 main courses, food served daily 12:00-15:00 & 18:00-22:00, afternoon tea served between lunch and dinner, bar open longer hours, on Thames Street near the bridge to Eton, tel. 01753/866-056).

Cornucopia Bistro, with a cozy, woody atmosphere, serves tasty international dishes (£10 two-course and £13 three-course lunch meals, £13-16 main courses at dinner, open daily 12:00-

14:30 & 18:00-21:30, Fri-Sat until 22:00, closed Sun night, 6 High Street, tel. 01753/833-009).

The Duchess of Cambridge's friendly staff serves up the normal grub in a pub that's right across from the castle walls, and with an open fireplace to boot (£10-14 meals, daily 10:00-22:30 or later, 3 Thames Street, tel. 01753/864-405). While the pub predates Kate, it was named in her honor following a recent remodel, and has the photos to prove her endorsement.

Meimo offers "Mediterranean/Moroccan" cuisine in a nicely subdued dining room at the quieter end of the pedestrian zone (£10-15 main dishes, several fixed-price meal options, daily 10:00-22:00, 69 Peascod Street, tel. 01753/862-222).

Saffron Restaurant, while a fairly long walk from the castle, is the local choice for South Indian cuisine, with a modern interior and attentive waiters who struggle with English but are fluent at bringing out tasty dishes. Their vegetarian *thali* is a treat (£8-12 dishes, daily 12:00-14:30 & 17:30-23:30, 99 St. Leonards Road, tel. 01753/855-467).

Cambridge

Cambridge, 60 miles north of London, is world-famous for its prestigious university. Wordsworth, Isaac Newton, Tennyson, Darwin, and Prince Charles are a few of its illustrious alumni. The university dominates—and owns—most of Cambridge, a historic town of about 125,000 people. Cambridge is the epitome of a university town, with busy bikers, stately residence halls, plenty of bookshops, and proud locals who can point out where DNA was originally modeled, the atom first split, and electrons discovered.

In medieval Europe, higher education was the domain of the Church and was limited to ecclesiastical schools. Scholars lived in "halls" on campus. This academic community of residential halls, chapels, and lecture halls connected by peaceful garden courtyards survives today in the colleges that make up the universities of Cambridge and Oxford. By 1350 (Oxford is roughly 100 years older), Cambridge had eight colleges, each with a monastic-type courtyard, chapel, library, and lodgings. Today, Cambridge has 31 colleges, each with its own facilities, and about 12,000 undergrads.

In the town center, these grand old halls date back centuries, with ornately decorated facades that try to one-up each other. While students' lives revolve around their independent colleges, the university organizes lectures, presents degrees, and promotes research.

The university schedule has three terms: Lent term from mid-January to mid-March, Easter term from mid-April to mid-June, and Michaelmas term from early October to early December. During exams (roughly the month of May), the colleges are closed to visitors, which can impede access to some of the town's picturesque little corners. But the main sights—King's College Chapel and the Wren Library at Trinity College—stay open, and Cambridge is never sleepy.

PLANNING YOUR TIME

Cambridge can easily be seen as a day trip from London. A good five-hour plan is to follow my self-guided walk, spend an hour on a punt ride, tour the Fitzwilliam Museum (closed Mon), and see the Wren Library at Trinity College (open Mon-Sat for only two hours a day, so plan ahead). For a little extra color, consider joining a walk through town with a local guide from the TI (2 hours, repeats much of my self-guided walk but splices in local flavor). The TI's town walk includes King's College Chapel, so don't do that on your own.

If you're in town for the evening, the evensong service at King's College Chapel (at 17:30) is a must. If you like plays and music, events are always happening in this thriving cultural hub.

GETTING TO CAMBRIDGE

By Train: It's an easy trip from London and less than an hour away. Catch the train from London's King's Cross Station (2/hour, trains leave King's Cross at :15 and :44 past the hour, 45 minutes, £23 one-way standard class, £24 same-day return after 9:30, tel. 0845-748-4950, www.firstcapitalconnect.co.uk or www.nationalrail.co.uk). Cheaper direct trains also run from London's Liverpool Street Station, but take longer (2/hour, 1.5 hours).

By Bus: National Express coaches run from London's Victoria Coach Station to the Parkside stop in Cambridge (every 60-90 minutes, 2-2.5 hours, £12, discounted fares may be available in advance online, tel. 0871-781-8181, www.nationalexpress.co.uk).

Orientation to Cambridge

Cambridge is small. Everything is within a pleasant walk. The town has two main streets, separated from the Cam River by the most interesting colleges. The town center, brimming with tearooms, has a TI and a colorful open-air market square. The train station is about a mile to the southeast.

TOURIST INFORMATION

Cambridge's TI is well run and well signposted, just off Market Square in the town center. They book rooms for £5, offer walking tours (see "Tours in Cambridge," later), and sell bus tickets and a £2 map/guide (Mon-Sat 10:00-17:00, Easter-Sept also Sun 11:00-15:00—otherwise closed Sun, phones answered from 9:00, Peas Hill, tel. 0871-226-8006, room-booking tel. 01223/457-581, www.visitcambridge.org). In the same building as the TI, you can duck into a former courtroom to catch a free video overview of the town and its history.

ARRIVAL IN CAMBRIDGE

By Train: Cambridge's train station doesn't have baggage storage or a TI. You can pick up a free map at the small info desk on the platform and other brochures on an interior wall just before the turnstiles.

To get from the station to downtown Cambridge, you can **walk** for about 25 minutes (exit straight ahead on Station Road, bear right at the war memorial onto Hills Road, and follow it into town); take public **bus** #1, #3, #7, or #8 (referred to as "Citi 1," "Citi 3," and so on in schedules, but buses are marked only with the number; £1.60, pay driver, runs every 5-10 minutes, turn left when exiting station and walk half a block to find bus stands, get off when you see Lion's Yard shopping mall on the left); pay about £6 for a **taxi;** or take a City Sightseeing **bus tour** (described later).

By Car: To park in the middle of town, follow signs from the M-11 motorway to any of the central short-stay parking lots. Or leave your car at one of five park-and-ride lots outside the city, then take the shuttle into town (parking-£1/4 hours; shuttle-£2.70 round-trip).

HELPFUL HINTS

Live Theater and Entertainment: With all the smart and talented students in town, there is always something going on. Make a point of enjoying a play or concert. The ADC **(Cambridge University Amateur Dramatic Club)** is Britain's oldest university playhouse, offering a steady stream of performances since 1855. It's lots of fun and casual, with easy-to-get and inexpensive tickets. This is your chance to see a future Emma Thompson or Ian McKellen—alums who performed here as students—before they become stars (tel. 01223/300-085, www.adctheatre.com).

    Cambridge Live Tickets is a very helpful service, offer-

Cambridge

DAY TRIPS

1. Hotel du Vin
2. Lensfield Hotel
3. The Eagle Pub; Bread & Meat
4. Michaelhouse Café
5. The Anchor Pub
6. Agora at The Copper Kettle
7. Fitzbillies
8. Marks & Spencer
9. Sainsbury's
10. Cambridge Chauffeur Punts
11. Scudamore's Punts (2)
12. Cambridge Live Tickets
13. Bus from Train Station
14. Bus to Train Station
15. Station Cycles

ing event info and ticket sales in person and online (Mon-Fri 12:00-18:00, Sat from 10:00, Sun from 18:00 until 30 minutes before showtime, 2 Wheeler Street, tel. 01223/357-851 answered Mon-Sat 12:00-18:00, www.cambridgelivetrust. co.uk). The TI also has lists of what's on.

Festivals: The **Cambridge Folk Festival** gets things humming and strumming in late July (tickets go on sale several months ahead and often sell out; www.cambridgefolkfestival.co.uk). From mid-July through August, the town's **Shakespeare Festival** attracts 25,000 visitors for outdoor performances in some of the college's gardens (£16, book tickets online, www. cambridgeshakespeare.com).

Bike Rental: Station Cycles, inside the Lion's Yard shopping mall, rents bikes and offers luggage lockers (bikes—£7/4 hours, £10/day, helmets-£1, £60 deposit, cash or credit card; lockers—£3-4 depending on size); Mon-Fri 8:00-18:00, Sat 9:00-18:00, Sun 10:00-17:00; tel. 01223/307-655, www. stationcycles.co.uk.

Tours in Cambridge

▲▲Walking Tour of the Colleges

A walking tour is the best way to understand Cambridge's mix of "town and gown." The walks can be more educational (read: dry) than entertaining, but they do provide a good rundown of the historic and scenic highlights of the university, some fun local gossip, and plenty of university trivia.

The TI offers **daily walking tours** that include the King's College Chapel, as well as another college—usually Queen's College (£18, 2 hours, includes entry fees; July-Aug daily at 11:00, 12:00, 13:00, and 14:00, no 11:00 tour on Sun; Sept-June Mon-Sat at 11:00 and 13:00, Sun at 13:00 only; tel. 01223/457-574, www. visitcambridge.org). Groups are limited to 20, so it's smart to call ahead or drop in at the TI in advance to reserve a spot. Note that the 12:00 tour overlaps with the limited opening times of the Wren Library, so you'll miss out on the library if you take the noon tour.

Private guides are available through the TI and affordable if you can assemble a group to share the cost (2-hour tour-£88; does not include individual college entrance fees, tel. 01223/457-574, tours@cambridge.gov.uk).

Walking Ghost Tour

If you're in Cambridge on the weekend, consider a £6 "ghost walk" to where spooky sightings have been reported (Fri-Sat at 18:00, organized by the TI, tel. 01223/457-574).

Cambridge Colleges 101

Of Cambridge's 31 colleges, some are free to visit and welcoming to the public, some are closed off and very private, and others are famous and make money by charging for visits. All have a similar design and etiquette. At their historic front gates, you'll find a porter's lodge where the porter keeps an eye on things. He delivers mail, monitors who comes and goes, and keeps people off the grass. The exclusive putting-green quality of the courtyard lawns is a huge deal here: Only fellows (senior professors) can walk on the courts, which are the centerpiece of each college campus. Whether a college is open to visitors or private, you can usually at least pop in through the gate, chat with the porter, and enjoy the view of the grassy court.

The court is ringed by venerable buildings. The dining hall is easy to identify by its big bay windows marking the location of the "high table," where VIPs eat. Dining halls are rarely open to the public, but you can look in from the main door. Other major buildings fronting the court are the chapel (often historic and with memorials to students who died in World War I and II). A college's chapel is the building that's most often open to the public. In the chapel, seating is usually arranged in several rows of pews that face each other to allow for antiphonal singing and chanting—where one side starts and the other responds. Libraries are treasured and generally not open to the public. There's also a Senior Common Room (like a teachers' lounge but much fancier), where fellows share ideas in an exclusive social hall, creating a fertile intellectual garden. Students live on campus not along halls but in "staircases" (narrow towers with one room per floor; not open to the public). Their address includes their college, their staircase, and their room number.

The college houses, feeds, and parents its students, while the university offers formal teaching and lectures. Colleges also have a "home professor," who coaches students as they navigate the higher education system.

DAY TRIPS

Bus Tours

City Sightseeing hop-on, hop-off bus tours are informative and cover the outskirts, including the American WWII Cemetery. But keep in mind that buses can't go where walking tours can—right into the center (£15, 80 minutes for full 19-stop circuit, buy ticket with credit card at the bus-stop kiosk—or pay cash to driver when you board, departs every 20 minutes in summer, every 40 minutes in winter, first bus leaves train station at 10:06, last bus around 17:30, recorded commentary, tel. 01223/433-250, www.city-sightseeing.

com). If arriving by train, you can buy your ticket from the kiosk directly in front of the station, then ride the bus into town.

Cambridge Town Walk

Cambridge is built along its dreamy little river and around its 31 colleges (the first, Peterhouse, was founded in the 1280s). It's easy to sort out. There's a small and youthful commercial center—quiet and traffic free (except for lots of bikes), one important museum (the Fitzwilliam), and lots of minor museums (all free). The Cam River has boat tours, three public bridges, and a strip of six colleges whose gardens basically own the river through the center of town and make it feel like an exclusive park. The university includes two dominant colleges (Trinity with its famous Wren Library, and King's College with its famous chapel), but also plenty of minor ones, each with a grand front gate. The city is filled with students year-round—scholars throughout the regular terms and visiting students enjoying summer programs.

In the following self-guided walk, I cover the essential town sights (including two less-visited colleges), finishing at Kings College Chapel. Trinity College and the Fitzwilliam Museum are covered in "Sights in Cambridge," later.

• *Start this self-guided walk on Market Hill Square (the TI is just half a block away). To find the square from the lively street called King's Parade—which feels like the center of town and is where this walk ends—go behind Great St. Mary's Church (with the tall tower).*

Market Hill Square

This square has been a center of commerce for more than a thousand years. Think of the history this place has seen: Romans first built a bridge over the Cam in 43 A.D., Anglo-Saxons and Danes established a market here in the Dark Ages, and Normans built a castle here (now gone) in the 11th century.

But the big year was 1209, when scholars and students first arrived. After scuffles in Oxford between its townsfolk and university (which is older than Cambridge), Oxford's students and professors fled here and settled. (The Oxford-Cambridge rivalry just seems natural.) Where's the university? Everywhere, mixed into the town, with the 31 individual colleges, university halls, and student dorms scattered about. Even on this square you can see dorms (the more modern, tasteless buildings around you). Cambridge suffered no bomb damage in World War II, so the older buildings you see are originals. As you walk, notice how peaceful the town is. Almost no cars, but bikes everywhere—be careful! They are silent and pack a punch.

The Guildhall facing this square (the seat of the city council today) overlooks market stalls. The big market is on Sunday (9:30-16:30) and features produce, arts, and crafts. On other days, you'll find mostly clothes and food (Mon-Sat generally 9:30-16:00).

• *Facing the Guildhall, exit the square to your left down Petty Curry Lane, a modern pedestrian shopping street. At its end (with my three favorite fast-food chains: Eat, Pret a Manger, and Wasabi) you hit St. Andrews Street. On the left is the fine 16th-century gatehouse of Christ's College. Step inside to enjoy the classic court, next to a bust of Charles Darwin (a notable alum). Although the college isn't open to the public, you can chat with the porter. Now continue down St. Andrews Street a long block to Emmanuel College.*

Emmanuel College

This college welcomes the public and offers a classic peek at a typical Cambridge college (free, open 9:00-6:00). Emmanuel was founded in 1584 as a Protestant college on land that had once been a Dominican friary. (Like many monasteries and convents in the 16th century, the friary had been dissolved by the English king in an epic power struggle that left England with its own version of Christianity and the government with lots of land once owned by the Catholic Church.)

Facing the court, with the big clock, is one of two chapels in town designed by Christopher Wren. Above the church is the Senior Common Room, a social hall for college fellows. On the left is the dining hall—marked by its big bay window.

At this point you could visit the church (find the portrait of John Harvard—the Emmanuel College student who went to America and founded another prestigious school—in the stained glass on the left), look through the doorway into the dining hall, enjoy the garden behind the chapel (typical of these colleges; the fish pond goes back to monastic days when the fish were part of the diet), or chat with the porter.

• *Leaving Emmanuel College, walk straight ahead, down Downing Street. You'll pass several museums that are owned by the university to support various fields of study (generally free to enter). Downing Street ends at King's Parade, with Pembroke College on the left and the recommended Fitzbillies Café on the right. (Fitzbillies is famous for its local cinnamon roll, the Chelsea Bun, and is a good place for a break).*

Pembroke College

Founded in 1347, Pembroke is the third-oldest college in Cambridge. Step into the court, past the porter's lodge—it's polite to say hello and ask whether you can wander around. Survey the court. Two chapels face it. The original chapel (on the left) was replaced by the bigger one on the right. Ahead of you is the medieval dining hall, and the fancy building with the pointed clock tower is the

DAY TRIPS

library (the statue in front is of alumnus William Pitt the Younger—a great 18th-century prime minister), with a charming garden beyond.

The highlight here is the chapel on the right. The chapel dates from about 1660 and is the first building that the famed architect Christopher Wren completed. Before stepping inside to enjoy the interior, pause for a moment at the somber WWI and WWII memorial.

• *From Pembroke College, cross King's Parade and follow Mill Lane directly down to the River Cam and its mill pond.*

River Cam, the Mill Pond, and Punting

From this perch you see the "harbor action" of Cambridge. The city was a sort of harbor in medieval times: Trading vessels from the North Sea could navigate to here. Today a weir divides the River Cam from the River Granta (on the left), which leads through idyllic countryside to the town of Grantchester (note that punts cannot cross the weir). Filling the actual mill pond is a commotion of the iconic Cambridge boats called punts. Students hustle to take visitors on a 45-minute trip along the parklike "backs" of the colleges that line the river from here to the far side of town (about £15, see page 503). You can share a boat with others and enjoy a colorful narration as you're poled past fine college architecture. Skilled residents rent boats for themselves, as do not-so-skilled tourists—much to the amusement of locals who sip their beer while watching clumsy visitors fumble with the boats (which are tougher to maneuver than they look).

Walk along the harbor past the recommended Anchor Pub (with waterfront tables and fancier seating upstairs) to the Silver Street Bridge. From here you can watch more punt action and check out the famous "Mathematical Bridge," which links the old and new buildings of Queens' College. This wooden bridge, although curved, is made of straight boards. (It was not designed by Isaac Newton, as a popular fable would have it—Newton died before the bridge was constructed.)

Gazing upstream past the wooden bridge, you see the start of the stretch of six colleges, each with a bridge that connects their campus complexes with the garden-like "backs."

• *Walk up Silver Street, back to King's Parade, and turn left toward this walk's finale—King's College. On the first corner, find the fancy gilded clock.*

The Corpus Clock, Benet Street, and Eagle Pub

Designed and commissioned by Corpus Christi College alum John Taylor, this clock was unveiled by Cambridge physicist Stephen Hawking in a 2008 ceremony. Perched on top is the Chronophage—the "time eater"—a grotesque giant grasshopper that keeps the clock moving and periodically winks at passersby. The message? Time is passing, so live every moment to the fullest.

The Eagle Pub, a venerable joint, is just down Benet Street on the left. This is Cambridge's oldest pub and a sight in itself. Poke into the courtyard and atmospheric rooms even if you don't eat or drink here.

From the courtyard outside, look up at the balcony of second-floor guest rooms that date back to when this was a coachmen's inn as well as a pub. (It's said that in Shakespeare's time, plays were performed from this perch to entertain guests below.) The faded *Bath* sign indicates that this was a posh place—you could even wash. Notice that the window on the right end is open; any local will love to tell you why.

Step past the "glancing stones" that protected the corner from careening coaches. During World War II, US Army Air Corps pilots famously hung out here before missions over Germany. The fun interior is plastered with stickers of air crews and WWII memorabilia. Next to the fireplace a photo and plaque remember two esteemed regulars—Francis Crick and James Watson—the scientists who first described the structure of DNA. They announced their finding here in 1953, and if you'd like to drink to that, there's a beer on tap for you—a bitter called DNA.

St. Benet's Church, across the street from the pub, is the oldest surviving building in Cambridgeshire. The Saxons who built the church in the 11th century included circular holes in its bell tower to encourage owls to roost there and keep the mouse population under control.

• *Return to the creepy grasshopper clock and turn right, continuing down King's Parade past the regal front facade of King's College Chapel (we'll return here shortly) to the...*

Senate House

This stately classical building with triangular pediments is the ceremonial and administrative heart of Cambridge University and the meeting place of the university's governing body. In June, you might notice green boxes lining the front of this house. Traditionally, at the end of the term, students came to these boxes to see whether they earned their degree; those not listed knew they had flunked. Amazingly, until 2010 this was the only notification students received about their status. (Now they first get an email.)

Looming across the street from the Senate House is **Great St. Mary's Church** (a.k.a. the University Church), with a climbable bell tower (£4, Mon-Sat 9:30-16:30, Sun 12:30-16:00, 123 stairs). On the corner nearby is **Ryder and Amies** (22 King's Parade), which has been the official university outfitter for 150 years.

DAY TRIPS

It's a great shop for college gear: sweaters, ties, and so on. Upstairs, if you ask, you can try on an undergraduate gown and mortar board.

• *Just after the Senate House, take the first left possible (on Senate House passage); at the end, bear left on Trinity Lane to reach the gate where you pay to enter...*

▲▲King's College Chapel

Built from 1446 to 1515 by Henrys VI through VIII, England's best example of Perpendicular Gothic architecture is the single most impressive building in Cambridge.

Cost and Hours: £8, erratic hours depending on school events; during academic term usually Mon-Fri 9:30-15:30, Sat 9:30-15:15, Sun 13:15-14:30; during breaks (see page 488) usually daily 9:30-16:30; recorded info tel. 01223/331-1212.

Evensong: When school's in session, you're welcome to enjoy an evensong service in this glorious space, with a famous choir made up of men and boys (free, Mon-Sat at 17:30, Sun at 15:30; for more on evensong, see page 450). Line up at the front entrance (on King's Parade) by 17:00 if you want prime seats in the choir.

Visiting the Chapel: Stand inside, look up, and marvel, as Christopher Wren did, at what was then the largest single span of **vaulted roof** anywhere. Built between 1512 and 1515, its 2,000 tons of incredible fan vaulting—held in place by the force of gravity—are a careful balancing act resting delicately on the buttresses visible outside the building.

While Henry VI—who began work on the chapel—wanted it to be austere, his descendants decided it should glorify the House of Tudor (of which his son, Henry VII, was the first king). Lining the walls are giant **Tudor coats-of-arms.** The shield is supported by

symbolism for each branch of the family: the fleur-de-lis because an earlier ancestor, Edward III, woke up one day and somewhat arbitrarily declared himself king of France; a rose and the dragon of Wales represent the family of Henry VII's father; and the greyhound holding the shield and the portcullis (the iron grate) symbolize the family of Henry VII's mother, Lady Margaret Beaufort.

The 26 **stained-glass windows** date from the 16th century. It's the most Renaissance stained glass anywhere in one spot. (Most

of the stained glass in English churches dates from Victorian times, but this glass is three centuries older.) The lower panes show scenes from the New Testament, while the upper panes feature corresponding stories from the Old Testament. Considering England's turbulent history, it's miraculous that these windows have survived for nearly half a millennium in such a pristine state. After Henry VIII separated from the Catholic Church in 1534, many such windows and other Catholic features around England were destroyed. (Think of all those ruined abbeys dotting the English countryside.) However, since Henry had just paid for these windows, he couldn't bear to destroy them. A century later, in the days of Oliver Cromwell, another wave of iconoclasm destroyed more windows around England. Though these windows were slated for removal, they stayed put. (Historians speculate that Cromwell's troops, who were garrisoned in this building, didn't want the windows removed in the chilly wintertime.) Finally, during World War II, the windows were taken out and hidden away for safekeeping, then painstakingly replaced after the war ended. The only non-medieval windows are on the west wall (opposite the altar). These are in the Romantic style from the 1880s; when Nazi bombs threatened the church, all agreed they should be left in place.

The **choir screen** that bisects the church was commissioned by King Henry VIII to commemorate his marriage to Anne Boleyn. By the time it was finished, so was she (beheaded). But it was too late to remove her initials, which were carved into the screen (look on the far left and right for *R.A.*, for *Regina Anna*—"Queen Anne"). Behind the screen is the **choir** area, where the King's College Choir performs a daily evensong (during school terms). On Christmas Eve, a special service is held here and broadcast around the world on the BBC—a tradition near and dear to British hearts.

Walk to the altar and admire Rubens' masterful *Adoration of the Magi* (1634). It's actually a family portrait: The admirer in the front (wearing red) is a self-portrait of Rubens, Mary looks an awful lot like his much-younger wife, and the Baby Jesus resembles their own newborn at the time. The chapel to the right of the altar is a moving memorial to those who died in the World Wars.

Finally, check out the long and fascinating series of rooms that run the length of the nave on the left. Dedicated to the history and art of the church, these are a great little King's College Chapel museum (including a model showing how the fan vaults were constructed).

• *Exit the church opposite where you entered, into the college court. From here you can stroll the rich grounds all the way to the River Cam and then back, passing through the grand entry gate and onto King's Parade.*

Sights in Cambridge

My self-guided walk takes you to most of the main sights in Cambridge, but not all. Your time is well spent visiting these places as well.

▲▲Trinity College and Wren Library

More than a third of Cambridge's 83 Nobel Prize winners have come from this richest and biggest of the town's colleges, founded in 1546 by Henry VIII. The college has three sights to see: the entrance gate, the grounds, and the magnificent Wren Library.

Cost and Hours: Grounds—£2, often free off-season, daily 10:00-17:00; library—free, Mon-Fri 12:00-14:00, during full term also Sat 10:30-12:30, closed Sun year-round; only 20 people allowed in at a time, tel. 01223/338-400, www.trin.cam.ac.uk.

Visiting the College: To see the Wren Library without paying for the grounds, access it from the riverside entrance (a long walk around the college via the Garret Hostel Bridge).

Trinity Gate: You'll notice gates like these adorning facades of colleges around town. Above the door is a statue of **King Henry VIII,** who founded Trinity because he feared that Cambridge's existing colleges were too cozy with the Church. Notice Henry's right hand holding a chair leg instead of the traditional scepter with the crown jewels. This is courtesy of Cambridge's Night Climbers, who first replaced the scepter a century ago, and continue to periodically switch it out for other items. According to campus legend, decades ago some of the world's most talented mountaineers enrolled at Cambridge...in one of the flattest parts of England. (Cambridge was actually a seaport until Dutch engineers drained the surrounding swamps.) Lacking

opportunities to practice their skill, they began scaling the frilly facades of Cambridge's college buildings under cover of darkness (if caught, they'd have been expelled). In the 1960s, climbers actually managed to haul an entire automobile onto the roof of the Senate House. The university had to bring in the army to cut it into pieces and remove it. Only 50 years later, at a class reunion, did the guilty parties finally fess up.

In the little park to the right, notice the lone **apple tree.** Supposedly, this tree is a descendant of the very one that once stood in the garden of Sir Isaac Newton (who spent 30 years at Trinity). According to legend, Newton was inspired to investigate gravity when an apple fell from the tree onto his head. This tree stopped bearing fruit long ago; if you do see apples, they've been tied on by mischievous students.

Beyond the gate are the Trinity grounds. Note that there's often a fine and free view of Trinity College courtyard—if the gate is open—from Trinity Lane (leading, under a uniform row of old chimneys, around the school to the Wren Library).

Trinity Grounds: The grounds are enjoyable to explore. Inside the **Great Court,** the clock (on the tower on the right) double-rings at the top of each hour. It's a college tradition to take off running from the clock when the high noon bells begin (it takes 43 seconds to clang 24 times), race around the courtyard, touching each of the four corners without setting foot on the cobbles, and try to return to the same spot before the ringing ends. Supposedly only one student (a young lord) ever managed the feat—a scene featured in *Chariots of Fire* (but filmed elsewhere).

The **chapel** (entrance to the right of the clock tower)—which pales in comparison to the stunning King's College Chapel—feels like a shrine to thinking, with statues honoring great Trinity minds both familiar (Isaac Newton, Alfred Lord Tennyson, Francis Bacon) and unfamiliar. Who's missing? The poet Lord Byron, who was such a hell-raiser during his time at Trinity that a statue of him was deemed unfit for Church property; his statue stands in the library instead.

Wren Library: Don't miss the 1695 Christopher Wren-designed library, with its wonderful carving and fascinating original manuscripts. Just outside the library entrance, Sir Isaac Newton clapped his hands and timed the echo to measure the speed of sound as it raced down the side of the cloister and back. In the library's 12 display cases (covered with cloth that you flip back), you'll see handwritten works by Sir Isaac Newton and John Milton, alongside A. A. Milne's original *Winnie the Pooh* (the real Christopher Robin attended Trinity College). Unlike the other libraries at Cambridge, Wren designed his to be used from the first floor up—instead of the damp, dark ground floor. As a result, Wren's library is flooded with light, rather than water (and it's also brimming with students during exam times).

▲▲Fitzwilliam Museum

Britain's best museum of antiquities and art outside London is the Fitzwilliam. Housed in a grand Neoclassical building, a 10-minute walk south of Market Square, it's a palatial celebration of beauty and humankind's ability to create it.

Cost and Hours: Free but £5 donation suggested, Tue-Sat 10:00-17:00, Sun 12:00-17:00, closed Mon, photos allowed without flash, lockers, Trumpington Street, tel. 01223/332-900, www.fitzmuseum.cam.ac.uk.

Visiting the Museum: The Fitzwilliam's broad collection is like a mini-British Museum/National Gallery rolled into one; you're bound to find something you like. Helpful docents—many with degrees or doctorates in art history—are more than willing to answer questions about the collection. The ground floor features an extensive range of antiquities and applied arts—everything from Greek vases, Mesopotamian artifacts, and Egyptian sarcophagi to Roman statues, fine porcelain, and suits of armor.

Upstairs is the painting gallery, with works that span art history: Italian Venetian masters (such as Titian and Canaletto), a worthy English section (featuring Gainsborough, Reynolds, Hogarth, and others), and a notable array of French Impressionist art (including Monet, Renoir, Pissarro, Degas, and Sisley). Rounding out the collection are old manuscripts, including some musical compositions from Handel.

Museum of Classical Archaeology

Although this museum contains no originals, it offers a unique chance to study accurate copies (19th-century casts) of virtually every famous ancient Greek and Roman statue. More than 450 statues are on display. If you've seen the real things in Greece, Istanbul, Rome, and elsewhere, touring this collection is like a high school reunion..."Hey, I know you!" But since it takes some time to get here, this museum is best left to devotees of classical sculpture.

Cost and Hours: Free, Mon-Fri 10:00-17:00, Sat 10:00-13:00 during term, closed Sun year-round, Sidgwick Avenue, tel. 01223/330-402, www.classics.cam.ac.uk/museum.

Getting There: The museum is a five-minute walk west of

Silver Street Bridge; after crossing the bridge, continue straight until you reach a sign reading *Sidgwick Site.*

▲Punting on the Cam

For a little levity and probably more exercise than you really want, try renting one of the traditional flat-bottom punts at the river

and pole yourself up and down (or around and around, more likely) the lazy Cam. This is one of the best memories the town has to offer, and once you get the hang of it, it's a fine way to enjoy the scenic side of Cambridge. It's less crowded in late afternoon (and less embarrassing).

Several companies rent punts and also offer punting tours with entertaining narration. Hawkers try to snare passengers in the thriving people zone in front of King's College. Prices are soft in slow times—try talking them down a bit before committing.

Scudamore's has two locations: on Mill Lane, just south of the central Silver Street Bridge, and at the less convenient Quayside at Magdalene Bridge, at the north end of town (£25/hour, credit-card deposit required; 45-minute tours-£18/person, ask for discount; open daily 9:00-dusk, tel. 01223/359-750, www.scudamores.com).

Cambridge Chauffeur Punts, just under the Silver Street Bridge, also rents punts. Take yourself and up to five friends for a spin, or they will chauffeur (£22/hour; passport, credit card, or £60 cash deposit required; 45-minute shared tours-£14/person; open daily March-Nov 9:00-dusk, tel. 01223/354-164, www.punting-in-cambridge.co.uk).

NEAR CAMBRIDGE

Imperial War Museum Duxford

This former airfield, nine miles south of Cambridge, is popular with aviation fans and WWII buffs. Wander through seven exhibition halls housing 200 vintage aircraft (including Spitfires, B-17 Flying Fortresses, a Concorde, and a Blackbird) as well as military land vehicles and special displays on Normandy and the Battle of Britain. On many weekends, the museum holds special events, such as air shows (extra fee)—check the website for details.

Cost and Hours: £17.50, show local bus ticket for discount, daily 10:00-18:00, off-season until 16:00, last entry one hour before closing; tel. 01223/835-000, www.iwm.org.uk/visits/iwm-duxford.

Getting There: The museum is located off the A-505 in Duxford. On Sundays, direct Myalls bus #132 runs to the museum from the train station (4/day, 30 minutes, www.travelineeastanglia.org.uk). On other days of the week, it's best to take a taxi from Cambridge. (Other buses do stop in Duxford, but too far from the museum to walk.)

Sleeping in Cambridge

While Cambridge is an easy side-trip from London (and you can enjoy an evening here before catching a late train back), its subtle charms might convince you to spend a night or two. Cambridge has few accommodations in the city center, and none in the tight maze of colleges and shops where you'll spend most of your time. These recommendations (each just past the Fitzwilliam Museum) are about a 10-minute walk south of the town center, toward the train station. (Though weak in hotel offerings, Cambridge does have plenty of B&Bs, which you can research and book online.)

$$$ Lensfield Hotel, popular with visiting professors, has 40 comfortable, old-fashioned rooms (Sb-£75, Db-£114, newer "deluxe" Db-£155, Tb-£139, spa and fitness room, 53 Lensfield Road, tel. 01223/355-017, www.lensfieldhotel.co.uk, enquiries@lensfieldhotel.co.uk).

$$$ Hotel du Vin is a pretentious place that rents 41 decent rooms at a high price. It has duck-your-head character and a good location (Db-£150-225, check online for special offers, breakfast-£14, Trumpington Street 15, tel. 01223/227-330 or 0844-736-4253, www.hotelduvin.com, reception.cambridge@hotelduvin.com).

Eating in Cambridge

The Eagle, near the TI and described earlier in my town walk, is the oldest pub in town. While the food is mediocre, the pub is a Cambridge institution with a history so rich that a visit here practically qualifies as sightseeing (£10-18 lunches and dinners, food served daily 11:00-22:00, 8 Benet Street, tel. 01223/505-020).

Michaelhouse Café is a heavenly respite from the crowds, tucked into the repurposed St. Michael's Church, just north of Great St. Mary's Church. At lunch, choose from salads and sandwiches, as well as a few hot dishes and a variety of tasty baked goods (£6-10 lunches, Mon-Sat 8:00-17:00, breakfast served 8:00-11:30, lunch served 12:00-15:30, closed Sun,

Trinity Street, tel. 01223/309-147). Between 14:30 and 15:30 you can pay £4.50 to fill your plate with whatever they have left.

The Anchor Pub's claim to fame is as the setting of Pink Floyd's first gig. Today it's known for the best people-watching—and some locals say best food—in Cambridge. Choose from its out-door riverside terrace, inside bar, or more romantic upstairs restaurant (all seating areas serve the same menu, but the upstairs menu has a few added specials; £6-8 starters, £13-16 main dishes, daily 12:00-21:30, on the riverfront at Silver Street, tel. 01224/353-554).

Bread & Meat serves simple soups and hearty sandwiches. Grab a signature *porchetta* sandwich to take away or snag a rustic table in the small dining room (£2 soups, £7 sandwiches, £2-3 sides, daily 9:00-21:00, Sun-Mon until 17:00, 4 Benet Street, tel. 0791/808-3057).

Agora at The Copper Kettle is a popular place for Greek and Turkish *meze*, beautifully situated facing King's College on King's Parade (£10-£12 dishes, also fish-and-chips at lunch, open for lunch and dinner, 4 King's Parade, tel. 01223/308-448).

Fitzbillies, long a favorite for cakes (Chelsea Buns) and coffee, offers an inviting lunch menu (£8-10) and a fancier one for dinner (£8 first courses, £17 main dishes, daily, 51 Trumpington Street).

Fast Food: For healthy fast-food chains, the corner of Petty Curry Lane and Sidney Street (a long block off Market Hill Square) has three good places: **Eat, Pret a Manger,** and **Wasabi.**

Supermarkets: There's a **Marks & Spencer Simply Food** at the train station (daily 7:00-23:00) and a larger Marks & Spencer department store on Market Hill Square (Mon-Tue 8:00-18:00, later Wed-Sat, Sun 11:00-17:00). **Sainsbury's** supermarket has longer hours (Mon-Sat 7:30-23:30, Sun 11:00-17:00, 44 Sidney Street, at the corner of Green Street).

A good picnic spot is Laundress Green, a grassy park on the river, at the end of Mill Lane near the Silver Street Bridge punts. There are no benches, so bring something to sit on. Remember, the college lawns are private property, so walking or picnicking on the grass is generally not allowed. When in doubt, ask at the college's entrance.

Cambridge Connections

From Cambridge by Train to: York (hourly, 2.5 hours, transfer in Peterborough), **Oxford** (2-3/hour, 2.5-3 hours, change in London involves Tube transfer between train stations), **London** (King's Cross Station: 2/hour, 45 minutes; Liverpool Street Station: 2/hour, 1.5 hours). Train info: Tel. 0345-748-4950, www.nationalrail.co.uk.

By Bus to: **London** (every 60-90 minutes, 2 hours), **Heathrow Airport** (1-2/hour, 2-3 hours), **Oxford** (2/hour, 3.5 hours). Bus info: Tel. 0871-781-8181, www.nationalexpress.com.

Stonehenge

As old as the pyramids, and older than the Acropolis and the Colosseum, this iconic stone circle amazed medieval Europeans, who figured it was built by a race of giants. And it still impresses visitors today. As one of Europe's most famous sights, Stonehenge, worth ▲▲, does a valiant job of retaining an air of mystery and majesty (partly because cordons, which keep hordes of tourists from trampling all over

it, foster the illusion that it stands alone in a field). Although some people are underwhelmed by Stonehenge, most of its almost one million annual visitors find that it's worth the trip. And the ancient site continues to reveal its mysteries: In 2010, within sight of Stonehenge, archaeologists discovered another 5,000-year-old henge, which they believe once encircled a wooden "twin" of the famous circle. Recent excavations revealed that people had been living on the site since around 3,000 B.C.—about five centuries earlier than anyone had realized.

GETTING TO STONEHENGE
Stonehenge is about 90 miles southwest of central London. To reach it from London, you can take a bus tour; go on a guided tour that uses public transportation; or do it on your own using public transit, connecting via Salisbury. It's not worth the hassle or expense to rent a car just for a Stonehenge day trip.

By Bus Tour from London: Several companies offer big-bus day trips to Stonehenge from London, often with stops in Bath, Windsor, Salisbury, and/or Avebury. These generally cost about £45-85 (including admission to Stonehenge), last 8-12 hours, and pack a 45-seat bus. Some include hotel pickup, admission fees, and meals; understand what's included before you book. The more destinations listed for a tour, the less time you'll have at any one stop. Well-known companies are **Evan Evans** (their bare-bones Stonehenge Express gets you there and back for £44, tel. 020/7950-1777 or US tel. 866-382-6868, www.evanevanstours.co.uk) and **Golden Tours** (£44, tel. 020/7630-2028 or US toll-free tel. 800-509-2507, www.goldentours.com). **International Friends** runs pricier but smaller 16-person tours that include Windsor and Bath (£119, tel. 01223/244-555, www.internationalfriends.co.uk).

By Guided Tour on Public Transport: London Walks offers a guided "Stonehenge and Salisbury Tour" by train and bus on Tuesdays from May through October (£60, includes all transportation, Salisbury walking tour, entry fees, and guided tours of Stonehenge and Salisbury Cathedral; buy all tickets from guide; cash only, Tue at 8:45, meet at Waterloo Station's main ticket office, opposite Platform 16, verify price and schedule by phone or online, advance booking not required, tel. 020/7624-3978, recorded info tel. 020/7624-9255, www.walks.com).

On Your Own on Public Transport: You can catch a train to Salisbury, then go by bus or taxi to Stonehenge. Trains to Salisbury run from London's Waterloo Station (around £38 for same-day return leaving weekdays after 9:30, 2/hour, 1.5 hours, tel. 0871-200-4950 or 0345-748-4950, www.southwesttrains.co.uk or www.nationalrail.co.uk).

Once in Salisbury, you can take **The Stonehenge Tour** bus to the site. Their distinctive double-decker buses leave from the Salisbury train station (also stops at bus station) and make a circuit to Stonehenge and Old Sarum, with lovely scenery and a decent light commentary along the way (£14, £27 with Stonehenge and Old Sarum admission; tickets good all day; buy ticket from driver; daily June-Aug 10:00-18:00, 2/hour; may not run June 21 because of solstice crowds, shorter hours and hourly departures off-season; 30 minutes from station to Stonehenge, tel. 01202/338-420, timetable at www.thestonehengetour.info).

A **taxi** from Salisbury to Stonehenge can make sense for groups (about £40-50). Try Value Cars Taxis (tel. 01722/505-050, www.salisbury-valuecars.co.uk) or a local cabbie named Brian (tel. 01722/339-781, briantwort@ntlworld.com).

ORIENTATION TO STONEHENGE

Cost: £17.20, best to buy in advance online (see next), covered by English Heritage Pass (see page 544), includes shuttle-bus ride to the stone circle. In summer, there's a £5 refundable parking fee for drivers.

Advance Tickets: Prebooking a timed-entry ticket at least 24 hours in advance is the only way to assure you'll actually get in to the site, which caps the number of visitors per day at 7,000. (Some same-day tickets may be available at the ticket window, but in high season, it's risky to count on this.) Purchase your ticket online at www.english-heritage.org.uk/stonehenge. After booking a 30-minute arrival window, you'll receive a confirmation email with your e-ticket. Either print your ticket

DAY TRIPS

Note: No vehicles other than
shuttle beyond this point.

B3086

A360
To Bath

GIFT
SHOP   ⓑ SHUTTLE
CAFÉ   PLATFORM   FARGO
TICKETS   SHUTTLE
            NEOLITHIC   STOP
            VILLAGE
            EXHIBIT
A360   VISITORS
         CENTER

P

To A-303
& Salisbury

200 Meters
200 Yards

to present at the site, or bring your booking reference number
with you.

    If tickets are sold out for the day you planned to visit,
consider a guided tour that includes entry (see various options
under "Getting to Stonehenge," earlier).

Hours: Daily June-Aug 9:00-20:00, mid-March-May and Sept-
mid-Oct 9:30-19:00, mid-Oct-mid-March 9:30-17:00. Note
that last entry is two hours before closing. Expect shorter
hours and possible closures June 20-22 due to huge, raucous
solstice crowds.

Tours: Audioguides are available behind the ticket counter (included with Heritage Pass, otherwise £2); the same audio content can be downloaded for free to your mobile device from the
English Heritage website using the visitors center's free Wi-Fi
(download before boarding the shuttle bus).

Visiting the Inner Stones: For the true Stonehenge fan, special
one-hour access to the stones' inner circle is available early in
the morning (times vary depending on sunrise, but the earliest
is 5:00 in June and July) or after closing to the general public.
Touching the stones is not allowed. Only 26 people are allowed at a time, so reservations must be made well in advance
(£30, allows you to revisit the site the same day at no extra
charge). Details are on the English Heritage website (under
"Visit Stonehenge," click "Prices and Opening Times," then
"Stone Circle Access Application Form").

Information: Tel. 0870-333-1181, www.english-heritage.org.uk/
stonehenge.

Services: The visitors center has WCs, a large gift shop, and free
Wi-Fi. Services at the circle itself are limited to emergency
WCs. Even in summer, carry a jacket, as there are no trees to
act as a wind-break and there's a reason the Salisbury plains
are so green.

Stonehenge Overview

BURIAL
MOUNDS

SHUTTLE
STOP
B

PATH

Note: From the Visitors Center to the
stone circle is 1.25 miles. If you choose
to disembark the shuttle at Fargo, it's a
20-minute walk to the circle.

STONEHENGE

DITCH

Eating: A large café within the visitors center serves hot drinks, soups, sandwiches, and salads along with hot light bites (£4-7).

Length of this Tour: Allow at least two hours to see everything.

◉ SELF-GUIDED TOUR

Whether you're using the audioguide or downloading the audio tour to your mobile device, this commentary will help make your visit even more meaningful. Start by touring the visitors center, then take a shuttle (or walk) to the stone circle.

• *Collect your ticket (and rent or download the audioguide) before heading to the excellent exhibit space.*

Visitors Center

The visitors center, located 1.25 miles west of the circle, is a minimalist steel structure with a subtly curved roofline, intended to replicate the Salisbury plains.

The **permanent exhibit** uses an artful combination of high-tech multimedia displays and prehistoric bones, tools, and pottery shards to explore the history of the people who built Stonehenge, how they lived, and why they might have built the stone circle.

Stand in the virtual center of Stonehenge, as 5,000 years pass by around you. Find the forensic reconstruction of a Neolithic man, based on a skeleton unearthed in 1863. Then step outside and visit his ancient neighborhood—a village of **Neolithic huts** modeled after the traces of a village discovered just northeast of Stonehenge.

If nature calls, be sure to use the WCs within the visitors center, as there are only emergency WCs at the circle itself.

• *Shuttle buses to the stone circle depart every 5-10 minutes from the platform behind the gift shop. The trip takes six minutes. If you'd prefer,*

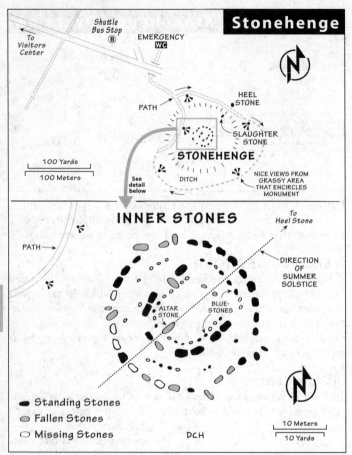

you can walk 1.25 miles through the fields to the site (use the map you receive with your ticket, or ask a staff member for directions).

Along the way, you have the option of stopping at **Fargo Plantation**, where you can see several burial mounds (tell the shuttle attendant if you want to disembark here). After wandering through the burial mounds, you'll need to walk the rest of the way to the stone circle (about 20 minutes).

Stone Circle

As you approach the massive structure, walk right up to the knee-high cordon and let your fellow 21st-century tourists melt away. It's just you and the druids...

England has hundreds of stone circles, but Stonehenge—which literally means "hanging stones"—is unique. It's the only one that has horizontal cross-pieces (called lintels) spanning the vertical monoliths, and the only one with stones that have been made smooth and uniform. What you see here is a bit more than half the original structure—the rest was quarried centuries ago for other buildings.

Now do a slow **clockwise spin** around the monument, and ponder the following points. As you walk, mentally flesh out the missing pieces and re-erect the rubble. Knowledgeable guides posted around the site are happy to answer your questions.

It's now believed that Stonehenge, which was built in phases between 3000 and 1500 B.C., was originally used as a cremation **cemetery.** But that's not the end of the story, as the monument was expanded over the millennia. This was a hugely significant location to prehistoric peoples. There are several hundred burial mounds within a three-mile radius of Stonehenge—some likely belonging to kings or chieftains. Some of the human remains are of people from far away, and others show signs of injuries—evidence that Stonehenge may have been used as a place of **medicine** or healing.

Whatever its original purpose, Stonehenge still functions as a celestial **calendar.** As the sun rises on the summer solstice (June 21), the **"heel stone"**—the one set apart from the rest, near the road—lines up with the sun and the altar at the center of the stone circle. A study of more than 300 similar circles in Britain found that each was designed to calculate the movement of the sun, moon, and stars, and to predict eclipses in order to help early societies know when to plant, harvest, and party. Even in modern times, as the summer solstice sun sets in just the right slot at Stonehenge, pagans boogie.

Some believe that Stonehenge is built at the precise point where six **"ley lines"** intersect. Ley lines are theoretical lines of magnetic or spiritual power that crisscross the globe. Belief in the power of these lines has gone in and out of fashion over time. They are believed to have been very important to prehistoric peoples, but then were largely ignored until the early 20th century, when the English writer Alfred Watkins popularized them (to the scorn of serious scientists). More recently, the concept has been embraced by the New Age movement. Without realizing it, you follow these ley lines all the time: Many of England's modern highways, following prehistoric paths, and churches, built over prehistoric monuments, are located where ley lines intersect. If you're a skeptic, ask one of the guides at Stonehenge to explain the mystique of this paranormal tradition that continued for centuries; it's creepy and convincing.

Notice that two of the stones (facing the entry passageway) are blemished. At the base of one monolith, it looks like someone has pulled back the stone to reveal a concrete skeleton. This is a clumsy **repair job** to fix damage done long ago by souvenir seekers, who actually rented hammers and chisels to take home a piece of Stonehenge. Look to the right of the repaired stone: The back of another stone is missing the same thin layer of protective lichen that covers the others. The lichen—and some of the stone itself—was sandblasted off to remove graffiti. (No wonder they've got Stonehenge roped off now.) The repairs were intentionally done in a different color, so as not to appear like the original stone.

Stonehenge's builders used two different types of stone. The tall, stout monoliths and lintels are sandstone blocks called **sarsen stones.** Most of the monoliths weigh about 25 tons (the largest is 45 tons), and the lintels are about 7 tons apiece. These sarsen stones were brought from "only" 20 miles away. The shorter stones in the middle, called **bluestones,** came from the south coast of Wales— 240 miles away (close if you're taking a train, but far if you're packing a megalith). Imagine the logistical puzzle of floating six-ton stones across Wales' Severn Estuary and up the River Avon, then rolling them on logs about 20 miles to this position...an impressive feat, even in our era of skyscrapers. We know the stones came from Wales because geologists have chemically matched the bluestones to specific outcrops there.

Why didn't the builders of Stonehenge use what seem like perfectly adequate stones nearby? This, like many other questions about Stonehenge, remains shrouded in mystery. Think again about the ley lines. Ponder the fact that many experts accept none of the explanations of how these giant stones were transported. Then imagine congregations gathering here 5,000 years ago, raising thought levels, creating a powerful life force transmitted along the ley lines. Maybe a particular kind of stone was essential for maximum energy transmission. Maybe the stones were levitated here. Maybe psychics really do create powerful vibes. Maybe not. It's as unbelievable as electricity used to be.

BRITAIN: PAST AND PRESENT

To fully appreciate the many fascinating sights you'll encounter in your travels, learn the basics of the sweeping story of this land and its people. (Generally speaking, the fascinating stories you'll hear from tour guides are not true...and the boring ones are.)

Regardless of the revolution we had nearly 240 years ago, many American travelers feel that they "go home" to Britain. This most popular tourist destination has a strange influence and power over us. The more you know of Britain's roots, the better you'll get in touch with your own.

This chapter starts with a once-over of Britain's illustrious history. It's speckled throughout with more in-depth information about current issues and this great country's future.

British History

ORIGINS (2000 B.C.-A.D. 500)

When Julius Caesar landed on the misty and mysterious isle of Britain in 55 B.C., England entered the history books. He was met by primitive Celtic tribes whose druid priests made human sacrifices and worshipped trees. (Those Celts were themselves immigrants, who had earlier conquered the even more mysterious people who built Stonehenge.) The Romans eventually settled in England (A.D. 43) and set about building towns and roads and establishing their capital at Londinium (today's London).

But the Celtic natives—consisting of Gaels, Picts, and Scots—were not easily subdued. Around A.D. 60, Boadicea, a queen of the

Isle's indigenous people, defied the Romans and burned Londinium before the revolt was squelched. Some decades later, the Romans built Hadrian's Wall near the Scottish border as protection against their troublesome northern neighbors. Even today, the Celtic language and influence are strongest in these far reaches of Britain.

Londinium became a bustling Roman river-and-sea trading port. The Romans built the original London Bridge and a city wall, encompassing one square mile, which set the city boundaries for 1,500 years. By A.D. 200, London was a thriving, Latin-speaking capital of Roman-dominated England.

Sights
- Boadicea statue near Westminster Bridge
- Roman Wall

DARK AGES (500-1000)

As Rome fell, so fell Roman Britain—a victim of invaders and internal troubles. Barbarian tribes from Germany, Denmark, and northern Holland, called Angles, Saxons, and Jutes, swept through the southern part of the island, establishing Angle-land. These were the days of the real King Arthur, possibly a Christianized Roman general who fought valiantly—but in vain—against invading barbarians.

In 793, England was hit with the first of two centuries of savage invasions by barbarians from Norway, called the Vikings or Norsemen. King Alfred the Great (849-899) liberated London from Danish Vikings, reunited England, reestablished Christianity, and fostered learning. Nevertheless, for most of this 500-year period, the island was plunged into a dark age—wars, plagues, and poverty—lit only by the dim candle of a few learned Christian monks and missionaries trying to convert the barbarians. Today, visitors see little from this Anglo-Saxon period.

Sights
- Lindisfarne Gospels, *Beowulf* manuscript (British Library)

WARS WITH FRANCE, WARS OF THE ROSES (1000-1500)

Modern England began with yet another invasion. In 1066, William the Conqueror and his Norman troops crossed the English Channel from France. William crowned himself king in Westminster Abbey (where all subsequent coronations would take place). He began building the Tower of London, as well as Windsor Castle, which would become the residence of many monarchs to come.

Over the succeeding centuries, French-speaking kings would rule England, and English-speaking kings invaded France as the two budding nations defined their modern borders. Richard the Lionheart (1157-1199) ruled as a French-speaking king who spent most of his energy on distant Crusades. This was the time of the legendary (and possibly real) Robin Hood, a bandit who robbed from the rich and gave to the poor—a populace that felt neglected by its francophone rulers. In 1215, King John (Richard's brother), under pressure from England's barons, was forced to sign the Magna Carta, establishing the principle that even kings must follow the rule of law.

London asserted itself as England's trade center. London Bridge—the famous stone version, topped with houses—was built (1209), and Old St. Paul's Cathedral was finished (1314).

Then followed two centuries of wars, chiefly the Hundred Years' War with France (1337-1443), in which France's Joan of Arc rallied the French to drive English forces back across the Channel. In 1348, the Black Death (bubonic plague) killed half of London's population.

In the 1400s, noble families duked it out for the crown. The York and Lancaster families fought the Wars of the Roses, so-called because of the white and red flowers the combatants chose as their symbols. Rife with battles and intrigues, and with kings, nobles, and ladies imprisoned and executed in the Tower, it's a wonder the country survived its rulers.

Sights

- Tower of London
- Westminster Abbey
- Windsor Castle
- Magna Carta, *The Canterbury Tales* (British Library)
- Temple Church

THE TUDOR RENAISSANCE (1500s)

England was finally united by the "third-party" Tudor family. Henry VIII, a Tudor, was England's Renaissance king. Powerful, charismatic, handsome, athletic, highly sexed, a poet, a scholar, and a musician, Henry VIII thrust England onto the world stage. He was also arrogant, cruel, gluttonous, and paranoid. He went through six wives in 40 years, divorcing, imprisoning, or executing them when they no longer suited his needs. (To keep track of each one's fate, British kids learn this rhyme: "Divorced, beheaded, died; divorced, beheaded, survived.")

When the Pope refused to grant Henry a divorce so he could marry his mistress Anne Boleyn, Henry "divorced" England from the Catholic Church. He established the Protestant Church of England (the Anglican Church), thus setting in motion a century of bitter Protestant/Catholic squabbles. Henry's own daughter, "Bloody" Mary, was a staunch Catholic who presided over the burning of hundreds of prominent Protestants. (For more on Henry VIII, see the sidebar on page 172.)

Henry was followed by another daughter (by Anne Boleyn)—Queen Elizabeth I. She reigned for 45 years, making England a great trading and naval power (defeating the Spanish Armada) and treading diplomatically over the Protestant/Catholic divide. Elizabeth presided over a cultural renaissance known (not surprisingly) as the "Elizabethan Age." Playwright William Shakespeare moved from Stratford-upon-Avon to London, beginning a remarkable career as the earth's greatest playwright. Sir Francis Drake circumnavigated the globe. Sir Walter Raleigh explored the Americas, and Sir Francis Bacon pioneered the scientific method. London's population swelled.

But Elizabeth—the "Virgin Queen"—never married or produced an heir. So the English Parliament invited Scotland's King James (Elizabeth's first cousin twice removed) to inherit the English throne. The two nations have been tied together ever since, however fitfully.

Sights
- Shakespeare's Globe
- Shakespeare folios (British Library)
- Tower of London execution site
- Chapel of Henry VII and Elizabeth I's tomb in Westminster Abbey
- Kings College Chapel in Cambridge

KINGS VS. PARLIAMENT (1600s)
The enduring quarrel between England's kings and Parliament's nobles finally erupted into the Civil War (1642). The war pitted (roughly speaking) the Protestant Puritan Parliament against the Catholic aristocracy. Parliament

forces under Oliver Cromwell defeated—and beheaded—King Charles I. After Cromwell died, Parliament invited Charles' son to take the throne—the "restoration of the monarchy." To emphasize the point, Cromwell's corpse was subsequently exhumed and posthumously beheaded.

This turbulent era was followed by back-to-back disasters—the Great Plague of 1665 (which killed 100,000) and the Great Fire of 1666 (which incinerated London). London was completely rebuilt in stone, centered around New St. Paul's Cathedral, which was built by Christopher Wren. With a population over 200,000, London was now Europe's largest city. At home, Isaac Newton watched an apple fall from a tree, leading him to discover the mysterious force of gravity.

In the war between kings and Parliament, Parliament finally got the last word, when it deposed Catholic James II and imported the Dutch monarchs William and Mary in 1688, guaranteeing a Protestant succession.

Sights

- Banqueting House (site of Charles I's beheading)
- Crown jewels (Tower of London)
- City of London
- Fire Monument
- St. Paul's and other Wren churches
- Isaac Newton's apple tree (outside Trinity College Gate, Cambridge)
- Kensington Palace (residence of William, Mary, and Anne)

COLONIAL EXPANSION (1700s)

Britain grew as a naval superpower, colonizing and trading with all parts of the globe. Eventually, Britannia ruled the waves, exploiting the wealth of India, Africa, and Australia. (And America...at least until they lost its most important colony when those ungrateful Yanks revolted in 1776 in the "American War.") Throughout the century, the country was ruled by the German Hanover family, including four kings named George.

The "Georgian Era" was one of great wealth. London's population was now half a million, and one in seven Brits lived in London. The nation's first daily newspapers hit the streets. The cultural scene was refined: painters (like William Hogarth, Joshua Reynolds, and Thomas Gainsborough), theater (with actors like David Garrick), music (Handel's *Messiah*), and literature (Samuel

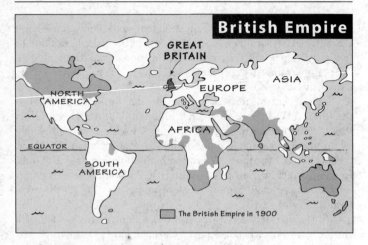

British Empire

GREAT BRITAIN
NORTH AMERICA
EUROPE
ASIA
AFRICA
EQUATOR
SOUTH AMERICA

☐ The British Empire in 1900

Johnson's dictionary). Scientist James Watt's steam engines laid the groundwork for a coming Industrial Revolution.

In 1789, the French Revolution erupted, sparking decades of war between France and Britain. Britain finally prevailed in the early 1800s, when Admiral Horatio Nelson defeated Napoleon's fleet at the Battle of Trafalgar and the Duke of Wellington stomped Napoleon at Waterloo. (Nelson and Wellington are memorialized by many arches, columns, and squares throughout England.)

By war's end, Britain had emerged as Europe's top power.

Sights

- Nelson's Column at Trafalgar Square
- Apsley House (Wellington Museum) and adjacent Wellington Arch
- Portraits by Reynolds and Gainsborough and slices of life by Hogarth (Tate Britain)
- Royal Observatory and National Maritime Museum, Greenwich
- Dr. Johnson's House in The City

VICTORIAN GENTILITY AND THE INDUSTRIAL REVOLUTION (1800s)

Britain reigned supreme, steaming into the Industrial Age with her mills, factories, coal mines, gas lights, and trains. By century's end, there was electricity, telephones, and the first Underground.

In 1837, eighteen-year-old Victoria became queen. She ruled for 64 years, presiding over an era of unprecedented wealth, peace, and middle-class ("Victorian") values. Britain was at its zenith of power, with a colonial empire that covered one-fifth of the world (for more on Victoria and her Age, see sidebar on page 102).

Meanwhile, there was another side to Britain's era of superiority and industrial might. A generation of Romantic poets (William Wordsworth, John Keats, Percy Shelley, and Lord Byron) longed for the innocence of nature. Jane Austen and the Brontë sisters wrote romantic tales about the landed gentry. Painters like J. M. W. Turner and William Constable immersed themselves in nature to paint moody landscapes.

The gritty modern world was emerging. Popular novelist Charles Dickens brought literature to the masses, educating them about Britain's harsh social and economic realities. Rudyard Kipling critiqued the colonial system. Charles Darwin questioned the very nature of humanity when he articulated the principles of natural selection and evolution. Jack the Ripper, a serial killer of prostitutes, terrorized east London and was never caught. Not even by Sherlock Holmes—a fictional detective living at 221B Baker Street who solved fictional crimes that the real Scotland Yard couldn't.

Sights
- Big Ben and Halls of Parliament
- Buckingham Palace, the Mall, and Hyde Park
- The Tube
- Paintings by Turner and Constable (Tate Britain)
- Writers' manuscripts in the British Library
- Poets' Corner in Westminster Abbey
- Victoria and Albert Museum
- Kensington Palace (Victoria Revealed exhibit)
- Sherlock Holmes Museum
- London's East End tenements (reminiscent of the Jack the Ripper days)

WORLD WARS AND RECOVERY (20TH CENTURY)
The 20th century was not kind to Britain. Two world wars and economic struggles whittled Britain down from a world empire to an island chain struggling to compete in a global economy.

In World War I, Britain joined France and other allies to battle Germany in trench warfare. A million British men died. Meanwhile, after decades of rebellion, Ireland finally gained its independence—except for the Protestant-leaning Northern Ireland, which remained tied to Britain. This division of the Emerald Isle would result in decades of bitter strife, protests, and terrorist attacks known as "The Troubles."

In the 1920s, London was home to a flourishing literary scene, including T. S. Eliot (American-turned-British), Virginia Woolf, and E. M. Forster. In 1936, the country was rocked and scandalized when King Edward VIII abdicated to marry a divorced American commoner, Wallis Simpson. He was succeeded by his brother, George VI—"Bertie" of *The King's Speech* fame, and father of Queen Elizabeth II.

In World War II, the Nazi Blitz (aerial bombing campaign) reduced much of London to rubble, sending residents into Tube stations for shelter and the government into a fortified bunker (now the Churchill War Rooms). Britain was rallied through its darkest hour by two leaders: Prime Minister Winston Churchill, a remarkable orator, and King George VI, who overcame a persistent stutter. Amid the chaos of war, the colonial empire began to dwindle to almost nothing, and Britain emerged from the war as a shell of its former superpower self.

The postwar recovery began, aided by the United States. Many cheap, concrete (ugly) buildings rose from the rubble.

Culturally, Britain remained world-class. Oxford professor J. R. R. Tolkien wrote *The Lord of the Rings* and his friend C. S. Lewis wrote *The Chronicles of Narnia*. In the 1960s, "Swinging London" became a center for rock music, film, theater, youth culture, and Austin Powers-style joie de vivre. America was conquered by a "British Invasion" of rock bands (The Beatles, The Rolling Stones, and The Who, followed later by Led Zeppelin, Elton John, David Bowie, and others), and James Bond ruled the box office.

The 1970s brought massive unemployment, labor strikes, and recession. A conservative reaction followed in the 1980s and 90s, led by Prime Minister Margaret Thatcher—the "Iron Lady." As proponents of traditional, Victorian values—community, family, hard work, thrift, and trickle-down economics—the Conservatives took a Reaganesque approach to Britain's serious social and economic problems. They cut government subsidies to old-fashioned heavy industries (closing many factories, earning working-class ire), as they tried to nudge Britain toward a more modern economy.

In 1981, the world was captivated by the spectacle of Prince Charles marrying Lady Diana in St. Paul's Cathedral. Their children, Princes William and Harry, grew up in the media spotlight, and when Diana died in a car crash (1997), the nation—and the world—mourned.

The 1990s saw Britain finally emerging from decades of economic stagnation and social turmoil. An energized nation prepared for the new millennium.

Sights
- Cabinet War Rooms
- Cenotaph

- Imperial War Museum
- Blitz photos at St. Paul's
- Beatles memorabilia (British Library)
- Harrods

EARLY 2000s

London celebrated the millennium with a new Ferris wheel (the London Eye), the Millennium Bridge, and the Millennium Dome exhibition (now "The O2"). In 2002, Queen Elizabeth II celebrated her 50-year Jubilee.

After two decades of Conservative politics, Britain was now ruled by a Labour (left-of-center) government under Prime Minister Tony Blair. Labour began shoring up a social-service system (health care, education, minimum wage) undercut by years of Conservative rule. But Blair's popularity was undermined when he joined the US invasion of Iraq. On the morning of July 7 ("7/7") in 2005, London's commuters were rocked by four terrorist bombs that killed dozens across the city. In subsequent years, Britain has had numerous terrorist plots that either caused destruction or were foiled by police.

Thankfully, one hot spot—Northern Ireland, plagued for decades by the "Troubles"—was healed. In the spring of 2007, the previously unthinkable happened when leaders of the ultra-nationalist party sat down with those of the ultra-unionist party. An agreement was reached and, after almost 40 years, the British Army withdrew.

In 2008, Britain suffered mightily in the global recession. The economy shrank more than 6 percent and faced a huge budget deficit. British voters turned for answers to the Conservative party under David Cameron, who was elected prime minister in 2010. Cameron's approach was "austerity"—cut government spending, raise the national sales tax, eliminate half a million public-sector jobs, and slash spending on unemployment benefits, public housing, police, and funding for the arts and the BBC. The question of whether these policies worked or hurt the economy has been a topic of great debate.

In 2012, in a one-two punch of festivity, the Brits hosted two huge events: the London Olympics and the Queen's Diamond Jubilee. The flurry of investment has left the country looking better than ever. This was just the latest of decades of renovation that have turned former urban wastelands and industrial waterfronts into hip, thriving people zones.

Sights

- The London Eye
- Millennium Bridge

- Tate Modern contemporary art exhibits
- West End theaters
- The Docklands skyscraper zone

Britain Today

The Britain you visit today is vibrant and alive. It's smaller, and no longer the superpower it once was, but it's still a cultural and economic powerhouse.

WHAT'S SO GREAT ABOUT BRITAIN?

Think of it. At its peak in the mid-1800s, Britain owned one-fifth of the world and accounted for more than half the planet's industrial output. Today, the Empire is down to the Isle of Britain itself and a few token scraps (the Falklands, Gibraltar, Northern Ireland) and a loose association of former colonies (Canada, Australia) called the "British Commonwealth."

Geographically, the Isle of Britain is small—smaller than the state of Oregon—and its highest mountain (Scafell Pike in the Lake District at 3,209 feet) is a foothill by US standards. The population is a fifth that of the United States.

It's small, but Britain is still Great.

Economically, Great Britain's industrial production is about 5 percent of the world's total. Ethnically, it's become quite diverse. It's a mix of Celtic (the natives of Scotland, Ireland, Wales, and Cornwall), Anglo-Saxon (the former "barbarians" from Dark Age times), the conquering Normans, and the many recent immigrants from around the world.

The Britain you visit today remains a global superpower of heritage, culture, and tradition. It's a major exporter of actors, movies, and theater; of rock and classical music; and of writers, painters, and sculptors. It's the perfect place for you to visit and make your own history.

CURRENT ISSUES AND POLITICAL LANDSCAPE

Britain is ruled by the House of Commons, with some guidance from the mostly figurehead Queen and House of Lords. Just as the United States Congress is dominated by Democrats and Republicans, Britain's Parliament has traditionally been dominated by two parties: left-leaning Labour and right-leaning Conservative ("Tories"). But other parties also attract votes (e.g., the center-left Liberal Democrats, or "Lib Dems"), and whoever rules must form some kind of coalition to remain strong.

Strangely, Britain's "constitution" is not one single document; the government's structures and policies are based on centuries of tradition, statutes, and doctrine, and much of it is not actually in

Get It Right

Americans tend to use "England," "Britain," and the "United Kingdom" (or "UK") interchangeably, but they're not quite the same.

- **England** is the country occupying the center and south-east part of the island.
- **Britain** is the name of the island.
- **Great Britain** is the political union of the island's three countries: England, Scotland, and Wales.
- The **United Kingdom** (UK) adds a fourth country, Northern Ireland.
- The **British Isles** (not a political entity) also includes the independent Republic of Ireland.
- The **British Commonwealth** is a loose association of possessions and former colonies (including Canada, Australia, and India) that profess at least symbolic loyalty to the Crown.

You can call the modern nation either the United Kingdom ("the UK"), "Great Britain," or simply "Britain."

---

writing. While this might seem potentially troublesome—if not dangerous—the British body politic takes pride in its ethos of civility and mutual respect, which has long made this arrangement work.

The prime minister is the chief executive but is not elected directly by voters; rather, he or she assumes power as the head of the party that wins a majority in parliamentary elections. While historically the prime minister could dissolve Parliament at will to make way for new elections, a law passed in 2011 now requires parliamentary elections to be held every five years.

The biggest issue in Britain today is the economy. The 2008 global downturn hurt Britain enormously, and it's been a long slog back. The dividing lines are similar to those in the States: should government nurture the economy through spending on social programs (Labour's platform), or cut programs and taxes to allow businesses to thrive (as Conservatives say)?

Wealth inequality is also a hot button. The 2008 downturn sharpened unemployment and slashed programs for the working class. This has resulted in protests and riots that pit poor young men against the police.

Like the US, Britain has suffered a number of terrorist threats and attacks. The question remains how to balance security with privacy concerns. The British have surveillance cameras everywhere—you'll frequently see signs warning you that you're being recorded. As Brits trade their privacy for security, many wonder if they've given up too much. Most Brits have accepted that terrorist acts are a fact of life—and that life must go on.

The terrorist threats have highlighted issues relating to Britain's large immigrant population (nearly 4 million). Brits are stunned that many terrorists (like the notorious "Jihadi John" of ISIS) speak the king's English and were born and raised in Britain. And some radical Islamic clerics seem to be preaching jihad in the mosque down the street. It raises the larger question: How well is the nation assimilating its many immigrants?

The large Muslim population is just one thread in the tapestry of today's Britain. While 9 out of 10 Brits are white, the country has large minority groups, mainly from Britain's former colonies: India, Pakistan, Bangladesh, Africa, the Caribbean, and many other places. Despite the tensions between some groups, for the most part Britain is relatively integrated, with minorities represented in most (if not all) walks of life.

Throughout the British Isles, you'll also see many Eastern Europeans (mostly Poles, Slovaks, and Lithuanians) working in restaurants, cafés, and B&Bs. These transplants—who started arriving after their home countries joined the EU in 2004—can make a lot more money working here than back home. British small-business owners have found them to be polite, hardworking, and affordable. While a few Brits complain that the new arrivals are taking their jobs or diluting English culture, most of Britain has absorbed this new set of immigrants gracefully.

The European Union is hotly debated. Labour embraces Britain's membership in the EU. Conservatives want to renegotiate the country's membership, or leave the EU altogether. A public referendum on the matter could be held sometime in 2016.

The issue of whether Scotland should be granted independence from rule from London has raised all kinds of thorny problems. Nationalists insist a free Scotland would be rich (on oil reserves) and free from the "shackles" of London-based problems. (Cynics call the "United" Kingdom an English Empire ruled by London, whose millions of ethnic Anglo-Saxons dominate their Celtic brothers and sisters.) Opponents insist it's the union of British peoples (and the strong pound currency) that make the country strong. Although Scottish voters rejected an independence referendum in 2014, the Scottish Nationalist Party has become a significant third-party kingmaker in British national elections.

In the May 2015 general election, polls had predicted an extremely tight race, but the Conservatives, led by David Cameron, won a working majority of seats in Parliament. The Labour Party lost seats (and now has its lowest total since 1987). The Scottish National Party, more popular since the independence referendum, became the third-largest party in the House of Commons, securing 56 of Scotland's 59 seats—taking many of these from the Labour Party.

Among social issues, binge-drinking is a serious problem. Since 2003, pubs can stay open past the traditional 23:00 closing time. An unintended consequence is that (according to one study) one in three British men and one in five British women routinely drinks to excess. Young adults routinely spend evenings drinking at pubs and carousing in the streets, then ratchet it up still more on weekends and stag and hen nights—bachelor and bachelorette parties. Sociologists and politicians debate whether this phenomenon is a serious problem or harmless fun, and tourists may find it either wonderful or obnoxious.

Then there's the eternal question of the royals. Is having a monarch (who's politically irrelevant) and a royal family (who fill the tabloids with their scandals and foibles) worth it? In decades past, many Brits wanted to toss the whole lot of them. But the recent marriage of the popular William and Kate and the birth of their two cute kids have boosted royal esteem. According to pollsters, four out of five Brits want to keep their Queen and let the tradition live on.

BRITISH TV

Although it has its share of lowbrow reality programming, much British television is still so good—and so British—that it deserves a mention as a sightseeing treat. After a hard day of castle climbing, watch the telly over tea in your B&B.

For many years there were only five free channels, but now nearly every British television can receive a couple of dozen. BBC television is government-regulated and commercial-free. Broadcasting of its eight channels (and of the five BBC radio stations) is funded by a mandatory £145.50-per-year-per-household television and radio license (hmmm, 60 cents per day to escape commercials and public-broadcasting pledge drives...not bad). Channels 3, 4, and 5 are privately owned, are a little more lowbrow, and have commercials—but those "adverts" are often clever and sophisticated, providing a fun look at British life. About 60 percent of households pay for cable or satellite television.

Whereas California "accents" fill US airwaves 24 hours a day, homogenizing the way our country speaks, Britain protects and promotes its regional accents by its choice of TV and radio announcers. See if you can tell where each is from (or ask a local for help).

Commercial-free British TV, while looser than it used to be, is still careful about what it airs and when. But after the 21:00 "watershed" hour, when children are expected to be in bed, some nudity and profanity are allowed, and may cause you to spill your tea.

Royal Families: Past and Present

Royal Lineage

802-1066	Saxon and Danish kings
1066-1154	Norman invasion (William the Conqueror), Norman kings
1154-1399	Plantagenet (kings with French roots)
1399-1461	Lancaster
1462-1485	York
1485-1603	Tudor (Henry VIII, Elizabeth I)
1603-1649	Stuart (civil war and beheading of Charles I)
1649-1653	Commonwealth, no royal head of state
1653-1659	Protectorate, with Cromwell as Lord Protector
1660-1714	Restoration of Stuart dynasty
1714-1901	Hanover (four Georges, William IV, Victoria)
1901-1910	Saxe-Coburg (Edward VII)
1910-present	Windsor (George V, Edward VIII, George VI, Elizabeth II)

The Royal Family Today

It seems you can't pick up a British newspaper without some mention of the latest event, scandal, or oddity involving the royal family. Here is the cast of characters:

Queen Elizabeth II wears the traditional crown of her great-great grandmother Victoria, who ruled for 63 years, 7 months, and 2 days. In September 2015, Queen Elizabeth officially overtook Victoria as England's longest-reigning monarch. Elizabeth's husband is Prince Philip, who's not considered king.

Their son, Prince Charles (the Prince of Wales), is next in line to become king—and already holds the title as the longest "heir in waiting." But it's Prince Charles' sons who generate the tabloid buzz. The older son, Prince William (b. 1982), is a graduate of Scotland's St. Andrews University and served as a search-and-rescue helicopter pilot with the Royal Air Force. In 2011, when William married Catherine "Kate" Middleton, the TV audience was estimated at one-quarter of the world's population—more than two billion people. Kate—a commoner William met at university—is now the Duchess of Cambridge and will eventually become Britain's queen. Their son, Prince George Alexander Louis, born in 2013—and voted the most powerful and influential person in London by a poll in the *Evening Standard* two months later—will

American programs (such as *Game of Thrones, CSI, Friends, Frasier, How I Met Your Mother, The Simpsons, Family Guy,* and trash-talk shows) are very popular. But the visiting viewer should be sure to tune the TV to more typically British shows, including a dose of British situation- and political-comedy fun, and the top-notch BBC evening news. British comedies have tickled the Amerultimately succeed William as sovereign. (A conveniently timed change in the law ensured that William and Kate's firstborn would inherit the throne, regardless of gender.) In 2015, the royal couple welcomed the arrival of their second child, daughter Princess Charlotte Elizabeth Diana.

William's brother, redheaded Prince Harry (b. 1984), has mostly shaken his earlier reputation as a bad boy: He's proved his mettle as a career soldier, completing a tour in Afghanistan, doing charity work in Africa, and serving as an Apache aircraft commander pilot with the Army Air Corps. Nonetheless, Harry's romances and high-wire party antics are popular tabloid topics.

For years, their parents' love life was also fodder for the British press: Charles' 1981 marriage to Princess Di, their bitter divorce, Diana's dramatic death in 1997, and the ongoing drama with Charles' longtime girlfriend—and now wife—Camilla Parker Bowles. Camilla, trying to gain the respect of the Queen and the public, doesn't call herself a princess—she uses the title Duchess of Cornwall. (And even when Charles becomes king, she will not be Queen Camilla—instead she plans to call herself the "Princess Consort.")

Charles' siblings are occasionally in the news: Princess Anne, Prince Andrew (who married and divorced Sarah "Fergie" Ferguson), and Prince Edward (who married Di look-alike Sophie Rhys-Jones).

Royal Sightseeing

You can see the trappings of royalty at Buckingham Palace (the Queen's London residence) with its Changing of the Guard; Kensington Palace—with a wing that's home to Will, Kate, and kids, and a cottage that serves as Harry's bachelor pad; Clarence House, the London home of Prince Charles and Camilla; Althorp Estate (80 miles from London), the childhood home and burial place of Princess Diana; Windsor Castle, a royal country home near London; and the crown jewels in the Tower of London.

Your best chances to actually see the Queen are on three public occasions: State Opening of Parliament (next in May 2016), Remembrance Sunday (early November, at the Cenotaph), or Trooping the Colour (one Saturday in mid-June, parading down Whitehall and at Buckingham Palace).

Otherwise, check the "Latest news and diary" section of www.royal.gov.uk, where you can search for future royal events.

ican funny bone for years, from sketch comedy *(Monty Python's Flying Circus)* to sitcoms *(Are You Being Served?, Fawlty Towers, Absolutely Fabulous,* and *The Office).* Quiz shows and reality shows are taken very seriously here *(American Idol, America's Got Talent, Dancing with the Stars, Who Wants to Be a Millionaire?,* and *The X Factor* are all based on British shows). Jonathan Ross is the Jimmy

Fallon of Britain for sometimes edgy late-night talk. Other popular late-night "chat show" hosts include Graham Norton and Alan
Carr. For a tear-filled, slice-of-life taste of British soaps dealing in
all the controversial issues, see the popular and remarkably long-
running *Emmerdale, Coronation Street,* or *EastEnders.* The costume
drama *Downton Abbey,* the long-running sci-fi serial *Doctor Who,*
the small-town dramedy *Doc Martin,* and the modern crime series
Sherlock have all become hits on both sides of the Atlantic.

NOTABLE BRITS OF TODAY AND TOMORROW

Only history can judge which British names will stand the test of
time, but these days big names in the UK include politicians (David
Cameron, Boris Johnson, Jeremy Corbyn, Nicola Sturgeon), actors
(Helen Mirren, Emma Thompson, Helena Bonham Carter, Jude
Law, Stephen Fry, Ricky Gervais, James Corden, Daniel Radcliffe,
Kate Winslet, Benedict Cumberbatch, Martin Freeman, Peter
Capaldi, Colin Firth), musicians (Adele, Chris Martin of Cold-
play, James Arthur, Ellie Goulding, One Direction, Ed Sheeran,
Sam Smith), writers (J. K. Rowling, E. L. James, Hilary Mantel,
Tom Stoppard, Nick Hornby, Ian McEwan, Zadie Smith), artists
(Damien Hirst, Rachel Whiteread, Tracey Emin, Anish Kapoor),
athletes (David Beckham, Bradley Wiggins, Andy Murray), entre-
preneurs (Sir Richard Branson, Lord Alan Sugar)...and, of course,
William, Kate, and their children, George and Charlotte.

Architecture in Britain

From Stonehenge to Big Ben, travelers are storming castle walls,
climbing spiral staircases, and snapping the pictures of 5,000 years
of architecture. Let's sort it out.

The oldest ruins—mysterious and prehistoric—date from
before Roman times back to 3000 B.C. The earliest sites, such as
Stonehenge and Avebury, were built during the Stone and Bronze
ages. The remains from these periods are made of huge stones or
mounds of earth, even man-made hills, and were created as celestial calendars and for worship or burial. Britain is crisscrossed
with imaginary lines said to connect these mysterious sights (ley
lines). Iron Age people (600 B.C.-A.D. 50) left desolate stone forts.
The Romans thrived in Britain from A.D. 50 to 400, building cities, walls, and roads. Evidence of Roman greatness can be seen in
lavish villas with ornate mosaic floors, temples uncovered beneath
great English churches, and Roman stones in medieval city walls.
Roman roads sliced across the island in straight lines. Today, un-
usually straight rural roads are very likely laid directly on these
ancient roads.

As Rome crumbled in the fifth century, so did Roman Britain.

Mysterious Ruins

Little architecture survives from Dark Ages England, the Saxon period from 500 to 1000. Architecturally, the light was switched on with the Norman Conquest in 1066. As William earned his title "the Conqueror," his French architects built churches and castles in the European Romanesque style.

English Romanesque is called Norman (1066-1200). Norman churches had round arches, thick walls, and small windows; Durham Cathedral and the Chapel of St. John in the Tower of London are prime examples. The Tower of London, with its square keep, small windows, and spiral stone stairways, is a typical Norman castle. You can see plenty of Norman castles around England—all built to secure the conquest of these invaders from Normandy.

Gothic architecture (1200-1600) replaced the heavy Norman style with light, vertical buildings, pointed arches, soaring spires, and bigger windows. English Gothic is divided into three stages. Early English Gothic (1200-1300) features tall, simple spires; beautifully carved capitals; and elaborate chapter houses (such as the Wells Cathedral). Decorated Gothic (1300-1400) gets fancier, with more elaborate tracery, bigger windows, and ornately carved pinnacles, as you see at Westminster Abbey. Finally, the Perpendicular Gothic style (1400-1600, also called "rectilinear") returns to square towers and emphasizes straight, uninterrupted vertical lines from ceiling to floor, with vast windows and exuberant decoration, including fan-vaulted ceilings (King's College Chapel at Cambridge). Through this evolution, the structural ribs (arches meeting at the top of the ceilings) became more and more decorative and fanciful (the most fancy being the star vaulting and fan vaulting of the Perpendicular style).

As you tour the great medieval churches of Britain, remember that almost everything is symbolic. For instance, on the tombs of knights, if the figure has crossed legs, he was a Crusader. If his feet rest on a dog, he died at home; but if his legs rest on a lion, he died

Typical Church Architecture

History comes to life when you visit a centuries-old church. Even if you wouldn't know your apse from a hole in the ground, learning a few simple terms will enrich your experience. Note that not every church has every feature, and that a "cathedral" isn't a type of church architecture, but rather a designation for a church that's a governing center for a local bishop.

Aisles: The long, generally low-ceilinged arcades that flank the nave.

Altar: The raised area with a ceremonial table (often adorned with candles or a crucifix), where the priest prepares and serves the bread and wine for Communion.

Apse: The space beyond the altar, often bordered with small chapels.

Barrel Vault: A continuous round-arched ceiling that resembles an extended upside-down U.

Choir ("quire" in British English): A cozy area, often screened off, located within the church nave and near the high altar where services are sung in a more intimate setting.

Cloister: Covered hallways bordering a square or rectangular open-air courtyard, traditionally where monks and nuns got fresh air.

Facade: The exterior surface of the church's main (west) entrance, viewable from outside and usually highly decorated.

Groin Vault: An arched ceiling formed where two equal barrel vaults meet at right angles. Less common usage: term for a medieval jock strap.

Narthex: The area (portico or foyer) between the main entry and the nave.

Nave: The long, central section of the church (running west to east, from the entrance to the altar) where the congregation sits or stands through the service.

Transept: In a traditional cross-shaped floor plan, the transept is one of the two parts forming the "arms" of the cross. The transepts run north-south, perpendicularly crossing the east-west nave.

West Portal: The main entry to the church (on the west end, opposite the main altar).

Typical Castle Architecture

Castles were fortified residences for medieval nobles. Castles come in all shapes and sizes, but knowing a few general terms will help you understand them.

Barbican: A fortified gatehouse, sometimes a stand-alone building located outside the main walls.

Crenellation: A gap-toothed pattern of stones atop the parapet.

Drawbridge: A bridge that could be raised or lowered using counterweights or a chain and winch.

Great Hall: The largest room in the castle, serving as throne room, conference center, and dining hall.

Hoardings (or Gallery or Brattice): Wooden huts built onto the upper parts of the stone walls. They served as watch towers, living quarters, and fighting platforms.

The Keep (or Donjon): A high, strong stone tower in the center of the castle complex; the lord's home and refuge of last resort.

Loopholes (or Embrasures): Narrow wall slits through which soldiers could shoot arrows.

Machicolation: A stone ledge jutting out from the wall, with holes through which soldiers could drop rocks or boiling oil onto wall-scaling enemies below.

Moat: A ditch encircling the wall, often filled with water.

Motte-and-Bailey: A type of early English castle, with a hilltop fort (motte) and an enclosed, fortified yard (bailey).

Parapet: Outer railing of the wall walk.

Portcullis: A heavy iron grille that could be lowered across the entrance.

Postern Gate: A small, unfortified side or rear entrance from which to launch attacks or escape.

Towers: Tall structures with crenellated tops or conical roofs serving as lookouts, chapels, living quarters, or dungeons.

Turret: A small lookout tower rising up from the top of the wall.

Wall Walk (or Allure): A pathway atop the wall where guards could patrol and where soldiers stood to fire at the enemy.

The Yard (or Bailey): An open courtyard inside the castle walls.

PAST & PRESENT

in battle. Local guides and books help us modern pilgrims under-stand at least a little of what we see.

Wales is particularly rich in English castles, which were need-ed to subdue the stubborn Welsh. Edward I built a ring of powerful castles in North Wales, including Conwy and Caernarfon.

Gothic houses were a simple mix of woven strips of thin wood, rubble, and plaster called wattle and daub. The famous black-and-white Tudor (or "half-timbered") look came simply from filling in heavy oak frames with wattle and daub.

The Tudor period (1485-1560) was a time of relative peace (the Wars of the Roses were finally over), prosperity, and renais-sance. But when Henry VIII broke with the Catholic Church and disbanded its monasteries, scores of Britain's greatest churches were left as gutted shells. These hauntingly beautiful abbey ruins (Glastonbury, Tintern, Whitby, Rievaulx, Battle, St. Augustine's in Canterbury, St. Mary's in York, and lots more), surrounded by lush lawns, are now pleasant city parks.

Although few churches were built during the Tudor period, this was a time of house and mansion construction. Heating a home was becoming popular and affordable, and Tudor buildings featured small square windows and many chimneys. In towns, where land was scarce, many Tudor houses grew up and out, get-ting wider with each overhanging floor.

The Elizabethan and Jacobean periods (1560-1620) were fol-lowed by the English Renaissance style (1620-1720). English ar-chitects mixed Gothic and classical styles, then Baroque and clas-sical styles. Although the ornate Baroque never really grabbed Britain, the classical style of the Italian architect Andrea Palladio did. Inigo Jones (1573-1652), Christopher Wren (1632-1723), and those they inspired plastered Britain with enough columns, domes, and symmetry to please a Caesar. The Great Fire of London (1666) cleared the way for an ambitious young Wren to put his mark on London forever with a grand rebuilding scheme, including the great St. Paul's Cathedral and more than 50 other churches.

The celebrants of the Boston Tea Party remember Britain's Georgian period (1720-1840) for its lousy German kings. But in architectural terms, "Georgian" is English for "Neoclassical." Its architecture was rich and showed off by being very classical. Grand ornamental doorways, fine cast-ironwork on balconies and railings, Chippendale furniture, and white-on-blue Wedgwood ceramics graced rich homes everywhere. John Wood Sr. and Jr. led the way, giving the trendsetting city of Bath its crescents and circles of aris-tocratic Georgian row houses.

The Industrial Revolution shaped the Victorian period (1840-1890) with glass, steel, and iron. Britain had a huge new erector set (so did France's Mr. Eiffel). This was also a Romantic period, reviving the "more Christian" Gothic style. London's Houses of Parliament are Neo-Gothic—they're just 140 years old but look 700, except for the telltale modern precision and craftsmanship. Whereas Gothic was stone or concrete, Neo-Gothic was often red brick. These were Britain's glory days, and there was more building in this period than in all previous ages combined.

The architecture of the mid-20th century obeyed the formula "form follows function"—it worried more about your needs than your eyes. But more recently, the dull "international style" has been nudged aside by a more playful style, thanks to cutting-edge architects such as Lord Norman Foster and Renzo Piano. In the last several years, London has added several creative buildings to its skyline: the City Hall (nicknamed "The Armadillo"), 30 St. Mary Axe ("The Gherkin"), 20 Fenchurch ("The Walkie-Talkie"), and the tallest building in the European Union, the pointy Shard London Bridge (called...um, "The Shard").

Even as it sets trends for the 21st century, Britain treasures its heritage and takes great pains to build tastefully in historic districts and to preserve its many "listed" (government-protected) buildings. With a booming tourist trade, these quaint reminders of its past—and ours—are becoming a valuable part of the British economy.

For more about British history, consider Europe 101: History and Art for the Traveler *by Rick Steves and Gene Openshaw, available at* www.ricksteves.com.

PAST & PRESENT

PRACTICALITIES

Tourist Information 534
Travel Tips 535
Money 536
Sightseeing 542
Sleeping 544
Eating 552
Staying Connected 560
Transportation 567
Resources 571

This chapter covers the practical skills of European travel: how to get tourist information, pay for purchases, sightsee efficiently, find good-value accommodations, eat affordably but well, use technology wisely, and get between destinations smoothly. To round out your knowledge, check out "Resources."

Tourist Information

Before your trip, start with the TI's official website, www. visitlondon.com. The Visit Britain website contains a wealth of knowledge on destinations, activities, accommodations, and transport in Great Britain. Families will especially appreciate the "Britain for Kids & Families" travel suggestions. Maps, airport transfers, sightseeing tours, and theater tickets can be purchased online (www.visitbritain.com, www.visitbritainshop.com/usa for purchases).

In London, a good first stop is generally the tourist information office (abbreviated **TI** in this book). London's fine TI, called the **City of London Information Centre,** is near St. Paul's Cathedral (see page 18).

Be aware that TIs are in business to help you enjoy spending money in their town. (Once upon a time, they were actually information services, but today some have become promoters masquerading as TIs.) While this corrupts much of their advice—and you can get plenty of information online—I still make a point to swing by the local TI upon arrival in a new town. Even if they are overly commercial, TIs continue to be good places to confirm opening times, pick up a city map, and get information on public transit (including bus and train schedules), walking tours, special events, and nightlife. Stop in with a list of questions and a proposed plan to double-check.

For all the help TIs offer, steer clear of their room-finding services (bloated prices, booking fees, no opinions, and commissions that come from the pocket of your B&B host).

Other Helpful Websites: www.timeout.com/london, www.londontown.com.

Travel Tips

Emergency and Medical Help: In Britain, dial 999 for police help or a medical emergency. If you get sick, do as the locals do: Go to a pharmacy and see a "chemist" (pharmacist) for advice. Or ask at your hotel for help—they know of the nearest medical and emergency services. St. Thomas' Hospital, across the river from Big Ben, has a fine reputation.

Theft or Loss: To replace a passport, you'll need to go in person to a US embassy (see page 575). If your credit and debit cards disappear, cancel and replace them (see "Damage Control for Lost Cards" on page 539). File a police report, either on the spot or within a day or two; you'll need it to submit an insurance claim for lost or stolen rail passes or travel gear, and it can help with replacing your passport or credit and debit cards. For more information, see www.ricksteves.com/help. To minimize the effects of loss, back up your digital photos and other files frequently.

Time Zones: Britain, which is one hour earlier than most of continental Europe, is five/eight hours ahead of the East/West Coasts of the US. The exceptions are the beginning and end of Daylight Saving Time: Britain and Europe "spring forward" the last Sunday in March (two weeks after most of North America), and "fall back" the last Sunday in October (one week before North America). For a handy online time converter, see www.timeanddate.com/worldclock.

Business Hours: Most stores are open Monday through Saturday (roughly 9:00 or 10:00 until 17:00 or 18:00), with a late

PRACTICALITIES

night on Wednesday or Thursday (until 19:00 or 20:00). Department stores are usually open later throughout the week (until about 21:00 Mon-Sat). On Sunday, when stores are closed or have shorter hours, many street markets are lively with shoppers.

Watt's Up? Britain's electrical system is 220 volts, instead of North America's 110 volts. Most newer electronics (such as laptops, battery chargers, and hair dryers) convert automatically, so you won't need a converter, but you will need an adapter plug with three square prongs, sold inexpensively at travel stores in the US. Avoid bringing older appliances that don't automatically convert voltage; instead, buy a cheap replacement in Britain. Low-cost hairdryers and other small appliances are sold at Superdrug and Boots (ask your hotelier for the closest branch). Or pop into a London department store (see the Shopping in London chapter).

Discounts: Discounts (called "concessions" or "concs" in Britain) are not listed in this book. However, many sights, buses, and trains offer discounts to youths (up to age 18), students (with proper identification cards, www.isic.org), families, seniors (loosely defined as retirees or those willing to call themselves seniors), and groups of 10 or more. Always ask. Some discounts are available only for citizens of the European Union (EU).

Money

This section offers advice on how to pay for purchases on your trip (including getting cash from ATMs and paying with plastic), dealing with lost or stolen cards, VAT (sales tax) refunds, and tipping.

WHAT TO BRING

Bring both a credit card and a debit card. You'll use the debit card at cash machines (ATMs) to withdraw local cash for most purchases, and the credit card to pay for larger items. Some travelers carry a third card, in case one gets demagnetized or eaten by a temperamental machine.

For an emergency stash, bring several hundred dollars in hard cash in $20 bills. If you need to exchange the bills, go to a bank; avoid using currency-exchange booths because of their lousy rates and/or outrageous (and often hard-to-spot) fees.

CASH

Cash is just as desirable in Britain as it is at home. Small businesses (B&Bs, mom-and-pop cafés, shops, etc.) prefer that you pay your bills with cash. Some vendors will charge you extra for using a credit card, some won't accept foreign credit cards, and some won't take any credit cards at all. Cash is the best—and sometimes only—way to pay for cheap food, bus fare, taxis, and local guides.

Exchange Rate

1 British pound (£1) = about $1.60

While the euro (€) is now the currency of most of Europe, Britain is sticking with its pound sterling. The British pound (£), also called a "quid," is broken into 100 pence (p). Pence means "cents." You'll find coins ranging from 1p to £2 and bills from £5 to £50.

To convert prices from pounds to dollars, add about 60 percent: £20 = about $32, £50 = about $80. (Check www.oanda.com for the latest exchange rates.) London is so expensive that some travelers try to kid themselves that pounds are dollars. But when they get home, that £1,000-pound Visa bill isn't asking for $1,000...it wants around $1,600.

Throughout Britain, ATMs are the standard way for travelers to get cash. They work just like they do at home. To withdraw money from an ATM (known as a "cashpoint" in Britain), you'll need a debit card (ideally with a Visa or MasterCard logo for maximum usability), plus a PIN code (numeric and four digits). For increased security, shield the keypad when entering your PIN code, and don't use an ATM if anything on the front of the machine looks loose or damaged (a sign that someone may have attached a "skimming" device to capture account information). Try to withdraw large sums of money to reduce the number of per-transaction bank fees you'll pay.

When possible, use ATMs located outside banks—a thief is less likely to target a cash machine near surveillance cameras, and if your card is munched by a machine, you can go inside for help. Stay away from "independent" ATMs such as Travelex, Euronet, YourCash, Cardpoint, and Cashzone, which charge huge commissions, have terrible exchange rates, and may try to trick users with "dynamic currency conversion" (described at the end of "Credit and Debit Cards," next). Although you can use a credit card to withdraw cash at an ATM, this comes with high bank fees and only makes sense in an emergency.

While traveling, if you want to monitor your accounts online to detect any unauthorized transactions, be sure to use a secure connection (see page 565).

Even in jolly olde England, pickpockets target tourists. To safeguard your cash, wear a money belt—a pouch with a strap that you buckle around your waist like a belt and tuck under your clothes. Keep your cash, credit cards, and passport secure in your money belt, and carry only a day's spending money in your front pocket.

PRACTICALITIES

CREDIT AND DEBIT CARDS

For purchases, Visa and MasterCard are more commonly accepted than American Express. Just like at home, credit or debit cards work easily at larger hotels, restaurants, and shops. I typically use my debit card to withdraw cash to pay for most purchases. I use my credit card sparingly: to book hotel reservations, to buy advance tickets for events or sights, to cover major expenses (such as car rentals or plane tickets), and to pay for things online or near the end of my trip (to avoid another visit to the ATM). While you could instead use a debit card for these purchases, a credit card offers a greater degree of fraud protection.

Ask Your Credit- or Debit-Card Company: Before your trip, contact the company that issued your debit or credit cards.

• Confirm that your **card will work overseas,** and alert them that you'll be using it in Europe; otherwise, they may deny transactions if they perceive unusual spending patterns.

• Ask for the specifics on transaction **fees.** When you use your credit or debit card—either for purchases or ATM withdrawals— you'll typically be charged additional "international transaction" fees of up to 3 percent (1 percent is normal) plus $5 per transaction. If your card's fees seem high, consider getting a different card just for your trip: Capital One (www.capitalone.com) and most credit unions have low-to-no international fees.

• Verify your daily ATM **withdrawal limit,** and if necessary, ask your bank to adjust it. I prefer a high limit that allows me to take out more cash at each ATM stop and save on bank fees; some travelers prefer to set a lower limit in case their card is stolen. Note that foreign banks also set maximum withdrawal limits for their ATMs (£300 is usually the maximum).

• Get your bank's emergency **phone number** in the US (but not its 800 number, which isn't accessible from overseas) to call collect if you have a problem.

• Ask for your credit card's **PIN** in case you need to make an emergency cash withdrawal or encounter Europe's chip-and-PIN system; the bank won't tell you your PIN over the phone, so allow time for it to be mailed to you.

Magnetic-Stripe versus Chip-and-PIN Credit Cards: Europeans are increasingly using chip-and-PIN credit cards embedded with an electronic security chip and requiring a four-digit PIN. Your American-style card (with just the old-fashioned magnetic stripe) will work fine in most places. But it might not work at unattended payment machines, such as those at train and subway stations, toll plazas, parking garages, bike-rental kiosks, and gas pumps. If you have problems, try entering your card's PIN, look for a machine that takes cash, or find a clerk who can process the transaction manually.

Major US banks are beginning to offer credit cards with chips. Many of these are not true chip-and-PIN cards, but instead are chip-and-signature cards, for which your signature verifies your identity. These cards should work for live transactions and at most payment machines, but won't work for offline transactions such as at unattended gas pumps. If you're concerned, ask if your bank offers a true chip-and-PIN card. Andrews Federal Credit Union (www.andrewsfcu.org) and the State Department Federal Credit Union (www.sdfcu.org) offer these cards and are open to all US residents.

No matter what kind of card you have, it pays to carry pounds; you can always use an ATM to withdraw cash with your magnetic-stripe debit card.

Dynamic Currency Conversion: If merchants or hoteliers offer to convert your purchase price into dollars (called dynamic currency conversion, or DCC), refuse this "service." You'll pay even more in fees for the expensive convenience of seeing your charge in dollars. If your receipt shows the total in dollars only, ask for the transaction to be processed in the local currency. If the clerk refuses, pay in cash—or mark the receipt "local currency not offered" and dispute the DCC charges with your bank.

Some ATMs and retailers try to confuse customers by presenting DCC in misleading terms. If an ATM offers to "lock in" or "guarantee" your conversion rate, choose "proceed without conversion." Other prompts might state, "You can be charged in dollars: Press YES for dollars, NO for GBP." Always choose the local currency in these situations.

DAMAGE CONTROL FOR LOST CARDS

If you lose your credit, debit, or ATM card, you can stop people from using your card by reporting the loss immediately to the respective global customer-assistance centers. Call these 24-hour US numbers collect: Visa (tel. 303/967-1096), MasterCard (tel. 636/722-7111), and American Express (tel. 336/393-1111). In Britain, to make a collect call to the US, dial 0-800-89-0011. Press zero or stay on the line for an operator. European toll-free numbers (listed by country) can be found at the websites for Visa and MasterCard. Diner's Club has offices in Britain (tel. 0845-862-2937) and the US (tel. 514/877-1577; call collect).

Try to have this information ready: full card number, whether you are the primary or secondary cardholder, the cardholder's name exactly as printed on the card, billing address, home phone number, circumstances of the loss or theft, and identification verification (your birth date, your mother's maiden name, or your Social Security number—memorize this, don't carry a copy). If you are the secondary cardholder, you'll also need to provide the primary cardholder's identification-verification details. You can generally receive a temporary card within two or three business days in Europe (see www.ricksteves.com/help for more).

If you report your loss within two days, you typically won't be responsible for any unauthorized transactions on your account, although many banks charge a liability fee of $50.

TIPPING

Tipping in Britain isn't as automatic and generous as it is in the US. For special service, tips are appreciated, but not expected. As in the US, the proper amount depends on your resources, tipping philosophy, and the circumstances, but some general guidelines apply.

Restaurants: If a service charge is included in the bill, it's not necessary to tip. Otherwise, it's appropriate to tip about 10-12.5 percent. (For more information, see page 552.)

Taxis: For a typical ride, round up your fare a bit (for instance, if the fare is £4.50, pay £5). If the cabbie hauls your bags and zips you to the airport to help you catch your flight, you might want to toss in a little more. But if you feel like you're being driven in circles or otherwise ripped off, skip the tip.

Services: In general, if someone in the service industry does a super job for you, a tip of a pound or so is appropriate...but not required. If you're not sure whether (or how much) to tip for a service, ask a local for advice.

GETTING A VAT REFUND

Wrapped into the purchase price of your British souvenirs is a Value-Added Tax (VAT) of about 20 percent. You're entitled to get most of that tax back if you purchase more than £30 (about $48) worth of goods at a store that participates in the VAT-refund scheme (although individual stores can require that you spend more—Harrods, for example, won't process a refund unless you spend £50). Typically, you must ring up the minimum at a single retailer—you can't add up your purchases from various shops to reach the required amount.

Getting your refund is straightforward and, if you buy a substantial amount of souvenirs, well worth the hassle. If you're lucky, the merchant will subtract the tax when you make your purchase. (This is more likely to occur if the store ships the goods to your home.) Otherwise, you'll need to:

Get the paperwork. Have the merchant completely fill out the necessary refund document (either an official VAT customs form, or the shop or refund company's own version of it). The newest ones look like a long receipt. You'll have to present your passport at the store. Get the paperwork done before you leave, the shop to ensure you'll have everything you need (including your original sales receipt).

Get your stamp at the border or airport. Process your VAT document at your last stop in the European Union (such as at the airport) with the customs agent who deals with VAT refunds. Arrive an additional hour early before you need to check in for your flight to allow time to find the local customs office—and to stand in line. It's best to keep your purchases in your carry-on. If they're too large or dangerous to carry on (such as knives), pack them in your checked bags and alert the check-in agent. You'll be sent (with your tagged bag) to a customs desk outside security; someone will examine your bag, stamp your paperwork, and put your bag on the belt. You're not supposed to use your purchased goods before you leave. If you show up at customs wearing your new Wellingtons, officials might look the other way—or deny you a refund.

Collect your refund. You'll need to return your stamped document to the retailer or its representative. Many merchants work with a service that has offices at major airports, ports, or border crossings (at Heathrow, Travelex counters and customs desks are located before and after security in terminals 2-5). These services, which extract a 4 percent fee, can refund your money immediately in cash or credit your card (within two billing cycles). If the retailer handles VAT refunds directly, it's up to you to contact the merchant for your refund. You can mail the documents from home, or more quickly, from your point of departure (using an envelope you've prepared in advance or one that's been provided by the merchant). You'll then have to wait—it can take months.

CUSTOMS FOR AMERICAN SHOPPERS

You are allowed to take home $800 worth of items per person duty-free, once every 31 days. You can also bring in duty-free a liter of alcohol. As for food, you can take home many processed and packaged foods: vacuum-packed cheeses, dried herbs, jams, baked goods, candy, chocolate, oil, vinegar, mustard, and honey. Fresh fruits and vegetables and most meats are not allowed, with exceptions for some canned items. As for alcohol, you can bring in one liter duty-free (it can be packed securely in your checked luggage, along with any other liquid-containing items).

To bring alcohol (or liquid-packed foods) in your carry-on bag on your flight home, buy it at a duty-free shop at the airport. You'll increase your odds of getting it onto a connecting flight if it's packaged in a "STEB"—a secure, tamper-evident bag. But stay away from liquids in opaque, ceramic, or metallic containers, which usually cannot be successfully screened (STEB or no STEB).

For details on allowable goods, customs rules, and duty rates, visit www.cbp.gov.

PRACTICALITIES

Sightseeing

Sightseeing can be hard work. Use these tips to make your visits to London's finest sights meaningful, fun, efficient, and painless.

PLAN AHEAD

Set up an itinerary that allows you to fit in all your must-see sights. For a one-stop look at opening hours, see "London at a Glance" on page 50; also see the "Daily Reminder" on page 20. Most sights keep stable hours, but you can easily confirm the latest by checking with the TI or visiting museum websites.

Don't put off visiting a must-see sight—you never know when a place will close unexpectedly for a holiday, strike, or royal audience. Many museums are closed or have reduced hours at least a few days a year, especially on holidays such as Christmas, New Year's, and Bank Holiday Mondays in May and August. A list of holidays is on page 576; check online for possible museum closures during your trip. Off-season, many museums have shorter hours.

Going at the right time helps avoid crowds. This book offers tips on the best times to see specific sights. Try visiting popular sights very early or very late. Evening visits are usually peaceful, with fewer crowds. In addition to the London Eye, at least one major London sight is open late every night (see the sidebar on page 76).

Study up. To get the most out of the self-guided tours and sight descriptions in this book, read them before you visit. The British Museum rocks if you understand the significance of the Rosetta Stone.

AT SIGHTS

Here's what you can typically expect:

Entering: Be warned that you may not be allowed to enter if you arrive 30 to 60 minutes before closing time. And guards start ushering people out well before the actual closing time, so don't save the best for last.

Some important sights have a security check, where you must open your bag or send it through a metal detector. Some sights require you to check daypacks and coats. (If you'd rather not check your daypack, try carrying it tucked under your arm like a purse as you enter.)

Admission Charges: Several major London museums are free, but they ask for a donation (which is completely optional). I see it as a good way to get rid of loose change while helping the arts. Admission at most museums includes a "voluntary donation" of about 10 percent, which is automatically tacked on. At these sights, you may see two prices listed—one with the donation added in and one without—and often the cashier will ask if you are able to include it. It's perfectly OK to pay the price without the donation. (You may also see references to "Gift Aid"—a tax-deduction scheme that benefits museums—but this only concerns British taxpayers.)

Photography: If the museum's photo policy isn't clearly posted, ask a guard. Generally, taking photos without a flash or tripod is allowed. Some sights ban photos altogether.

Special Exhibits: Museums may show special exhibits in addition to their permanent collection. An extra fee, which may not be optional, might be assessed for these shows.

Expect Changes: Artwork can be on tour, on loan, out sick, or shifted at the whim of the curator. Pick up a floor plan as you enter, and ask museum staff if you can't find a particular item.

Audioguides and Apps: Many sights rent audioguides, which generally offer excellent recorded descriptions (about £4). If you bring your own earbuds, you can enjoy better sound and avoid holding the device to your ear. To save money, bring a Y-jack and share one audioguide with your travel partner. Increasingly, museums and sights offer apps—often free—that you can download to your mobile device (check their websites). I've produced free, downloadable audio tours for my Westminster Walk, the British Museum, the British Library, St. Paul's Cathedral, and The City Walk; look for the ∩ symbol in this book. For more on my audio tours, see page 5.

Guided tours are most likely to occur during peak season (usually £3-8 and widely ranging in quality). Some sights also run short introductory videos featuring their highlights and history. These are generally well worth your time and a great place to start your visit.

Services: Important sights and cathedrals may have an on-site café or cafeteria (usually a handy place to rejuvenate during a long visit—try a cheap "cream tea" to pick up your energy in midafternoon, like Brits do). The WCs at sights are free and nearly always clean.

Before Leaving: At the gift shop, scan the postcard rack or thumb through a guidebook to be sure that you haven't overlooked something that you'd like to see.

Every sight or museum offers more than what is covered in this book. Use the information in this book as an introduction—not the final word.

SIGHTSEEING PASSES

The following sightseeing passes are sold online and at the City of London Information Centre, near St. Paul's Cathedral; see page 18.

The **London Pass,** which covers many big sights and lets you skip some lines, is expensive but potentially worth the investment for extremely busy sightseers. Among the many sights it includes are the Tower of London, Westminster Abbey, Churchill War Rooms, and Windsor Castle, as well as many temporary exhibits and audioguides at otherwise "free" biggies. Think through your sightseeing plans, study their website to see what's covered, and do the math before you buy (£52/1 day, £71/2 days, £85/3 days, £159/6 days; days are calendar days rather than 24-hour periods; comes with 160-page guidebook, also sold at major train stations and airports, tel. 020/7293-0972, www.londonpass.com).

The **English Heritage** society sells passes and memberships that include free entry to its 400 sights (which are exclusive to England); they're worth it only if you'll be thoroughly exploring England, not just London. You can buy passes or memberships at any participating sight. For most travelers, the Overseas Visitor Pass is a better choice than the pricier one-year membership (Visitor Pass: £30/9 days, £35/16 days, discounts for couples and families, www.english-heritage.org.uk/ovp; membership: £50 for one person, £88 for two, discounts for families, seniors, and students, children under 19 free, www.english-heritage.org.uk/membership; tel. 0370-333-1181).

Sleeping

I favor hotels and restaurants that are handy to your sightseeing activities. Rather than list hotels scattered throughout a city, I choose hotels in my favorite neighborhoods. My recommendations run the gamut, from dorm beds to fancy rooms with all of the comforts.

A major feature of the Sleeping sections in this book is my extensive and opinionated listing of good-value rooms. I like places that are clean, central, relatively quiet at night, reasonably priced, friendly, small enough to have a hands-on owner and stable staff, run with a respect for British traditions, and not listed in other guidebooks. (In London, for me, meeting six out of these eight criteria means it's a keeper.) I'm more impressed by a convenient location and a fun-loving philosophy than flat-screen TVs and a pricey laundry service.

Book your accommodations well in advance, especially if you want to stay at one of my top listings or if you'll be traveling during busy times. See page 576 for a list of major holidays and festivals; for tips on making reservations, see page 550.

RATES AND DEALS

I've described my recommended accommodations using a Sleep Code (see sidebar). The prices I list are for one-night stays in peak season, include a hearty breakfast unless otherwise noted, and assume you're booking directly with the hotel (not through a TI or online hotel-booking engine). Booking services extract a commission from the hotel, which logically closes the door on special deals. Book direct.

My recommended hotels each have a website (often with a built-in booking form) and an email address; you can expect a response within a day (and often sooner).

If you're on a budget, it's smart to email several hotels to ask for their best price. Comparison-shop and make your choice. This is especially helpful when dealing with the larger hotels that use "dynamic pricing," a computer-generated system that predicts the demand for particular days and sets prices accordingly: High-demand days can be more than double the price of low-demand days. This makes it impossible for a guidebook to list anything more accurate than a wide range of prices. I regret this trend. While you can assume that hotels listed in this book are good, it's difficult to say which ones are the better value unless you email to confirm the price.

As you look over the listings, you'll notice that some accommodations promise special prices to Rick Steves readers. To get these rates, you must book direct (that is, not through a booking site like TripAdvisor or Booking.com), mention this book when you reserve, and then show the book upon arrival. Rick Steves discounts apply to readers with ebooks as well as printed books. Because I trust hotels to honor this, please let me know if you don't receive a listed discount. Note, though, that discounts understandably may not be applied to promotional rates.

It's harder to negotiate a discount in London than it is elsewhere in Britain, but it doesn't hurt to try: Offer to pay cash, stay at least three nights, or mention this book. You can also try asking for a cheaper room or a discount, or offer to skip breakfast.

Staying in B&Bs and small hotels can save money over sleeping in big hotels. Big, impersonal chain hotels can be even cheaper, but they don't include breakfast. When comparing prices between chain hotels and B&Bs, remember you're getting two breakfasts (about a £25 value) for each double room at a B&B. Some fancy hotels rent for a third off if you arrive late on a slow day and ask for a deal. Official "rack rates" (the highest rates a hotel charges) can be misleading, because they often omit cheaper oddball rooms and special promo deals.

In general, prices can soften if you do any of the following: offer to pay cash, stay at least three nights, or mention this book. You can also try asking for a cheaper room or a discount, or offer to skip breakfast.

PRACTICALITIES

Sleep Code

(£1 = about $1.60)

Price Rankings

To help you easily sort through my listings, I've divided the accommodations into three categories based on the highest price for a basic double room with bath during high season:

$$$ Higher Priced

$$ Moderately Priced

$ Lower Priced

I always rate hostels as $, whether or not they have double rooms, because they have the cheapest beds in town.

Prices can change without notice; verify the hotel's current rates online or by email. For the best prices, always book directly with the hotel.

Abbreviations

To pack maximum information into minimum space, I use the following code to describe accommodations in this book. Prices are listed per room, not per person. When a price range is given for a type of room (such as double rooms listing for £80-120), it means the price fluctuates with the season, size of room, or length of stay; expect to pay the upper end for peak-season stays.

S = Single room (or price for one person in a double)

D = Double or twin room. "Double beds" can be two twins sheeted together and are usually big enough for nonromantic couples.

T = Triple (generally a double bed with a single)

Q = Quad (usually two double beds; adding an extra child's bed to a T is usually cheaper)

b = Private bathroom with toilet and shower or tub

According to this code, a couple staying at a "Db-£90" hotel would pay a total of £90 (about $145) per night for a double room with a private bathroom. Unless otherwise noted, breakfast is included, and credit cards are accepted. For most places, the rates I list include the 20 percent VAT tax—but it's smart to ask when you book your room.

There's almost always Wi-Fi and/or a guest computer available, and it's generally free.

TYPES OF ACCOMMODATIONS
Hotels

Many of my recommended hotels have three or more floors of rooms and steep stairs. Elevators are rare except in the larger hotels. If you're concerned about stairs, call and ask about ground-floor rooms or pay for a hotel with a lift (elevator). Air-conditioning is rare (I've noted which of my listings have it), but most places have fans. On hot summer nights, you'll want your window open—and unfortunately, in this big city, street noise is a fact of life. If concerned, request a room on the back side or on an upper floor.

"Twin" means two single beds, and "double" means one double bed. If you'll take either one, let them know, or you might be needlessly turned away. Most hotels offer family deals, which means that parents with young children can easily get a room with an extra child's bed or a discount for larger rooms. Call to negotiate the price. Teenagers are generally charged as adults. Kids under five sleep almost free.

An "en suite" room has a bathroom (toilet and shower/tub) inside the room; a room with a "private bathroom" can mean that the bathroom is all yours, but it's across the hall; and a "standard" room has access to a bathroom down the hall that's shared with other rooms. Figuring there's little difference between "en suite" and "private" rooms, some places charge the same for both. If you want your own bathroom inside the room, request "en suite."

If money's tight, ask for a standard room. You'll almost always have a sink in your room, and as more rooms go "en suite," the hallway bathroom is shared with fewer standard rooms.

Confusingly, pricey hotels might call an en suite room "standard" to differentiate it from a fancier "superior" or "deluxe" room. If you're not sure, ask for clarification.

Note that to be called a "hotel," a place technically must have certain amenities, including a 24-hour reception (though this rule is loosely applied). TVs are standard in rooms, but may come with limited channels (no cable). Note that all of Britain's accommodations are now non-smoking.

If you're arriving early in the morning, your room probably won't be ready. Drop your bag safely at the hotel and dive right into sightseeing.

Hoteliers can be a great help and source of advice. Most know their city well, and can assist you with everything from public transit and airport connections to finding a good restaurant, the nearest launderette, or a Wi-Fi hotspot.

Even at the best places, mechanical breakdowns occur: Air-conditioning malfunctions, sinks leak, hot water turns cold, and toilets gurgle and smell. Report your concerns clearly and calmly at the front desk. For more complicated problems, don't expect instant results.

If you suspect night noise will be a problem (if, for instance, your room is over a noisy pub), ask for a quieter room in the back or on an upper floor. To guard against theft in your room, keep valuables out of sight. Some rooms come with a safe, and other hotels have safes at the front desk. I've never bothered using one.

Checkout can pose problems if surprise charges pop up on

The Good and Bad of Online Reviews

User-generated travel review websites—such as TripAdvisor, Booking.com, and Yelp—have quickly become a huge player in the travel industry. These sites give you access to actual reports—good and bad—from travelers who have experienced the hotel, restaurant, tour, or attraction.

My hotelier friends in Europe are in awe of these sites' influence. Small hoteliers who want to stay in business have no choice but to work with review sites—which often charge fees for good placement or photos, and tack on commissions if users book through the site instead of directly with the hotel.

While these sites work hard to weed out bogus users, my hunch is that a significant percentage of reviews are posted by friends or enemies of the business being reviewed. I've even seen hotels "bribe" guests (for example, offer a free breakfast) in exchange for a positive review. Also, review sites are uncurated and can become an echo chamber, with one or two flashy businesses camped out atop the ratings, while better, more affordable, and more authentic alternatives sit ignored farther down the list. (For example, I find review sites' restaurant recommendations skew to very touristy, obvious options.) And you can't always give credence to the negative reviews: Different people have different expectations.

Remember that a user-generated review is based on the experience of one person. That person likely stayed at one hotel and ate at a few restaurants, and doesn't have much of a basis for comparison. A guidebook is the work of a trained researcher who has exhaustively visited many alternatives to assess their relative value. I recently checked out some top-rated TripAdvisor listings in various towns; when stacked up against their competitors, some are gems, while just as many are duds.

Both types of information have their place, and in many ways, they're complementary. If a hotel or restaurant is well-reviewed in a guidebook or two, and also gets good ratings on one of these sites, it's likely a winner.

your bill. If you settle up your bill the afternoon before you leave, you'll have time to discuss and address any points of contention (before 19:00, when the night shift usually arrives).

Above all, keep a positive attitude. Remember, you're on vacation. If your hotel is a disappointment, spend more time out enjoying the city you came to see.

Small Hotels and B&Bs

Places with "townhouse" or "house" in their name (such as "London House") are like big B&Bs or small family-run hotels—with fewer amenities but more character than a hotel. Places named

"B&B"—rare in big and bustling London—typically have six rooms or fewer.

Small hotels and B&Bs come with their own etiquette and quirks. Keep in mind that owners are at the whim of their guests—if you're getting up early, so are they; and if you check in late, they'll wait up for you. Be considerate.

Small places usually serve a hearty fried breakfast of eggs and much more (for details on breakfast, see the Eating section, later). Because your B&B or small-hotel owner is often also the cook, there's usually a quite limited time span when breakfast is served (typically about an hour—make sure you know when it is before you turn in for the night). It's an unwritten rule that guests shouldn't show up at the very end of the breakfast period and expect a full cooked breakfast. If you do arrive late (or if you need to leave before breakfast is served), most establishments are happy to let you help yourself to cereal, fruit or juice, and coffee; ask politely if it's possible.

Most places stock rooms with an electric kettle, along with cups, tea bags, and coffee packets (if you prefer decaf, buy a jar at a grocery and dump the contents into a baggie for easy packing).

Electrical outlets sometimes have switches that turn the current on or off; if your electrical appliance isn't working, flip the switch at the outlet. When you unplug your appliance, don't forget your adapter—most B&Bs have boxes of various adapters and converters that guests have left behind (which is handy if you left yours at the last place).

You're likely to encounter unusual bathroom fixtures. The "pump toilet" has a flushing handle or button that doesn't kick in unless you push it just right: too hard or too soft, and it won't go. (Be decisive but not ruthless.) There's also the "dial-a-shower," an electronic box under the shower head where you'll turn a dial to select the heat of the water and (sometimes with a separate dial or button) turn on or shut off the flow of water. If you can't find the switch to turn on the shower, it may be just outside the bathroom.

Many B&Bs and small hotels come with thin walls and doors that can make for a noisy night. If you're a light sleeper, bring earplugs. And please be quiet in the halls and in your rooms at night (talk softly, and keep the TV volume low)...those of us getting up early will thank you for it.

Hostels and Dorms

A hostel provides cheap beds where you sleep alongside strangers for about £20-30 per night. Travelers of any age are welcome if they don't mind dorm-style accommodations and meeting other travelers. Cheap meals are sometimes available. Most hostels offer kitchen facilities, guest computers, Wi-Fi, and a self-service laun-

Making Hotel Reservations

Reserve your rooms several weeks in advance—or as soon as you've pinned down your travel dates. Note that some national holidays merit your making reservations far in advance (see page 576).

Requesting a Reservation: It's easiest to book your room through the hotel's website. (For the best rates, always use the hotel's official site and not a booking agency's site.) If there's no reservation form, or for complicated requests, send an email (see below for a sample request).

The hotelier wants to know:
- the number and type of rooms you need
- the number of nights you'll stay
- your date of arrival
- your date of departure
- any special needs (such as bathroom in the room or down the hall, twin beds vs. double bed)

Mention any discounts—for Rick Steves readers or otherwise—when you make the reservation.

Confirming a Reservation: Most places will request a credit-card number to hold your room. If they don't have a secure online reservation form—look for the *https*—you can email your card number (I do), but it's safer to share that confidential info via a phone call or two emails (splitting your number between them).

Canceling a Reservation: If you must cancel, it's courteous—and smart—to do so with as much notice as possible, especially for smaller family-run places. Be warned that cancellation policies

dry. Nowadays, concerned about bedbugs, hostels are likely to provide all bedding, including sheets. Family and private rooms may be available on request.

Independent hostels tend to be easygoing, colorful, and informal (no membership required). For London independent hostel listings, try www.hostellondon.com; www.hostelworld.com is the standard way backpackers search and book hostels, but also try www.hostels.com and www.hostelz.com.

Official hostels are part of Hostelling International (HI) and share an online booking site (www.hihostels.com). In Britain, these official hostels are run by the YHA (www.yha.org.uk). Official hostels typically require that you either have a membership card or pay extra per night.

Many London **colleges** rent out their dorms during school holidays, mainly during July, August, and early September. Types of accommodations vary, but are usually somewhat spartan (no phones or TVs in the rooms) and come with single or twin beds. For listings, see "Dorms" on page 392.

From:	rick@ricksteves.com
Sent:	Today
To:	info@hotelcentral.com
Subject:	Reservation request for 19-22 July

Dear Hotel Central,

I would like to reserve a room for 2 people for 3 nights, arriving 19 July and departing 22 July. If possible, I would like a quiet room with a double bed and a bathroom inside the room.

Please let me know if you have a room available and the price.

Thank you!
Rick Steves

can be strict; read the fine print or ask about these before you book. Internet deals may require prepayment, with no refunds for cancellations.

Reconfirming a Reservation: Always call or email to reconfirm your room reservation a few days in advance. For B&Bs or very small hotels, I call again on my day of arrival to tell my host what time I expect to get there (especially important if arriving late—after 17:00).

Phoning: For tips on calling hotels overseas, see page 562.

Apartments

Renting an apartment (or "flat," as the Brits call them) can be a fun and cost-effective way to go local. Usually equipped with a modest kitchen and living room, apartments can be a good option for families and groups on a budget, and anyone looking for more space and the option of cooking your own meals.

Websites such as Booking.com, Airbnb, VRBO, and FlipKey let you browse properties and correspond directly with property owners or managers. Or, for more guidance, you can book through an agency that specializes in London rentals (see page 393 for a list of agencies). Agency-represented apartments may cost more, but this method often offers more help and safeguards than booking direct. Reading reviews from past guests can also help with your choice (but keep in mind that a booking agency's posted reviews may have been "curated" to weed out negativity).

Apartment prices vary depending on size, amenities, and location. Some places have a minimum-stay requirement (typically 4-5 nights). Read the contract carefully so you are aware of additional fees (a one-time cleaning fee is standard) and cancellation policies, which are usually less flexible than at a hotel (for example, a nonrefundable 50 percent deposit).

Ask about amenities that are important to you (elevator, laundry, coffee maker, etc.) If it's a private residence, be clear on whether you're getting the place to yourself while the owner is away—or just a spare bed. To find out more about an apartment's location, plot the address on a mapping site. Virtually "explore" the neighborhood using the Street View feature on Google Maps. Determine how close the nearest Tube stop is, and factor transportation costs into the overall price.

In most cases, you'll need to let the owner or property manager know your arrival time so they can meet you for check-in. Or they may give you a door code for self check-in.

Other Options: If a whole apartment is overkill, Airbnb and Roomorama also list rooms in private homes. Beds range from air-mattress-in-living-room basic to plush-B&B-suite posh. If you want a place to sleep that's free, Couchsurfing.org is a vagabond's alternative to Airbnb. It lists millions of outgoing members, who host fellow "surfers" in their homes.

Eating

These days, the stereotype of "bad food in Britain" is woefully dated. Britain is on the leading edge of the foodie revolution, and I find it's easy to eat very well here.

British cooking has embraced international influences and good-quality ingredients, making "modern British" food quite delicious. While some dreary pub food still exists, you'll generally find the cuisine scene here lively, trendy, and pleasantly surprising (but expensive). Basic pubs are more likely to dish up homemade, creative dishes than microwaved pies, soggy fries, and mushy peas. Even traditional pub grub has gone upmarket, with gastropubs that serve locally sourced meats and fresh vegetables.

All of Britain is smoke-free. Expect restaurants and pubs that sell food to be non-smoking indoors, with smokers occupying patios and doorways outside.

When restaurant-hunting, choose a spot filled with locals, not tourists. Venturing even a block or two off the main drag leads to higher-quality food for a better price. Locals eat better at lower-rent locales. Rely on my recommendations in the Eating in London chapter.

Tipping: At pubs and places where you order at the counter, you don't have to tip. Regular customers ordering a round sometimes say, "Add one for yourself" as a tip for drinks ordered at the bar—but this isn't expected. At restaurants and fancy pubs with waitstaff, tip about 10-12.5 percent. Most restaurants in London now add a 12.5 percent "optional" tip onto the bill. Tip only what you think the service warrants, and be careful not to tip double.

BREAKFAST (FRY-UP)

The traditional fry-up or full English breakfast—generally included in the cost of your room—is famous as a hearty way to start the day. Also known as a "heart attack on a plate," your standard fry-up is a heated plate with eggs, Canadian-style bacon and/or sausage, a grilled tomato, sautéed mushrooms, baked beans, and sometimes potatoes, kippers (herring), or fried bread (sizzled in a greasy skillet). Toast comes in a rack (to cool quickly and crisply) with butter and marmalade. The meal is typically topped off with tea or coffee. At a B&B or hotel, it may start with juice and cereal or porridge. Many progressive B&B owners offer vegetarian, organic, gluten-free, or other creative variations on the traditional breakfast.

Much as the full English breakfast is a traditional way to start the day, these days most hotels serve a healthier continental breakfast—with a buffet of everything you'd expect, such as yogurt, cereal, scrambled eggs, fruit, and veggies.

LUNCH AND DINNER ON A BUDGET

Eating in London can be pricey, but plenty of inexpensive choices are available: pub grub, daily lunch and early-bird dinner specials, ethnic restaurants, cafeterias, fast food, picnics, greasy-spoon cafés, cheap chain restaurants, and pizza.

I've found that portions are huge, and with locals feeling the economic pinch, **sharing plates** is generally just fine. Ordering two drinks, a soup or side salad, and splitting a £10 meat pie can make a good, filling meal. If you're on a limited budget, share a main course in a more expensive place for a nicer eating experience.

Pub grub is the most atmospheric budget option. You'll usually get hearty lunches and dinners priced reasonably at £8-12 under ancient timbers (see "Pubs," later). Gastropubs, with better food, are more expensive.

Classier restaurants have some affordable deals. Lunch is usually cheaper than dinner; a top-end, £25-for-dinner-type restaurant often serves the same quality two-course lunch deals for about half the price. Look for early-bird dinner specials, allowing you to eat well and affordably (about 17:30-19:00, last order by around 19:00).

Many restaurants advertise **early bird** or **pre-theater specials** of two or three courses, often for significant savings. They are usually available only before 18:30 or 19:00, but are good for bargain hunters willing to eat a bit earlier.

PRACTICALITIES

Ethnic restaurants add spice to Britain's cuisine scene. Eating Indian, Bangladeshi, Chinese, or Thai is cheap (even cheaper if you do takeout). Middle Eastern stands sell gyro sandwiches, falafel, and *shwarmas* (grilled meat in pita bread). An Indian samosa (greasy, flaky meat-and-vegetable pie) costs
about £2 and makes a very cheap, if small, meal. (For more, see "Indian Cuisine," later.) You'll find all-you-can-eat Chinese and Thai places serving £6 meals and offering even cheaper takeaway boxes. While you can't "split" a buffet, you can split a takeaway box. Stuff the box full, and you and your partner can eat in a park for under £2 each—making this London's cheapest hot meal.

Most large **museums** (and many historic **churches**) have handy, moderately priced cafeterias with forgettably decent food.

Picnicking saves time and money. Fine park benches and polite pigeons abound in most neighborhoods. You can easily get prepared food to go. The modern chain eateries on nearly every corner often have simple seating but are designed for takeout. Bakeries serve a wonderful array of fresh sandwiches. Munch a relaxed "meal on wheels" picnic during your open-top bus tour or river cruise to save 30 precious minutes for sightseeing.

PUBS

Pubs are a fundamental part of the British social scene, and whether you're a teetotaler or a beer guzzler, they should be a part of your travel here. "Pub" is short for "public house." It's an extended common room where, if you don't mind the stickiness, you can feel the pulse of London. Smart travelers use pubs to eat, drink, get out of the rain, watch sporting events, and make new friends.

It's interesting to consider the role pubs filled for Britain's working class in more modest times: For workers with humble domestic quarters and no money for a vacation, a beer at the corner pub was the closest they'd get to a comfortable living room, a place to entertain, and a getaway. And locals could meet people from far away in a pub—today, that's you!

Though hours vary, pubs generally serve beer daily from 11:00-23:00, though many are open later, particularly on Friday and Saturday. As it nears closing time, you'll hear shouts of "Last orders." Then comes the 10-minute warning bell. Finally, they'll call "Time!" to pick up your glass, finished or not, when the pub closes.

A cup of darts is free for the asking. People go to a public house to be social. They want to talk. Get vocal with a local. This is easiest at the bar, where people assume you're in the mood to talk (rather than at a table, where you're allowed a bit of privacy). The pub is the next best thing to having relatives in town. Cheers!

Pub Grub: For £8-12, you'll get a basic budget hot lunch or dinner in friendly surroundings. In high-priced London, this is your best indoor eating value. (For something more refined, try a gastropub, which serves higher-quality meals for £12-18.) The *Good Pub Guide* is an excellent resource (www.thegoodpubguide. co.uk). Pubs that are attached to restaurants, advertise their food, and are crowded with locals are more likely to have fresh food and a chef—and less likely to sell only lousy microwaved snacks.

Pubs generally serve traditional dishes, such as fish-and-chips, roast beef with Yorkshire pudding (batter-baked in the oven), and assorted meat pies, such as steak-and-kidney pie or shepherd's pie (stewed lamb topped with mashed potatoes) with cooked vegetables. Side dishes include salads, vegetables, and—invariably— "chips" (French fries). "Crisps" are potato chips. A "jacket potato" (baked potato stuffed with fillings of your choice) can almost be a meal in itself. A "ploughman's lunch" is a "traditional English meal" of bread, cheese, and sweet pickles that nearly every tourist tries...once. These days, you'll likely find more pasta, curried dishes, and quiche on the menu than traditional fare.

Meals are usually served 12:00-14:00 and 18:00-20:00—with a break in the middle (rather than straight through the day). Since they make more money selling beer, many pubs stop serving meals early in the evening—especially on weekends. There's generally no table service. Order at the bar, then take a seat. Either they'll bring the food when it's ready or you'll pick it up at the bar. Pay at the bar (sometimes when you order, sometimes after you eat). Don't tip unless it's a place with full table service. Servings are hearty, and service is quick. If you're on a tight budget, it's OK to share a meal. A beer, cider, or dram of whisky adds another couple of pounds. Free tap water is always available. For a list of recommended historic pubs in London, see page 400. For details on ordering beer and other drinks, see the "Beverages" section, later.

GOOD CHAIN RESTAURANTS

I know—you're going to Britain to enjoy characteristic little hole-in-the-wall pubs, so mass-produced food is the furthest thing from your mind. But several excellent chains with branches across the UK can be a nice break from pub grub. My favorites are Pret, Wasabi, and Eat.

Pret (a.k.a. Pret à Manger) is perhaps the most pervasive of these modern convenience eateries. Some are takeout only, and others have seating ranging from simple stools to restaurant-quality tables. The service is fast, the price is great, and the food is healthy and fresh. Their slogan: "Made today. Gone today. No 'sell-by' date, no nightlife."

Côte Brasserie is a contemporary French chain serving good-value French cuisine in reliably pleasant settings (£10-14 main dishes, early dinner specials). Côte's London locations include Soho, Covent Garden, Leicester Square, Oxford Circus, Fitzrovia, Kensington, Bayswater, and near St. Paul's on Ludgate Hill.

Byron Hamburgers, an upscale-hamburger chain with hip interiors, is worth seeking out if you need a burger fix. While British burgers aren't exactly like American ones—they tend to be a bit overcooked by our standards—Byron's burgers are your best bet (£7-10 burgers). London locations include Soho, Covent Garden, Leicester Square, between Piccadilly Circus and Trafalgar Square, near St. Paul's, Fitzrovia, South Kensington, Kensington, and Greenwich.

Wagamama Noodle Bar, serving up pan-Asian cuisine (udon noodles, fried rice, and curry dishes), is a noisy, organic slurpathon. Portions are huge and splittable. There's one in almost every mid-size city in Britain, usually located in sprawling halls filled with long shared tables and busy servers who scrawl your order on the placemat. In London, you'll find branches in Soho, Piccadilly Circus, Leicester Square, Covent Garden, Kensington, near the British Museum, near the Holborn Tube stop, next to the Tower of London, on the South Bank near the Southwark Cathedral, and in The City (along Fleet Street and near the Mansion House Tube stop).

Loch Fyne Fish Restaurant is a Scottish chain that raises its own oysters and mussels. Its branches offer an inviting, lively atmosphere with a fine fishy energy and no pretense (£12-20 main dishes, two- and three-course specials often available before 19:00). In London, there's one near Covent Garden, and another in The City (near Leadenhall Market).

Marks & Spencer department stores have a new feature: inviting deli sections with cheery sit-down eating (along with their popular sandwiches-to-go section). There's a handy one across from the Covent Garden Tube station.

Thai Square is a dependable Thai option with a nice atmosphere (£9-13 salads, noodle dishes, and curries; £14-19 meat dishes; £10 daily lunch box specials). Most branches are in London, with locations in Soho, Trafalgar Square, Covent Garden, the Strand, South Kensington, near Oxford Circus, and The City (one on The Strand at Fleet Street and another near the Mansion House Tube stop).

Masala Zone is a London chain providing a good, predictable alternative to the many one-off, hole-in-the-wall Indian joints around town. Try a curry-and-rice dish, a *thali* (platter with several small dishes), or their street food specials. Each branch has its own personality (£9-14 meals). Locations include Soho, Covent Garden, Bayswater, and in the Selfridges department store on Oxford Street.

Ask and **Pizza Express** serve quality pasta and pizza in a pleasant, sit-down atmosphere that's family-friendly. **Jamie's Italian** (from celebrity chef Jamie Oliver) is hipper and pricier, and feels more upmarket.

Japanese: Three popular chains serve fresh and inexpensive Japanese food. **Itsu** and **Wasabi** are two bright and competitive chains that let you assemble your own plate in a fun and efficient way while **Yo! Sushi** lets you pick your dish off a conveyor belt and pay according to the color of your plate. If you're in the mood for sushi, all are great.

Carry-Out Chains: While the following places may have some seating, they're best as an easy place to grab prepackaged food on the run.

Major supermarket chains have smaller, offshoot branches that specialize in sandwiches, salads, and other prepared foods to go. These can be a picnicker's dream come true. Some shops are stand-alone, while others are located inside a larger store. The most prevalent—and best—is **M&S Simply Food** (an offshoot of Marks & Spencer; there's one in every major train station). **Sainsbury's Local** grocery stores also offer decent prepared food; **Tesco Express** and **Tesco Metro** run a distant third.

Some "cheap and cheery" chains provide office workers with good, healthful sandwiches, salads, and pastries to go. These include **Apostróphe, Pod,** and **Eat** (with slightly higher-quality food and higher prices).

INDIAN CUISINE

Eating Indian food is "going local" in cosmopolitan, multiethnic Britain. Take the opportunity to sample food from Britain's former colony. Indian cuisine is as varied as the country itself. In general, they use more exotic spices than British or American cuisine—some hot, some sweet. Indian food is very vegetarian-friendly, offering many meatless dishes to choose from on any given menu.

For a simple meal that costs about £10-12, order one dish with rice and naan (Indian flatbread). Generally one order is plenty for two people to share. A serving of rice costs £2-3 extra. Many Indian restaurants offer a fixed-price combination that offers more variety, and is simpler and cheaper than ordering à la carte. For about £20, you can make a mix-and-match platter out of several shareable dishes, including dal (simmered lentils) as a starter, one or two meat or vegetable dishes with sauce (for example, chicken curry, chicken *tikka masala* in a creamy tomato sauce, grilled fish tandoori, chickpea *chana masala*, or a spicy vindaloo dish), *raita* (a cooling yogurt that's added to spicy dishes), rice, naan, and an Indian beer (wine and Indian food don't really mix) or chai (cardamom/cinnamon-spiced tea, usually served with milk). An easy way to taste a variety of dishes is to order a thali—a sampler plate, generally served on a metal tray, with small servings of various specialties.

AFTERNOON TEA

Once the sole province of genteel ladies in fancy hats, afternoon tea has become more democratic in the 21st century. These days, people of leisure punctuate their day with an afternoon tea at a tearoom. You'll get a pot of tea, small finger foods (like sandwiches with the crusts cut off), homemade scones, jam, and thick clotted cream. A lighter "cream tea" gets you tea and a scone or two. Tearooms, which often serve appealing light meals, are usually open for lunch and close at about 17:00, just before dinner.

The cheapest "tea" on the menu is generally a "cream tea"; the most expensive is the "champagne tea." **Cream tea** is simply a pot of tea and a homemade scone or two with jam and thick clotted cream. (For maximum pinkie-waving taste per calorie, slice your scone thin like a miniature loaf of bread.) **Afternoon tea**—what many Americans would call "high tea"—generally is a cream tea plus a tier of three plates holding small finger foods (such as cucumber sandwiches) and an assortment of small pastries. **Champagne tea** includes all of the goodies, plus a glass of bubbly. **High tea** to the English generally means a more substantial late-afternoon or early-evening meal, often served with meat or eggs.

DESSERTS (SWEETS)

To the British, the traditional word for dessert is "pudding," although it's also referred to as "sweets" these days. Sponge cake, cream, fruitcake, and meringue are key players.

Trifle is the best-known British concoction, consisting of sponge cake soaked in brandy or sherry (or orange juice for children), then covered with jam and/or fruit and custard cream. Whipped cream can sometimes put the final touch on this "light" treat.

The English version of custard is a smooth, yellow liquid. Cream tops most everything that custard does not. There's single cream for coffee. Double cream is really thick. Whipped cream is familiar, and clotted cream is the consistency of whipped butter.

Fool is a dessert with sweetened pureed fruit (such as rhubarb, gooseberries, or black currants) mixed with cream or custard and chilled. Elderflower is a popular flavoring for sorbet.

British Chocolate

My chocoholic readers are enthusiastic about British chocolates. As with other dairy products, chocolate seems richer and creamier here than it does in the US, so even the basics like Mars, Kit Kat, and Twix have a different taste. Some favorites include Cadbury Gold bars (filled with liquid caramel), Cadbury Crunchie bars, Nestlé's Lion bars (layered wafers covered in caramel and chocolate), Cadbury's Boost bars (a shortcake biscuit with caramel in milk chocolate), Cadbury Flake (crumbly folds of melt-in-your-mouth chocolate), Aero bars (with "aerated" chocolate filling), and Galaxy chocolate bars (especially the ones with hazelnuts). Thornton shops (in larger train stations) sell a box of sweets called the Continental Assortment, which comes with a tasting guide. (The highlight is the mocha white-chocolate truffle.) British M&Ms, called Smarties, are better than American ones. Many Brits feel that the ultimate treat is a box of either Nestlé Quality Street or Cadbury Roses—assortments of filled chocolates in colorful wrappers. (But don't mention the Kraft takeover of Cadbury—many Brits believe the American company changed the recipe for their beloved Dairy Milk bars, and they're not happy about it). At ice-cream vans, look for the beloved traditional "99p"—a vanilla soft-serve cone with a small Flake bar stuck right into the middle.

Flapjacks here aren't pancakes, but are dense, sweet oatmeal cakes (a little like a cross between a granola bar and a brownie). They come with toppings such as toffee and chocolate.

Scones are tops, and many inns and restaurants have their secret recipes. Whether made with fruit or topped with clotted cream, scones take the cake.

BEVERAGES
Beer: The British take great pride in their beer. Many locals think that drinking beer cold and carbonated, as Americans do, ruins the taste. Most pubs will have **lagers** (cold, refreshing, American-style beer), **ales** (amber-colored, cellar-temperature beer), **bitters** (hop-flavored ale, perhaps the most typical British beer), and **stouts** (dark and somewhat bitter, like Guinness).

At pubs, long-handled pulls (or taps) are used to pull the traditional, rich-flavored "real ales" up from the cellar. These are the connoisseur's favorites and often come with fun names. Served straight from the brewer's cask at cellar temperature, real ales finish fermenting naturally and are not pasteurized or filtered, so they must be consumed within two or three days after the cask is tapped. Naturally carbonated, real ales have less gassiness and head; they vary from sweet to bitter, often with a hoppy or nutty flavor.

Short-handled pulls mean colder, fizzier, mass-produced, and less interesting keg beers. Mild beers are sweeter, with a creamy malt flavoring. Irish cream ale is a smooth, sweet experience. Try the draft cider (sweet or dry)...carefully.

Order your beer at the bar and pay as you go, with no need to tip. An average beer costs £3. Part of the experience is standing before a line of hand pulls, and wondering which beer to choose.

As dictated by British law, draft beer and cider are served by the pint (20-ounce imperial size) or the half-pint (9.6 ounces). (It's almost feminine for a man to order just a half; I order mine with quiche.) In 2011, the government sanctioned an in-between serving size—the schooner, or two-thirds pint—hoping that more choice will woo more beer drinkers (a steady decline in beer consumption, which is taxed, has had a negative effect on tax revenues). Proper English ladies like a **shandy** (half beer and half 7-Up).

Other Alcoholic Drinks: Besides beer, many pubs have a good selection of wines by the glass, a fully stocked bar for the gentleman's "G and T" (gin and tonic), and the increasingly popular bottles of alcohol-plus-sugar (such as Bacardi Breezers) for the younger working-class set. **Pimm's** is a refreshing and fruity summer cocktail, traditionally popular during Wimbledon. It's an upper-class drink—a rough bloke might insult a pub by claiming it sells more Pimm's than beer.

Non-Alcoholic Drinks: Teetotalers can order from a wide variety of soft drinks—both the predictable American sodas and other more interesting bottled drinks, such as ginger beer (similar to ginger ale but with more bite), root beers, or other flavors (Fentimans brews some unusual options that are stocked in many English pubs). Note that in Britain, "lemonade" is lemon-lime soda (like 7-Up). Children are served food and soft drinks in pubs, but you must be 18 to order a beer.

Staying Connected

Staying connected in Europe gets easier and cheaper every year. The simplest solution is to bring your own device—mobile phone, tablet, or laptop—and use it just as you would at home (following the tips below, such as connecting to free Wi-Fi whenever possible). Another option is to buy a European SIM card for your mobile phone—either your US phone or one you buy in Europe. Or you can travel without a mobile device and use European landlines and computers to connect. Each of these options is described below, and you'll find even more details at www.ricksteves.com/phoning.

USING YOUR OWN MOBILE DEVICE IN EUROPE

Without an international plan, typical rates from major service providers (AT&T, Verizon, etc.) for using your device abroad are about $1.50/minute for voice calls, 50 cents to send text messages, 5 cents to receive them, and $20 to download one megabyte of data. But at these rates, costs can add up quickly. Here are some budget tips and options.

Use free Wi-Fi whenever possible. Unless you have an unlimited-data plan, you're best off saving most of your online tasks for Wi-Fi. You can access the Internet, send texts, and even make voice calls over Wi-Fi.

Many cafés (including Starbucks and McDonald's) have hotspots for customers; look for signs offering it and ask for the Wi-Fi password when you buy something. You'll also often find Wi-Fi at TIs, city squares, major museums, public-transit hubs, airports, and aboard trains and buses. In Britain, another option is to sign up for Wi-Fi access through a company such as BT (one hour-£5, one day-£10, www.btwifi.co.uk) or The Cloud (free though sometimes slow, www.thecloud.net/free-wifi).

Sign up for an international plan. Most providers offer a global calling plan that cuts the per-minute cost of phone calls and texts, and a flat-fee data plan that includes a certain amount of megabytes. Your normal plan may already include international coverage (T-Mobile's does).

Before your trip, call your provider or check online to confirm that your phone will work in Europe, and research your provider's international rates. A day or two before you leave, activate the plan by calling your provider or logging on to your mobile phone account. Remember to cancel your plan (if necessary) when your trip's over.

Minimize the use of your cellular network. When you can't find Wi-Fi, you can use your cellular network—convenient but slower and potentially expensive—to connect to the Internet, text, or make voice calls. When you're done, avoid further charges by manually switching off "data roaming" or "cellular data" (in your device's Settings menu; if you don't know how to switch it off, ask your service provider or Google it). Another way to make sure you're not accidentally using data roaming is to put your device in "airplane" or "flight" mode (which also disables phone calls and texts, as well as data), and then turn on Wi-Fi as needed.

Don't use your cellular network for bandwidth-gobbling tasks, such as Skyping, downloading apps, and watching YouTube—save

How to Dial

Many Americans are intimidated by dialing European phone numbers. You needn't be. It's simple, once you break the code.

Dialing Rules

Here are the rules for dialing, along with examples of how to call one of my recommended hotels in London (tel. 020/7730-8191). The 020 is London's area code.

Dialing Internationally to Britain

Whether you're phoning from a US landline, your own mobile phone, a Skype account, or a number in another European country (e.g., France to Britain), you're making an international call. Here's how to do it:

1. Dial the **international access code** (011 if calling from a US or Canadian phone; 00 if calling from any European phone number outside of Britain). If dialing from a mobile phone, you can enter a + in place of the international access code (press and hold the 0 key).
2. Dial the **country code** (44 for Britain).
3. Dial the **phone number** (drop the initial 0).

Examples:
- To call my recommended hotel from a **US or Canadian phone,** dial 011, then 44, then 20/7730-8191.
- To call from **any European phone number** (outside of Britain), dial 00, then 44, then 20/7730-8191.
- To call from any **mobile phone** (except a British one), dial +, then 44, then 20/7730-8191.

Dialing Within Britain

To make a domestic call (either from a British mobile phone or landline), you'll generally dial both the area code (including the initial 0) and the local number. If you're calling within the same

these for when you're on Wi-Fi. Using a navigation app such as Google Maps can take lots of data, so use this sparingly.

Limit automatic updates. By default, your device is constantly checking for a data connection and updating apps. It's smart to disable these features so they'll only update when you're on Wi-Fi, and to change your device's email settings from "auto-retrieve" to "manual" (or from "push" to "fetch").

It's also a good idea to keep track of your data usage. On your device's menu, look for "cellular data usage" or "mobile data" and reset the counter at the start of your trip.

Use Skype or other calling/messaging apps for cheaper calls and texts. Certain apps let you make voice or video calls or send texts over the Internet for free or cheap. If you're bringing a tab-area code, you could drop the area code and just dial the local number. But because British area codes vary in length, and mobile phones utilize their own sets of prefixes, I keep things simple by always dialing the full phone number, including the area code or prefix.

Example: To call my recommended hotel from any British landline or mobile phone, dial 020/7730-8191. If dialing from within the same 020 area code, you can just enter 7730-8191.

Calling from any European Country to the US

To call the US or Canada from Europe (either from a mobile phone or landline), dial 00 (Europe's international access code), 1 (US/Canada country code), and the phone number, including the area code. If calling from a mobile phone, you can enter a + instead of 00.

Example: To call my office in Edmonds, Washington, from anywhere in Europe, I dial 00-1-425-771-8303; or, from a mobile phone, +-1-425-771-8303.

More Dialing Tips

British Phone Numbers: Numbers beginning with 074, 075, 076, 077, 078, and 079 are mobile numbers, which are more expensive to call than a landline. For directory assistance, dial 118-500 (£3.99/call and £1.99/minute).

Toll and Toll-Free Calls: Numbers starting with 080 are toll-free, but those beginning with 084, 087, or 03 are inexpensive toll numbers (£0.10/minute maximum from a landline, £0.20-40/minute from a mobile). Numbers beginning with 09 are pricey toll lines. If you have questions about a prefix, call 100 for free help.

More Resources: The "Phoning Cheat Sheet" on page 566 shows how to dial per country, or you can check www.countrycallingcodes.com or www.howtocallabroad.com.

let or laptop, you can also use them for voice calls and texts. All you have to do is log on to a Wi-Fi network, then contact any of your friends or family members who are also online and signed into the same service. You can make voice and video calls using Skype, Viber, FaceTime, and Google+ Hangouts. If the connection is bad, try making an audio-only call.

You can also make voice calls from your device to telephones worldwide for just a few cents per minute using Skype, Viber, or Hangouts if you prebuy credit.

To text for free over Wi-Fi, try apps like Google+ Hangouts, What's App, Viber, and Facebook Messenger. Apple's iMessage connects with other Apple users, but make sure you're on Wi-Fi to avoid data charges.

USING A EUROPEAN SIM CARD IN A MOBILE PHONE

This option works well for those who want to make a lot of voice calls at cheap local rates. Either buy a phone in Europe (as little as $40 from mobile-phone shops anywhere), or bring an "unlocked" US phone (check with your carrier about unlocking it). With an unlocked phone, you can replace the original SIM card (the microchip that stores info about the phone) with one that will work with a European provider.

In Europe, buy a European SIM card. Inserted into your phone, this card gives you a European phone number—and European rates. SIM cards are sold at mobile-phone shops, department-store electronics counters, some newsstands, and even at vending machines. Costing about $5-10, they usually include about that much prepaid calling credit, with no contract and no commitment. You can still use your phone's Wi-Fi function to get online. To get a SIM card that also includes data costs (including roaming), figure on paying $15-30 for one month of data within the country you bought it. This can be cheaper than data roaming through your home provider. To get the best rates, buy a new SIM card whenever you arrive in a new country.

I like to buy SIM cards at a mobile-phone shop where there's a clerk to help explain the options and brands. Certain brands—including Lebara and Lycamobile, both of which operate in multiple European countries—are reliable and economical. Ask the clerk to help you insert your SIM card, set it up, and show you how to use it. In some countries you'll be required to register the SIM card with your passport as an antiterrorism measure (which may mean you can't use the phone for the first hour or two).

When you run out of credit, you can top it up at newsstands, tobacco shops, mobile-phone stores, or many other businesses (look for your SIM card's logo in the window), or online.

USING LANDLINES AND COMPUTERS IN EUROPE

It's easy to travel in Europe without a mobile device. You can check email or browse websites using public computers and Internet cafés, and make calls from your hotel room and/or public phones.

Phones in your **hotel room** can be inexpensive for local calls and calls made with cheap international phone cards (sold at newsstands, street kiosks, and train stations). You'll get a prepaid card with a toll-free number and a scratch-to-reveal PIN code; to make a call, dial the toll-free number, follow the prompts, enter the code, then dial your number.

Most hotels charge a fee for placing local and "toll-free" calls, as well as long-distance or international calls—ask for the rates

Tips on Internet Security

Using the Internet while traveling brings added security risks, whether you're getting online with your own device or at a public terminal using a shared network.

First, make sure that your device is running the latest version of its operating system and security software. Next, ensure that your device is password- or passcode-protected so thieves can't access your information if your device is stolen. For extra security, set passwords on apps that access key info (such as email or Facebook).

On the road, use only legitimate Wi-Fi hotspots. Ask the hotel or café staff for the specific name of their Wi-Fi network, and make sure you log on to that exact one. Hackers sometimes create a bogus hotspot with a similar or vague name (such as "Hotel Europa Free Wi-Fi"). The best Wi-Fi networks require entering a password.

Be especially cautious when checking your online banking, credit-card statements, or other personal-finance accounts. Internet security experts advise against accessing these sites while traveling. Even if you're using your own mobile device at a password-protected hotspot, any hacker who's logged on to the same network may be able to see what you're doing. If you do need to log on to a banking website, use a hard-wired connection (such as an Ethernet cable in your hotel room) or a cellular network, which is safer than Wi-Fi.

Never share your credit-card number (or any other sensitive information) online unless you know that the site is secure. A secure site displays a little padlock icon, and the URL begins with *https* (instead of the usual *http*).

before you dial. Since you're never charged for receiving calls, it's better to have someone from the US call you in your room.

Phones are rare in **B&Bs,** but if your room has one, the advice above applies. If there's no phone in your B&B room, and you have an important, brief call to make, politely ask your hosts if you can use their personal phone. Ideally use a cheap international phone card with a toll-free access number, or offer to pay your host for the call.

While **public pay phones** are relatively easy to find in Britain, they're expensive. Unlike most of Europe, British pay phones don't use dedicated, insertable phone cards; instead, you'll pay with a major credit card (which you insert into the phone—minimum charge for a credit-card call is £1.20) or coins (have a bunch handy; minimum fee is £0.60). The phone clearly shows how your money supply's doing. Only unused coins will be returned, so put in biggies with caution. Avoid using an international phone card at a

Phoning Cheat Sheet

Just smile and dial, using these rules.

Calling a European number

• **From a mobile phone** (whether you're in the US or in Europe):
Dial + (press and hold 0), then country code and number*

• **From a US/Canadian number:** Dial 011, then country code and number*

• **From a different European country** (e.g., German number to French
number): Dial 00, then country code and number*

• **Within the same European country** (e.g., German number to another
German number): Dial the number as printed, including initial 0 if there
is one

** Drop initial 0 (if present) from phone number
in all countries except Italy*

Calling the US or Canada from Europe

Dial 00, then 1 (country code for US/Canada), then area code and number;
on mobile phones, enter + in place of 00

Country	Country Code	Country	Country Code
Austria	43	Italy	39 [2]
Belgium	32	Latvia	371
Bosnia-Herzegovina	387	Montenegro	382
Croatia	385	Morocco	212
Czech Republic	420	Netherlands	31
Denmark	45	Norway	47
Estonia	372	Poland	48
Finland	358	Portugal	351
France	33	Russia	7 [3]
Germany	49	Slovakia	421
Gibraltar	350	Slovenia	386
Great Britain & N. Ireland	44	Spain	34
Greece	30	Sweden	46
Hungary	36 [1]	Switzerland	41
Ireland	353	Turkey	90

[1] For long-distance calls within Hungary, dial 06, then the area code and number.
[2] When making international calls to Italy, do not drop the initial 0 from the
phone number.
[3] For long-distance calls within Russia, dial 8, then the area code and number.
To call the US or Canada from Russia, dial 8, then 10, then 1, then the area
code and number.

PRACTICALITIES

The English Accent

In the olden days, an English person's accent indicated his or her social standing. Eliza Doolittle had the right idea—elocution could make or break you. Wealthier families would send their kids to fancy private schools to learn proper pronunciation. But these days, in a sort of reverse snobbery that has gripped the nation, accents are back. Politicians, newscasters, and movie stars are favoring deep accents over the Queen's English. While it's hard for American ears to pick out all of the variations, most English people can determine where a person is from based on their accent...not just the region, but often the village, and even the part of town.

British pay phone—a surcharge for their use effectively eliminates any savings.

Cheap **call shops,** often located in train-station neighborhoods, advertise low international rates. Before making your call, be completely clear on the rates (e.g., if there's a charge per unit, find out how long a unit is).

It's always possible to find **public computers:** at your hotel (many have one in their lobby for guests to use), or at an Internet café or library (ask your hotelier or the TI for the nearest location). If typing on a European keyboard, use the "Alt Gr" key to the right of the space bar to insert the extra symbol that appears on some keys. If you can't locate a special character (such as @), simply copy it from a Web page and paste it into your email message.

MAIL

You can mail one package per day to yourself worth up to $200 duty-free from Europe to the US (mark it "personal purchases"). If you're sending a gift to someone, mark it "unsolicited gift." For details, visit www.cbp.gov and search for "Know Before You Go."

The British postal service works fine, but for quick transatlantic delivery (in either direction), consider services such as DHL (www.dhl.com). For postcards, get stamps at the neighborhood post office, newsstands within fancy hotels, and some mini-marts and card shops.

Transportation

If your trip will cover more of Britain than just London, you may need to take a long-distance train or bus, rent a car, or fly. Buses are an alternative to trains (and may be your only option for reaching some small British towns), but they are generally slower and less efficient. Renting a car is great for touring rural areas, such as the Cotswolds, east of London. I give some specifics on trains, buses, and flights here. For more information on these options, plus details on renting a car and driving, see www.ricksteves.com/transportation.

BY TRAIN

Regular tickets on Britain's great train system (15,000 departures from 2,400 stations daily) are the most expensive per mile in all of Europe. For the greatest savings, book online in advance and leave after rush hour (after 9:30).

Since Britain's railways have been privatized, it can be tricky to track down all your options; a single train route can be operated by multiple companies. However, one British website covers all train lines (www.nationalrail.co.uk), and another covers all bus and train routes (www.traveline.org.uk—for information, not ticket sales). Another good resource, which also has schedules for trains throughout Europe, is German Rail's timetable (www.bahn.com).

As with airline tickets, British train tickets can come at many different prices for the same journey. A clerk at any station can figure out the cheapest fare for your trip.

Buying Train Tickets in Advance: To book ahead, go in person to any station, book online at www.nationalrail.co.uk, or call 0345-748-4950 (from the US, dial 011-44-20-7278-5240, phone answered 24 hours) to find out the schedule and best fare for your journey; you'll then be referred to the appropriate vendor—depending on the particular rail company—to book your ticket. If you order online, be sure you know what you want; it's tough to reach a person who can change your online reservation. You'll pick up your ticket at the station, or you may be able to print it at home. (BritRail passholders, however, cannot use the Web to make reservations.)

A company called **Megabus** (through their subsidiary Mega-train) sells some discounted train tickets well in advance on a few specific routes, though their focus is mainly on selling bus tickets (info tel. 0871-266-3333, www.megatrain.com).

Buying Train Tickets as You Travel: If you'd rather have the flexibility of booking tickets as you go, you can save a few pounds by buying a round-trip ticket, called a "return ticket" (a same-day round-trip, called a "day return," is particularly cheap); buying before 18:00 the day before you depart; traveling after the morning rush hour (this usually means after 9:30 Mon-Fri); and going standard class instead of first class. Preview your options at www.nationalrail.co.uk.

Rail Passes: For train travel outside London, consider getting a BritRail pass. Choose between England-only BritRail passes and ones that cover Scotland and Wales as well. More BritRail options

Public Transportation Routes in Britain

Legend:
- Rail
- Eurostar
- Bus
- (8H) Ferry with crossing time

Ferry Note:
Dover – Calais–1.5H
Dover – Boul–1.5 H

Orkney Islands
Burwick
Thurso • John o' Groats
Lewis
Skye
Portree • Inverness
Kyle • Culloden
Loch • Aviemore
Mallaig • Ness • Aberdeen
Fort William
SCOTLAND
Mull • Pitlochry
Iona • Oban • Perth • Dundee
Leuchars
Stirling • St. Andrews
Edinburgh
Glasgow • Berwick
Holy Island

50 Kilometers
50 Miles

(2H) • Cairnryan • Hexham
Larne • (2.5H) • Stranraer • Carlisle • Newcastle • To Amsterdam (15H)
Belfast • Durham • North Sea
NORTHERN IRELAND • Keswick • Penrith • Whitby
Danby
Windermere • North York Moors • Scarborough
Isle of Man • ENGLAND
Irish Sea • Blackpool • York • Hull
Leeds • To Zeebrugge (10H)
Dublin • Preston • Grimsby
Dun • (7H) • Holyhead • Conwy • Liverpool • Manchester
Laoghaire • (2-3H) • Bangor • Chester • Lincoln
Caernarfon • Betws-y-Coed • Stoke • Derby • Peter-borough • King's Lynn • Norwich
REPUBLIC • Pwllheli • Blaenau Ffest. • Telford • Wolv. • Birmingham • Ely
OF • Harlech • Ironbridge Gorge • Coventry • Cambridge
IRELAND • Aberystwyth • Stratford • Warwick • Harwich
(3.5H) • WALES • Cheltenham • Moreton • To Hoek van Holland (6H)
Rosslare • Carmarthen • Stow • Oxford • London • Ebbs-fleet
Fishguard • Newport • Reading • Canterbury
Swansea • Bath • STONEHENGE • Woking • Ashford • Dover (1.5H)
Cardiff • Bristol • West-bury • Salisbury • Brighton • Calais
Wells • Glastonbury • Southampton • Newhaven • EUROSTAR (2.5H)
Atlantic Ocean • Exeter • Portsmouth
Dartmoor • To Dieppe (4H) • To Paris & Brussels
Truro • Plymouth
St. Ives • English Channel • To Ouistreham (6H) • FRANCE
Penzance • Falmouth
To Roscoff (6H) • To St-Malo (11H)

PRACTICALITIES

include "London Plus" passes (good for travel in most of southeast England but not in London itself), and South West passes (good for the Cotswolds, Bath, Dorset, Devon, Cornwall, plus part of South Wales). These BritRail passes, as well as Eurail passes, get you a discount on the Eurostar train that zips you to continental Europe under the English Channel. These passes are sold outside of Europe only. For specifics, see www.ricksteves.com/rail.

BY BUS

Most domestic buses are operated by **National Express** (tel. 0871-781-8181, www.nationalexpress.com); their international departures are called **Eurolines** (www.eurolines.co.uk).

A smaller company called **Megabus** undersells National Express with deeply discounted promotional fares—the farther ahead you buy, the less you pay (some trips for just £1.50, toll tel. 0900-160-0900, www.megabus.com). While Megabus can be much cheaper than National Express, they tend to be slower than their competitor and their routes mainly connect cities, not smaller towns. They also sell discounted train tickets on selected routes.

Try to avoid bus travel on Friday and Sunday evenings, when weekend travelers are more likely to make buses sell out.

To ensure getting a ticket—and to save money with special promotions—book your ticket in advance online or over the phone. The cheapest pre-purchased tickets can usually be changed (for a £5 fee), but not refunded. Check if the ticket is only "amendable" or also "refundable" when you buy. If you have a mobile phone, you can order online and have a "text ticket" sent right to your phone for a small fee.

FLIGHTS

The best comparison search engine for both international and intra-European flights is www.kayak.com. For inexpensive flights within Europe, try www.skyscanner.com or www.hipmunk.com; for inexpensive international flights, try www.vayama.com.

Flying to Europe: Start looking for international flights four to five months before your trip, especially for peak-season travel. Off-season tickets can be purchased a month or so in advance. Depending on your itinerary, it can be efficient to fly into one city and out of another. If your flight requires a connection in Europe, see my hints on navigating Europe's top hub airports at www.ricksteves.com/hub-airports.

Flying Within Europe: London is the hub for many cheap, no-frills airlines, which affordably connect the city with other destinations in the British Isles and throughout Europe. If you're considering a train ride that's more than five hours long, a flight may save you both time and money. When comparing your options, factor in the time it takes to get to the airport and how early you'll need to arrive to check in.

Well-known cheapo airlines include easyJet (www.easyjet.com) and Ryanair (www.ryanair.com). **EasyJet** flies from Gatwick, Luton, Stansted, and Southend while **Ryanair** flies mostly from Stansted Airport, as well as Gatwick and Luton. Other airlines to consider include **CityJet** (based at London City Airport, www.cityjet.com), **Monarch** (specializes in connecting to Mediterranean resorts, www.monarch.co.uk), **Thomson** (similar to Monarch, www.thomsonfly.com), **Flybe** (www.flybe.com), and **Brussels Airlines** (with frequent connections from Heathrow to its Brussels hub, www.brusselsairlines.com).

But be aware of the potential drawbacks of flying with a discount airline: nonrefundable and nonchangeable tickets, minimal or nonexistent customer service, pricey and time-consuming treks to secondary airports, and stingy baggage allowances with steep overage fees. If you're traveling with lots of luggage, a cheap flight can quickly become a bad deal. To avoid unpleasant surprises, read the small print before you book. These days you can also fly within Europe on major airlines affordably—and without all the aggressive restrictions—for around $100 a flight.

Flying to the US and Canada: Because security is extra tight for flights to the US, be sure to give yourself plenty of time at the airport. It's also important to charge your electronic devices before you board because security checks may require you to turn them on (see www.tsa.gov for the latest rules).

Resources

PRACTICALITIES

RESOURCES FROM RICK STEVES

Rick Steves London 2016 is one of many books in my series on European travel, which includes country and regional guidebooks

(including Great Britain, Scotland, and England), city guidebooks, Snapshot guides (excerpted chapters from my country guides), Pocket Guides (full-color little books on big cities, including London), and my budget-travel skills handbook, *Rick Steves Europe Through the Back Door*. Most of my titles are available as ebooks. My phrase books—for Italian, French, German, Spanish, and Portuguese—are practical and budget-oriented. My other books include *Europe 101* (a crash course on art and history designed for travelers); *Mediterranean Cruise Ports* and *Northern European Cruise Ports* (how to make the most of your time in port); and *Travel as a Political Act* (a travelogue sprinkled with tips for bringing home a global perspective). A more complete list of my titles appears near the end of this book.

Video: My public television series, *Rick Steves' Europe,* covers Europe from top to bottom with over 100 half-hour episodes. To watch full episodes online for free, see www.ricksteves.com/tv. Or to raise your travel I.Q. with video versions of our popular classes (including my talks on travel skills, packing smart, European art for travelers, travel as a political act, and individual talks covering most European countries), see www.ricksteves.com/travel-talks.

Audio: My weekly public radio show, *Travel with Rick Steves,* features interviews with travel experts from around the world. A complete archive of 10 years of programs (over 400 in all) is available at www.ricksteves.com/radio. I've also produced free, self-guided **audio tours** of the top sights in London. Most of this audio content is available for free through my **Rick Steves Audio Europe app,** an extensive online library organized by destination. For more on my app, see page 5.

MAPS

The black-and-white maps in this book are concise and simple, designed to help you locate recommended places and get to local TIs, where you can pick up more in-depth maps of cities and regions (usually free). Better maps are sold at newsstands and bookstores. *The Handy London Map & Guide* from Bensons MapGuides is excellent. The *Rough Guide* map to London is well-designed (£5, sold at London bookstores). The *Rick Steves Britain, Ireland & London City Map* has a good map of London ($9, www.ricksteves.com). Many Londoners, along with obsessive-compulsive tourists, rely on the highly detailed *London A-Z* map book (generally £5-7, called "A to Zed" by locals, available at newsstands). The color city maps and Tube map at the front of this book are also useful. Even the vending-machine maps sold in Tube stations are good. Before you buy a map, look at it to be sure it has the level of detail you want.

If you use Google Maps or Apple Maps on your mobile device, pulling up maps on the fly or looking up turn-by-turn walking directions requires you to go online—so it's smart to get an international data plan (see page 561). In either app, it's possible to download a map while on Wi-Fi, then navigate with it all day long without incurring data-roaming charges—though you can't search for an address or get directions. A number of well-designed apps, including City Maps 2Go, OffMaps, and Navfree, allow you much of the convenience of online maps without any costly data demands.

Begin Your Trip at
www.RickSteves.com

My mobile-friendly **website** is *the* place to explore Europe. You'll find thousands of fun articles, videos, photos, and radio interviews organized by country; a wealth of money-saving tips for planning your dream trip; monthly travel news dispatches; my travel talks and travel blog; my latest guidebook updates (www.ricksteves.com/update); and my free Rick Steves Audio Europe app. You can also follow me on Facebook and Twitter.

Our **Travel Forum** is an immense yet well-groomed collection of message boards, where our travel-savvy community answers questions and shares their personal travel experiences—and our well-traveled staff chimes in when they can be helpful (www.ricksteves.com/forums).

Our **online Travel Store** offers travel bags and accessories that I've designed specifically to help you travel smarter and lighter. These include my popular bags (rolling carry-on and backpack versions, which I helped design...and live out of four months a year), money belts, totes, toiletries kits, adapters, other accessories, and a wide selection of guidebooks and planning maps.

Choosing the right **rail pass** for your trip—amid hundreds of options—can drive you nutty. Our website will help you find the perfect fit for your itinerary and your budget: We offer easy, one-stop shopping for rail passes, seat reservations, and point-to-point tickets.

Want to travel with greater efficiency and less stress? We organize **tours** with more than three dozen itineraries and more than 900 departures reaching the best destinations in this book...and beyond. Three of our tours include London: our seven-day in-depth London city tour, our 14-day England tour, and our 13-day Family Europe: London to Florence tour. You'll enjoy great guides, a fun bunch of travel partners (with small groups of 24 to 28 travelers), and plenty of room to spread out in a big, comfy bus when touring between towns. You'll find European adventures to fit every vacation length. For all the details, and to get our Tour Catalog and a free Rick Steves Tour Experience DVD (filmed on location during an actual tour), visit www.ricksteves.com or call us at 425/608-4217.

PRACTICALITIES

APPENDIX

Useful Contacts 575
Holidays and Festivals 576
Recommended Books
and Films 577
Conversions and Climate 581
Packing Checklist 584
British-Yankee Vocabulary 585

Useful Contacts

Emergency Needs
Police and Ambulance: Tel. 999

Embassies and Consulates
US Consulate and Embassy: Tel. 020/7499-9000 (all services), no walk-in passport services; for emergency 36-hour passport service, email LondonEmergencyPPT@state.gov or call all-services number (24 Grosvenor Square, Tube: Bond Street, http://london.usembassy.gov)

Canadian High Commission: Tel. 020/7004-6000, passport services available Mon-Fri 9:30-12:30 (Canada House, Trafalgar Square; Tube: Charing Cross, www.unitedkingdom.gc.ca)

Travel Advisories
US Department of State: Tel. 888-407-4747, from outside US tel. 1-202-501-4444, www.travel.state.gov

Canadian Department of Foreign Affairs: Canadian tel. 800-387-3124, from outside Canada call 1-613-944-6788, www.travel.gc.ca

US Centers for Disease Control and Prevention: US tel. 800-CDC-INFO (800-232-4636), www.cdc.gov/travel

Directory Assistance
Operator Assistance: Tel. 100 (free)
Directory Assistance: Toll tel. 118-500 (£0.59/minute, plus £0.23/minute connection charge from fixed lines)
International Directory Assistance: Toll tel. 118-505 (£2.99/minute, plus £0.99 connection charge)

Holidays and Festivals

This list includes selected festivals in London, major events in Windsor and Cambridge, plus national holidays observed throughout Great Britain. Many sights and banks close on national holidays—keep this in mind when planning your itinerary. Before planning a trip around a festival, verify its dates by checking the festival's website or TI sites (www.visitlondon.com and www.visitbritain.com).

In London, hotels get booked up on major holidays—New Year's Day, Easter weekend, Christmas, and Boxing Day—and on Fridays and Saturdays year-round. Some hotels require you to book the full three-day weekend around Bank Holiday Mondays.

Jan 1	New Year's Day
Feb 19-23	London Fashion Week (www.londonfashionweek.co.uk)
March 25	Good Friday
March 27-28	Easter Sunday and Monday
May 2	Early May Bank Holiday (first Monday in May)
May 30	Spring Bank Holiday (last Monday in May)
Late May	Chelsea Flower Show, London (book tickets ahead for this popular event at www.rhs.org.uk/chelsea)
June 11	Trooping the Colour, London (military bands and pageantry, Queen's birthday parade; www.trooping-the-colour.co.uk)
Late June	Royal Ascot Horse Race, Ascot (near Windsor; www.ascot.co.uk)
Late June-early July	Wimbledon Tennis Championship, London (www.wimbledon.com)

Late July-early Aug	Cambridge Folk Festival, Cambridge (buy tickets early at www.cambridgefolkfestival.co.uk)
Late Aug	Notting Hill Carnival, London (costumes, Caribbean music, www.thenottinghillcarnival.com)
Aug 29	Summer Bank Holiday (last Monday in August)
Sept 16-20	London Fashion Week (www.londonfashionweek.co.uk)
Nov 5	Bonfire Night (bonfires, fireworks, effigy burning of 1605 traitor Guy Fawkes)
Nov 13	Remembrance Sunday (second Sunday in November, royals lay wreaths at Cenotaph for WWI dead)
Mid-Nov	Lord Mayor's Show, London (second Saturday in November; huge parade in The City with fireworks, www.lordmayorsshow.org)
Dec 24-26	Christmas holidays (many sights close; limited or no public transport)

Recommended Books and Films

To learn more about London past and present, check out a few of these books and films. For kids' recommendations, see page 420.

Nonfiction

84, Charing Cross Road (Helene Hanff, 1970). Correspondence between a proper London bookseller and an outspoken New York writer turns into a trans-Atlantic friendship (also a 1987 movie with Anthony Hopkins and Anne Bancroft). In the sequel, *The Duchess of Bloomsbury Street*, the writer travels to London.

Elizabeth's London (Liza Picard, 2005). The author re-creates 16th-century life in the era of England's first great queen.

Fever Pitch (Nick Hornby, 1992). Hornby's memoir illuminates the British obsession with soccer.

A History of London (Stephen Inwood, 1998). Two thousand years of city history is laid out over 1,000 pages.

The Last Lion (William Manchester, final book completed by Paul Reid; 1983, 1988, and 2012). This superb, three-volume biography recounts the amazing life of Winston Churchill from 1874 to 1965.

Letters from London (Julian Barnes, 1995). The *New Yorker*'s former London correspondent captures life in the city in the early 1990s.

London: The Biography (Peter Ackroyd, 2001). The author uses an imaginative biographical approach to tell London's story.

Longitude (Dava Sobel, 1995). A London clockmaker solves the problem of keeping time aboard a ship—a timely read for visitors to Greenwich.

Notes from a Small Island (Bill Bryson, 1995). In this irreverent and delightful memoir, US expat Bryson writes about his travels through Britain—his home for two decades.

St Pancras Station (Simon Bradley, 2007). Bradley presents a treasure trove of history about London's iconic gateway to Europe.

A Traveller's History of England (Christopher Daniell, revised 2005). A British archaeologist and historian provides a comprehensive yet succinct overview of English history.

With Wings Like Eagles (Michael Korda, 2009). An English-born writer gives a historical analysis of Britain's pivotal WWII air battles versus the German Luftwaffe.

Fiction

For the classics of British fiction, read anything—and everything—by Charles Dickens, Jane Austen, and the Brontës. Some favorites that feature London include *Persuasion,* the beloved Austen book partially set in Bath, and Charles Dickens' tale of a workhouse urchin, *Oliver Twist.* Here are some other good reads:

Brick Lane (Monica Ali, 2003). A Bangladeshi woman in an arranged marriage to an older man raises her family—and starts an affair with a young radical—in contemporary London (also a 2007 film).

Bridget Jones's Diary (Helen Fielding, 1996). A year in the life of a single 30-something woman in London is humorously chronicled in diary form (also a motion picture).

The Buddha of Suburbia (Hanif Kureishi, 1990). The son of a self-proclaimed suburban guru gets swept up in the fast lane of 1970s London.

Confessions of a Shopaholic (Sophie Kinsella, 2001). A London woman lives beyond her means in this funny tale of modern English life.

The Great Stink (Clare Clark, 2005). A Crimean War veteran seeks refuge working in the London sewer system, but is sucked into a murder mystery.

High Fidelity (Nick Hornby, 1995). This humorous novel traces the romantic misadventures and musical musings of a 30-something record-store owner. Another good read is Hornby's 1998 coming-of-age story, *About a Boy*. (Both books were also made into films.)

In the Presence of the Enemy (Elizabeth George, 1996). London's movers and shakers commit sins and scandals in this detective story.

The Jupiter Myth (Lindsey Davis, 2002). In A.D. 75, an investigator from Rome probes a murder in what was then known as Londinium.

London (Edward Rutherfurd, 1997). This big and sprawling historical novel begins in ancient times and continues through to the 20th century.

Mapp and Lucia (E. F. Benson, 1931). A rural village in the 1930s becomes a social battlefield. In *Lucia in London* (1927), the protagonist attempts social climbing in the big city.

The Paying Guests (Sarah Waters, 2014). This realistic and suspenseful tale of love, obsession, and murder plays out amid the shifting culture of post-WWII upper-class London.

Pygmalion (George Bernard Shaw, 1913). This stage play, on which the film *My Fair Lady* is based, tells the story of a young Cockney girl groomed for high society.

Rumpole of the Bailey (Sir John Mortimer, 1978). Mortimer's popular detective story about an aging London barrister spawned a series of books and TV shows.

Saturday (Ian McEwan, 2005). The protagonist endures a series of strange events in London during a day of protest over the invasion of Iraq.

SS-GB (Len Deighton, 1979). In Nazi-occupied Great Britain, a Scotland Yard detective finds there's more to a murder than meets the eye.

A Study in Scarlet (Sir Arthur Conan Doyle, 1888). This mystery novel introduced the world to detective Sherlock Holmes and his trusty sidekick, Dr. Watson.

Thank You, Jeeves (P. G. Wodehouse, 1934). The author's first full-length novel is about the competent valet to a wealthy and foolish Londoner (also many short stories and sequels).

White Teeth (Zadie Smith, 2000). The postwar lives of two army buddies, a native Englishman and a Bengali Muslim, are chronicled in this acclaimed novel.

Film and TV

Alfie (1966). In 1960s London, a womanizer (Michael Caine) eventually must face up to his boorish behavior (also a 2004 remake with Jude Law). Other "swinging London" films include *Blow-up* (1966) and *Georgy Girl* (1966).

Battle of Britain (1969). An all-star cast and marvelous aerial combat scenes tell the story of Britain's "finest hour" of World War II.

Blackadder (1983-1989). This wickedly funny BBC sitcom starring Rowan Atkinson skewers various periods of English history over the course of four series (also several TV specials).

Call the Midwife (2012-). London's poor East End comes to gritty, poignant life in this BBC drama tracing the lives of a team of nurse midwives in the late 1950s and early 1960s.

The Elephant Man (1980). A severely disfigured man reveals his sensitive soul in this stark portrayal of Victorian London.

GoldenEye (1995). This James Bond film features the first look at the iconic MI6 headquarters, located in the center of London.

A Hard Day's Night (1964). The Beatles star in their debut film, a comedy depicting several days in the life of the band.

Hope and Glory (1987). John Boorman directed this semi-autobio-graphical story of a boy growing up during World War II and the London Blitz.

The King's Speech (2010). Colin Firth stars as the stuttering King George VI on the eve of World War II.

My Beautiful Laundrette (1985). This gritty, compelling movie tells the story of two gay men in urban London.

My Fair Lady (1964). Audrey Hepburn stars as a poor, Cockney flower seller who is transformed into a lady of high society by an arrogant professor.

Notting Hill (1999). Hugh Grant and Julia Roberts star in this romantic comedy set in the London neighborhood of...you guessed it.

The Queen (2006). Helen Mirren expertly channels Elizabeth II in the days after Princess Diana's death. Its prequel, *The Deal* (2003), probes the relationship between Tony Blair and Gordon Brown.

Sammy and Rosie Get Laid (1987). An unconventional middle-class couple's promiscuous adventures expose racial tensions in multiethnic London.

Shakespeare in Love (1999). Tudor-era London comes to life in this clever, romantic film set in the original Globe Theater.

Sherlock (2010-). Holmes (Benedict Cumberbatch) and Watson (Martin Freeman) are excellent in this BBC-TV update of the detective's story, set in present-day London.

To Sir, with Love (1967). Sidney Poitier grapples with social and racial issues in an East End inner-city school.

Upstairs, Downstairs (1971-1975). This TV series follows an aristocratic family and their servants in their new home at 165 Eaton Place.

Waterloo Bridge (1940). This Academy Award-nominated romantic drama recalls the lost love between a ballerina (Vivien Leigh) and a WWI army officer.

Conversions and Climate

NUMBERS AND STUMBLERS

- Some British people write a few of their numbers differently than we do: 1 = 1, 4 = 4, 7 = 7.
- In Europe, dates appear as day/month/year, so Christmas 2016 is 25/12/16.
- What Americans call the second floor of a building is the first floor in Britain.
- On escalators and moving sidewalks, Brits keep the left "lane" open for passing. Keep to the right.
- To avoid the British version of giving someone "the finger," don't hold up the first two fingers of your hand with your palm facing you. (It looks like a reversed victory sign.)
- And please...don't call your waist pack a "fanny pack" (see the British-Yankee Vocabulary list at the end of this appendix).

UNITS OF MEASUREMENT

Britain is becoming more metric, but imperial units are still used in a few official measurements.

Metric Conversions

Weight and volume are typically calculated in metric: A kilogram is 2.2 pounds, and a liter is about a quart (almost four to a gallon). Temperatures are generally given in Celsius, although some newspapers also list them in Fahrenheit.

1 foot = 0.3 meter	1 square yard = 0.8 square meter
1 yard = 0.9 meter	1 square mile = 2.6 square kilometers
1 mile = 1.6 kilometers	1 ounce = 28 grams
1 centimeter = 0.4 inch	1 quart = 0.95 liter
1 meter = 39.4 inches	1 kilogram = 2.2 pounds
1 kilometer = 0.62 mile	32°F = 0°C

Imperial Weights and Measures

Driving distances and speed limits are measured in miles. Beer is sold as pints (though milk can be measured in pints or liters), and a person's weight is measured in stone (a 168-pound person weighs 12 stone).

1 stone = 14 pounds
1 British pint = 1.2 US pints
1 imperial gallon = 1.2 US gallons or about 4.5 liters

APPENDIX

582 Rick Steves London

CLOTHING SIZES

When shopping for clothing, use these US-to-UK comparisons as general guidelines (but note that no conversion is perfect).

- Women's dresses and blouses: Add 4 (US women's size 10=UK size 14)
- Men's suits, jackets, and shirts: US and UK use the same sizing
- Women's shoes: Subtract 2½ (US size 8=UK size 5½)
- Men's shoes: Subtract about ½ (US size 9=UK size 8½)

London's Climate

First line, average daily high; second line, average daily low; third line, average days without rain. For more detailed weather statistics for destinations throughout Britain (as well as the rest of the world), check www.wunderground.com.

J	F	M	A	M	J	J	A	S	O	N	D
43°	44°	50°	56°	62°	69°	71°	71°	65°	58°	50°	45°
36°	36°	38°	42°	47°	53°	56°	56°	52°	46°	42°	38°
16	15	20	18	19	19	19	20	17	18	15	16

FAHRENHEIT AND CELSIUS CONVERSION

For Weather   For Health

Britain uses both Celsius and Fahrenheit to take its temperature. For a rough conversion from Celsius to Fahrenheit, double the number and add 30. For weather, remember that 28°C is 82°F—perfect. For health, 37°C is just right. At a launderette, 30°C is cold, 40°C is warm (usually the default setting), 60°C is hot, and 95°C is boiling.

APPENDIX

Packing Checklist

Whether you're traveling for five days or five weeks, you won't need more than this. Pack light to enjoy the sweet freedom of true mobility.

Clothing

- ❏ 5 shirts: long- & short-sleeve
- ❏ 2 pairs pants or skirt
- ❏ 1 pair shorts or capris
- ❏ 5 pairs underwear & socks
- ❏ 1 pair walking shoes
- ❏ Sweater or fleece top
- ❏ Rainproof jacket with hood
- ❏ Tie or scarf
- ❏ Swimsuit
- ❏ Sleepwear

Money

- ❏ Debit card
- ❏ Credit card(s)
- ❏ Hard cash ($20 bills)
- ❏ Money belt or neck wallet

Documents & Travel Info

- ❏ Passport
- ❏ Airline reservations
- ❏ Rail pass/train reservations
- ❏ Car-rental voucher
- ❏ Driver's license
- ❏ Student ID, hostel card, etc.
- ❏ Photocopies of all the above
- ❏ Hotel confirmations
- ❏ Insurance details
- ❏ Guidebooks & maps
- ❏ Notepad & pen
- ❏ Journal

Toiletries Kit

- ❏ Toiletries
- ❏ Medicines & vitamins
- ❏ First-aid kit
- ❏ Glasses/contacts/sunglasses (with prescriptions)
- ❏ Earplugs
- ❏ Packet of tissues (for WC)

Miscellaneous

- ❏ Daypack
- ❏ Sealable plastic baggies
- ❏ Laundry soap
- ❏ Spot remover
- ❏ Clothesline
- ❏ Sewing kit
- ❏ Travel alarm/watch

Electronics

- ❏ Smartphone or mobile phone
- ❏ Camera & related gear
- ❏ Tablet/ereader/media player
- ❏ Laptop & flash drive
- ❏ Earbuds or headphones
- ❏ Chargers
- ❏ Plug adapters

Optional Extras

- ❏ Flipflops or slippers
- ❏ Mini-umbrella or poncho
- ❏ Travel hairdryer
- ❏ Belt
- ❏ Hat (for sun or cold)
- ❏ Picnic supplies
- ❏ Water bottle
- ❏ Fold-up tote bag
- ❏ Small flashlight
- ❏ Small binoculars
- ❏ Insect repellent
- ❏ Small towel or washcloth
- ❏ Inflatable pillow
- ❏ Some duct tape (for repairs)
- ❏ Tiny lock
- ❏ Address list (to mail postcards)
- ❏ Postcards/photos from home
- ❏ Extra passport photos
- ❏ Good book

APPENDIX

BRITISH-YANKEE VOCABULARY

For a longer list, plus a dry-witted primer on British culture, see *The Septic's Companion* (Chris Rae). Note that instead of asking, "Can I help you?" many Brits offer a more casual, "You alright?" or "You OK there?"

advert: advertisement

afters: dessert

anticlockwise: counterclockwise

Antipodean: An Australian or New Zealander

aubergine: eggplant

banger: sausage

bangers and mash: sausages and mashed potatoes

bank holiday: legal holiday

bap: small roll

bespoke: custom-made

billion: a thousand of our billions (a million million)

biro: ballpoint pen

biscuit: cookie

black pudding: sausage made from dried blood

bloody: damn

blow off: fart

bobby: policeman ("the Bill" is more common)

Bob's your uncle: there you go (with a shrug), naturally

boffin: nerd, geek

bollocks: testicles (used in many colorful expressions)

bolshy: argumentative

bomb: success or failure

bonnet: car hood

booking: reservation

boot: car trunk

braces: suspenders

bridle way: path for walkers, bikers, and horse riders

brilliant: cool

brolly: umbrella

bubble and squeak: cabbage and potatoes fried together

builder: construction worker

bum: butt

candy floss: cotton candy

caravan: trailer

car boot sale: temporary flea market, often for charity

car park: parking lot

cashpoint: ATM

casualty: emergency room

cat's eyes: road reflectors

ceilidh (KAY-lee): informal evening of song and folk fun (Scottish and Irish)

cheap and cheerful: budget but adequate

cheap and nasty: cheap and bad quality

cheers: good-bye or thanks; also a toast

chemist: pharmacist

chicory: endive

chippie: fish-and-chip shop; carpenter (see also "joiner")

chips: French fries

chock-a-block: jam-packed

chuffed: pleased

cider: alcoholic apple cider

clearway: road where you can't stop

coach: long-distance bus

concession: discounted admission

concs (pronounced "conks"): short for "concession"

cos: romaine lettuce

cot: baby crib

cotton buds: Q-tips

council estate: public housing

courgette: zucchini

craic (pronounced "crack"): fun, good conversation (Irish and spreading to England)

crisps: potato chips

cuppa: cup of tea

curry: any Indian meal flavored with curry, popular with Brits

dear: expensive

dicey: iffy, risky

digestives: round graham cookies

dinner: lunch or dinner

diversion: detour

donkey's years: ages, a long time

draughts: checkers

draw: marijuana

dual carriageway: divided highway (four lanes)

dummy: pacifier

elevenses: coffee-and-biscuits break before lunch

elvers: baby eels

engaged tone: busy signal

estate car: station wagon

face flannel: washcloth

faff: bumble (about)

fag: cigarette

fagged: exhausted

faggot: meatball

fairy cake: cupcake

fancy: to like, to be attracted to (a person)

fanny: vagina

fell: hill or high plain (Lake District)

first floor: second floor

fixture: sports schedule

fizzy drink: pop or soda

flat: apartment

flutter: a bet

football: soccer

force: waterfall (Lake District)

fortnight: two weeks

fringe: hair bangs

Frogs: French people

fruit machine: slot machine

full Monty: whole shebang; everything

gallery: balcony

gammon: ham

gangway: aisle

gaol: jail (same pronunciation)

gateau (or gateaux): cake

gear lever: stick shift

geezer: dude (slang for young man)

ginger-haired: redhead

give way: yield

glen: narrow valley (Scotland)

goods wagon: freight truck

green fingers: green thumbs

grizzle: grumble, fuss (especially by a baby)

gutted: deeply disappointed

half eight: 8:30 (not 7:30)

hash sign: pound sign, as on a phone

heath: open treeless land

hen night: bachelorette party

High Street: Main Street (in a generic sense)

hire: rent, as in a car or bike

hire car: rental car

hob: stove burner

holiday: vacation

homely: homey or cozy

hoover: vacuum cleaner

ice lolly: popsicle

interval: intermission

ironmonger: hardware store

ish: more or less

jacket potato: baked potato

jelly: Jell-O

Joe Bloggs: John Q. Public

joiner: carpenter (see also "chippie")

jumble sale: rummage sale

jumper: sweater
just a tick: just a second
kipper: smoked herring
knackered: exhausted (Cockney: cream crackered)
knickers: ladies' panties
knocking shop: brothel
knock up: wake up or visit (old-fashioned)
ladybird: ladybug
lady fingers: flat, spongy cookie
lady's finger: okra
lager: light, fizzy beer
left luggage: baggage check
lemon squash: lemonade, not fizzy
lemonade: lemon-lime pop, fizzy
let: rent, as in property
licenced: restaurant authorized to sell alcohol
lie-in, having a: sleeping in late
lift: elevator
listed: protected historic building
loo: toilet or bathroom
lorry: truck
mac: mackintosh raincoat
main: entrée
mains: electrical outlet
mangetout: snow peas
Marmite: yeast paste, spread on sandwiches
marrow: summer squash
mate: buddy (boy or girl)
mean: stingy
mental: wild, memorable
mews: former stables converted to two-story rowhouses (London)
mince: hamburger meat
mobile: cell phone
moggie: cat

M.O.T.: mandatory annual car safety certificate
motorway: freeway
naff: dorky
nappy: diaper
natter: talk on and on
neep: Scottish for turnip
newsagent: corner store
nought: zero
noughts & crosses: tic-tac-toe
O.A.P.: old-age pensioner, retiree
off-licence: liquor store
on offer: for sale
one-off: unique; one-time event
panto, pantomime: fairy-tale play performed at Christmas (silly but fun)
pants: (noun) underwear, briefs; (adj.) terrible, ridiculous
paracetamol: acetaminophen, Tylenol
pasty (PASS-tee): crusted savory (usually meat) pie from Cornwall
pavement: sidewalk
people mover: minivan
pear-shaped: messed up, gone wrong
pensioner: senior citizen, retiree
petrol: gas
pillar box: mailbox
pissed (rude), paralytic, bevvied, wellied, popped up, merry, trollied, ratted, rat-arsed, pissed as a newt: drunk
pitch: playing field
plaster: Band-Aid
pram: baby carriage
publican: pub manager (old-fashioned)

588 Rick Steves London

public school: private "prep" school (e.g., Eton)

pudding: dessert in general

pull, to be on the: looking for love

punter: customer, especially in gambling

pushchair: stroller

put a sock in it: shut up

queue: line

queue up: line up

quid: a pound (money)

randy: horny

rasher: slice of bacon

redundant, made: laid off

Remembrance Day: Veterans' Day

return ticket: round-trip

revising; doing revisions: studying for exams

ring up: call (telephone)

rocket: arugula

roundabout: traffic circle

rubber: eraser

rubbish: bad

salad cream: mayo, mustard, and vinegar dressing

Sat Nav: GPS device

sausage roll: sausage wrapped in a flaky pastry

Scotch egg: hard-boiled egg wrapped in sausage meat

scrumpy: type of hard cider

self-catering: accommodation with kitchen

Sellotape: Scotch tape

services: freeway rest area

serviette: napkin

settee: couch

shag: intercourse (cruder than in the US)

shandy: lager and 7-Up

silencer: car muffler

single ticket: one-way ticket

skip: dumpster

sleeping policeman: speed bumps

smalls: underwear

snogging: kissing, making out

sod: mildly offensive insult

sod it, sod off: screw it, screw off

soda: soda water (not pop)

solicitor: lawyer (a.k.a. barrister)

spanner: wrench

sparkie: electrician

spend a penny: urinate

stag night: bachelor party

starkers: buck naked

starters: appetizers

state school: public school

sticking plaster: Band-Aid

sticky tape: Scotch tape

stone: 14 pounds (measurement of weight)

stroppy: bad-tempered

subway: underground walkway

suet: fat from animal rendering (sometimes used in cooking)

sultanas: golden raisins

surgical spirit: rubbing alcohol

suspenders: garters

suss out: figure out

swede: rutabaga

ta: thank you

take the mickey: tease

tatty: worn out or tacky

taxi rank: taxi stand

telly: TV

tenement: stone apartment house (not necessarily a slum)

tenner: £10 bill

theatre: live stage

tick: a check mark

tight as a fish's bum: cheapskate (watertight)

tights: panty hose

tin: can

tip: public dump
tipper lorry: dump truck
top hole: first rate
top up: refill a drink
torch: flashlight
towel, press-on: panty liner
towpath: path along a river
trainers: sneakers
Tube: subway
twee: quaint, cute
twitcher: bird watcher
Underground: subway
verge: grassy edge of road
verger: church official
way out: exit
wee (adj.): small (Scottish)
wee (verb): urinate
Wellingtons, wellies: rubber
    boots
whacked: exhausted
whinge (rhymes with hinge):
    whine
wind up: tease, irritate
witter on: gab and gab
yob: hooligan
zebra crossing: crosswalk
zed: the letter Z

INDEX

A

Abbey Road: 69
Abbeys: *See* Westminster Abbey
Abstract art, at Tate Modern: 312, 313–315
Accents, English: 567. *See also* Cockneys
Accommodations: *See* Sleeping
Actors' Church (St. Paul's Church): 55, 188
Adam and Eve (Cranach the Elder): 196
Adams, Douglas: 112
Admission fees ("voluntary donations"), about: 43
Adoration of the Magi (Rubens): 499–500
Affordability: London's sights, 70–71. *See also* Money-saving tips
Afternoon tea: *See* Tea
Airbnb.com: 551, 552
Airfares (airlines): 7, 570–571
Airports: 19, 457–462; baggage storage, 22; map, 458; sleeping near, 393; VAT refunds, 427, 540–541. *See also specific airports*
Albert, Prince: 98, 101, 102–103, 121, 179–180, 319, 452, 482
Albert Memorial Chapel (Windsor Castle): 482
Allegory with Venus and Cupid (Bronzino): 158
Almanac, London: 6
Althorp Estate: 527
Amenhotep III, Colossal Head of: 209
American Memorial Chapel (St. Paul's): 270
Amsterdam, transportation: 468–469
Anchor, The: 301–302
Anglican Communion: about, 269
Annunciation, with Saint Emidius (Crivelli): 156
Antiques: auctions, 435; markets, 431
Apartment rentals: 393, 551–552
Apple Store: 36, 434, 436
Apps: 21–22
Apsley House: 96–98
Aquarium: 422

Archaeological museums: Museum of Classical Archaeology (Cambridge), 502–503; Museum of London, 74–77, 421; Museum of London Docklands, 106, 371–372. *See also* British Museum
Archaeological sites: *See* Romans, ancient; Stonehenge
Architecture: 528–533. *See also* Castles and palaces; Churches and cathedrals
Ardabil Carpet: 328
Arnolfini Portrait (Van Eyck): 154
Arrival: *See* Traveling
Art: technology of painting, 159. *See also* Archaeological museums; Art museums; *and specific artists, artworks and periods*
Art museums: daily reminder, 20–21; free, 70; passes, 543–544; shopping at, 426; Apsley House, 96–98; Fitzwilliam Museum (Cambridge), 502; Geffrye Museum, 83, 453; Guildhall Art Gallery, 73–74, 259; Museum of Classical Archaeology (Cambridge), 502–503; Queen's Gallery (Buckingham Palace), 59; Sir John Soane's Museum, 67–68; Wallace Collection, 51, 64–66. *See also* British Museum; Courtauld Gallery; National Gallery; National Portrait Gallery; Tate Britain; Tate Modern; Victoria and Albert Museum
Ascot Racecourse: 456, 484, 486, 576
Ashurnasirpal II: 213–215
Assyrian art, at British Museum: 212–217
ATMs: 536–537, 538–539
Auctions: 435
Auden, W. H.: 139
Audio Europe, Rick Steves: 5, 9, 32–33, 543, 572
Austen, Jane: 178, 228, 235, 519, 578
Australia House: 110, 244

B

Back Door travel philosophy: 11
Bacon, Francis: 313, 347, 516
Baggage storage: 22, 463
Baker Street: 69, 72
Ballet: 451
"Banglatown": 81, 414, 433
Banking: *See* Money
Bank Junction: 259–261
Bank Museum: 260
Bank of England: 260
Bankside: 290–305; map, 292–293;
    walking tour, 291–305. *See also*
    Tate Modern
Bankside Pier: 40, 41
Bankside Road: 301–302
Banqueting House: 52, 124–128
Bar at the Folies-Bergère (Manet): 197
Barbican Centre: 447
Baroque art, at National Gallery:
    161–163
Bars: *See* Pubs
Bateaux London: 451
Bates Hats: 439
Bathers (Cézanne): 167
Bathers at Asnières (Seurat): 166
Battle of Britain: 109, 138, 272–273
Battle of San Romano (Uccello):
    153–154
Bayswater: eating, 411–413; sleeping,
    382–383
Beatles, the: 69, 190, 237–238; guided
    walks, 36
Beatles Store: 69
Beauchamp Tower (Tower of Lon-
    don): 284–285
Becket Casket: 323–324
Bed-and-breakfasts (B&Bs): over-
    view, 548–549; rates and deals,
    544–545; telephones, 565. *See also*
    Sleeping
Beefeaters: 276, 282, 284; tours of
    Tower of London, 277–278
Beer: about, 559–560. *See also* Pubs
Belfast, HMS: 94, 424
Belgravia: eating, 408–409; sleeping,
    376–377
Belshazzar's Feast (Rembrandt): 160
Benet Street (Cambridge): 496–497
Bensons London Street Map: 19, 572
Beowulf: 235
Berwick Street: 192
Beuys, Joseph: 317
Beverages: 559–560

BFI Southbank: 452
Bibles, at the British Library:
    230–233
Big Ben: 45, 110, 115
Big Bus London Tours: 33–34
Biking (bike rentals): 31–32; Cam-
    bridge, 492; tours, 38; Windsor,
    475
Billy Elliot (musical): 446
Black Friar, The: 400–401
Blackfriars Pier: 40
Blackpool, transportation: 464, 466
Blake, William: 339–340
Blitz, the: 72, 87, 138, 147, 241, 266,
    366, 520; and St. Paul's, 272–273
Bloomsbury: *See* British Library;
    British Museum
Bloomsbury Group: 200, 342–343,
    343
Blue Badge Tourist Guides: 37–38
Boadicea, Queen of the Iceni: 118,
    513–514
Boar and Bear Hunt Tapestry: 324
Boating: 98, 423; Cambridge, 496,
    503
Boat travel and cruises: 39–42, 425;
    Channel crossings, 466–470; cruise
    ports, 469–470; discounts, 24;
    Docklands, 41, 365; Greenwich,
    40–41, 349–350; maps, 465, 569;
    at night, 451; Regent's Canal, 42,
    424; Windsor, 484
Bog Man: 225
Boleyn, Anne: 136, 170, 172–173,
    280, 283, 499, 516
Bonfire Night: 577
Book of Mormon (musical): 446
Books, recommended: 577–579; for
    children, 420
Bookstores: 22, 189
Borough High Street: 291, 294,
    297–298
Borough Market: 111, 298–299, 434,
    454
Boswell, James: 249, 250, 251
Botticelli, Sandro: 155–156
Boucher, François: 163
Bow Lane: 258–259
Bracknell: 110
Brass rubbings: 54, 325, 421
Bread Street: 257
Breakfast: about, 553

Brewer Street: 192
Brick Lane: 81–82; eating, 414; markets, 82, 433
Brighton, transportation: 465, 466
"Britain," use of term: 523
British East India Company: 330–331
British Empire, overview: 517–518
British Impressionism: 342–343
British Library: 64, 227–238; eating, 228, 413; map, 229; orientation, 50, 64, 227–228; self-guided tour, 228–238
British Museum: 63–64, 201–226; eating, 203, 407; guided tours, 202–203; maps, 202, 204, 205, 213, 218, 221; orientation, 50, 63–64, 201–203; self-guided tour, 203–226
British pound: 6, 536–537
British Romantic art: 163–164, 340–342
British-Yankee vocabulary: 585–589
Brit Movie Tours: 485
BritRail: See Train travel
Brixton Market: 435
Broadway Market: 433–434
Brontë sisters: 180, 519
Bronzino: 158
Browning, Robert: 139
Brummell, Beau: 439
Brune Street: 82
BT Tower: 293
Buckingham Palace: 58–63; Changing of the Guard, 34, 51, 60–63, 422; map, 60; tickets, 58–59
Budgeting: 7–8
Bull's Head Passage: 110
Burberry: 438
Buses: 26–30, 465–466, 570; to airports, 460, 461–462; Cambridge, 489, 490; crossing the Channel, 469; Greenwich, 350; handy routes, 28–29; to London, 19; maps, 465, 569; Stonehenge, 506–507; tickets and passes, 22–24; tours, 33–35, 425, 493–494; Windsor, 473
Bush House: 244
Business hours: 426, 535–536
Byron, George Gordon: 139, 178, 501

C
Cabinet War Rooms: 46–47
Cabot Square: 371

Cabs: See Taxis
Cambridge: 472, 488–506; eating, 504–505; helpful hints, 490, 492; map, 491; sights/activities, 500–504; sleeping, 504; tourist information, 490; tours, 492–494; traveling to, 489, 490, 505; walking tour, 494–500
Cambridge Circus: 189
Cambridge Folk Festival: 492, 577
Cambridge University: 488–489, 493; helpful hints, 490, 492, 493; sights/activities, 496, 500–503; tours, 492–494; walking tour, 494–500
Cambridge University Amateur Dramatic Club: 490, 492
Camden Lock Market: 42, 422, 431–432
Camden Town: cruises, 42; markets, 431–432
Camera obscura: 361
Cameron, David: 122, 123, 124, 521, 524
Campin, Robert: 196
Cam River (Cambridge): 489, 494, 496; punting, 496, 503
Canada Square: 368–369
Canaletto: 68
Canary Wharf Pier: 40, 291–292, 350
Canary Wharf Tower: 364, 368–369
Canterbury, transportation: 464, 466
Canterbury Tales (Chaucer): 139, 235
Capital Radio London: 185–187
Caravaggio: 162–163
Carnaby Street: 192, 436
Car rentals: 9
Carroll, Lewis: 139, 235
Cartoon Museum: 68
Car travel: Cambridge, 490; congestion pricing, 32; driver-guides, 35; Stonehenge, 507; Windsor, 473–475
Castles and palaces: architecture, 531; Dover Castle, 470; Hampton Court Palace, 108–109; Highclere Castle, 485; Kensington Palace, 99–101; Winchester Palace, 300; Windsor Castle, 475–482. See also Buckingham Palace
Cathedrals: See Churches and cathedrals; St. Paul's Cathedral
Catherine, Duchess of Cambridge (Kate Middleton): 53, 99, 134, 135–136, 488, 525, 526–527

INDEX

Cell phones: 9, 19–21, 560–564

Cenotaph: 121–122

Central London: 13; with children, 421–423; eating, 395–407; maps, 46–47, 396–397; sight highlights, 43–63; sleeping, 388–390. *See also* West End; Westminster

Ceremony of the Keys (Tower of London): 282

Cézanne, Paul: 167, 199–200, 310

Changing of the Guard: Buckingham Palace, 34, 51, 60–63, 422; Windsor Castle, 477

Channel crossings: 466–470

Chapter House (Westminster Abbey): 140

Charing Cross monument: 242

Charing Cross Road: 186, 189, 190, 427

Charing Cross Station: 130, 241–242, 463

Charles Cornwallis Monument: 271–272

Charles I: 52, 108, 125–126, 127, 130, 146, 147, 175, 480, 482, 517

Charles II: 127, 175–176, 253, 359, 479

Charles I on Horseback (van Dyck): 97, 162

Chaucer, Geoffrey: 139, 235, 301

Cheapside: 256–257

Chelsea Flower Show: 576

Chihuly, Dale: 321

Children: 417–425; general tips, 417–419; top sights/activities, 419, 421–425

Chinatown: 55, 83, 191; eating, 395, 402

Chocolate: 559

Christ Church: 80

Christie's: 435

Christmas: special events, 453–455, 577; travel strategies, 454

Christmas crackers: 454–455

Christmas Day: 455

Christmas Market: 455

Churches and cathedrals: architecture, 530; concerts, 449–450; Christ Church, 80; Great St. Mary's Church (Cambridge), 497; St. Benet's Church (Cambridge), 497; St. Bride's Church, 253–254, 293, 449; St. Clement Danes, 244–245; St. Dunstan-in-the-West, 248–249; St. James's Church, 438, 449; St. Margaret's Church, 119; St. Martin-in-the-Fields, 54, 129, 421, 449; St. Martin-within-Ludgate, 255; St. Mary-le-Bow, 257; St. Mary-le-Strand, 244; St. Paul's Church, 55, 188; Southwark Cathedral, 92–93, 295–296; Temple Church, 246–247; Westminster Cathedral, 76, 95–96. *See also* Evensong; St. Paul's Cathedral; Westminster Abbey

Churchill, Winston: 119–120, 134, 138, 147, 182, 273, 412, 520; biographical sketch, 48–49; Museum, 47–49; War Rooms, 45–49, 50

City Cruises: 39, 40–41

City of London: 13, 239–275; guided walks, 37; information centre, 18, 240, 535; maps, 74–75, 242–243; markets, 110, 261, 432; pubs, 400–401; sight highlights, 72–78; views of, 117; walking tour, 241–262. *See also* St. Paul's Cathedral

City of London Information Centre: 18, 240, 535

Clarence House: 63, 527

Climate: 8, 583

Clink Prison Museum: 76, 92, 300–301

Clocktower Market (Greenwich): 351

Clothing sizes: 582

Cockneys: 258–259

Codex Alexandrinus: 230–231

Codex Sinaiticus: 230

Coleridge, Samuel Taylor: 178

Columbia Road Flower Market: 433

Conceptual Art: 317

Concerts: *See* Music

Concessions: *See* Money-saving tips

Constable, John: 163–164, 345–346

Consulates: 575

Cool Britannia: 438

Corner of a Café-Concert (Manet): 165

Cornwallis (Charles) Monument: 271–272

Coronation Chair (Westminster Abbey): 135–136, 141

Coronation Spot (Westminster Abbey): 135–136

Corpus Clock (Cambridge): 496–497

Costs of trip: 7–8

Counting House Pub: 261, 401

Courtauld Gallery: 58, 194–200,

244; eating, 195; orientation, 51, 58, 194–195; self-guided tour, 196–200

Covent Garden: 51, 55, 187–189; with children, 421; eating near, 405–407; map, 186–187; market, 188, 434

Covent Garden Market: 188, 434

Coward, Noel: 182

Cranach the Elder, Lucas: 196

Credit cards: 9, 535, 538–540

Crivelli, Carlo: 156

Cromwell, Oliver: 125, 127, 138, 175, 288, 482, 499, 517

Crown Jewels: 285–287

Cruises: *See* Boat travel and cruises

Cubism: 310

Cuisine: 553–557; Indian, 557–558. *See also* Eating

Currency and exchange: 6, 536–537

Customs regulations: 427, 541

Cutty Sark (Greenwich): 352, 354, 424

D

Dadaism: 311

Daily Express: 248

Daily Telegraph: 248

Dalí, Salvador: 312

Dance: 451

Darwin, Charles: 104, 181, 459, 519

Da Vinci, Leonardo: 155, 156–157, 234, 325, 475

Da Vinci Code: 247

Day trips: 471–512; Cambridge, 488–506; map, 471; Stonehenge, 506–512; Windsor, 471–488

Debit cards: 9, 535, 538–540

Degas, Edgar: 197, 198

Dejeuner sur l'Herbe, Le (Manet): 197

Delaroche, Paul: 164

Denmark Street: 189–190

Department stores: 426, 427–431; light displays, 453

Desserts (sweets): 558–559

Diana, Princess of Wales: 99, 101, 135, 183, 267, 412, 429–430, 520, 527; Memorial Fountain, 98

Diana, Princess of Wales Memorial Playground: 98, 423

Dickens, Charles: 140, 180–181, 239, 244, 252, 294, 338, 358, 406, 455, 519, 578; guided tours, 37, 455

Dining: *See* Eating

Dinosaurs: 104–105, 423

Directory assistance: 576

Discounts: 536; TKTS Booth, 71, 185, 444–445. *See also* Money-saving tips

Discover Greenwich: 351, 354–355

Docklands: 13, 15, 106, 364–373; cruises, 40, 365; eating, 365; maps, 366–367, 369; overview, 365–368; walking tour, 368–373

Docklands, Museum of London: 106, 371–372

Docklands Light Railway (DLR): 24, 349, 350, 365

Dolls' House, Queen Mary's (Windsor Castle): 480

Donne, John: 271

Dorm accommodations: 392–393, 549–550

Dover Castle: 470

Dover Cruise Port: 469–470

Downing Street, no. 10: 122, 124

Downton Abbey (TV series): 472, 485, 528

Drake, Francis: 92, 299–300, 516

Driving: *See* Car travel

Dublin, transportation: 466

Duchamp, Marcel: 311

Durham, transportation: 464, 466

Duxford: 503–504

Dynamic currency conversion (DCC): 427, 539

E

Eagle Pub (Cambridge): 497, 504

Earth Art: 317

East End: 13; Cockneys, 258–259; maps, 74–75, 79; markets, 82, 432–434; pubs, 400–401; sight highlights, 78–83; walking tour, 79–83

East London: 13; with children, 419, 421; map, 74–75; sight highlights, 78–83. *See also* City of London; East End

EasyHotel: 380, 387, 391, 393

EasyJet: 462, 571

Eating: 394–416, 552–560; Bayswater, 411–413; Belgravia, 408–409; British Library, 228, 413; British Museum, 203, 407; budgeting, 7; Cambridge, 504–505; Central London, 395–407; chain restaurants, 555–557; with children,

417–418; Chinatown, 395, 402; Courtauld Gallery, 195; near Covent Garden, 405–407; Docklands, 365; Fitzrovia, 407; fun food facts, 6; Greenwich, 355; money-saving tips, 394–395, 553–554; National Gallery, 150; National Portrait Gallery, 169; Notting Hill, 411–413; near Piccadilly, 404–405; Pimlico, 409–410; St. Paul's Cathedral, 264–265, 413; Soho, 395, 398–399, 402–403; South Kensington, 410–411; Tate Britain, 335; Tate Modern, 307; tipping, 540, 552–553; Tower of London, 278, 413–414; Victoria and Albert Museum, 320; near Victoria Station, 408–410; West London, 408–413; Westminster Abbey, 132–133; Windsor, 487–488

Edinburgh, transportation: 464, 466

Edward the Confessor: 119, 122, 133, 136, 144, 286, 287

Edward VI: 171, 173, 281, 284

Edward VIII: 182, 519–520

Egyptian art, at British Museum: 204–212

Electricity: 536

Elgin Marbles: 220–225

Eliot, George: 112

Eliot, T. S.: 139, 183, 519

Elizabeth I: 77, 108, 138, 171, 173, 249, 280, 289, 299–300, 332, 516; tomb, 136–137

Elizabeth II: 59–60, 115, 135, 182, 282, 285, 286, 370, 471, 521, 526, 527

E-mail: *See* Internet access

Embankment Pier: 40, 42

Embassies: 575

Emergencies: 19, 535, 575

Emirates Air Line Cable Car: 373

Emmanuel College (Cambridge): 495

"England," use of term: 523

English Heritage: 507, 508, 544

Entertainment: 441–456; budgeting, 7–8; Cambridge, 490, 492; current schedule, 18, 441; winter diversions, 452–455. *See also* Evensong; Music; Theater

Entombment, The (Michelangelo): 157–158

Epsom Derby: 456

Eton College: 483

Eton High Street: 483

Eurolines: 466, 570

Eurostar: 9, 466–468

Euston Station: 463, 464

Evensong: 450; Cambridge, 498; St. Paul's Cathedral, 72–73, 264, 450; Southwark Cathedral, 93, 450; Westminster Abbey, 44, 132, 450; Windsor Castle, 477

Exchange rate: 537

Excursion areas: *See* Day trips

Execution of Lady Jane Grey, The (Delaroche): 164

Expressionism: 311

Eye, London: *See* London Eye

F

Families: *See* Children

Family of Jan Brueghel the Elder (Rubens): 196–197

Faraday, Michael: 181

Fashion Street: 82

Fast Track tickets: 18

Father Christmas: 453–454

Fat Tire Bike Tours: 38

Fawkes, Guy: 146, 280, 577

Ferries, across the Channel: 468–469

Ferris wheel: *See* London Eye

Festival Pier: 40

Festivals: 576–577; Cambridge, 492

Fighting Téméraire, The (Turner): 164

Fitzrovia: eating, 407. *See also* British Museum

Fitzwilliam Museum (Cambridge): 502

Five Foot Walk (Greenwich): 357–358

Flamsteed House (Greenwich): 361–362

Flea markets: *See* Markets

Fleet River: 254–255

Fleet Street: 246, 247–249, 251–252

Floral Street: 187, 427

Forster, E. M.: 200, 519

Fortnum & Mason: 415, 430, 438–439

Fournier Street: 80–81

Foyles Books: 189

Fragonard, Jean-Honoré: 65

French Rococo art: 163

Freud, Lucian: 348

Futurism: 311

G

Gainsborough, Thomas: 339, 502

Gandhi, Mahatma: 120, 330

Gardens: 77, 83, 98, 101, 108, 418. *See also* Hyde Park; Kew Gardens

Gare St. Lazare (Monet): 165

Garrick, David: 249–250

Garrick Street: 187

Gatwick Airport: 461; sleeping near, 393

Gauguin, Paul: 198

Geffrye Museum: 83, 453

George III: 177

George Inn: 298

George VI: 182, 481–482, 519–520

German Christmas Market: 455

Gerrard Street: 191

Gherkin, the (30 St. Mary Axe): 274

Ghost tours: Cambridge, 492; London, 451

Giacometti, Alberto: 313

Giambologna: 322–323

Gibraltar House: 243

Gilbert and George: 348

Glasgow, transportation: 464, 466

Globe Theatre: *See* Shakespeare's Globe

Golden Hinde Replica: 92, 299–300

Golden Jubilee Bridge: 92

Gough Square: 249–251

Gower, John: 296

Goya, Francisco: 97

Grave of the Unknown Warrior: 134

"Great Britain," use of term: 523

Great Fire of 1666: 73, 77, 241, 246, 249, 250, 253, 263, 271, 303, 517, 532; Monument, 77, 261

Great Marlborough Street: 436

Great Plague of 1665: 251, 517

Great St. Mary's Church (Cambridge): 497

Greek art, at British Museum: 217–225

Greek Street: 190, 191

Greenwich: 15, 51, 105–106, 349–363; cruises, 40–41, 349–350; eating, 355; guided tours, 351; map, 353; markets, 351, 355; sights/activities, 352–363; tourist information, 351; transportation, 349–350

Greenwich Market: 351, 355

Greenwich Mean Time (GMT): 359

Grey, Jane: 164, 281, 284

Groucho Club: 191

Guidebooks, Rick Steves: 571–572; updates, 3, 22

Guided tours: *See* Tours

Guildhall: 73–74, 259

Guildhall (Cambridge): 494–495

Guildhall Art Gallery: 73–74, 259

Gutenberg Bible: 232–233

H

Hackett: 438

Hals, Frans: 65–66

Hamleys: 422, 437–438

Hampstead Heath: 109, 112

Hampton Court Palace: 108–109; cruises, 41

Handel, George Frideric: 140, 176, 238

Harrods: 422, 427–430, 453–454

Harry Potter sights: 110–111, 112–113, 423

Harvard (John) Chapel (Southwark Cathedral): 296

Harvey Nichols: 430

Hay Wain, The (Constable): 163–164

Heathrow Airport: 457–461, 474; sleeping near, 393

Heathrow Express: 460

Heathrow Shuttle: 460

Henry II: 324, 327–328

Henry VII Chapel (Westminster Abbey): 137

Henry VIII: 45, 78, 82, 98, 108, 124–125, 136, 140, 144, 170–171, 332, 352, 500, 515–516, 532; biographical sketch, 172–173

Hepworth, Barbara: 347

Hereford Screen: 321–322

Hertford House: 64–66

Highclere Castle: 485

Highgate Cemetery: 112

History: 513–522

HMS *Belfast*: 94, 424

Hockney, David: 347–348

Hogarth, William: 68, 336–338, 502

Holbein, Hans: 481

Holidays: 576–577

Holland Park: sleeping near, 386

Horse Guards: 49, 52, 128, 422

Horse racing: 456, 484, 486, 576

Hospitals: 19, 535

Hostels: 391–392, 549–550

Hotels: overview, 546–549; rates and deals, 544–545; reservations, 9,

550–551; telephones, 564–565. *See also* Sleeping

Houses of Parliament: 44–45, 110, 119–120, 142–148; guided tours, 45, 143; map, 145; orientation, 44–45, 50, 142–143; self-guided tour, 144–148; views of, 115, 117, 119

Hunt, William Holman: 268–270, 341

Hyde Park: 98, 423; Winter Wonderland, 453

I

Ibis Hotels: 391

Ice skating: 453

Imperial War Museum: 51, 86–88

Imperial War Museum Duxford: 503–504

Impressionism: 165–166, 197, 309, 342–343, 502

India, British in: 330–331

Indian cuisine: about, 557–558. *See also* Eating

Information sources: *See* Tourist information

Inns of Court: 247

Internet access: 19–21, 417, 561–563; Heathrow Airport, 459; Windsor, 475

Internet security: 565

Islamic art, at V&A Museum: 328–331

Itineraries: 15–17

J

Jack the Ripper: 80–81, 82, 519; guided walks, 37

James I: 52, 58, 126, 174, 358

Jamme Masjid: 81

Jenny Wren: 42

Jermyn Street: 427, 439

Jersey Boys (musical): 446

Jewel Tower (Houses of Parliament): 45

John, Elton: 190, 446

John Harvard Chapel (Southwark Cathedral): 296

John Lewis: 415

John Lobb: 439

Johnson, Samuel: 140, 252, 302; House, 249–251

Jones, Inigo: 52, 124–127, 188, 352, 358, 532

Jubilee Gardens, playground: 421–422

Jubilee Hall Market: 434

Jubilee Place Park: 370

Jubilee Walkway: 16, 83–84, 117, 452

Judgment of Paris (Rubens): 161

Jugged Hare, The: 401, 410

K

Keats, John: 178

Kensington Gardens: map, 384–385; sleeping, 382–386

Kensington Palace: 99–101; afternoon tea, 101, 414

Kew Gardens: 107–108, 424; cruises, 41

Keynes, John Maynard: 200

Kids: *See* Children

King's College: 244

King's College Chapel (Cambridge): 492, 498–500

King's Cross Station: 110–111, 463, 464

King's Parade (Cambridge): 495, 496

Knightsbridge, shopping: 427, 430

L

Lady Chapel (Westminster Abbey): 137

La Montagne Sainte-Victoire (Cézanne): 199–200

Land and Sea Tours: 35

Language: 6; British-Yankee vocabulary, 585–589

Laughing Cavalier, The (Hals): 65–66

Laundress Green: 505

Leadenhall Market: 110, 261, 432

Leavesden Film Studios: 111, 112–113

Le Dejeuner sur l'Herbe (Manet): 197

Legible London: 19

Legoland Windsor: 425, 482–483

Leicester Square: 12, 111, 185–187; map, 186–187; TKTS Booth, 71, 185, 444–445

Leonardo da Vinci: 155, 156–157, 234, 325, 475

Les Misérables (musical): 446–447

Lexington Street, eating: 402–403

Liberty of London: 430–431, 436

Lichtenstein, Roy: 316

Light of the World, The (Hunt): 268–270

Lillywhites: 438

Lincoln, Abraham: 120

Lindisfarne Gospels: 231
Lindow Man: 225
Lion King, The (musical): 447
Little Opera House: 451
Live music: *See* Evensong; Music
Liverpool, transportation: 464, 466
Liverpool Street: 83
Liverpool Street Station: 83, 463
Locke, John: 176
Lodgings: *See* Sleeping
London Bicycle Tour Company: 38
London Bridge: 262, 291–292, 514; view of, 294–295
London Bridge Experience: 425
London Bridge Pier: 40
London Bridge Station: 463
London by Night Sightseeing Tour: 34–35, 451
London City Airport: 462
London City Hall: 94–95
London Coliseum: 451
London Dungeon: 71, 425
London Eye: 84–86; with children, 421–422; crowd-beating tips, 86; cruises, 39, 40; late hours, 76, 452; orientation, 51, 85–86; views, 88, 117
London (Waterloo) Eye Pier: 40, 41, 117–118
London Fashion Week: 576, 577
London for Children: 419
London Hilton, Park Lane: 89
London Museum of Water and Steam: 425
London Natural History Museum: 51, 104–105, 423
London Pass: 544
London Planner: 18, 441
London plays: *See* Theater
London School of Economics, sleeping: 393
London Science Museum: 105, 423
London Showboat: 451
London Tombs: 425
London Transport Museum: 56–58, 188–189, 426
London Walks: 36, 70–71, 455, 472, 507
London Zoo: 424; Reptile House, 110
Longitude Problem: 360
Lord Mayor's Show: 577
Ludgate: 254–255
Luggage storage: 22, 463

Luton Airport: 462

M
McCartney, Paul: 191, 238; current home, 69
Mackenzie Walk: 370
McLaren, Malcolm: 112
Madame Tussauds Waxworks: 66–67, 71, 76, 423
Magna Carta: 233–234, 327–328, 515
Mail: 567
Making of Harry Potter: 112–113, 424
Maltby Street Market: 434–435
Mamma Mia! (musical): 447
Mandela, Nelson: 120
Manet, Édouard: 165, 197
Mansion House: 260–261
Mappin and Webb: 438
Maps: apps, 21–22; buying, 19, 572; legend, 2. *See also* Map Index
Market Hill Square (Cambridge): 494–495
Markets: 431–435; Cambridge, 494–495; with children, 422; Christmas, 455; daily reminder, 20; Greenwich, 351, 355. *See also specific markets*
Marks & Spencer: 395, 407, 413, 426, 556; Cambridge, 505; Greenwich, 355; Windsor, 475
Marx, Karl: 63, 112, 203, 204
Mary, Queen of Scots, tomb: 138
Mary I, tomb: 136–137
Marylebone Station: 463
Matilda (musical): 447
Matisse, Henri: 309
Maze, at Hampton Court Palace: 108
Medical help: 19, 535
Medieval Banquet: 413–414
Megabus: 568, 570
Menier Chocolate Factory: 448
Meridian Building (Greenwich): 362
Mermaid Tavern: 257
Metric system: 581–582
Metro: *See* Tube
Michelangelo: 157–158, 225–226, 326, 480
Middlesex Street: 82–83
Middleton, Catherine "Kate": *See* Catherine, Duchess of Cambridge
Millbank Pier: 40, 41
Millennium Bridge: 90, 92, 111, 304–305

Mill Pond (Cambridge): 496
Milne, A. A.: 502
Ministry of Defence (MOD): 124
Mobile (cell) phones: 9, 19–21,
 560–564
Mondrian, Piet: 313
Monet, Claude: 165, 309
Money: 536–541; budgeting, 7–8
Money belts: 7, 19, 419, 537
Money-saving tips: 536; eating,
 394–395, 553–554; sightsee-
 ing, 70–71, 543–544; sleeping,
 544–545; theater tickets, 71, 185,
 444–445; transportation, 22–25
Montgomery, Bernard Law: 124, 182,
 289, 478
Moore, Henry: 182, 270, 346–347
Mother and Child (Moore): 270
Movies, recommended: 579–581; for
 children, 420
Movie theaters: 185, 452
Mummies, at British Museum:
 208–209
Museum of Classical Archaeology
 (Cambridge): 502–503
Museum of London: 74–77, 421
Museum of London Docklands: 106,
 371–372
Museums: with children, 418–419;
 daily reminder, 20–21; for early
 birds and night owls, 76; free, 70;
 general tips, 542–543; money-
 saving tips, 70–71, 543–544; passes,
 543–544; shopping at, 426. *See
 also* Archaeological museums; Art
 museums; *and specific museums*
Music: 449–451; Cambridge, 492,
 577; Denmark Street, 189–190;
 St. Martin-in-the-Fields, 54, 129,
 449; St. Paul's Cathedral, 72–73,
 264, 450; Southwark Cathedral, 93,
 450; West End musicals, 446–447;
 Westminster Abbey, 44, 132, 450

N
National Army Museum: 96
National Express: 460, 461, 462, 489,
 570
National Gallery: 53, 129, 149–167;
 afternoon tea, 415; with children,
 421; eating, 150, 403–404; map,
 152–153; orientation, 50, 53, 149–
 150; self-guided tour, 151–167

National Maritime Museum (Greenwich): 358–359
National Portrait Gallery: 53–54,
 88–89, 168–183; eating, 169;
 maps, 170, 179; orientation, 50,
 54, 168–169; self-guided tour,
 169–183
National Theatre: 447
Natural History Museum: 51,
 104–105, 423
Neal's Yard Dairy: 189, 298
Nebamun: 207–208
Neighborhoods: 12–15; maps, 13, 14,
 46–47; overview of sights, 43–113.
 See also specific neighborhoods
Nelson, Horatio: 52, 140, 177, 358,
 518; column, in Trafalgar Square,
 52, 128–130; Monument, 271;
 tomb, 274
Nenkheftka, Statue of: 211
Nereid Monument: 219–220
Nevermore (Gauguin): 198
New Change Street: 256–257
Newton, Isaac: 176, 234, 496,
 501–502, 517
New Year: 455, 576
Nightingale, Florence: 180, 274
Nightlife: *See* Entertainment; Theater
Night sightseeing tours: 34–35, 451
Nimrud Gallery (British Museum):
 213–215
Norfolk Square, sleeping: 387
North Bank: 292–293
Northern Protestant art: 159–161
North London: 13; with children,
 423–424; map, 65; sight highlights,
 63–72; sleeping, map, 388–389.
 See also British Library; British
 Museum
Northumberland Street: 130
Notting Hill: eating, 411–413; map,
 384–385; market, 431; sleeping,
 386
Notting Hill Carnival: 577
#10 Downing Street: 122, 124

O
O₂ Arena (Greenwich): 357–358, 368
O₂ Express: 41
Odeon Theater: 185
Old Admiralty: 128
Old Bailey: 73, 255
Old Bank of England Pub: 246, 401
Old Compton Street: 191–192

Old Operating Theatre Museum and Herb Garret: 93, 296–297
Old Royal Naval College (Greenwich): 355–357
Oliver, Jamie: 140, 182, 406, 557
Olivier, Laurence: 182
Olympic Park (Stratford): 106, 365
One Canada Square: *See* Canary Wharf Tower
One New Change: 73, 257
Op Art: 316, 348
Opera: 451
Orangery at Kensington Palace: 101, 414
Order of the Garter: 478
Organized tours: *See* Tours
Original London Sightseeing Bus Tour: 33–34
Origin of the Milky Way (Tintoretto): 158–159
Oxford, transportation: 463, 466
Oxford Street: 422, 427, 435
OXO Tower: 89
Oyster cards: 23–24

P
Packing checklist: 584
Paddington Station: 463; sleeping near, 386–388
Painting, changes in technology of: 159
Palace of Westminster: *See* Houses of Parliament
Palaces: *See* Buckingham Palace; Castles and palaces
Pan and Syrinx (Boucher): 163
Pantomimes: 453
Paris, transportation: 466–469
Parking, Victoria Station: 376
Parks: Jubilee Place Park, 370; Olympic Park (Stratford), 106, 365. *See also* Hyde Park
Parliament: *See* Houses of Parliament
Parliament Square: 119–120
Parr, Catherine: 171, 173
Parr, Thomas: 140
Parthenon, Elgin Marbles: 220–225
Passports: 8–9, 535
Paternoster Square: 256
Pedestrian safety: 19
Pembroke College (Cambridge): 495–496
Penhaligon's: 438
Peter Harrison Planetarium (Greenwich): 361, 362
Peter Pan Cup Swim Race: 455
Petticoat Lane Market: 82, 433
Phantom of the Opera (musical): 447
Pharmacies: 535
Phones: *See* Telephones
Picasso, Pablo: 310
Piccadilly Circus: 12, 54–55, 111, 192–193; with children, 422; eating near, 404–405; shopping, 438, 440
Piccadilly Street: 438–439
Picnics (picnicking): 395, 418, 554
Pimlico: eating, 409–410; sleeping, 377–380
Pimm's: 560
Planetarium, in Greenwich: 361, 362
Playgrounds: 421–422, 423
Poe, Edgar Allan: 289
Poets' Corner (Westminster Abbey): 138–140
Police: 575
Politics: 522–525
Pollock, Jackson: 314
Pollock's Toy Museum: 68–69, 424
Pop Art: 316
Pope Julius II (Raphael): 158
Portobello Road Market: 431
Post-Impressionism: 166–167, 197–200, 310
Post offices: 567
Pound, British: 536–537
Premier Inn: 390–391
Pre-Raphaelites: 341–342
Prime meridian: 361, 362
Primrose Hill: 89
Princess Diana Memorial Fountain: 98
Princess Louise Pub: 400
Prom Concerts: 451
Pubs: 400–401, 554–555; Bayswater, 412; Belgravia, 408–409; Cambridge, 497, 504–505; Covent Garden, 406–407; eating at, 395, 553, 555; Greenwich, 355; map, 401; Pimlico, 410; South Kensington, 411; Trafalgar Square, 403–404; Windsor, 487–488
Punch Tavern: 254
Punting, in Cambridge: 496, 503
Pyx Chamber: 140

Q
Queen Elizabeth Olympic Park

(Stratford): 106, 365
Queen Mary's Dolls' House (Windsor Castle): 480
Queen's Gallery (Buckingham Palace): 59
Queen's House (Greenwich): 358
Queen's State Apartments (Kensington Palace): 99–100
Queensway, eating: 413

R
Rail passes: 568, 570, 573
Raleigh, Walter: 257, 287–288, 516
Ramesses II, Colossal Statue of: 206
Raphael: 158, 331–332
Reader feedback: 9
Red Lion Pub: 440
Regent's Canal: 42, 424
Regent's Park: 424; summer theater, 449
Regent Street: 427, 435, 436–438; map, 437
Rembrandt van Rijn: 160–161
Renaissance art: 151–159, 323, 331–332
Renoir, Pierre Auguste: 165–166
Rental properties: 393, 551–552
Restaurants: *See* Eating
Restrooms: 6, 419
Reynolds, Joshua: 251, 274, 338, 502
Rick Steves Audio Europe: 5, 9, 32–33, 543, 572
Rick Steves resources: 571–572, 573
Riley, Bridget: 348
Ripley's Believe It or Not: 192, 422
Ritz Hotel: 439
Robin Hood: 233, 327
Rokeby Venus (Velázquez): 161–162
Rolling Stones: 104, 190, 520
Romans, ancient: 73, 74, 76–77, 78, 81, 117, 118, 126, 241, 262, 278, 290, 294, 326–327, 494, 513–514, 528
Ronnie Scott's Jazz Club: 191
Ropewalk (Maltby Street Market): 434–435
Rosetta Stone: 204–205
Rothko, Mark: 314–315
Royal Air Force Chapel (St. Clement Danes): 244
Royal Air Force Chapel (Westminster Abbey): 138
Royal Air Force Museum London: 109

Royal Albert Hall: 451, 453
Royal Armory (Tower of London): 281
Royal Ascot Horse Race: 456, 484, 486, 576
Royal Ballet: 451
Royal Botanic Gardens of Kew: *See* Kew Gardens
Royal Courts of Justice: 245
Royal Court Theatre: 447–448
Royal Exchange: 260
Royal families: overview, 526–527. *See also specific members*
Royal Fusiliers Regimental Museum: 289
Royal Mews (Buckingham Palace): 59–60
Royal Observatory Greenwich: 89, 105, 359–363
Royal Opera House: 189, 451
Royal Shakespeare Company: 448
Royal Windsor Racecourse: 484
Rubens, Peter Paul: 52, 126, 161, 196–197, 481, 499–500
Ryanair: 466, 571
Ryder and Amies (Cambridge): 497

S
Sadler's Wells Theatre: 451
St. Benet's Church (Cambridge): 497
St. Bride's Church: 253–254, 293, 449
St. Clement Danes: 244–245
St. Dunstan-in-the-West: 248–249
St. George's Chapel (Windsor Castle): 481–482
St. James's Church: 438, 449
St. John's Chapel (Tower of London): 281
St. Katharine Dock: 78
St. Katharine's Pier: 40
St. Margaret's Church: 119
St. Martin-in-the-Fields: 54, 129, 421; eating, 403; music, 54, 129, 449
St. Martin-within-Ludgate: 255
St. Mary-le-Bow: 257
St. Mary-le-Strand: 244
St. Pancras International Station: 461–465, 467–468
St. Paul's Cathedral: 72–73, 255–256, 263–275; climbing the dome, 88, 264, 272–274; eating, 264–265, 413; map, 266; music, 72–73, 264, 450; orientation, 50, 72–73, 263–

266; self-guided tour, 266–275; views of, 73, 88, 252–253

St. Paul's Church: 55, 188

St. Peter ad Vincula (Tower of London): 277, 282

Sts. Peter and St. Paul Chapel (Greenwich): 357

St. Stephen's Hall (Houses of Parliament): 146

Salt Tower (Tower of London): 289

Samson Slaying a Philistine (Giambologna): 322–323

Sandemans New London "Free Royal London Tour": 36

Sargent, John Singer: 87, 342

Savoy Hotel: 242–243

Savoy Theatre: 242–243

Science Museum: 105, 423

Scoop, the: 452

SeaCity Museum (Southampton): 469

Sealife Aquarium: 422

Seasons: 8

Seilern Triptych (Campin): 196

Self-guided tours: British Library, 227–238; British Museum, 201–226; Courtauld Gallery, 194–200; Houses of Parliament, 142–148; National Gallery, 149–167; National Portrait Gallery, 168–183; St. Paul's Cathedral, 263–275; Tate Britain, 334–348; Tate Modern, 306–318; Tower of London, 276–289; Victoria and Albert Museum, 319–333; Westminster Abbey, 131–141

Self-Portrait at the Age of 63 (Rembrandt): 161

Self-Portrait with Bandaged Ear (Van Gogh): 199

Senate House (Cambridge): 497

Serpentine Gallery: 98

Serpentine Lake: 98, 423

Seurat, Georges: 166, 199

Seven Dials: 189

Sex Pistols: 112, 190

Shaftesbury Avenue: 55, 442

Shah Jahan: 329

Shakespeare, William: 139–140, 174, 235–237, 302–303, 516; biographical sketch, 236–237; Monument (Southwark Cathedral), 295–296

Shakespeare Festival (Cambridge): 492

Shakespeare's Globe: 51, 90–92, 302–303; eating, 91–92; plays and tickets, 51, 91, 448–449

Shard, the: 89, 93–94

Shaw, George Bernard: 182

Shelley, Mary Wollstonecraft: 178

Shelley, Percy Bysshe: 178

Sherlock Holmes: 37, 130, 519, 579; Museum, 69, 72

Sherlock Holmes Pub: 130

Shiva Nataraja: 328–329

Shopping: 426–440; best streets, 427; budgeting, 8; Carnaby Street, 192, 436; Charing Cross Road, 189, 427; with children, 422; clothing sizes, 582; department stores, 427–431; Docklands, 365; general tips, 426–427; hours, 426, 535–536; Jermyn Street, 427, 439; map, 428–429; Oxford Street, 422, 427, 435; Piccadilly Street, 438–439; Regent Street, 427, 435, 436–438; VAT refunds, 427, 540–541. *See also* Markets

Short's Gardens: 189

Shrek's Adventure: 422

Sightseeing (sights): 43–373; at a glance, 50–51; affording the sights, 70–71; to avoid, 71, 425; best views, 88–89; budgeting, 7–8; Cambridge, 500–504; with children, 418–425; daily reminder, 20–21; for early birds, 76; Fast Track tickets, 18; general tips, 542–543; itineraries, 15–17; money-saving tips, 543–544; for night owls, 76, 451–452; passes, 543–544; Windsor, 475–486. *See also specific sights*

SIM cards: 564

Sir John Soane's Museum: 67–68

Skiff, The (Renoir): 165–166

Sleep code: 375, 546

Sleeping: 374–393, 544–552; near airports, 393; Bayswater, 382–383; budgeting, 7; Cambridge, 504; chain hotels, 390–391; with children, 417; Kensington Gardens north, 382–386; Notting Hill, 386; online reviews, 548; near Paddington Station, 386–388; rates and deals, 544–545; reservations, 9, 550–551; South Kensington, 380–382; telephones, 564–565; types of

accommodations, 546–552; near Victoria Station, 375–380; Windsor, 486–487
Smartphones: 9, 19–21, 560–564
Soane's (Sir John) Museum: 67–68
Soccer: 438, 456
Soho: 55, 190–192; eating, 395, 398–399, 402–403
Soho Square: 190–191
Soho Square Gardens: 191
Somerset House: 58, 194, 243–244. *See also* Courtauld Gallery
Sotheby's: 435; afternoon tea, 415–416
Southampton Cruise Port: 469
South Bank: 13, 293–294; with children, 424; map, 84–85; markets, 434–435; sight highlights, 83–95; summer evenings, 452. *See also* Bankside
Southend Airport: 462
South Kensington: eating, 410–411; map, 381; sleeping, 380–382
South Quay: 368
Southwark: 13; map, 84–85; sight highlights, 88–95. *See also* Bankside
Southwark Bridge: 302
Southwark Cathedral: 92–93, 295–296; map, 296; music, 93, 450
Speakers' Corner (Hyde Park): 98
Spitalfields Market: 80, 432–433
Sporting events: 456
Stanfords Travel Bookstore: 22, 187
Stansted Airport: 461–462
State Department, U.S.: 575
State Rooms (Buckingham Palace): 59
Steves, Andy, tour packages: 42
Stonehenge: 472, 506–512, 528; guided tours, 506–507; maps, 508–509, 510; orientation, 507–509; reservations, 9, 507–508; self-guided tour, 509–512; traveling to, 506–507
Strand, the: 130, 241–247; map, 242–243
Stratford-upon-Avon, transportation: 464, 466
Street markets: *See* Markets
Stubbs, George: 338
Subway: *See* Tube
Sunflowers (Van Gogh): 166
Supermarkets: *See* Marks & Spencer
Supper at Emmaus (Caravaggio): 162–163

Supreme Court: 120
Surrealism: 312
Sussex Gardens: sleeping, 387–388
Sutton Hoo Ship-Burial: 225

T
Tate Boat: 41, 307, 334
Tate Britain: 95, 334–348; cruises, 41, 334; eating, 335; map, 337; orientation, 51, 95, 334–335; self-guided tour, 336–348
Tate Modern: 88, 89–90, 304, 306–318; cruises, 41, 307; eating, 307; orientation, 51, 90, 307–308; self-guided tour, 308–318
Taverns: *See* Pubs
Taxis: 30–31; Gatwick Airport, 461; Heathrow Airport, 460–461; Highclere Castle, 485; Stansted Airport, 462; Stonehenge, 507; tipping, 540
Tax refund, VAT: 427, 540–541
Tea: 414–416, 558; Greenwich, 355; places to sip, 414–416; terms, 558; Twinings, 245; Windsor, 487
Teddy bears: 68
Telephone numbers, useful: 575–576
Telephones: 560–567; cheat sheet, 566
Temperatures, average monthly: 583
Temple Bar Monument: 246
Temple Church: 246–247
Ten Bells Pub: 80
Tennis: 456, 576
Tennyson, Alfred, Lord: 139, 181, 252
Thames Clippers: 24, 39, 41, 307, 334, 365
Thames River: 12, 117–118, 291–293, 357–358, 442; boat piers, 40, 117–118; footbridges, 90, 92, 304–305; views of, 117–118, 304–305. *See also* Boat travel and cruises
Thames River Services: 39, 40–41
Thatcher, Margaret: 317, 520
Theater: 441–449; Cambridge, 490, 492; with children, 421, 423; current schedule, 18, 441, 444, 446–447; map, 442–443; money-saving tips, 71; outdoor and fringe, 449; seating terminology, 441–442; tickets, 9, 444–446; TKTS Booth, 71, 185, 444–445. *See also* Shakespeare's Globe

Theft alert: 19, 535, 537
Thomas, Dylan: 139, 182–183
Ticketmaster: 444, 456
Time Out London: 21–22, 35, 419
Time zones: 535
Tintoretto: 158–159
Tipping: 540
Tippoo's Tiger: 330–331
Titanic: 469
Titian: 502
TKTS Booth: 71, 185, 444–445
Toilets: 419
Tolkien, R. R.: 520
Tomb of the Unknown Warrior: 134
Tour guides: 9, 37–38; Cambridge, 492; tipping, 540
Tourist information: 18, 534–545; Cambridge, 490; Greenwich, 351; Windsor, 474
Tours: 32–42, 70–71; by bike, 38; by bus, 33–35, 425, 493–494; Cambridge, 492–494; by car, 35; with children, 425; Highclere Castle, 485; at night, 34–35, 451; Rick Steves, 573; Stonehenge, 506–507; for students, 42. *See also* Boat travel and cruises; Self-guided tours; Walking tours
Tower 42: 274
Tower Bridge: 78, 288, 291
Tower Bridge Exhibition: 78
Tower Green (Tower of London): 282–283
Tower of London: 77–78, 276–289, 529; with children, 419; eating, 278, 413–414; map, 279; orientation, 50, 78, 276–278; self-guided tour, 278–289
Tower Pier: 39, 40, 277
Toy Museum, Pollock's: 68–69, 424
Toy store: *See* Hamleys
Trafalgar Square: 12, 50, 52–53, 128–130; with children, 421; Christmas tree, 453; eating, 403–404; map, 129; sight highlights, 52–54
Trafalgar Tavern (Greenwich): 358
Train stations: 18–19, 463–465; baggage storage, 22; map, 464. *See also specific stations*
Train travel: 463–465, 472, 568, 570; Cambridge, 489, 490, 505; Eurostar, 9, 466–468; Gatwick Airport, 461; Greenwich, 350; Heathrow Airport, 460; Highclere Castle,

485; maps, 464, 465, 569; Stonehenge, 507; tickets, 568; Windsor, 473, 474
Traitor's Gate (Tower of London): 280
Trajan's Column Casts: 326–327
Transportation: 22–32, 457–462, 567–571; apps, 21–22; budgeting, 7; with children, 425; discounts, 24–25; maps, 464, 465, 569; tickets and passes, 22–24. *See also* Buses; Taxis; Tube
Transport Museum: 56–58, 188–189, 426
Travel advisories: 575–576
Travelcards: 15, 24–25
Traveling: to Cambridge, 489, 490, 505; Gatwick Airport, 461; to Greenwich, 349–350; Heathrow Airport, 459–461; to Highclere Castle, 485; to London, 19–20, 457–466; to Stonehenge, 506–507; to Windsor, 472, 473–475. *See also* Airports; Buses; Train travel
Travel insurance: 9
Travelodge: 391
Travel smarts: 4–5, 7
Travel tips: 535–536
Tricker's: 439
Trinity College (Cambridge): 500–502
Trip costs: 7–8
Trooping the Colour: 527, 576
Truman Brewery: 82, 433
Truman Markets: 82, 433
Tube: 25–26; apps, 21–22; budgeting, 7; etiquette, 26; Heathrow Airport, 459–460; tickets and passes, 22–24; Wi-Fi, 20–21
Turnbull & Asser: 439
Turner, J.M.W.: 164, 274, 343–345
TV (television): 525–528, 579–580
Twinings Tea Shop: 245
Two Dancers on the Stage (Degas): 197

U

Uccello, Paolo: 153–154
Underground: *See* Tube
Unicorn Theatre: 421
"United Kingdom (UK)," use of term: 523
University College London, sleeping: 393

University of Westminster, sleeping: 392–393
Urinal (Duchamp): 311

V

Van Dyck, Anthony: 97, 162, 481
Van Eyck, Jan: 154
Van Gogh, Vincent: 166, 199
Van Hoogstraten: 160
VAT refunds: 427, 540–541
Velázquez, Diego: 97, 161–162
Venus and Mars (Botticelli): 155–156
Vermeer, Jan: 160
Victoria, Queen: 99–101, 179–180, 286–287, 518–519; biographical sketch, 102–103
Victoria and Albert Museum: 101, 104, 319–333; afternoon tea, 415; eating, 320, 410; map, 322–323; orientation, 50, 104, 320; self-guided tour, 321–333
Victoria Coach Station: 19, 465–466
Victoria Station: 95, 463; eating near, 408–410; map, 378–379; sleeping near, 375–380
Views, best: 88–89
Virgin and Child with St. Anne and St. John the Baptist (da Vinci): 156–157
Virgin of the Rocks (da Vinci): 155
Visit London: 18, 534
Visitor information: *See* Tourist information

W

Walker's Quay: 42
Walking tours: Bankside, 290–305; Cambridge, 494–500; City of London, 239–262; Docklands, 364–373; East End, 79–83; Greenwich, 352–363; guided, 35–38, 451, 455; West End, 184–193; Westminster, 114–130
Wallace Collection: 51, 64–66
Wardour Street, eating: 398–399
Warhol, Andy: 316
Warner Bros. Studio Tour London: 112–113, 424
Washington, George: 177, 272, 274
Water-Lily Pond, The (Monet): 165
Waterloo Bridge: 243
Waterloo Pier: 40, 41, 117–118
Waterloo Station: 463

Waterstones Bookstores: 22, 89, 416, 438
Watt, James: 176
Waxworks, Madame Tussauds: 66–67, 71, 76, 423
Weather: 8, 583
Weekend Student Adventures (WSA Europe): 42
Weller Astronomy Galleries (Greenwich): 361, 362
Wellington, Duke of: 96–98, 177, 481, 518; Monument, 267; tomb, 274
Wellington Arch: 98
Wellington Barracks: 61–62
Wellington boots: 97–98
Wellington Museum: 96–98
West End: 12, 184–193; bike tour, 38; eating, 395–405; maps, 56–57, 186–187, 396–397; markets, 434; shopping, 427; sight highlights, 54–58; theater, 442–447; walking tour, 185–193
West India Quay: 371
West London: 13; with children, 423; department stores, 427–431; eating, 408–413; map, 97; sight highlights, 95–105; sleeping, 375–388
Westminster: 12, 114–130; map, 116; sight highlights, 43–52; walking tour, 115–130
Westminster Abbey: 43–44, 131–141; eating, 132–133; map, 134; music, 44, 132, 450; orientation, 44, 50, 131–133; self-guided tour, 133–141; view of, 119
Westminster Abbey Museum: 140–141
Westminster Bridge: 115, 117
Westminster Cathedral: 76, 95–96
Westminster Hall: 144–146
Westminster Palace: *See* Houses of Parliament
Westminster Pier: 40, 117, 425
Whistler, James McNeill: 342–343
Whitehall: 120–122
Whitehall Mural Cartoon: 170–171
White Tower (Tower of London): 280
White Tower Museum (Tower of London): 281–282
Wicked (musical): 447
Wi-Fi: *See* Internet access

Wilde, Oscar: 204, 244, 255
William I (the Conqueror): 136, 241, 276, 280, 281, 286, 472, 479, 514–515, 529
Wilton Diptych: 151–152
Wimbledon Tennis Championship: 456, 576
Winchester Palace: 300
Windsor: 471–488; eating, 487–488; helpful hints, 475; map, 476; sights/activities, 475–486; sleeping, 486–487; tourist information, 474; traveling to, 472, 473–475
Windsor and Royal Borough Museum: 483–484
Windsor Castle: 475–482
Winter events: 452–455
Wolseley, The: 404, 414, 439
Woolf, Virginia: 182, 200, 519
Wordsworth, William: 118, 178
World War I: 87, 121–122, 134, 181, 311, 346, 519
World War II: 87–88, 121, 134, 254, 313, 497, 520; Cabinet War Rooms, 46–47; HMS *Belfast,* 94, 424; memorials, 124, 270; and St. Paul's, 272–273. *See also* Blitz, the
Wren, Christopher: 72, 77, 99, 108, 176, 244, 253–257, 261, 263, 267–268, 280, 355, 501–502, 517, 532; biographical sketch, 253; tomb, 274. *See also* St. Paul's Cathedral
Wren Library (Cambridge): 501–502
WSA Europe: 42

Y
Ye Olde Cheshire Cheese Tavern: 252, 400
Yeoman Warders: *See* Beefeaters
York, transportation: 464, 466
Young Woman Standing at a Virginal, A (Vermeer): 160

Z
Zoo: *See* London Zoo

MAP INDEX

Color Maps
West London: v
East London: vii
The Underground: ix
England: xi

Introduction
Map Legend: 2

Orientation to London
London's Neighborhoods: 13
London Map Overview: 14
Greater London: 16
Handy Bus Routes: 28

Sights
London: 46
West End & Nearby: 56
Buckingham Palace Area: 60
North London: 65
The City, The Tower & East London: 74
East End Walk: 79
The South Bank: 84
West London: 97

Westminster Walk
Westminster Walk: 116
Trafalgar Square Area: 129

Westminster Abbey Tour
Westminster Abbey Tour: 134

Houses of Parliament Tour
Houses of Parliament: 145

National Gallery Tour
National Gallery: 153

National Portrait Gallery
National Portrait Gallery—Second Floor: 170
National Portrait Gallery—First Floor: 179

West End Walk
West End Walk: 186

British Museum Tour
British Museum Overview: 202
The Ancient World: 204
British Museum—Egypt: 205
British Museum—Assyria: 213
British Museum—Greece: 218
British Museum—Parthenon Galleries: 221

British Library Tour
British Library Tour: 229

The City Walk
The City Walk: 242

St. Paul's Cathedral Tour
St. Paul's Cathedral: 266

Tower of London Tour
Tower of London Tour: 279

Bankside Walk
Bankside Walk: 293
Southwark Cathedral: 296

Victoria & Albert Museum Tour
Victoria & Albert Museum Tour: 323

Tate Britain Tour
Tate Britain Overview: 337

Greenwich Tour
Greenwich: 353

The Docklands Walk
Docklands Area: 366
Docklands Walk: 369

Sleeping
London's Hotel Neighborhoods: 376
Victoria Station Neighborhood: 378
South Kensington Neighborhood: 381
North of Kensington Gardens: 384
North London Accommodations: 388

Eating
Central London Eateries: 396
Historic Pubs: 401

Shopping in London
Shopping in London: 428
Regent Street Shopping Walk: 437

Entertainment in London
London's Major Theaters: 442

London Connections
London's Airports: 458
London's Major Train Stations: 464
Public Transportation near London: 465
Eurostar Routes: 467

Day Trips
London Day Trips: 471
Windsor: 476

Cambridge: 491
Stonehenge Overview: 509
Stonehenge: 510

Britain: Past and Present
British Empire: 518
Mysterious Ruins: 529
Church Diagram: 530
Castle Diagram: 531

Practicalities
Public Transportation Routes in Britain: 569

Our website enhances this book and turns

Explore Europe

At ricksteves.com you can browse through thousands of articles, videos, photos and radio interviews, plus find a wealth of money-saving travel tips for planning your dream trip. And with our mobile-friendly website, you can easily access all this great travel information anywhere you go.

TV Shows

Preview the places you'll visit by watching entire half-hour episodes of Rick Steves' Europe (choose from all 100 shows) on-demand, for free.

your travel dreams into affordable reality

Radio Interviews

Enjoy ready access to Rick's vast library of radio interviews covering travel

tips and cultural insights that relate specifically to your Europe travel plans.

Travel Forums

Learn, ask, share! Our online community of savvy travelers is a great resource for first-time travelers to Europe, as well as seasoned pros. You'll find forums on each country, plus travel tips and restaurant/hotel reviews. You can even ask one of our well-traveled staff to chime in with an opinion.

Travel News

Subscribe to our free Travel News e-newsletter, and get monthly updates from Rick on what's happening in Europe.

Rick's Free Travel App

Get your FREE **Rick Steves Audio Europe**™ app to enjoy…

- Dozens of self-guided tours of Europe's top museums, sights and historic walks
- Hundreds of tracks filled with cultural insights and sightseeing tips from Rick's radio interviews
- All organized into handy geographic playlists
- For iPhone, iPad, iPod Touch, Android

With Rick whispering in your ear, Europe gets even better.

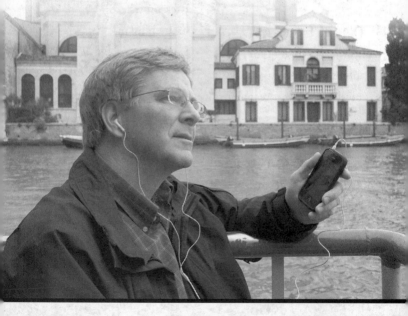

Gear up for your next adventure at ricksteves.com

Light Luggage
Pack light and right with Rick Steves' affordable, custom-designed rolling carry-on bags, backpacks, day packs and shoulder bags.

Accessories
From packing cubes to moneybelts and beyond, Rick has personally selected the travel goodies that will help your trip go smoother.

Experience maximum Europe

Save time and energy

This guidebook is your independent-travel toolkit. But for all it delivers, it's still up to you to devote the time and energy it takes to manage the preparation and logistics that are essential for a happy trip. If that's a hassle, there's a solution.

Rick Steves Tours

A Rick Steves tour takes you to Europe's most interesting places with great

with minimum stress

guides and small groups of 28 or less. We follow Rick's favorite itineraries, ride in comfy buses, stay in family-run hotels, and bring you intimately close to the Europe you've traveled so far to see. Most importantly, we take away the logistical headaches so you can focus on the fun.

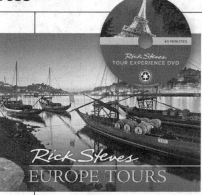

customers—along with us on 40 different itineraries, from Ireland to Italy to Istanbul. Is a Rick Steves tour the right fit for your travel dreams? Find out at ricksteves.com, where you can also get Rick's latest tour catalog and free Tour Experience DVD.

Join the fun

This year we'll take 18,000 free-spirited travelers— nearly half of them repeat

Europe is best experienced with happy travel partners. We hope you can join us.

Rick Steves

EUROPE GUIDES

Best of Europe
Eastern Europe
Europe Through the Back Door
Mediterranean Cruise Ports
Northern European Cruise Ports

COUNTRY GUIDES

Croatia & Slovenia
England
France
Germany
Great Britain
Ireland
Italy
Portugal
Scandinavia
Spain
Switzerland

CITY & REGIONAL GUIDES

Amsterdam & the Netherlands
Belgium: Bruges, Brussels, Antwerp & Ghent
Barcelona
Budapest
Florence & Tuscany
Greece: Athens & the Peloponnese
Istanbul
London
Paris
Prague & the Czech Republic
Provence & the French Riviera
Rome
Venice
Vienna, Salzburg & Tirol

SNAPSHOT GUIDES

Basque Country: Spain & France
Berlin
Copenhagen & the Best of Denmark
Dublin
Dubrovnik
Hill Towns of Central Italy
Italy's Cinque Terre
Kraków, Warsaw & Gdansk
Lisbon
Loire Valley
Madrid & Toledo
Milan & the Italian Lakes District
Naples & the Amalfi Coast
Northern Ireland
Norway
Scotland
Sevilla, Granada & Southern Spain
St. Petersburg, Helsinki & Tallinn
Stockholm

POCKET GUIDES

Amsterdam
Athens
Barcelona
Florence
London
Munich & Salzburg
Paris
Rome
Venice
Vienna

Maximize your travel skills with a good guidebook.

TRAVEL CULTURE

Europe 101
European Christmas
Postcards from Europe
Travel as a Political Act

eBOOKS

Nearly all Rick Steves guides are available as ebooks. Check with your favorite bookseller.

RICK STEVES' EUROPE DVDs

12 New Shows 2015–2016
Austria & the Alps
The Complete Collection 2000-2016
Eastern Europe
England & Wales
European Christmas
European Travel Skills & Specials
France
Germany, BeNeLux & More
Greece, Turkey & Portugal
The Holy Land: Israelis & Palestinians Today
Iran
Ireland & Scotland
Italy's Cities
Italy's Countryside
Scandinavia
Spain
Travel Extras

PHRASE BOOKS & DICTIONARIES

French
French, Italian & German
German
Italian
Portuguese
Spanish

PLANNING MAPS

Britain, Ireland & London
Europe
France & Paris
Germany, Austria & Switzerland
Ireland
Italy
Spain & Portugal

Photo © Patricia Feaster

Credits

RESEARCHERS
To help update this book, Rick and Gene relied on...

Robyn Stencil

Robyn credits the origin of her love affair with England to the Thames, supporting her motto "where there's a river, there's a run." Her ideal British adventure involves the call of gulls, plenty of flat whites, and friendly people from rocky coastline to green hills. When she's not researching, guiding, or pursuing the perfect burger, Robyn calls Seattle home, where she works as a tour operations specialist for Rick Steves' Europe.

PHOTO CREDITS

Front Cover: House of Parliament with Big Ben and Westminster Bridge spanning the River Thames © Sebastian Wasek/Getty Images

Title Page: p. i, Millennium Bridge and St. Paul's Cathedral © Dominic Arizona Bonuccelli

Front Matter Color: p. xii, Guards outside Buckingham Palace © Dominic Arizona Bonuccelli

Additional Photography: Dominic Arizona Bonuccelli, Rich Earl, Barb Geisler, Jennifer Hauseman, Cameron Hewitt, David C. Hoerlein, Lauren Mills, Sarah Murdoch, Pat O'Connor, Gene Openshaw, Sarah Slauson, Robyn Stencil, Rick Steves, Gretchen Strauch, Bruce VanDeventer, Wikimedia Commons (PD-Art/PD-US)

Additional Credits: p. 137, Lady Chapel © Jon Arnold Images Ltd/Alamy; p. 165, Monet-Gare St. Lazare © National Gallery, London/Art Resource, NY; p. 175, Charles II © National Portrait Gallery, London; p. 183, Princess Diana © National Portrait Gallery, London; p. 231, Lindisfarne Gospels © The British Library Board; p. 232, The Gutenberg Bible © North Wind Picture Archives/Alamy; p. 233, Magna Carta © The British Library Board; p. 268, The Choir and High Altar © Johnny Greig/istockphoto.com, p. 271, John Donne © Angelo Hornak/Alamy; p. 287, crown jewels © ImageState/Alamy; p. 306, Tate Modern © Cathy Yeulet/123rf.com; p. 352, Cutty Sark © Cutty Sark Trust

Photos are used by permission and are the property of the original copyright owners.